SIX RENAISSANCE TRAGEDIES

WITHDRAWN FROM
THE LIBRARY

UNIVERSITY OF
WiNCHESTER

D0452281

The Swan Theatre
(Source: The Mansell Collection, London)

Six Renaissance Tragedies

The Spanish Tragedy
The Tragical History of Doctor Faustus
The Revenger's Tragedy
The Duchess of Malfi
The Changeling
'Tis Pity She's a Whore

Edited by

COLIN GIBSON
Donald Collie Professor of English
University of Otago, New Zealand

MACMILLAN
in association with
The Department of English
University of Otago

Editorial matter and selection © Colin Gibson 1997

All rights reserved. No reproduction, copy or transmission of
this publication may be made without written permission.

No paragraph of this publication may be reproduced, copied or
transmitted save with written permission or in accordance with
the provisions of the Copyright, Designs and Patents Act 1988,
or under the terms of any licence permitting limited copying
issued by the Copyright Licensing Agency, 90 Tottenham Court
Road, London W1P 9HE.

Any person who does any unauthorised act in relation to
this publication may be liable to criminal prosecution and civil
claims for damages.

The author has asserted his rights to be identified as the author of this
work in accordance with the Copyright, Designs and Patents Act 1988.

First published 1997 by
MACMILLAN PRESS LTD
Houndmills, Basingstoke, Hampshire RG21 6XS
and London
Companies and representatives
throughout the world

ISBN 0–333–60922–0 hardcover
ISBN 0–333–60923–9 paperback

A catalogue record for this book is available
from the British Library.

This book is printed on paper suitable for recycling and
made from fully managed and sustained forest sources.

10 9 8 7 6 5 4 3 2 1
06 05 04 03 02 01 00 99 98 97

Typeset by Forewords, Oxford/Longworth Editorial Services
Longworth, Oxfordshire.

Printed in Malaysia

KING ALFRED'S COLLEGE
WINCHESTER

822.3 GIB | 0207878

Contents

Acknowledgements

I would like to thank Mary Sullivan, Justine Thompson, and Fiona McDonald for expert assistance in preparing the typescript of this anthology. Thanks are due to the Division of Humanities and the University of Otago for generous research grants and research leave, and to Clare Hall, Cambridge, and the Folger Shakespeare Library for visiting fellowships. I am grateful for the willing assistance of the librarians and staff of my own university and of the libraries where I have researched material for this edition. Particular thanks go to the British Library, the Folger Shakespeare Library, the Library of Congress, the University of Cambridge Library and the Bodleian Library, Oxford. I gratefully acknowledge the patience and professional assistance of Macmillan and its staff, in particular, Cathryn Tanner and Margaret Bartley. Valery Rose and Nick Allen scrupulously attended to the copy-editing and setting of the text. More personal but deeply felt thanks are due to Muriel King and Jeanette Gibson for their daily encouragement and unfailing support.

COLIN GIBSON
Dunedin, New Zealand

General Introduction

The six plays in this anthology have been chosen to represent a remarkable flowering of tragic dramatic writing during one of the most prolific periods of theatrical activity in any culture, the period known as the English Renaissance, dating from about 1590 to 1640.

The tragedies of the two greatest English dramatists of the period, Shakespeare and Jonson, are not represented here, both because they are readily available and because their absence allows the individual talents of the many writers who were their predecessors, contemporaries and successors to be more clearly displayed. But each of the plays included is both a major work in the dramatic output of its author (or principal author) and – with the possible exception of Kyd's *The Spanish Tragedy*, important in its own right as a seminal drama for the period – has held its place in the theatre until the present day.

The Tragic Scene

Tragedy has always enjoyed a senior position in the hierarchy of dramatic kinds, and the interest of the writers and critics of the English Renaissance in the heritage of classical Greek and Roman drama, fostered by school and university study as well as by the publication of texts and translations, ensured that many writers attempted what was widely regarded as the most challenging and important kind of dramatic writing. Comedies might be more popular and enjoyable, but tragedy was admired for its gravity and the seriousness of its subject matter. Thomas Middleton, the co-author of *The Changeling*, and himself a prolific writer of both tragedies and comedies, contributed a commendatory verse in learned Latin (here given in translation) on the occasion of the publication of Webster's *Duchess of Malfi* (1623); titled 'Upon Tragedy' it declared that 'Just as light springs from darkness at a blow from the Thunderer [Jupiter, king of the gods], so Tragedy, ruinous for bad poets, becomes lasting life for good and famous poets.' To which John Ford, another author of comedies and tragedies including '*Tis Pity She's a Whore*, in yet another commendatory verse prefixed to *The Duchess of Malfi*, added the final accolade for a Renaissance writer, 'Crown him a poet, whom nor Rome nor Greece/Transcend in all theirs, for a masterpiece.'

For such reasons of literary prestige (and doubtless the more pragmatic reason that tragedies could draw audiences), large numbers of such plays were written between 1590 and 1640. Alfred Harbage's *Annals of English Drama 975–1700* documents the existence of about 1300 plays datable to the span of fifty years which sets the chronological frame for this collection, with some two hundred claiming the generic name of tragedy. In many cases, the plays are only known by title or from some other fragmentary piece of evidence; and there can be little doubt that many more have vanished, leaving no record whatever. While the six tragedies chosen powerfully present many of the common tragic themes of the period and display something of its variety of forms, within the limits of this anthology it has not been possible to cover the full range of subject matter or comprehensively display the variations within a form explored by so many writers. It will be useful to draw attention to some of the more significant omissions.

Tragedies of state, that is, dramas in which the focus is on the tragic experience of high-ranking individuals within the tumultuous currents of great political events, are not to be found here: plays such as Marlowe's *Edward II*, dealing with the fall from power and brutal destruction of a weak king, Shakespeare's *Coriolanus*, with its account of the life and death of a charismatic but deeply flawed military leader made the tool of political manipulators, Jonson's description in *Sejanus* of the human effects of a corrupt and tyrannical system of political government, or Massinger's depiction in *Believe As You List* of the politically expedient extermination of a royal claimant. As in Shakespeare's *Othello*, Kyd's tragic protagonist Hieronimo, in *The Spanish Tragedy*, works out his personal conflicts in the shadow of a greater war, just as Marlowe can exploit the conflict between Catholicism and the Protestant faith in *The Tragical History of Doctor Faustus*, but the destruction of a Faustus, or a Giovanni, of a Beatrice-Joanna or a Duchess of Malfi, does not cause or resolve a political crisis.

Nor are there any examples of what have been called 'domestic tragedies', plays in which human disasters occur within the framework of bourgeois or middle-class family life realistically portrayed, as in the anonymous tragedy *Arden of Faversham*, or Heywood's *A Woman Killed with Kindness*. Not that the majority of plays selected locate themselves exclusively in royal courts or focus on the affairs of kings and nations. Hieronimo is a senior judge associated with the Spanish crown; Faustus occasionally shows off his magic powers in papal and royal settings; Italian dukedoms provide the tragic arena for Vindice in *The Revenger's Tragedy* and for the Duchess of Malfi. But the action of *The Changeling* takes place in a nobleman's castle and a doctor's asylum, and the tragic protagonists in Ford's play *'Tis Pity She's a Whore* are the children of a well-to-do citizen of Parma.

Although several of the dramatists represented here set the action of their plays at a time before the present time of their audiences (a typical strategy in tragic writing), their primary interests do not lie in the simple reconstruction of remote historical events, either as intrinsically interesting in themselves or as thinly disguised reflections of contemporary realities. The universal capacities and defects of their characters are more important to them than the manners of a past age; there is no representative included here of the many Renaissance tragedies dealing in the style of a dramatised chronicle with the historical lives and deaths of famous Greek, Roman or early medieval figures. (In 1602, early in their careers as playwrights, Webster and Middleton contributed to the team-writing of such a play (now lost) called *Caesar's Fall*.)

Finally, though several of the plays selected reflect the English taste for mixed theatrical modes by their inclusion of clown figures, parodic comic scenes or sub-plots, or instances of black humour, none of them exemplifies the tragi-comic forms that became prominent in the last years of the period: plays in which events drive their principal characters towards a total catastrophe which is avoided at the last possible moment, to veer into the reassuring world of comedy and a happy close to lives which have experienced 'the danger but not the death'.

Carnal, Bloody and Unnatural Acts

It would be easy to make a case for the uniqueness of each of the chosen plays as the expression of their authors' individual sensibility and vision of the world. As Gamini Salgādo points out, 'literary categories are always arbitrary and creative artists have always shown a healthy disrespect for them (if, indeed, they have been aware of their existence)' (*Three Jacobean Tragedies* [Harmondsworth, 1965] p. 11). But there are significant common elements in these plays, already recognised in their own time.

The first is simply a preoccupation with violence and excess, whether of emotion or action, among the most powerful, cultured and high-ranking members of society. 'The argument of tragedy', declared a hostile Puritan writer, Stephen Gosson, 'is wrath, cruelty, incest, injury, murder either violent by sword or voluntary by poison. The persons gods, goddesses, juries, friends, kings, queens, and mighty men.' Gosson was writing in 1582, but it would be easy to match his list of topics to these plays. There is indeed a paradoxical relationship between the subject matter of even the greatest tragedies of the period and the genre's reputed gravity and seriousness of theme, well displayed in Horatio's summary of the action of *Hamlet* (1600):

> So shall you hear
> Of carnal, bloody, and unnatural acts,
> Of accidental judgements, casual slaughters,
> Of deaths put on by cunning and forced cause,
> And in this upshot, purposes mistook
> Fallen on th' inventors' heads.
> (5.2.359–64, New Cambridge edition)

This paradox is also recognised by an unknown dramatist of the period, who in the Induction to *A Warning for Fair Women* (1599) puts into the mouth of Comedy a highly irreverent view of Tragedy. The subject of tragic plays, declares the scoffer, is

> How some damned tyrant, to obtain a crown,
> Stabs, hangs, imprisons, smothers, cutteth throats,
> And then a Chorus, too, comes howling in,
> And tells us of the worrying of a cat,
> Then of a filthy, whining ghost,
> Lapped in some foul sheet, or leather pilch,
> Comes screaming in like a pig half-sticked,
> And cries '*Vindicta*, revenge, revenge'.
> With that a little resin flasheth forth,
> Like smoke out of a tobacco pipe, or a boy's squib.

> Then comes in two or three, like to drovers,
> With tailors' bodkins, stabbing one another.
> Is not this trim? is not here goodly things
> That you should be so much accounted of?
> (ll. 50–63)

For all the partial truth in such accounts, it is not difficult to recognise that these tragic plays actually have much in common with the comedies of the period. Indeed, some of the tragedies subsume a comic and jeering perspective objectified in characters like Robin and Rafe (*Doctor Faustus*), aspects of Vindice, Ambitioso and Supervacuo (*The Revenger's Tragedy*), Bosola (*The Duchess of Malfi*), Antonio and Franciscus (*The Changeling*), and Bergetto (*'Tis Pity She's a Whore*). In particular, they share with comedy an interest in social boundary-breaking (though where the comedies mock, ridicule and reform offenders, tragic stories typically apply the most extreme penalties for such behaviour). Kyd's play concerns itself with the imperative social and religious sanctions against taking human life; Marlowe deals with his (and our own) culture's nervousness about unlimited scientific and philosophical inquiry. *The Revenger's Tragedy* draws out the consequences of sexual violation and unchecked self-indulgence; in both *The Duchess of Malfi* and *The Changeling* the fatal boundary crossed is that of social class distinction and blood line, though the offenders are held within the circle of the audience's sympathies in the first tragedy and moved out to its limits in the second play. Beatrice-Joanna acknowledges her marginalisation in a dying speech to her betrayed husband:

> Oh, come not near me, sir, I shall defile you,
> I am that of your blood was taken from you
> For your better health; look no more upon't,
> But cast it to the ground regardlessly:
> Let the common sewer take it from distinction . . .
> Alsemero, I am a stranger to your bed.
> (5.3.149–59)

In *'Tis Pity She's a Whore*, Ford plays off an enervated conventional moral and social order of courtship and marriage against the anti-social behaviour of the faithless but possessive Soranzo, and the incestuous brother and sister whose romantic, idealising love for each other breaks the strongest of all sexual taboos.

Why This Is Hell, Nor Am I Out of It

In all of these tragedies, social sanctions are reinforced with appeals to religious sanctions and invocations addressed to divine authority, though only in *Doctor Faustus* is God's displeasure at the boundary-crosser's challenge unambiguously declared. However, their grand theme is not so much the mysterious working out of the will of the gods, or the imaginative, emotional and intellectual capacity of some human beings to experience and comprehend the full repertoire of physical and psychological suffering. It is rather the terrifying ability of the human spirit to bring into being and endure hell on earth for itself and others. Such a theme in turn mirrors the dark creative powers of the dramatist, just as it reflects the theatre audience's perennial willingness to enter imaginatively into scenes of agonised suffering or triumphant iniquity.

It is hardly surprising that the greatest tragedies of the period address in such metaphysical terms the experience of the worst that can befall humanity. As a form, tragedy has always located human life and action within the framework of the whole of the natural world and the jurisdiction of whatever powers lie beyond the visible universe. Hieronimo, Faustus, the Duchess of Malfi and Giovanni cry to heaven, challenge the power or apparent indifference of the gods, or puzzle over the ways of providence, just as do Oedipus, Lear, Hamlet, Juno Boyle or Estragon and Vladimir. Ghosts, blazing stars, peals of thunder, the appearance of angels and demons and stage representations of death such as Vindice's 'bony lady' or Bosola's Tomb-maker and Bellman signify the mysterious co-existence of worlds beyond the present one.

It must also be remembered that the playwrights of the English Renaissance were heirs to a vigorous medieval tradition of religious drama, in which the powers of Good and Evil beset and fought to win the souls of humankind, and allegorical figures might hold the stage with representative human characters. The dramaturgical techniques of that tradition are still to be seen in the work of the earliest writers in this anthology: for instance, in the figures of Revenge and the ghost of Andrea brought on stage to brood over the human action of *The Spanish Tragedy,* or in the appearance of the Good and Bad Angel or the show of the Seven Deadly Sins in *The*

Tragical History of Doctor Faustus. Later dramatists work with similar frames of thought but abandon such external stage representation as old-fashioned. When hell is evoked some forty years later in Ford's *'Tis Pity She's a Whore*, it is described in vivid pictorial images in the friar's terrifying sermon to Annabella (3.6.8–30), but not introduced as a stage property.

The plays in this anthology are distinguished not so much by their incorporation of such an explicit or implied metaphysical framework of the polar opposites of heaven and hell, the domains of God and the Devil, as the context for human life, as they are by their authors' deliberate disablement of the usual sources of moral and religious authority, to allow the maximum freedom for (unwise) human choice, and to test to the utmost their protagonists' capacity to endure and respond to a tragic world in which evil is predominant and active.

The choice of an Italian or Spanish setting for five of the six tragedies (Faustus visits the Papal court at Rome, but the centre of his activities is the German university town of Wittenberg) already signals the characteristic focus of much Renaissance English tragic writing on disordered societies displaying extremes of passion, corruption and violence. Both Italy and Spain were associated in English audiences' minds with stereotypical extravagance of emotion, rigid codes of honour demanding private and comprehensive revenge for insult or injury, family feuds, extreme cruelty and violence. The Cambridge scholar Fynes Morrison solemnly reported the Italians' furious jealousy, their predilection for poison and bloodthirsty revenge, their lechery and their flattery. Thomas Nashe, in a famous passage in his fictional work *The Unfortunate Traveller* published in 1594, describes Italy as 'the paradise of the earth and the epicure's heaven'. It teaches impressionable young Englishmen, says Nashe, 'the art of atheism, the art of epicurising, the art of whoring, the art of poisoning, the art of sodomitry. . . . It is now a privy note among the better sort of men, when they would set a singular mark or brand on a notorious villain, to say, he hath been in Italy.' In Ford's *'Tis Pity She's a Whore*, when the injured husband Soranzo declares 'the less I speak, the more I burn,/And blood shall quench that flame', his Spanish servant Vasques (who will later rejoice that a Spaniard outdid an Italian in revenge) congratulates him with the words, 'Now you begin to turn Italian'.

In the unsettled and fragile social world of these tragedies, children throw off parental restraint, servants bring about the destruction of their superiors, dukes and nobles neglect their public obligations in order to satisfy their personal ends. Antonio's glowing praise of the French court, with its 'fixed order' and 'judicious king', is positioned at the beginning of *The Duchess of Malfi* to set off by contrast the tyrannical and vicious rule of Ferdinand and his Cardinal brother. The conventionally ordered world of arranged marriages between social equals is everywhere disrupted: Bel-Imperia takes successive lovers; Faustus seeks a wife to satisfy his lust and is offered 'a hot whore', a devil woman sputtering fire and smoke; Gratiana can be persuaded to prostitute her daughter to Lussorioso; the servant De Flores finds an unlikely but natural partner in Beatrice-Joanna, while the courtiers Antonio and Franciscus seek to corrupt Alibius's wife. The Duchess of Malfi defies her brothers' authority and finds for herself a lover and a husband in her major-domo; Giovanni and Annabella break their father's heart with the discovery of their incestuous adulterous passion. Characters of simple faith or virtue, like the Old Man in *Doctor Faustus* or Castiza in *The Revenger's Tragedy*, are briefly tested then dismissed, with little or no moral effect on the world around them. Philotis in *'Tis Pity She's a Whore* is made the tool of her uncle's revenge, then dismissed to a nunnery.

The religious landscape of these tragedies is dark and apocalyptic; life is lived out under the eye of a wrathful god or gods, and for many of the characters closes in punitive suffering and 'confusion', Ford's favourite word for final ruin and perdition. Webster's Duchess of Malfi and Ford's own Annabella meet their deaths with something like Hamlet's readiness, but the dramatists for the most part deny their characters dignity, clarity or self-knowledge in the hour of death. The world of *The Spanish Tragedy* is openly controlled by the spirit of Revenge, licensed by the King of Hell at the urging of his consort Proserpina. Despite the brief appearances of the Good Angel in *Doctor Faustus*, demons dominate the scenes and God is perceived only at an unreachable distance. It is possible to argue that Marlowe is projecting the world as seen through the haunted imagination of Faustus himself, but it is a perspective which denies any sense of equality between the forces of good and evil, religion and anti-religion, salvation and damnation. The strongest ethical and moral imperative in *The Revenger's Tragedy* is a medieval awareness of mortality, yet its most eloquent spokesman, Vindice, busily and paradoxically commits himself to winning a triumph over his enemies in the very pride of life whose futility he elsewhere denounces. It is possible to read the trials of the Duchess of Malfi as a prolonged process of spiritual purification through inordinate suffering, with Bosola's Judgement-Day fable of the Salmon and the Dogfish (3.5.121–37) occupying a crucial thematic position. But such a reading requires a position close to that of the contemporary Puritan divine William Perkins, who expresses the tough-minded belief that 'when God will send his own servants to heaven, he sends them in a contrary way, even by the gates of hell'. Certainly, the official representative of the Church, the Cardinal, is in many respects a stereotypical corrupt Catholic churchman, sensual and power-hungry, the persecutor rather than the protector of his own sister. Ford's Cardinal is little better. His protection of the assassin Grimaldi outrages both Donado and Florio, and his confiscation of the property of those slain at the end of the play, together with his brutal sentence of execution on Putana and his protection of Vasques is meant to outrage the audience. The Friar, who acts as spiritual adviser to both Giovanni and Annabella, fails to match his charges intellectually, and can do little more than threaten the erring couple with conventional images of hell-fire and damnation. Crucially, when he sees his own failure and 'the bad, fearful end' that lies before Giovanni, he leaves him to despair and hurries out of Parma to 'shun this coming blow', leaving Giovanni to find what moral strength he can draw from himself.

The Spanish Tragedy, the earliest play in this collection, begins the explicit exploration of the theme of hell on earth when in its opening lines the revengeful ghost of Andrea describes how after death in battle it descended to the court of Pluto and returned to earth accompanied by the hellish spirit of Revenge to watch out the convoluted destruction of his enemies and others. The play closes with their return 'to deepest hell' to complete the reward of the guiltless, and the torment of the guilty. Marlowe's Doctor Faustus 'confounds hell in Elysium' and commits himself to the demonic powers. When he naïvely asks Mephostophilis about the location of hell, he is told 'Hell hath no limits, nor is circumscribed /In one self place, for where we are is hell, / And where hell is must we ever be.' At the close of the play, a real hell gapes for him, and screaming to the demon who has companioned him for twenty-four years, he is borne away by devils. There is a memorable echo of this passage at the close of *The Changeling*, when De Flores holds the dying Beatrice-Joanna in his arms and acknowledges to the husband he has cuckolded, 'I coupled with your mate/At barley-break. Now we are left in hell.' Her father Vermandero, in a moment of general recognition characteristic of the close of a tragic play, comments, 'We are all there; it circumscribes us here.'

The Revenger's Tragedy offers a vision of what human life might be at its worst, deprived of all social, legal and moral restraints. Its mordant and revengeful observer, Vindice, introduces us to its doomed characters in language resonant with ideas of sin, damnation and the fires of hell:

> go, grey-haired adultery,
> And thou his son, as impious steeped as he,
> And thou his bastard, true-begot in evil,
> And thou his duchess, that will do with devil.
> Four excellent characters! O that marrowless age
> Would stuff the hollow bones with damned desires,
> And 'stead of heat, kindle infernal fires
>
> (1.1.1–7)

Life in such a world lived out under the wrath of God, signalled by blazing stars and rolling thunder, becomes a living torment; the agonised and dying duke, held down and forced to watch his bastard son meeting his own wife 'for damned clips', asks, 'Is there a hell beside this, villains?'

The Duchess of Malfi, enduring the psychological tortures imposed on her by her brothers, perceives the continuation of life itself as the torment endured by the damned:

> BOSOLA: Come, you must live.
> DUCHESS: That's the greatest torture souls feel in hell,
> In hell; that they must live and cannot die.
>
> (4.1.68–70)

In a stream of images of her imprisonment as a theatre, a cage, a tomb, a charnel-house, she describes the heaven over her head as 'made of molten brass,/The earth of flaming sulphur'. In a further image directly applicable to her torments, the second Madman tells the audience that 'Hell is a mere glasshouse, where the devils are continually blowing up women's souls on hollow irons, and the fire never goes out'. Bosola, watching her death throes invokes her 'fair soul' to return from darkness, 'and lead mine/Out of this sensible hell.' And the Cardinal, whose mind is much preoccupied with questions about hell, advises him to 'Throw to the devil/Thy melancholy; the fire burns well,/What need we keep a stirring of it, and make/A greater smother?' It is a remark among many which suggestively associate the two brothers with evil and diabolical forces, setting out to destroy the goodness of their sister.

In Ford's *'Tis Pity She's a Whore*, the Friar represents the orthodox religious view of their behaviour to the two young lovers: he associates Giovanni with those forward wits who 'Discovered first the nearest way to hell,/And filled the world with devilish atheism', and terrifies Annabella with a long set-piece description of the torments of an infernal hell. When his servant Vasques taunts Annabella's make-shift husband Soranzo with the question 'what do you think of your heaven of happiness now, sir?' the enraged husband declares, 'I carry hell about me; all my blood/Is fired in swift revenge.' At the close of the play, in a moment reminiscent of Othello's final questioning of Iago, the Cardinal demands of Vasques 'what incarnate fiend/Hath led thee on to this?' to which Vasques replies in terms disclaiming all association with a metaphysical evil, 'Honesty and pity of my master's wrongs'. We need not accept his profession of offended virtue – it is undercut by his delight in deception and his savagery – but it signals that there is no longer any need for stage demons of the kind Marlowe introduces; in the later tragedies of the period 'confusion' (a repeated word in this play) is brought down upon the characters by themselves.

If hell is the common metaphor in these plays for a world brought into existence by unchecked self-seeking expressed as a craving for power, control over others, sexual, emotional or intellectual self-satisfaction, tragic experience in such a world is focused on the consequent assault on the integrity of individual human personality and the hard-won wisdom progressively acquired both by the characters and the watching audience as more and more is lost.

In Hieronimo, we see a judge, finally unable to control his grief for the loss of his son, turning into a savage revenger no better than his enemies. The grand scholar Faustus, who aspires to deity itself and boasts of his 'manly fortitude' to Mephostophilis, finally rises to a frenzy of fear and despair, cursing his parents and envying the soulless, mindless life of the brute beasts. Vindice and his brother revenger Hippolito, at the beginning of *The Revenger's Tragedy* capable of moral horror and caustic indignation at the viciousness and lustfulness of the court, are gradually drawn into the lifestyle of scheming and self-gratification they condemn, progressively becoming more and more like those they hate. At the close of the play the audience is invited neither to pity nor to fear their fall, but to smile grimly as their self-adulatory cleverness overreaches itself. In the final moments of *The Changeling*, Beatrice-Joanna at last clearly recognises her own corruption, and the bewildered surviving characters led by Alsemero can do little more than list the astonishing transformations which have taken place in their lives beneath the changes of the moon. In Ford's *'Tis Pity She's a Whore*, Giovanni, the brilliant student, the 'miracle of wit' solemnly challenged by his sister to 'Love me, or kill me', finally and defiantly acts out a terrible 'rape of life and beauty', murdering and mutilating a love 'for whose each drop of blood/I would have pawned my heart'. Only the Duchess of Malfi outfaces the worst her brothers can inflict on her, and earns the final tribute of the play, 'Integrity of life is fame's best friend,/Which nobly, beyond death, shall crown the end.'

While the authors of most of these plays endorse the judgement of Vindice that 'When the bad bleeds, then is the tragedy good' (3.5.199) and gratify their audiences with scenes of physical and bloody violence, such manifestations of death and mutilation also serve to symbolise the assault on the integrity of personality which is the deeper theme of these tragedies. From Hieronimo's self mutilation to Giovanni's impalement of his sister's heart, the human body is brutalised, tortured and dismembered. Sometimes the violence is projected verbally rather than actualised, as when Ferdinand instructs the Duchess of Malfi to 'cut out thine own tongue' least it betray her lover, or when Vindice orders his brother to 'Let our two other hands tear up his lids/And make his eyes, like comets. shine through blood' if their victim refuses to look at the sight of his own wife's adultery they are forcing him to watch and acknowledge. But shocking stage spectacles in these tragedies are seldom merely gratuitous; they are mounted to force home both the appalling destructiveness of human wrongdoing and its moral implications. The body of Faustus is cut and bleeds, it loses a leg in a magic 'trick', it is torn apart by devils in actions analogous to and anticipating the final loss of his soul. Beatrice-Joanna is confronted with the all too physical evidence of the murder she has brought about in the ring-finger De Flores cuts from Piracquo, and in his turn De Flores is haunted by the image of his mutilated victim.

But in a culture which tolerated much physical pain and brutality (plays could be performed in bear-baiting amphitheatres) yet held reason to be the primary human faculty, the greatest threat to the integrity of the protagonists of these tragedies is the loss or subversion of rationality. Insistently in these tragedies an eruption of passionate emotion (associated in the Elizabethans' mind with 'blood') overthrows all the controls of reason and leads both to disaster and to madness. Kyd traces the destructive effects of obsessive grief on the mind of an old judge, Hieronimo, and his wife Isabella; both make deranged attacks on their unreachable enemies, the one in a court of law, the other at the scene of the crime, before Hieronimo succeeds in destroying his son's murderers in an ingenious but bloodthirsty way. Marlowe and his collaborator display the vacillating progress of a superb and adventurous mind driven towards the unthinkable by unexamined ambition, framing Faustus's tortured conscience with mindless admirers and exploiters of his powers. Like Hieronimo, Vindice, consumed by murderous grief, is arguably half-crazed; the thought of his wrongs 'Turns [his] abusèd heart-strings into fret'. Consequently, much of the bleakly comic power of *The Revenger's Tragedy* lies in its presentation of a corrupt, self-seeking group of aristocrats totally unaware of the activities of the psychopathic killer among them. *The Changeling* explicitly parallels the quest for emotional and sexual satisfaction in Vermandero's castle with sexual intrigues among the managers and patients of a hospital for the insane. The tragedy works by ironic inversion. In the apparent safety and stability of the castle world, the supposedly clear-eyed and coldly unattainable Beatrice-Joanna discovers her hidden capacity for criminality and sexual transgression. In the asylum, on the other hand, the stubbornly virtuous and clear-sighted Isabella exposes the mad folly of her disguised aristocratic lovers.

Webster's Duchess of Malfi is subjected to psychological torture in a deliberate and sustained assault on her reason. When a 'wild consort of madmen' from the common hospital fails to unsettle her mind she is strangled. Webster then proceeds to expose the irrational impulses driving her twin brothers' tyrannical and murderous behaviour. Ferdinand descends into absolute insanity; even the icily self-controlled Cardinal is troubled by the vision of 'a thing, armed with a rake,/That seems to strike at me'. Ford's Giovanni, characterised like Faustus as a brilliant student, commits himself to an absolute but incestuous love for his sister. Throughout the tragedy a vein of commentary describes both this and other lawless passions as a kind of madness: Giovanni is 'a frantic madman';

Soranzo's liaison with Hippolita is the result of 'distracted lust', provoked by his 'sensual rage of blood', and both these extremes are contrasted with the childish affection of the simpleton Bergetto for the innocent Philotis. Eventually Giovanni is trapped in the ways of the society he despises and murders his sister in a vain attempt to take revenge as others do. Ford daringly images his loss of all sense of reality as he brings on stage Annabella's heart, torn from her body and spitted on his dagger to display the 'truth' of a love he can find no other way to communicate to a disbelieving world. 'Rip up my bosom; there thou shalt behold/A heart in which is writ the truth I speak', he had earlier told his sister; his own final act is at once an affirmation and destruction of that truth, a tragic gesture of irrationality constructing itself as heroic defiance.

When the Bad Bleeds, then is the Tragedy Good

In the unjust world isolating the tragic pair of lovers, Vasques, the cunning and brutal Spanish servant who has brought about the poisoning of Hippolita, the dishonourable assassination of Giovanni and the blinding of Annabella's nurse Putana, is allowed to leave Parma without punishment, rejoicing that 'a Spaniard outwent an Italian in revenge'. So Ford makes his own distinctive use of a key narrative and thematic element in many of the tragedies of this period, a quest for bloody retributive justice.

Revenge plots have a universal appeal: they are found in such Greek and Roman tragedies as Euripides' *Medea* or Seneca's *Thyestes*, and they have enjoyed an enormous resurgence of popularity in the films, television dramas and detective stories of our own age. Kyd's *Spanish Tragedy* made such successful use of the theme in his own theatre that later writers took the arousal and satisfaction of revenge as a given narrative component of the form; in *The Revenger's Tragedy* Vindice describes vengeance as 'Murder's quit-rent' and 'tenant to Tragedy'.

Kyd's inventive play institutes the crucial elements of delay and frustration (for the audience as well as the protagonist) as the old judge Hieronimo first struggles to discover the identity of his murderous enemies and is then baulked in his attempts to reach them. The effects of frustration on the psyche of the avenger are registered in terms of desperate but apparently fruitless appeals to higher powers and an emotional apprehension of the world as wholly corrupt and degenerate, leading to incipient madness. The avenger is opposed by cruel and cunning enemies, who must be out-witted before they can be destroyed in a satisfyingly bloody and elaborate way. Kyd further delighted his audience by creating ironic situations and episodes of sudden and extreme violence brought about by complex cross-plotting (both in the sense of counter-intrigues and the interlacing of separate revenge stories). Finally, he developed the intellectual aspect of the revenge theme through his characters' eloquent speculations about human and divine justice and the ethics of revenge.

Marlowe used the revenge theme more insistently in tragedies other than *Doctor Faustus* – notably in his bleakly comic play *The Jew of Malta* – but in *Doctor Faustus* the audience is aware from the start of the play of the slow gathering of divine retribution. The author of *The Revenger's Tragedy* exploits both the satiric possibilities of the theme in powerful monologues expressing Vindice's Hamlet-like melancholy and disgust at the corruption and mortality he sees all around him, and exciting narrative effects such as the biter–bitten pattern, deriving these from braided revenge plots springing out of two major crimes, the poisoning of Vindice's lover Gloriana and the rape of Antonio's wife.

In Middleton and Rowley's *The Changeling*, the traditional iconic figures of revenge are marginalised. Tomazo, Piracquo's avenging brother, does not arrive on stage until Act Five, Scene Two, with little opportunity to display his by now conventional profession of loss of all relish for the benefits of life; it is only in the very last scene of the play that Beatrice-Joanna's confession of her responsibility for the murder of Piracquo draws from her deceived husband Alsemero the kind of horror-stricken utterance which rings throughout *The Spanish Tragedy*:

> O, the place itself e'er since
> Has been crying for vengeance: the temple
> Where blood and beauty first unlawfully
> Fired their devotion, and quenched the right one.
>   (5.3.72–5)

But the two dramatists have chosen to internalise the experience of retribution. It is Beatrice-Joanna's punishment to become 'the deed's creature'; in the arms of De Flores, as she recognises, 'Vengeance begins;/Murder is followed by more sins.' And at the close of the play it is not in the grip of stage demons or the spectre of Revenge but in the imagination of those left behind that her soul and that of her lover, transformed into 'black fugitives', are hurried away 'to take a second vengeance'.

Webster, too, chooses to delay the onset of revenge, allowing for two successive waves of retribution and placing the dark crime which initiates the second wave of retribution as late as the fourth act of his tragedy. First, the Cardinal and his brother fall upon their sister, after a long delay supposedly required to discover the identity of her lover Antonio. Having destroyed his sister, Ferdinand seeks to hunt down Antonio, feeding 'a fire great as my revenge,/Which ne'er will slack, till it have spent his fuel'. In a sequential counter-movement, the chief murderers are finally destroyed, but through a confused sequence of intentional plotting and accidental events which also take the lives of Antonio and Bosola. The dying Bosola may see his killing of Ferdinand as the perfection of his revenge on the main cause of his undoing, but Webster's world is one in which the powers of good and evil are almost equally balanced and retribution brings no satisfying triumphs for justice. In his friend John Ford's play *'Tis Pity She's a Whore*, revenge-taking has become simply the normal response of passionate men and women in a society corrupt and lawless under its surface conventionalities; when Giovanni adopts the behaviour of the revenger he characteristically outgoes all others in the ritual cruelty of his actions and signifies his fall from fervent idealism to common corruption. Only his victimised sister, like the Duchess of Malfi, is left to claim the audience's pity.

In all of these tragedies Nemesis strikes at the lives of the characters, often brought down by their own or others' deliberate schemes of revenge. But in a way typical of tragedy, catastrophe is both explicable in terms of willed human action and incomprehensible in its apparently random invasion of human life. In these tragedies, revenge stories are the dramatists' principal means of dramatising the grand and universal theme of tragedy, the ancient mystery of evil, suffering and violent death.

Public and Private Playhouses

The plays in this anthology are all closely connected with the commercial theatre scene in London; they were written by authors who for the most part lived and worked in London, performed by resident London companies and printed for London publishers.

More is known about the London theatres than about other theatrical venues outside the capital, but it should be remembered that many of the plays were also toured to provincial towns or given private performances in great country houses by travelling companies of actors; they were given command performances at court, they were acted by schoolboys and later by professional companies of young actors (known as 'Children'); they were staged by students at the universities of Oxford and Cambridge or the Inns of Court in London where lawyers were educated for their profession, and were sometimes taken to Europe by roving English companies.

In so many and such different locations, performance conditions might ranging from a makeshift stage on trestles in the courtyard of an inn or the floor-space of the large communal hall of a country house or university college to the arena of a public amphitheatre also used for bull or bear-baiting, or the specially constructed stage with its tiered seating in the Banqueting Hall in the palace at Whitehall. As they have always done, actors worked with whatever conditions they could find, and in his study of the much-performed *Spanish Tragedy*, D. F. Rowan usefully points out that 'some productions . . . must have been mounted on the barest of scaffolds with perhaps only a traverse [curtain] at the back, while others were presented on permanent stages with trapdoors, backed by a two- or three-door tiring house façade, and topped with an upper acting area' (*The Elizabethan Theatre V*, ed. G. R. Hibbard [Ontario, London and Basingstoke, 1975] p. 114).

The first three plays in this collection, *The Spanish Tragedy, Doctor Faustus* and *The Revenger's Tragedy*, were originally performed in large public playhouses capable of holding almost 3000 people; circular or octagonal buildings, open to the sky, with a yard audience of about 800 standing in the open, crowded round the stage. More expensive seated accommodation was available in the three tiers of roofed galleries ranged round the standing yard and accessed from it by steps; later playhouses allowed for independent admission to the galleries by means of stairwells above the entrance-ways. Divided from these galleries and across the façade above the stage were high-priced 'lords' rooms' which offered a degree of privacy and a cushioned seat or stool and were accessed through the players' changing rooms. Contemporary evidence suggests that playgoers paid one penny to enter the yard, a further penny to be admitted to the galleries, and a third penny for a good view from the upper galleries. The lords' rooms cost sixpence.

A large platform stage (sometimes edged with a low railing) jutted out into the yard, raised about four feet above the yard floor and occupying almost a third of the space. For tragedies, it may have been draped with black. The contract for the Fortune Theatre, built in 1600, and modelled on the Globe, specified a stage 43 feet wide and 27 feet deep (12.9 × 8.1 metres). A well-equipped stage had a trapdoor in the centre or towards the front of the stage, leading down to a notional hell below stage-level, or opening to allow actors or stage properties to rise into sight. On such a stage, surrounded on three sides by the standing audience, actors could establish a more immediate relationship with their audience than is possible on a stage separated from the auditorium by a proscenium arch; soliloquies and asides, frequent in Renaissance playtexts, show the dramatists and the actors exploiting the possibilities of such a relationship.

At the rear of the stage, facing the audience was the façade of the 'tiring-house' or actors' changing rooms. Two or three large doors led out onto the stage-space from this facade. At first-gallery level in the same façade, there was a gallery or balcony which could serve as an upper acting space or a place where musicians could play, or provide further seating for the wealthiest members of the audience. Earlier theatre historians argued for the general existence of an alcove or 'discovery space' at the centre of the façade, which could be closed off by a curtain (or 'traverse') or opened up as an inner stage area. The Globe certainly seems to have had such a shallow space for the display of static tableaux and other purposes, but a curtained booth with a rigid and firmly supported top set up between the two outer stage doors could serve equally well for such a purpose.

From above the highest gallery, covering and protecting the main stage from the weather, extended a canopy supported on two pillars; it was called 'the heavens', and its underside was painted with a sun, moon, stars, and possibly also the signs of the zodiac. Like the flies in a modern theatre, above it there was an enclosed space where sound and lighting effects could be produced, and from which properties like a heavenly throne could be winched down or the descent of a supernatural being safely managed.

The interior of the theatre was richly decorated and painted, but on stage there was a minimum of scenery and no attempt to create

the detailed and realistic impression of a room or exterior usual in
early modern theatres. Painted back-cloths or an arras could be
hung up, and if required a stage property such as a 'state' (a throne
set on a dais) could be quickly set out and removed again by
stage-hands. The theatre manager Philip Henslowe's 1598 inventory
of his stage-properties included a hell mouth, a 'dragon in fostes'
(that is, for use in *Doctor Faustus*), a City of Rome (perhaps a
back-cloth which, like 'a pope's mitre', might also have been used in
the play), a tomb, a bay tree, a wooden canopy, a little altar and
assorted foils. On a relatively bare and unlocalised stage, the
audience's attention and imaginative involvement could be focused
on the action rather than on the factitious lifelikeness of the set.
Night scenes could be signalled by the introduction of lanterns or
'lights' (flaming torches). Both are used, for instance, in *The Duchess
of Malfi*, and Hieronimo probably carried on a torch to signify the
discovery of his murdered son by night. Stage effects of a
spectacular kind were frequently introduced. In 1620, John Melton
describes a visit to the Fortune in Golding Lane to see the tragedy of
Doctor Faustus: 'There indeed a man may behold shag-haired devils
run roaring over the stage with squibs in their mouths, while
drummers make thunder in the tiring-house, and the twelve-penny
hirelings make artificial lightning in the heavens.'
   Performances usually began at 2 p.m. to take full advantage of
daylight – a practice followed also in the private indoors theatres –
and in the absence of curtains to mask off the whole stage from the
audience for a scene change, were continuous, allowing uninter-
rupted attention to the unfolding narrative. Not that the theatre
audience lacked distractions: food and drink was on sale throughout
the performance, tobacco smoking and noisy nut-cracking was
common, there were outbursts of laughter, applause or hissing, the
usual crowd noises, and disturbances occasioned by drunken behaviour or the activities of cutpurses (pickpockets) and prostitutes.
   On the English stage, only male actors were permitted to perform,
with boys or young men taking women's roles; in 1629 a visiting
troupe of French actresses were 'hissed, hooted, and pippin-pelted
from the stage' at the Blackfriars Theatre. Early actors caught and
held their large audiences' attention with oratorical gesturing,
full-voiced delivery, and stalking movements across the stage. The
famous Edward Alleyn, who played the roles of Faustus and
Tamburlaine, created an heroic gestural style of acting which
lingered in the most plebeian public theatres like the Fortune and

the Red Bull but was rapidly displaced among the leading public theatre companies as well as among those performing in the smaller and more sophisticated private playhouses by a more life-sized personation of individual character, particularly associated with Alleyn's famous contemporary, Richard Burbage, who played the roles of Hieronimo, Hamlet, Lear, and Ferdinand in Webster's *Duchess of Malfi*. The difference may be illustrated by a passage in a 1607 play describing an Alleyn-like 'stalking-stamping player, that will raise a tempest with his tongue, and thunder with his heels' compared with Thomas May's description in 1620 of Burbage's performance as Hieronimo in *The Spanish Tragedy*:

> I have seen the knave paint grief
> In such a lively colour, that for false
> And acted passion he has drawn true tears
> From the spectators. Ladies in the boxes
> Kept time with sighs and tears to his sad accents,
> As had he truly been the man he seemed.
>
> (*The Heir*, 1.1)

But the players also held the eye with splendid and exotic costuming (sometimes given or sold to the actors at second or third hand by noble patrons or their servants). In a 1598 inventory of costumes in Alleyn's hand, 'faustus Jerkin his clok' is listed along with a scarlet cloak laid down with silver lace and silver buttons, a black silk gown with red flush, a yellow silk gown, french hose of silver panes laced with carnation satins laced over with silver, and cloth of gold for a boy. Little attention was paid to historical or ethnic accuracy in costuming (though it is likely that in Hieronimo's play the participants wore Turkish bonnets), but performers often donned familiar vocational costumes, like a friar's 'gown of gray', a cardinal's scarlet gown, or a soldier's coat. Edward Alleyn, who played the part of Doctor Faustus, did so 'in a surplice, with a cross upon his breast'; the woodcut in the 1616 edition of the play shows a more conventional scholarly costume, resembling the 'crimson gown striped with gold faced with ermine' in Alleyn's 1598 inventory of costumes. The boy playing Isabella in *The Changeling*, for the scene in which she pretends to be a madwoman, wore the 'habit' (costume) of 'a wild unshapen antic' (4.3.116).

As early as 1576 a new type of commercial indoors theatre appeared in London, the first Blackfriars Theatre. It was followed in

1600 by the more famous second Blackfriars Theatre, acquired in 1609 by the King's Men as their winter home. Webster's *Duchess of Malfi* was played both there and at their public playhouse the Globe. *The Changeling* and *'Tis Pity She's a Whore* were performed in yet another private playhouse, the Cockpit or Phoenix Theatre in Drury Lane, opened in 1617.

These were much smaller theatres than the public playhouses, usually taking the rectangular shape of an enclosed hall, and seating 600–700 spectators. The Blackfriars Theatre stage occupied the full width of the south end of the hall, though with boxes or lords' rooms at stage level on each side of the stage reducing its dimensions to about 28 square feet (8.4 metres square). For two shillings, ten or so members of the audience could hire stools and sit on each side of the stage itself; boxes cost half-a-crown. On the floor of the hall were padded bench seats, the most expensive of them immediately in front of the stage. Along the sides of the hall and across the rear wall ran two or three galleries; the cheapest seats cost sixpence and were in the top rear gallery at the furthest distance from the stage.

Such theatres were for a select and wealthy clientele: merchants and wealthier citizens and their wives, fashionable young men ('gallants'), law students, courtiers and members of the nobility and their attendants. Performances were given in the afternoon, and were interrupted by the need to regularly trim the candles which lit the hall. It became customary to provide string and woodwind chamber music before the beginning of the performance and in between the acts; the Blackfriars musicians played from a music-room above the stage, which could also double as a small upper stage from which a complacent Giovanni could watch his sister Annabella resist Soranzo's courtship on the main stage below. The Cockpit had a small tiring-house façade gallery from which Lollio watched an amorous Antonio court a frosty Isabella, and where madmen made their appearance acting out their own fantasies (3.3). Like the public theatres, these playhouses were equipped with trapdoors, and the tiring-house façade commonly provided a central double-doored entrance flanked by single-door entrances. A 'heaven' with concealed machinery could be suspended above the stage without the use of supporting pillars. A booth construction, or a curtain across the central entrance could create a discovery space serving as a shop, a tomb, a cell, a study, a closet or a display space for tableaux and static displays. On the stage of the

Cockpit Theatre, Beatrice-Joanna was thrust into such an inner space with Alsemero's words 'Enter my closet;/I'll be your keeper yet' (*The Changeling*, 5.3 86–7).

While the smoke and din associated with the cannon and fireworks used in the open-air public theatres were inappropriate in the confined space of an interior theatre, stage properties and effects were used much as in the public theatres and could be even more elaborate, intended as they were for a more sophisticated audience. *The Duchess of Malfi*, performed in both public and private theatre venues, requires the discovery of an altar and shrine for the dumb-show in 3.4, life-sized effigies of Antonio and his children *'appearing as if they were dead'* (4.1) and a tomb marking the Duchess's grave (5.3) from which the voice of the dead woman speaks, echoing Antonio's words. It is possible that for this scene the King's Men used a property-tomb already employed in *The Second Maiden's Tragedy* (1611) which allowed for a noise like a wind, clattering doors, the sudden opening of the tombstone and a great light appearing in the midst of the tomb to reveal 'his lady . . . standing just before him all in white, stuck with jewels, and a great crucifix on her breast'.

Note on the Texts

This anthology is intended for use by undergraduate students of English Renaissance drama, general readers and theatre practitioners rather than by scholars and research students needing access to exhaustive historical, bibliographical and textual information. Accordingly, the six play texts collected in this anthology are presented for reading with a minimum of editorial and explanatory intervention. Square brackets are used in the texts to indicate substantive emendation or addition; the existence of explanatory notes is signalled within the texts by a superscript circle (°); the notes themselves are supplied at the end of each text.

In each instance I have selected as copytext a representative of the first (and usually unique) authoritative edition; the accretions and unauthorised changes made during the working life of the companies which performed the plays are not recorded, with the exception of two major and representative examples from *The Spanish Tragedy* and *Doctor Faustus* (see Appendix I and II). In editing the texts, I have consulted the most recent textual scholarship, in particular the editions listed in the introductory notes to each play, but I do not record textual variants between individual copies of the plays (quartos) or between successive editions; nor in general do I record the history of and authority for necessary and substantive corrections made to the original texts. These may be conveniently studied in the textual collations provided in the Revels editions of the six plays concerned here, or in the very full collations supplied in such new standard collected editions as the Clarendon Press Marlowe (1987–) or the Cambridge Webster (1995–).

With the exception of the prefatory material appearing with two plays, *The Duchess of Malfi* (1623) and *'Tis Pity She's a Whore* (1633), the complete texts of the original quarto editions are given in this anthology. Webster's and Ford's tragedies were equipped with prose dedications by their authors to potential or actual aristocratic patrons, and with commendatory poems by friends and supporters. Webster addressed his tragedy to George Harding, the thirteenth Baron Berkeley (1601–58), whose maternal grandfather and father had been patrons of the Lord Chamberlain's Men, the company taken under the patronage of King James in 1603 as the King's Men, and the players who first performed his tragedy. Ford dedicated his play to John Mordaunt (*c*.1599–1643), who had recently been created first Earl of Peterborough (1628) and from the dedication seems to have given particular but unknown favours to the dramatist. Webster's poetic supporters were Thomas Middleton, William Rowley and John Ford, with all of whom at various times Webster worked on team-written plays, a common practice in the theatre industry then as now. Little is known of Thomas Ellice, Ford's single admirer, other than that he was the brother of an Inns of Court man who shared the dedication of another of Ford's plays, *The Lover's Melancholy* (1629).

The play-texts are presented in a normalised and modernised form. That is, standardised layout, font and print conventions in the use of italics and capitals for act and scene indications, speech headings and scene directions have been imposed on the variety of practices in the original texts. Act and scene directions are given a standard form (as, Act One, Scene One) and editorial intervention to mark new scene divisions following standard modern practice is not noted in the Commentary. All original asides are printed in italics within curved brackets; asides added by the editor are distinguished by square brackets. The various forms of past participles in these texts are reduced to *-ed* or *-èd*; the first is not pronounced as an extra syllable, the second is.

A number of other changes are made silently. Spellings are modernised (*burthen* becomes *burden*, *ile* becomes *I'll*), and names are given a consistent and usual modern-spelling form, both to avoid what Gāmini Salgādo calls a bogus 'archaism' in the reader's response and to regularise different spelling practices among authors and printing-house compositors. (For instance, the various spellings of the name of Doctor Faustus's familiar spirit are reduced to Mephostophilis.)

The frequent seventeenth-century practice of introducing capital letters to mark an emphasis or signal a grammatical form is replaced by modern print conventions. Wherever possible, the original punctuation of the dialogue is retained since it may preserve valuable indications of how the actor was meant to deliver the lines, as well as providing grammatical indicators. However, Elizabethan and Jacobean punctuation can be erratic or obscure to modern readers and actors, and in many cases it reflects the inconsistent practice of printers rather than that of the author. Accordingly, punctuation is silently modernised where the original pointing of the texts is plainly deficient or misleading.

Where they are missing in the original text (and no Renaissance publisher thought it necessary to supply a full record of contemporary stage practice), necessary or implied stage directions are supplied in square brackets, and although such familiar Latin directions as *Exit* and *Exeunt omnes* ('the stage is cleared of all actors') are retained, more elaborate or unfamiliar Latin directions are translated into English. Passages in a language other than English are retained in the body of the text, but a translation is supplied in the notes on the play.

The general intention is provide readers, performers and playgoers with readily accessible texts, accompanied with sufficient information to create, in John Webster's words, in the dedication of his first great tragedy, *The White Devil* (1612) 'that which is the only grace and setting out of a tragedy, a full and understanding auditory'.

The Spanish Tragedy

THOMAS KYD

INTRODUCTORY NOTE

Authorship, date of composition and stage history

No manuscript of *The Spanish Tragedy* has survived, its author went
unnamed in printed editions during the sixteenth and seventeenth
centuries, and although Thomas Heywood in his *Apology for Actors*
(1612) had attributed it to 'M. Kid', until 1773 the play was taken to
be by an unknown author. It is now accepted that *The Spanish
Tragedy* was written about 1590 by Thomas Kyd (1558–94); a more
precise date of composition has not yet been established. From at
least 1592 to 1597 it was performed with great success by an
amalgamated company of Lord Strange's Men and the Admiral's
Men at the Rose Theatre, on the Bankside, London. Twenty-nine
performances during those years are recorded in the diary of the
Elizabethan theatre manager Philip Henslowe; the title-page of the
first known edition (1592) suggests that the play's appeal lay in 'the
lamentable end of Don Horatio and Bel-Imperia: with the pitiful
death of old Hieronimo'. It is likely that the Admiral's Men and their
successors continued to play the tragedy at their theatre, the
Fortune, until at least 1615, and possibly until the closing of the
theatres in 1642. Other companies may have presented the play at
several other London theatres, including the first Globe Theatre.
There were European performances well into the seventeenth
century, and the ten editions published in England before 1640, as
well as a rich literary tradition of references and parodies of the
tragedy, establish its status as an early stage triumph. Modern

1

performances began with revivals by university dramatic societies in 1921 and 1931, but the play's potential impact in the theatre was not fully realised until three professional productions, at the Mercury Theatre, London (1973), the Citizens' Theatre, Glasgow (1978), and the National (Cottesloe) Theatre, London (1982), demonstrated its enduring power to shock and astonish modern audiences.

Text

The first extant edition of the tragedy was printed by Edward Allde for the publisher Edward White in 1592. Apart from some corrupt passages in the later scenes of the play, perhaps carried over from a now lost unauthorised and defective edition, the text is a relatively sound one, probably based on Kyd's own manuscript, since there is little sign of preparation for practical use in the theatre. The title-page describes 1592 as 'Newly corrected and amended of such gross faults as passed in the first impression'. All subsequent editions, including the present one, are based on the one surviving copy of 1592, now in the British Library. A second important early edition of Kyd's tragedy was printed by William White for Thomas Pavier in 1602, 'Newly corrected, amended and enlarged, with new additions of the Painter's part, and others, as it hath of late been divers times acted'. Five passages, amounting to some 320 lines, are added to the original text. Since none of this material can be Kyd's work or part of the original conception of the play, these additions are excluded from the present text, but one remarkable scene (the so-called 'Painter' scene, inserted between 3.12 and 3.13) is printed as Appendix I, to illustrate the familiar theatre practice of revising an older text to attract new audiences. Ben Jonson was paid for additional script material for *The Spanish Tragedy*, but his contributions to the working development of the text have not survived: the author of the additions remains unidentified.

Sources

No major source for the tragedy has so far been discovered. The inset play of Soliman and Perseda (4.4) appears to be based on a story in Henry Wotton's *A Courtly Controversy of Cupid's Cautels* (1578), a translation of tales by Jacqes Yver; parallels have been noted between Lorenzo's treatment of his agent Pedringano and the

Earl of Leicester's manner of removing one of his criminal accomplices, while pretending to act as his protector. There is a general debt to the tragedies of the classsical writer Seneca. But in our current state of knowledge it is impossible to tell whether Kyd himself invented the braided revenge plots which constitute his tragedy or worked up his script from some as yet unknown historical or fictional source.

Further reading

A facsimile edition of the 1592 copy of *The Spanish Tragedy* is published by the Scolar Press (Menston, 1966). The fullest single-volume edition of *The Spanish Tragedy* is in the Revels series, edited by Philip Edwards (London, 1959). Other scholarly editions are provided by Andrew S. Cairncross in the Regents Renaissance Drama Series (London, 1967) and J. R. Mulryne, in the New Mermaid Series (London and New York, 1989); the tragedy is also included in the volume *Minor Elizabethan Tragedies*, edited by T. W. Craik (London, 1974). The little that is known about Kyd's life is assembled by Arthur Freeman, *Thomas Kyd: Facts and Problems* (Oxford, 1967); see also Peter B. Murray's *Thomas Kyd* (New York, 1970). D. F. Rowan discusses the original staging of *The Spanish Tragedy*, in *The Elizabethan Theatre V*, edited by G. R. Hibbard (London and Basingstoke, 1975). The theatrical impact of the 1978 Robert David MacDonald Glasgow production and the 1982 Michael Bogdanov National (Cottesloe) Theatre production is discussed by Michael Hattaway in *Elizabethan Popular Theatre: Plays in Performance* (London, 1982) and Tony Howard, 'Renaissance Drama Productions', *Research Opportunities in Renaissance Drama*, 21 (1978), and 26 (1983). See also Emrys Jones's extensive review of the 1982 National Theatre production, 'Stage-managing Revenge' in the *Times Literary Supplement* October 15 (1982), and Frank R. Ardolino's *Thomas Kyd's Mystery Play: Myth and Ritual in 'The Spanish Tragedy'* (New York, 1985).

Dramatis Personae

GHOST OF ANDREA
REVENGE

KING OF SPAIN
CYPRIAN, DUKE OF CASTILLE, *his brother*
LORENZO, *the Duke's son*   5
BEL-IMPERIA, *Lorenzo's sister*
GENERAL *of the Spanish Army*

VICEROY OF PORTUGAL
PEDRO, *his brother*
BALTHAZAR, *his son*   10
ALEXANDRO } *Portuguese noblemen*
VILLUPPO°
AMBASSADOR *of Portugal to the Spanish court*

HIERONIMO, *Knight Marshal of Spain*
ISABELLA, *his wife*   15
HORATIO, *their son*

PEDRINGANO, *servant to* BEL-IMPERIA
SERBERINE, *servant to Belthazar*
CHRISTOPHIL,° *servant to Lorenzo*
BAZULTO, *an old man*   20

Page *to Lorenzo*, Three Watchmen, Messenger, Deputy, Hangman, Maid *to Isabella*, Two Portuguese, Servant, Three Citizens.
Portuguese Nobles, Soldiers, Officers, Attendants, Halberdiers.°

Three Knights, Three Kings, a Drummer *in the Dumb-show.*°
Hymen,° Two Torch-bearers *in the second Dumb-show.*   25

In HIERONIMO'S play:
SOLIMAN,° *Sultan of Turkey* (BALTHAZAR)
ERASTO ('Erastus'),° *Knight of Rhodes* (LORENZO)
BASHAW° (HIERONIMO)
PERSEDA (BEL-IMPERIA)   30

In the Additions:
PEDRO   } *Hieronimo's servants*
JACQUES
BAZARDO, *a Painter*

Act One, Scene One

Enter the Ghost of ANDREA, *and with him* REVENGE.

ANDREA: When this eternal substance of my soul
    Did live imprisoned in my wanton flesh,
    Each in their function serving other's need,
    I was a courtier in the Spanish court.
    My name was Don Andrea, my descent,   5
    Though not ignoble, yet inferior far
    To gracious° fortunes of my tender youth:
    For there in prime and pride° of all my years,
    By duteous service and deserving love,
    In secret I possessed° a worthy dame,°   10
    Which hight° sweet Bel-imperia by name.
    But in the harvest of my summer joys
    Death's winter nipped° the blossoms of my bliss,
    Forcing divorce betwixt my love and me.
    For in the late conflict with Portingale°   15
    My valour drew me into danger's mouth,
    Till life to death made passage through my wounds.
    When I was slain, my soul descended straight
    To pass the flowing stream of Acheron:°
    But churlish Charon, only boatman there,   20
    Said that my rites of burial not performed,
    I might not sit amongst his passengers.
    Ere Sol° had slept three nights in Thetis's° lap
    And slaked° his smoking chariot in her flood,°
    By Don Horatio, our Knight Marshal's° son,   25
    My funerals and obsequies were done.
    Then was the ferryman of hell content
    To pass me over to the slimy strond°
    That leads to fell° Avernus' ugly waves.
    There, pleasing Cerberus° with honeyed speech,   30
    I passed the perils of the foremost porch.°
    Not far from hence, amidst ten thousand souls,
    Sat Minos, Aeacus, and Rhadamanth,°
    To whom no sooner 'gan I make approach,
    To crave a passport° for my wandering ghost,   35
    But Minos, in graven leaves of lottery,°
    Drew forth the manner of my life and death.
    'This knight', quoth he, 'both lived and died in love,
    And for his love tried fortune of the wars,
    And by war's fortune lost both love and life.'   40
    'Why then,' said Aeacus, 'convey him hence,

To walk with lovers in our fields of love,
And spend the course of everlasting time
Under the green myrtle trees and cypress shades.'°
'No, no,' said Rhadamanth, 'it were not well   45
With loving souls to place a martialist.°
He died in war, and must to martial fields,
Where wounded Hector lives in lasting pain,
And Achilles' Myrmidons do scour the plain.'°
The Minos, mildest censor° of the three,   50
Made this device to end the difference:
'Send him,' quoth he, 'to our infernal° king,
To doom° him as best seems his majesty.'
To this effect my passport straight was drawn.
In keeping on my way to Pluto's° court,   55
Through dreadful shades of ever-glooming° night,
I saw more sights than thousand tongues can tell,
Or pens can write, or mortal hearts can think.
Three ways there were: that on the right-hand side
Was ready way unto the foresaid fields   60
Where lovers live and bloody martialists,
But either sort contained within his° bounds.
The left hand path, declining° fearfully,
Was ready downfall° to the deepest hell,
Where bloody Furies° shake their whips of steel,   65
And poor Ixion° turns an endless wheel;
Where usurers° are choked with melting gold,
And wantons are embraced with ugly snakes,
And murderers groan with never-killing wounds,
And perjured wights° scalded in boiling lead,   70
And all foul sins with torments overwhelmed.
'Twixt these two ways I trod the middle path,
Which brought me to the fair Elysian green,°
In midst whereof there stands a stately tower,
The walls of brass, the gates of adamant.°   75
Here finding Pluto with his Proserpine,°
I showed my passport, humbled on my knee;
Whereat fair Proserpine began to smile,
And begged that only she might give my doom.°
Pluto was pleased, and sealed it with a kiss.   80
Forthwith, Revenge, she rounded° thee in th'ear,
And bade thee lead me through the gates of horn,°
Where dreams have passage in the silent night.
No sooner had she spoke but we were here,
I wot° not how, in twinkling of an eye.   85
REVENGE: Then know, Andrea, that thou art arrived

Where thou shalt see the author of thy death,
Don Balthazar, the prince of Portingale,
Deprived of life by Bel-imperia.
Here sit we down° to see the mystery,°   90
And serve for Chorus in this tragedy.

Act One, Scene Two

Enter SPANISH KING, GENERAL, CASTILE, HIERONIMO.

KING: Now say, Lord General, how fares our camp?°
GENERAL: All well, my sovereign liege, except some few
    That are deceased by fortune of the war.
KING: But what portends thy cheerful countenance,
    And posting° to our presence thus in haste?   5
    Speak, man, hath Fortune given us victory?
GENERAL: Victory, my liege, and that with little loss.
KING: Our Portingals° will pay us tribute° then?
GENERAL: Tribute and wonted° homage therewithal.
KING: Then blest be heaven, and guider of the heavens,   10
    From whose fair influence such justice flows.
CASTILE: *O multum dilecte Deo, tibi militat aether,*
    Et conjuratae curvato poplite gentes
    Succumbunt: recti soror est victoria juris.°
KING: Thanks to my loving brother of Castile.   15
    But, General, unfold in brief discourse
    Your form of battle and your war's success,
    That adding all the pleasure of thy news
    Unto the height of former happiness,
    With deeper wage° and greater dignity°   20
    We may reward thy blissful chivalry.°
GENERAL: Where Spain and Portingale do jointly knit
    Their frontiers, leaning on each other's bound,°
    There met our armies in their proud array:
    Both furnished° well, both full of hope and fear,   25
    Both menacing alike with daring shows,
    Both vaunting sundry colours of device,°
    Both cheerly sounding trumpets, drums and fifes,
    Both raising dreadful° clamours to the sky,
    That valleys, hills, and rivers made rebound,   30
    And heaven itself was frightened with the sound.
    Our battles° both were pitched in squadron form,°
    Each corner strongly fenced° with wings of shot;°
    But ere we joined and came to push of pike,°

I brought a squadron of our readiest° shot   35
From out our rearward to begin the fight:
They brought another wing to encounter us.
Meanwhile, our ordnance° played° on either side,
And captains strove to have their valours tried.
Don Pedro, their chief horsemen's colonel,°   40
Did with his cornet° bravely make attempt
To break the order of our battle ranks:
But Don Rogero, worthy man of war,
Marched forth against him with our musketeers,
And stopped the malice of his fell approach.   45
While they maintain hot skirmish to and fro,
Both battles join and fall to handy° blows,
Their violent shot° resembling th'ocean's rage
When, roaring loud, and with a swelling tide,
It beats upon the rampiers° of huge rocks,   50
And gapes to swallow neighbour-bounding° lands.
Now while Bellona° rageth here and there,
Thick storms of bullets rain like winter's hail,
And shivered° lances dark° the troubled air.
   Pede pes et cuspide cuspis;   55
   Arma sonant armis, vir petiturque viro.°
On every side drop captains to the ground,
And soldiers, some ill-maimed,° some slain outright.
Here falls a body scindered° from his head,
There legs and arms lie bleeding on the grass,   60
Mingled with weapons and unbowellèd° steeds,
That scattering overspread the purple° plain.
In all this turmoil, three long hours and more,
The victory to neither part inclined,
Till Don Andrea with his brave lanciers°   65
In their main battle made so great a breach
That, half dismayed, the multitude retired:
But Balthazar, the Portingales' young prince,
Brought rescue, and encouraged them to stay.
Here-hence° the fight was eagerly renewed,   70
And in that conflict was Andrea slain —
Brave man at arms, but weak to Balthazar.
Yet while the prince, insulting° over him,
Breathed out proud vaunts, sounding° to our reproach,
Friendship and hardy° valour joined in one,   75
Pricked° forth Horatio, our Knight Marshal's son,
To challenge forth that prince in single fight.
Not long between these twain the fight endured,
But straight the prince was beaten from his horse,

And forced to yield him° prisoner to his foe.   80
When he was taken, all the rest they fled,
And our carbines° pursued them to the death,
Till, Phoebus° waning to the western deep,°
Our trumpeters were charged° to sound retreat.
KING: Thanks, good Lord General, for these good news;   85
    And for some argument° of more to come,
    Take this and wear it for thy sovereign's sake.   *Give[s] him his chain.*
    But tell me now, hast thou confirmed a peace?
GENERAL: No peace, my liege, but peace conditional,
    That if with homage tribute be well paid,   90
    The fury of your forces will be stayed:°
    And to this peace their viceroy hath subscribed,°
                             Give[s] the KING *a paper.*
    And made a solemn vow that, during life,
    His tribute shall be paid truly to Spain.
KING: These words, these deeds, become thy person well.   95
    But now, Knight Marshal, frolic° with thy king,
    For 'tis thy son that wins this battle's prize.
HIERONIMO: Long may he live to serve my sovereign liege,
    And soon decay° unless he serve my liege.   *A tucket° afar off.*
KING: Nor thou, nor he, shall die without reward.   100
    What means the warning of this trumpet's sound?
GENERAL:
    This tells me that your grace's men of war,
    Such as war's fortune hath reserved from death,
    Come marching on towards your royal seat,°
    To show themselves before your majesty,   105
    For so I gave in charge at my depart.
    Whereby by demonstration shall appear
    That all (except three hundred or few more)
    Are safe returned and by their foes enriched.

The Army enters; BALTHAZAR, *between* LORENZO *and* HORATIO,
captive.

KING: A gladsome sight! I long to see them here.   110

They enter and pass by.

    Was that the warlike prince of Portingale,
    That by our nephew was in triumph led?
GENERAL: It was, my liege, the prince of Portingale.
KING: But what was he that on the other side

Held him by th'arm as partner of the prize?   115
HIERONIMO: That was my son, my gracious sovereign,
    Of whom, though from his tender infancy
    My loving thoughts did never hope but well,
    He never pleased his father's eyes till now,
    Nor filled my heart with overcloying° joys.   120
KING: Go let them march once more about these walls,
    That staying° them we may confer and talk
    With our brave prisoner and his double guard.
    Hieronimo, it greatly pleaseth us,
    That in our victory thou have a share,   125
    By virtue of thy worthy son's exploit.

Enter [the Army] again.

Bring hither the young prince of Portingale.
The rest march on, but ere they be dismissed,
We will bestow on every soldier
Two ducats, and on every leader ten,   130
That they may know our largess° welcomes them.
        Exeunt all [the Army] but BALTHAZAR, LORENZO, HORATIO.
Welcome, Don Balthazar, welcome, nephew,
And thou, Horatio, thou art welcome too.
Young prince, although thy father's hard° misdeeds
In keeping back the tribute that he owes   135
Deserve but evil measure at our hands,
Yet shalt thou know that Spain is honourable.
BALTHAZAR: The trespass that my father made in peace
    Is now controlled° by fortune of the wars;
    And cards once dealt, it boots° not ask why so.   140
    His men are slain, a weakening to his realm,
    His colours° seized, a blot unto his name,
    His son distressed,° a corsive° to his heart:
    Those punishments may clear his late° offence.
KING: Ay, Balthazar, if he observe this truce,   145
    Our peace will grow the stronger for these wars.
    Meanwhile live thou, though not in liberty,
    Yet free from bearing any servile yoke;
    For in our hearing thy deserts were great,
    And in our sight thyself art gracious.   150
BALTHAZAR: And I shall study to deserve this grace.
KING: But tell me, for their holding° makes me doubt,
    To which of these twain art thou prisoner?
LORENZO: To me, my liege
HORATIO: To me, my sovereign.

LORENZO: This hand first took his courser by the reins.　　　155
HORATIO: But first my lance did put him from his horse.
LORENZO: I seized his weapon, and enjoyed it first.
HORATIO: But first I forced him lay his weapons down.
KING: Let go his arm, upon our privilege.°　　　[*They*] *let him go.*
　　　Say, worthy prince, to whether° didst thou yield?　　160
BALTHAZAR: To him in courtesy, to this perforce:
　　　He spake me fair, this other gave me strokes;
　　　He promised life, this other threatened death;
　　　He wan° my love, this other conquered me;
　　　And truth to say I yield myself to both.　　　165
HIERONIMO: But that I know your Grace for just and wise,
　　　And might seem partial in the difference,°
　　　Enforced by nature and by law of arms
　　　My tongue should plead for young Horatio's right.
　　　He hunted well that was a lion's death,　　　170
　　　Not he that in a garment wore his skin:
　　　So hares may pull dead lions by the beard.
KING: Content thee, Marshal, thou shalt have no wrong,
　　　And for thy sake thy son shall want° no right.
　　　Will both abide the censure of my doom?°　　　175
LORENZO: I crave no better than your Grace awards.
HORATIO: Nor I, although I sit beside° my right.
KING: Then by my judgement thus your strife shall end:
　　　You both deserve, and both shall have reward.
　　　Nephew, thou took'st his weapon and his horse,　　180
　　　His weapons and his horse are thy reward.
　　　Horatio, thou didst force him first to yield,
　　　His ransom therefore is thy valour's fee:
　　　Appoint the sum as you shall both agree.
　　　But nephew, thou shalt have the prince in guard,　　185
　　　For thine estate best fitteth such a guest:
　　　Horatio's house were small for all his train.°
　　　Yet in regard thy substance° passeth his,
　　　And that just guerdon° may befall desert,
　　　To him° we yield the armour of the prince.　　　190
　　　How likes Don Balthazar of this device?°
BALTHAZAR: Right well my liege, if proviso were,
　　　That Don Horatio bear us company,
　　　Whom I admire and love for chivalry.
KING: Horatio, leave him not that loves thee so.　　　195
　　　Now let us hence to see our soldiers paid,
　　　And feast our prisoner as our friendly guest.　　　*Exeunt.*

Act One, Scene Three

Enter VICEROY, ALEXANDRO, VILLUPPO [, Attendants].

VICEROY: Is our ambassador despatched for Spain?
ALEXANDRO: Two days, my liege, are passed since his depart.
VICEROY: And tribute payment gone along with him?
ALEXANDRO: Ay, my good lord.
VICEROY: Then rest we here awhile in our unrest,   5
    And feed our sorrows with some inward sighs,
    For deepest cares break never into tears.
    But wherefore sit I in a regal throne?
    This better fits a wretch's endless moan.   *Falls to the ground.*
    Yet this is higher than my fortunes reach,   10
    And therefore better than my state° deserves.
    Ay, ay, this earth, image of melancholy,°
    Seeks him whom fates adjudge to misery:
    Here let me lie, now am I at the lowest.
    Qui jacet in terra, non habet unde cadat.   15
    In me consumpit vires fortuna nocendo,
    Nil superest ut iam possit obesse magis.°
    Yes, Fortune may bereave me of my crown —
    Here, take it now.° Let Fortune do her worst,
    She will not rob me of this sable weed:°   20
    O no, she envies none but pleasant things.
    Such is the folly of despiteful° chance!
    Fortune is blind and sees not my deserts,
    So is she deaf and hears not my laments:
    And could she hear, yet is she wilful mad,°   25
    And therefore will not pity my distress.
    Suppose that she could pity me, what then?
    What help can be expected at her hands,
    Whose foot is standing on a rolling stone,°
    And mind more mutable than fickle winds?   30
    Why wail I then, where's hope of no redress?
    O yes, complaining° makes my grief seem less.
    My late ambition hath distained° my faith,
    My breach of faith occasioned bloody wars,
    Those bloody wars have spent my treasure,°   35
    And with my treasure° my people's blood,
    And with their blood, my joy and best beloved,
    My best beloved, my sweet and only son.
    O wherefore went I not to war myself?
    The cause was mine, I might have died for both: 40

My years were mellow, his but young and green,
   My death were natural, but his was forced.°
ALEXANDRO: No doubt, my liege, but still the prince survives.
VICEROY: Survives! ay, where?
ALEXANDRO: In Spain, a prisoner by mischance of war.   45
VICEROY: Then they have slain him for his father's fault.°
ALEXANDRO: That were a breach to common law of arms.
VICEROY: They reck° no laws that meditate revenge.
ALEXANDRO: His ransom's worth will stay from foul revenge.
VICEROY: No, if he lived the news would soon be here.   50
ALEXANDRO: Nay, evil news fly faster still° than good.
VICEROY: Tell me no more of news, for he is dead.
VILLUPPO: My sovereign, pardon the author of ill news,
   And I'll bewray° the fortune of thy son.
VICEROY: Speak on, I'll guerdon thee whate'er it be: 55
   Mine ear is ready to receive ill news,
   My heart grown hard 'gainst mischief's° battery.
   Stand up, I say, and tell thy tale at large.°
VILLUPPO: Then hear that truth which these mine eyes have seen.
   When both the armies were in battle joined,   60
   Don Balthazar, amidst the thickest troops,
   To win renown did wondrous feats of arms.
   Amongst the rest I saw him hand to hand
   In single fight with their Lord General;
   Till Alexandro, that here counterfeits°   65
   Under the colour of a duteous friend,
   Discharged his pistol at the prince's back,
   As though he would have slain their general.
   But therewithal Don Balthazar fell down,
   And when he fell, then we began to fly: 70
   But had he lived, the day had sure been ours.
ALEXANDRO: O wicked forgery!° O traitorous miscreant!°
VICEROY: Hold thou thy peace! But now, Villuppo, say,
   Where then became° the carcase of my son?
VILLUPPO: I saw them drag it to the Spanish tents.   75
VICEROY: Ay, ay, my nightly dreams have told me this.
   Thou false, unkind, unthankful, traitorous beast,
   Wherein had Balthazar offended thee,
   That thou shouldst thus betray him to our foes?
   Was't Spanish gold that blearèd° so thine eyes   80
   That thou couldst see no part of our deserts?
   Perchance because thou art Terceira's° lord,
   Thou hadst some hope to wear this diadem,
   If first my son and then myself were slain:
   But thy ambitious thought shall break thy neck.   85

Ay, this was it that made thee spill his blood,
                    Take[s] the crown and put[s] it on again.
But I'll now wear it till thy blood be spilt.
ALEXANDRO: Vouchsafe, dread sovereign, to hear me speak.
VICEROY: Away with him, his sight is second hell;
   Keep him till we determine of° his death.   90
                    [*Exeunt* Attendants *with* ALEXANDRO.]
If Balthazar be dead, he shall not live.
Villuppo, follow us for thy reward.   *Exit* VICEROY.
VILLUPPO: Thus have I with an envious,° forgèd tale
   Deceived the king, betrayed mine enemy,
   And hope for guerdon° of my villainy.   *Exit.* 95

Act One, Scene Four

Enter HORATIO *and* BEL-IMPERIA.

BEL-IMPERIA: Signior Horatio, this is the place and hour
   Wherein I must entreat thee to relate
   The circumstance of Don Andrea's death,
   Who, living, was my garland's sweetest flower,
   And in his death hath buried my delights.   5
HORATIO: For love of him and service to yourself,
   I nill° refuse this heavy doleful charge.
   Yet tears and sighs I fear will hinder me.
   When both our armies were enjoined in fight,
   Your worthy chevalier° amidst the thick'st,   10
   For glorious cause still aiming at the fairest,°
   Was at the last by young Don Balthazar
   Encountered hand to hand: their fight was long,
   Their hearts were great, their clamours menacing,
   Their strength alike, their strokes both dangerous.   15
   But wrathful Nemesis,° that wicked power,
   Envying at° Andrea's praise and worth,
   Cut short his life, to end his praise and worth.
   She, she herself, disguised in armour's mask
   (As Pallas° was before proud Pergamus),°   20
   Brought in a fresh supply of halberdiers,
   Which paunched° his horse, and dinged° him to the ground.
   Then young Don Balthazar with ruthless rage,
   Taking advantage of his foe's distress,
   Did finish what his halberdiers begun,   25
   And left not till Andrea's life was done.

Then, though too late, incensed with just remorse,°
I with my band set forth against the prince,
And brought him prisoner from his halberdiers.
BEL-IMPERIA: Would thou hadst slain him that so slew my love! 30
But then was Don Andrea's carcase lost?
HORATIO: No, that was it for which I chiefly strove,
Nor stepped I back till I recovered him.
I took him up, and wound° him in mine arms,
And welding° him unto my private tent, 35
There laid him down, and dewed him with my tears,
And sighed and sorrowed as became a friend.
But neither friendly sorrow, sighs nor tears,
Could win pale Death from his usurpèd right.°
Yet this I did, and less I could not do: 40
I saw him honoured with due funeral.
This scarf° I plucked from off his lifeless arm,
And wear it in remembrance of my friend.
BEL-IMPERIA: I know the scarf, would he had kept it still,
For had he lived he would have kept it still, 45
And worn it for his Bel-imperia's sake:
For 'twas my favour at his last depart.
But now wear thou it both for him and me,
For after him thou hast deserved it best.
But, for thy kindness in his life and death, 50
Be sure while Bel-imperia's life endures,
She will be Don Horatio's thankful friend.
HORATIO: And, madam, Don Horatio will not slack
Humbly to serve fair Bel-imperia.
But now, if your good liking stand thereto,° 55
I'll crave your pardon to go seek the prince,
For so the duke your father gave me charge. *Exit.*
BEL-IMPERIA: Ay, go Horatio, leave me here alone,
For solitude best fits my cheerless mood.
Yet what avails to wail Andrea's death, 60
From whence Horatio proves my second love?
Had he not loved Andrea as he did,
He could not sit in Bel-imperia's thoughts.
But how can love find harbour in my breast,
Till I revenge the death of my beloved? 65
Yes, second love shall further my revenge.
I'll love Horatio, my Andrea's friend,
The more to spite the prince that wrought his end.
And where Don Balthazar, that slew my love,
Himself now pleads for favour at my hands, 70
He shall in rigour of my just disdain°

Reap long repentance for his murderous deed.
For what was't else but murderous cowardice,
So many to oppress° one valiant knight,
Without respect of honour in the fight?   75
And here he comes that murdered my delight.

Enter LORENZO *and* BALTHAZAR.

LORENZO: Sister, what means this melancholy walk?
BEL-IMPERIA: That for a while I wish no company.
LORENZO: But here the prince is come to visit you.
BEL-IMPERIA: That argues that he lives in liberty.   80
BALTHAZAR: No, madam, but in pleasing servitude.°
BEL-IMPERIA: Your prison then belike is your conceit.
BALTHAZAR: Ay, by conceit° my freedom is enthralled.°
BEL-IMPERIA: Then with conceit enlarge° yourself again.
BALTHAZAR: What if conceit have laid my heart to gage?°   85
BEL-IMPERIA: Pay that you borrowed and recover it.
BALTHAZAR: I die if it return from whence it lies.
BEL-IMPERIA: A heartless man, and live? A miracle!
BALTHAZAR: Ay lady, love can work such miracles.
LORENZO: Tush, tush, my lord, let go these ambages,°   90
　　　And in plain terms acquaint her with your love.
BEL-IMPERIA: What boots° complaint, when there's no remedy?
BALTHAZAR: Yes, to your gracious self must I complain,
　　　In whose fair answer lies my remedy,
　　　On whose perfection all my thoughts attend,   95
　　　In whose aspèct° mine eyes find beauty's bower,
　　　In whose translucent breast my heart is lodged.
BEL-IMPERIA: Alas, my lord, these are but words of course,°
　　　And but device° to drive me from this place.

She, in going in, lets fall her glove, which HORATIO, *coming out,
takes up.*

HORATIO: Madam, your glove.   100
BEL-IMPERIA: Thanks good Horatio; take it for thy pains.
BALTHAZAR: Signior Horatio stooped in happy time.°
HORATIO: I reaped more grace than I deserved or hoped.
LORENZO: My lord, be not dismayed for what is past,
　　　You know that women oft are humorous:°   105
　　　These clouds will overblow with little wind.
　　　Let me alone, I'll scatter them myself.
　　　Meanwhile let us devise to spend the time
　　　In some delightful sports and revelling.

HORATIO: The king, my lords, is coming hither straight,°   110
    To feast the Portingale ambassador:
    Things were in readiness before I came.
BALTHAZAR: Then here it fits° us to attend the king,
    To welcome hither our ambassador,
    And learn my father and my country's health.   115

      Enter the Banquet,° Trumpets, the KING, *and* AMBASSADOR.

KING: See, Lord Ambassador, how Spain entreats°
    Their prisoner Balthazar, thy viceroy's son:
    We pleasure° more in kindness than in wars.
AMBASSADOR: Sad is our king, and Portingale laments,
    Supposing that Don Balthazar is slain.   120
BALTHAZAR [*aside*]: So am I slain by beauty's tyranny. —
    You see, my lord, how Balthazar is slain:
    I frolic with the Duke of Castile's son,
    Wrapped every hour in pleasures of the court,
    And graced° with favours of his majesty.   125
KING: Put off your greetings till our feast be done;
    Now come and sit with us and taste our cheer.
                                [*They*] *sit to the banquet.*
    Sit down, young prince, you are our second guest;
    Brother sit down and nephew take your place;
    Signior Horatio, wait thou upon° our cup,   130
    For well thou hast deservèd to be honoured.
    Now, lordings, fall to; Spain is Portugal,
    And Portugal is Spain, we both are friends,
    Tribute is paid, and we enjoy our right.
    But where is old Hieronimo, our marshal?   135
    He promised us, in honour of our guest,
    To grace° our banquet with some pompous jest.°

      Enter HIERONIMO *with a* Drum,° *three* Knights, *each* [*hangs up*]
    his scutcheon; °*then he fetches three* Kings, [*the* Knights] *take their*
                      crowns and them captive.

    Hieronimo, this masque contents mine eye,
    Although I sound° not well the mystery.°
HIERONIMO: The first armed knight, that hung his scutcheon up,   140
                    He takes the scutcheon and gives it to the KING.
    Was English Robert, Earl of Gloucester,
    Who when King Stephen bore sway in Albion,°
    Arrived with five and twenty thousand men
    In Portingale, and by success of war

Enforced the king, then but a Saracen,   145
  To bear the yoke of the English monarchy.°
KING: My lord of Portingale, by this you see
  That which may comfort both your king and you,
  And make your late discomfort seem the less.
  But say, Hieronimo, what was the next?   150
HIERONIMO: The second knight, that hung his scutcheon up,
                                  He doth as he did before.

  Was Edmund, Earl of Kent in Albion,°
  When English Richard wore the diadem;
  He came likewise, and razèd Lisbon walls,
  And took the King of Portingale in fight: 155
  For which, and other suchlike service done,
  He after was created Duke of York.°
KING: This is another special° argument,
  That Portingale may deign to bear our yoke,
  When it by little England hath been yoked.   160
  But now Hieronimo, what were the last?
HIERONIMO: The third and last, not least in our account,   *Doing as before.*
  Was as the rest a valiant Englishman,
  Brave John of Gaunt, the Duke of Lancaster,
  As by his scutcheon plainly may appear.   165
  He with a puissant° army came to Spain,
  And took our King of Castile prisoner.°
AMBASSADOR: This is an argument for° our viceroy,
  That Spain may not insult for her success,
  Since English warriors likewise conquered Spain,   170
  And made them bow their knees to Albion.
KING: Hieronimo, I drink to thee for this device,°
  Which hath pleased both the ambassador and me;
  Pledge me, Hieronimo, if thou love the king.   *Takes the cup of* °HORATIO.
  My lord, I fear we sit but over-long,   175
  Unless our dainties were more delicate:°
  But welcome are you to the best we have.
  Now let us in, that you may be despatched;°
  I think our council is already set.°   *Exeunt omnes.*

Act One, Scene Five

[*Enter* ANDREA, REVENGE.]

ANDREA: Come we for this from depth of underground,
  To see him feast that gave me my death's wound?

These pleasant sights are sorrow to my soul:
Nothing but league, and love, and banqueting!
REVENGE: Be still, Andrea; ere we go from hence,   5
    I'll turn their friendship into fell despite,°
    Their love to mortal hate, their day to night,
    Their hope into despair, their peace to war,
    Their joys to pain, their bliss to misery.

Act Two, Scene One

Enter LORENZO *and* BALTHAZAR.

LORENZO: My lord, though Bel-imperia seem thus coy,°
    Let reason hold° you in your wonted joy:
    'In time the savage bull sustains the yoke,
    In time all haggard° hawks will stoop to lure,°
    In time small wedges cleave° the hardest oak,   5
    In time the flint is pierced with softest shower' —
    And she in time will fall from her disdain,
    And rue the sufferance of your friendly pain.°
BALTHAZAR: 'No, she is wilder, and more hard withal,
    Than beast, or bird, or tree, or stony wall'.   10
    But wherefore blot I Bel-imperia's name?
    It is my fault,° not she, that merits blame.
    My feature° is not to content her sight,
    My words are rude° and work her no delight.
    The lines I send her are but harsh and ill,   15
    Such as do drop from Pan and Marsyas' quill.°
    My presents are not of sufficient cost,
    And being worthless all my labour's lost.
    Yet might she love me for my valiancy;°
    Ay, but that's slandered° by captivity.   20
    Yet might she love me to content her sire;
    Ay, but her reason masters his desire.
    Yet might she love me as her brother's friend;
    Ay, but her hopes aim at some other end.
    Yet might she love me to uprear her state;°   25
    Ay, but perhaps she hopes some nobler mate.
    Yet might she love me as her beauty's thrall;
    Ay, but I fear she cannot love at all.
LORENZO: My lord, for my sake leave these ecstasies,°
    And doubt not but we'll find some remedy.   30
    Some cause there is that lets you not be loved:°
    First that must needs be known, and then removed.

What if my sister love some other knight?
BALTHAZAR: My summer's day will turn to winter's night.
LORENZO: I have already found a stratagem   35
    To sound the bottom° of this doubtful theme.
    My lord, for once you shall be ruled by me:
    Hinder me not whate'er you hear or see.
    By force or fair means will I cast about°
    To find the truth of all this question out.   40
    Ho, Pedringano!
PEDRINGANO [*within*]: Signior!
LORENZO: *Vien qui presto.*°

Enter PEDRINGANO.

PEDRINGANO: Hath your lordship any service to command me?
LORENZO: Ay, Pedringano, service of import;
    And not to spend the time in trifling words,
    Thus stands the case: it is not long, thou know'st,   45
    Since I did shield thee from my father's wrath
    For thy conveyance° in Andrea's love,
    For which thou wert adjudged to punishment.
    I stood betwixt thee and thy punishment;
    And since, thou know'st how I have favoured thee.   50
    Now to these favours will I add reward,
    Not with fair words, but store° of golden coin,
    And lands and living joined with dignities,
    If thou but satisfy my just demand.
    Tell truth and have me for thy lasting friend.   55
PEDRINGANO: Whate'er it be your lordship shall demand,
    My bounden duty bids me tell the truth,
    If case it lie in me° to tell the truth.
LORENZO: Then, Pedringano, this is my demand:
    Whom loves my sister Bel-imperia?   60
    For she reposeth all her trust in thee.
    Speak man, and gain both friendship and reward:
    I mean, whom loves she in Andrea's place?
PEDRINGANO: Alas, my lord, since Don Andrea's death,
    I have no credit° with her as before,   65
    And therefore know not if she love or no.
LORENZO: Nay, if thou dally then I am thy foe,   [*Draws his sword.*]
    And fear shall force what friendship cannot win.
    Thy death shall bury what thy life conceals.
    Thou diest for more esteeming her than me.   70
PEDRINGANO: O stay, my lord!
LORENZO: Yet speak the truth and I will guerdon° thee,

And shield thee from whatever can ensue,
And will conceal whate'er proceeds from thee:
But if thou dally once again, thou diest.   75
PEDRINGANO: If Madam Bel-imperia be in love —
LORENZO: What, villain! ifs and ands?   [*Offers to kill him.*]
PEDRINGANO: O stay, my lord, she loves Horatio.   BALTHAZAR *starts back.*
LORENZO: What, Don Horatio our Knight Marshal's son?
PEDRINGANO: Even him my lord.   80
LORENZO: Now say but how know'st thou he is her love,
And thou shalt find me kind and liberal:
Stand up, I say, and fearless tell the truth.
PEDRINGANO: She sent him letters which myself perused,
Full-fraught° with lines and arguments of love,   85
Preferring him before Prince Balthazar.
LORENZO: Swear on this cross° that what thou say'st is true,
And that thou wilt conceal what thou hast told.
PEDRINGANO: I swear to both by him that made us all.
LORENZO: In hope thine oath is true, here's thy reward,
                                        [*Gives him money.*] 90
But if I prove thee perjured and unjust,°
This very sword whereon thou took'st thine oath
Shall be the worker of thy tragedy.
PEDRINGANO: What I have said is true, and shall for me
Be still° concealed from Bel-imperia.   95
Besides, your honour's liberality
Deserves my duteous service even till death.
LORENZO: Let this be all that thou shalt do for me:
Be watchful when, and where, these lovers meet,
And give me notice in some secret sort.°   100
PEDRINGANO: I will my lord.
LORENZO: Then shalt thou find that I am liberal.
Thou know'st that I can more advance thy state°
Than she, be therefore wise and fail me not.
Go and attend her as thy custom is,   105
Lest absence make her think thou dost amiss.   *Exit* PEDRINGANO.
Why so, *tam armis quam ingenio:*°
Where words prevail not, violence prevails.
But gold doth more than either of them both.
How likes Prince Balthazar this stratagem?   110
BALTHAZAR: Both well, and ill: it makes me glad and sad.
Glad, that I know the hinderer of my love;
Sad, that I fear she hates me whom I love.
Glad, that I know on whom to be revenged;
Sad, that she'll fly me if I take revenge.   115
Yet must I take revenge or die myself,

For love resisted grows impatient.
I think Horatio be my destined plague:
First, in his hand he brandished a sword,
And with that sword he fiercely wagèd war,   120
And in that war he gave me dangerous wounds,
And by those wounds he forcèd me to yield,
And by my yielding I became his slave.
Now in his mouth he carries pleasing words,
Which pleasing words do harbour sweet conceits,°   125
Which sweet conceits are limed° with sly deceits,
Which sly deceits smooth° Bel-imperia's ears,
And through her ears dive down into her heart,
And in her heart set him where I should stand.
Thus hath he ta'en my body by his force,   130
And now by sleight° would captivate my soul:
But in his fall° I'll tempt the destinies,
And either lose my life, or win my love.
LORENZO: Let's go, my lord, your staying stays° revenge.
Do you but follow me and gain your love: 135
Her favour must be won by his remove.   *Exeunt.*

Act Two, Scene Two

Enter HORATIO *and* BEL-IMPERIA.

HORATIO: Now, madam, since by favour of your love
Our hidden smoke is turned to open flame,
And that with looks and words we feed our thoughts
(Two chief contents,° where more cannot be had),
Thus in the midst of love's fair blandishments,   5
Why show you sign of inward languishments?

PEDRINGANO *showeth all to the* PRINCE *and* LORENZO,
placing them in secret [*above*].°

BEL-IMPERIA: My heart, sweet friend,° is like a ship at sea:
She wisheth port, where riding all at ease,
She may repair° what stormy times have worn,
And leaning on the shore, may sing with joy   10
That pleasure follows pain, and bliss annoy.°
Possession of thy love is th' only port
Wherein my heart, with fears and hopes long tossed,

Each hour doth wish and long to make resort,
There to repair the joys that it hath lost,   15
And sitting safe, to sing in Cupid's choir
That sweetest bliss is° crown of love's desire.
BALTHAZAR: O sleep mine eyes, see not my love profaned,
    Be deaf my ears, hear not my discontent,
    Die heart, another joys° what thou deserv'st.   20
LORENZO: Watch still mine eyes, to see this love disjoined,
    Hear still mine ears, to hear them both lament,
    Live heart, to joy at fond° Horatio's fall.
BEL-IMPERIA: Why stands Horatio speechless all this while?
HORATIO: The less I speak, the more I meditate.   25
BEL-IMPERIA: But whereon dost thou chiefly meditate?
HORATIO: On dangers past, and pleasures to ensue.
BALTHAZAR: On pleasures past, and dangers to ensue.
BEL-IMPERIA: What dangers and what pleasures dost thou mean?
HORATIO: Dangers of war, and pleasures of our love.   30
LORENZO: Dangers of death, but pleasures none at all.
BEL-IMPERIA: Let dangers go; thy war shall be with me,
    But such a war, as breaks no bond of peace.
    Speak thou fair words, I'll cross° them with fair words,
    Send thou sweet looks, I'll meet them with sweet looks,   35
    Write loving lines, I'll answer° loving lines,
    Give me a kiss, I'll countercheck° thy kiss:
    Be this our warring peace, or peaceful war.
HORATIO: But gracious madam, then appoint the field
    Where trial of this war shall first be made.   40
BALTHAZAR: Ambitious villain, how his boldness grows!
BEL-IMPERIA: Then be thy father's pleasant bower° the field,
    Where first we vowed a mutual amity:
    The court were dangerous, that place is safe.
    Our hour shall be when Vesper° 'gins to rise,   45
    That summons home distressful travellers.°
    There none shall hear us but the harmless birds:
    Happily° the gentle nightingale°
    Shall carol us asleep ere we be ware,
    And singing with the prickle at her breast,   50
    Tell our delight and mirthfull dalliance.
    Till then each hour will seem a year and more.
HORATIO: But honey sweet, and honourable love,
    Return we now into your father's sight:
    Dangerous suspicion waits on° our delight.   55
LORENZO: Ay, danger mixed with jealous despite°
    Shall send thy soul into eternal night.   *Exeunt.*

Act Two, Scene Three

Enter KING *of Spain, Portingale* AMBASSADOR, DON CYPRIAN, *etc.*

KING: Brother of Castile, to the prince's love
    What says your daughter Bel-imperia?
CASTILE: Although she coy it as becomes her kind,°
    And yet dissemble that she loves the prince,
    I doubt not, I, but she will stoop° in time.   5
    And were she froward,° which she will not be,
    Yet herein shall she follow my advice,
    Which is to love him or forgo my love.
KING: Then, Lord Ambassador of Portingale,
    Advise thy king to make this marriage up,   10
    For strengthening of our late-confirmèd league:
    I know no better means to make us friends.
    Her dowry shall be large and liberal:
    Besides that she is daughter and half-heir
    Unto our brother here, Don Cyprian,   15
    And shall enjoy the moiety° of his land,
    I'll grace her marriage with an uncle's gift,
    And this it is: in case° the match go forward,
    The tribute which you pay shall be released,
    And if by Balthazar she have a son,   20
    He shall enjoy the kingdom after us.
AMBASSADOR: I'll make the motion° to my sovereign liege,
    And work it if my counsel may prevail.
KING: Do so, my lord, and if he give consent,
    I hope his presence here will honour us   25
    In celebration of the nuptial day;
    And let himself determine of the time.
AMBASSADOR: Will 't please your Grace command me aught beside?
KING: Commend me to the king, and so farewell.
    But where's Prince Balthazar to take his leave?   30
AMBASSADOR: That is performed already, my good lord.
KING: Amongst the rest of what you have in charge,
    The prince's ransom must not be forgot.
    That's none of mine, but his that took him prisoner,
    And well his forwardness° deserves reward: 35
    It was Horatio, our Knight Marshal's son.
AMBASSADOR: Between us there's a price already pitched,°
    And shall be sent with all convenient speed.°
KING: Then once again farewell, my lord.
AMBASSADOR: Farewell, my lord of Castile and the rest.   *Exit.*   40
KING: Now, brother, you must take some little pains

To win fair Bel-imperia from her will:°
Young virgins must be rulèd by their friends.
The prince is amiable and loves her well;
If she neglect him and forgo his love,   45
She both will wrong her own estate and ours:
Therefore, whiles I do entertain the prince
With greatest pleasure that our court affords,
Endeavour you to win your daughter's thought:
If she give back,° all this will come to naught.   *Exeunt.* 50

Act Two, Scene Four

Enter HORATIO, BEL-IMPERIA, *and* PEDRINGANO.

HORATIO: Now that the night begins with sable° wings
     To overcloud the brightness of the sun,
     And that in darkness pleasures may be done,
     Come Bel-imperia, let us to the bower,
     And there in safety pass a pleasant hour.   5
BEL-IMPERIA: I follow thee, my love, and will not back,
     Although my fainting° heart controls° my soul.
HORATIO: Why, make you doubt of Pedringano's faith?
BEL-IMPERIA: No, he is as trusty as my second self.
     Go Pedringano, watch without° the gate,   10
     And let us know if any make approach.
PEDRINGANO [*aside*]: Instead of watching, I'll deserve more gold
     By fetching Don Lorenzo to this match.°   *Exit* PEDRINGANO.
HORATIO: What means my love?
BEL-IMPERIA: I know not what myself;
     And yet my heart foretells me some mischance.   15
HORATIO: Sweet say not so; fair Fortune is our friend,
     And heavens have shut up day to pleasure us.
     The stars, thou seest, hold back their twinkling shine,
     And Luna° hides herself to pleasure us.
BEL-IMPERIA: Thou hast prevailed, I'll conquer my misdoubt,   20
     And in thy love and counsel drown my fear:
     I fear no more, love now is all my thoughts.
     Why sit we not? for pleasure asketh° ease.
HORATIO: The more thou sit'st within these leavy bowers,
     The more will Flora° deck it with her flowers.   25
BEL-IMPERIA: Ay, but if Flora spy Horatio here,
     Her jealous eye will think I sit too near.
HORATIO: Hark, madam, how the birds record° by night,
     For joy that Bel-imperia sits in sight.

BEL-IMPERIA: No, Cupid counterfeits° the nightingale,   30
    To frame° sweet music to Horatio's tale.
HORATIO: If Cupid sing, then Venus is not far:
    Ay, thou art Venus or some fairer star.
BEL-IMPERIA: If I be Venus thou must needs be Mars,
    And where Mars reigneth there must needs be wars.   35
HORATIO: Then thus begin our wars: put forth thy hand,
    That it may combat with my ruder° hand.
BEL-IMPERIA: Set forth thy foot to try the push° of mine.
HORATIO: But first my looks shall combat against thine.
BEL-IMPERIA: Then ward° thyself, I dart this kiss at thee.   40
HORATIO: Thus I retort° the dart thou threw'st at me.
BEL-IMPERIA: Nay then, to gain the glory° of the field,
    My twining arms shall yoke and make thee yield.
HORATIO: Nay then, my arms are large and strong withal:
    Thus elms by vines are compass'd till they fall.°   45
BEL-IMPERIA: O let me go, for in my troubled eyes
    Now may'st thou read that life in passion dies.
HORATIO: O stay awhile and I will die with thee,
    So shalt thou yield and yet have conquered me.

Enter LORENZO, BALTHAZAR, SERBERINE, PEDRINGANO, *disguised.*

BEL-IMPERIA: Who's there? Pedringano! We are betrayed!   50
LORENZO: My lord, away with her, take her aside.
    O sir, forbear,° your valour is already tried.°
    Quickly despatch, my masters.   *They hang him in the arbour.*
HORATIO: What, will you murder me?
LORENZO: Ay, thus, and thus; these are the fruits of love.   *They stab him.* 55
BEL-IMPERIA: O save his life and let me die for him!
    O save him, brother, save him Balthazar:
    I loved Horatio but he loved not me.
BALTHAZAR: But Balthazar loves Bel-imperia.
LORENZO: Although his life were still ambitious proud,°   60
    Yet is he at the highest° now he is dead.
BEL-IMPERIA: Murder! murder! Help, Hieronimo, help!
LORENZO: Come stop her mouth, away with her.
                    Exeunt [, *leaving* HORATIO's *body*].

Enter HIERONIMO *in his shirt,*° *etc.*°

HIERONIMO: What outcries pluck me from my naked° bed,
    And chill my throbbing heart with trembling fear,   65
    Which never danger yet could daunt before?
    Who calls Hieronimo? Speak, here I am.

I did not slumber, therefore 'twas no dream,
No, no, it was some woman cried for help,
And here within this garden did she cry,   70
And in this garden must I rescue her. —
But stay, what murd'rous spectacle is this?
A man hanged up and all the murderers gone,
And in my bower, to lay the guilt on me:
This place was made for pleasure, not for death. *He cuts him down.* 75
Those garments that he wears I oft have seen —
Alas, it is Horatio my sweet son!
O no, but he that whilom° was my son.
O was it thou that call'dst me from my bed?
O speak, if any spark of life remain: 80
I am thy father. Who hath slain my son?
What savage monster, not of human kind,
Hath here been glutted with thy harmless blood,
And left thy bloody corpse dishonoured° here,
For me amidst this° dark and deathful shades°   85
To drown thee with an ocean of my tears?
O heavens, why made you night to cover sin?
By day this deed of darkness had not been.
O earth, why didst thou not in time devour
The vild° profaner of this sacred bower?   90
O poor Horatio, what hadst thou misdone,
To leese° thy life ere life was new begun?°
O wicked butcher, whatsoe'er thou wert,
How could thou strangle virtue and desert?
Ay me most wretched, that have lost my joy,   95
In leesing° my Horatio, my sweet boy!

Enter ISABELLA.

ISABELLA: My husband's absence makes my heart to throb. —
    Hieronimo!
HIERONIMO: Here, Isabella, help me to lament,
    For sighs are stopped, and all my tears are spent.   100
ISABELLA: What world of grief — My son Horatio!
    O where's the author of this endless woe?
HIERONIMO: To know the author were some ease of grief,
    For in revenge my heart would find relief.
ISABELLA: Then is he gone? and is my son gone too?   105
    O gush out, tears, fountains and floods of tears;
    Blow, sighs, and raise an everlasting storm,
    For outrage° fits our cursed wretchedness.
HIERONIMO: Sweet lovely rose, ill-plucked before thy time,

Fair worthy son, not conquered but betrayed: 110
I'll kiss thee now, for words with° tears are stayed.°
ISABELLA: And I'll close up the glasses of his sight,°
For once these eyes were only my delight.°
HIERONIMO: Seest thou this handkercher° besmeared with blood?
It shall not from me till I take revenge.   115
Seest thou those wounds that yet are bleeding fresh?
I'll not entomb them till I have revenged:
Then will I joy amidst my discontent;°
Till then my sorrow never shall be spent.
ISABELLA: The heavens are just, murder cannot be hid;   120
Time is the author both of truth and right,
And time will bring this treachery to light.
HIERONIMO: Meanwhile, good Isabella, cease thy plaints,°
Or at the least dissemble them awhile:
So shall we sooner find the practice° out,   125
And learn by whom all this was brought about.
Come, Isabel, now let us take him up,   *They take him up.°*
And bear him in from out this cursèd place.
I'll say his dirge;° singing fits not this case.

O aliquis mihi quas pulchrum ver educat herbas   130
                          HIERONIMO *sets his breast unto his sword.°*
Misceat, et nostor detur medicina dolori;
Aut, si qui faciunt animis oblivia, succos
Praebeat; ipse metam magnum quaecunque per orbem
Gramina Sol pulchras effert in luminis oras;
Ipse bibam quicquid meditatur saga veneni,   135
Quicquid et herbarum vi caeca nenia nectit:
Omnia perpetiar, lethum quoque, dum semel omnis
Noster in extincto moriatur pectore sensus.
Ergo tuos oculos nunquam, mea vita, videbo,
Et tua perpetuus sepelivit lumina somnus?   140
Emoriar tecum, sic, sic juvat ire sub umbras.
At tamen absistam properato cedere letho,
Ne mortem vindicta tuam tum nulla sequatur.°
                    Here he throws it from him and bears the body away.

Act Two, Scene Five

[*Enter* ANDREA, REVENGE.]

ANDREA: Brought'st thou me hither to increase my pain?

I looked° that Balthazar should have been slain:
But 'tis my friend Horatio that is slain,
And they abuse fair Bel-imperia,
On whom I doted more than all the world,   5
Because she loved me more than all the world.
REVENGE: Thou talk'st of harvest when the corn is green:
The end is crown of every work well done;
The sickle comes not till the corn be ripe.
Be still, and ere I lead thee from this place,   10
I'll show thee Balthazar in heavy case.°

Act Three, Scene One

Enter VICEROY *of Portingale,* NOBLES, VILLUPPO.

VICEROY: Infortunate° condition of kings,
Seated amidst so many helpless doubts!°
First we are placed upon extremest height,
And oft supplanted with exceeding heat,°
But ever subject to the wheel of chance:°   5
And at our highest never joy we so,
As we both doubt and dread our overthrow.
So striveth not the waves with sundry° winds
As Fortune toileth in the affairs of kings,
That would be° feared, yet fear to be beloved,   10
Sith° fear or love to kings is flattery:
For instance, lordings,° look upon your king,
By hate deprivèd of his dearest son,
The only hope of our successive line.°
1 NOBLE: I had not thought that Alexandro's heart   15
Had been envenomed with such extreme hate;
But now I see that words have several works,°
And there's no credit° in the countenance.
VILLUPPO: No; for, my lord, had you beheld the train
That feignèd love had coloured in his looks,°   20
When he in camp consorted° Balthazar,
Far more inconstant had you thought the sun,
That hourly coasts the centre of the earth,°
Than Alexandro's purpose° to the prince.
VICEROY: No more, Villuppo, thou hast said enough,   25
And with thy words thou slay'st our wounded thoughts.
Nor shall I longer dally with the world,
Procrastinating Alexandro's death:
Go some of you and fetch the traitor forth,

That as he is condemnèd he may die.   30

       Enter ALEXANDRO *with a* NOBLEMAN *and* Halberts.°

2 NOBLE: In such extremes will naught but patience° serve.
ALEXANDRO: But in extremes what patience shall I use?
    Nor discontents it me to leave the world,
    With whom there nothing can prevail but wrong.
2 NOBLE: Yet hope the best.
ALEXANDRO: 'Tis Heaven is my hope.   35
    As for the earth, it is too much infect°
    To yield me hope of any of her mould.°
VICEROY: Why linger ye? Bring forth that daring fiend
    And let him die for his accursèd deed.
ALEXANDRO: Not that I fear the extremity of death,   40
    For nobles cannot stoop to servile fear,
    Do I, O king, thus discontented live.
    But this, O this, torments my labouring soul,
    That thus I die suspected of a sin,
    Whereof, as heavens have known my secret thoughts,   45
    So am I free from this suggestion.°
VICEROY: No more, I say! to the tortures! when!°
    Bind him, and burn his body in those flames   *They bind him to the stake.*
    That shall prefigure those unquenched fires
    Of Phlegethon° prepared for his soul.   50
ALEXANDRO: My guiltless death will be avenged on thee,
    On thee, Villuppo, that hath maliced° thus,
    Or for thy meed° hast falsely me accused.
VICEROY: Nay Alexandro, if thou menace me,
    I'll lend a hand to send thee to the lake°   55
    Where those thy words shall perish with thy works,
    Injurious traitor, monstrous homicide!

               Enter AMBASSADOR.

AMBASSADOR: Stay, hold a while,
    And here, with pardon of his majesty,
    Lay hands upon Villuppo.
VICEROY: Ambassador,   60
    What news hath urged this sudden entrance?°
AMBASSADOR: Know, sovereign lord, that Balthazar doth live.
VICEROY: What say'st thou? liveth Balthazar our son?
AMBASSADOR: Your highness' son, Lord Balthazar, doth live;
    And, well entreated° in the court of Spain,   65
    Humbly commends° him to your majesty.

These eyes beheld, and these my followers,
With these, the letters of the king's commends,   *Gives him letters.*
Are happy witnesses of his highness' health.
      The [VICEROY] *looks on the letters, and proceeds.*
VICEROY: 'Thy son doth live, your tribute is received,   70
    Thy peace is made, and we are satisfied.
    The rest resolve upon as things proposed
    For both our honours and thy benefit.'
AMBASSADOR: These are his highness' farther articles.
      He gives him more letters.
VICEROY: Accursed wretch, to intimate these ills   75
    Against the life and reputation
    Of noble Alexandro! — Come, my lord,
    Let him unbind thee that is bound to death,
    To make a quital° for thy discontent.°   *They unbind him.*°
ALEXANDRO: Dread lord, in kindness° you could do no less,   80
    Upon report of such a damnèd fact:°
    But thus we see our innocence hath saved
    The hopeless life which thou, Villuppo, sought
    By thy suggestions° to have massacred.°
VICEROY: Say, false Villuppo! wherefore didst thou thus   85
    Falsely betray Lord Alexandro's life?
    Him whom thou know'st that no unkindness° else,
    But even the slaughter of our dearest son,
    Could once have moved us to have misconceived?
ALEXANDRO: Say, treacherous Villuppo, tell the king,   90
    Or wherein hath Alexandro used thee ill?
VILLUPPO: Rent with remembrance of so foul a deed,
    My guilty soul submits me to thy doom:°
    For, not for Alexandro's injuries,
    But for reward, and hope to be preferred,   95
    Thus have I shamelessly hazarded his life.
VICEROY: Which, villain, shall be ransomed with thy death,
    And not so mean° a torment as we here
    Devised for him, who thou said'st slew our son,
    But with the bitterest torments and extremes   100
    That may be yet invented for thine end.   ALEXANDRO *seems to entreat.*
    Entreat me not, go take the traitor hence.   *Exit* VILLUPPO [*guarded*].
    And, Alexandro, let us honour thee
    With public notice of thy loyalty.
    To end those things articulated° here   105
    By our great lord, the mighty King of Spain,
    We with our council will deliberate.
    Come, Alexandro, keep us company.   *Exeunt.*

Act Three, Scene Two

Enter HIERONIMO.

HIERONIMO: O eyes, no eyes, but fountains fraught° with tears;
    O life, no life, but lively° form of death;
    O world, no world, but mass of public wrongs,
    Confused° and filled with murder and misdeeds;
    O sacred heavens! if this unhallowed deed,   5
    If this inhuman and barbarous attempt,
    If this incomparable murder thus
    Of mine, but now no more my son,
    Shall unrevealed and unrevengèd pass,
    How should we term your dealings to be just,   10
    If you unjustly deal with those that in your justice trust?
    The night, sad secretary° to my moans,
    With direful visions wake my vexèd soul,°
    And with the wounds of my distressful° son
    Solicit me for notice of his death.   15
    The ugly fiends do sally forth of hell,
    And frame° my steps to unfrequentèd paths,
    And fear° my heart with fierce inflamèd thoughts.
    The cloudy day my discontents records,
    Early begins to register my dreams   20
    And drive me forth to seek the murderer.
    Eyes, life, world, heavens, hell, night, and day,
    See, search, shew, send, some man, some mean,° that may —
                      A letter falleth, [written in red ink].
    What's here? a letter? tush, it is not so!
    A letter written to Hieronimo!   25
    'For want of ink, receive this bloody writ.°
    Me hath my hapless° brother hid from thee:
    Revenge thyself on Balthazar and him,
    For these were they that murderèd thy son.
    Hieronimo, revenge Horatio's death,   30
    And better fare than Bel-imperia doth.'
    What means this unexpected miracle?
    My son slain by Lorenzo and the prince!
    What cause had they Horatio to malign?°
    Or what might move thee, Bel-imperia,   35
    To accuse thy brother, had he been the mean?
    Hieronimo beware, thou art betrayed,
    And to entrap thy life this train° is laid.
    Advise thee therefore, be not credulous:
    This is devised to endanger thee,   40

That thou by this Lorenzo shouldst accuse,
And he, for thy dishonour done,° should draw
Thy life in question, and thy name in hate.
Dear was the life of my belovèd son,
And of his death behoves me be revenged: 45
Then hazard not thine own, Hieronimo,
But live t'effect thy resolution.°
I therefore will by circumstances° try
What I can gather to confirm this writ,
And, heark'ning near the Duke of Castile's house,   50
Close if I can with° Bel-imperia,
To listen more, but nothing to bewray.°

Enter PEDRINGANO.

Now, Pedringano!
PEDRINGANO: Now, Hieronimo!
HIERONIMO: Where's thy lady?
PEDRINGANO: I know not; here's my lord.

Enter LORENZO.

LORENZO: How now, who's this? Hieronimo?
HIERONIMO: My lord.   55
PEDRINGANO: He asketh for my lady Bel-imperia.
LORENZO: What to do, Hieronimo? The duke my father hath
    Upon some disgrace awhile removed her hence,
    But if it be aught I may inform her of,
    Tell me, Hieronimo, and I'll let her know it.   60
HIERONIMO: Nay, nay, my lord, I thank you, it shall not need;
    I had a suit° unto her, but too late,
    And her disgrace makes me unfortunate.
LORENZO: Why so, Hieronimo? use me.°
HIERONIMO: O no, my lord, I dare not, it must not be.   65
    I humbly thank your lordship.
LORENZO: Why then, farewell.
HIERONIMO: My grief no heart, my thoughts no tongue can tell.   *Exit.*
LORENZO: Come hither, Pedringano, seest thou this?
PEDRINGANO: My lord, I see it, and suspect it too.
LORENZO: This is that damned villain Serberine,   70
    That hath, I fear, revealed Horatio's death.
PEDRINGANO: My lord, he could not, 'twas so lately done,
    And since, he hath not left my company.
LORENZO: Admit he have not, his condition's° such,
    As fear or flattering words may make him false.   75

I know his humour,° and therewith repent
That e'er I used him in this enterprise.
But Pedringano, to prevent the worst,
And 'cause I know thee secret as my soul,
Here for thy further satisfaction take thou this, *Gives him more gold.* 80
And hearken to me — thus it is devised:
This night thou must, and prithee so resolve,
Meet Serberine at Saint Luigi's Park —°
Thou know'st 'tis here hard° by behind the house;
There take thy stand, and see thou strike him sure, 85
For die he must, if we do mean to live.
PEDRINGANO: But how shall Serberine be there, my lord?
LORENZO: Let me alone, I'll send to him to meet
The prince and me, where thou must do this deed.
PEDRINGANO: It shall be done, my lord, it shall be done, 90
And I'll go arm myself to meet him there.
LORENZO: When things shall alter, as I hope they will,
Then shalt thou mount° for this: thou know'st my mind.

Exit PEDRINGANO.

Chi l'e?° *Jeron!*

Enter PAGE.

PAGE: My lord?
LORENZO: Go, sirrah, to Serberine,
And bid him forthwith meet the prince and me 95
At Saint Luigi's Park, behind the house —
This evening, boy.
PAGE: I go, my lord.
LORENZO: But sirrah, let the hour be eight o' clock:
Bid him not fail.
PAGE: I fly, my lord.
LORENZO: Now, to confirm the complot° thou hast cast° 100
Of all these practices,° I'll spread the watch,°
Upon precise commandment from the king,
Strongly to guard the place where Pedringano
This night shall murder hapless° Serberine.
Thus must we work that will avoid distrust,° 105
Thus must we practise° to prevent mishap,
And thus one ill another must expulse.°
This sly enquiry of Hieronimo
For Bel-imperia breeds suspicion,
And this suspicion bodes a further ill. 110
As for myself, I know my secret fault,
And so do they, but I have dealt for them.

They that for coin their souls endangerèd,
To save my life, for coin shall venture theirs:
And better tis that base companions° die,   115
Than by their life to hazard our good haps.°
Nor shall they live, for me to fear their faith:°
I'll trust myself, myself shall be my friend,
For die they shall, slaves° are ordained to no other end.

Act Three, Scene Three

Enter PEDRINGANO *with a pistol.*

PEDRINGANO: Now, Pedringano, bid thy pistol hold,°
    And hold on,° Fortune! once more favour me,
    Give but success to mine attempting spirit,
    And let me shift for taking of mine aim!°
    Here is the gold,° this is the gold proposed: 5
    It is no dream that I adventure for,
    But Pedringano is possessed thereof.°
    And he that would not strain his conscience
    For him that thus his liberal purse hath stretched,
    Unworthy such a favour, may he fail,°   10
    And, wishing, want,° when such as I prevail.
    As for the fear of apprehension,
    I know, if need should be, my noble lord
    Will stand between me and ensuing harms:
    Besides, this place is free from all suspect.°   15
    Here therefore will I stay and take my stand.

Enter the WATCH.

1 WATCH: I wonder much to what intent it is
    That we are thus expressly charged to watch.
2 WATCH: 'Tis by commandment in the king's own name.
3 WATCH: But we were never wont to watch and ward°   20
    So near the duke his brother's house before.
2 WATCH: Content yourself, stand close,° there's somewhat in't.

Enter SERBERINE.

SERBERINE: Here, Serberine, attend and stay thy pace,°
    For here did Don Lorenzo's page appoint
    That thou by his command shouldst meet with him.   25
    How fit a place, if one were so disposed;

Methinks this corner is to close with one.°
PEDRINGANO: Here comes the bird that I must seize upon:
  Now, Pedringano, or never play the man!
SERBERINE: I wonder that his lordship stays so long,   30
  Or wherefore should he send for me so late?
PEDRINGANO: For this, Serberine, and thou shalt ha't.
                              Shoots the dag°[*killing* SERBERINE].
  So, there he lies, my promise is performed.

                        The WATCH.

1 WATCH: Hark, gentlemen, this is a pistol shot.
2 WATCH: And here's one slain; stay the murderer.   35
PEDRINGANO: Now by the sorrows of the souls in hell,
                              He strives with the WATCH.
  Who first lays hand on me, I'll be his priest.°
3 WATCH: Sirrah, confess,° and therein play the priest,
  Why hast thou thus unkindly° killed the man?
PEDRINGANO: Why? because he walked abroad° so late.   40
3 WATCH: Come, sir, you had been better kept your bed,
  Than have committed this misdeed so late.
2 WATCH: Come, to the Marshal's with the murderer!
  On to Hieronimo's! Help me here
  To bring the murdered body with us too.   45
PEDRINGANO: Hieronimo! Carry me before whom you will:
  Whate'er he be, I'll answer him and you,
  And do your worst, for I defy you all.   *Exeunt.*

Act Three, Scene Four

            Enter LORENZO *and* BALTHAZAR.

BALTHAZAR: How now, my lord, what makes you rise so soon?
LORENZO: Fear of preventing° our mishaps too late.
BALTHAZAR: What mischief° is it that we not mistrust?°
LORENZO: Our greatest ills we least mistrust, my lord,
  And inexpected harms do hurt us most.   5
BALTHAZAR: Why, tell me, Don Lorenzo, tell me, man,
  If aught concerns our honour and your own.
LORENZO: Nor you nor me, my lord, but both in one,
  For I suspect, and the presumption's great,
  That by those base confederates in our fault°   10
  Touching the death of Don Horatio,

We are betrayed to old Hieronimo.
BALTHAZAR: Betrayed, Lorenzo? tush, it cannot be.
LORENZO: A guilty conscience, urged with the thought
    Of former evils, easily cannot err: 15
    I am persuaded, and dissuade me not,
    That all's revealed to Hieronimo.
    And therefore know that I have cast° it thus —

[*Enter* PAGE.]

But here's the page. How now, what news with thee?
PAGE: My lord, Serberine is slain. 20
BALTHAZAR: Who? Serberine, my man?
PAGE: Your highness' man, my lord.
LORENZO: Speak, page; who murdered him?
PAGE: He that is apprehended for the fact.°
LORENZO: Who? 25
PAGE: Pedringano.
BALTHAZAR: Is Serberine slain, that loved his lord so well?
    Injurious villain, murderer of his friend!
LORENZO: Hath Pedringano murdered Serberine?
    My lord, let me entreat you to take the pains 30
    To exasperate° and hasten his revenge
    With your complaints° unto my lord the king.
    This their dissension breeds a greater doubt.°
BALTHAZAR: Assure thee, Don Lorenzo, he shall die,
    Or else his highness hardly shall deny.° 35
    Meanwhile, I'll haste the marshal-sessions:°
    For die he shall for this his damnèd deed.   *Exit* BALTHAZAR.
LORENZO: Why so, this fits our former policy,
    And thus experience bids the wise to deal.
    I lay the plot, he prosecutes the point;° 40
    I set the trap, he breaks the worthless twigs
    And sees not that wherewith the bird was limed.°
    Thus hopeful° men, that mean to hold their own,
    Must look like fowlers° to their dearest friends.
    He runs to kill whom I have holp° to catch, 45
    And no man knows it was my reaching fatch.°
    'Tis hard to trust unto a multitude,
    Or anyone, in mine opinion,
    When men themselves their secrets will reveal.

Enter a MESSENGER *with a letter.*

Boy!   50
PAGE: My lord.
LORENZO: What's he?
MESSENGER: I have a letter to your lordship.
LORENZO: From whence?
MESSENGER: From Pedringano that's imprisoned.
LORENZO: So, he is in prison then?
MESSENGER: Ay, my good lord.
LORENZO: What would he with us? He writes us here   55
     To stand good lord° and help him in distress.
     Tell him I have his letters, know his mind,
     And what we may, let him assure him of.
     Fellow, begone: my boy shall follow thee.   *Exit* MESSENGER.
     This works like wax,° yet once more try thy wits.°   60
     Boy, go convey this purse to Pedringano:
     Thou know'st the prison, closely° give it him,
     And be advised° that none be there about.
     Bid him be merry still, but secret;°
     And though the marshal-sessions be today,   65
     Bid him not doubt of his delivery.
     Tell him his pardon is already signed,
     And thereon bid him boldly be resolved:°
     For were he ready to be turnèd off°
     (As 'tis my will the uttermost be tried),   70
     Thou with his pardon shalt attend him still.
     Show him this box, tell him his pardon's in't,
     But open't not, and if° thou lov'st thy life,
     But let him wisely keep his hopes unknown;
     He shall not want while Don Lorenzo lives. [*Gives the* PAGE *a box.*] 75
     Away!
PAGE: I go my lord, I run.
LORENZO: But sirrah, see that this be cleanly° done.   *Exit* PAGE.
     Now stands our fortune on a tickle° point,
     And now or never ends Lorenzo's doubts.°
     One only thing is uneffected yet,   80
     And that's to see the executioner.
     But to what end? I list° not trust the air
     With utterance of our pretence° therein,
     For fear the privy whisp'ring of the wind
     Convey our words amongst unfriendly ears,   85
     That lie too open° to advantages.
     E quel che voglio io, nessun lo sa;
     Intendo io: quel mi basterà.°

Act Three, Scene Five

Enter [PAGE] *with the box.*

PAGE: My master hath forbidden me to look in this box, and by my
   troth° 'tis likely, if he had not warned me, I should not have had so
   much idle time; for we men's-kind in our minority° are like women
   in their uncertainty:° that they are most forbidden, they will
   soonest attempt: so I now. [*Opens box.*] By my bare honesty, here's   5
   nothing but the bare empty box: were it not sin against secrecy, I
   would say it were a piece of gentlemanlike knavery. I must go to
   Pedringano, and tell him his pardon is in this box, nay, I would
   have sworn it, had I not seen the contrary. I cannot choose but
   smile to think how the villain will flout° the gallows, scorn   10
   the audience, and descant° on the hangman, and all presuming of
   his pardon from hence. Will't not be an odd jest for me to stand and
   grace every jest he makes, pointing my finger at this box, as who
   would say, 'Mock on, here's thy warrant.' Is't not a scurvy° jest,
   that a man should jest himself to death? Alas, poor Pedringano,   15
   I am in a sort sorry for thee, but if I should be hanged with thee,
   I cannot weep.   *Exit.*

Act Three, Scene Six

Enter HIERONIMO *and the* DEPUTY.°

HIERONIMO: Thus must we toil in other men's extremes,°
   That know not how to remedy our own,
   And do them justice, when unjustly we,
   For all our wrongs, can compass no redress.
   But shall I never live to see the day   5
   That I may come, by justice of the heavens,
   To know the cause° that may my cares allay?
   This toils° my body, this consumeth age,°
   That only I to all men just must be,
   And neither gods nor men be just to me.   10
DEPUTY: Worthy Hieronimo, your office asks°
   A care to punish such as do transgress.
HIERONIMO: So is't my duty to regard° his death
   Who, when he lived, deserved my dearest blood:°
   But come, for that we came for, let's begin,   15
   For here lies that which bids me to be gone.°

Enter [HANGMAN *and other*] Officers, [PAGE] *and* PEDRINGANO,
with a letter in his hand, bound.

DEPUTY: Bring forth the prisoner, for the court is set.
PEDRINGANO: Gramercy,° boy, but it was time to come,
    For I had written to my lord anew
    A nearer° matter that concerneth him,   20
    For fear his lordship had forgotten me;
    But sith he hath remembered me so well —
    Come, come, come on, when shall we to this gear?°
HIERONIMO: Stand forth, thou monster, murderer of men,
    And here, for satisfaction of the world,°   25
    Confess thy folly and repent thy fault,°
    For there's thy place of execution.
PEDRINGANO: This is short work: well, to your marshalship
    First I confess, nor fear I death therefore,
    I am the man, 'twas I slew Serberine.   30
    But sir, then you think this shall be the place
    Where we shall satisfy you for this gear?°
DEPUTY: Ay, Pedringano.
PEDRINGANO: Now I think not so.
HIERONIMO: Peace, impudent, for thou shalt find it so:
    For blood with blood shall, while I sit as judge,   35
    Be satisfied, and the law discharged;
    And though myself cannot receive the like,
    Yet will I see that others have their right.
    Despatch! the fault's approvèd° and confessed,
    And by our law he is condemned to die.   40
HANGMAN: Come on sir, are you ready?
PEDRINGANO: To do what, my fine officious knave?
HANGMAN: To go to this gear.°
PEDRINGANO: O sir, you are too forward; thou wouldst fain furnish me
    with a halter, to disfurnish me of my habit,° so I should go out of   45
    this gear, my raiment, into that gear, the rope. But, hangman, now
    I spy your knavery, I'll not change° without boot,° that's flat.
HANGMAN: Come sir.
PEDRINGANO: So then, I must up?
HANGMAN: No remedy.   50
PEDRINGANO: Yes, but there shall be for my coming down.
HANGMAN: Indeed, here's a remedy for that.
PEDRINGANO: How? be turned off?
HANGMAN: Ay truly; come, are you ready? I pray sir, despatch:° the day
    goes away.   55

PEDRINGANO: What, do you hang by the hour?° If you do, I may chance
to break your old custom.
HANGMAN: Faith, you have reason, for I am like to break your young
neck.
PEDRINGANO: Dost thou mock me, hangman? Pray God I be not   60
preserved to break your knave's pate° for this!
HANGMAN: Alas, sir, you are a foot too low to reach it, and I hope you
will never grow so high while I am in the office.°
PEDRINGANO: Sirrah, dost see yonder boy with the box in his hand?
HANGMAN: What, he that points to it with his finger?   65
PEDRINGANO: Ay, that companion.°
HANGMAN: I know him not, but what of him?
PEDRINGANO: Dost thou think to live till his old doublet will make thee
a new truss?°
HANGMAN: Ay, and many a fair year after, to truss up° many an   70
honester man than either thou or he.
PEDRINGANO: What hath he in his box, as thou think'st?
HANGMAN: Faith, I cannot tell, nor I care not greatly. Methinks you
should rather hearken° to your soul's health.
PEDRINGANO: Why, sirrah hangman? I take it, that that is good for the 75
body is likewise good for the soul; and it may be, in that box is
balm for both.
HANGMAN: Well, thou art even the merriest piece of man's flesh that
e'er groaned at my office door.
PEDRINGANO: Is your roguery become an office,° with a knave's name?   80
HANGMAN: Ay, and that shall all they witness that see you seal it° with
a thief's name.
PEDRINGANO: I prithee request this good company to pray with me.
HANGMAN: Ay, marry, sir, this is a good motion:° my masters, you see
here's a good fellow.   85
PEDRINGANO: Nay, nay, now I remember me, let them alone till some
other time, for now I have no great need.
HIERONIMO: I have not seen a wretch so impudent!
    O monstrous times, where murder's set so light,
    And where the soul, that should be shrined in heaven,   90
    Solely delights in interdicted° things,
    Still° wand'ring in the thorny passages°
    That intercepts itself of happiness.°
    Murder, O bloody monster! — God forbid
    A fault° so foul should scape unpunishèd.   95
    Despatch, and see this execution done:
    This makes me to remember thee, my son.   *Exit* HIERONIMO.
PEDRINGANO: Nay, soft, no haste.
DEPUTY: Why, wherefore stay you? have you hope of life?
PEDRINGANO: Why, ay.   100

HANGMAN: As how?
PEDRINGANO: Why, rascal, by my pardon from the King.
HANGMAN: Stand° you on that? then you shall off with this.

He turns him off.

DEPUTY: So, executioner; convey him hence,
    But let his body be unburièd.   105
    Let not the earth be chokèd or infect°
    With that which heaven contemns° and men neglect.   *Exeunt.*

Act Three, Scene Seven

Enter HIERONIMO.

HIERONIMO: Where shall I run to breathe abroad° my woes,
    My woes, whose weight hath wearièd the earth?
    Or mine exclaims,° that have surcharged the air
    With ceaseless plaints for my deceasèd son?
    The blust'ring winds, conspiring with my words,   5
    At my lament have moved the leaveless trees,
    Disrobed the meadows of their flowered green,
    Made mountains marsh with spring-tides of my tears,
    And broken through the brazen gates of hell.
    Yet still tormented is my tortured soul   10
    With broken sighs and restless passions,°
    That wingèd mount, and, hovering in the air,
    Beat at the windows of the brightest heavens,
    Soliciting for justice and revenge:
    But they are placed in those empyreal heights°   15
    Where, countermured° with walls of diamond,
    I find the place impregnable, and they
    Resist my woes, and give my words no way.

Enter HANGMAN *with a letter.*°

HANGMAN: O lord, sir, God bless you, sir, the man, sir, Petergade,° sir,
    he that was so full of merry conceits —°   20
HIERONIMO: Well, what of him?
HANGMAN: O lord, sir, he went the wrong way; the fellow had a fair
    commission° to the contrary. Sir, here is his passport; I pray you sir,
    we have done him wrong.
HIERONIMO: I warrant thee, give it me.   25
HANGMAN: You will stand between the gallows and me?
HIERONIMO: Ay, ay.

HANGMAN: I thank your lord-worship.   *Exit* HANGMAN.
HIERONIMO: And yet, though somewhat nearer me concerns,
    I will, to ease the grief that I sustain,   30
    Take truce with sorrow while I read on this.
    'My lord, I writ as mine extremes° required,
    That you would labour° my delivery:
    If you neglect, my life is desperate,°
    And in my death I shall reveal the troth.°   35
    You know, my lord, I slew him for your sake,
    And as confederate with the prince and you,
    Won by rewards and hopeful promises,
    I holp° to murder Don Horatio, too.'
    Holp he to murder mine Horatio?   40
    And actors in th' accursèd tragedy
    Wast thou, Lorenzo, Balthazar and thou,
    Of whom my son, my son, deserved so well?
    What have I heard, what have mine eyes beheld?
    O sacred heavens, may it come to pass   45
    That such a monstrous and detested deed,
    So closely smothered,° and so long concealed,
    Shall thus by this be vengèd or revealed?
    Now see I what I durst not then suspect,
    That Bel-imperia's letter was not feigned,   50
    Nor feignèd she, though falsely they have wronged
    Both her, myself, Horatio and themselves.
    Now may I make compare, 'twixt hers and this,°
    Of every accident;° I ne'er could find°
    Till now, and now I feelingly° perceive,   55
    They did what heaven unpunished would not leave.
    O false Lorenzo, are these thy flattering looks?
    Is this the honour that thou didst my son?
    And Balthazar, bane° to thy soul and me,
    Was this the ransom he reserved thee for?   60
    Woe to the cause of these constrainèd° wars,
    Woe to thy baseness and captivity,
    Woe to thy birth, thy body and thy soul,
    Thy cursèd father, and thy conquered self!
    And banned° with bitter execrations be   65
    The day and place where he did pity thee!
    But wherefore waste I mine unfruitful words,
    When naught but blood will satisfy my woes?
    I will go plain me° to my lord the king,
    And cry aloud for justice through the court,   70
    Wearing the flints with these my withered feet,
    And either purchase° justice by entreats

Or tire them all with my revenging threats.   *Exit.*

Act Three, Scene Eight

Enter ISABELLA *and her* MAID.

ISABELLA: So that you say this herb will purge° the eye,
    And this the head?
    Ah, but none of them will purge the heart:
    No, there's no medicine left for my disease,
    Nor any physic to recure° the dead.   *She runs lunatic.* 5
    Horatio! O where's Horatio?
MAID: Good madam, affright not thus yourself
    With outrage° for your son Horatio:
    He sleeps in quiet in the Elysian fields.°
ISABELLA: Why, did I not give you gowns and goodly things,   10
    Bought you a whistle and a whipstalk° too,
    To be revengèd on their villainies?
MAID: Madam, these humours° do torment my soul.
ISABELLA: My soul? poor soul, thou talks of things
    Thou know'st not what — my soul hath silver wings   15
    That mounts me up unto the highest heavens.
    To heaven, ay, there sits my Horatio,
    Backed with a troop of fiery cherubins,
    Dancing about his newly-healèd wounds,
    Singing sweet hymns and chanting heavenly notes,   20
    Rare° harmony to greet° his innocence,
    That died, ay, died, a mirror° in our days.
    But say, where shall I find the men, the murderers,
    That slew Horatio? Whither shall I run
    To find them out that murderèd my son?   *Exeunt.* 25

Act Three, Scene Nine

BEL-IMPERIA *at a window.*°

BEL-IMPERIA: What means this outrage that is offered me?
    Why am I thus sequestered° from the court?
    No notice?° Shall I not know the cause
    Of this, my secret° and suspicious ills?
    Accursèd brother, unkind° murderer,   5
    Why bends° thou thus thy mind to martyr me?

Hieronimo, why writ I of thy wrongs,
Or why art thou so slack in thy revenge?
Andrea, O Andrea, that thou sawest
Me for thy friend Horatio handled thus,   10
And him for me thus causeless murderèd.
Well, force perforce,° I must constrain myself
To patience, and apply me to the time,°
Till heaven, as I have hoped, shall set me free.

Enter CHRISTOPHIL.°

CHRISTOPHIL: Come, Madam Bel-imperia, this may not be.   *Exeunt.* 15

Act Three, Scene Ten

Enter LORENZO, BALTHAZAR, *and the* PAGE.

LORENZO: Boy, talk no further, thus far things go well.
    Thou art assured that thou sawest him dead?
PAGE: Or else, my lord, I live not.
LORENZO: That's enough.
    As for his resolution° in his end,
    Leave that to him with whom he sojourns now.   5
    Here, take my ring, and give it Christophil,
    And bid him let my sister be enlarged,°
    And bring her hither straight. —   *Exit* PAGE.
    This that I did was for a policy°
    To smooth° and keep the murder secret,°   10
    Which as a nine-days' wonder being o'er-blown,
    My gentle° sister will I now enlarge.
BALTHAZAR: And time, Lorenzo, for my lord the duke,
    You heard, enquirèd for her yester-night.
LORENZO: Why, and, my lord, I hope you heard me say   15
    Sufficient reason why she kept away:
    But that's all one. My lord, you love her?
BALTHAZAR: Ay.
LORENZO: Then in your love beware, deal cunningly,
    Salve° all suspicions, only soothe me up;°
    And if she hap to stand on terms° with us,   20
    As for her sweetheart, and concealment so,
    Jest with her gently: under feignèd jest
    Are things concealed that else would breed unrest.
    But here she comes.

Enter BEL-IMPERIA.

Now, sister —
BEL-IMPERIA: Sister? No,
    Thou art no brother, but an enemy;   25
    Else wouldst thou not have used thy sister so:
    First, to affright me with thy weapons drawn,
    And with extremes° abuse my company:
    And then to hurry me, like whirlwind's rage,
    Amidst a crew of thy confederates,   30
    And clap me up° where none might come at me,
    Nor I at any to reveal my wrongs.
    What madding fury° did possess thy wits?
    Or wherein is't that I offended thee?
LORENZO: Advise you better, Bel-imperia,   35
    For I have done you no disparagement,°
    Unless, by more discretion than deserved,°
    I sought to save your honour and mine own
BEL-IMPERIA: Mine honour! why Lorenzo, wherein is't
    That I neglect my reputation so,   40
    As you, or any, need to rescue it?
LORENZO: His highness and my father were resolved
    To come confer with old Hieronimo,
    Concerning certain matters of estate
    That by the viceroy was determinèd.°   45
BEL-IMPERIA: And wherein was mine honour touched in that?
BALTHAZAR: Have patience, Bel-imperia; hear the rest.
LORENZO: Me next in sight° as messenger they sent,
    To give him notice that they were so nigh:
    Now when I came, consorted with° the prince,   50
    And unexpected in an arbour there
    Found Bel-imperia with Horatio —
BEL-IMPERIA: How then?
LORENZO: Why then, remembering that old disgrace°
    Which you for Don Andrea had endured,   55
    And now were likely longer to sustain,
    By being found so meanly accompanied,°
    Thought rather, for I knew no readier mean,
    To thrust Horatio forth° my father's way.
BALTHAZAR: And carry you obscurely° somewhere else,   60
    Lest that his highness should have found you there.
BEL-IMPERIA: Even so, my lord? And you are witness
    That this is true which he entreateth of?
    You, gentle brother, forged° this for my sake,
    And you, my lord, were made his instrument: 65

A work of worth, worthy the noting too!
But what's the cause that you concealed me since?
LORENZO: Your melancholy, sister, since the news
    Of your first favourite Don Andrea's death,
    My father's old wrath hath exasperate.°   70
BALTHAZAR: And better was't for you, being in disgrace,
    To absent yourself and give his fury place.°
BEL-IMPERIA: But why had I no notice of his ire?
LORENZO: That were to add more fuel to your fire,
    Who burnt like Aetna° for Andrea's loss.   75
BEL-IMPERIA: Hath not my father then enquired for me?
LORENZO: Sister, he hath, and thus excused I thee.   *He whispereth in her ear.*
    But Bel-imperia, see the gentle° prince,
    Look on thy love, behold young Balthazar,
    Whose passions by thy presence are increased,   80
    And in whose melancholy thou mayst see
    Thy hate, his love; thy flight, his following thee.
BEL-IMPERIA: Brother, you are become an orator,
    I know not, I, by what experience,
    Too politic° for me, past all compare,   85
    Since last I saw you; but content yourself,
    The prince is meditating higher things.
BALTHAZAR: 'Tis of thy beauty then, that conquers kings:
    Of those thy tresses, Ariadne's twines,°
    Wherewith my liberty thou hast surprised:°   90
    Of that thine ivory front,° my sorrow's map,
    Wherein I see no haven to rest my hope.
BEL-IMPERIA: To love, and fear, and both at once, my lord,
    In my conceit,° are things of more import
    Than women's wits are to be busied with.   95
BALTHAZAR: 'Tis I that love.
BEL-IMPERIA: Whom?
BALTHAZAR: Bel-imperia.
BEL-IMPERIA: But I that fear.
BALTHAZAR: Whom?
BEL-IMPERIA: Bel-imperia.
LORENZO: Fear yourself?
BEL-IMPERIA: Ay, brother.
LORENZO: How?
BEL-IMPERIA: As those
    That what they love are loath and fear to lose.
BALTHAZAR: Then, fair, let Balthazar your keeper be.   100
BEL-IMPERIA: No, Balthazar doth fear as well as we:
    Et tremulo metui pavidum junxere timorem,
    Et vanum stolidae proditionis opus.°

LORENZO: Nay, and you argue things so cunningly,
    We'll go continue this discourse at court.   105
BALTHAZAR: Led by the loadstar° of her heavenly looks,
    Wends poor oppressèd Balthazar,
    As o'er the mountains walks the wanderer,
    Incertain to effect° his pilgrimage.   *Exeunt.*

Act Three, Scene Eleven

Enter two PORTINGALES, *and* HIERONIMO *meets them.*

1 PORTINGALE: By your leave, sir.
HIERONIMO: Good leave have you, nay, I pray you go,
    For I'll leave you, if you can leave me, so.
2 PORTINGALE: Pray you, which is the next° way to my lord the duke's?
HIERONIMO: The next way from me.
1 PORTINGALE: To his house, we mean.   5
HIERONIMO: Oh, hard° by, 'tis yon house that you see.
2 PORTINGALE: You could not tell us if his son were there?
HIERONIMO: Who, my lord Lorenzo?
1 PORTINGALE: Ay, sir.
             He goeth in at one door and comes out at another.°
HIERONIMO: Oh, forbear,
    For other talk for us far fitter were.
    But if you be importunate° to know   10
    The way to him, and where to find him out,
    Then list to me, and I'll resolve your doubt.
    There is a path upon your left-hand side,
    That leadeth from a guilty conscience
    Unto a forest of distrust and fear,   15
    A darksome place and dangerous to pass:
    There shall you meet with melancholy thoughts,
    Whose baleful humours° if you but uphold,°
    It will conduct you to despair and death:
    Whose rocky cliffs when you have once beheld,   20
    Within a hugy dale° of lasting night,
    That, kindled with the world's iniquities,
    Doth cast up filthy and detested fumes,
    Not far from thence, where murderers have built
    A habitation for their cursèd souls,   25
    There, in a brazen cauldron fixed by Jove°
    In his fell° wrath upon a sulphur flame,
    Yourselves shall find Lorenzo bathing him

In boiling lead and blood of innocents.°
1 PORTINGALE: Ha, ha, ha!
HIERONIMO: Ha, ha, ha!   30
   Why, ha, ha, ha! Farewell, good, ha, ha, ha!   *Exit.*
2 PORTINGALE: Doubtless this man is passing° lunatic,
   Or imperfection of his age doth make him dote.
   Come, let's away to seek my lord the duke.   [*Exeunt.*]

Act Three, Scene Twelve

Enter HIERONIMO *with a poniard in one hand, and a rope*
in the other.°

HIERONIMO: Now, sir, perhaps I come and see the king,
   The king sees me, and fain° would hear my suit:
   Why, is not this a strange and seld-seen° thing,
   That standers-by with toys° should strike me mute?
   Go to, I see their shifts,° and say no more.   5
   Hieronimo, 'tis time for thee to trudge.°
   Down by the dale that flows with purple° gore
   Standeth a fiery tower: there sits a judge
   Upon a seat of steel and molten brass,
   And 'twixt his teeth he holds a firebrand,   10
   That leads° unto the lake where hell doth stand.
   Away, Hieronimo, to him be gone:
   He'll do thee justice for Horatio's death.
   Turn down this path,° thou shalt be with him straight,°
   Or this,° and then thou need'st not take thy breath: 15
   This way, or that way? Soft and fair, not so:
   For if I hang or kill myself, let's know
   Who will revenge Horatio's murder then?
   No, no! fie, no! pardon me, I'll none of that:
            He flings away the dagger and halter.°
   This way I'll take, and this way comes the king,
               He takes them up again.   20
   And here I'll have a fling° at him, that's flat;
   And, Balthazar, I'll be with thee to bring,°
   And thee, Lorenzo! Here's the king, nay, stay,
   And here, ay here, there goes the hare away.°

Enter KING, AMBASSADOR, CASTILE *and* LORENZO.

KING: Now show, ambassador, what our viceroy saith: 25
   Hath he received the articles we sent?

HIERONIMO: Justice, O justice to Hieronimo!
LORENZO: Back! seest thou not the king is busy?
HIERONIMO: Oh, is he so?
KING: Who is he that interrupts our business?   30
HIERONIMO: Not I. Hieronimo, beware! go by, go by.°
AMBASSADOR: Renownèd king, he hath received and read
    Thy kingly proffers, and thy promised league,
    And, as a man extremely overjoyed
    To hear his son so princely entertained,   35
    Whose death he had so solemnly bewailed,
    This, for thy further satisfaction
    And kingly love, he kindly lets thee know:
    First, for the marriage of his princely son
    With Bel-imperia, thy belovèd niece,   40
    The news are more delightful to his soul
    Than myrrh or incense to the offended heavens.
    In person therefore will he come himself,
    To see the marriage rites solemnized,
    And, in the presence of the court of Spain,   45
    To knit a sure, inexplicable° band
    Of kingly love, and everlasting league,
    Betwixt the crowns of Spain and Portingale.
    There will he give his crown to Balthazar,
    And make a queen of Bel-imperia.   50
KING: Brother, how like you this our viceroy's love?
CASTILE: No doubt, my lord, it is an argument°
    Of honourable care to keep his friend,
    And wondrous zeal to Balthazar his son:
    Nor am I least indebted to his Grace,   55
    That bends° his liking to my daughter thus.
AMBASSADOR: Now last, dread lord, here hath his highness sent
    (Although he send not that° his son return)
    His ransom due to Don Horatio.
HIERONIMO: Horatio? who calls Horatio?   60
KING: And well remembered, thank his majesty.
    Here, see it given to Horatio.
HIERONIMO: Justice, O justice, justice, gentle° king!
KING: Who is that? Hieronimo?
HIERONIMO: Justice, O justice! O my son, my son,   65
    My son, whom naught can ransom or redeem!
LORENZO: Hieronimo, you are not well-advised.
HIERONIMO: Away, Lorenzo, hinder me no more,
    For thou hast made me bankrupt of my bliss.
    Give me my son! You shall not ransom him.°   70
    Away! I'll rip the bowels of the earth,   *He diggeth with his dagger.*

And ferry over to th'Elysian plains,°
And bring my son to show his deadly wounds.
Stand from about me!
I'll make a pickaxe of my poniard, 75
And here surrender up my marshalship;
For I'll go marshal up the fiends in hell,
To be avengèd on you all for this.
KING: What means this outrage?°
Will none of you restrain his fury? 80
HIERONIMO: Nay, soft and fair: you shall not need to strive,
Needs must he go that the devils drive. *Exit.*
KING: What accident hath happed° Hieronimo?
I have not seen him to demean him° so.
LORENZO: My gracious lord, he is with extreme pride, 85
Conceived of young Horatio his son,
And covetous of having to himself
The ransom of the young prince Balthazar,
Distract, and in a manner lunatic.
KING: Believe me, nephew, we are sorry for't: 90
This is the love that fathers bear their sons:
But gentle brother, go give to him this gold,
The prince's ransom; let him have his due,
For what he hath, Horatio shall not want:°
Haply° Hieronimo hath need thereof. 95
LORENZO: But if he be thus helplessly distract,
'Tis requisite his office be resigned,
And given to one of more discretion.°
KING: We shall increase his melancholy so.
'Tis best that we see further in° it first, 100
Till when, ourself will not exempt the place.°
And brother, now bring in the ambassador,
That he may be a witness of the match
'Twixt Balthazar and Bel-imperia,
And that we may prefix a certain time, 105
Wherein the marriage shall be solemnized,
That we may have thy lord the viceroy here.
AMBASSADOR: Therein your highness highly shall content
His majesty, that longs to hear from hence.
KING: On then, and hear you, lord ambassador. *Exeunt.* 110

Act Three, Scene Thirteen

Enter HIERONIMO *with a book° in his hand.*

HIERONIMO: '*Vindicta mihi!*'°
>   Ay, heaven will be revenged of every ill,°
>   Nor will they suffer murder unrepaid:
>   Then stay, Hieronimo, attend° their will,
>   For mortal men may not appoint their time.   5
>   '*Per scelus semper tutum est sceleribus iter.*'°
>   Strike, and strike home, where wrong is offered thee,
>   For evils unto ills conductors be,
>   And death's the worst of resolution.°
>   For he that thinks with patience to contend°   10
>   To quiet life, his life shall easily end.
>   '*Fata si miseros juvant, habes salutem;*
>   *Fata si vitam negant, habes sepulchrum.*'°
>   If destiny thy miseries do ease,
>   Then hast thou health, and happy shalt thou be: 15
>   If destiny deny thee life, Hieronimo,
>   Yet shalt thou be assurèd of a tomb:
>   If neither, yet let this thy comfort be,
>   Heaven covereth him that hath no burial.
>   And to conclude, I will revenge his death!   20
>   But how? not as the vulgar° wits of men,
>   With open, but inevitable ills,°
>   As by a secret, yet a certain mean,°
>   Which under kindship° will be cloakèd best.
>   Wise men will take their opportunity,   25
>   Closely° and safely fiting things to time:
>   But in extremes advantage hath no time,°
>   And therefore all times fit not for revenge.
>   Thus therefore will I rest me in unrest,
>   Dissembling quiet in unquietness,   30
>   Not seeming that I know their villainies,
>   That my simplicity° may make them think
>   That ignorantly I will let all slip:
>   For ignorance, I wot,° and well they know,
>   *Remedium malorum iners est.*°   35
>   Nor aught avails it me to menace them,
>   Who, as a wintry storm upon a plain,
>   Will bear me down with their nobility.°
>   No, no, Hieronimo, thou must enjoin°
>   Thine eyes to observation, and thy tongue   40
>   To milder speeches than thy spirit affords,
>   Thy heart to patience, and thy hands to rest,
>   Thy cap to courtesy,° and thy knee to bow,
>   Till to revenge thou know, when, where, and how.   *A noise within.*
>   How now, what noise? what coil is that you keep?°   45

Enter a SERVANT.

SERVANT: Here are a sort° of poor petitioners,
    That are importunate, and° it shall please you, sir,
    That you should plead their cases to the king.
HIERONIMO: That I should plead their several actions?°
    Why, let them enter, and let me see them.   50

Enter three CITIZENS *and an* OLD MAN.

1 CITIZEN: So I tell you this, for learning and for law,
    There's not any advocate in Spain
    That can prevail, or will take half the pain
    That he will, in pursuit of equity.
HIERONIMO: Come near, you men that thus importune me. —   55
    [*Aside.*] Now must I bear a face of gravity,
    For thus I used, before my marshalship,
    To plead in causes as corregidor. —°
    Come on sirs, what's the matter?
2 CITIZEN: Sir, an action.
HIERONIMO: Of battery?
1 CITIZEN: Mine of debt.
HIERONIMO: Give place.°   60
2 CITIZEN: No sir, mine is an action of the case.°
3 CITIZEN: Mine an *ejectione firmae* by a lease.°
HIERONIMO: Content you, sirs, are you determinèd
    That I should plead your several actions?
1 CITIZEN: Ay sir, and here's my declaration.°   65
2 CITIZEN: And here is my band.°
3 CITIZEN: And here is my lease. *They give him papers.*
HIERONIMO: But wherefore stands yon silly° man so mute,
    With mournful eyes and hands to heaven upreared?
    Come hither, father, let me know thy cause.
SENEX: O worthy sir, my cause but slightly known   70
    May move the hearts of warlike Myrmidons°
    And melt the Corsic rocks° with ruthful tears.
HIERONIMO: Say, father, tell me what's thy suit?
SENEX: No, sir, could my woes
    Give way unto my most distressful words,   75
    Then should I not in paper, as you see,
    With ink bewray° what blood° began in me.
HIERONIMO: What's here? 'The humble supplication
    Of Don Bazulto for his murdered son.'
SENEX: Ay, sir.
HIERONIMO: No, sir, it was my murdered son,   80

O my son, my son, O my son Horatio!
But mine, or thine, Bazulto, be content.
Here, take my handkercher and wipe thine eyes,
Whiles wretched I in thy mishaps may see
The lively° portrait of my dying self.
                              He draweth out a bloody napkin.°   85
O no, not this: Horatio, this was thine,
And when I dyed it in thy dearest blood,
This was a token 'twixt thy soul and me
That of thy death revengèd I should be.
But here, take this,° and this — what, my purse? —
                              [*Gives him money.*]   90
Ay, this and that, and all of them are thine,
For all as one are our extremities.°
1 CITIZEN: O see the kindness of Hieronimo!
2 CITIZEN: This gentleness shows him a gentleman.
HIERONIMO: See, see, O see thy shame, Hieronimo,   95
    See here a loving father to his son!
    Behold the sorrows and the sad laments
    That he delivereth for his son's decease!
    If love's effects so strives° in lesser things,
    If love enforce such moods in meaner° wits,   100
    If love express such power in poor estates:°
    Hieronimo, whenas° a raging sea,
    Tossed with the wind and tide, o'erturneth then
    The upper billows, course of waves to keep,°
    Whilst lesser waters labour in the deep:°   105
    Then sham'st thou not, Hieronimo, to neglect
    The sweet revenge of thy Horatio?
    Though on this earth justice will not be found,
    I'll down to hell, and in this passion
    Knock at the dismal gates of Pluto's° court,   110
    Getting by force, as once Alcides° did,
    A troop of Furies and tormenting hags
    To torture Don Lorenzo and the rest.
    Yet lest the triple-headed porter should
    Deny my passage to the slimy strond,°   115
    The Thracian poet° thou shalt counterfeit:
    Come on, old father, be my Orpheus,
    And if thou canst no notes° upon the harp,
    Then sound the burden° of thy sore heart's grief,
    Till we do gain that Proserpine may grant —   120
    Revenge on them that murderèd my son:
    Then will I rent° and tear them thus and thus,
    Shivering° their limbs in pieces with my teeth.   *Tear[s] the papers.*

1 CITIZEN: O sir, my declaration!
2 CITIZEN: Save my bond!
3 CITIZEN: Alas, my lease! it cost me ten pound,   125
   And you, my lord, have torn the same.
HIERONIMO: That cannot be, I gave it never a wound;
   Shew me one drop of blood fall from the same:
   How is it possible I should slay it then?
   Tush, no; run after, catch me if you can.
                    Exeunt all but the OLD MAN.   130
                    BAZULTO *remains till* HIERONIMO *enters again,*
                    who, staring him in the face, speaks.
HIERONIMO: And art thou come, Horatio, from the depth,
   To ask for justice in this upper earth?
   To tell thy father thou art unrevenged,
   To wring more tears from Isabella's eyes,
   Whose lights° are dimmed with over-long laments?   135
   Go back, my son, complain to Aeacus,°
   For here's no justice: gentle boy be gone,
   For justice is exiled from the earth.
   Hieronimo will bear thee company.   .
   Thy mother cries on righteous Rhadamanth   140
   For just revenge against the murderers.
SENEX: Alas my lord, whence springs this troubled speech?
HIERONIMO: But let me look on my Horatio:
   Sweet boy, how art thou changed in death's black shade!
   Had Proserpine no pity on thy youth?   145
   But suffered thy fair crimson-coloured spring
   With withered winter to be blasted thus?
   Horatio, thou art older than thy father:
   Ah, ruthless fate, that favour° thus transforms!
SENEX: Ah, my good lord, I am not your young son.   150
HIERONIMO: What, not my son? thou, then, a Fury° art,
   Sent from the empty kingdom of black night
   To summon me to make appearance
   Before grim Minos and just Rhadamanth,
   To plague Hieronimo that is remiss   155
   And seeks not vengeance for Horatio's death.
SENEX: I am a grievèd man, and not a ghost,
   That came for justice for my murdered son.
HIERONIMO: Ay, now I know thee, now thou nam'st thy son,
   Thou art the lively° image of my grief: 160
   Within thy face my sorrows I may see.
   Thy eyes are gummed with tears, thy cheeks are wan,
   Thy forehead troubled, and thy mutt'ring lips
   Murmur sad words abruptly broken off,

By force of windy sighs thy spirit breathes,   165
And all this sorrow riseth for thy son:
And selfsame sorrow feel I for my son.
Come in, old man, thou shalt to Isabel;
Lean on my arm: I thee, thou me shalt stay,°
And thou, and I, and she, will sing a song,   170
Three parts in one, but all of discords framed —
Talk not of cords,° but let us now be gone,
For with a cord Horatio was slain.

Act Three, Scene Fourteen

Enter KING *of Spain, the* DUKE, VICEROY, *and* LORENZO,
BALTHAZAR, DON PEDRO, *and* BEL-IMPERIA.

KING: Go, brother, it is the Duke of Castile's cause,°
    Salute the Viceroy in our name.
CASTILE: I go.
VICEROY: Go forth, Don Pedro, for thy nephew's sake,
    And greet the Duke of Castile.
PEDRO: It shall be so.
KING: And now to meet these Portuguese,   5
    For as we now are, so sometimes were these,
    Kings and commanders of the western Indies.°
    Welcome, brave Viceroy, to the court of Spain,
    And welcome, all his honourable train!°
    'Tis not unknown to us for why you come,   10
    Or have so kingly crossed the seas:°
    Sufficeth it, in this we note the troth°
    And more than common love you lend to us.
    So is it that mine honourable niece
    (For it beseems us now that it be known)   15
    Already is betrothed to Balthazar:
    And by appointment and our condescent°
    To-morrow are they to be marrièd.
    To this intent we entertain thyself,
    Thy followers, their pleasure° and our peace: 20
    Speak, men of Portingale, shall it be so?
    If ay, say so: if not, say flatly no.
VICEROY: Renownèd King, I come not as thou think'st,
    With doubtful followers, unresolvèd men,
    But such as have upon thine articles   25
    Confirmed thy motion° and contented me.

Know, sovereign, I come to solemnize
The marriage of thy beloved niece,
Fair Bel-imperia, with my Balthazar —
With thee, my son, whom sith° I live to see,   30
Here take my crown, I give it her and thee;
And let me live a solitary life,
In ceaseless prayers,
To think how strangely heaven hath thee preserved.   [*He weeps.*]
KING: See brother, see, how nature strives in him!   35
   Come, worthy Viceroy, and accompany
   Thy friend with thine extremities:°
   A place more private fits this princely mood.
VICEROY: Or here or where your highness thinks it good.
                  Exeunt all but CASTILE *and* LORENZO.
CASTILE: Nay stay, Lorenzo, let me talk with you.   40
   Seest thou this entertainment° of these kings?
LORENZO: I do, my lord, and joy to see the same.
CASTILE: And knowest thou why this meeting is?
LORENZO: For her, my lord, whom Balthazar doth love,
   And to confirm their promised marriage.   45
CASTILE: She is thy sister?
LORENZO: Who, Bel-imperia?
   Ay, my gracious lord, and this is the day
   That I have longed so happily to see.
CASTILE: Thou wouldst be loath that any fault of thine
   Should intercept° her in her happiness.   50
LORENZO: Heavens will not let Lorenzo err so much.
CASTILE: Why then, Lorenzo, listen to my words:
   It is suspected and reported too,
   That thou, Lorenzo, wrong'st Hieronimo,
   And in his suits towards his majesty   55
   Still° keep'st him back, and seeks to cross° his suit.
LORENZO: That I, my lord —?
CASTILE: I tell thee, son, myself have heard it said,
   When to my sorrow I have been ashamed
   To answer for thee, though thou art my son.   60
   Lorenzo, know'st thou not the common° love
   And kindness° that Hieronimo hath won
   By his deserts within the court of Spain?
   Or seest thou not the king my brother's care
   In his behalf, and to procure his health?   65
   Lorenzo, shouldst thou thwart his passions,°
   And he exclaim against° thee to the king,
   What honour were't in this assembly,
   Or what a scandal were't among the kings

To hear Hieronimo exclaim on thee? 70
Tell me, and look thou tell me truly too,
Whence grows the ground of this report in court?
LORENZO: My lord, it lies not in Lorenzo's power
To stop the vulgar,° liberal° of their tongues:
A small advantage° makes a water-breach,° 75
And no man lives that long contenteth all.
CASTILE: Myself have seen thee busy to keep back
Him and his supplications from the King.
LORENZO: Yourself, my lord, hath seen his passions,
That ill-beseemed° the presence of a king, 80
And for I pitied him in his distress,
I held him thence with kind and courteous words,
As free from malice to Hieronimo
As to my soul, my lord.
CASTILE: Hieronimo, my son, mistakes thee then. 85
LORENZO: My gracious father, believe me so he doth.
But what's a silly° man, distract in mind,
To think upon the murder of his son?
Alas, how easy is it for him to err!
But for his satisfaction and the world's, 90
'Twere good, my lord, that Hieronimo and I
Were reconciled, if he misconster° me.
CASTILE: Lorenzo, thou hast said, it shall be so;
Go one of you and call Hieronimo.

Enter BALTHAZAR *and* BEL-IMPERIA.

BALTHAZAR: Come Bel-imperia, Balthazar's content, 95
My sorrow's ease and sovereign of my bliss,
Sith heaven hath ordained thee to be mine:
Disperse those clouds and melancholy looks,
And clear them up with those thy sun-bright eyes
Wherein my hope and heaven's fair beauty lies. 100
BEL-IMPERIA: My looks, my lord, are fitting for my love,
Which, new begun, can show no brighter yet.
BALTHAZAR: New-kindled flames should burn as morning sun.
BEL-IMPERIA: But not too fast, lest heat and all be done.°
I see my lord my father.
BALTHAZAR: Truce, my love; 105
I will go salute° him.
CASTILE: Welcome, Balthazar,
Welcome brave prince, the pledge of Castile's peace;
And welcome Bel-imperia. How now, girl?
Why com'st thou sadly° to salute us thus?

Content thyself, for I am satisfied,   110
It is not now as when Andrea lived,
We have forgotten and forgiven that,
And thou art gracèd with a happier love.
But Balthazar, here comes Hieronimo,
I'll have a word with him.   115

Enter HIERONIMO *and a* SERVANT.

HIERONIMO: And where's the duke?
SERVANT: Yo nder.
HIERONIMO: Even so:
    What new device° have they devised, trow?°
    Pocas palabras,° mild as the lamb,
    Is't I will be revenged? no, I am not the man.
CASTILE: Welcome, Hieronimo.   120
LORENZO: Welcome, Hieronimo.
BALTHAZAR: Welcome, Hieronimo.
HIERONIMO: My lords, I thank you for Horatio.
CASTILE: Hieronimo, the reason that I sent
    To speak with you, is this.
HIERONIMO: What, so short?   125
    Then I'll be gone, I thank you for't.   *[He goes to leave.]*
CASTILE: Nay, stay, Hieronimo! Go call him, son.
LORENZO: Hieronimo, my father craves a word with you.
HIERONIMO: With me, sir? why my lord, I thought you had done.
LORENZO [*aside*]: No; would he had!
CASTILE: Hieronimo, I hear   130
    You find yourself aggrievèd at my son
    Because you have not access unto the king,
    And say 'tis he that intercepts° your suits.
HIERONIMO: Why, is not this a miserable thing, my lord?
CASTILE: Hieronimo, I hope you have no cause,   135
    And would be loath that one of your deserts
    Should once have reason to suspect my son,
    Considering how I think of you myself.
HIERONIMO: Your son, Lorenzo? whom, my noble lord?
    The hope of Spain, mine honourable friend?   140
    Grant me the combat of them,° if they dare.   *Draws out his sword.*
    I'll meet him face to face to tell me so.
    These be the scandalous reports of such
    As love not me, and hate my lord too much.
    Should I suspect Lorenzo would prevent°   145
    Or cross my suit, that loved my son so well?
    My lord, I am ashamed it should be said.

LORENZO: Hieronimo, I never gave you cause.
HIERONIMO: My good lord, I know you did not.
CASTILE: There then pause;
  And for the satisfaction of the world,   150
  Hieronimo, frequent my homely° house,
  The Duke of Castile, Cyprian's ancient seat,
  And when thou wilt, use me, my son, and it:
  But here, before Prince Balthazar and me,
  Embrace each other, and be perfect friends.   155
HIERONIMO: Ay, marry,° my lord, and shall:
  Friends, quoth he? see, I'll be friends with you all:
  Specially with you, my lovely lord.
  For divers causes it is fit for us
  That we be friends; the world is suspicious,   160
  And men may think what we imagine not.
BALTHAZAR: Why, this is friendly done, Hieronimo.
LORENZO: And thus, I hope, old grudges are forgot.
HIERONIMO: What else? it were a shame it should not be so.
CASTILE: Come on, Hieronimo, at my request;   165
  Let us entreat your company today.   *Exeunt [all but* HIERONIMO].
HIERONIMO: Your lordship's to command. — Pha!° keep your way.
  Chi mi fa più carezze che non suole,
  Tradito mi ha, o tradir mi vuole.°   *Exit.*

Act Three, Scene Fifteen

Ghost [of ANDREA] *and* REVENGE.

ANDREA: Awake, Erichtho!° Cerberus,° awake!
  Solicit Pluto, gentle Proserpine;°
  To combat, Acheron and Erebus!°
  For ne'er by Styx and Phlegethon in hell
  ....°   5
  Nor ferried Charon° to the fiery lakes
  Such fearful sights as poor Andrea sees!
  Revenge, awake!
REVENGE: Awake? for why?
ANDREA: Awake, Revenge, for thou art ill-advised
  To sleep; awake! what, thou art warned to watch!   10
REVENGE: Content thyself, and do not trouble me.
ANDREA: Awake, Revenge, if love, as love hath had,
  Have yet the power or prevalence in hell!
  Hieronimo with Lorenzo is joined in league

And intercepts° our passage to revenge: 15
Awake, Revenge, or we are woe-begone!
REVENGE: Thus worldlings ground° what they have dreamed upon.
Content thyself, Andrea; though I sleep,
Yet is my mood° soliciting° their souls.
Sufficeth thee that poor Hieronimo   20
Cannot forget his son Horatio.
Nor dies Revenge, although he sleep awhile;
For in unquiet quietness is feigned,
And slumb'ring is a common worldly wile.
Behold, Andrea, for an instance how   25
Revenge hath slept, and then imagine thou
What 'tis to be subject to destiny.

Enter a Dumb Show.°

ANDREA: Awake, Revenge; reveal this mystery.°
REVENGE: The two first, the nuptial torches bore,
As brightly burning as the mid-day's sun: 30
But after them doth Hymen° hie° as fast,
Clothed in sable, and a saffron robe,°
And blows them out and quencheth them with blood,
As discontent that things continue so.
ANDREA: Sufficeth me; thy meaning's understood,   35
And thanks to thee and those infernal powers
That will not tolerate a lover's woe.
Rest thee, for I will sit to see the rest.
REVENGE: Then argue not, for thou hast thy request.

Act Four, Scene One

Enter BEL-IMPERIA *and* HIERONIMO.

BEL-IMPERIA: Is this the love thou bear'st Horatio?
Is this the kindness that thou counterfeits?
Are these the fruits of thine incessant tears?
Hieronimo, are these thy passions,°
Thy protestations and thy deep laments,   5
That thou wert wont to weary men withal?°
O unkind° father, O deceitful world!
[With what excuses canst thou shield thyself]
From this dishonour and the hate of men?°
Thus to neglect the loss and life of him   10
Whom both my letters and thine own belief
Assures thee to be causeless slaughtered!
Hieronimo, for shame, Hieronimo,

Be not a history° to after-times
Of such ingratitude unto thy son.   15
Unhappy mothers of such children then,
But monstrous fathers, to forget so soon
The death of those whom they with care and cost
Have tendered° so, thus careless° should be lost.
Myself, a stranger in respect of° thee,   20
So loved his life, as still I wish their deaths,
Nor shall his death be unrevenged by me,
Although I bear it out for fashion's sake:°
For here I swear in sight of heaven and earth,
Shouldst thou neglect the love thou shouldst retain   25
And give it over and devise° no more,
Myself should send their hateful souls to hell,
That wrought his downfall with extremest° death.
HIERONIMO: But may it be that Bel-imperia
Vows such revenge as she hath deigned to say?   30
Why then, I see that heaven applies our drift,°
And all the saints do sit soliciting
For vengeance on those cursèd murderers.
Madam, 'tis true, and now I find it so,
I found a letter, written in your name,   35
And in that letter, how Horatio died.
Pardon, O pardon, Bel-imperia,
My fear and care° in not believing it,
Nor think I thoughtless° think upon a mean°
To let his death be unrevenged at full.   40
And here I vow (so you but give consent,
And will conceal my resolution)
I will ere long determine of° their deaths,
That causeless thus have murderèd my son.
BEL-IMPERIA: Hieronimo, I will consent, conceal,   45
And aught that may effect for thine avail,°
Join with thee to revenge Horatio's death.
HIERONIMO: On, then; and whatsoever I devise,
Let me entreat you grace my practices;°
For why,° the plot's already in mine head.   50
Here they are.

Enter BALTHAZAR *and* LORENZO.

BALTHAZAR: How now, Hieronimo?
What, courting Bel-imperia?
HIERONIMO: Ay, my lord,
Such courting as, I promise you,

She hath my heart, but you, my lord, have hers.
LORENZO: But now, Hieronimo, or never,   55
    We are to entreat your help.
HIERONIMO: My help?
    Why, my good lords, assure yourselves of me,
    For you have given me cause,
    Ay, by my faith have you.
BALTHAZAR: It pleasèd you
    At the entertainment of the ambassador   60
    To grace° the king so much as with a show.
    Now, were your study° so well furnishèd,
    As for the passing of the first night's sport
    To entertain my father with the like,
    Or any such-like pleasing motion,°   65
    Assure yourself it would content them well.
HIERONIMO: Is this all?
BALTHAZAR: Ay, this is all.
HIERONIMO Why then I'll fit you;° say no more.
    When I was young, I gave my mind
    And plied myself to fruitless poetry: 70
    Which though it profit the professor° naught,
    Yet is it passing° pleasing to the world.
LORENZO: And how for that?°
HIERONIMO: Marry, my good lord, thus —
    And yet methinks you are too quick° with us —
    When in Toledo° there I studièd,   75
    It was my chance to write a tragedy:
    See here my lords,   *He shows them a book.*
    Which long forgot, I found this other day.
    Now would your lordships favour me so much
    As but to grace° me with your acting it —   80
    I mean each one of you to play a part —
    Assure you it will prove most passing strange,°
    And wondrous plausible° to that assembly.
BALTHAZAR: What, would you have us play a tragedy?
HIERONIMO: Why, Nero thought it no disparagement,°   85
    And kings and emperors have ta'en delight
    To make experience° of their wits in plays!
LORENZO: Nay, be not angry, good Hieronimo;
    The prince but asked a question.
BALTHAZAR: In faith, Hieronimo, and° you be in earnest,   90
    I'll make one.
LORENZO: And I another.
HIERONIMO: Now, my good lord, could you entreat
    Your sister Bel-imperia to make one?

For what's a play without a woman in it?
BEL-IMPERIA: Little entreaty shall serve me, Hieronimo,   95
    For I must needs be employèd in your play.
HIERONIMO: Why, this is well; I tell you, lordings,
    It was determinèd to have been acted
    By gentlemen, and scholars too,
    Such as could° tell what to speak.   100
BALTHAZAR: And now it shall be played by princes and courtiers,
    Such as can tell how to speak,°
    If, as it is our country manner,
    You will but let us know the argument.°
HIERONIMO: That shall I roundly.° The chronicles of Spain   105
    Record this written of a knight of Rhodes:
    He was betrothed and wedded at the length
    To one Perseda, an Italian dame,°
    Whose beauty ravished all that her beheld,
    Especially the soul of Soliman,°   110
    Who at the marriage was the chiefest guest.
    By sundry means sought Soliman to win
    Perseda's love, and could not gain the same.
    Then gan he break° his passions to a friend,
    One of his bashaws° whom he held full dear;   115
    Her had this bashaw long solicited,°
    And saw she was not otherwise to be won
    But by her husband's death, this knight of Rhodes,
    Whom presently by treachery he slew.
    She, stirred with an exceeding hate therefore,   120
    As cause of this slew Soliman,
    And to escape the bashaw's tyranny
    Did stab herself: and this the tragedy.
LORENZO: O excellent!
BEL-IMPERIA: But say, Hieronimo,
    What then became of him that was the bashaw?   125
HIERONIMO: Marry thus, moved with remorse of his misdeeds,
    Ran to a mountain top and hung himself.
BALTHAZAR: But which of us is to perform that part?
HIERONIMO: Oh, that will I, my lords, make no doubt of it:
    I'll play the murderer, I warrant you,   130
    For I already have conceited that.°
BALTHAZAR: And what shall I?
HIERONIMO: Great Soliman, the Turkish emperor.
LORENZO: And I?
HIERONIMO: Erastus, the knight of Rhodes.
BEL-IMPERIA: And I?
HIERONIMO: Perseda, chaste and resolute.

And here, my lords, are several abstracts drawn,° 135
For each of you to note your parts,
And act it as occasion's offered you.
You must provide a Turkish cap,
A black mustachio and a fauchion;° *Gives a paper to* BALTHAZAR.
You with a cross like to a knight of Rhodes;
                                       Gives another to LORENZO. 140
And madam, you must attire yourself   *He giveth* BEL-IMPERIA *another.*
Like Phoebe, Flora, or the Huntress,°
Which to your discretion shall seem best.
And as for me, my lords, I'll look to° one,
And with the ransom that the viceroy sent 145
So furnish and perform this tragedy,
As all the world shall say Hieronimo
Was liberal in gracing° of it so.
BALTHAZAR: Hieronimo, methinks a comedy were better.
HIERONIMO: A comedy? 150
    Fie! comedies are fit for common wits.°
    But to present a kingly troop° withal,
    Give me a stately-written tragedy,
    Tragedia cothurnata,° fitting kings,
    Containing matter,° and not common things. 155
    My lords, all this must be performed
    As fitting for the first night's revelling.
    The Italian tragedians° were so sharp of wit,
    That in one hour's meditation°
    They would perform anything in action. 160
LORENZO: And well it may, for I have seen the like
    In Paris, 'mongst the French tragedians.
HIERONIMO: In Paris? mass,° and well rememberèd!
    There's one thing more that rests° for us to do.
BALTHAZAR: What's that, Hieronimo? forget not anything. 165
HIERONIMO: Each one of us must act his part
    In unknown° languages,
    That it may breed the more variety.
    As you, my lord, in Latin, I in Greek,
    You in Italian, and for because I know 170
    That Bel-imperia hath practised the French,
    In courtly French shall all her phrases be.
BEL-IMPERIA: You mean to try my cunning° then, Hieronimo.
BALTHAZAR: But this will be a mere° confusion,
    And hardly° shall we all be understood. 175
HIERONIMO: It must be so, for the conclusion
    Shall prove the invention° and all was good:
    And I myself in an oration,

And with a strange and wondrous show besides,
That I will have there behind a curtain,   180
Assure yourself, shall make the matter° known.
And all shall be concluded in one scene,
For there's no pleasure ta'en in tediousness.
BALTHAZAR [*aside to* LORENZO]: How like you this?
LORENZO [*aside to* BALTHAZAR]:   Why thus, my lord,
We must resolve to soothe his humours up.°   185
BALTHAZAR: On then, Hieronimo, farewell till soon.
HIERONIMO: You'll ply this gear?°
LORENZO: I warrant you.   *Exeunt all but* HIERONIMO.
HIERONIMO: Why, so:
Now shall I see the fall of Babylon,°
Wrought by the heavens in this confusion.
And if the world like not this tragedy,   190
Hard is the hap° of old Hieronimo.   *Exit.*

Act Four, Scene Two

Enter ISABELLA *with a weapon.*°

ISABELLA: Tell me no more! O monstrous homicides!
Since neither piety nor pity moves
The king to justice or compassion,
I will revenge myself upon this place
Where thus they murdered my belovèd son. *She cuts down the arbour.* 5
Down with these branches and these loathsome boughs
Of this unfortunate° and fatal pine!
Down with them, Isabella; rent° them up
And burn the roots from whence the rest is sprung:
I will not leave a root, a stalk, a tree,   10
A bough, a branch, a blossom, nor a leaf,
No, not an herb within this garden plot —
Accursèd complot° of my misery.
Fruitless for ever may this garden be,
Barren the earth, and blissless whosoever   15
Imagines° not to keep it unmanured!°
An eastern wind commixed with noisome° airs
Shall blast the plants and the young saplings;
The earth with serpents shall be pesterèd,°
And passengers,° for fear to be infect,°   20
Shall stand aloof, and looking at it, tell,
'There, murdered, died the son of Isabel.'

Ay, here he died, and here I him embrace:
See where his ghost solicits with his wounds
Revenge on her that should revenge his death. 25
Hieronimo, make haste to see thy son,
For sorrow and despair hath cited° me
To hear Horatio plead with Rhadamanth:°
Make haste, Hieronimo, to hold excused°
Thy negligence in pursuit of their deaths, 30
Whose hateful wrath bereaved him of his breath.
Ah, nay, thou dost delay their deaths,
Forgives the murderers of thy noble son,
And none but I bestir me — to no end.
And as I curse this tree from further fruit, 35
So shall my womb be cursèd for his sake,
And with this weapon will I wound the breast, *She stabs herself.*
The hapless° breast, that gave Horatio suck. [*Exit.*]

Act Four, Scene Three

Enter HIERONIMO; *he knocks up the curtain.*°
Enter the DUKE *of* CASTILE.

CASTILE: How now, Hieronimo, where's your fellows,°
    That you take all this pain?
HIERONIMO: O sir, it is for the author's credit
    To look that all things may go well.
    But, good my lord, let me entreat your Grace 5
    To give the king the copy of the play:°
    This is the argument° of what we show.
CASTILE: I will, Hieronimo.
HIERONIMO: One thing more, my good lord.
CASTILE: What's that?
HIERONIMO: Let me entreat your Grace,
    That when the train° are passed into the gallery° 10
    You would vouchsafe to throw me down° the key.
CASTILE: I will, Hieronimo. *Exit* CASTILE.
HIERONIMO: What, are you ready, Balthazar?
    Bring a chair and a cushion for the King.

Enter BALTHAZAR *with a chair.*

Well done, Balthazar! Hang up the title,°
    Our scene is Rhodes; what, is your beard on? 15
BALTHAZAR: Half on; the other is in my hand.

HIERONIMO: Despatch,° for shame; are you so long?   *Exit* BALTHAZAR.
    Bethink thyself, Hieronimo,
    Recall thy wits, recompt° thy former wrongs
    Thou hast received by murder of thy son,   20
    And lastly, not least, how Isabel,
    Once his mother and thy dearest wife,
    All woe-begone for him hath slain herself.
    Behoves thee then, Hieronimo, to be revenged.
    The plot is laid of dire revenge: 25
    On then, Hieronimo, pursue revenge,
    For nothing wants° but acting° of revenge.   *Exit* HIERONIMO.

Act Four, Scene Four

Enter Spanish KING, VICEROY, *the* DUKE *of* CASTILE, *and their train.*

KING: Now, Viceroy, shall we see the tragedy
    Of Soliman the Turkish emperor,
    Performed of pleasure° by your son the prince,
    My nephew, Don Lorenzo, and my niece.
VICEROY: Who? Bel-imperia?   5
KING: Ay, and Hieronimo our marshal,
    At whose request they deign to do't themselves:
    These be our pastimes in the court of Spain.
    Here, brother, you shall be the book-keeper:
    This is the argument° of that they show.   *He giveth him a book.* 10

        Gentlemen, this play of Hieronimo in sundry languages, was
           thought good to be set down in English more largely,°
              for the easier understanding to every
                  public reader.°

       Enter BALTHAZAR, BEL-IMPERIA, *and* HIERONIMO.

BALTHAZAR: *Bashaw, that Rhodes is ours, yield heavens the honour,*
    And holy Mahomet, our sacred prophet;
    And be thou graced with every excellence
    That Soliman can give, or thou desire.
    But thy desert in conquering Rhodes is less   15
    Than in reserving° this fair Christian nymph,
    Perseda, blissful lamp of excellence,
    Whose eyes compel, like powerful adamant,°
    The warlike heart of Soliman to wait.°

KING: See, Viceroy, that is Balthazar your son, 20
    That represents the emperor Soliman:
    How well he acts his amorous passion.
VICEROY: Ay, Bel-imperia hath taught him that.
CASTILE: That's because his mind runs all on Bel-imperia.
HIERONIMO: *Whatever joy earth yields betide your majesty.* 25
BALTHAZAR: *Earth yields no joy without Perseda's love.*
HIERONIMO: *Let then Perseda on your grace attend.*
BALTHAZAR: *She shall not wait on me, but I on her:*
    Drawn by the influence of her lights, °I yield.
    But let my friend, the Rhodian knight, come forth, 30
    Erasto, dearer than my life to me,
    That he may see Perseda, my beloved.

Enter [LORENZO *as*] ERASTO.

KING: Here comes Lorenzo; look upon the plot,°
    And tell me, brother, what part plays he?
BEL-IMPERIA: *Ah, my Erasto, welcome to Perseda.*
LORENZO: *Thrice happy is Erasto that thou liv'st,*
    Rhodes' loss is nothing to° Erasto's joy:
    Sith° his Perseda lives, his life survives.
BALTHAZAR: *Ah, Bashaw, here is love between Erasto*
    And fair Perseda, sovereign of my soul. 40
HIERONIMO: *Remove Erasto, mighty Soliman,*
    And then Perseda will be quickly won.
BALTHAZAR: *Erasto is my friend, and while he lives*
    Perseda never will remove her love.
HIERONIMO: *Let not Erasto live to grieve great Soliman.* 45
BALTHAZAR: *Dear is Erasto in our princely eye.*
HIERONIMO: *But if he be your rival, let him die.*
BALTHAZAR: *Why, let him die, so love commandeth me.*
    Yet grieve I that Erasto should so die.
HIERONIMO: *Erasto, Soliman saluteth thee,* 50
    And lets thee wit° by me his highness' will,
    Which is, thou shouldst be thus employed. *Stab*[s] *him.*
BEL-IMPERIA: *Ay me,*
    Erasto! see, Soliman, Erasto's slain!
BALTHAZAR: *Yet liveth Soliman to comfort thee.*
    Fair queen of beauty, let not favour° die, 55
    But with a gracious eye behold his grief,
    That with Perseda's beauty is increased,
    If by Perseda grief be not released.
BEL-IMPERIA: *Tyrant, desist soliciting vain suits,*
    Relentless° are mine ears to thy laments, 60

As thy butcher is pitiless and base,
Which seized on my Erasto, harmless knight.
Yet by thy power thou thinkest to command,
And to thy power Perseda doth obey:
But were she able, thus she would revenge 65
Thy treacheries on thee, ignoble prince: *Stab[s] him.*
And on herself she would be thus revenged. *Stab[s] herself.*
KING: Well said,° old Marshal, this was bravely° done!
HIERONIMO: But Bel-imperia plays Perseda well.
VICEROY: Were this in earnest, Bel-imperia, 70
 You would be better° to my son than so.
KING: But now what follows for Hieronimo?
HIERONIMO: Marry, this follows for Hieronimo:
 Here break we off our sundry languages
 And thus conclude I in our vulgar° tongue. 75
 Haply° you think — but bootless° are your thoughts, —
 That this is fabulously counterfeit,°
 And that we do as all tragedians do:
 To die today, for fashioning our scene,°
 The death of Ajax,° or some Roman peer, 80
 And in a minute starting up again,
 Revive to please tomorrow's audience.
 No, princes, know I am Hieronimo,
 The hopeless father of a hapless° son,
 Whose tongue is tuned to tell his latest° tale, 85
 Not to excuse gross errors in the play.
 I see your looks urge instance° of these words:
 Behold the reason urging me to this! *Shows his dead son.°*
 See here my show, look on this spectacle:
 Here lay my hope, and here my hope hath end; 90
 Here lay my heart, and here my heart was slain;
 Here lay my treasure, here my treasure lost;
 Here lay my bliss, and here my bliss bereft:
 But hope, heart, treasure, joy and bliss,
 All fled, failed, died, yea, all decayed with this. 95
 From forth these wounds came breath that gave me life;°
 They murdered me that made these fatal marks.
 The cause was love, whence grew this mortal hate:
 The hate, Lorenzo and young Balthazar,
 The love, my son to Bel-imperia. 100
 But night, the coverer of accursèd crimes,
 With pitchy silence hushed° these traitors' harms°
 And lent them leave, for they had sorted° leisure
 To take advantage in my garden plot
 Upon my son, my dear Horatio: 105

There, merciless, they butchered up my boy,
In black dark night, to pale dim cruel death.
He shrieks: I heard, and yet methinks I hear,
His dismal outcry echo in the air.
With soonest speed I hasted to the noise, 110
Where hanging on a tree I found my son,
Through-girt° with wounds, and slaughtered as you see.
And grieved I, think you, at this spectacle?
Speak, Portuguese, whose loss resembles mine:
If thou canst weep upon thy Balthazar, 115
'Tis like I wailed for my Horatio.
And you, my lord, whose reconcilèd son
Marched in a net,° and thought himself unseen,
And rated° me for brainsick lunacy,
With 'God amend° that mad Hieronimo!' — 120
How can you brook our play's catastrophe?°
And here behold this bloody handkercher,
Which at Horatio's death I weeping dipped
Within the river of his bleeding wounds:
It, as propitious, see, I have reserved, 125
And never hath it left my bloody heart,
Soliciting remembrance of my vow
With these, O these accursèd murderers,
Which now performed, my heart is satisfied.
And to this end the bashaw I became 130
That might revenge me on Lorenzo's life,
Who therefore was appointed to the part
And was to represent the knight of Rhodes,
That I might kill him more conveniently.
So, Viceroy, was this Balthazar, thy son, 135
Soliman, which Bel-imperia,
In person of Perseda, murdered:
Solely appointed to that tragic part,
That she might slay him that offended° her.
Poor Bel-imperia missed her part° in this, 140
For though the story saith she should have died,
Yet I of kindness, and of care to her,
Did otherwise determine of her end:
But love of him whom they did hate too much
Did urge her resolution to be such. 145
And princes, now behold Hieronimo,
Author and actor in this tragedy,
Bearing his latest fortune in his fist;°
And will as resolute conclude his part
As any of the actors gone before. 150

And gentles,° thus I end my play:
Urge no more words, I have no more to say.   *He runs to hang himself.*
KING: O hearken, Viceroy! Hold,° Hieronimo!
    Brother, my nephew and thy son are slain!
VICEROY: We are betrayed! My Balthazar is slain!   155
    Break ope° the doors, run, save Hieronimo!
                                    [*They break in, and hold* HIERONIMO.]
    Hieronimo, do but inform the king of these events,
    Upon mine honour thou shalt have no harm.
HIERONIMO: Viceroy, I will not trust thee with my life,
    Which I this day have offered to my son.   160
    Accursèd wretch,
    Why stayest thou him that was resolved to die?
KING: Speak, traitor: damned, bloody murderer, speak!
    For now I have thee I will make thee speak.
    Why hast thou done this undeserving deed?   165
VICEROY: Why hast thou murderèd my Balthazar?
CASTILE: Why hast thou butchered both my children thus?
HIERONIMO: O good words!
    As dear to me was my Horatio
    As yours, or yours, or yours, my lord, to you.   170
    My guiltless son was by Lorenzo slain,
    And by° Lorenzo and that Balthazar
    Am I at last revengèd thoroughly,
    Upon whose souls may heavens be yet avenged
    With greater far than these afflictions.   175
CASTILE: But who were thy confederates in this?
VICEROY: That was thy daughter Bel-imperia,
    For by her hand my Balthazar was slain:
    I saw her stab him.
KING: Why speak'st thou not?
HIERONIMO: What lesser liberty can kings afford   180
    Than harmless silence? then afford it me.
    Sufficeth I may not, nor I will not tell thee.
KING: Fetch forth the tortures!
    Traitor, as thou art, I'll make thee tell.
HIERONIMO: Indeed, thou may'st torment me, as his wretched son   185
    Hath done in murdering my Horatio,
    But never shalt thou force me to reveal
    The thing which I have vowed inviolate:
    And therefore, in despite of all thy threats,
    Pleased with their deaths, and eased with their revenge,   190
    First take my tongue, and afterwards my heart. [*He bites out his tongue.*]
KING: O monstrous resolution of a wretch!
    See, Viceroy, he hath bitten forth his tongue

Rather than to reveal what we required.
CASTILE: Yet can he write. 195
KING: And if in this he satisfy us not,
    We will devise th'extremest kind of death
    That ever was invented for a wretch.°
                     Then he makes signs for a knife to mend his pen.°
CASTILE: Oh, he would have a knife to mend his pen.
VICEROY [*gives* HIERONIMO *a knife*]: Here, and advise thee that thou write
    the troth.°
               [HIERONIMO] *with a knife stabs the* DUKE *and himself.* 200
KING: Look to my brother! save Hieronimo.°
    What age hath ever heard such monstrous deeds?
    My brother, and the whole succeeding hope
    That Spain expected after my decease!
    Go bear his body hence, that we may mourn 205
    The loss of our belovèd brother's death,
    That he may be entombed whate'er befall:
    I am the next, the nearest, last of all.
VICEROY: And thou, Don Pedro, do the like for us:
    Take up our hapless son, untimely slain. 210
    Set me with him, and he with woeful me,
    Upon the mainmast of a ship unmanned,
    And let the wind and tide haul° me along
    To Scylla's barking° and untamèd gulf,
    Or to the loathsome pool of Acheron,° 215
    To weep my want for my sweet Balthazar:
    Spain hath no refuge for a Portingale.

    The trumpets sound a dead march, the KING *of* Spain, *mourning,*
    after his brother's body, and the KING *of* Portingale *bearing the*
    body of his son.

Act Four, Scene Five

Ghost [of ANDREA] *and* REVENGE

ANDREA: Ay, now my hopes have end in their effects,
    When blood and sorrow finish my desires:
    Horatio murdered in his father's bower,
    Vild° Serberine by Pedringano slain,
    False Pedringano hanged by quaint° device, 5
    Fair Isabella by herself misdone,°
    Prince Balthazar by Bel-imperia stabbed,
    The Duke of Castile and his wicked son

Both done to death by old Hieronimo,
My Bel-imperia fall'n as Dido fell,°   10
And good Hieronimo slain by himself:
Ay, these were spectacles to please my soul.
Now will I beg at lovely Proserpine,
That by the virtue° of her princely doom°
I may consort° my friends in pleasing sort,   15
And on my foes work just and sharp revenge.
I'll lead my friend Horatio through those fields
Where never-dying wars are still inured;°
I'll lead fair Isabella to that train°
Where pity weeps but never feeleth pain;   20
I'll lead my Bel-imperia to those joys
That vestal virgins° and fair queens possess;
I'll lead Hieronimo where Orpheus° plays,
Adding sweet pleasure to eternal days.
But say, Revenge, for thou must help or none,   25
Against the rest how shall my hate be shown?
REVENGE: This hand shall hale them down to deepest hell,
        Where none but furies, bugs° and tortures dwell.
ANDREA: Then, sweet Revenge, do this at my request:
        Let me be judge, and doom them to unrest.   30
        Let loose poor Tityus° from the vulture's gripe,
        And let Don Cyprian supply his room;°
        Place Don Lorenzo on Ixion's° wheel,
        And let the lover's endless pains surcease°
        (Juno forgets old wrath and grants him ease);   35
        Hang Balthazar about Chimaera's° neck,
        And let him there bewail his bloody love,
        Repining at our joys that are above;
        Let Serberine go roll the fatal stone,
        And take from Sisyphus° his endless moan;   40
        False Pedringano, for his treachery,
        Let him be dragged through boiling Acheron,°
        And there live, dying still° in endless flames,
        Blaspheming gods and all their holy names.
REVENGE: Then haste we down to meet thy friends and foes;   45
        To place thy friends in ease, the rest in woes:
        For here, though death hath end° their misery,
        I'll there begin their endless tragedy.   *Exeunt.*

Finis

Notes to the Play

Dramatis Personae

12 VILLUPPO: from Italian *inviluppo*, 'entanglement'

19 CHRISTOPHIL: 'lover of Christ'; an ironic name for Lorenzo's servant

23 Halberdiers: soldiers armed with halberds, a combined spear point and battle-axe mounted on a long pole

24 Dumb-show: pageant without dialogue

25 Hymen: Roman god of marriage

27 SOLIMAN: an historical figure, Suleiman the Magnificent, ruler of the Ottoman Turks (1520–1566).

28 ERASTO: from Latin *erastes*, 'lover' Knight of Rhodes: a member of the Knights of the Order of St John, a Christian military order, famous for its defence of Rhodes and Malta against the forces of Suleiman

29 Bashaw: Turkish military commander (Pasha)

Act One, Scene One

0 SD Enter...REVENGE: it is probable that in an Elizabethan theatre Andrea and Revenge entered from beneath the stage (the traditional theatrical 'hell') by means of a trapdoor, and left in the same way at the end of the play.

7 gracious: (1) happy, fortunate; (2) well-favoured, suggesting a lover's 'grace'

8 prime and pride: spring-time and best

10 possessed: took as my lover worthy dame: nobly-born lady

11 hight: was named

13 nipped: killed with frost

15 Portingale: Portugal

19 Acheron: a river of the underworld, here identified

with the Styx, where Charon was the ferryman

23 Sol: the sun
Thetis: the sea

24 slaked: extinguished the flames flood: waters

25 Knight Marshal: Marshal of the King's House (an English title); a law officer of the royal household with responsibility for hearing pleas and suits, and punishing any crimes committed within twelve miles of the king's palace.

28 strond: shore

29 fell: cruel

30 Cerberus: the monstrous three-headed dog which guarded access to the underworld

31 porch: place of entry

33 Minos, Aeacus and Rhadamanth: the three judges of the underworld. Minos had the casting vote (see lines 50–1).

35 passport: safe-conduct

36 leaves of lottery: (1) records of allotted life; (2) lottery slips (the after-life of the dead was decided by drawing lots from an urn). Kyd seems to have both ideas in mind.

44 myrtle trees and cypress: symbolising love and sorrow

46 martialist: warrior

48–9 wounded...plain: The Trojan hero Hector was killed by the Greek warrior Achilles and his followers, the Myrmidons.

50 censor: judge

52 infernal: underworld

53 doom: pass sentence on

55 Pluto: king of the underworld

56 ever-glooming: always dark and threatening

62 his: its

63 declining: sloping down

64 downfall: sudden descent

65 Furies: three female deities who avenged wrong and punished crime

65 Ixion: condemned to an everlasting treadmill, for the

attempted rape of Hera, queen of the gods

67   usurers: money-lenders taking interest on their loans
70   wights: people
73   Elysian green: Elysium, the abode of blessed spirits, located in the underworld by classical writers such as Virgil
75   adamant: hard stone, diamond
76   Proserpine: Persephone, consort of the king of the underworld, stolen by him from her mother Demeter.
79   doom: sentence
81   rounded: whispered to
82   gates of horn: In Virgil's *Aeneid*, there are two gates of sleep; true visions emerge from the gate of horn, false visions from a gate made of ivory.
85   wot: know
90   here sit we down: In Kyd's theatre, the actors probably sat on stools on the main stage, rather than on the upper stage. mystery: events with a secret meaning

Act One, Scene Two

1   camp: army on campaign
5   posting: hurrying
8   Portingals: Portuguese tribute: money paid in token of submission. The implication is that this military campaign has re-subjugated a previously subject nation.
9   wonted: accustomed
12–14 *O multum...juris*: 'O man beloved by God, the heavens fight for you, and conspiring peoples fall on bended knee: victory is the sister of just rights.' Lines adapted by Kyd from a late-classical poem by Claudian.
20   deeper wage: greater rewards dignity: rank
21   blissful chivalry: successful skill in battle
23   bound: boundary
25   furnished: equipped

27   vaunting...device: proudly displaying various heraldic banners
29   dreadful: terrifying
32   battles: military forces squadron form: squares
33   fenced: protected, reinforced shot: soldiers equipped with firearms
34   push of pike: hand-to-hand fighting; literally thrusting with lances
35   readiest: most expert
38   ordnance: artillery played: directed their fire
40   colonel: pronounced as three syllables
41   cornet: squadron of cavalry
47   handy: hand-to-hand
48   shot: exchange of fire
50   rampiers: ramparts
51   neighbour-bounding: adjacent to the shore
52   Bellona: Roman goddess of war
54   shivered: splintered dark: darken
55–6 *Pede...viro*: 'Foot against foot, lance against lance; arms clash on arms, and each man seeks out an opponent.'
58   ill-maimed: badly wounded
59   scindered: separated
61   unbowellèd: disembowelled
62   purple: blood-red
65   lanciers: lancers
70   Here-hence: as a consequence of this
73   insulting: insolently exulting
74   sounding: tending
75   hardy: couragious
76   Pricked: spurred
80   him: himself
82   carbines: mounted musketeers
83   Phoebus: the sun
83   deep: ocean
84   charged: ordered
86   argument: token
91   stayed: held back, halted
92   subscribed: signed his name
96   frolic: rejoice
99   decay: fail in health and fortunes
99 SD *tucket*: trumpet call
104 seat: throne

120	overcloying: satiating
122	staying: stopping
131	largess: royal generosity
134	hard: serious
139	controlled: brought to an end
140	boots: profits
142	colours: standards, flags
143	distressed: taken prisoner
	corsive: corrosive agent
144	late: recent, previous
152	their holding: the way they
	hold you (cf. lines 111–15)
159	privilege: absolute authority
160	whether: which of the two
164	wan: won
167	difference: my distinction
174	want: lack
175	censure...doom: outcome of my
	judgement
177	sit beside: forgo
187	train: attendants
188	substance: wealth and property
189	guerdon: reward
190	him: Horatio
191	device: idea

Act One, Scene Three

11	state: situation
12	earth...melancholy: In medieval thought, earth, one of the four elements that made up all created things, corresponded with melancholy, one of the four bodily humours that determined each individual human temperament.
15–17	*Qui iacet...magis*: 'Who lies on the ground has no further to fall. In me, Fortune has exhausted her powers to harm. There is nothing left that can affect me further.'
19	Take it now: The Viceroy may place his crown on the ground, or pass it to one of his attendants.
20	sable weed: black garb
22	despiteful: malicious
25	wilful mad: deliberately irrational
29	whose foot...stone: Contemporary images of Fortune commonly showed a blind goddess standing on a

	rolling sphere, expressing her impartiality and fickleness.
32	complaining: lamenting
33	distained: sullied
35, 36	treasure: pronounced as three syllables
42	forced: unnatural
46	fault: crime
48	reck: pay heed to
51	still: always
54	bewray: reveal
57	mischief's: misfortune's
58	at large: in detail
65	counterfeits: acts deceitfully
72	forgery: fabrication
	miscreant: villain
74	became: was taken
80	blearèd: blinded
82	Terceira: an island in the Azores group. Alexandro apparently held the position of Capitano Donatario, or absolute ruler of a territory annexed by Portugal.
90	determine of: come to a decision about
93	envious: malicious
95	guerdon: reward, profit

Act One, Scene Four

7	nill: will not
10	chevalier: knight
11	For...fairest: 'always striving to perform the finest deeds for his glorious cause (Bel-Imperia's favour)'
16	Nemesis: goddess of retribution, especially against presumption
17	Envying at: begrudging
20	Pallas: Athene, patron goddess of Athens, who fought on the Greek side at the siege of Troy. But Kyd confuses her with Juno, whom Virgil describes as 'girt with steel' (*Aeneid*, 2. 615–16).
	Pergamus: Troy
22	paunched: stabbed in the belly
	dinged: struck
27	just remorse: righteous indignation and sorow
34	wound: embraced
35	welding: carrying
39	right: authority, rule (over Horatio's life)

42   This scarf: Knights wore such tokens of a lover's affection into battle. The same bloodstained scarf is later taken from Horatio's body by his father and worn by him, possibly on his sleeve: see 2. 5. 114–15.

55   stands thereto: gives support to it

71   disdain: indignation

74   oppress: overwhelm with sheer numbers

81   servitude: the typical posture of the courtly lover

83   conceit: sheer imagination enthralled: enslaved

84   enlarge: set free

85   laid...to gage: (1) given as a pledge (of love); (2) placed in pawn

90   ambages: roundabout ways of talking

92   boots complaint: use lies in pleading your love

96   aspèct: appearance

98   words of course: conventional phrases

99   but device: merely a device

102   in happy time: at a fortunate moment

105   humorous: temperamental

110   straight: immediately

113   fits: befits

115 SD   *Enter the Banquet*: Servants might carry on dishes; on the Elizabethan stage a property representing a sumptuously set table and stools could be carried on.

116   entreats: treats, deals with

118   pleasure: take pleasure

125   graced: honoured

130   wait...upon: attend; Horatio is to act as the royal cup-bearer.

137   grace: lend pleasure to pompous jest: stately entertainment

137 SD   *Drum*: drummer *scutcheon*: shield with armorial bearings

139   sound: perceive, understand mystery: inner meaning, significance

140–6   The first...monarchy: Kyd's history is patriotic but inaccurate. English crusaders assisted the Portuguese in the capture of Lisbon, then under Saracen rule (1147), but Robert of Gloucester was never in Portugal.

141   when...Albion: King Stephen ruled England ('Albion') from 1135–1154.

152–7   Edmund...York: In 1381–2 the historical Edmund Langley, Earl of Kent, went to the assistance of the Portuguese crown against the Spanish, but the expedition achieved nothing, and Edmund later received the title of Duke of York for his part in an expedition to Scotland.

158   special: particular, appropriate

164–7   Brave...prisoner: Gaunt led an expedition to Spain in 1386–7 and briefly claimed the Castilian throne. Popular belief magnified this event into a partial or complete conquest of Spain.

166   puissant: powerful

169   insult for: boast over

172   device: masque, show

174 SD   of: from

176   Unless...delicate: unless we could offer for your pleasure more sophisticated food

178   you...despatched: your business may be dealt with

179   set: in sitting

Act One, Scene Five

6   fell despite: ferocious hatred

Act Two, Scene One

1   coy: unresponsive, disdainful

2   hold: uphold

4   haggard: wild stoop to lure: A technical phrase; hawks were taught to return to the lure held by their trainer.

5   cleave: split open

8   rue...pain: take pity on your

patient endurance of the pain you feel as her lover
12 fault: deficiencies
13 feature: outward appearance
14 rude: unpolished
16 Such...quill: Pan the goat-god and the satyr Marsyas each challenged and failed to match the god Apollo in artistic skill in flute-playing.
quill: (1) reed flute; (2) quill pen
19 valiancy: valour
20 slandered: brought into disrepute
25 uprear her state: improve her social rank
29 ecstasies: transports of passion
31 lets...loved: prevents you from being loved
36 sound the bottom: get to the bottom (a metaphor from taking soundings to navigate unknown or dangerous waters)
39 cast about: like a hunting dog sniffing out a trail
41 *Vien qui presto*: 'come here quickly' (Italian)
47 conveyance: underhand service
52 store: abundance
58 If...in me: if I am able to
65 credit: trust
72 guerdon: reward
85 fraught: loaded
87 this cross: the hilt of Lorenzo's sword
91 unjust: dishonest
95 still: forever
100 sort: fashion, way
103 state: social rank
107 *tam...ingenio*: 'as much by force as by guile'
125 sweet conceits: pleasing expressions, figures of speech
126 limed: made into traps; birds were caught by smearing branches with a glue called bird-lime
127 smooth: flatter
131 sleight: deceit
132 in his fall: by bringing about his destruction
134 stays: delays, holds back

Act Two, Scene Two

4 contents: sources of contentment
6 SD *above*: the lovers are watched from the gallery above the stage.
7 friend: lover
9 repair: restore
11 annoy: discomfort
17 is: which is
20 joys: enjoys
23 fond: foolish, infatuated
34 cross: (1) meet; (2) counter
36 answer: reply with (in a military sense)
37 countercheck: check in return (with an answering kiss)
42 bower: an arbour, or garden-seat with an over-arching trellis. The lovers sit in it together at 2. 4. 23.
45 Vesper: Venus, the evening star
46 distressful travellers: weary labourers
48 Happily: perhaps
48 nightingale: A bird associated in Greek legend with love and grief; according to folklore it sang with its breast against a thorn (*prickle*, line 50) to keep its memory of sorrow keen.
55 waits on: attends
56 jelious despite: watchful malice; *jelious* is pronounced as three syllables

Act Two, Scene Three

3 coy...kind: affects reserve, as it is her natural disposition as a woman to do
5 stoop: become obedient (cf. note to 2.1.4)
6 froward: refractory
16 moiety: half-share
18 in case: provided that
22 make the motion: put the proposal
35 forwardness: enterprise
37 pitched: settled
38 with...speed: as quickly as possible
42 will: wilfulness
50 give back: refuse

Act Two, Scene Four

1	sable: black
7	fainting: timid, fearful
	controls: overmasters
10	without: outside
13	match: meeting
19	Luna: the moon (associated with female virginity)
23	asketh: needs
25	Flora: goddess of flowers and nature
28	record: sing
30	counterfeits: imitates
31	frame: compose
37	ruder: rougher, coarser
38	push: suggesting the military sense of the word (cf. 1.2.34 and note)
40	ward: guard
41	retort: throw back
42	glory: fame due to the victor
45	Thus...fall: Conventionally, the vine was an emblem of everlasting friendship, embracing and holding up an elm tree after its death. But Horatio suggests an embrace leading to sexual union: *fall* and *die* (line 48) were common Elizabethan puns for intercourse and orgasm.
52	forbear: give up struggling
	tried: (1) tested and proved; (2) brought to legal trial
60	still ambitious proud: always ambitous to reach a position befitting his sense of pride
61	at the highest: a brutal pun
63 SD	shirt: nightshirt
	etc: A near-contemporary (1615) woodcut illustration of this scene shows Hieronimo carrying a sword (used at line 75) and a torch.
64	naked: lacking outer clothing (a transferred adjective)
78	whilom: once
84	dishonoured: Hanging was regarded as a felon's death, degrading to a nobleman.
85	this: these
	shades: shadows of night
90	vild: vile
92	leese: lose

	new begun: recommenced (perhaps, after the wars)
96	leesing: losing
108	outrage: passionate outburst
111	with: by
	stayed: stopped, choked up
112	the glasses...sight: his eyes
113	only my delight: my whole delight
114	handkercher: scarf (cf. 1.4.42)
118	discontent: desolation
123	plaints: lamentations
125	practice: plot
127 SD	*They...up*: it has been suggested that this direction belongs to a shortened version of the text in which the body is carried out by the two parents (at line 128) and the dirge is omitted. However, the full text is actable, if Isabella supports the body while Hieronimo recites the dirge, before he throws away the sword and himself lifts and carries the corpse off-stage.
129	dirge: funeral song
130–43	*'O aliquis...sequatur*: Let someone mingle for me the herbs which beautiful spring brings forth, and a salve be given for our grief; or let him offer juices, if there are any which will bring oblivion to our minds. I myself shall gather anywhere in the great world whatever herbs the sun draws forth into the fair realms of light. I myself shall drink whatever potion the wise-woman devises; whatever herbs, too, the goddess of spells weaves together by her secret power. I shall essay all things, even death, until the moment all feeling dies in my dead breast. And so, my life, shall I never again see your eyes; has everlasting sleep buried your light of life? I shall perish with you—thus, thus would I rejoice to go into the shades below. Nonetheless, I shall keep myself from yielding to

an early death, lest in that case no revenge should follow your death.'

130 SD   *sets...sword*: as if in preparation for suicide, which is finally rejected at line 142; emblematically, Hieronimo himself now resembles the nightingale singing 'with the prickle at her breast' (2. 2. 50).

Act Two, Scene Five

2   looked: expected, hoped
11   heavy case: grievous state

Act Three, Scene One

1   Infortunate: hapless
2   helpless doubts: inescapable fears, suspicions
4   heat: fury
5   wheel of chance: Fortune was imaged as controlling a wheel on which humans rose in a cyclical movement, up to success and down to suffering and death
8   sundry: conflicting
10   would be: wish to be
11   Sith: since
12   lordings: my lords
14   successive line: line of succession
17   words...works: what is said may differ from what is done
18   credit: trust to be placed
19–20 the train...looks: the inner treachery which pretended love had disguised in his looks
21   consorted: accompanied
23   hourly...earth: regularly (hour by hour) circles the earth, centre of the universe. Kyd uses the old cosmology, in which the sun's apparent circling of the earth symbolised absolute constancy.
24   purpose: relationship
30 SD Halberts: halberdiers; see Dramatis Personae 23 and note
31   patience: endurance, long-suffering
36   infect: corrupt, diseased

37   her mould: earth's making (and therefore corrupt)
46   suggestion: false accusation
47   when: an exclamation of impatience
50   Phlegethon: burning river of hell
52   maliced: behaved maliciously
53   meed: reward
55   the lake: the lake of hell, Acheron, into which flowed Phlegethon
61   entrance: pronounced as three syllables
65   entreated: looked after
66   commends: greetings
79   quital: recompense discontent: vexation
79 SD *They unbind him*: He is unbound by Villuppo.
80   in kindness: by your very nature (as a king)
81   damnèd fact: damnable deed
84   suggestions: false accusations massacred: cruelly murdered
87   unkindness: unnatural deed
93   doom: judgement
98   mean: moderate, mild
105 things articulated: formal proposals set out as articles

Act Three, Scene Two

1   fraught: filled
2   lively: living
4   Confused: chaotic
12   secretary: confidant
12–13 night...wake: false concords of this kind are quite common in Elizabethan English; cf. *Solicit* (line 15) and *drive* (line 21).
14   distressful: unhappy
17   frame: direct
18   fear: put fear into
23   mean: means
26   writ: written document
27   hapless: ill-fortuned
34   malign: hate
38   train: trap, plot
42   thy dishonour done: for the dishonour you have done him
47   effect thy resolution: carry out what you have resolved
48   circumstances: seeking circumstantial evidence

51	Close...with: meet, come to an understanding with
52	bewray: disclose
62	suit: request
64	use me: put your request to me
74	condition: nature, disposition
76	humour: disposition
83	Saint Liugi's Park: unknown, but not a Spanish name
84	hard: close
93	mount: (1) rise by preferment; (2) be hung
94	*Chi l'e*: who is there?
100	complot: conspiracy
	cast: devised
101	practices: deceits
	spread the watch: position the night-watch
104	hapless: luckless
105	distrust: suspicion
106	practise: behave deceitfully
107	expulse: drive out
115	base companions: low fellows
116	good haps: success, good fortune
117	faith: trustworthiness, loyalty
119	slaves: servile wretches

Act Three, Scene Three

1	hold: function properly
2	hold on: continue as before
4	let...aim: 'I'll look after taking aim with the pistol'
5	Here...gold: Pedringano may flourish a purse.
	proposed: offered to me
7	is possessed thereof: actually has the dreamt-of gold
10	fail: fall into poverty
11	want: go lacking
15	suspect: suspicion
20	watch and ward: keep guard
22	close: hidden
23	stay thy pace: stop walking
27	this...one: this corner is an appropriate place for an attack
32 SD	*dag*: heavy pistol
37	be his priest: attend his death as his priest; that is, kill him
38	confess: (1) admit your crime; (2) hear confession
39	unkindly: inhumanly
40	abroad: outside

Act Three, Scene Four

2	preventing: forestalling
3	mischief: evil
	not mistrust: do not suspect or anticipate
10	confederates in our fault: partners in our crime
18	cast: planned
24	fact: deed, crime
31	exasperate: make harsh
32	complaints: legal charges, statements of injury
33	doubt: fear
35	hardly shall deny: will act harshly in denying me
36	marshal-sessions: sitting of the court of the Knight-Marshal; cf. 1.1.25 and note
40	prosecutes the point: achieves the end
42	limed: snared (with bird-lime)
43	hopeful: ambitious
44	look like fowlers: take on the guise of bird-trappers
45	holp: helped
46	my reaching fatch: the tentacles of my plot
56	stand good lord: act as his patron and protector
60	like wax: easily (since wax was pliable and easily moulded)
	try thy wits: test your cleverness
62	closely: secretly
63	be advised: take care
64	secret: revealing nothing; the word is pronounced as three syllables
68	boldly be resolved: act with complete self-assurance
69	turnèd off: hung (when the the support on which the prisoner stands before execution is removed)
73	and if: if
76	cleanly: efficiently
77	tickle: precarious, delicately balanced
79	doubts: fears
82	list not: am not willing to
83	pretence: intention
86	open: receptive
87–8	*E quel...basterà*: 'And what I

wish no one knows; I
understand, and
that's enough for me.'

Act Three, Scene Five

1   troth: faith
3   in our minority: while still
     children
4   uncertainty: unreliability,
     changeableness
10   flout: scorn
11   descant on: hold forth about
14   scurvy: low, base

Act Three, Scene Six

0 SD DEPUTY: the official title of the
      Knight-Marshal's legal assistant.
1   extremes: difficulties, desperate
      situations
7   cause: reason for the crime
8   toils: burdens
      consumeth age: wears out my
      old life
11   asks: requires
13   regard: show concern for
14   my...blood: [the giving of] my
      life-blood
16   here...gone: Hieronimo touches
      his head or heart; or possibly
      the bloodstained scarf of
      Horatio that he wears (see
      1.4.42 and note).
18   Gramercy: thank you
20   nearer: more serious
23   gear: business
25   for...world: for public
      satisfaction that you are guilty
26   fault: crime
32   gear: deed
39   approvèd: proved
43   gear: business, taken by
      Pedringano in the punning
      sense of 'clothing'
45   disfurnish...habit: remove my
      clothing (which it was
      customary to give to the
      hangman as a fee)
47   change: exchange (my clothes
      for a halter)
      boot: compensation
54   despatch: (1) hasten; (2) die
56   by the hour: at set times

61   break...pate: strike your
      villainous head
63   office: occupation
66   companion: fellow
69   truss: close-fitting jacket
70   truss up: (1) fit with a doublet;
      (2) hang
74   hearken: pay attention
79   office: profession. Pedringano
      mocks the hangman's use of
      such an elevated word for the
      lowest of occupations.
81   seal it: confirm the grant of my
      office as hangman by signing
      the document
84   motion: proposal
91   interdicted: forbidden; with a
      reference to the biblical
      commandment against murder
92   Still: for ever
      passages: pathways
93   intercepts...happiness: prevents
      the soul (*itself*) from reaching
      happiness
95   fault: crime
103   Stand: (1) rely; (2) stand
      (literally)
106   infect: corrupted
107   contemns: scorns

Act Three, Scene Seven

1   breathe abroad: give public
      expression to
3   exclaims: cries
11   passions: sufferings,
      pronounced as three syllables
15   empyreal heights: in the old
      cosmology the sphere of fire;
      the highest heaven and the
      dwelling place of God and the
      angels
16   countermured: double-walled
18 SD *with a letter*: See 3. 6. 16 SD,
      where Pedringano introduces
      the letter.
19   Petergade: the hangman's
      approximation to 'Pedringano'
20   conceits: jests
22–3 fair commission: properly
      constituted commission
32   extremes: desperate situation
33   labour: work hard to achieve
34   desperate: without hope

35	troth: truth
39	holp: helped
47	closely smothered: completely hidden
53	hers and this: the letters of Bel-Imperia and Pedringano
54	accident: occurrence, event find: come to a considered conclusion (as a judge might do)
55	feelingly: with deep understanding and emotion
59	bane: ruin
61	constrainèd: forced, unnecessary
65	banned: cursed
69	plain me: make my plea or complaint
72	purchase: obtain

Act Three, Scene Eight

1	purge: cleanse, heal
5	physic to recure: medicine to restore to health
8	outrage: passionate outburst
9	Elysian fields: the dwelling place in the afterworld of the blessed spirits
11	whipstalk: whip handle (stock), used in children's games, for instance to spin tops. But alluding also to the whips of the Furies who punished human crimes.
13	humours: extravagant moods
21	Rare: choice, perfect greet: honour, acclaim
22	mirror: model of excellence

Act Three, Scene Nine

0 SD	*at a window*: This implies that the scene takes place on the upper stage.
2	sequestered: kept apart in seclusion
3	No notice: am I to be told nothing?
4	secret: kept secret
5	unkind: unnatural
6	bends: applies, directs
12	force perforce: of necessity

13	apply...time: submit to things as they are
14 SD	*Enter* CHRISTOPHIL: The servant must enter on the upper stage, to join and lead off Bel-Imperia.

Act Three, Scene Ten

4	resolution: courage
7	enlarged: released
9	policy: cunning purpose
10	smooth: smooth over secret: pronounced as three syllables
12	gentle: 'nobly-born', unless Lorenzo is being ironic about his sister's nature
19	Salve: allay, heal over only...up: above all back me up in all I say
20	stand on terms: insist on conditions, raise difficulties
28	extremes: harsh behaviour
31	clap me up: unceremoniously imprison me
33	madding fury: furious madness
36	disparagement: dishonour, humiliation
37	Unless...deserved: unless it were that, acting with more consideration than you deserved
44–5	matters...determinèd: The phrase might mean 'important matters (matters of state) raised by the viceroy', or 'issues concerning possessions brought to a conclusion by the viceroy'.
48	next in sight: the nearest person to be seen
50	consorted with: in the company of
54	that old disgrace: see 1.1.10–11
57	meanly acompanied: in the company of a man of low rank (Horatio is her social inferior)
59	forth: out of
60	obscurely: in secret
64	forged: fabricated
70	exasperate: increased, strengthened

72	place: room to spend itself
75	Aetna: a famous active volcano in Sicily
78	gentle: noble
85	politic: cunning, clever
89	Ariadne's twines: Kyd may mean Arachne, a famous Lydian weaver who challenged Athene and was turned into a spider; Ariadne, the daughter of Minos of Crete, used a thread to guide the Greek hero Theseus through the Labyrinth. It was a commonplace in Elizabethan love poetry to compare a woman's hair to nets trapping her lover's heart.
90	surprised: captured
91	front: forehead, whose whiteness (a conventional feature of female beauty) suggests a paper map charting the way to his disdainful mistress for the grieving lover
94	In my conceit: to my mind
102–3	*Et tremulo...opus*: 'They joined craven fear to trembling dread, a futile act of stupid betrayal.'
106	loadstar: star to steer by
109	Incertain to effect: doubtful that he will be able to complete

Act Three, Scene Eleven

4	next: nearest
6	hard: close
8 SD	*He goeth...another*: implying a fruitless visit to a nearby house; a stage movement suited to the Elizabethan stage which normally had two entrances opening in the rear wall.
10	be importunate: insist
18	baleful humours: harmful moods uphold: persist in
21	hugy dale: enormous gulf
26	Jove: king of the gods
27	fell: cruel
28–9	Lorenzo...innocents: Cf. 1.1.64–70, where in 'deepest hell' murderers suffer and perjurers are scalded in boiling lead
32	passing: exceedingly

Act Three, Scene Twelve

0 SD	*with...the other*: A dagger and noose were the standard stage properties associated with a suicidal state of mind.
2	fain: gladly, eagerly
3	seld: seldom
4	toys: trifling matters
5	shifts: tricks
6	trudge: get moving (the word does not imply slowness)
7	purple: blood-red
11	leads: shows the way
14	this path: Hieronimo indicates the dagger straight: immediately
15	this: Hieronimo indicates the noose
19 SD	*halter*: noose
21	fling: go, try
22	I'll...bring: I'll get even with you
24	there...away: Hieronimo sees his opportunity eluding him as the King passes, preoccupied with state business.
31	go by: keep out of trouble
46	inexplicable: unable to be untied
52	argument: proof
56	bends: directs
58	that: so that
63	gentle: noble
70	You...him: no payment of ransom will bring him back alive
72	th'Elysian plains: Cf. 3.8.9 and note.
79	outrage: passionate outburst
83	happed: befallen
84	demean him: conduct himself
94	want: feel the lack
95	Haply: perhaps
98	more discretion: sounder judgement
100	in: into
101	exempt the place: bar him from the position (of Knight Marshal). I accept Edwards' emendation *not exempt* for 1592's *exempt*.

Act Three, Scene Thirteen

0 SD	*a book*: Later quotations from the book show that Hieronimo is

1 *Vindicta mihi*: 'vengeance is mine', a biblical quotation which continues,' I will repay, saith the Lord' (Romans 17: 19).

2 ill: evil action

4 attend: wait for

6 *Per scelus...iter*: 'the safe way for crime is always through further crimes' (Seneca, *Agamemnon*, line 115).

9 death's...resolution: death is the worst outcome of decisive action

10 contend: battle through

12–13 *Fata...sepulchrum*: From Seneca's *Troades*, lines 511–12, and loosely translated in lines 14–15.

21 vulgar: ordinary, common

22 With...ills: with unconcealed (and therefore avoidable) bad deeds, but with unavoidable ones

23 mean: course of action

24 kindship: kindness, friendliness

26 Closely: secretively

27 But...time: but there are no special opportunities in times of crisis

32 simplicity: apparent artlessness

34 wot: know

35 *Remedium...est*: 'is an inactive remedy for evils'

38 nobility: high rank

39 enjoin: apply

43 Thy cap to courtesy: Men removed their hats (worn indoors as well as outside) as a mark of respect for their superiors.

45 what coil...keep: what fuss is going on there?

46 sort: group

47 and: if

49 several actions: individual lawsuits

58 corregidor: advocate (a Spanish term, actually meaning 'chief magistrate')

60 Give place: 'make room',

spoken as the suitors crowd round him

61 an action...case: an action which normally lay outside the limited jurisdiction of the Court of Common Pleas needed a special writ, called 'an action on the case' to be brought before it.

62 *ejectione*...lease: a writ of early ejection (of a tenant, before the expiry of his lease), in the matter of a lease

65 declaration: statement of legal claim

66 band: bond

67 silly: simple, pitiable

71 Myrmidons: the brutal followers of Achilles in the Trojan War

72 Corsic rocks: rocks of Corsica, renowned for their hardness

77 bewray: express
blood: passion

85 lively: living

85 SD *napkin*: cloth; the object first taken from Don Andrea

90 take this: Hieronimo offers a coin, then a second coin, and finally his whole purse.

92 extremities: depths of suffering

99 strives: work

100 meaner: of lower social position

101 poor estates: people of humble condition

102 whenas: when

104 course...keep: to keep a succession of waves rolling

105 Whilst...deep: 'while (even) less grand masses of water in the depths of the ocean are disturbed'; the implied comparison is with lower-born Bazulto's expressive grief

110 Pluto: ruler of the underworld

111 Alcides: the Greek hero Hercules, whose twelfth labour was to descend to the underworld and conquer Cerberus the monstrous three-headed watchdog of hell (line 114).

115 strond: shore (cf. 1.1.27–30 and notes)

116 Thracian poet: Orpheus, the legendary poet and musician who sought his dead wife Eurydice in the underworld and through his music moved Proserpine (Persephone), the queen of the underworld, to release her.
counterfeit: imitate

118 canst no notes: have no skill in playing music

119 burden: (1) musical refrain; (2) oppressiveness

122 rent: rend

123 Shivering: tearing apart

135 lights: eyes

136 Aeacus: with Minos and Rhadamanth, one of the three judges of the underworld (see 1.1.33 and note)

149 favour: physical appearance

151 Fury: avenging spirit

160 lively: living

169 stay: support

172 cords: (1) musical chords; (2) ropes

Act Three, Scene Fourteen

1 cause: responsibility

7 western Indies: Unless Kyd has simply confused the East and West Indies, the king refers to Portuguese Brazil, taken over by Spain in the late sixteenth century.

9 train: company of followers

11 crossed the seas: a rhetorical flourish, or a geographical error on Kyd's part; cf. 1.2.22–3

12 troth: loyalty

17 condescent: agreement

20 their pleasure: referring to Bel-Imperia and Balthazar

26 motion: proposal

30 sith: since

37 extremities: extreme emotions

41 entertainment: reception

50 intercept: obstruct

56 Still: forever
cross: prevent, interrupt

61 common: popular

62 kindness: sympathy

66 passions: complaints

67 exclaim against: denounce

74 vulgar: common folk
liberal: scurrilous

75 advantage: exploitable weakness
breach: break-through in a dyke or wall

80 beseemed: suited, were fitted to

87 silly: simple, ignorant

92 misconster: misunderstands, misinterprets

104 done: consumed and ended

106 salute: greet

109 sadly: with serious looks

117 device: plot
trow: think you?

118 *Pocas palabras*: 'say little' (literally, 'few words')

133 intercepts: stands in the way of

141 combat of them: permission to fight them in a duel

145 prevent: forestall

151 homely: hospitable

156 marry: to be sure

167 Pha!: an expression of disgust

168–9 *Chi mi...vuole*: 'Who ever caresses me more than usual has betrayed me, or wants to do so.'

Act Three, Scene Fifteen

1 Erichtho: the name of an infamous Thessalian witch
Cerberus: the watch-dog of hell

2 Pluto...Proserpine: king and queen of the underworld

3 Acheron and Erebus: the lake of hell, and the spirit of primeval darkness

5 The text at this point is corrupt, and at least one line has been omitted by the compositor. Edwards suggests something like, 'Was I distressed with outrage sore as this'. It is likely that another line has been lost after line 5.

6 Charon: the ferryman of the underworld

15 intercepts: thwarts

17 ground: make substantial, real

19 mood: angry state of mind
soliciting: incite, stirring up

27 SD *Dumb Show*: Revenge's

28   description shows what the
      audience saw in the course of
      this wordless pageant.
28   reveal this mystery: explain
      the inner significance of this
      mysterious show
31   Hymen: Roman god of
      marriage
      hie: hasten
32   sable...saffron: Saffron (yellow)
      was the usual colour of
      Hymen's marriage robe; sable
      (black) signifies death.

Act Four, Scene One

4   passions: passionate outbursts
6   withal: with
7   unkind: unnatural
8–9   With...men: 1592 reads here,
      'With what excuses canst thou
      show thyself, / With what
      dishonour, and the hate of
      men'. Some of the original text
      has certainly been lost,
      probably by the mistaken
      conflation by the compositor
      of two lines. What is proposed
      here is no more than
      guesswork, which allows the
      passage to make some sense
      with a minimum of
      emendation.
14   history: exemplary story
19   tendered: cherished
      careless: with indifference
20   in respect of: compared to
23   bear...sake: put on an outward
      show (of acceptance) for the
      sake of appearances
26   devise: plot revenge
28   extremest: most cruel
31   applies our drift: assists us in
      achieving our goal
38   care: excessive caution
39   thoughtless think upon: give
      no thought to
      mean: means
43   determine of: bring about
46   effect...avail: work to assist you
49   grace my practices: support
      my schemes
50   For why: because
61   grace: honour
62   study: library

65   motion: theatrical
      entertainment
68   fit you: (1) provide what you
      need; (2) punish you as you
      deserve
71   professor: practitioner
72   passing: exceedingly
73   how for that: so what?
74   too quick: (1) too urgent; (2) in
      much too good health, too
      alive
75   Toledo: location of a famous
      Spanish university
80   grace: favour
82   strange: remarkable
83   plausible: agreeable
85   Nero...disparagement: 'the
      Roman emperor Nero did not
      think it demeaning to perform
      in plays'; historically this was
      so, but Nero also had a
      reputation for murderous
      deeds.
87   experience: trial
90   and: if
100   could: knew about, were
      skilful in
102   how to speak: how to deliver
      their lines well
104   argument: story
105   roundly: plainly, directly
108   dame: gentlewoman
110   Soliman: the Ottoman ruler,
      Suleiman the Magnificent
114   gan he break: he disclosed
115   bashaws: pashas, officers of
      high rank
116   solicited: wooed
131   conceited that: imagined,
      thought that out
135   abstracts drawn: story outlines
      written out
139   fauchion: falchion, a Turkish
      broad curved sword
142   Phoebe...Huntress: the moon
      goddess, the goddess of
      flowers and nature, Diana the
      virgin goddess and huntress
144   look to: see to preparing
148   gracing: furnishing, richly
      adorning
151   common wits: ordinary
      people's intelligences
152   kingly troop: royal company,
      audience

154   *Tragedia cothurnata*: the most serious and stately kind of tragedy, performed in classical Greece and Rome by actors wearing thick-soled boots (*cothurnus*)
155   matter: serious subject-matter
158   tragedians: tragic actors; referring to the theatre of the Italian *commedia dell-arte*, in which performers improvised short plays from given simple scenarios.
159   meditation: concentrated action
163   mass: by the mass
164   rests: remains
167   unknown: not understood by the audience. Cf. the publisher's note at 4.4.10.
173   cunning: (1) skill (in French); (2) craftiness
174   mere: total, absolute
175   hardly: with difficulty
177   invention: conception, basic idea
181   matter: true subject
185   resolve...up: make up our minds to indulge his whims
187   ply this gear: carry out this business
188   Babylon: the biblical city symbolising absolute corruption and tyrannical power; see Isaiah 13, Jeremiah 51, and Revelation 18. Hieronimo may also have in mind God's judgement on the tower of Babel (a name used for both city and tower in the contemporary Genevan translation of the Bible), associated with the confusion of languages; see Genesis 11.
191   hap: fortune

Act Four, Scene Two

0 SD   *weapon*: a dagger (cf. line 37); possibly the instrument used to 'cut down the arbour' at line 5ff.
7   unfortunate: disastrous
8   rent: tear
13   complot: (1) associated garden plot; (2) plot, scheme
16   Imagines: thinks
       unmanured: uncultivated
17   noisome: pestilential

19   pesterèd: plagued
20   passengers: passers-by
       infect: infected
27   cited: summoned (before a court)
28   Rhadamanth: one of the judges of the underworld
29   hold excused: have held excused
38   hapless: luckless
38 SD There is no stage direction printed in 1592 for Isabella's exit ; it is possible that Hieronimo constructed his curtain (see 4. 3. 0 SD and note) in front of the 'body', concealing the exit of the actor from the audience.

Act Four, Scene Three

0 SD   *knocks...curtain*: Hieronimo probably hangs up a curtain in front of one of the two large stage-entrances usually placed in the rear wall of an Elizabethan stage; this would allow the actor playing Isabella to leave unseen, and the body of Horatio to be brought in behind it; cf. 4.1.79–80.
1   fellows: assistants
6   copy of the play: the play-book, usually held by the stage manager and prompt (book-keeper) during a performance. Horatio may pass over such a script to Castile here. The King receives it and passes it over to the Viceroy at 4.4.9–10.
7   argument: plot summary
10   train: royal assembly
       gallery: not the upper gallery of the theatre, but the hall or 'long gallery' in a typical grand Elizabethan house. It is clear that the King and the court must sit on-stage to watch Hieronimo's play.
11   throw me down: 'drop me'; Castile may pass the key to Hieronimo rather than literally throw it down on the floor for him when the court enter.
14   Hang...title: a literal direction.

There is other evidence that title and locality boards were used in the Elizabethan theatre.

17   Despatch: hurry up, be quick
19   recompt: recollect
27   wants: is lacking
        acting: (1) putting into action; (2) theatrical performance

Act Four, Scene Four

3   of pleasure: at their pleasure; neither royalty nor the nobility would normally take part in such a menial pursuit as theatrical acting.
10   argument: plot-summary
10 SD   *Gentlemen...reader*: a printer's note, which implies that the stage performance was briefer than the published 'translation'.
        more largely: at greater length
16   *reserving*: preserving, protecting
18   *adamant*: stone with magnetic properties (loadstone)
19   *wait*: attend as a servant
29   *lights*: eyes
33   plot: book of the play, with a secondary sense for the audience of Hieronimo's 'plot'
37   *to*: compared with
38   *Sith*: since
51   *wit*: know, learn
55   *favour*: your love for me
60   *Relentless*: inflexible
68   Well said: excellently done bravely: splendidly
71   better: more lovingly disposed
75   vulgar: native
76   Haply: perhaps bootless: unavailing
77   fabulously counterfeit: a fictitious theatrical imitation
79   fashioning our scene: enacting our play
80   Ajax: a Greek hero in the Trojan War
84   hapless: luckless
85   latest: final
87   instance: concrete evidence
88 SD   *Shows...son*: Hieronimo draws

back the curtain to reveal the corpse of Horatio.
96   breath...life: my own breath of life
102   hushed: hushed up harms: crimes
103   sorted: sought out
112   Through-girt: pierced through
118   Marched in a net: practised deceit
119   rated: berated
120   amend: heal
121   catastrophe: (1) dènouement; (2) disastrous outcome
139   offended: wronged
140   missed her part: imperfectly played her role
148   Bearing...fist: controlling his own destiny
151   gentles: noble people
153   Hold: It is not clear whether the King means 'wait' or 'arrest'.
153–201 O hearken...Hieronimo: several scholars have suggested that this passage with its inconsistencies and repetitive information constitutes an alternative ending to the play incorporated into the main text.
156   ope: open; the doors have been previously locked by Hieronimo with Castile's key; cf. 4.3.9–12. Guards or attendants ('*They*') break in, according to a stage direction found first in the 1602 text of the play.
172   by: through, through the deaths of
198   wretch: vile creature
198 SD *pen*: a quill pen, which required recutting to sharpen it
200   advise...troth: take care you write down the truth
213   haul: hale, drag
214   Scylla's barking: Scylla was one of two dangerous rocks between Italy and Sicily. In classical legend, Scylla, the goddess of the rock, was surrounded by barking dogs.
215   Acheron: the fiery lake of hell

Act Four, Scene Five

4   Vild: vile
5   quaint: ingenious
6   misdone: slain
10 as Dido fell: Dido, queen of
    Carthage, committed suicide
    when her lover Aeneas left her.
14 virtue: power
    doom: judgement
15 consort: accompany
18 inured: carried on
19 train: company
22 vestal virgins: priestesses of the
    Roman goddess of fire, Vesta,
    consecrated to chastity

23 Orpheus: see 3.13.116 and note
28 bugs: horrors
31 Tityus: doomed to have his liver
    perpetually torn by vultures
32 supply his room: take his place
33 Ixion: see 1.1.65 and note
34 surcease: come to an end
36 Chimaera: a fire-breathing
    monster of Greek mythology
40 Sisyphus: legendary cruel king
    of Crete, condemned in the
    underworld to forever rolling a
    huge stone uphill
42 Acheron: see 4.4.215 and note
43 still: forever
47 end: ended

The Tragical History of Doctor Faustus

CHRISTOPHER MARLOWE

INTRODUCTORY NOTE

Authorship, date of composition and stage history

The Tragical History of Doctor Faustus (the play's first printed title) was written by Christopher Marlowe (1564–93) and an unnamed collaborator, perhaps the dramatist Henry Porter. There is general scholarly agreement that the serious and tragic scenes (the Prologue, 1.1, 1.3, 2.1, 2.3, the Act 3 and 4 Choruses, and 5.1 to the close of the play) are Marlowe's; the remaining comic scenes are the work of his collaborator. Porter was associated with the Lord Admiral's Men, who gave the first recorded performances of the tragedy at the Rose Theatre in 1594 with Edward Alleyn in the role of Faustus, two years after the first known production there of Kyd's *Spanish Tragedy*. There is some evidence to suggest that *Doctor Faustus* was written in 1588/9 and its earliest performances given at the Belsavage Theatre, London, though a number of scholars argue for a later date of composition in 1592.

Doctor Faustus remained in the repertory of the Lord Admiral's Men and their successors until the closing of all theatres by the Puritans in 1642. It received European performances, and its continuing popularity in England is attested by the publication of nine editions between 1604 and 1631 and a rich tradition of literary allusions and theatre stories. After the Restoration there were performances in 1662 at the Red Bull, with Betterton and Mountford playing Faustus and Mephostophilis, and in 1675 the Duke of York's company performed the play at court. The stage history of the play from this time to the end of the nineteenth century is one of neglect and decline, with theatre managers concentrating on its comic and spectacular elements, but since Poel's Elizabethan Stage Society revived the play in 1896 this century has seen a succession of professional and university productions reinterpreting it in many ways, often highly experimental, for modern audiences. Notable British productions include the work of directors such as Michael Benthall (Edinburgh, 1961), Neville Coghill (Oxford, 1966), Clifford Williams (Stratford, 1968), Gareth Morgan (Dublin, 1970), John Barton (Stratford and elsewhere, 1974–5), Christopher Fettes (Hammersmith, London, 1980), Adrian Noble (Manchester, 1981), and Barry Kyle (Stratford, 1989). Kyle's production at the Swan Theatre, Stratford-upon-Avon, was one of the first to take the A text as its script base. European and American revivals began in 1903 (Heidelberg) and 1907 (Princeton), with later outstanding productions by Orson Welles (1937, New York) and Jerzy Grotowski (1963, Opole, Poland). Distinguished actors, including Welles himself, Paul Daneman, Richard Burton, Eric Porter, Ian McKellen, and Ben Kingsley have taken the role of Faustus; Hugh Griffith, Paul Scofield, Alan Howard, Emrys Jones, and David Bradley have interpreted the role of Mephostophilis. In addition, there have been a number of radio and television productions and a 1968 film based on Coghill's 1966 Oxford Playhouse production. These adaptations for other media and many other stage productions are given detailed descriptive listings in the 1993 Revels edition of the play (see below). Marlowe's play continues to hold its place in the British and international theatre: in 1992 there were productions at the Nottingham Playhouse, and Duke's Theatre, Lancaster; in 1994 at the Bridewell Theatre, London, with Mephostophilis simultaneously played by two actors, one male, one female; in 1995 at the Greenwich Theatre, London, the New Venture Theatre, Brighton, and the University of Tennessee, and in 1996 (with a female Mephostophilis) at the Fifth Third Bank Theatre, Cincinnati, Ohio.

Text

No manuscript of *Doctor Faustus* has survived, and the play was not published in Marlowe's lifetime. The first surviving print record of the original version of the play is the edition of 1604 (known to scholars as the A text), printed by Valentine Simmes for Thomas Bushell, who had in 1601 acquired rights to what was probably the authors' original manuscript. It was reissued in 1609 and 1611. A longer and substantially different version of the text of *Doctor Faustus* (known as the B text) was printed in 1616 for John Wright, with a woodcut possibly based on a stage performance, showing Faustus raising the devil, on the title-page. It incorporates material by Samuel Rowley and William Birde who are known to have been paid by the theatre manager Philip Henslowe in 1602 for additions to the text, but there are other layers of rewriting, including possible authorial revisions. The edition of 1616 records the working development of the text in the theatre, and preserves a number of evidently superior readings. Although the present edition is based on the A text, as closest to Marlowe and his collaborator's original conception, such readings from the B text are accepted into the text, and the whole of Act 5 in the B text version is printed as Appendix II to illustrate the many major and minor differences between the two texts. Five subsequent editions of the B text (1619, 1620, 1624, 1628 and 1631) carried the sub-title 'With new additions'; the last seventeenth-century edition advertised 'several New Scenes' which amount to the replacement of 3.1 with a scene at the court of the Soldan of Babylon and the extension of 4.1. The text printed in this anthology closely follows the authoritative new Revels edition of the tragedy, edited by David Bevington and Eric Rasmussen (Manchester and New York, 1993).

Sources

Marlowe and his collaborator's main source for the story of Faustus was *The History of the Damnable Life and Deserved Death of Doctor John Faustus*, a free translation by 'P.F.' of a German work first published in 1587, but Marlowe brought to bear on this material a rich acquaintance with classical learning and contemporary theology, as well as the English tradition of the Morality play.

Further reading

The new Revels edition of *Doctor Faustus* (which prints modernised versions of both the A and B texts as separate entities), edited by David Bevington and Eric Rasmussen (Manchester and New York, 1993) is the fullest single-volume edition to date. See further, W. W.

Greg's parallel-text edition, *Marlowe's "Doctor Faustus" 1604–1616*, (Oxford, 1950), and the facsimile of both texts of the play, *Doctor Faustus 1604 and 1616*, published by the Scolar Press (Menston, 1970). There are well-annotated editions of the A text by David Ormerod and Christopher Wortham (Nedlands, Western Australia, 1985). Roma Gill (London and New York, 1989, and Oxford, 1990), and Michael Keefer (Peterborough, Ontario, 1991). J. D. Jump's scholarly Revels edition of the play (London, and Cambridge, Mass., 1962) is based on the B text and remains the fullest single-volume edition of that text. Other useful B version editions include those by Irving Ribner (*Christopher Marlowe's Dr Faustus: Text and Major Criticism*, New York, 1966), E. D. Pendry and J. C. Maxwell (*Christopher Marlowe: Complete Plays and Poems*, London, 1976) and Sylvan Barnet (Signet, New York, 2nd edn 1980). Michael Scott studies the staging of modern productions of the play in *Renaissance Drama and a Modern Audience* (London and Basingstoke, 1982). For book-length studies with a focus on Marlowe's tragedies and *Doctor Faustus* in particular, see Paul H. Kocher, *Christopher Marlowe: A Study in his Thought, Learning, and Character* (Chapel Hill, NC, 1946), Harry Levin, *The Overreacher: A Study of Christopher Marlowe* (Cambridge, Mass., 1952), J. P. Brockbank, *Marlowe: Dr Faustus* (London, 1962), Douglas Cole, *Suffering and Evil in the Plays of Christopher Marlowe* (Princeton, NJ, 1962), J. B. Steane, *Marlowe: A Critical Study* (Cambridge, 1964), *Marlowe: Doctor Faustus: A Casebook*, edited by J. D. Jump (London, 1969), Clifford Leech, *Christopher Marlowe: Poet for the Stage* (edited by Anne Lancaster, New York, 1986), William Empson, *Faustus and the Censor: The English Faustbook and Marlowe's 'Doctor Faustus'* (edited by J. H. Jones, Oxford, 1987) and Michael Mangin, *'Doctor Faustus': A Critical Study* (Harmondsworth, 1987).

Dramatis Personae

THE CHORUS
DOCTOR JOHN FAUSTUS°
WAGNER°
GOOD ANGEL
EVIL ANGEL   5
VALDES
CORNELIUS
THREE SCHOLARS
MEPHOSTOPHILIS°
ROBIN, *the Clown*   10
DEVILS
RAFE
LUCIFER°
BEELZEBUB°

PRIDE   15
COVETOUSNESS
WRATH
ENVY   }   *The Seven Deadly Sins*
GLUTTONY
SLOTH   20
LECHERY

THE POPE°
THE CARDINAL OF LORRAINE
FRIARS
A VINTNER°   25

THE EMPEROR OF GERMANY, CHARLES V°
A KNIGHT
ATTENDANTS

ALEXANDER THE GREAT° } *Spirits*
HIS PARAMOUR°   30

A HORSE-COURSER.°
THE DUKE OF VANHOLT
THE DUCHESS OF VANHOLT
HELEN OF TROY,° *a spirit*
AN OLD MAN   35

Scene: *Wittenberg, Rome, Innsbruck, Anholt*

Prologue

Enter CHORUS.

CHORUS: Not marching now in fields of Trasimene,
    Where Mars did mate° the Carthaginians,°
    Nor sporting in the dalliance of love
    In courts of kings, where state° is overturned,
    Nor in the pomp of proud audacious deeds,   5
    Intends our muse° to vaunt° his heavenly verse.
    Only this, gentlemen: we must perform
    The form° of Faustus' fortunes, good or bad.
    To patient judgements we appeal our plaud,°
    And speak for Faustus in his infancy.   10
    Now is he born, his parents base of stock,
    In Germany, within a town called Rhodes.°
    Of riper years, to Wittenberg° he went,
    Whereas° his kinsmen° chiefly brought him up.
    So soon he profits in divinity,°   15
    The fruitful plot of scholarism graced,°
    That shortly he was graced° with doctor's name,
    Excelling all whose sweet delight disputes°
    In heavenly matters of theology;
    Till, swoll'n with cunning of a self-conceit,°   20
    His waxen wings° did mount above his reach,
    And melting heavens conspired° his overthrow.
    For, falling to° a devilish exercise,°
    And glutted more with learning's golden gifts,
    He surfeits° upon cursed necromancy;°   25
    Nothing so sweet as magic is to him,
    Which he prefers before his chiefest bliss.°
    And this the man° that in his study sits.   *Exit.*

Act One, Scene One

Enter FAUSTUS, *in his study.*

FAUSTUS: Settle° thy studies, Faustus, and begin
    To sound the depth of that thou wilt profess.°
    Having commenced,° be a divine in show,°
    Yet level at the end of every art,°
    And live and die in Aristotle's works.°   5
    Sweet *Analytics*,° 'tis thou hast ravished me.

[*He reads.*] *Bene disserere est finis logices.*°
Is to dispute well logic's chiefest end?
Affords this art° no greater miracle?
Then read no more; thou hast attained the end.°   10
A greater subject fitteth Faustus' wit.°
Bid *On kai me on* ° farewell; Galen,° come!
Seeing *ubi desinit philosophus, ibi incipit medicus,*°
Be a physician, Faustus. Heap up gold,
And be eternised° for some wondrous cure.   15
[*He reads.*] *Summum bonum medicinae sanitas:*°
The end of physic° is our body's health.
Why, Faustus, hast thou not attained that end?
Is not thy common talk sound aphorisms?°
Are not thy bills° hung up as monuments,°   20
Whereby whole cities have escaped the plague,
And thousand desp'rate maladies been eased?
Yet art thou still but Faustus, and a man.
Wouldst thou make men to live eternally?
Or, being dead, raise them to life again?°   25
Then this profession were to be esteemed.
Physic, farewell! Where is Justinian?
[*He reads.*] *Si una eademque res legatur duobus,*
Alter rem, alter valorem rei,° etcetera.
A pretty case of paltry legacies!   30
[*He reads.*] *Exhaereditare filium non potest pater nisi:*°
Such is the subject of the Institute,
And universal body of the Law.°
This study fits a mercenary drudge,
Who aims at nothing but external trash —   35
Too servile and illiberal° for me.
When all is done,° divinity° is best.
Jerome's Bible,° Faustus, view it well.
[*He reads.*] *Stipendium peccati mors est.*° Ha!
Stipendium, etcetera.   40
The reward of sin is death. That's hard.
[*He reads.*] *Si peccasse negamus, fallimur*
Et nulla est in nobis veritas.
If we say that we have no sin,
We deceive ourselves, and there's no truth in us.°   45
Why then, belike,° we must sin,
And so consequently die.
Ay, we must die an everlasting death.
What doctrine call you this? *Che serà, serà:*°
What will be, shall be? Divinity, adieu!°   [*He takes a book of magic.*] 50
These metaphysics° of magicians,

And necromantic books, are heavenly;°
Lines, circles, schemes,° letters, and characters:
Ay, these are those that Faustus most desires.
O, what a world of profit and delight,   55
Of power, of honour, of omnipotence,
Is promised to the studious artisan!°
All things that move between the quiet poles°
Shall be at my command. Emperors and kings
Are but° obeyed in their several° provinces,   60
Nor can they raise the wind or rend the clouds;°
But his dominion that exceeds° in this
Stretcheth as far as doth the mind of man.
A sound magician is a mighty god.
Here, Faustus, try° thy brains to gain a deity.   65
Wagner!

Enter WAGNER.

       Commend me to my dearest friends,
The German Valdes and Cornelius.
Request them earnestly to visit me.
WAGNER. I will, sir.   *Exit.*
FAUSTUS: Their conference° will be a greater help to me   70
   Than all my labours, plod I ne'er so fast.

Enter the GOOD ANGEL *and the* EVIL ANGEL.

GOOD ANGEL: O Faustus, lay that damnèd book aside
   And gaze not on it, lest it tempt thy soul,
   And heap God's heavy wrath upon thy head.
   Read, read the Scriptures. That° is blasphemy.   75
EVIL ANGEL: Go forward, Faustus, in that famous art,
   Wherein all nature's treasury is contained.
   Be thou on earth as Jove° is in the sky,
   Lord and commander of these elements.°   *Exeunt* [ANGELS].
FAUSTUS: How am I glutted with conceit of this!°   80
   Shall I make spirits fetch me what I please,
   Resolve me° of all ambiguities,
   Perform what desperate° enterprise I will?
   I'll have them fly to India° for gold,
   Ransack the ocean for orient° pearl,   85
   And search all corners of the new-found world
   For pleasant fruits and princely delicates.°
   I'll have them read me strange philosophy,
   And tell the secrets of all foreign kings.

I'll have them wall all Germany with brass,   90
And make swift Rhine circle fair Wittenberg.°
I'll have them fill the public schools° with silk,°
Wherewith the students shall be bravely° clad.
I'll levy° soldiers with the coin they bring,
And chase the Prince of Parma from our land,°   95
And reign sole king of all our provinces;
Yea, stranger engines° for the brunt° of war
Than was the fiery keel at Antwerp's bridge°
I'll make my servile° spirits to invent.
Come, German Valdes and Cornelius,   100
And make me blest° with your sage conference!

Enter VALDES *and* CORNELIUS.

Valdes, sweet Valdes, and Cornelius,
Know that your words have won me at the last
To practise magic and concealèd° arts.
Yet not your words only, but mine own fantasy,°   105
That will receive no object,° for my head
But ruminates on necromantic skill.
Philosophy is odious and obscure;
Both law and physic are for petty wits;°
Divinity is basest of the three,   110
Unpleasant, harsh, contemptible, and vile.
'Tis magic, magic that hath ravished me.
Then, gentle° friends, aid me in this attempt,
And I, that have with concise syllogisms
Gravelled° the pastors of the German Church,   115
And made the flow'ring pride° of Wittenberg
Swarm to my problems° as the infernal spirits
On sweet Musaeus, when he came to hell,°
Will be as cunning° as Agrippa° was,
Whose shadows made all Europe honour him.   120
VALDES: Faustus, these books, thy wit,° and our experience
Shall make all nations to canonise° us.
As Indian Moors° obey their Spanish lords,
So shall the spirits° of every element
Be always serviceable to us three.   125
Like lions shall they guard us when we please,
Like Almaine rutters with their horsemen's staves,°
Or Lapland giants,° trotting by our sides;
Sometimes like women, or unwedded maids,
Shadowing° more beauty in their airy° brows   130
Than in the white breasts of the Queen of Love.
From Venice shall they drag huge argosies,°

And from America the golden fleece
That yearly stuffs old Philip's treasury,°
If learned Faustus will be resolute.   135
FAUSTUS: Valdes, as resolute am I in this
As thou to live; therefore object° it not.
CORNELIUS: The miracles that magic will perform
Will make thee vow to study nothing else.
He that is grounded in astrology,°   140
Enriched with tongues,° well seen in° minerals,
Hath all the principles magic doth require.
Then doubt not, Faustus, but to be renowned,
And more frequented° for this mystery°
Than heretofore the Delphian oracle.°   145
The spirits tell me they can dry the sea,
And fetch the treasure of all foreign wrecks;
Ay, all the wealth that our forefathers hid
Within the massy° entrails of the earth.
Then tell me, Faustus, what shall we three want?°   150
FAUSTUS: Nothing, Cornelius. O, this cheers my soul!
Come, show me some demonstrations magical,
That I may conjure in some lusty° grove,
And have these joys in full possession.
VALDES: Then haste thee to some solitary grove,   155
And bear wise Bacon's and Albanus'° works,
The Hebrew Psalter, and New Testament;°
And whatsoever else is requisite
We will inform thee ere our conference° cease.
CORNELIUS: Valdes, first let him know the words of art,°   160
And then, all other ceremonies learned,
Faustus may try his cunning° by himself.
VALDES: First, I'll instruct thee in the rudiments,
And then wilt thou be perfecter° than I.
FAUSTUS: Then come and dine with me, and after meat°   165
We'll canvass° every quiddity° thereof,
For ere I sleep I'll try what I can do.
This night I'll conjure, though I die therefore.   *Exeunt.*

Act One, Scene Two

Enter two SCHOLARS.

1 SCHOLAR: I wonder what's become of Faustus, that was wont to make
our schools° ring with '*sic probo*'.°

2 SCHOLAR: That shall we know, for see, here comes his boy.

Enter WAGNER [*, carrying wine*].

1 SCHOLAR: How now, sirrah,° where's thy master?
WAGNER: God in heaven knows.   5
2 SCHOLAR: Why, dost not thou know?
WAGNER: Yes, I know, but that follows not.°
1 SCHOLAR: Go to, sirrah! Leave your jesting, and tell us where he is.
WAGNER: That follows not necessary° by force of argument, that you,
    being licentiate,° should stand upon't.° Therefore acknowledge   10
    your error, and be attentive.
2 SCHOLAR: Why, didst thou not say thou knew'st?
WAGNER: Have you any witness on't?°
1 SCHOLAR: Yes, sirrah, I heard you.
WAGNER: Ask my fellow if I be a thief.°   15
2 SCHOLAR: Well, you will not tell us.
WAGNER: Yes, sir, I will tell you. Yet if you were not dunces,° you would
    never ask me such a question. For is not he *corpus naturale*? And is
    not that *mobile*?° Then wherefore should you ask me such a
    question? But that I am by nature phlegmatic, slow to wrath,° and   20
    prone° to lechery — to love, I would say — it were not for you to
    come within forty foot of the place of execution,° although I do not
    doubt to see you both hanged the next sessions.° Thus, having
    triumphed over you, I will set my countenance like a precisian°
    and begin to speak thus: Truly, my dear brethren, my master is   25
    within at dinner with Valdes and Cornelius, as this wine, if it could
    speak, it would inform your worships.° And so the Lord bless you,
    preserve you, and keep you,° my dear brethren, my dear brethren.
                                                                       Exit.
1 SCHOLAR: Nay, then, I fear he is fallen into that damned art for which
    they two are infamous through the world.   30
2 SCHOLAR: Were he a stranger, and not allied° to me, yet should I grieve
    for him. But come, let us go and inform the Rector,° and see if he,
    by his grave counsel, can reclaim him.
1 SCHOLAR: O, but I fear me nothing can reclaim him.
2 SCHOLAR: Yet let us try what we can do.   *Exeunt.* 35

Act One, Scene Three

Enter FAUSTUS *to conjure* [*,with a book*].

FAUSTUS: Now that the gloomy shadow of the earth,°
    Longing to view Orion's drizzling look,°

Leaps from th'Antarctic world unto the sky
And dims the welkin° with her pitchy° breath,
Faustus, begin thine incantations,   5
And try if devils will obey thy hest,°
Seeing thou hast prayed and sacrificed to them.

                                                                          [*He draws a circle.*]

Within this circle° is Jehovah's name,
Forward and backward anagrammatised,°
The breviated° names of holy saints,   10
Figures of every adjunct to the heavens,
And characters of signs and erring° stars,°
By which the spirits are enforced to rise.
Then fear not, Faustus, but be resolute,
And try the uttermost magic can perform.   15
Sint mihi dei Acherontis° propitii! Valeat numen triplex Jehovae!° Ignei,
aerii, aquatici, terreni, spiritus, salvete! Orientis princeps° Lucifer,
Beelzebub, inferni ardentis monarcha, et Demogorgon,° propitiamus vos,
ut appareat et surgat Mephostophilis! Quid tu moraris? Per Jehovam,
Gehennam, °et consecratam aquam quam nunc spargo, signumque crucis   20
quod nunc facio, et per vota nostra, ipse nunc surgat nobis dicatus
Mephostophilis!°

                    [FAUSTUS *sprinkles holy water and makes a sign of the cross.*]

                    Enter [MEPHOSTOPHILIS *as a devil*].

I charge thee to return and change thy shape;
Thou art too ugly to attend on me.
Go, and return an old Franciscan friar;   25
That holy shape becomes a devil best.°   *Exit* [MEPHOSTOPHILIS].
I see there's virtue° in my heavenly words:°
Who would not be proficient in this art?
 How pliant is this Mephostophilis,
Full of obedience and humility!   30
Such is the force of magic and my spells.
Now, Faustus, thou art conjurer laureate, °
That canst command great Mephostophilis.
Quin redis, Mephostophilis, fratris imagine!°

                    Enter MEPHOSTOPHILIS [*as a friar*].

MEPHOSTOPHILIS: Now, Faustus, what wouldst thou have me do?   35
FAUSTUS: I charge thee wait upon me whilst I live,
     To do whatever Faustus shall command,
     Be it to make the moon drop from her sphere,°
     Or the ocean to overwhelm the world.

MEPHOSTOPHILIS: I am a servant to great Lucifer,   40
   And may not follow thee without his leave.
   No more than he commands must we perform.
FAUSTUS: Did not he charge thee to appear to me?
MEPHOSTOPHILIS: No, I came now hither of mine own accord.
FAUSTUS: Did not my conjuring speeches raise thee? Speak.   45
MEPHOSTOPHILIS: That was the cause, but yet *per accidens,*°
   For when we hear one rack the name of God,
   Abjure the Scriptures and his Saviour Christ,
   We fly in hope to get his glorious° soul;
   Nor will we come, unless he use such means   50
   Whereby he is in danger to be damned.
   Therefore, the shortest cut for conjuring
   Is stoutly° to abjure the Trinity,
   And pray devoutly to the prince of hell.
FAUSTUS: So Faustus hath already done, and holds this principle: 55
   There is no chief but only Beelzebub,°
   To whom Faustus doth dedicate himself.
   This word 'damnation' terrifies not him,
   For he confounds hell in Elysium.°
   His ghost° be with the old philosophers! —°   60
   But leaving these vain trifles of men's souls,
   Tell me what is that Lucifer, thy lord?
MEPHOSTOPHILIS: Arch-regent and commander of all spirits.
FAUSTUS: Was not that Lucifer an angel once?
MEPHOSTOPHILIS: Yes, Faustus, and most dearly loved of God.   65
FAUSTUS: How comes it then that he is prince of devils?
MEPHOSTOPHILIS: O, by aspiring pride and insolence,
   For which God threw him from the face of heaven.
FAUSTUS: And what are you that live with Lucifer?
MEPHOSTOPHILIS: Unhappy spirits that fell with Lucifer,   70
   Conspired against our God with Lucifer,
   And are for ever damned with Lucifer.
FAUSTUS: Where are you damned?
MEPHOSTOPHILIS: In hell.
FAUSTUS: How comes it then that thou art out of hell?
MEPHOSTOPHILIS: Why, this is hell, nor am I out of it.   75
   Think'st thou that I, who saw the face of God,
   And tasted the eternal joys of heaven,
   Am not tormented with ten thousand hells
   In being deprived of everlasting bliss?
   O Faustus, leave these frivolous demands,   80
   Which strike a terror to my fainting soul!
FAUSTUS: What, is great Mephostophilis so passionate°
   For being deprived of the joys of heaven?

Learn thou of Faustus manly fortitude,
And scorn those joys thou never shalt possess.   85
Go bear these tidings to great Lucifer,
Seeing Faustus hath incurred eternal death
By desp'rate° thoughts against Jove's deity.
Say he surrenders up to him his soul,
So° he will spare him four-and-twenty years,   90
Letting him live in all voluptuousness,
Having thee ever to attend on me,
To give me whatsoever I shall ask,
To tell me whatsoever I demand,
To slay mine enemies, and aid my friends,   95
And always be obedient to my will.
Go, and return to mighty Lucifer,
And meet me in my study at midnight,
And then resolve° me of thy master's mind.
MEPHOSTOPHILIS: I will, Faustus.   100
FAUSTUS: Had I as many souls as there be stars,
    I'd give them all for Mephostophilis.
    By him I'll be great emperor of the world,
    And make a bridge through the moving air
    To pass° the ocean with a band of men;   105
    I'll join the hills that bind° the Afric shore,
    And make that land continent° to Spain,
    And both contributory° to my crown.
    The Emperor shall not live but by my leave,
    Nor any potentate of Germany.   110
    Now that I have obtained what I desire,
    I'll live in speculation° of this art
    Till Mephostophilis return again.   *Exit.*

Act One, Scene Four

Enter WAGNER *and* [ROBIN] *the* CLOWN.°

WAGNER: Sirrah boy, come hither.
ROBIN: How, 'boy'? 'Swounds,° 'boy'! I hope you have seen many boys
    with such pickedevants° as I have. 'Boy', quotha?°
WAGNER: Tell me, sirrah, hast thou any comings in?°
ROBIN: Ay, and goings out° too, you may see else.°   5
WAGNER: Alas, poor slave; see how poverty jesteth in his nakedness!
    The villain is bare and out of service,° and so hungry that I know

he would give his soul to the devil for a shoulder of mutton,
though it were blood raw.

ROBIN: How? My soul to the devil for a shoulder of mutton, though   10
'twere blood raw? Not so, good friend. By'r Lady,° I had need have
it well roasted, and good sauce to it, if I pay so dear.

WAGNER: Well, wilt thou serve me, and I'll make thee go° like *Qui mihi
discipulus?*°

ROBIN: How, in verse?   15

WAGNER: No, sirrah, in beaten° silk° and stavesacre.°

ROBIN: How, how, knave's acre?° [*Aside*] Aye, I thought that was all the
land his father left him. — Do ye hear? I would be sorry to rob you
of your living.

WAGNER: Sirrah, I say in stavesacre.   20

ROBIN: Oho, oho, 'stavesacre'! Why then, belike,° if I were your man, I
should be full of vermin.°

WAGNER: So thou shalt, whether thou beest with me or no. But sirrah,
leave your jesting, and bind yourself° presently° unto me for seven
years, or I'll turn all the lice about thee into familiars,° and they   25
shall tear thee in pieces.

ROBIN: Do you hear, sir? You may save that labour. They are too
familiar° with me already. 'Swounds, they are as bold with my
flesh° as if they had paid for my meat and drink.

WAGNER: Well, do you hear, sirrah? Hold, take these guilders.°   30

[*Offering money.*]

ROBIN: Gridirons?° What be they?

WAGNER: Why, French crowns.°

ROBIN: Mass, but for the name of French crowns a man were as good
have as many English counters.° And what should I do with these?

WAGNER: Why now, sirrah, thou art at an hour's warning whensoever   35
or wheresoever the devil shall fetch thee.

ROBIN: No, no! Here, take your gridirons again.

[*He attempts to return the money.*]

WAGNER: Truly, I'll none of them.

ROBIN: Truly, but you shall.

WAGNER [*to the audience*]: Bear witness I gave them him.   40

ROBIN: Bear witness I give them you again.

WAGNER: Well, I will cause two devils presently° to fetch thee away. —
Baliol° and Belcher!

ROBIN: Let your Balio° and your Belcher come here, and I'll knock°
them. They were never so knocked since they were devils. Say I   45
should kill one of them, what would folks say? 'Do ye see yonder
tall° fellow in the round slop?° He has killed the devil.' So I should
be called 'Kill devil'° all the parish over.

Enter two Devils, *and* [ROBIN] *the* CLOWN *runs up and down crying.*

WAGNER: Balioll and Belcher! Spirits, away!   *Exeunt* [Devils].

ROBIN: What, are they gone? A vengeance on them! They have vile   50
     long nails. There was a he-devil and a she-devil. I'll tell you how
     you shall know them: all he-devils has horns,° and all she-devils
     has clefts° and cloven feet.

WAGNER: Well, sirrah, follow me.

ROBIN: But do you hear? If I should serve you, would you teach me to   55
     raise up Banios° and Belcheos?

WAGNER: I will teach thee to turn thyself to anything; to a dog, or a cat,
     or a mouse, or a rat, or anything.

ROBIN: How? A Christian fellow to a dog or a cat, a mouse or a rat? No,
     no, sir. If you turn me into anything, let it be in the likeness of a   60
     little, pretty, frisking flea, that I may be here and there and
     everywhere. O, I'll tickle the pretty wenches' plackets!° I'll be
     amongst them, i'faith!

WAGNER: Well, sirrah, come.

ROBIN: But do you hear, Wagner?   65

WAGNER: How? — Baliol and Belcher!

ROBIN: O Lord, I pray sir, let Banio and Belcher go sleep.

WAGNER: Villain, call me Master Wagner, and let thy left eye be
     diametarily° fixed upon my right heel, with *quasi vestigiis nostris
     insistere.*°   *Exit.* 70

ROBIN: God forgive me, he speaks Dutch fustian.° Well, I'll follow him,
     I'll serve him, that's flat.°

Exit.

Act Two, Scene One

Enter FAUSTUS, *in his study.*

FAUSTUS: Now, Faustus, must thou needs be damned,
     And canst thou not be saved.
     What boots° it then to think of God or heaven?
     Away with such vain fancies, and despair!
     Despair in God and trust in Beelzebub.   5
     Now go not backward.° No, Faustus, be resolute.
     Why waverest thou? O, something soundeth in mine ears:
     'Abjure this magic, turn to God again!'
     Ay, and Faustus will turn to God again.
     To God? He loves thee not.   10

The god thou servest is thine own appetite,
Wherein is fixed the love of Beelzebub.
To him I'll build an altar and a church,
And offer lukewarm blood of new-born babes.

Enter GOOD ANGEL *and* EVIL [ANGEL].

GOOD ANGEL: Sweet Faustus, leave that execrable art. 15
FAUSTUS: Contrition, prayer, repentance — what of them?
GOOD ANGEL: O, they are means to bring thee unto heaven.
EVIL ANGEL: Rather illusions, fruits of lunacy,
    That makes men foolish that do trust them most.
GOOD ANGEL: Sweet Faustus, think of heaven and heavenly things. 20
EVIL ANGEL: No, Faustus, think of honour and of wealth.   *Exeunt* [ANGELS].
FAUSTUS: Of wealth?
    Why, the seigniory of Emden° shall be mine.
    When Mephostophilis shall stand by me,
    What god can hurt thee,° Faustus? Thou art safe; 25
    Cast° no more doubts. Come, Mephostophilis,
    And bring glad tidings° from great Lucifer!
    Is't not midnight? Come, Mephostophilis!
    Veni, veni, Mephostophile!°

Enter MEPHOSTOPHILIS.

    Now tell me, what says Lucifer thy lord? 30
MEPHOSTOPHILIS: That I shall wait on Faustus whilst he lives,
    So° he will buy my service with his soul.
FAUSTUS: Already Faustus hath hazarded that for thee.
MEPHOSTOPHILIS: But, Faustus, thou must bequeath it solemnly
    And write a deed of gift with thine own blood; 35
    For that security craves great Lucifer.
    If thou deny it, I will back to hell.
FAUSTUS: Stay, Mephostophilis, and tell me, what good
    Will my soul do thy lord?
MEPHOSTOPHILIS: Enlarge his kingdom.
FAUSTUS: Is that the reason why he tempts us thus? 40
MEPHOSTOPHILIS: *Solamen miseris socios habuisse doloris.*°
FAUSTUS: Have you any pain, that° tortures others?
MEPHOSTOPHILIS: As great as have the human souls of men.
    But tell me, Faustus, shall I have thy soul?
    And I will be thy slave, and wait on thee, 45
    And give thee more than thou hast wit to ask.
FAUSTUS: Ay, Mephostophilis, I give it thee.
MEPHOSTOPHILIS: Then stab thine arm courageously,

And bind° thy soul that at some certain° day
Great Lucifer may claim it as his own,   50
And then be thou as great as Lucifer.
FAUSTUS: Lo, Mephostophilis, for love of thee   [*Cuts his arm.*]
    I cut mine arm, and with my proper° blood
    Assure° my soul to be great Lucifer's,
    Chief lord and regent of perpetual night.   55
    View here the blood that trickles from mine arm,
    And let it be propitious for my wish.
MEPHOSTOPHILIS: But Faustus, thou must write it in manner of a deed of
    gift.
FAUSTUS: Ay, so I will. [*He writes.*] But Mephostophilis,
    My blood congeals, and I can write no more.   60
MEPHOSTOPHILIS: I'll fetch thee fire to dissolve it straight.°   *Exit.*
FAUSTUS: What might the staying of my blood portend?
    Is it unwilling I should write this bill?°
    Why streams it not, that I may write afresh?
    'Faustus gives to thee his soul' — ah, there it stayed!   65
    Why shouldst thou not? Is not thy soul thine own?
    Then write again: 'Faustus gives to thee his soul.'

Enter MEPHOSTOPHILIS, *with a chafer° of coals.*

MEPHOSTOPHILIS: Here's fire. Come, Faustus, set it on.°
FAUSTUS: So; now the blood begins to clear again;
    Now will I make an end immediately.   [*He writes.*] 70
MEPHOSTOPHILIS [*aside*]: O, what will not I do to obtain his soul?
FAUSTUS: *Consummatum est.*° This bill is ended,
    And Faustus hath bequeathed his soul to Lucifer.
    But what is this inscription on mine arm?
    '*Homo, fuge!*'° Whither should I fly?   75
    If unto God, he'll throw thee down to hell.°
    My senses are deceived; here's nothing writ.
    I see it plain. Here in this place is writ
    '*Homo, fuge!*' Yet shall not Faustus fly.
MEPHOSTOPHILIS [*aside*]: I'll fetch him somewhat to delight his mind.
                                                                              Exit. 80

Enter [MEPHOSTOPHILIS] *with* Devils, *giving crowns and rich
apparel to* FAUSTUS. [*The* Devils] *dance and then depart.*

FAUSTUS: Speak, Mephostophilis. What means this show?
MEPHOSTOPHILIS: Nothing, Faustus, but to delight thy mind withal°
    And to show thee what magic can perform.
FAUSTUS: But may I raise up spirits when I please?

MEPHOSTOPHILIS: Ay, Faustus, and do greater things than these.   85
FAUSTUS: Then there's enough for a thousand souls.
    Here, Mephostophilis, receive this scroll,°
    A deed of gift of body and of soul.
    But yet conditionally, that thou perform
    All articles prescribed between us both.   90
MEPHOSTOPHILIS: Faustus, I swear by hell and Lucifer
    To effect all promises between us made.
FAUSTUS: Then hear me read them.
    'On these conditions following:
    First, that Faustus may be a spirit in form and substance.   95
    Secondly, that Mephostophilis shall be his servant, and at his
    command.
    Thirdly, that Mephostophilis shall do for him, and bring him
    whatsoever.
    Fourthly, that he shall be in his chamber or house invisible.   100
    Lastly, that he shall appear to the said John Faustus at all times, in
    what form or shape soever he please.
    I, John Faustus of Wittenberg, Doctor, by these presents, °do give both
    body and soul to Lucifer, Prince of the East, and his minister
    Mephostophilis; and furthermore grant unto them that four-and-   105
    twenty years being expired, the articles above written inviolate, °full
    power to fetch or carry the said John Faustus, body and soul, flesh, blood,
    or goods, into their habitation wheresoever.
                               By me, John Faustus.'
MEPHOSTOPHILIS: Speak, Faustus. Do you deliver this as your deed?   110
FAUSTUS [*giving the deed*]: Ay. Take it, and the devil give thee good on't.°
MEPHOSTOPHILIS: Now, Faustus, ask what thou wilt.
FAUSTUS: First will I question with thee about hell.
    Tell me, where is the place that men call hell?
MEPHOSTOPHILIS: Under the heavens.
FAUSTUS: Ay, but whereabout?   115
MEPHOSTOPHILIS: Within the bowels of these elements,°
    Where we are tortured and remain for ever.
    Hell hath no limits, nor is circumscribed
    In one self° place, for where we are is hell,
    And where hell is must we ever be.   120
    And, to conclude, when all the world dissolves,
    And every creature shall be purified,°
    All places shall be hell that is not heaven.
FAUSTUS: Come, I think hell's a fable.
MEPHOSTOPHILIS: Ay, think so still, till experience change thy mind.   125
FAUSTUS: Why, think'st thou then that Faustus shall be damned?
MEPHOSTOPHILIS: Ay, of necessity, for here's the scroll
    Wherein thou hast given thy soul to Lucifer.

FAUSTUS: Ay, and body too. But what of that?
    Think'st thou that Faustus is so fond°   130
    To imagine that after this life there is any pain?
    Tush, these are trifles and mere old wives' tales.
MEPHOSTOPHILIS: But, Faustus, I am an instance to prove the contrary,
    For I am damned and am now in hell.
FAUSTUS: How? Now in hell? Nay, an° this be hell, I'll willingly be   135
    damned here. What? Walking, disputing, etcetera? But leaving off
    this, let me have a wife, the fairest maid in Germany, for I am
    wanton and lascivious, and cannot live without a wife.
MEPHOSTOPHILIS: How, a wife? I prithee, Faustus, talk not of a wife.°
FAUSTUS: Nay, sweet Mephostophilis, fetch me one, for I will have one. 140
MEPHOSTOPHILIS: Well, thou wilt have one. Sit there till I come. I'll
    fetch thee a wife, in the devil's name.   [*Exit.*]

        [*Re-enter* MEPHOSTOPHILIS *with*] *a* Devil *dressed*
            like a woman, with fireworks.°

MEPHOSTOPHILIS: Tell, Faustus, how dost thou like thy wife?
FAUSTUS: A plague on her for a hot whore!
MEPHOSTOPHILIS: Tut, Faustus,
    Marriage is but a ceremonial toy.°   145
    If thou lovest me, think no more of it.   [*Exit* Devil.]
    I'll cull thee out° the fairest courtesans,
    And bring them ev'ry morning to thy bed.
    She whom thine eye shall like, thy heart shall have,
    Be she as chaste as was Penelope,°   150
    As wise as Saba,° or as beautiful
    As was bright Lucifer before his fall.   [*Presents a book.*]
    Hold, take this book. Peruse it thoroughly.
    The iterating° of these lines brings gold;
    The framing of this circle on the ground   155
    Brings whirlwinds, tempests, thunder, and lightning.°
    Pronounce this thrice devoutly to thyself,
    And men in armour shall appear to thee,
    Ready to execute what thou desir'st.
FAUSTUS: Thanks, Mephostophilis. Yet fain° would I have a book   160
    wherein I might behold all spells and incantations, that I might
    raise up spirits when I please.
MEPHOSTOPHILIS: Here they are in this book.   [*Turns*] *to them.*
FAUSTUS: Now would I have a book where I might see all characters°
    and planets of the heavens, that I might know their motions and   165
    dispositions.°
MEPHOSTOPHILIS: Here they are too.   *Turns to them.*
FAUSTUS: Nay, let me have one book more — and then I have done —

wherein I might see all plants, herbs, and trees that grow upon the
earth.   170
MEPHOSTOPHILIS: Here they be.   *Turns to them.*
FAUSTUS: O, thou art deceived.°
MEPHOSTOPHILIS: Tut, I warrant° thee.   [*Exeunt.*]

Act Two, Scene Two

Enter ROBIN *the ostler,° with a book in his hand.*

ROBIN: O, this is admirable! Here I ha' stol'n one of Doctor Faustus'
conjuring books, and, i'faith, I mean to search some circles° for my
own use.° Now will I make all the maidens in our parish dance at
my pleasure stark naked before me, and so by that means I shall
see more than e'er I felt or saw yet.   5

Enter RAFE, *calling* ROBIN.

RAFE: Robin, prithee, come away! There's a gentleman tarries to have
his horse, and he would have his things rubbed° and made clean;
he keeps such a chafing° with my mistress about it, and she has
sent me to look thee out. Prithee, come away.
ROBIN: Keep out, keep out, or else you are blown up, you are   10
dismembered, Rafe! Keep out, for I am about° a roaring° piece of work.
RAFE: Come, what dost thou with that same book? Thou canst not read.
ROBIN: Yes, my master and mistress shall find that I can read — he for
his forehead,° she for her private° study. She's born to bear with
me,° or else my art fails.   15
RAFE: Why, Robin, what book is that?
ROBIN: What book? Why the most intolerable° book for conjuring that
e'er was invented by any brimstone° devil.
RAFE: Canst thou conjure with it?
ROBIN: I can do all these things easily with it: first, I can make thee   20
drunk with hippocras° at any tavern in Europe for nothing. That's
one of my conjuring works.
RAFE: Our Master Parson says that's nothing.°
ROBIN: True, Rafe; and more, Rafe, if thou hast any mind to Nan Spit,
our kitchen maid, then turn her and wind her to thy own use° as   25
often as thou wilt, and at midnight.
RAFE: O, brave Robin! Shall I have Nan Spit, and to mine own use? On
that condition, I'll feed thy devil with horse-bread° as long as he
lives,° of free cost.
ROBIN: No more, sweet Rafe. Let's go and make clean our boots, which   30

lie foul upon our hands,° and then to our conjuring, in the devil's
name.   *Exeunt.*

Act Two, Scene Three

[*Enter* FAUSTUS *in his study, and* MEPHOSTOPHILIS.]°

FAUSTUS: When I behold the heavens,° then I repent
      And curse thee, wicked Mephostophilis,
      Because thou hast deprived me of those joys.
MEPHOSTOPHILIS: Why Faustus,
      Think'st thou heaven is such a glorious thing?   5
      I tell thee, 'tis not half so fair as thou,
      Or any man that breathes on earth.
FAUSTUS: How provest thou that?
MEPHOSTOPHILIS: It was made for man;° therefore is man more excellent.
FAUSTUS: If it were made for man, 'twas made for me.   10
      I will renounce this magic and repent.

          Enter GOOD ANGEL *and* EVIL ANGEL.

GOOD ANGEL: Faustus, repent yet; God will pity thee.
EVIL ANGEL: Thou art a spirit;° God cannot pity thee.
FAUSTUS: Who buzzeth in mine ears I am a spirit?
      Be I a devil, yet God may pity me;   15
      Ay, God will pity me if I repent.
EVIL ANGEL: Ay, but Faustus never shall repent.   *Exeunt* [ANGELS].
FAUSTUS: My heart's so hardened° I cannot repent.
      Scarce can I name salvation, faith, or heaven
      But fearful echoes thunder in mine ears: 20
      'Faustus, thou art damned!' Then swords and knives,
      Poison, guns, halters,° and envenomed steel°
      Are laid before me to dispatch myself;
      And long ere this I should have slain myself
      Had not sweet pleasure conquered deep despair.   25
      Have not I made blind Homer° sing to me
      Of Alexander's love, and Oenone's death?°
      And hath not he that built the walls of Thebes°
      With ravishing sound of his melodious harp
      Made music with my Mephostophilis?   30
      Why should I die, then, or basely despair?
      I am resolved Faustus shall ne'er repent.
      Come, Mephostophilis, let us dispute again,

And argue of divine astrology.
Tell me, are there many heavens° above the moon?   35
Are all celestial bodies but one globe,
As is the substance of this centric° earth?
MEPHOSTOPHILIS: As are the elements, such are the spheres,
Mutually folded in each others' orb;°
And, Faustus, all jointly move upon one axletree,   40
Whose terminine° is termed the world's wide pole.
Nor are the names of Saturn, Mars, or Jupiter
Feigned,° but are erring stars.°
FAUSTUS: But tell me, have they all one motion, both *situ et tempore*?°
MEPHOSTOPHILIS: All jointly move from east to west in four-and twenty   45
hours upon the poles of the world, but differ in their motion upon
the poles of the zodiac.
FAUSTUS: Tush, these slender trifles Wagner can decide.
Hath Mephostophilis no greater skill?°
Who knows not the double motion of the planets?°   50
The first is finished in a natural day,
The second thus, as Saturn in thirty years,
Jupiter in twelve, Mars in four, the sun, Venus, and Mercury in a
year, the moon in twenty-eight days. Tush, these are freshmen's
suppositions.° But tell me, hath every sphere a dominion or   55
intelligentia?°
MEPHOSTOPHILIS: Ay.
FAUSTUS:How many heavens or spheres are there?
MEPHOSTOPHILIS: Nine: the seven planets, the firmament, and the
empyreal heaven.°   60
FAUSTUS: Well, resolve me in° this question: why have we not
conjunctions, oppositions, aspects,° eclipses all at one time, but in
some years we have more, in some less?
MEPHOSTOPHILIS: *Per inaequalem motum respectu totius.*°
FAUSTUS: Well, I am answered. Tell me, who made the world?   65
MEPHOSTOPHILIS: I will not.
FAUSTUS: Sweet Mephostophilis, tell me.
MEPHOSTOPHILIS: Move° me not, for I will not tell thee.
FAUSTUS: Villain, have I not bound thee to tell me anything?
MEPHOSTOPHILIS: Ay, that is not against our kingdom, but this is. Think   70
thou on hell, Faustus, for thou art damned.
FAUSTUS: Think, Faustus, upon God, that made the world.
MEPHOSTOPHILIS: Remember this.°   *Exit.*
FAUSTUS: Ay, go, accursed spirit, to ugly hell!
'Tis thou hast damned distressed Faustus' soul.   75
Is't not too late?

Enter GOOD ANGEL *and* EVIL [ANGEL].

EVIL ANGEL: Too late.

GOOD ANGEL: Never too late, if Faustus can repent.

EVIL ANGEL: If thou repent, devils shall tear thee in pieces.

GOOD ANGEL: Repent, and they shall never raze° thy skin.　*Exeunt* [ANGELS].

80

FAUSTUS: Ah, Christ, my Saviour,
　　Seek to save° distressèd Faustus' soul!

Enter LUCIFER, BEELZEBUB, *and* MEPHOSTOPHILIS.

LUCIFER: Christ cannot save thy soul, for he is just.
　　There's none but I have int'rest° in the same.

FAUSTUS: O, who art thou that look'st so terrible?　　　　　　　85

LUCIFER: I am Lucifer,
　　And this is my companion prince in hell.

FAUSTUS: O Faustus, they are come to fetch away thy soul!

[BEELZEBUB:] We come to tell thee thou dost injure us.

[LUCIFER:] Thou talk'st of Christ, contrary to thy promise.　　　　90

[BEELZEBUB:] Thou shouldst not think of God.

[LUCIFER:]　　　　　　　　　　　　　Think of the devil,

[BEELZEBUB:] And of his dam,° too.

FAUSTUS: Nor will I henceforth. Pardon me in this,
　　And Faustus vows never to look to heaven,
　　Never to name God, or to pray to him,　　　　　　　　　　95
　　To burn his Scriptures, slay his ministers,
　　And make my spirits pull his churches down.

LUCIFER: Do so, and we will highly gratify thee. Faustus, we are come
　　from hell to show thee some pastime. Sit down, and thou shalt see
　　all the Seven Deadly Sins° appear in their proper° shapes.　　100

FAUSTUS: That sight will be as pleasing unto me as paradise was
　　to Adam, the first day of his creation.

LUCIFER: Talk not of paradise nor creation, but mark this show. Talk of
　　the devil, and nothing else. — Come away!　　　　[FAUSTUS *sits*.]

Enter the SEVEN DEADLY SINS.

Now, Faustus, examine them of their several° names and　　　105
　　dispositions.

FAUSTUS: What art thou, the first?

PRIDE: I am Pride. I disdain to have any parents. I am like to Ovid's
　　flea:° I can creep into every corner of a wench. Sometimes, like a
　　periwig,° I sit upon her brow, or like a fan of feathers I kiss her lips.　110
　　Indeed I do! What do I not? But fie, what a scent is here! I'll not

speak another word, except° the ground were perfumed and covered with cloth of arras.°

FAUSTUS: What art thou, the second?

COVETOUSNESS: I am Covetousness, begotten of an old churl in an old   115
leathern bag;° and might I have my wish, I would desire that this house and all the people in it were turned to gold, that I might lock you up in my good chest. O, my sweet gold!

FAUSTUS: What art thou, the third?

WRATH: I am Wrath. I had neither father nor mother. I leaped out of a   120
lion's° mouth when I was scarce half an hour old, and ever since I have run up and down the world with this case° of rapiers, wounding myself when I had nobody to fight withal. I was born in hell, and look to it, for some of you shall be my father.

FAUSTUS: What art thou, the fourth?   125

ENVY: I am Envy, begotten of a chimney-sweeper and an oyster-wife.° I cannot read, and therefore wish all books were burnt. I am lean with seeing others eat. O, that there would come a famine through all the world, that all might die, and I live alone! Then thou shouldst see how fat I would be. But must thou sit and I stand?   130
Come down,° with a vengeance!

FAUSTUS: Away, envious rascal! — What are thou, the fifth?

GLUTTONY: Who, I, sir? I am Gluttony. My parents are all dead, and the devil a penny they have left me but a bare pension,° and that is thirty meals a day, and ten bevers:° a small trifle to suffice nature. O, I come of a royal parentage. My grandfather was a gammon of   135
bacon, my grandmother a hogshead° of claret wine. My godfathers were these: Peter Pickle-herring° and Martin Martlemas beef.° O, but my godmother, she was a jolly gentlewoman, and well beloved in every good town and city; her name was Mistress Margery March-beer.° Now, Faustus, thou hast heard all my progeny,° wilt   140
thou bid me to supper?

FAUSTUS: No, I'll see thee hanged. Thou wilt eat up all my victuals.

GLUTTONY: Then the devil choke thee!

FAUSTUS: Choke thyself, glutton! — What art thou, the sixth?

SLOTH: I am Sloth. I was begotten on a sunny bank, where I have lain   145
ever since, and you have done me great injury to bring me from thence. Let me be carried thither again by Gluttony and Lechery. I'll not speak another word, for a king's ransom.

FAUSTUS: What are you, Mistress Minx,° the seventh and last?

LECHERY: Who, I, sir? I am one that loves an inch of raw mutton° better   150
than an ell of fried stockfish,° and the first letter of my name begins with lechery.

LUCIFER: Away, to hell, to hell!   *Exeunt the* SINS.
Now, Faustus, how dost thou like this?

FAUSTUS: O, this feeds my soul!   155

LUCIFER: Tut, Faustus, in hell is all manner of delight.
FAUSTUS: O, might I see hell and return again, how happy were
    I then!
LUCIFER: Thou shalt. I will send for thee at midnight. [*Presents a book.*]
    In meantime, take this book. Peruse it throughly,° and thou shalt   160
    turn thyself into what shape thou wilt.
FAUSTUS [*taking the book*]: Great thanks, mighty Lucifer. This will I keep
    as chary° as my life.
LUCIFER: Farewell, Faustus, and think on the devil.
FAUSTUS: Farewell, great Lucifer. Come, Mephostophilis.   16⁵
                              Exeunt omnes, [different ways].

Act Three Chorus

Enter WAGNER *solus.*°

WAGNER: Learned Faustus,
    To know the secrets of astronomy
    Graven° in the book of Jove's high firmament,
    Did mount himself° to scale Olympus'° top,
    Being seated in a chariot burning bright,   5
    Drawn by the strength of yoky° dragons' necks.
    He now is gone to prove cosmography,°
    And, as I guess, will first arrive at Rome,
    To see the Pope, and manner of his court,
    And take some part of holy Peter's feast°   10
    That to this day is highly solemnised.   *Exit* WAGNER.

Act Three, Scene One

Enter FAUSTUS *and* MEPHOSTOPHILIS.

FAUSTUS: Having now, my good Mephostophilis,
    Passed with delight the stately town of Trier,°
    Environed round° with airy mountain-tops,
    With walls of flint, and deep intrenchèd lakes,°
    Not to be won by any conquering prince;   5
    From Paris next, coasting° the realm of France,
    We saw the river Maine° fall into Rhine,
    Whose banks are set with groves of fruitful vines.
    Then up to Naples, rich Campania,°
    Whose buildings, fair and gorgeous to the eye,   10

The streets straight forth,° and paved with finest brick,
Quarters the town in four equivalents.
There saw we learnèd Maro's° golden tomb,
The way° he cut an English mile in length
Thorough a rock of stone in one night's space.   15
From thence to Venice, Padua, and the rest,
In midst of which° a sumptuous temple° stands,
That threats the stars with her aspiring top.
Thus, hitherto, hath Faustus spent his time.
But tell me now, what resting place is this?   20
Hast thou, as erst° I did command,
Conducted me within the walls of Rome?
MEPHOSTOPHILIS: Faustus, I have. And because we will not be unprovi-
   ded, I have taken up° his Holiness' privy chamber° for our use.
FAUSTUS: I hope his Holiness will bid us welcome.   25
MEPHOSTOPHILIS: Tut, 'tis no matter, man. We'll be bold with his good
   cheer.
   And now, my Faustus, that thou mayst perceive
   What Rome containeth to delight thee with,
   Know that this city° stands upon seven hills   30
   That underprops the groundwork of the same.
   Just through the midst runs flowing Tiber's stream,
   With winding banks that cut it in two parts,
   Over the which four stately bridges lean,
   That makes safe passage to each part of Rome.   35
   Upon the bridge called Ponte Angelo
   Erected is a castle passing° strong,°
   Within whose walls such store of ordnance are,
   And double cannons,° framed of carved brass,
   As match the days within one complete year —   40
   Besides the gates and high pyramides°
   Which Julius Caesar brought from Africa.
FAUSTUS: Now, by the kingdoms of infernal rule,
   Of Styx, Acheron, and the fiery lake
   Of ever-burning Phlegethon,° I swear   45
   That I do long to see the monuments
   And situation of bright splendent° Rome.
   Come, therefore, let's away!
MEPHOSTOPHILIS: Nay, Faustus, stay. I know you'd fain° see the Pope
   And take some part of° holy Peter's feast,   50
   Where thou shalt see a troupe of bald-pate° friars
   Whose *summum bonum*° is in belly cheer.
FAUSTUS: Well, I am content to compass° then some sport,
   And by their folly make us merriment.
   Then charm me that I may be invisible, to do what I please unseen   55

of any whilst I stay in Rome.

MEPHOSTOPHILIS [*placing a robe° on* FAUSTUS]: So, Faustus, now do what
thou wilt, thou shalt not be discerned.

Sound a sennet.° Enter the POPE *and the* CARDINAL OF LORRAINE
to the banquet, with FRIARS *attending.*

POPE: My lord of Lorraine, will't please you draw near?

FAUSTUS: Fall to,° and the devil choke you an you spare.°   60

POPE: How now, who's that which spake? Friars, look about.

FRIAR: Here's nobody, if it like° your Holiness.

POPE: My lord, here is a dainty° dish was sent me from the Bishop of
Milan.   [*He presents a dish.*]

FAUSTUS: I thank you, sir.   [*Snatches it.*] 65

POPE: How now, who's that which snatched the meat° from me? Will no
man look? — My lord, this dish was sent me from the Cardinal of
Florence.

FAUSTUS [*snatching the dish*]: You say true. I'll ha't.

POPE: What again? — My lord, I'll drink to your Grace.   70

FAUSTUS [*snatching the cup*]: I'll pledge your Grace.

LORRAINE. My lord, it may be some ghost, newly crept out of
purgatory,° come to beg a pardon° of your Holiness.

POPE: It may be so. Friars, prepare a dirge° to lay° the fury of this ghost.
Once again, my lord, fall to.   *The* POPE *crosseth °himself.* 75

FAUSTUS: What, are you crossing of yourself? Well, use that trick no
more, I would advise you.   [*The* POPE] *cross[es himself] again.*
Well, there's a second time. Aware° the third; I give you fair warning.
                              [*The* POPE] *cross[es himself] again, and* FAUSTUS
                              hits him a box of° the ear, and they all run away.
Come on, Mephostophilis. What shall we do?

MEPHOSTOPHILIS: Nay, I know not. We shall be cursed with bell, book,   80
and candle.°

FAUSTUS: How? Bell, book, and candle; candle, book, and bell;
Forward and backward, to curse Faustus to hell.
Anon you shall hear a hog grunt, a calf bleat, and an ass bray,
Because it is Saint Peter's holy day.   85

Enter all the FRIARS, *to sing the dirge.*

FRIAR: Come, brethren, let's about our business with good devotion.

[*The* FRIARS] *sing this:*

Cursèd be he that stole away his Holiness' meat from the table.

Maledicat Dominus!°
Cursèd be he that struck his Holiness a blow on the face.
  Maledicat Dominus!   90
Cursèd be he that took Friar Sandelo° a blow on the pate.°
  Maledicat Dominus!
Cursèd be he that disturbeth our holy dirge.
  Maledicat Dominus!
Cursed be he that took away his Holiness' wine.   95
  Maledicat Dominus!
Et omnes sancti. °*Amen.*   [FAUSTUS *and* MEPHOSTOPHILIS] *beat the* FRIARS,
                             and fling fireworks among them, and so exeunt.

Act Three, Scene Two°

Enter ROBIN [*with a book*] *and* RAFE *with a silver goblet.*

ROBIN: Come, Rafe, did not I tell thee we were for ever made° by this
  Doctor Faustus' book? *Ecce signum!*° Here's a simple purchase° for
  horse-keepers. Our horses shall eat no hay° as long as this lasts.

Enter the VINTNER.°

RAFE: But Robin, here comes the Vintner.
ROBIN: Hush, I'll gull° him supernaturally. — Drawer,° I hope all   5
  is paid. God be with you. Come, Rafe.   [*They start to go.*]
VINTNER [*to* ROBIN]: Soft,° sir, a word with you. I must yet have a goblet
  paid from you ere you go.
ROBIN: I, a goblet? Rafe, I, a goblet? I scorn you, and you are but an
  etcetera.° I, a goblet? Search me.   10
VINTNER: I mean so, sir, with your favour.°   [*He searches* ROBIN.]
ROBIN: How say you now?
VINTNER: I must say somewhat to your fellow. — You, sir.
RAFE: Me, sir? Me, sir? Search your fill. [*He gives the goblet to* ROBIN *as the*
  VINTNER *searches him.*] Now, sir, you may be ashamed to   15
  burden honest men with a matter of truth.
VINTNER: Well, t'one of you hath this goblet about you.°
ROBIN [*producing the goblet*]: You lie, drawer, 'tis afore me. Sirrah, you,
  I'll teach ye to impeach° honest men. Stand by. I'll scour° you for a
  goblet. Stand aside, you had best, I charge you in the name of   20
  Beelzebub. [*Tosses the goblet to* RAFE.] Look to the goblet, Rafe.
VINTNER: What mean you, sirrah?
ROBIN: I'll tell you what I mean.   [*He reads.*]

Sanctobulorum Periphrasticon! Nay, I'll tickle° you, Vintner. Look to
the goblet, Rafe. *Polypragmos Belseborams framanto pacostiphos*   25
tostu Mephostopheles!° etc.

Enter MEPHOSTOPHILIS.°

[*Exit the* VINTNER, *running.*]
MEPHOSTOPHILIS: Monarch of hell, under whose black survey
    Great potentates do kneel with awful° fear,
    Upon whose altars thousand souls do lie,
    How am I vexèd° with these villains' charms!°   30
    From Constantinople° am I hither come
    Only for pleasure of these damnèd slaves.
ROBIN: How, from Constantinople? You have had a great journey. Will
    you take sixpence in your purse to pay for your supper and be
    gone?   35
MEPHOSTOPHILIS: Well, villains, for your presumption I transform thee°
    [*to* ROBIN] into an ape, and thee [*to* RAFE] into a dog. And so, begone!
                                           Exit.
ROBIN: How, into an ape? That's brave.° I'll have fine sport with the
    boys; I'll get nuts and apples enough.
RAFE: And I must be a dog.   40
ROBIN: I'faith, thy head will never be out of the pottage pot.°   *Exeunt.*

Act Four Chorus

Enter CHORUS.°

CHORUS: When Faustus had with pleasure ta'en the view
    Of rarest things, and royal courts of kings,
    He stayed his course° and so returned home,
    Where such as bear his absence but with grief —
    I mean his friends and nearest companions —   5
    Did gratulate° his safety with kind words.
    And in their conference° of what befell,
    Touching his journey through the world and air,
    They put forth questions of astrology,
    Which Faustus answered with such learnèd skill   10
    As° they admired and wondered at his wit.°
    Now is his fame spread forth in every land.
    Amongst the rest the Emperor is one,
    Carolus the Fifth,° at whose palace now
    Faustus is feasted 'mongst his noblemen.   15

What there he did in trial of his art°
I leave untold; your eyes shall see performed.   *Exit.*

Act Four, Scene One

Enter EMPEROR, FAUSTUS, [MEPHOSTOPHILIS,] *and a* KNIGHT,
with Attendants.

EMPEROR: Master Doctor Faustus, I have heard strange° report of thy
knowledge in the black art: how that none in my empire, nor in the
whole world, can compare with thee for the rare° effects of magic.
They say thou hast a familiar spirit,° by whom thou canst
accomplish what thou list.° This, therefore, is my request: that thou   5
let me see some proof of thy skill, that mine eyes may be witnesses
to confirm what mine ears have heard reported. And here I swear
to thee, by the honour of mine imperial crown, that whatever thou
dost, thou shalt be no ways prejudiced or endamaged.°
KNIGHT (*aside*): I'faith, he looks much like a conjurer.°   10
FAUSTUS: My gracious sovereign, though I must confess myself far
inferior to the report men have published, and nothing
answerable° to the honour of your Imperial Majesty, yet, for that°
love and duty binds me thereunto, I am content to do whatsoever
your Majesty shall command me.   15
EMPEROR: Then, Doctor Faustus, mark what I shall say.
As I was sometime° solitary set
Within my closet,° sundry° thoughts arose
About the honour of mine ancestors;
How they had won by prowess such exploits,   20
Got such riches, subdued so many kingdoms
As we that do succeed° or they that shall
Hereafter possess our throne shall,
I fear me, never attain to that degree
Of high renown and great authority.   25
Amongst which kings is Alexander the Great,
Chief spectacle of the world's pre-eminence,°
The bright shining of whose glorious acts
Lightens the world with his reflecting° beams,
As when I hear but motion° made of him,   30
It grieves my soul I never saw the man.
If, therefore, thou by cunning° of thine art
Canst raise this man from hollow vaults below,
Where lies entombed this famous conqueror,
And bring with him his beauteous paramour,°   35
Both in their right° shapes, gesture, and attire

They used to wear during their time of life,
Thou shalt both satisfy my just desire
And give me cause to praise thee whilst I live.

FAUSTUS: My gracious lord, I am ready to accomplish your request, so   40
far forth as by art and power of my spirit I am able to perform.

KNIGHT (*aside*): I'faith, that's just nothing at all.

FAUSTUS: But if it like° your Grace, it is not in my ability to present
before your eyes the true substantial bodies of those two deceased
princes, which long since are consumed to dust.   45

KNIGHT (*aside*): Ay, marry,° Master Doctor, now there's a sign of grace in
you, when you will confess the truth.

FAUSTUS: But such spirits as can lively° resemble Alexander and his
paramour shall appear before your Grace, in that manner that they
best lived in, in their most flourishing estate —° which I doubt not   50
shall sufficiently content your Imperial Majesty.

EMPEROR: Go to, Master Doctor. Let me see them presently.°

KNIGHT: Do you hear, Master Doctor? You bring Alexander and his
paramour before the Emperor?

FAUSTUS: How then,° sir?   55

KNIGHT: I'faith, that's as true as Diana turned me to a stag.°

FAUSTUS: No, sir, but when Actaeon died, he left the horns° for you.
[*Aside to* MEPHOSTOPHILIS] Mephostophilis, begone!

Exit MEPHOSTOPHILIS.

KNIGHT: Nay, an° you go to conjuring, I'll be gone.   *Exit* KNIGHT.

FAUSTUS [*aside*]: I'll meet° with you anon for interrupting me so. —   60
Here they are, my gracious lord.

Enter MEPHOSTOPHILIS, *with* ALEXANDER *and his* Paramour.

EMPEROR: Master Doctor, I heard this lady, while she lived, had a wart
or mole in her neck. How shall I know whether it be so or no?

FAUSTUS: Your Highness may boldly go and see.
[*The* EMPEROR *makes an inspection, then*] ALEXANDER [*and his* Paramour] *exit.*

EMPEROR: Sure, these are no spirits, but the true substantial bodies of   65
two those deceased princes.

FAUSTUS: Will't please your Highness now to send for the knight that
was so pleasant° with me here of late?

EMPEROR: One of you call him forth.

[*An* Attendant *leaves to summon the* KNIGHT.]

Enter the KNIGHT *with a pair of horns on his head.*

How now, sir knight? Why, I had thought thou hadst been a   70
bachelor,° but now I see thou hast a wife, that not only gives thee
horns but makes thee wear them. Feel on thy head.

KNIGHT [*to* FAUSTUS]: Thou damned wretch and execrable dog,
    Bred in the concave° of some monstrous rock,
    How dar'st thou thus abuse a gentleman?   75
    Villain, I say, undo what thou hast done.
FAUSTUS: O, not so fast, sir. There's no haste but good.°
    Are you remembered° how you crossed me in my conference° with
    the Emperor? I think I have met° with you for it.
EMPEROR: Good Master Doctor, at my entreaty release him. He hath   80
    done penance sufficient.
FAUSTUS: My gracious lord, not so much for the injury° he offered me
    here in your presence as to delight you with some mirth hath
    Faustus worthily requited this injurious knight; which being all I
    desire, I am content to release° him of his horns. — And, sir knight, 85
    hereafter speak well of scholars. — [*Aside to* MEPHOSTOPHILIS.]
    Mephostophilis, transform him straight.°   [*The horns are removed.*]
    Now, my good lord, having done my duty, I humbly take my leave.
EMPEROR: Farewell, Master Doctor. Yet, ere you go,
    Expect from me a bounteous reward.   90
                  Exeunt EMPEROR, [KNIGHT, *and* Attendants].
FAUSTUS: Now, Mephostophilis, the restless course
    That time doth run with calm and silent foot,
    Short'ning my days and thread° of vital life,
    Calls for the payment° of my latest years.   95
    Therefore, sweet Mephostophilis, let us
    Make haste to Wittenberg.
MEPHOSTOPHILIS: What, will you go on horseback or on foot?
FAUSTUS: Nay, till I am past this fair and pleasant green,°
    I'll walk on foot.

Enter a HORSE-COURSER.

HORSE-COURSER: I have been all this day seeking one Master Fustian.°   100
    Mass!° see where he is. — God save you, Master Doctor.
FAUSTUS: What, Horse-courser! You are well met.°
HORSE-COURSER: Do you hear, sir? I have brought you forty dollars° for
    your horse.   [*He offers money.*]
FAUSTUS: I cannot sell him so. If thou lik'st him for fifty, take him.   105
HORSE-COURSER: Alas, sir, I have no more. [*To* MEPHOSTOPHILIS] I pray
    you, speak for me.
MEPHOSTOPHILIS [*to* FAUSTUS]: I pray you, let him have him. He is an
    honest fellow,° and he has a great charge,° neither wife nor child.
FAUSTUS: Well, come, give me your money. [*He takes the money.*] My boy° 110
    will deliver him to you. But I must tell you one thing before you
    have him: ride him not into the water,° at any hand.
HORSE-COURSER: Why, sir, will he not drink of all waters?°

FAUSTUS: O, yes, he will drink of all waters, but ride him not into the
    water. Ride him over hedge, or ditch, or where thou wilt, but not   115
    into the water.
HORSE-COURSER: Well, sir. [*Aside*] Now am I made man° for ever. I'll not
    leave° my horse for forty.° If he had but the quality of hey, ding,
    ding, hey, ding, ding,° I'd make a brave° living on him; he has a
    buttock as slick as an eel. [*To* FAUSTUS] Well, goodbye,° sir. Your boy   120
    will deliver him me? But hark ye, sir: if my horse be sick or ill at
    ease, if I bring his water° to you, you'll tell me what it is?
FAUSTUS: Away, you villain! What, dost think I am a horse-doctor?
                                            Exit the HORSE-COURSER.
    What art thou, Faustus, but a man condemned to die?°
    Thy fatal time° doth draw to final end.   125
    Despair doth drive distrust unto my thoughts.
    Confound these passions° with a quiet sleep.
    Tush! Christ did call the thief upon the cross;°
    Then rest thee, Faustus, quiet in conceit.°   [*He sleeps*] *in his chair.*

                Enter HORSE-COURSER *all wet, crying.*

HORSE-COURSER: Alas, alas! Fustian, quotha!° Mass, Doctor Lopus° was   130
    never such a doctor. H'as given me a purgation,° h'as° purged me of
    forty dollars. I shall never see them more. But yet, like an ass as I
    was, I would not be ruled by him, for he bade me I should ride him
    into no water. Now I, thinking my horse had had some rare quality
    that he would not have had me known of,° I, like a venturous   135
    youth, rid him into the deep pond at the town's end. I was no
    sooner in the middle of the pond but my horse vanished away, and
    I sat upon a bottle of hay,° never so near drowning in my life. But
    I'll seek out my doctor and have my forty dollars again, or I'll
    make it the dearest° horse! O, yonder is his snipper-snapper. —°   140
    Do you hear? You, hey-pass,° where's your master?
MEPHOSTOPHILIS: Why, sir, what would you? You cannot speak with him.
HORSE-COURSER: But I will speak with him.
MEPHOSTOPHILIS: Why, he's fast asleep. Come some other time.
HORSE-COURSER: I'll speak with him now, or I'll break his glass   145
    windows° about his ears.
MEPHOSTOPHILIS: I tell thee he has not slept this eight nights.°
HORSE-COURSER: An° he have not slept this eight weeks, I'll speak with
    him.
MEPHOSTOPHILIS: See where he is, fast asleep.   150
HORSE-COURSER: Ay, this is he. — God save ye, Master Doctor. Master
    Doctor, Master Doctor Fustian! Forty dollars, forty dollars for a
    bottle of hay!

MEPHOSTOPHILIS: Why, thou seest he hears thee not.

HORSE-COURSER (*holler[s] in his ear*): So, ho, ho!° So, ho, ho! No, will you   155
not not wake? I'll make you wake ere I go.

                           [*He pulls*] *him by the leg, and pull[s] it away.*
Alas, I am undone! What shall I do?

FAUSTUS: O my leg, my leg! Help, Mephostophilis! Call the officers!° My   1
leg, my leg!

MEPHOSTOPHILIS [*seizing the* HORSE-COURSER]: Come, villain, to the   160
constable.

HORSE-COURSER: O Lord, sir, let me go, and I'll give you forty dollars
more.

MEPHOSTOPHILIS: Where be they?

HORSE-COURSER: I have none about me. Come to my hostry,° and I'll   165
give them you.

MEPHOSTOPHILIS: Begone, quickly.   [*The*] HORSE-COURSER *runs away.*

FAUSTUS: What, is he gone? Farewell, he! Faustus has his leg again,
and the horse-courser, I take it, a bottle of hay for his labour. Well,
this trick shall cost him forty dollars more.   170

Enter WAGNER.

How now, Wagner, what's the news with thee?

WAGNER: Sir, the Duke of Vanholt° doth earnestly entreat your
company.

FAUSTUS: The Duke of Vanholt! An honourable gentleman, to whom I
must be no niggard of my cunning.° Come, Mephostophilis, let's
away to him.   *Exeunt.* 175

Act Four, Scene Two

[*Enter* FAUSTUS *with* MEPHOSTOPHILIS.] *Enter to them the* DUKE [OF
VANHOLT] *and the* DUCHESS. *The* DUKE *speaks.*

DUKE: Believe me, Master Doctor, this merriment hath much
pleased me.

FAUSTUS: My gracious lord, I am glad it contents you so well. — But it
may be, madam, you take no delight in this. I have heard that
great-bellied° women do long for some dainties° or other. What is it,   5
madam? Tell me, and you shall have it.

DUCHESS: Thanks, good Master Doctor. And, for I see your courteous
intent to pleasure° me, I will not hide from you the thing my heart
desires. And were it now summer, as it is January and the dead
time of the winter, I would desire no better meat° than a dish of   10
ripe grapes.

FAUSTUS: Alas, madam, that's nothing. [*Aside to* MEPHOSTOPHILIS]
    Mephostophilis, begone!   *Exit* MEPHOSTOPHILIS.
    Were it a greater thing than this, so it would content you, you
    should have it.   15

Enter MEPHOSTOPHILIS, *with the grapes.*

    Here they be, madam. Will't please you taste on° them?
                              [*The* DUCHESS *tastes the grapes.*]
DUKE: Believe me, Master Doctor, this makes me wonder above the rest,
    that, being in the dead time of winter and in the month of January,
    how you should come by these grapes.
FAUSTUS: If it like° your Grace, the year is divided into two circles over   20
    the whole world, that when it is here winter with us, in the
    contrary circle it is summer with them, as in India, Saba,° and
    farther countries in the East; and by means of a swift spirit that I
    have, I had them brought hither, as ye see. — How do you like
    them, madam? Be they good?   25
DUCHESS: Believe me, Master Doctor, they be the best grapes that e'er I
    tasted in my life before.
FAUSTUS: I am glad they content you so, madam.
DUKE: Come, madam, let us in,
    Where you must well reward this learnèd man   30
    For the great kindness he hath showed to you.
DUCHESS: And so I will, my lord, and whilst I live
    Rest beholding° for this courtesy.
FAUSTUS: I humbly thank your Grace.
DUKE: Come, Master Doctor, follow us and receive your reward. *Exeunt.* 35

Act Five, Scene One

Enter WAGNER *solus.*

WAGNER: I think my master means to die shortly,
    For he hath given to me all his goods.
    And yet methinks° if that death were near
    He would not banquet, and carouse, and swill°
    Amongst the students, as even now he doth,   5
    Who are at supper with such belly-cheer
    As Wagner ne'er beheld in all his life.
    See where they come; belike° the feast is ended.   [*Exit.*]

Enter FAUSTUS [*and* MEPHOSTOPHILIS,]°
with two or three SCHOLARS.

1 SCHOLAR: Master Doctor Faustus, since our conference° about fair
    ladies — which was the beautifullest in all the world — we have   10
    determined with° ourselves that Helen of Greece° was the
    admirablest lady that ever lived. Therefore, Master Doctor, if you
    will do us that favour as to let us see that peerless dame° of Greece,
    whom all the world admires for majesty, we should think
    ourselves much beholding unto you.   15
FAUSTUS: Gentlemen,
    For that° I know your friendship is unfeigned,
    And Faustus' custom is not to deny
    The just requests of those that wish him well,
    You shall behold that peerless dame of Greece,   20
    No otherways° for pomp and majesty
    Than when Sir Paris crossed the seas with her,
    And brought the spoils to rich Dardania.°
    Be silent, then, for danger is in words.

Music sounds and HELEN *passeth over the stage.*°

2 SCHOLAR: Too simple is my wit° to tell her praise,   25
    Whom all the world admires for majesty.
3 SCHOLAR: No marvel though the angry Greeks pursued°
    With ten years' war the rape° of such a queen,
    Whose heavenly beauty passeth all compare.°
1 SCHOLAR: Since we have seen the pride of nature's works   30
    And only paragon of excellence,

Enter an OLD MAN.

    Let us depart; and for this glorious deed
    Happy° and blest be Faustus evermore.
FAUSTUS: Gentlemen, farewell. The same I wish to you.   *Exeunt* SCHOLARS.
OLD MAN: Ah, Doctor Faustus, that I might prevail   35
    To guide thy steps unto the way of life,
    By which sweet path thou mayst attain the goal
    That shall conduct thee to celestial rest!
    Break heart, drop blood, and mingle it with tears,
    Tears falling from repentant heaviness°   40
    Of thy most vile and loathsome filthiness,
    The stench whereof corrupts the inward soul
    With such flagitious° crimes of heinous sins

As no commiseration may expel
But mercy, Faustus, of thy Saviour sweet,   45
Whose blood alone must wash away thy guilt.
FAUSTUS: Where art thou, Faustus?° Wretch, what hast thou done?
Damned art thou, Faustus, damned! Despair and die!
Hell calls for right, and with a roaring voice°
Says, 'Faustus, come! Thine hour is come.'°   50
                   MEPHOSTOPHILIS *gives him a dagger.*°
And Faustus will come to do thee right.
                        [FAUSTUS *prepares to stab himself.*]
OLD MAN: Ah, stay, good Faustus, stay thy desperate steps!
I see an angel hovers o'er thy head,
And with a vial full of precious grace
Offers to pour the same into thy soul.   55
Then call for mercy, and avoid despair.
FAUSTUS: Ah, my sweet friend, I feel thy words
To comfort my distressèd soul.
Leave me a while to ponder on my sins.
OLD MAN: I go, sweet Faustus, but with heavy cheer,°   60
Fearing the ruin of thy hopeless soul.   [*Exit.*]
FAUSTUS: Accursèd Faustus, where is mercy now?
I do repent, and yet I do despair.
Hell strives with grace for conquest in my breast.
What shall I do to shun the snares of death?   65
MEPHOSTOPHILIS: Thou traitor, Faustus, I arrest thy soul
For disobedience to my sovereign lord.
Revolt,° or I'll in piecemeal tear thy flesh!
FAUSTUS: Sweet Mephostophilis, entreat thy lord
To pardon my unjust presumption,   70
And with my blood again I will confirm
My former vow I made to Lucifer.
MEPHOSTOPHILIS: Do it then quickly, with unfeignèd heart,
Lest greater danger do attend thy drift.°
FAUSTUS: Torment, sweet friend, that base and crooked age°   75
That durst dissuade me from thy Lucifer,
With greatest torments that our hell affords.
MEPHOSTOPHILIS: His faith is great. I cannot touch his soul.
But what I may afflict his body with
I will attempt, which is but little worth.   80
FAUSTUS: One thing, good servant, let me crave of thee
To glut the longing of my heart's desire,
That I might have unto my paramour°
That heavenly Helen which I saw of late,
Whose sweet embracings may extinguish clean°   85
These thoughts that do dissuade me from my vow,

And keep mine oath I made to Lucifer.
MEPHOSTOPHILIS: Faustus, this, or what else thou shalt desire,
    Shall be performed in twinkling of an eye.

Enter HELEN.

FAUSTUS: Was this the face that launched a thousand ships,°   90
    And burnt the topless° towers of Ilium?°
    Sweet Helen, make me immortal with a kiss.   [*They kiss.*]
    Her lips sucks forth my soul. See where it flies!°
    Come, Helen, come, give me my soul again.   [*They kiss again.*]
    Here will I dwell, for heaven be in these lips,   95
    And all is dross that is not Helena.

Enter OLD MAN.

    I will be Paris, and, for love of thee,
    Instead of Troy shall Wittenberg° be sacked;
    And I will combat with weak Menelaus,°
    And wear thy colours on my plumèd crest.   100
    Yea, I will wound Achilles in the heel,°
    And then return to Helen for a kiss.
    O, thou art fairer than the evening air,
    Clad in the beauty of a thousand stars.
    Brighter art thou than flaming Jupiter,   105
    When he appeared to hapless Semele,°
    More lovely than the monarch of the sky
    In wanton Arethusa's azured° arms;°
    And none but thou shalt be my paramour.
                 Exeunt [FAUSTUS *and* HELEN].
OLD MAN: Accursèd Faustus, miserable man,   110
    That from thy soul exclud'st the grace of heaven,
    And fliest the throne of His tribunal seat!°

Enter the Devils. [*They menace the* OLD MAN.]

    Satan begins to sift me° with his pride.
    As in this furnace° God shall try my faith,
    My faith, vile hell, shall triumph over thee.   115
    Ambitious fiends, see how the heavens smiles
    At your repulse, and laughs your state to scorn!°
    Hence, hell! For hence I fly° unto my God.   *Exeunt.*

Act Five, Scene Two

Enter FAUSTUS, *with the* SCHOLARS.

FAUSTUS: Ah, gentlemen!

1 SCHOLAR: What ails Faustus?

FAUSTUS: Ah, my sweet chamber-fellow! Had I lived with thee, then had
I lived still, but now I die eternally.° Look, comes he not? Comes he
not?   5

2 SCHOLAR: What means Faustus?

3 SCHOLAR: Belike° he is grown into some sickness by being over-solitary.

1 SCHOLAR: If it be so, we'll have physicians to cure him. [*To* FAUSTUS]
'Tis but a surfeit.° Never fear, man.

FAUSTUS: A surfeit of deadly sin that hath damned both body and soul.   10

2 SCHOLAR: Yet, Faustus, look up to heaven. Remember God's mercies
are infinite.

FAUSTUS: But Faustus' offence can ne'er be pardoned. The serpent that
tempted Eve may be saved,° but not Faustus. Ah, gentlemen, hear me
with patience, and tremble not at my speeches. Though my heart   15
pants° and quivers to remember that I have been a student here
these thirty years, O, would I had never seen Wittenberg, never
read book! And what wonders I have done all Germany can
witness, yea, all the world; for which Faustus hath lost both
Germany and the world,° yea, heaven itself — heaven, the seat of   20
God, the throne of the blessed, the kingdom of joy — and must
remain in hell for ever. Hell, ah, hell for ever! Sweet friends, what
shall become of Faustus, being in hell for ever?

3 SCHOLAR: Yet, Faustus, call on God.

FAUSTUS: On God, whom Faustus hath abjured? On God, whom   25
Faustus hath blasphemed? Ah, my God, I would weep, but the
devil draws in my tears. Gush forth blood instead of tears, yea, life
and soul. O, he stays my tongue! I would lift up my hands, but see,
they hold them, they hold them.

ALL: Who, Faustus?   30

FAUSTUS: Lucifer and Mephostophilis. Ah, gentlemen! I gave them my
soul for my cunning.°

ALL: God forbid!

FAUSTUS: God forbade it indeed, but Faustus hath done it. For vain°
pleasure of four-and-twenty years hath Faustus lost eternal joy and   35
felicity. I writ them a bill° with mine own blood. The date is
expired, the time will come, and he will fetch me.

1 SCHOLAR: Why did not Faustus tell us of this before, that divines°
might have prayed for thee?

FAUSTUS: Oft have I thought to have done so, but the Devil threatened   40
to tear me in pieces if I named God, to fetch both body and soul if

I once gave ear to divinity.° And now 'tis too late. Gentlemen,
   away, lest you perish with me.
2 SCHOLAR: O, what shall we do to save Faustus?
FAUSTUS: Talk not of me, but save yourselves and depart.   45
3 SCHOLAR: God will strengthen me. I will stay with Faustus.
1 SCHOLAR [*To the third* SCHOLAR]: Tempt not God,° sweet friend, but let us
into the next room and there pray for him.
FAUSTUS: Ay, pray for me, pray for me! And what noise soever ye hear,
   come not unto me, for nothing can rescue me.   50
2 SCHOLAR: Pray thou, and we will pray that God may have mercy upon
   thee.
FAUSTUS: Gentlemen, farewell. If I live till morning, I'll visit you; if not,
   Faustus is gone to hell.
ALL: Faustus, farewell.   *Exeunt* SCHOLARS. 55
                                     The clock strikes eleven.

FAUSTUS: Ah, Faustus,
   Now hast thou but one bare hour to live,
   And then thou must be damned perpetually.
   Stand still, you ever-moving spheres of heaven,
   That time may cease and midnight never come!   60
   Fair nature's eye,° rise, rise again, and make
   Perpetual day; or let this hour be but
   A year, a month, a week, a natural day,
   That Faustus may repent and save his soul!
   O lente, lente currite noctis equi!°   65
   The stars move still; time runs; the clock will strike;
   The devil will come, and Faustus must be damned.
   O, I'll leap up to my God! Who pulls me down?
   See, see where Christ's blood° streams in the firmament!
   One drop would save my soul, half a drop. Ah, my Christ!   70
   Ah, rend not my heart for naming of my Christ!
   Yet will I call on him. O, spare me, Lucifer!
   Where is it now? 'Tis gone; and see where God
   Stretcheth out his arm and bends his ireful brows!
   Mountains and hills, come, come and fall on me,   75
   And hide me from the heavy wrath of God!°
   No, no?
   Then will I headlong run into the earth.
   Earth, gape! O, no, it will not harbour me.
   You stars that reigned at my nativity,°   80
   Whose influence° hath allotted death and hell,
   Now draw up Faustus like a foggy mist
   Into the entrails of yon labouring° cloud,
   That when you vomit forth° into the air,
   My limbs may issue from your smoky mouths,   85

So that my soul may but ascend to heaven.   *The watch° strikes.*
Ah, half the hour is past!
'Twill all be past anon.
O God,
If thou wilt not have mercy on my soul,   90
Yet for Christ's sake, whose blood hath ransomed me,
Impose some end to my incessant pain.
Let Faustus live in hell a thousand years,
A hundred thousand, and at last be saved.
O, no end is limited° to damnèd souls.   9⁻
Why wert thou not a creature wanting° soul?
Or why is this immortal that thou hast?
Ah, Pythagoras' *metempsychosis;°* were that true,
This soul should fly from me and I be changed
Unto some brutish beast.   100
All beasts are happy,° for, when they die,
Their souls are soon dissolved in elements.°
But mine must live still° to be plagued in hell.
Curst be the parents that engendered me!
No, Faustus, curse thyself. Curse Lucifer,   105
That hath deprived thee of the joys of heaven.   *The clock striketh twelve.*
O, it strikes, it strikes! Now, body, turn to air,
Or Lucifer will bear thee quick° to hell.   *Thunder and lightning.*
O soul, be changed into little waterdrops,
And fall into the ocean, ne'er be found!   110
My God, my God, look not so fierce on me!

Enter [LUCIFER, MEPHOSTOPHILIS, *and other*] Devils.

Adders and serpents,° let me breathe a while!
Ugly hell, gape not! Come not, Lucifer!
I'll burn my books.° Ah, Mephostophilis!   [*The* Devils] *exeunt with him.*

Epilogue

Enter CHORUS.

CHORUS: Cut is the branch that might have grown full straight,
          And burnèd is Apollo's laurel bough°
          That sometime° grew within this learnèd man.
          Faustus is gone. Regard his hellish fall,

Whose fiendful° fortune may exhort the wise   5
Only to wonder° at unlawful things,
Whose deepness doth entice such forward wits°
To practise more than heavenly power permits.   [*Exit.*]

       Terminat hora diem; terminat author opus.°

Notes to the Play

Dramatis Personae

2   DOCTOR JOHN FAUSTUS: based on the historical wandering scholar and professed magician Georgius of Helmstadt (*c.* 1466–*c.* 1537), who took a Master's degree at Heidelberg in 1487, and assumed the humanist surname Faustus ('auspicious').

3   WAGNER: described as a handsome but vicious young servant in Marlowe's source, *The History of the damnable life and deserved death of Doctor John Faustus* (London, 1592).

9   MEPHOSTOPHILIS: perhaps meaning 'no friend to Faustus'; the name of an evil spirit, first appearing in Marlowe's source as 'a prince, but servant to Lucifer'.

13   LUCIFER: the chief rebel archangel, also known as Satan and the Devil

14   BEELZEBUB: 'Lord of the Flies', one of the fallen angels, and 'prince of devils' (Matthew 12:24)

22   THE POPE: named as Adrian in the 1616 text; Pope Adrian VI (1522–3), a contemporary of the historical Faustus

25   VINTNER: innkeeper selling wine

26   THE EMPEROR: Charles V (1500–58), King of Spain and Holy Roman Emperor from 1519 to 1555

29   ALEXANDER THE GREAT: the world conqueror, Alexander III of Macedon (356–323 BC)

30   HIS PARAMOUR: the famous beauty, Roxana, Alexander's wife (327–311 BC); *paramour* may mean 'consort' or 'mistress'

31   HORSE-COURSER: a jobbing dealer in horses

34   HELEN OF TROY: the beautiful wife of Menelaus, king of Sparta, whose abduction by Paris, prince of Troy, brought on the Trojan War

The Prologue

1–2   Trasimene...Carthaginians: in 217 BC the Carthaginian army under Hannibal inflicted a crushing defeat on the Romans at Lake Thrasymenus, preceded by spectactular portents in which the Roman war god Mars figured prominently.

2   mate: joined with

4   state: government

6   muse: dramatic poet
vaunt: proudly display

8   form: representation

9   appeal our plaud: appeal for approval, applause

12   Rhodes: Roda (now Stadtroda) in Weimar, in central Germany

13   Wittenberg: German university, famous as a centre for Protestant learning

14   Whereas: where
kinsmen: According to Marlowe's source, a wealthy uncle supported Faustus's early studies.

15   profits in divinity: does well in theology

16   plot...graced: brought distinction to the area, 'garden' of academic scholarship

17   graced: a University of Cambridge term, the official 'grace' permitting the candidate to proceed to the award of his degree

18   sweet delight disputes: took keen pleasure in academic argument

20   cunning...self-conceit: arrogant pride in his own cleverness

21   waxen wings: like those of Icarus, whose makeshift wings melted when he flew

too near the sun in his attempt to escape from Crete

22   conspired: plotted, devised
23   falling to: (1) having recourse to; (2) tumbling down to; (3) beginning to feed on
      exercise: activity
25   surfeits: feeds to over-repletion
      necromancy: divination through communication with the dead
27   chiefest bliss: that is, his hope of salvation and the final joy of heaven
28   this the man: perhaps the cue for the Chorus to draw aside a curtain and reveal Faustus sitting in the inner alcove stage, in his study

Act One, Scene One

1   Settle: decide on
2   profess: claim expertise in order to teach
3   commenced: (1) begun; (2) graduated as a Doctor of Divinity (another Cambridge term)
      a divine in show: to outward appearance a student of theology
4   level...art: aim at the (1) purpose, (2) uttermost limit of every academic discipline
5   Aristotle's works: The sixteenth-century university curriculum was based on the study of the writings of this Greek philosopher-scientist.
6   *Analytics*: the name given to two works by Aristotle on the science of reasoning
7   *Bene...logices*: translated in the following line; a definition derived from the Roman philosopher Cicero and quoted from a work on logic by Petrus Ramus (1515–72), known at Cambridge as a controversial anti-Aristotelian philosopher, during Marlowe's time there.
9   art: academic discipline
10   end: (1) purpose; (2) limit
11   wit: intelligence
12   *On...on*: 'being and non-being', a

phrase from a Greek philosopher, Georgias of Leontini
      Galen: Claudius Galenus (AD 129–99), a Greek doctor still regarded as the leading authority on medicine.
13   *ubi...medicus*: 'where the philosopher ends, the doctor begins', a phrase from Aristotle
15   eternised: made forever famous
16   *Summum...sanitas*: 'the greatest good provided by medicine is health', a phrase from Aristotle's *Nicomachean Ethics*. In scholastic theology, the phrase *summum bonum* was used to denote the infinite goodness of the nature of God.
17   physic: medical science
19   aphorisms: medical precepts; Faustus is in effect equating himself with Hippocrates, the fifth-century BC Greek author of the *Aphorisms*, the most famous of all medical textbooks.
20   bills: prescriptions, advertisements
      monuments: famous records
24–5 Wouldst...again: capacities attributed, according to the Christian faith, to Jesus Christ and the religion Faustus rejects
27   Justinian: Byzantine Roman Emperor (AD 527–65) associated with a famous codification of Roman Law known as *The Institutes of Justinian* (the 'Institute', line 32)
28   *Si....rei*: 'If one and the same thing is bequeathed to two persons, one shall have the thing itself, the other the equivalent value of the thing.' An inaccurate quotation from the *Institutes*, 2.20.8, which directs equal division of the inheritance.
31   *Exhaereditare...nisi*: 'A father cannot disinherit his son unless...' An inaccurately remembered phrase from the *Institutes*, 2.13.
33   universal: entire

36 illiberal: (1) unfitting a student of the liberal arts; (2) menial

37 when...done: after all
divinity: (1) theology; (2) godhead

38 Jerome's Bible: the Vulgate (Latin) translation compiled by St Jerome in the fourth century, the canonical text of the Bible for Western Christendom until the Reformation

39 *Stipendium...est*: translated at line 41, though Faustus does not quote the full context (Romans 6:23), which continues, 'but the gift of God is eternal life through Jesus Christ our Lord'.

42–5 *Si...* in us: the text (from 1 John 1:8) is given in a Latin version which appears to be Marlowe's own; the translation is taken from the 1599 Book of Common Prayer. Again, Faustus makes no reference to a crucial element in the context: the next verse reads (in the King James version) ' If we confess our sins, he is faithful and just to forgive us our sins, and to cleanse us from all unrighteousness.'

46 belike: in all likelihood

49 *Che serà, serà*: 'what shall be, shall be'

50 adieu: (1) farewell; (2) to God (*à Dieu*)

51 metaphysics: studies of the supernatural

52 heavenly: offering the delights of heaven

53 schemes: diagrams used in astrology, showing the configuration of the heavenly bodies

57 artisan: practitioner

58 quiet poles: the motionless poles of the universe

60 but: merely
several: respective

61 raise...clouds: powers attributed to God (see Jeremiah 10:13)

62 exceeds: excells

65 try: (1) apply; (2) test

70 conference: conversation

75 That: the book of magic (cf. line 50 SD)

78 Jove: the pagan (Greek) name for the supreme God

79 elements: the fundamental constituents of the universe as conceived in medieval and Renaissance thought, earth, air, fire, and water

80 glutted...this: filled with greedy longing at the thought of this

82 Resolve me: clear away for myself

83 desperate: extravagant, outrageous

84 India: the term could refer to any distant country; Faustus may have in mind the fabled gold of the East Indies or America

85 orient: from the Indian seas, hence brilliant or lustrous

87 delicates: delicacies

91 make...Wittenberg: Actually Wittenberg stands on the banks of the Elbe, some 200 miles from the Rhine.

92 public schools: university lecture-rooms
silk: in defiance of dress codes such as those in force at Cambridge, where students were to dress in sober colours and were forbidden to wear silk

93 bravely: handsomely, dashingly

94 levy: raise a military force

95 chase...land: an English ambition; Parma was the oppressive Spanish (hence Catholic) governor-general of the Netherlands from 1579 to 1592, and commander of the Armada troops

97 stranger engines: more ingenious military weapons
brunt: violent assault

98 the...bridge: In 1585 the Netherlands forces used a fireship (*fiery keel*) to destroy a

99 servile: subject (not 'slavish')

101 blest: (1) prosperous, happy; (2) (ironically) filled with heavenly grace

104 concealèd: occult

105 fantasy: (1) power of perception of objects; (2) imagination

106 receive no object: (1) perceive nothing else; (2) accept no objection

109 wits: brains

113 gentle: (1) kind; (2) well-born

115 Gravelled: perplexed, confounded

116 the flow'ring pride: the finest and most active scholars

117 problems: questions proposed for academic discussion and debate

118 Musaeus...hell: In his *Aeneid* (6.666–7) Virgil describes how the poet Musaeus visited the underworld (*hell*) as Aeneas's guide and was surrounded by spirits.

119 cunning: clever, skilful
Agrippa: Henry Cornelius Agrippa of Nettesheim (1486–1535), the most famous of Renaissance magicians, who was credited with the power to summon up phantoms (*shadows*) of the dead.

121 wit: intelligence, genius

122 canonise: grant us sainthood (with the power to do miracles)

123 Indian Moors: the American Indians ('Moor' was a term used for all dark-skinned peoples)

124 spirits: elemental beings

127 Almaine...staves: German cavalrymen with their lances

128 Lapland giants: Marlowe elsewhere refers to arctic giants, 'big as hugy Polypheme' (*2 Tamburlaine*, 1.1.28)

130 Shadowing: imaging forth
airy: ethereal, heavenly

132 huge argosies: The largest vessel in the Venetian trading empire's fleets was the *ragusa*, from which 'argosy' is derived; Marlowe associates the name with that of the *Argo*, in which Jason and his companions sailed to Colchis to seize the Golden Fleece.

133–4 from...treasury: The annual plate-fleet bringing the tribute of America to Spain, then under the rule of Philip II.

137 object: raise as a problem

140 astrology: the science of prediction based on a knowledge of the stars and their occult influences

141 Enriched with tongues: conversant with many languages; Faustus uses Hebrew, Greek and Latin (cf. line 157 below)
seen in: versed in the properties of

144 frequented: visited
mystery: secret art

145 the Delphian oracle: the famous oracle of Apollo at Delphi

149 massy: massive, solid

150 want: lack

153 lusty: pleasant

156 Bacon...Albanus: Roger Bacon (*c.* 1212–92) a Franciscan philosopher at Oxford, reputed to be a magician; Pietro d'Abano (*c.* 1250–1316), an Italian humanist and physician, also reputed to be a sorcerer

157 Hebrew...Testament: Verses from both the Old Testament Book of Psalms and the New Testament were used in magic spells.

159 conference: conversation

160 words of art: technical language of incantation

162 cunning: skill

164 perfecter: more skilful

165 meat: meal

166 canvass: discuss, explore
quiddity: (1) fundamental element; (2) nicety of argument

Act One, Scene Two

2 schools: lecture-rooms
sic probo: 'I prove it thus', the

triumphant declaration of the winner in a scholastic debate

4   sirrah: form of address to a social inferior or servant

7   follows not: does not logically follow, is a *non sequitur*

9   That...necessary: I am not compelled to do so

10   licentiate: graduates trained in logic
stand upon: rely on

13   on't: of it (that I did say so)

15   Ask...thief: a proverbial saying. Wagner means that one scholar cannot be considered a credible witness for another scholar (they will support each other with lies, as do thieves).

17   dunces: (1) hair-splitting logicians; (2) blockheads, dolts

18–19 For...*mobile*: 'Isn't Faustus a natural being, and isn't such a being capable of motion (so why should I know where he is)?' *Corpus naturale seu mobile* (a body that is natural and liable to change) was the current Aristotelian-scholastic definition of the subject-matter of physics.

20   I am...wrath: a parody of James 1:19, 'let every man be swift to hear, slow to speak, slow to wrath'

21   prone: (1) naturally inclined; (2) flat on his back, ready for

22   the place of execution: (1) the room where Faustus, Valdes and Cornelius are enjoying a meal (cf. 1.1.165); (2) the public gallows

23   sessions: sitting of the court

24   set...precisian: put on the serious face of a puritan; that is, having mocked the academic language of scholars, Wagner will now mock the pious phrases of the devoutly religious

27   your worships: your honours

27–8 the Lord...you: a familiar blessing from the Anglican Book of Common Prayer

31   allied: bound in friendship

32   Rector: head of the University of Wittenberg

Act One, Scene Three

1   shadow of the earth: night, so thought of in pre-Copernican science

2   Orion's drizzling look: the constellation of Orion, considered a 'rainy' sign, since it appears in northern latitudes at the onset of winter

4   welkin: sky
pitchy: (1) pitch-black; (2) viscous and stinking

6   hest: command

8   circle: the magician's magic circle, which both compelled spirits to appear and protected the conjurer

8–9   Jehovah's name...anagrammatised: the Hebrew name of God, usually rendered in English as 'Yahweh', considered too sacred for Jews to utter. Cabalist mystics believed that hidden meanings were present in every possible recombination of the letters in the Hebrew scriptures.

10   breviated: shortened

11–12 Figures...stars: charts of every heavenly body fixed in the firmament, astrological diagrams of constellations and the planets (*erring stars*).

12   erring: wandering

16–22 'Let the gods of Acheron be propitious to me! Farewell to the threefold power of Jehovah! All hail, spirits of fire, air, water and earth! Lucifer, prince of the East, Beelzebub, monarch of burning hell, and Demogorgon, grant us that grace that Mephostophilis may appear and rise up! Why do you delay? By Jehovah, and Gehenna, and the holy water I now sprinkle. and the sign of the cross I now make, and by our vows, let

16 *Acherontis*: Acheron is one of the rivers of the underworld
numen triplex Jehovae: the Christian God in three persons, the trinity of Father, Son and Holy Spirit, replaced by the infernal trinity of Lucifer, Beelzebub and Demogorgon

17 *Orientis princeps*: 'sun of the morning' is a title given to Lucifer in Isaiah 14:12

18 *Demogorgon*: a powerful primeval god, described as 'prince of hell' in Marlowe's *1 Tamburlaine*, 4.1.18

20 *Gehennam*: the Jewish hell

25–6 return...best: an anti-Catholic joke for a Protestant audience

27 virtue: (1) supernatural power; (2) moral goodness
heavenly words: (1) scriptural language; (2) divine utterance

32 conjuror laureate: supreme magician

34 *Quin...imagine*: 'Why don't you return, Mephostophilis, in the shape of a friar?'

38 her sphere: the crystalline sphere within which the moon revolved, according to pre-Copernican astronomy

46 *per accidens*: a scholastic phrase for a casual event providing the occasion for the operation of some external agency

49 glorious: (1) radiantly beautiful; (2) vainglorious

53 stoutly: (1) resolutely; (2) arrogantly

56 Beelzebub: used interchangeably for Lucifer or Satan, as in the Bible

59 confounds...Elysium: makes no distinction between a Christian hell and the pagan afterlife; (2) undoes the idea of hell through a belief in Elysium, the pagan paradise

60 ghost: spirit
old philosophers: the pre-Christian philosophers, who according to Christian theology spend eternity in Limbo, an

Mephostophilis himself arise at our command!'

intermediate condition between heaven and hell.

82 passionate: stirred by strong emotions

88 desp'rate: reckless, outrageous

90 So: provided that

99 resolve: inform, advise

105 pass: cross over

106 bind: gird

107 continent: joined

108 contributory: offering tribute

112 speculation: deep study

Act One, Scene Four

0 SD ROBIN *the* CLOWN: The fool is named Robin in the B text equivalent of this scene. See lines 5 and 47 for the fool's traditional costume.

2 'Swounds: by God's wounds

3 pickedevants: short beards trimmed to a point
quotha: said he

4 comings in: income

5 goings out: (1) expenses; (2) stickings-out (through his tattered clothes)
else: otherwise, if you don't believe me

7 out of service: (1) unemployed; (2) in rags

11 By'r Lady: by the Virgin Mary

13 go: (1) be dressed ; (2) take the poetic rhythm of

13–14 *Qui...discipulus*: 'one who is my pupil'; a Latin tag from a well-known poem of the time, William Lyly's *Ad discipulos carmen de moribus*, widely used in grammar schools of the period

16 beaten: (1) embroidered; (2) thrashed
silk: the material forbidden to undergraduate students
stavesacre: (1) a medical preparation against lice; (2) 'staff ache', the pain of a thrashing

17 knave's acre: a deliberate mishearing. The phrase means 'ruination', after the name given to a poor London district, a haven for criminals.

21   belike: probably
22   full of vermin: left in lousy poverty
24   bind yourself: apprentice yourself (seven years was the standard term for an apprenticeship)
      presently: at once
25   familiars: personal demons, often taking the form of domestic animals
27–8 too familiar: (1) too intimate with; (2) too much the demon
28–9 my flesh: me as their food
30   guilders: Dutch florins (as wages)
31   Gridirons: another deliberate mishearing; instruments of torture by roasting over a fire, possibly suggested by the fact that foreign coins often had holes struck through them
32   French crowns: (1) French coins called *ècus*; (2) the regalia of royalty. There may also be a punning reference to heads (*crowns*) made bald by venereal disease
34   counters: merchants' monetary tokens
42   presently: immediately
43   Baliol: comic version of Belial
44   Balio: suggesting 'belly-o'
      knock: beat
46   tall: (1) courageous; (2) man-killing
47   round slop: baggy trousers, which would become traditional wear for clowns
48   Kill devil: recklessly daring man
52   horns: (1) devils' horns; (2) penises
53   clefts: (1) cleft feet; (2) vulvas
56   Banios: (1) mispronunciation of 'Balliols'; (2) brothels (*bagnios*)
62   plackets: (1) side-slits in a skirt or petticoat; (2) vaginas
69   diametarily: a mispronunciation of 'diametrically', directly
69–70 *quasi...insistere*: 'as if to follow in our footsteps'

71   Dutch fustian: Dutch (or German) gibberish
72   that's flat: that's for sure

Act Two, Scene One

3   boots: avails
6   go not backward: don't falter, retreat
23   seigniory of Emden: governorship of Emden, a German port on the North Sea, and a busy centre of trade with England
24–5 When...thee: an ironic inversion of Romans 8: 31, 'If God be on our side, who can be against us?'
26   Cast: produce, or consider
27   glad tidings: an ironic echo of the declaration of Christ's birth, 'I bring you good tidings of great joy' (Luke 2:10)
29   *Veni...Mephostophile*: 'come, O come, Mephostophilis'; a blasphemous echo of Latin hymns of invocation, such *Veni, veni, Emmanuel* (O come, O come Emmanuel) and *Veni, veni rex gloriae* (O come, O come, king of glory)
32   So: provided that
41   *Solamen...doloris*: 'It is a comfort to the wretched to have companions in misery'
42   that: who
48   bind: give a bond for
49   certain: fixed
53   proper: own
54   Assure: convey by deed
61   straight: at once
63   bill: deed
67 SD *chafer*: portable grate
68   set it on: place the blood on the chafer (perhaps in a saucer, as in Marlowe's source)
72   *Consummatum est*: 'It is finished'; the final words of Christ on the cross (John 19: 30), taken to mark the completion of divine atonement for human sin
75   *Homo, fuge*: 'flee, O man'; from 1 Timothy 6: 11, where the passage continues, 'fight the

good fight of faith, lay hold on eternal life'

75–6 Whither...hell: an echo of Psalm 139: 7–8, 'Whither shall I go from thy spirit, or whither shall I free from thy presence? If I ascend into heaven, thou art there; if I make my bed in hell, thou art there'

82 withal: with

87 receive this scroll: Faustus offers the deed to the eager demon, only to withhold it while he reads from it.

103 *by these presents*: a legal phrase, 'by this present document'

106 *inviolate*: not having been violated

112 on't: of it

116 these elements: the four elements constituting all things beneath the sphere of the moon

119 one self: one and the same

121–2 when...purified: There are echoes here of 2 Peter's description of the final Day of the Lord and the fiery dissolution of the world ('all these things shall be dissolved'); also of the end of time as described in Daniel 12: 9–10, 'many shall be purified'.

130 fond: foolish

135 an: if

139 talk...wife: Since marriage was a religious sacrament, Mephostophilis cannot provide a wife or bear talk of marriage.

142 SD *fireworks*: probably exploding squibs, which were commonly used for scenes introducing devils

145 toy: trifle

147 cull thee out: pick out for you

150 Penelope: the faithful wife of Odysseus, in the *Odyssey*

151 Saba: the Queen of Sheba, who tested even Solomon with difficult questions (1 Kings 10:1)

154 iterating: repetition

156 lightning: pronounced as three syllables

160 fain: eagerly

164 characters: occult symbols

166 dispositions: positions in

relation to each other (an astrological term)

172 deceived: mistaken

173 warrant: assure

Act Two, Scene Two

0 SD *ostler*: stableman, groom

2 circles: (1) magic circles; (2) vaginas

3 use: (sexual) purposes

7 have...rubbed: (1) have his riding equipment polished; (2) receive a sexual massage

8 chafing with: (1) fretting at; (2) rubbing erotically against

11 about: busy with

roaring: (1) violent, noisy; (2) devilish

14 forehead: alluding to the deceived husband's cuckold's horns

private: personal, in private; with an allusion to 'private parts' (genitals)

bear with: (1) tolerate; (2) support in sexual intercourse; (3) bear a child

17 intolerable: unbearable (though the word could also mean 'irrestistible')

18 brimstone: sulphurous

21 hippocras: a spiced wine (filtered through a cloth bag known as Hippocrates' sleeve, after the name of the famous Greek physician)

23 nothing: (1) no cost; (2) not difficult

25 turn...wind...use: terms appropriate to both the action of a spit and sexual intercourse

28 horse-bread: (1) poorest-quality bread made of beans, bran, etc to feed horses; (2) whore's-bread

28–9 as long...lives: ironically, until the end of time

31 lie...hands: lie dirty, waiting for our attention

Act Two, Scene Three

0 SD Enter...MEPHOSTOPHILIS: found in the B text only

1 When...heavens: from Psalm 8:

3, which continues with praise of God as supreme creator

9   for man: (1) to serve human needs; 2) for human beings to attain

13   spirit: devil

18   hardened: rendered resistant to spiritual impulse

22   halters: nooses
steel: steel blades

26   blind Homer: traditionally the author of the *Iliad* and *Odyssey*, and poor and blind in his old age

27   Alexander's love...death: Paris of Troy (known in the *Iliad* as Alexandros) deserted the nymph Oenone for Helen; Oenone in turn refused to cure him when he was wounded to death by a poisoned arrow, then died of remorse. The story is told in post-Homeric poems.

28   he...Thebes: Amphion, ruler of Thebes, whose marvellous harp playing drew stones to form a wall around the city

35   heavens: used in Ptolemaic astronomy to mean the crystalline concentric spheres within which celestial bodies were thought to revolve

37   centric: in the Ptolemaic system, the earth lay at the centre of the universe

38–9   As...orb: the four fundamental elements were thought to be contained in concentric spheres (or orbs), with the heavier elements, earth and water, at the centre, surrounded by air and fire.

41   terminine: end, boundary point

43   Feigned: fictional
erring stars: wandering celestial bodies (referring to the apparently irregular motions of the planets)

44   *situ et tempore:* in direction and period of revolution

49   skill: knowledge

50   the double...planets: as Mephostophilis has said, the sun, moon and planets appear to revolve round the earth each day, but also shift through the constellations of the zodiac over a much longer period of time, as Faustus remarks (lines 50–4).

54–5   freshmen's suppositions: elementary facts for first-year students to argue about

55–6   hath...*intelligentia:* Faustus probes the teaching of scholastic philosophers that each celestial orb was moved or guided by an intelligence or angelic spirit (*dominions* were one of the angelic orders).

59–60   the firmament...heaven: the sphere of the fixed stars (here identified with the Primum Mobile, which imparted motion to the rest), and the final sphere, the unmoving Empyrean

61   resolve me in: give me an answer to

62   conjunctions...aspects: astrological terms, meaning the relative position of planets (*aspects*), appearing nearly together (*conjunctions*) or exactly opposite to each other (*oppositions*)

64   *Per...totius:* 'because of their unequal motion with respect to the whole'; an obscure answer to a major problem with the Ptolemaic system

68   Move: anger (because the answer is to name God)

73   this (1) that you said this; (2) that you are damned

80   raze: lightly scratch

82   Seek to save: according to Calvinist theology, salvation could only be initiated by God; in Catholic theology, Christ descended into hell to release those imprisoned there

84   int'rest in: legal and financial claim on

92   dam: (1) witch woman; (2) damnation

100 Seven Deadly Sins: in catholic theology the capital sins, bringing damnation to the sinner
proper: very own
105 several: various
108 Ovid's flea: refering to a medieval poem, *Carmen de Pulice*, attributed to the Roman erotic poet Ovid, in which the poet envies the flea's freedom of access to his mistress's body
110 periwig: wig
112 except: unless
112–13 cloth of arras: the finest tapestry work, made in Arras, Flanders, and far too costly to be used as a floor covering
116 leathern bag: the traditional money-bag of the miser
121 lion: associated with furious rage
122 case: pair
126 oyster-wife: woman who prepares and sells oysters; with such parentage Envy is black and stinking, the offspring of squalid poverty
131 Come down: Envy may pull at the sitting Faustus.
134 pension: payment for board and lodging
135 bevers: in-between-meal snacks or drinks
136 hogshead: sixty-three-gallon cask; with a play on 'hog'
137 Pickle-herring: (1) pickled-herring; (2) buffoon
Martin Martlemas beef: Cattle were commonly slaughtered and salted down for winter use about 11 November, the occasion of Martinmass, or the feast of St Martin
140 March-beer: a strong beer, brewed in March and left to mature for two years before drinking
progeny: parentage
149 Minx: prostitute, wanton woman
150 raw mutton: (1) undressed meat; (2) pure lust; (3) virile penis
151 an ell...stock-fish: (1) forty-five inches of fried dried cod; (2) a

lot of impotence; (3) a long listless penis
160 throughly: thoroughly
163 chary: carefully

Act Three Chorus

0 SD *solus*: alone
3 Graven: engraved
4 mount himself: set himself up
Olympus: in Greek mythology, the sacred mountain-home of the gods
6 yoky: coupled in a yoke
7 prove cosmography: to put to the test the mapping of the universe
10 holy Peter's feast: held on 29 June

Act Three, Scene One

2 Trier: a German town on the Mosel; in Marlowe's time an important administrative, comercial and cultural centre
3 Environed round: surrounded
4 intrenchèd lakes: moats
6 coasting: exploring
7 Maine: a river in West Germany
9 Campania: the district of Italy in which Naples is set
11 straight forth: in straight lines
13 Maro: Virgil, or Publius Vergilius Maro (70–19 BC), the great Roman epic poet, known also in the Renaissance as a magician and wonder worker.
14 way: road
17 of which: Venice
temple: the domed Church of St Mark, which stands near to a tall bell tower
21 erst: earlier
23 because...not: so that we will not
24 taken up: taken possession of privy chamber: private apartment (of a royal or papal palace)
30 this city: The Revels editors of this play point out that the Admiral's Men, one of the first companies to perform the play, owned what may have been a

backcloth showing the City of Rome for use in this scene.

36–7   Upon...strong: The reference is to the papal fortress of St Angelo (formerly the Roman emperor Hadrian's mausoleum) which faces the Roman bridge now known as Ponte Angelo.

37   passing: exceedingly

39   double cannons: guns of very large calibre

41   pyramides: Marlowe is following his source here, but the reference is to an obelisk still standing before St Peter's, brought from Thebes to Rome in AD 353 by the Emperor Constantius.

44–5   Styx...Phlegethon: three of the four rivers of the classical underworld; Styx divided the upper from the lower world, Acheron was the river of woe, Phlegethon the river (rather than 'lake') of liquid fire

47   bright splendent: shining and resplendent

49   fain: willingly

50   of: in

51   bald-pate: tonsured

52   *summum bonum*: supreme good; see 1. 1. 16 and note

53   compass: contrive

57 SD   *a robe*: The Admiral's Men's stage-properties included 'a robe to go invisible'. In the 1616 text of the play, a magic girdle is used.

58 SD   *sennet*: a flourish on a trumpet or cornet to announce a ceremonious entry

60   Fall to: begin eating an you spare: if you eat sparingly

62   like: please

63   dainty: fine, choice

66   meat: food

72   purgatory: in Catholic theology, a place of waiting, where souls are purged of their venial sins.

73   pardon: papal indulgence, or remission of sins

74   dirge: a service for the burial of the dead, a requiem mass lay: put to rest

75 SD   *crosseth*: makes the sign of the cross as a protective action

78   Aware: beware

78 SD   *of*: on

80–1   bell...candle: that is, by a service of excomunication, at the end of which a bell is tolled, the Bible closed and a candle extinguished. This ritual is confused here with the office of exorcism.

87   *Maledicat Dominus*: 'May the Lord curse him'; from the ritual for excommunication

91   took Friar Sandelo: gave Friar Sandal. Only Franciscans were permitted to wear sandals, and Mephostophilis was instructed to appear as an old Franciscan friar (1.3.25). Members of the order were much criticised for failure to obey their own vows of poverty and simplicity. pate: head. This implies that Faustus disrupts the ceremony by striking one of the singing friars.

97   *Et omni sancti*: 'And may all the saints (curse him).'

Act Three, Scene Two

SH   ACT...TWO: In 1603, 3.1 is immediately and continuously followed by what is printed in this edition as the Chorus to Act Four, the scene printed in this edition as 2.2, and the present scene.

1   for ever made: assured of perpetual wealthy and prosperity

2   *Ecce signum*: 'Behold the proof.' A phrase taken from the Catholic Mass. a simple purchase: (1) an honest profit; (2) a real haul

3   eat no hay: be richly fed

3 SD   VINTNER: innkeeper

5   gull: make a fool of Drawer: tapster, who serves drinks to the customers. Robin

7   Soft: wait a moment

10   etcetera: possibly a direction to the actor to improvise insults; or meaning 'a mere whatever'

11   with your favour: (sarcastically) by your leave

17   about you: somewhere on your person; leading to Robin's quibble, 'false, it's in front of me'

19   impeach: accuse
     scour you: (1) give you a thrashing; (2) thoroughly polish you

24–5   *Sanctobolorum...Mephostopheles*: gibberish, scraps of liturgical phrases in a mixture of Latin and Greek. The actor is directed to improvise further, with an 'etc'.

24   tickle: euphemism for 'thrash'

26 SD   *Enter...MEPHOSTOPHILIS*: I follow the Revels editors in rejecting as a cancelled first draft of the conclusion of this scene a passage in which Mephostophilis enters and sets all three characters running about the stage with firecrackers (squibs) exploding behind them. In a panic Rafe hands over the goblet to the Vintner and promises never to rob the devil's library again. Mephostophilis sends each of them off, transformed into an ape, a bear and an ass, 'for doing this enterprise'.

28   awful: dreadful

30   vexèd: tormented

30   charms: magic spells

31   from Constantinople: In the 1616 version of the play, this scene ends with Mephostophilis vowing to fly to Faustus at the Great Turk's court (at Constantinople). There is such an episode in Marlowe's source, but no surviving early version of the play includes such a scene.

36   I transform thee: The business of transformation may be conducted on stage (the Admiral's Men had as a stage property one black dog); but the actors may simply mimic animal behaviour, or walk off ready for their prospective change to take effect.

38   brave: fine, great

41   thy head...pot: dogs were proverbially hungry scavengers: cf. 'The cook's head is no sooner gone than the dog's head is in the porridge pot'.

Act Four Chorus

0 SD   *Enter* CHORUS: This speech is misplaced in 1604, where it follows the first scene of Act three.

3   stayed his course: put an end to his travels

6   gratulate: welcome

7   conference: discussion

11   As: that
     wit: knowledge, intelligence

14   Carolus the Fifth: Charles V of Spain, the Holy Roman Emperor (1519–56), whose court was at Innsbruck.

16   art: magical skills

Act Four, Scene One

1   strange: remarkable

3   rare: splendid

4   familiar spirit: demonic associate

5   list: desire

9   endamaged: endangered

10   conjuror: magician

12–13   nothing answerable: in no way commensurable

13   for that: because

17   sometime: on one occasion

18   closet: private room
     sundry: various

22   succeed: follow them on the throne

27   of...pre-eminence: among the most pre-eminent of world-famous men

29   reflecting: shining forth

30   motion: mention, suggestion

32	cunning: cleverness	112	ride...water: water was believed to cancel a magic spell
35	paramour: consort, mistress		
36	right: real, true		
43	like: please		at any hand: on any account
46	marry: by the Virgin Mary! (a mild exclamation)	113	drink...waters: go anywhere
		117	made man: prosperous and successful (cf. 'a made man')
48	lively: to the life		
50	estate: condition of life	118	leave: sell, quit
52	presently: at once		forty: forty other horses
55	How then: what if I do?	118–19	the quality...ding: sexual virility; the horse-courser hopes to make a living from the magic steed as a stud horse
56	Diana...stag: According to Greek myth, the goddess Diana turned the huntsman Actaeon into a stag when he witnessed her bathing nude with her nymphs. His own hounds tore him apart.		
		119	brave: fine, excellent
		120	goodbye: a shortened form of 'God be with you'
		122	water: urine, for analysis, with a final quibble on 'water'
57	horns: symbols of cuckoldry	124	At this point Faustus is presumed to have reached his study, which might be the previously curtained-off inner stage area in Marlowe's theatre.
59	an: if		
60	meet: get even		
68	pleasant: facetious		
71	bachelor: (1) knight (knight-bachelor); (2) unmarried man		
		125	fatal time: (1) time of death; (1) fated time
74	concave: cavity, hollow	127	Confound these passions: destroy these disturbing emotions
77	There's...good: proverbially, 'No haste but good speed'		
78	Are you remembered: do you recall?	128	Christ...cross: alluding to Luke 23:43. Faustus comforts himself with the thought that at the last moment, Christ declared the salvation of one of the two thieves crucified with him.
	conference: conversation		
79	have met : got even		
82	injury: insult		
85	release: relieve		
87	straight: at once		
93	thread: the classical Greek image of the thread of life, spun, measured and finally cut by the three Fates.	129	conceit: (1) state of mind; (2) fancy
		130	quotha: indeed
94	payment: death as a debt to nature, and in Faustus's case to the devils		Lopus: Doctor Roderigo Lopez, a Portuguese appointed as Queen Elizabeth's personal physician in 1586. He was later accused of attempting to poison the queen and executed in June 1594, more than a year after Marlowe's own death.
98	green: public grassy area		
100	Fustian: 'bombast, nonsense', the horse-dealer's version of 'Faustus'		
101	Mass: by the Mass!		
102	You...met: I am pleased to see you		
		131	purgation: purge
			h'as: he has
103	dollars: large silver coins	135	known of: aware of
109	honest fellow: ironic, for horse-dealers were notoriously dishonest charge: burden (of family expenses and responsibilities)	138	bottle of hay: hay bundle, traditionally all that was left when a witch's horse was ridden into water
111	boy: servant		

140	dearest: most expensive
	snipper-snapper: cheeky young
	fellow. The horse-dealer takes
	Mephostophilis as Faustus's
	manservant, which is doubly
	ironic if he retains his original
	form as an 'old Franciscan'.
141	hey-pass: juggler; from the
	command used by fairground
	magicians to make objects
	appear to move
145–6	glass windows: spectacles
147	this eight nights: for the last
	week
148	An: although
155	So, ho, ho: a cry used by
	huntsmen in the chase
158	the officers: oficers of the law
165	hostry: hostelry, inn
172	Vanholt: Anhalt, in Marlowe's
	source, a central German duchy,
	not far from Wittenberg.
175	cunning: skill

Act Four, Scene Two

4–5	great-bellied: pregnant
5	dainties: special food
8	pleasure: please
10	meat: food
16	taste on: taste of
20	like: please
22	Saba: the land of the Queen of
	Sheba (now the Yemen)
33	Rest beholding: remain indebted

Act Five, Scene One

3	methinks: spelled 'methinkes' in
	1603, and pronounced as three
	syllables
4	carouse, and swill: drink noisily
	and heavily
8	belike: in all likelihood
8 SD	*and* MEPHOSTOPHILIS: although
	Mephostophilis must be on
	stage by line 50 to offer Faustus
	a dagger, 1603 gives no
	indication of a previous entry.
	1616 brings him on with
	Faustus at line 8, which may
	reflect early stage practice. It is
	possible, though not necessary,
	that Mephostophilis exits at line
	25 to bring Helen on with him

	(so the Revels editors); in one
	contemporary production
	Mephostophilis entered for the
	first time after line 25, masked
	as Helen himself.
9	conference: discussion
11	determined with: decided
	among
	Helen of Greece: the beautiful
	daughter of Leda and Jupiter
	and wife of Menelaus, King of
	Sparta, whose abduction by the
	Trojan prince Paris led to the
	Trojan War
13	dame: lady
17	For that: because
21	otherways: otherwise
23	Dardania: the city of Troy,
	founded by Dardanus
24 SD	*passeth...stage*: a common stage
	direction in the Elizabethan
	theatre, calling for an entry at
	one stage door and an exit by
	another, or possibly a
	movement from the yard up
	across the stage and out
	through the yard again on the
	other side.
25	wit: intellect
27	pursued: avenged
28	rape: forceful abduction
29	compare: comparison
33	Happy: fortunate
40–1	heaviness Of: sorrow at
43	flagitious: extremely evil
47	Where...Faustus: an echo of
	God's accusing call at the time
	of the Fall (Genesis 3:9)
49	with...voice: the entrance to hell
	was commonly imaged as the
	gaping mouth of a roaring beast
	(see 5.2.114) , and roaring was
	associated with the devils, after
	1 Peter 5:8, 'the devil, as a
	roaring lion'.
50	Thine...come: an ironic echo of
	John 13:1, 'And Jesus knew that
	his hour was come, that he
	should depart out of this world'.
50 SD	*a dagger*: traditional symbol of
	suicidal despair, the deadly sin
	against hope for God's mercy
60	heavy cheer: downcast mood
68	Revolt: return (to your
	allegiance to the devil)

74   drift: wavering

75   age: old man

83   unto my paramour: as my lover

85   clean: 'completely', with a quible on 'purified'

90   a thousand ships: traditionally the size of the Greek fleet that sailed to Troy to begin the War

91   topless: immeasurably high Ilium: Troy, so named after its founder Ilos

92–3   Sweet...flies: the hyperbolic language of love poetry becomes ironic, given Faustus's imminent damnation.

98   Wittenberg: see Prologue 13 and note

99   weak Menelaus: another scornful hyperbole. According to the *Iliad*, book 3, Menelaus, husband of Helen and King of Sparta, actually fought with Paris who was only saved by the intervention of his patroness, Aphrodite.

101–2   wound...heel: Achilles was the greatest warrior among the Greeks, made invulnerable by his goddess-mother Thetis, except for one heel, where he was shot by Paris.

105–6   flaming Jupiter...Semele: when Semele, one of Jupiter's human mistresses, presumptuously asked her divine lover to appear in his full glory, she was destroyed by his fire.

107–8   the monarch...arms: the nymph Arethusa excited the river-god Alpheus's lust when she bathed in his stream; she fled him and was transformed into a fountain by Diana. No classical myth links Arethusa with Jupiter or the sun god, as Marlowe does here.

108   azured: made blue as water reflecting the sky

112   tribunal seat: seat of judgement

113   Satan...sift me: Christ warned his disciples that 'Satan hath

earnestly desired to have you, that he may sift you as wheat' (Luke 22:31).

114   this furnace: the fires of hell, but also alluding to the fiery furnace of Daniel 3, which tested the faith of Shadrach, Meshak and Abednigo.

117   laughs...scorn: an echo of Psalms 2:4, ' He that dwelleth in heaven will laugh them to scorn'.

118   fly: both 'flee for refuge' and 'take flight' are appropriate meanings here

Act Five, Scene Two

4   eternally: in a state of everlasting damnation

7   Belike: probably

9   surfeit: over-indulgence, excess

13–14   The serpent...saved: the reference is to the biblical story of the primal Fall into sin, through the agency of the serpent (Genesis 3).

16   pants: throbs, palpitates

20   Faustus...world: cf. Mark 8:36, 'For what shall it profit a man, if he shall win the world, and lose his own soul?'

32   cunning: knowledge

34   vain: worthless, empty

36   bill: deed

38   divines: priests

42   divinity: religion

47   Tempt not God: do not test, try the patience of God; cf. Christ's rejection of the Devil's temptation in the wilderness, 'Thou shalt not tempt the Lord thy God' (Matthew 4:7)

61   Fair nature's eye: the sun

65   *O lente...equi*: 'O gallop slowly, slowly, you horses of the night.' From the Roman erotic poet Ovid's *Amores*, 1.13.40; in its original context spoken by a lover asking the goddess of the dawn to think of her own reluctance to leave the arms of her lover Tithonus, and so to grant him more time with his Corinna.

69   Christ's blood: in Christian thought, the symbol of the crucified Christ's power to save all believers (cf. line 92 below)

75–6 Mountains...God: the language of terrified humanity at the time of the Last Judgement; '[They] said to the mountains and rocks, Fall on us, and hide us from the face of him that sitteth on the throne, and from the wrath of the Lamb' (Revelation 6:16–17)

80   stars...nativity: the dominant planetary powers at the time of Faustus's birth

81   influence: an etherial fluid streaming from the heavenly bodies to act upon the characters and destinies of human beings

83   labouring: convulsing in the act of emission

84   vomit forth: in the form of a thunderbolt. Renaissance science (based on Aristotle's *Metaphysics*) held that lightning resulted from an exhalation exploding within a enclosing cloud. Faustus asks for his body to be utterly destroyed, so releasing his soul to rise to heaven.

86 SD *watch*: clock
95   limited: appointed
96   wanting: lacking
98   Pythagoras' *metempsychosis*: the sixth-century BC Greek philosopher Pythagoras's doctrine of the transmigration of souls, which argued that at

the moment of death the human soul assumed some other life-form

101   happy: fortunate (in that they have no afterlife, so no experience of hell)

102   in elements: into their constituent elements

103   still: for ever

108   quick: alive

112   Adders and serpents: creatures associated with the demonic, and possibly incorporated in the costumes of Lucifer and his companion devils

114   burn my books: so renouncing the magic arts

Epilogue

2   Apollo's laurel bough: the laurel was sacred to Apollo, god of light, prophecy, the healing arts, poetry and music. Laurel wreaths were symbols of eminence in the arts.

3   sometime: previously

5   fiendful: (1) terrible; (2) full of devils

6   Only to wonder: to be content with wondering

7   forward wits: the clever and daring

9   *Terminat...opus*: 'The hour ends the day; the author finishes his work.' A conventional motto which may have been added by the printer.

The Revenger's Tragedy

AN UNKNOWN JACOBEAN DRAMATIST

INTRODUCTORY NOTE

Authorship, date of composition and stage history

Unreliable lists of plays issued as advertisements by two publishers, Edward Archer in 1656 and Francis Kirkman in 1661 and 1671, many years after the original stage production and publication of *The Revenger's Tragedy*, provide virtually the only seventeenth-century attribution of authorship for this otherwise anonymous play. A manuscript ascription to 'John W' (possibly John Webster) in a single copy of the tragedy now in the British Library has been generally discounted. Archer, followed by Kirkman, named Cyril Tourneur (*c.* 1575–1626) as the writer of the tragedy, but in 1926 the scholar E. H. C. Oliphant initiated an as yet unresolved debate by arguing for Thomas Middleton (1580–1627) as its author. The linguistic and stylistic case for Middleton has been strongly put by bibliographers such as George R. Price and MacD. P. Jackson but it is not yet conclusively established or universally accepted. The author's evident familiarity with a number of plays datable to 1602–7, by Marston (*The Malcontent* and *The Fawn*), Shakespeare (*Hamlet* and *King Lear*), and Jonson (*Volpone*), strongly suggests that the tragedy was written within a year or so of its publication in 1607/8; it may have been the work of an otherwise unknown but gifted amateur dramatist.

The only surviving seventeenth-century printing of the tragedy 'As it hath been sundry times acted by the King's Majesty's Servants', fails to name the writer, but does connect the play with the

King's Men. This indicates performances at both the company's large public playhouse, the second Globe Theatre, and at their smaller private playhouse, the Blackfriars Theatre, recently acquired by the King's Men in 1608. There is no evidence to suggest more than average success with Jacobean audiences. The play fell out of use in the theatre until late nineteenth- and early twentieth-century readers' and critics' response to its mordant and powerful poetry led to its revival on stage. Probably the first professional production since 1608 was given at Pitlochry in 1965. In 1966 the Royal Shakespeare Company mounted an influential production at its Stratford-upon-Avon Theatre (and later the Aldwych Theatre, London). Since that time, there have been at least ten professional productions in Britain, including a 1980 production at the Liverpool Playhouse, productions in 1981 at the Cockpit Theatre, London, and the Gulbenkian Theatre, Hull, and in 1982 and 1992 performances at the Bear Gardens, London, as well as a 1992 production at Quarry (West Yorkshire) Playhouse. In 1987 the Royal Shakespeare Company staged a fresh production at the Swan Theatre, Stratford-upon-Avon, with Anthony Sher as Vindice and Nicholas Farrell as Lussorioso. In the same period there have been at least eleven student productions, beginning at Wadham College, Oxford (1962) and Cambridge (1965), and the play has retained its attraction for student and amateur companies, with performances at the Oxford Playhouse (1978), Magdalen College, Oxford (1985), Manchester University (1986), and the Theatre Royal, Bath (1992) followed by eight other venues. North America has seen at least six professional revivals, with major student productions at Yale, the University of California (Santa Barbara), and Toronto. Professional productions have been given in 1981 and 1991 in Australia, with student productions in Melbourne and Canberra, and in 1995 the tragedy was revived in a professional production at the Fortune Theatre, Dunedin, New Zealand.

Text

The Revenger's Tragedy was issued by the printer George Eld in 1607 and again in 1608 (only the title-pages are variant). Although its crowded setting gives rise to questions of correct lineation and distinction between verse and prose, the text is in general a sound one, likely to have been set from an authorial manuscript that had neither been carefully transcribed for publication nor prepared for use in the theatre. As the only surviving authoritative edition, it forms the copy-text basis for the present edition.

Sources

The plot is based on historical events associated with the assassination of Alessandro de' Medici in 1537, relayed through an Italian source such as Benedetto Varchi's *Storia Fiorentina*, or an English version such as William Painter's *Palace of Pleasure* (1567) or Barnabe Rich's *Farewell to His Military Profession* (1581). The episode of Lussorioso's mistaken attack on his stepmother (2.3) has been traced to a late classical work, Heliodorus' *Aethiopica*, translated by Thomas Underdowne in 1587, while the rape of Antonio's wife and its revenge may derive from the story of the rape of Lucretia. In addition to such literary sources, the play accurately reflects many details of contemporary Jacobean court life and social conditions.

Further reading

The Revels edition of *The Revenger's Tragedy*, edited by R. A. Foakes (London, 1966), provides the fullest single-volume account of the play. See also the facsimile edition of the play introduced by MacD. P. Jackson (London and Toronto, 1983), where the case for the attribution of the play to Middleton is strongly argued on stylistic grounds, Lawrence J. Ross's edition in the Regents Renaissance Drama Series (London, 1967), *The Plays of Cyril Tourneur*, edited by George Parfitt (Cambridge, 1978), and the revised New Mermaid edition, edited by Brian Gibbons (London and New York, 1990). R. V. Holdsworth's *Three Jacobean Revenge Tragedies* (London, 1989) and Michael Scott's *Renaissance Drama and a Modern Audience* (London and Basingstoke, 1982) provide useful accounts of the play in performance. General critical studies of the play are listed variously under the name of Tourneur or Middleton. See, for instance, S. Schoenbaum, *Middleton's Tragedies: A Critical Study* (New York, 1955), J. D. Peter, *Complaint and Satire in Early English Literature* (Oxford, 1956), R. H. Barker, *Thomas Middleton* (New York, 1958), B. Murray, *A Study of Cyril Tourneur* (Philadelphia, 1964), David M. Holmes, *The Art of Thomas Middleton* (Oxford, 1970), S. Schuman, *Cyril Tourneur* (Boston, 1977), R. A. Foakes, *Marston and Tourneur* (Harlow, 1978), and L. G. Salingar, 'Tourneur and the Tragedy of Revenge', in *The Age of Shakespeare*, edited by Boris Ford (Harmondsworth, 1982).

Dramatis Personae

THE DUKE
LUSSURIOSO,° *the Duke's son*
SPURIO,° *a bastard* [*son of the Duke*]
AMBITIOSO,° *the Duchess' eldest son*
SUPERVACUO,° *the Duchess' second son*   5
YOUNGER SON *of the Duchess*

VINDICE,° *a revenger, also called* PIATO° *in disguise* ⎫ *brothers to*
HIPPOLITO,° *also called* CARLO   ⎰ CASTIZA

ANTONIO
PIERO   10

NENCIO°   ⎫ *followers of* LUSSORIOSO
SORDIDO°   ⎰

DONDOLO,° *a gentleman-usher attending* CASTIZA

Nobles, Judges, Gentlemen, Officers, Keeper, Servants

THE DUCHESS   15

CASTIZA°
GRATIANA,° *mother of* CASTIZA

Scene: *a city in Italy*

Act One, Scene One

Enter VINDICE [*carrying a skull; he watches as*] *the* DUKE, DUCHESS,
LUSSURIOSO *her son,* SPURIO *the bastard, with a train, pass over the
stage with torchlight.*

VINDICE: Duke; royal lecher; go, grey-haired adultery,°
    And thou his son, as impious steeped as he;
    And thou his bastard, true-begot in evil;
    And thou his duchess, that will do° with devil:
    Four excellent characters! —° O that marrowless age   5
    Would stuff the hollow bones with damned desires,
    And 'stead of heat° kindle infernal fires
    Within the spendthrift veins° of a dry° duke,

A parched and juiceless luxur.° O God! one
That has scarce blood enough to live upon,   10
And he to riot it° like a son and heir?
Oh, the thought of that
Turns my abusèd heart-strings into fret.°
Thou sallow picture° of my poisoned love,
My study's ornament,° thou shell of death,   15
Once the bright face of my betrothèd lady,
When life and beauty naturally filled out
These ragged imperfections;
When two heaven-pointed° diamonds were set
In those unsightly° rings — then 'twas a face   20
So far beyond the artificial shine
Of any woman's bought complexion
That the uprightest man (if such there be,
That sin but seven times a day) broke custom
And made up eight with looking after her.   25
O, she was able to ha' made a usurer's son
Melt all his patrimony° in a kiss,
And what his father fifty years° told°
To have consumed, and yet his suit been cold.°
But O, accursèd palace!   30
Thee, when thou wert apparelled in thy flesh,
The old duke poisoned,
Because thy purer part would not consent
Unto his palsy-lust;° for old men lustful
Do show like young men angry — eager, violent,   35
Out-bid° like their limited performances.
O 'ware an old man hot and vicious:°
'Age, as in gold, in lust is covetous.'
Vengeance, thou Murder's quit-rent,° and whereby
Thou show'st thyself tenant to Tragedy,   40
O keep thy day, hour, minute, I beseech,
For those thou hast determined.° Hum, who e'er knew
Murder unpaid? Faith, give Revenge her due;
She's kept touch° hitherto — be merry, merry.
Advance thee, O thou terror° to fat folks   45
To have their costly three-piled° flesh worn off
As bare as this; for banquets, ease and laughter
Can make great° men, as greatness goes by clay,
But wise men, little, are more great than they.

Enter [his] brother HIPPOLITO.

HIPPOLITO: Still sighing o'er Death's vizard?°

VINDICE: Brother, welcome,   50
　　What comfort bring'st thou? How go things at court?
HIPPOLITO: In silk and silver, brother: never braver.°
VINDICE: Puh,
　　Thou play'st upon my meaning. Prithee say,
　　Has that bald° madam, Opportunity,   55
　　Yet thought upon's? Speak, are we happy° yet?
　　Thy wrongs and mine are for one scabbard fit.
HIPPOLITO: It may prove happiness.
VINDICE: What is't may prove?
　　Give me to taste.
HIPPOLITO: Give me your hearing then.
　　You know my place at court.
VINDICE: Ay, the duke's chamber;   60
　　But 'tis a marvel thou'rt not turned out yet!
HIPPOLITO: Faith, I have been shoved at, but 'twas still my hap°
　　To hold by the duchess' skirt. You guess at that;
　　Whom such a coat keeps up can ne'er fall flat.
　　But to the purpose.   65
　　Last evening, predecessor unto this,
　　The duke's son warily inquired for me,
　　Whose pleasure I attended. He began
　　By policy° to open and unhusk me
　　About the time and common rumour;   70
　　But I had so much wit° to keep my thoughts
　　Up° in their built houses, yet afforded him
　　An idle satisfaction without danger.
　　But the whole aim and scope of his intent
　　Ended in this: conjuring me in private   75
　　To seek some strange-digested° fellow forth
　　Of ill-contented nature, either disgraced
　　In former times, or by new grooms° displaced
　　Since his step-mother's nuptials; such a blood,°
　　A man that were for evil only good —   80
　　To give you the true word, some base-coined° pandar.
VINDICE: I reach° you, for I know his heat is such
　　Were there as many concubines as ladies
　　He would not be contained, he must fly out.
　　I wonder how ill-featured, vild-proportioned°   85
　　That one should be,° if she were made for woman,
　　Whom at the insurrection° of his lust
　　He would refuse for once: heart, I think none;
　　Next to a skull, though more unsound than one,
　　Each face he meets he strongly dotes upon.   90
HIPPOLITO: Brother, you've truly spoke° him!

He knows not you, but I'll swear you know him.
VINDICE: And therefore I'll put on° that knave for once,
And be a right° man then, a man o' the time;
For to be honest is not to be i' the world. 95
Brother, I'll be that strange-composèd fellow.
HIPPOLITO: And I'll prefer° you, brother.
VINDICE: Go to, then;
The small'st advantage fattens wrongèd men.
It may point out Occasion;° if I meet her
I'll hold her by the fore-top fast° enough, 100
Or, like the French mole°, heave up hair and all.
I have a habit° that will fit it quaintly —°
Here comes our mother.

[*Enter* GRATIANA *and* CASTIZA.]

HIPPOLITO: And sister.
VINDICE: We must coin.°
Women are apt, you know, to take false money,
But I dare stake my soul for these two creatures — 105
Only excuse excepted: that they'll swallow
Because their sex is easy in belief.°
GRATIANA: What news from court, son Carlo?°
HIPPOLITO: Faith, mother,
'Tis whispered there the duchess' youngest son
Has played° a rape on Lord Antonio's wife. 110
GRATIANA: On that religious lady!
CASTIZA: Royal blood! monster! He deserves to die,
If° Italy had no more hopes° but he.
VINDICE: Sister, you've sentenced most direct, and true;
The law's a woman,° and would she were you. 115
Mother, I must take leave of you.
GRATIANA: Leave for what?
VINDICE: I intend speedy travel.°
HIPPOLITO: That he does, madam.
GRATIANA: Speedy indeed!
VINDICE: For since my worthy father's funeral,
My life's unnatural to me, e'en compelled,° 120
As if I lived now when I should be dead.
GRATIANA: Indeed he was a worthy gentleman,
Had his estate° been fellow to his mind.
VINDICE: The duke did much deject° him.
GRATIANA: Much?
VINDICE: Too much.
And through disgrace oft smothered in his spirit 125

When it would mount. Surely I think he died
Of discontent, the nobleman's consumption.
GRATIANA: Most sure he did.
VINDICE: Did he? 'Lack, you know all;
    You were his midnight secretary.°
GRATIANA: No,
    He was too wise to trust me with his thoughts.   130
VINDICE [*aside*]: I' faith then, father, thou wast wise indeed;
    'Wives° are but made to go to bed and feed'. —°
    Come mother, sister: you'll bring me onward, brother?
HIPPOLITO: I will.
VINDICE [*aside*]:   I'll quickly turn into another.   *Exeunt.*

Act One, Scene Two

Enter the old DUKE, LUSSURIOSO *his son, the* DUCHESS, [SPURIO] *the
bastard, the duchess's two sons* AMBITIOSO *and* SUPERVACUO, *the
third, her youngest, brought out with* Officers *for the* [*trial for*]
rape, [*and*] *two* JUDGES.

DUKE: Duchess, it is your youngest son. We're sorry
    His violent act has e'en drawn blood of honour
    And stained our honours;
    Thrown ink upon the forehead° of our state,
    Which envious° spirits will dip their pens into   5
    After our death, and blot us in our tombs.
    For that which would seem treason in our lives
    Is laughter when we're dead. Who dares now whisper
    That dares not then speak out, and e'en proclaim
    With loud words and broad pens our closest° shame.   10
1 JUDGE: Your Grace hath spoke like to your silver years,°
    Full of confirmed gravity; for what is it to have
    A flattering false insculption° on a tomb,
    And in men's hearts reproach? The 'bowelled° corpse
    May be cered° in, but — with free tongue I speak —   15
    'The faults of great men through their cerecloths break'.
DUKE: They do. We're sorry for't; it is our fate
    To live in fear, and die to live in hate.
    I leave him to your sentence: doom° him, lords,
    The fact° is great — whilst I sit by and sigh.   20
DUCHESS [*kneels*]: My gracious lord, I pray be merciful,
    Although his trespass far exceed his years;
    Think him to be your own as I am yours.

Call him not son-in-law;° the law I fear
Will fall too soon upon his name and him. 25
Temper his fault with pity.
LUSSURIOSO: Good my lord,
Then 'twill not taste so bitter and unpleasant
Upon the judge's palate; for offences
Gilt° o'er with mercy show like fairest women,
Good only for their beauties, which washed off, 30
No sin is uglier.
AMBITIOSO: I beseech your Grace,
Be soft and mild, let not relentless law
Look with an iron forehead on our brother.
SPURIO [*aside*]: He yields small comfort yet. Hope he shall die;
And if a bastard's wish might stand in force, 35
Would all the court were turned into a corse.°
DUCHESS: No pity yet? Must I rise fruitless then —
A wonder in a woman? Are my knees
Of such low metal° that without respect —
1 JUDGE: Let the offender stand forth. 40
'Tis the duke's pleasure that impartial doom°
Shall take fast hold of his unclean attempt.°
A rape! Why 'tis the very core of lust,
Double adultery!
YOUNGER SON: So, sir.
2 JUDGE: And which was worse,
Committed on the Lord Antonio's wife, 45
That general-honest° lady. Confess, my lord:
What moved you to't?
YOUNGER SON: Why, flesh and blood, my lord;
What should move men unto a woman else?
LUSSURIOSO: O do not jest thy doom, trust not an axe
Or sword too far; the law is a wise serpent° 50
And quickly can beguile thee of thy life.
Though marriage only has made thee my brother,
I love thee so far; play not with thy death.
YOUNGER SON: I thank you, troth;° good admonitions, faith,
If I'd the grace now to make use of them. 55
1 JUDGE: That lady's name has spread such a fair wing
Over all Italy that if our tongues
Were sparing toward the fact, judgement itself
Would be condemned and suffer in men's thoughts.
YOUNGER SON: Well then, 'tis done,° and it would please me well 60
Were it to do again. Sure she's a goddess,
For I'd no power to see her and to live;°
It falls out true in this for I must die.

Her beauty was ordained to be my scaffold,
And yet methinks I might be easier ceased;°   65
My fault being sport,° let me but die in jest.
1 JUDGE: This be the sentence —
DUCHESS: O keep't upon your tongue, let it not slip;°
Death too soon steals out of a lawyer's lip.
Be not so cruel-wise.
1 JUDGE: Your Grace must pardon us,   70
'Tis but the justice of the law.
DUCHESS: The law
Is grown more subtle than a woman should be.
SPURIO [*aside*]: Now, now he dies; rid 'em away.
DUCHESS [*aside*]: O what it is to have an old-cool duke
To be as slack in tongue as in performance.°   75
1 JUDGE: Confirmed, this be the doom irrevocable.
DUCHESS: O!
1 JUDGE: Tomorrow early —
DUCHESS: Pray be abed,° my lord.
1 JUDGE: Your Grace much wrongs° yourself.
AMBITIOSO: No, tis that tongue;
Your too much right° does do us too much wrong.   80
1 JUDGE: Let that offender —
DUCHESS: Live, and be in health.
1 JUDGE: Be on a scaffold —
DUKE: Hold, hold, my lord.
SPURIO [*aside*]:   Pox on't,
What makes my dad speak now?
DUKE: We will defer the judgement till next sitting.
In the meantime let him be kept close prisoner: 85
Guard, bear him hence.
AMBITIOSO [*aside*]:   Brother, this makes for thee;°
Fear not, we'll have a trick to set thee free.
YOUNGER SON [*aside*]: Brother, I will expect it from you both,
And in that hope I rest.
SUPERVACUO: Farewell; be merry.
                        Exit [YOUNGER SON] *with a guard.*
SPURIO [*aside*]: Delayed, deferred. Nay then, if judgement have   90
Cold blood, flattery and bribes will kill it.
DUKE: About it then, my lords, with your best powers,
More serious business calls upon our hours.
                        Exeunt [*all but the*] DUCHESS.
DUCHESS: Was't ever known step-duchess was so mild
And calm as I? Some now would plot his death   95
With easy° doctors, those loose-living men,
And make his withered Grace fall to his grave,

And keep° church better.
Some second wife would do this, and dispatch
Her double-loathèd lord at meat° and sleep. 100
Indeed 'tis true an old man's twice a child.
Mine cannot speak! One of his single words
Would quite have freed my youngest dearest son
From death or durance,° and have made him walk
With a bold foot upon the thorny law, 105
Whose prickles should bow under him; but 'tis not,
And therefore wedlock faith shall be forgot.
I'll kill him in his forehead,° hate there feed;
That wound is deepest though it never bleed.
And here comes he whom my heart points unto, 110
His bastard son, but my love's true-begot.
Many a wealthy letter have I sent him,
Swelled up with jewels, and the timorous man
Is yet but coldly kind.°

[*Enter* SPURIO.]

That jewel's mine that quivers in his ear, 115
Mocking his master's chillness and vain fear. —
He's spied me now.
SPURIO: Madam? Your Grace so private?
My duty on your hand.   [*Kisses her hand.*]
DUCHESS: Upon my hand, sir, troth I think you'd fear
To kiss my hand too, if my lip stood there. 120
SPURIO: Witness I would not, madam.   [*Kisses her.*]
DUCHESS: 'Tis a wonder,
For ceremony° has made many fools.
It is as easy way unto a duchess
As to a hatted° dame, if her love answer,
But that° by timorous honours, pale respects, 125
Idle degrees of fear, men make their ways
Hard of themselves. What have you thought of me?
SPURIO: Madam I ever think of you, in duty,
Regard and —
DUCHESS: Puh! Upon my love, I mean.
SPURIO: I would 'twere love, but 't'as° a fouler name 130
Than lust. You are my father's wife; your Grace may guess now
What I could call it.
DUCHESS: Why th'art his son, but falsely;°
'Tis a hard° question whether he begot thee.
SPURIO: I' faith 'tis true too; I'm an uncertain man
Of more uncertain woman. Maybe his groom 135

O' the stable begot me — you know I know not.
He could ride a horse° well, a shrewd suspicion, marry!
He was wondrous tall, he had his length i' faith
For peeping over half-shut holiday windows:°
Men would desire him 'light.° When he was afoot°   140
He made a goodly show under a penthouse,°
And when he rid, his hat would check the signs°
And clatter barbers' basins.
DUCHESS: Nay, set you a horseback once
You'll ne'er 'light off.
SPURIO: Indeed I am a beggar.°
DUCHESS: That's more the sign thou art great — but to our love.   145
Let it stand firm° both in thought and mind
That the duke was thy father (as no doubt then
He bid fair° for't). Thy injury is the more;
For had he cut thee a right diamond,°
Thou had'st been next set in the dukedom's ring,   150
When his worn self, like age's easy slave,
Had dropped out of the collet° into the grave.
What wrong can equal this? Canst thou be tame
And think upon't?
SPURIO: No, mad and think upon't.
DUCHESS: Who would not be revenged of° such a father,   155
E'en the worst way? I would thank that sin
That could most injure him, and be in league with it.
O what a grief 'tis that a man should live
But once i' the world, and then to live a bastard,
The curse o' the womb, the thief of Nature,   160
Begot against the seventh commandment,°
Half damned in the conception by the justice
Of that unbribèd everlasting law.
SPURIO: O I'd a hot-backed devil to° my father.
DUCHESS: Would not this mad° e'en patience, make blood rough?°   165
Who but an eunuch would not sin, his bed
By one false minute disinherited?
SPURIO: Ay, there's the vengeance that my birth was wrapped in.
I'll be revenged for all. Now hate begin;
I'll call foul incest but a venial sin.   170
DUCHESS: Cold still? in vain then must a duchess woo?
SPURIO: Madam, I blush to say what I will do.
DUCHESS: Thence flew sweet comfort. Earnest° and farewell. [*She kisses him.*]
SPURIO: Oh, one incestuous kiss picks open hell.
DUCHESS: Faith now, old duke, my vengeance shall reach high;   175
I'll arm° thy brow with woman's heraldry.°   *Exit.*
SPURIO: Duke, thou did'st do me wrong and by thy act

Adultery is my nature;
Faith, if the truth were known, I was begot
After some gluttonous dinner — some stirring° dish   180
Was my first father, when deep healths went round
And ladies' cheeks were painted red with wine,
Their tongues as short and nimble as their heels,°
Uttering words sweet and thick; and when they rose
Were merrily disposed to fall again.°   185
In such a whispering and withdrawing hour,
When base male bawds kept sentinel at stair-head,
Was I stol'n softly; O, damnation met
The sin of feasts, drunken adultery.
I feel it swell me, my revenge is just;   190
I was begot in impudent wine and lust.
Stepmother, I consent to thy desires;
I love thy mischief° well, but I hate thee,
And those three cubs thy sons, wishing confusion,
Death and disgrace may be their epitaphs.   195
As for my brother, the duke's only° son,
Whose birth is more beholding to report
Than mine, and yet perhaps as falsely sown
— Women must not be trusted with their own —
I'll loose my days upon him, hate all I!   200
Duke, on thy brow I'll draw my bastardy:
For indeed a bastard by nature should make cuckolds,°
Because he is the son of a cuckold maker.   *Exit.*

Act One, Scene Three

Enter VINDICE *and* HIPPOLITO, VINDICE *in disguise to attend*
LUSSURIOSO *the duke's son.*

VINDICE: What, brother, am I far enough from myself?°
HIPPOLITO: As if another man had been sent whole
    Into the world and none wist° how he came.
VINDICE: It will confirm me bold — the child o' the court.
    Let blushes dwell i' the country. Impudence,   5
    Thou goddess of the palace, mistress of mistresses,
    To whom the costly-perfumed people pray,
    Strike thou my forehead into dauntless marble,
    Mine eyes to steady sapphires; turn° my visage,
    And if I must needs glow let me blush inward   10
    That this immodest season may not spy
    That scholar in my cheeks, fool-bashfulness,

That maid in the old time, whose flush of grace
Would never suffer her to get° good clothes.
Our maids are wiser and are less ashamed;   15
Save Grace the bawd,° I seldom hear grace named!
HIPPOLITO: Nay, brother, you reach out o' the verge° now —

[*Enter* LUSSURIOSO, *attended by* Servants.]

'Sfoot,° the duke's son! Settle your looks.
VINDICE: Pray let me not be doubted.°   [*Withdraws to one side.*]
HIPPOLITO: My lord.
LUSSURIOSO: Hippolito? — [*To* Servants] Be absent, leave us.   20
                                                              [*Exeunt* Servants.]
HIPPOLITO: My lord, after long search, wary enquiries
And politic siftings,° I made choice of yon fellow,
Whom I guess rare° for many deep employments.
This our age swims within him; and if Time
Had so much hair° I should take him for Time,   25
He is so near kin to this present minute.
LUSSURIOSO: 'Tis enough,
We thank thee; yet words are but great men's blanks.°
Gold, though it be dumb, does utter the best thanks. [*Gives him money.*]
HIPPOLITO: Your plenteous honour! — an excellent fellow, my lord.   30
LUSSURIOSO: So, give us leave. —°   [*Exit* HIPPOLITO.]
                     Welcome, be not far off;
We must be better acquainted. Push,° be bold
With us; thy hand.
VINDICE: With all my heart i' faith!
How dost sweet musk-cat?° When shall we lie together?
                                              [*Embraces* LUSSORIOSO]
LUSSURIOSO [*aside*]: Wondrous knave!   35
Gather him into boldness? 'Sfoot, the slave's
Already as familiar as an ague,°
And shakes me at his pleasure. — Friend, I can
Forget myself in private, but elsewhere
I pray do you remember me.°   40
VINDICE: Oh, very well, sir. — I conster° myself saucy.
LUSSURIOSO: What hast been? Of what profession?
VINDICE: A bone-setter.
LUSSURIOSO: A bone setter!
                     A bawd, my lord;
One that sets bones together.
LUSSURIOSO: Notable bluntness! —
[*Aside*] Fit, fit for me, e'en trained up to my hand. —   45
Thou hast been scrivener° to much knavery then?

VINDICE: Fool° to abundance, sir; I have been witness
    To the surrenders of a thousand virgins,
    And not so little;°
    I have seen patrimonies washed a-pieces,°   50
    Fruit fields turned into bastards,
    And, in a world of acres,
    Not so much dust due to the heir 'twas left, too,
    As would well gravel a petition.°
LUSSURIOSO [*aside*]: Fine villain! Troth, I like him wondrously;   55
    He's e'en shaped for my purpose. — Then thou know'st
    In the world strange lust?
VINDICE: Oh, Dutch° lust, fulsome lust!
    Drunken procreation, which begets so many drunkards.
    Some fathers dread not, gone to bed in wine,
    To slide from the mother and cling° the daughter-in-law;   60
    Some uncles are adulterous with their nieces,
    Brothers with brothers' wives. Oh, hour of incest!
    Any kin now next to the rim° o' the sister
    Is man's meat in these days, and in the morning,
    When they are up and dressed and their mask on,   65
    Who can perceive this, save that eternal eye
    That sees through flesh and all? Well, if anything
    Be damned, it will be twelve o'clock at night:
    That twelve will never 'scape;
    It is the Judas° of the hours, wherein   70
    Honest salvation is betrayed to sin.
LUSSURIOSO: In troth it is, too; but let this talk glide.
    It is our blood to err, though hell gaped° loud:
    Ladies know Lucifer fell,° yet still are proud!
    Now, sir, wert thou as secret as thou'rt subtle,   75
    And deeply fathomed into all estates,°
    I would embrace thee for a near employment,°
    And thou should'st swell in money and be able
    To make lame beggars crouch to thee.
VINDICE: My lord?
    Secret? I ne'er had that disease o' the mother,°   80
    I praise my father. Why are men made close°
    But to keep thoughts in best? I grant you this:
    Tell but some woman a secret overnight,
    Your doctor may find it in the urinal i' the morning.°
    But, my lord —
LUSSURIOSO: So, thou'rt confirmed in me,°   85
    And thus I enter° thee.   [*Gives him money.*]
VINDICE: This Indian° devil
    Will quickly enter any man — but a usurer;

He prevents° that by entering° the devil first!

LUSSURIOSO: Attend me. I am past my depth in lust,
  And I must swim or drown. All my desires   90
  Are levelled at a virgin not far from court,
  To whom I have conveyed by messenger
  Many waxed lines° full of my neatest spirit,°
  And jewels that were able to ravish her
  Without the help of man; all which, and more,   95
  She, foolish-chaste, sent back, the messengers
  Receiving frowns for answers.

VINDICE: Possible?
  'Tis a rare phoenix,° whoe'er she be.
  If your desires be such, she so repugnant,°
  In troth, my lord, I'd be revenged and marry her.   100

LUSSURIOSO: Push! the dowry of her blood° and of her fortunes
  Are both too mean; good enough to be bad withal.
  I am one of that number can defend
  Marriage is good; yet rather keep a friend.°
  Give me my bed by stealth — there's true delight;   105
  What breeds a loathing in't but night by night?

VINDICE: A very fine religion!

LUSSURIOSO: Therefore thus:
  I'll trust thee in the business of my heart
  Because I see thee well-experienced
  In this luxurious day° wherein we breathe.   110
  Go thou, and with a smooth enchanting tongue
  Bewitch her ears and cozen° her of all grace;
  Enter upon the portion° of her soul,°
  Her honour, which she calls her chastity,
  And bring it into expense;° for honesty   115
  Is like a stock of money laid to sleep,
  Which, ne'er so little broke, does never keep.

VINDICE: You have given it the tang,° i' faith, my lord.
  Make known the lady to me, and my brain
  Shall swell with strange invention: I will move it°   120
  Till I expire with speaking, and drop down
  Without a word to save me; but I'll work —

LUSSURIOSO: We thank thee and will raise° thee; receive her name.
  It is the only daughter to Madam Gratiana,
  The late widow.

VINDICE [*aside*]:   Oh, my sister, my sister!   125

LUSSURIOSO: Why dost walk aside?°

VINDICE: My lord, I was thinking how I might begin,
  As thus — 'oh lady' — or twenty hundred devices:
  Her very bodkin° will put a man in.

LUSSURIOSO: Ay, or the wagging of her hair.   130
VINDICE: No, that shall put you in,° my lord.
LUSSURIOSO: Shall't? Why, content. Dost know the daughter then?
VINDICE: O, excellent well — by sight.
LUSSURIOSO: That was her brother
   That did prefer thee to us.
VINDICE: My lord, I think so;
   I knew I had seen him somewhere.   135
LUSSURIOSO: And therefore prithee let thy heart to him
   Be as a virgin, close.°
VINDICE: O my good lord.
LUSSURIOSO: We may laugh at that simple age° within him —
VINDICE: Ha! Ha! Ha!
LUSSURIOSO: — Himself being made the subtle instrument   140
   To wind up° a good fellow —
VINDICE: That's I, my lord.
LUSSURIOSO: That's thou —
   To entice and work° his sister.
VINDICE: A pure novice!
LUSSURIOSO: 'Twas finely managed.
VINDICE: Gallantly carried: a pretty-perfumed villain!   145
LUSSURIOSO: I've bethought me.
   If she prove chaste still and immoveable,
   Venture upon the mother, and with gifts,
   As I will furnish thee, begin with her.
VINDICE: O fie, fie, that's the wrong end, my lord.   150
   'Tis mere impossible that a mother, by any gifts,
   Should become a bawd to her own daughter!
LUSSURIOSO: Nay then I see thou'rt but a puny°
   In the subtle mystery of a woman.
   Why, 'tis held now no dainty dish: the name°   155
   Is so in league with age that nowadays
   It does eclipse three quarters of a mother.
VINDICE: Does it so, my lord?
   Let me alone then to eclipse the fourth.
LUSSURIOSO: Why, well said; come I'll furnish thee: but first   160
   Swear to be true in all.
VINDICE: True?
LUSSURIOSO: Nay, but swear!
VINDICE: Swear? I hope your honour little doubts my faith.
LUSSURIOSO: Yet, for my humour's sake, 'cause I love swearing —
VINDICE: 'Cause you love swearing, 'slud° I will.
LUSSURIOSO: Why, enough.
   Ere long look to be made of better stuff.   165
VINDICE: That will do well indeed, my lord.

LUSSURIOSO: Attend me.°   [*Exit.*]
VINDICE: Oh,
    Now let me burst. I've eaten noble poison!
    We are made strange fellows,° brother, innocent villains:
    Wilt not be angry when thou hear'st on't, think'st thou?   170
    I' faith thou shalt. Swear me to foul° my sister!
    Sword, I durst make a promise of him to thee;
    Thou shalt dis-heir him, it shall be thine honour.
    And yet, now angry froth is down in me,
    It would not prove the meanest policy   175
    In this disguise to try the faith of both;
    Another might have had the self-same office,
    Some slave that would have wrought effectually,
    Ay and perhaps o'erwrought° 'em. Therefore I,
    Being thought travelled, will apply myself   180
    Unto the self-same form, forget my nature,
    As if no part about me were kin to 'em,
    So touch° 'em — though I durst almost for good
    Venture my lands in heaven upon their blood.°   *Exit.*

Act One, Scene Four

Enter the discontented lord ANTONIO (*whose wife the Duchess'
youngest son ravished*); *he discovering*° [*her dead body*] *to certain
lords and* [*to* PIERO *and*] HIPPOLITO.

ANTONIO: Draw nearer, lords, and be sad witnesses
    Of a fair comely building newly fallen,
    Being falsely undermined. Violent rape
    Has played a glorious° act: behold, my lords,
    A sight that strikes man out of me.   5
PIERO: That virtuous lady!
ANTONIO: Precedent for wives!
HIPPOLITO: The blush of many women, whose chaste presence
    Would e'en call shame up to their cheeks, and make
    Pale wanton sinners have good colours.
ANTONIO: Dead!
    Her honour first drank poison, and her life,   10
    Being fellows in one house, did pledge her honour.
PIERO: O grief of many!
ANTONIO: I marked not this before:
    A prayer book the pillow to her cheek;
    This was her rich confection,° and another

Placed in her right hand, with a leaf tucked up,   15
Pointing to these words:
Melius virtute mori, quam per dedecus vivere.°
True and effectual it is indeed.
HIPPOLITO: My lord, since you invite us to your sorrows,
Let's truly taste 'em, that with equal comfort   20
As to ourselves we may relieve your wrongs.
We have grief too, that yet walks without tongue:
Curae leves loquuntur, maiores stupent.°
ANTONIO: You deal with truth, my lord.
Lend me but your attentions and I'll cut   25
Long grief into short words. Last revelling night,
When torchlight made an artificial noon
About the court, some courtiers in the masque,
Putting on better faces than their own,°
Being full of fraud and flattery, amongst whom   30
The duchess' youngest son — that moth° to honour —
Filled up a room;° and with long lust to eat
Into my wearing,° amongst all the ladies
Singled out that dear form, who ever lived
As cold in lust as she is now in death —   35
Which that step-duchess' monster knew too well —
And therefore in the height of all the revels,
When music was heard loudest, courtiers busiest,
And ladies great with laughter — O vicious minute!
Unfit, but for relation,° to be spoke of —   40
Then, with a face more impudent than his vizard,
He harried° her, amidst a throng of pandars
That live upon damnation of both kinds,°
And fed the ravenous vulture of his lust.
O, death to think on't! She, her honour forced,   45
Deemed it a nobler dowry for her name
To die with poison than to live with shame.
HIPPOLITO: A wondrous lady of rare fire compact;
She's made her name an empress° by that act.
PIERO: My lord, what judgement follows the offender?   50
ANTONIO: Faith none, my lord; it cools and is deferred.
PIERO: Delay the doom° for rape?
ANTONIO: O you must note who 'tis should die —
The duchess' son. She'll look to be a saver;
'Judgement in this age is near kin to favour'.   55
HIPPOLITO: Nay then, step forth thou bribeless officer.   [*Draws his sword.*]
I bind you all in steel to bind you surely;
Here let your oaths meet, to be kept and paid,
Which else will stick like rust and shame the blade.

Strengthen my vow, that if at the next sitting   60
Judgement speak all in gold, and spare the blood
Of such a serpent, e'en before their seats
To let his soul out, which long since was found
Guilty in heaven.
ALL: We swear it and will act it.
ANTONIO: Kind gentlemen, I thank you in mine ire.   65
HIPPOLITO: 'Twere pity the ruins of so fair a monument
  Should not be dipped in the defacer's blood.
PIERO: Her funeral shall be wealthy, for her name
  Merits a tomb of pearl. My lord Antonio,
  For this time wipe your lady from your eyes;   70
  No doubt our grief and yours may one day court it,°
  When we are more familiar with revenge.
ANTONIO: That is my comfort, gentlemen, and I joy
  In this one happiness above the rest,
  Which will be called a miracle at last;   75
  That, being an old man, I'd a wife so chaste.   *Exeunt.*

Act Two, Scene One

Enter CASTIZA, *the sister.*

CASTIZA: How hardly shall that maiden be beset,°
  Whose only fortunes are her constant thoughts;
  That has no other child's-part° but her honour,
  That keeps her low and empty in estate.
  Maids and their honours are like poor beginners: 5
  Were not sin rich there would be fewer sinners.
  Why had not virtue a revenue? Well,
  I know the cause: 'twould have impoverished hell.

[Enter DONDOLO.*]°*

How now Dondolo?
DONDOLO: Madonna, there is one, as they say, a thing of flesh and   10
  blood — a man I take him by his beard — that would very
  desirously mouth to mouth with you.
CASTIZA: What's that?
DONDOLO: Show his teeth in your company.
CASTIZA: I understand thee not.   15
DONDOLO: Why, speak with you, Madonna.
CASTIZA: Why, say so, madman, and cut off a great deal of dirty way.

Had it not been better spoke in ordinary words, that one would
speak with me?

DONDOLO: Ha, ha, that's as ordinary as two shillings; I would strive a   20
little to show myself° in my place.° A gentleman-usher° scorns to
use the phrase and fancy° of a servingman.

CASTIZA: Yours be your own, sir; go direct him hither.   [*Exit* DONDOLO.]
I hope some happy tidings from my brother,
That lately travelled, whom my soul affects.°   25
Here he comes.

Enter VINDICE *her brother, disguised.*

VINDICE: Lady, the best of wishes to your sex;
Fair skins and new gowns.   [*Gives her a letter.*]

CASTIZA: O, they shall thank you, sir —
Whence this?

VINDICE: Oh, from a dear and worthy friend,
Mighty!

CASTIZA: From whom?

VINDICE: The duke's son.

CASTIZA: Receive that!   30
[*Gives*] *a box o' the ear to her brother.*
I swore I'd put anger in my hand
And pass the virgin limits of myself
To him that next appeared in that base office,
To be his sin's attorney. Bear to him
That figure of my hate upon thy cheek   35
Whilst 'tis yet hot, and I'll reward thee for't;
Tell him my honour shall have a rich name
When several harlots shall share his with shame.
Farewell; commend me to him in my hate!   *Exit.*

VINDICE: It is the sweetest box° that e'er my nose came nigh;   40
The finest drawn-work cuff° that e'er was worn!
I'll love this blow forever, and this cheek
Shall still henceforward take the wall° of this.
Oh, I'm above my tongue!° Most constant sister,
In this thou hast right honourable shown.   45
Many are called by their honour that have none;
Thou art approved forever in my thoughts.
It is not in the power of words to taint thee,
And yet for the salvation of my oath,
As my resolve in that point, I will lay   50
Hard siege unto my mother, though I know
A siren's tongue° could not bewitch her so.

[*Enter* GRATIANA.]

	Mass,° fitly, here she comes. Thanks, my disguise.	
	Madam, good afternoon.	

GRATIANA: You're welcome, sir.
VINDICE: The next of Italy° commends him to you;   55
    Our mighty expectation, the duke's son.   [*Gives her a letter.*]
GRATIANA: I think myself much honoured that he pleases
    To rank me in his thoughts.
VINDICE: So may you, lady.
    One that is like to be our sudden duke —
    The crown gapes for him every tide —° and then   60
    Commander o'er us all; do but think on him.
    How blest were they now that could pleasure him,
    E'en with anything almost.
GRATIANA: Ay, save° their honour.
VINDICE: Tut, one would let a little of that go too,
    And ne'er be seen in't:° ne'er be seen in't, mark you.   65
    I'd wink and let it go.
GRATIANA: Marry,° but I would not.
VINDICE: Marry, but I would, I hope; I know you would too
    If you'd that blood now which you gave your daughter.
    To her indeed 'tis, this wheel° comes about;
    That man that must be all this, — perhaps ere morning,   70
    For his white° father does but mould away, —
    Has long desired your daughter.
GRATIANA: Desired?
VINDICE: Nay but hear me:
    He desires now that will command hereafter,
    Therefore be wise; I speak as more a friend   75
    To you than him. Madam, I know you're poor,
    And 'lack the day,
    There are too many poor ladies already;
    Why should you vex° the number? 'Tis despised.
    Live wealthy, rightly understand the world,   80
    And chide away that foolish country girl
    Keeps company with your daughter, Chastity.
GRATIANA: O fie, fie, the riches of the world cannot hire
    A mother to such a most unnatural task.
VINDICE: No, but a thousand angels° can.   85
    Men have no power; angels must work you to it.
    The world descends into such base-born evils
    That forty angels can make fourscore devils.
    There will be fools still, I perceive, still fools.
    Would I be poor, dejected,° scorned of greatness,   90

Swept from the palace, and see other daughters
Spring° with the dew o'the court, having mine own
So much desired and loved — by the duke's son!
No, I would raise my state° upon her breast,
And call her eyes my tenants; I would count   95
My yearly maintenance upon her cheeks,
Take coach° upon her lip, and all her parts
Should keep men after men,° and I would ride
In pleasure upon pleasure.
    You took great pains for her, once when it was;   100
Let her requite it now, though it be but some.
You brought her forth; she may well bring you home.°
GRATIANA: O heavens, this overcomes me!
VINDICE [*aside*]: Not, I hope, already?
GRATIANA [*aside*]: It is too strong for me. Men know, that know us,   105
We are so weak their words can overthrow us.
He touched me nearly,° made my virtues bate,°
When his tongue struck upon my poor estate.
VINDICE [*aside*]: I e'en quake to proceed, my spirit turns edge,°
I fear me she's unmothered,° yet I'll venture:°   110
'That woman is all male whom none can enter!' —
What think you now lady, speak, are you wiser?
What said advancement to you? Thus it said:
The daughter's fall lifts up the mother's head.
Did it not, madam? But I'll swear it does,   115
In many places. Tut, this age fears no man;
' 'Tis no shame to be bad, because 'tis common.'
GRATIANA: Ay that's the comfort on't.
VINDICE: The comfort on't!
    I keep the best for last; can these persuade you
To forget heaven — and —   [*Gives her gold.*]
GRATIANA: Ay, these are they —
VINDICE [*aside*]:   O!   120
GRATIANA: That enchant our sex; these are the means
    That govern our affections. That woman
    Will not be troubled with the mother° long
    That sees the comfortable shine of you;
    I blush to think what for your sakes I'll do.   125
VINDICE [*aside*]: O suffering heaven, with thy invisible finger
    E'en at this instant turn the precious side
    Of both mine eyeballs inward, not to see myself.°
GRATIANA: Look you, sir.
VINDICE: Holla.
GRATIANA: Let this° thank your pains.
VINDICE: Oh, you're a kind madam.°   130

GRATIANA: I'll see how I can move.°
VINDICE: Your words will sting.
GRATIANA: If she be still chaste, I'll ne'er call her mine.
VINDICE [*aside*]: Spoke truer than you meant it.
GRATIANA: Daughter Castiza.

[*Enter* CASTIZA.]

CASTIZA: Madam.
VINDICE: O, she's yonder.
Meet her.
[*Aside*] Troops of celestial soldiers guard her heart: 135
Yon dam° has devils enough to take her part.
CASTIZA: Madam, what makes° yon evil-officed man
In presence of you?
GRATIANA: Why?
CASTIZA: He lately brought
Immodest writing, sent from the duke's son
To tempt me to dishonourable act. 140
GRATIANA: Dishonourable act? Good honourable fool,
That wouldst be honest° 'cause thou wouldst be so,
Producing no one reason but thy will.
And 't'as a good report, prettily commended,
But pray, by whom? Mean people, ignorant people; 145
The better° sort I'm sure cannot abide it,
And by what rule should we square out our lives
But by our betters' actions? Oh, if thou knew'st
What 'twere to lose it, thou would never keep it.
But there's a cold curse laid upon all maids: 150
Whilst others clip the sun, they clasp the shades.°
Virginity is paradise, locked up.
You cannot come by yourselves without fee,°
And 'twas decreed that man should keep the key.
Deny advancement, treasure, the duke's son? 155
CASTIZA: I cry you mercy, lady, I mistook you.
Pray did you see my mother? Which way went she?
Pray God I have not lost her.
VINDICE [*aside*]: Prettily put by.
GRATIANA: Are you as proud to me as coy° to him? [*She slaps her.*]
Do you not know me now?
CASTIZA: Why, are you she? 160
The world's so changed, one shape into another,
It is a wise child now that knows her mother.
VINDICE [*aside*]: Most right, i' faith.
GRATIANA: I owe your cheek my hand°

For that presumption now, but I'll forget it;
Come you shall leave those childish 'haviours   165
And understand your time. Fortunes flow to you;
What, will you be a girl?
'If all feared drowning that spy waves ashore,°
Gold would grow rich, and all the merchants poor.'°
CASTIZA: It is a pretty saying of a wicked one,   170
But methinks now it does not show so well
Out of your mouth.
Better in his.
VINDICE [*aside*]: Faith, bad enough in both,
Were I in earnest — as I'll seem no less. —
I wonder, lady, your own mother's words   175
Cannot be taken, nor stand in full force.
'Tis honesty° you urge: what's honesty?
'Tis but heaven's beggar; and what woman is
So foolish to keep honesty
And be not able to keep° herself? No,   180
Times are grown wiser, and will keep less charge.°
A maid that has small portion now intends°
To break up house and live upon her friends.
How blest are you: you have happiness alone;
Others must fall to thousands, you to one   185
Sufficient in himself to make your forehead
Dazzle the world with jewels, and petitionary people°
Start at your presence.
GRATIANA: Oh, if I were young
I should be ravished!°
CASTIZA: Ay, to lose your honour.
VINDICE: 'Slid, how can you lose your honour to deal with my lord's
      Grace?   190
He'll add more honour to it by his title;
Your mother will tell you how.
GRATIANA: That I will.
VINDICE: O think upon the pleasure of the palace,
Securèd ease and state; the stirring meats,°
Ready to move out of the dishes,   195
That e'en now quicken° when they're eaten;
Banquets abroad° by torchlight, music, sports;
Bare-headed vassals that had ne'er the fortune
To keep on their own hats, but let horns wear 'em;°
Nine coaches waiting, — hurry, hurry, hurry —   200
CASTIZA: Ay, to the devil!
VINDICE [*aside*]: Ay, to the devil. — To the duke, by my faith!
GRATIANA: Ay, to the duke. Daughter, you'd scorn to think

O' the devil an° you were there once.
VINDICE [*aside*]:   True, for most
   There are as proud as he for his heart,° i' faith. —   205
   [*To* CASTIZA] Who'd sit at home in a neglected room,
   Dealing° her short-lived beauty to the pictures
   That are as useless as old men, when those
   Poorer in face and fortune than herself
   Walk with a hundred acres on their backs —°   210
   Fair meadows cut into green foreparts.° O,
   It was the greatest blessing ever happened to women
   When farmers' sons agreed, and met again,
   To wash their hands and come up° gentlemen;
   The commonwealth has flourished ever since.   215
   Lands that were mete° by the rod,° that labour's spared;
   Tailors ride down and measure 'em by the yard.°
   Fair trees, those comely foretops° of the field,
   Are cut to maintain head-tires:° much untold.°
   All thrives but Chastity; she lies a-cold.   220
   Nay, shall I come nearer to you? mark but this:
   Why are there so few honest women but
   Because 'tis the poorer profession?°
   That's accounted best that's best followed;
   Least in trade, least in fashion —   225
   And that's not honesty, believe it; and do
   But note the low and dejected price of it:
   'Lose but a pearl, we search and cannot brook° it;
   But that once gone, who is so mad to look° it?'
GRATIANA: Troth he says true.
CASTIZA: False! I defy you both.   230
   I have endured you with an ear of fire;
   Your tongues have struck hot irons on my face.
   Mother, come from that poisonous woman there!
GRATIANA: Where?
CASTIZA: Do you not see her? She's too inward° then.   235
   [*To* VINDICE] Slave, perish in thy office! You heavens, please
   Henceforth to make the mother° a disease
   Which first begins with me; yet I've outgone you.   *Exit.*
VINDICE [*aside*]: O angels, clap your wings upon the skies,
   And give this virgin crystal plaudities!°   240
GRATIANA: Peevish,° coy, foolish! But return this answer:
   My lord shall be most welcome when his pleasure
   Conducts him this way. I will sway mine own;°
   Women with women can work best alone.   *Exit.*
VINDICE: Indeed I'll tell him so.   245
   Oh, more uncivil,° more unnatural

Than those base-titled creatures that look downward!°
Why does not heaven turn black, or with a frown
Undo the world? Why does not earth start up
And strike the sins that tread upon it?   250
Were't not for gold and women there would be no damnation.
Hell would look like a lord's great kitchen without fire in't.
But 'twas decreed before the world began
That they should be the hooks to catch at man.   *Exit.*

Act Two, Scene Two

Enter LUSSURIOSO *with* HIPPOLITO (VINDICE'S *brother*).

LUSSURIOSO: I much applaud thy judgement; thou art well read in a
    fellow,°
  And 'tis the deepest art to study man.
  I know this, which I never learned in schools,
  The world's divided into knaves and fools.
HIPPOLITO [*aside*]: Knave° in your face, my lord — behind your back!   5
LUSSURIOSO: And I much thank thee that thou hast preferred°
  A fellow of discourse,° well-mingled,
  And whose brain time hath seasoned.
HIPPOLITO: True, my lord;
  We shall find season° once,° I hope. — [*Aside*] O villain,
  To make such an unnatural slave of me! — But —   10

[*Enter* VINDICE *disguised.*]

LUSSURIOSO: Mass, here he comes.
HIPPOLITO [*aside*]: And now shall I have free leave to depart.
LUSSURIOSO: Your absence — leave us.
HIPPOLITO [*aside*]:   Are not my thoughts true?
  I must remove,° but brother you may stay.
  Heart, we are both made bawds a new-found way!   *Exit.* 15
LUSSURIOSO: Now, we're an even number: a third man's
  Dangerous, especially her brother.
  Say, be free, have I a pleasure toward?°
VINDICE: Oh, my lord.
LUSSURIOSO: Ravish° me in thine answer: art thou rare,°
  Hast thou beguiled her of salvation,   20
  And rubbed hell o'er with honey? Is she a woman?
VINDICE: In all but in desire.
LUSSURIOSO: Then she's in nothing —
  I bate in courage° now.

VINDICE: The word I brought
   Might well have made indifferent honest naught;°
   A right good woman in these days is changed   25
   Into white money° with less labour far.
   Many a maid has turned to Mahomet°
   With easier working. I durst undertake,
   Upon the pawn and forfeit of my life,
   With half those words to flat° a Puritan's wife.   30
   But she is close° and good; yet 'tis a doubt
   By this time — O the mother, the mother!
LUSSURIOSO: I never thought their sex had been a wonder
   Until this minute. What fruit from the mother?
VINDICE [*aside*]: Now must I blister my soul, be forsworn,   35
   Or shame the woman that received me° first.
   I will be true;° thou liv'st not to proclaim;°
   Spoke to a dying man shame has no shame. —
   My lord.
LUSSURIOSO: Who's that?
VINDICE: Here's none but I, my lord.
LUSSURIOSO: What would thy haste utter?
VINDICE: Comfort.
LUSSURIOSO: Welcome.   40
VINDICE: The maid being dull, having no mind to travel
   Into unknown lands, what did me straight°
   But set spurs to the mother; golden spurs
   Will put her to a false gallop in a trice.
LUSSURIOSO: Is't possible that in this the mother should be damned   45
   Before the daughter?
VINDICE: Oh, that's good manners, my lord:
   The mother for her age must go foremost,° you know.
LUSSURIOSO: Thou'st spoke that true! But where comes in this comfort?
VINDICE: In a fine place, my lord. The unnatural mother
   Did with her tongue so hard beset° her honour   50
   That the poor fool was struck to silent wonder;
   Yet still the maid, like an unlighted taper,
   Was cold and chaste, save that her mother's breath
   Did blow fire on her cheeks. The girl departed,
   But the good ancient madam, half mad,° threw me   55
   These promising words which I took deeply note of:
   'My lord shall be most welcome,' —
LUSSURIOSO: Faith, I thank her!
VINDICE: 'When his pleasure conducts him this way.'
LUSSURIOSO: That shall be soon, i' faith!
VINDICE: 'I will sway mine own' —
LUSSURIOSO: She does the wiser; I commend her for't.   60

VINDICE: 'Women with women can work best alone.'
LUSSURIOSO: By this light, and so they can; give 'em
    Their due, men are not comparable to 'em.
VINDICE: No, that's true, for you shall have one woman
    Knit° more, in a hour, than any man   65
    Can ravel° again in seven and twenty year.
LUSSURIOSO: Now my desires are happy, I'll make 'em freemen now.°
    Thou art a precious fellow;° faith, I love thee.
    Be wise, and make it thy revenue.° Beg, leg;°
    What office° couldst thou be ambitious for?   70
VINDICE: Office, my lord? Marry, if I might have my wish
    I would have one that was never begged yet.
LUSSURIOSO: Nay then thou canst have none.
VINDICE: Yes, my lord,
    I could pick out another office yet;
    Nay, and keep a horse and drab° upon it.   75
LUSSURIOSO: Prithee, good bluntness, tell me.
VINDICE: Why, I would desire but this, my lord:
    To have all the fees behind the arras,° and all
    The farthingales° that fall plump° about
    Twelve o'clock at night upon the rushes.°   80
LUSSURIOSO: Thou'rt a mad apprehensive° knave;
    Dost think to make any great purchase° of that?
VINDICE: Oh, 'tis an unknown thing, my lord; I wonder
    'T'as been missed so long!
LUSSURIOSO: Well, this night I'll visit her, and 'tis till then   85
    A year in my desires. Farewell, attend,
    Trust me with thy preferment.   *Exit.*
VINDICE: My loved lord. —
    Oh, shall I kill him o' the wrong-side now? No,   *[Draws his sword.]*
    Sword thou wast never a back-biter° yet.
    I'll pierce him to his face, he shall die looking upon me.   90
    Thy veins are swelled with lust, this shall unfill 'em;
    Great men were gods if beggars could not kill 'em. *[Sheathes his sword.]*
    Forgive me, heaven, to call my mother wicked;
    Oh, lessen not my days° upon the earth!
    I cannot honour her; by this I fear me°   95
    Her tongue has turned my sister into use.°
    I was a villain not to be forsworn
    To this our lecherous hope,° the duke's son;
    For lawyers, merchants, some divines and all,°
    Count beneficial perjury a sin small.   100
    It shall go hard yet, but I'll guard her honour
    And keep the ports° sure.

Enter HIPPOLITO.

HIPPOLITO: Brother, how goes the world? I would know news
    Of you, but I have news to tell you.
VINDICE: What, in the name of knavery?
HIPPOLITO: Knavery, faith.   105
    This vicious old duke's worthily abused,
    The pen° of his bastard writes him cuckold!
VINDICE: His bastard?
HIPPOLITO: Pray believe it. He and the duchess
    By night meet in their linen; they have been seen
    By stair-foot pandars.
VINDICE: O sin foul and deep!   110
    Great faults are winked at when the duke's asleep.
    See, see, here comes the Spurio —

                    [*Enter* SPURIO *with two* SERVANTS.]

HIPPOLITO: Monstrous luxur!°
VINDICE: Unbraced;° two of his valiant bawds with him.
    Oh, there's a wicked whisper; hell is in his ear.
    Stay, let's observe his passage.   [*They retire.*]
SPURIO: Oh, but are you sure on't?   115
SERVANT: My lord most sure on't, for 'twas spoke by one
    That is most inward with the duke's son's lust;
    That he intends within this hour to steal
    Unto Hippolito's sister, whose chaste life
    The mother has corrupted for his use.   120
SPURIO: Sweet word, sweet occasion! Faith then, brother,
    I'll disinherit you in as short time
    As I was when I was begot in haste,
    I'll damn you at your pleasure — precious deed!
    After your lust, O, 'twill be fine to bleed!   125
    Come, let our passing out° be soft and wary.
                 Exeunt [SPURIO *and the two* SERVANTS.]
VINDICE: Mark, there, there, that step! Now to the duchess;
    This their second meeting writes the duke cuckold
    With new additions,° his horns newly revived.
    Night, thou that look'st like funeral herald's fees°   130
    Torn down betimes° i' the morning, thou hang'st fitly°
    To grace those sins that have no grace at all.
    Now 'tis full sea abed° over the world,
    There's juggling° of all sides. Some that were maids
    E'en at sunset are now perhaps i' the toll-book;°   135
    This woman in immodest thin apparel

Lets in her friend by water;° here a dame,
Cunning, nails leather hinges to a door
To avoid proclamation. Now cuckolds are
A-coining, apace, apace, apace, apace;   140
And careful sisters° spin that thread i' the night
That does maintain them and their bawds i' the day.
HIPPOLITO: You flow well, brother.
VINDICE: Puh, I'm shallow yet,
   Too sparing and too modest; shall I tell thee,
   If every trick were told that's dealt by night,   145
   There are few here that would not blush outright.
HIPPOLITO: I am of that belief, too.
VINDICE: Who's this comes?

[*Enter* LUSSURIOSO.]

The duke's son up so late? Brother, fall back
And you shall learn some mischief. —° My good lord.
LUSSURIOSO: Piato! Why, the man I wished for; come,   150
   I do embrace this season for the fittest
   To taste of that young lady.
VINDICE [*aside*]:   Heart and hell!
HIPPOLITO [*aside*]: Damned villain!
VINDICE [*aside*]: I ha' no way now to cross° it; but to kill him.
LUSSURIOSO: Come, only thou and I.
VINDICE: My lord, my lord!   155
LUSSURIOSO: Why dost thou start us?°
VINDICE: I'd almost forgot —
   The bastard!
LUSSURIOSO: What of him?
VINDICE: This night, this hour —
   This minute, now —
LUSSURIOSO: What? What?
VINDICE: Shadows° the duchess —
LUSSURIOSO: Horrible word!
VINDICE: And like strong poison, eats
   Into the duke your father's forehead.°
LUSSURIOSO: Oh!   160
VINDICE: He makes horn-royal.°
LUSSURIOSO: Most ignoble slave!
VINDICE: This is the fruit of two beds.°
LUSSURIOSO: I am mad.
VINDICE: That passage he trod warily.
LUSSURIOSO: He did!
VINDICE: And hushed his villains every step he took.

LUSSURIOSO: His villains! I'll confound them.   165
VINDICE: Take 'em finely, finely now.
LUSSURIOSO: The duchess' chamber door shall not control me.
                              Exeunt [LUSSURIOSO *and* VINDICE].
HIPPOLITO: Good, happy, swift, there's gunpowder i' the court,
    Wildfire° at midnight! In this heedless fury,
    He may show violence to cross himself: 170
    I'll follow the event.°   *Exit.*

Act Two, Scene Three

[*The* DUKE *and* DUCHESS *discovered in a curtained bed.*]° *Enter*
again [LUSSURIOSO *and* VINDICE *disguised.*]

LUSSURIOSO: Where is that villain?
VINDICE: Softly, my lord, and you may take 'em twisted.
LUSSURIOSO: I care not how.
VINDICE: Oh, twill be glorious,
    To kill 'em doubled, when they're heaped. Be soft,°
    My lord.
LUSSURIOSO: Away! My spleen° is not so lazy;   5
    Thus, and thus, I'll shake their eyelids ope,
    And with my sword shut 'em again for ever. —
    Villain! Strumpet! [*They approach the bed;* LUSSURIOSO *opens the curtains.*]
DUKE: You upper° guard defend us!
DUCHESS: Treason, treason!
DUKE: Oh, take me not in sleep;
    I have great sins, I must have days,   10
    Nay months, dear son, with penitential heaves°
    To lift 'em out, and not to die unclear.°
    O, thou wilt kill me both in heaven and here.
LUSSURIOSO: I am amazed to death.
DUKE: Nay, villain, traitor,
    Worse than the foulest epithet, now I'll grip thee   15
    E'en with the nerves° of wrath, and throw thy head
    Amongst the lawyers. — Guard!

Enter [Guard], NOBLES *and* [AMBITIOSO *and* SUPERVACUO *the*
Duke's] *sons* [*with* HIPPOLITO].°

1 NOBLE: How comes the quiet of your Grace disturbed?
DUKE: This boy, that should be myself° after me,
    Would be myself before me, and in heat   20

Of that ambition bloodily rushed in,
    Intending to depose me in my bed.
2 NOBLE: Duty and natural loyalty forfend!°
DUCHESS: He called his father villain, and me strumpet,
    A word that I abhor to 'file° my lips with.   25
AMBITIOSO: That was not so well done, brother!
LUSSURIOSO: I am abused.°
    I know there's no excuse can do me good.
VINDICE [*aside to* HIPPOLITO]: 'Tis now good policy to be from sight;
    His vicious purpose to our sister's honour
    Is crossed beyond our thought.
HIPPOLITO: You little dreamt   30
    His father slept here?
VINDICE: O 'twas far beyond me.
    But since it fell so — without frightful word —°
    Would he had killed him, 'twould have eased our swords.
                             [VINDICE *and* HIPPOLITO *dissemble a flight.*]°
DUKE: Be comforted, our duchess, he shall die.°
LUSSURIOSO: Where's this slave-pandar now? Out of mine eye,°   35
    Guilty of this abuse.

            Enter SPURIO, *with* [*two* SERVANTS,] *his villains.*

SPURIO: You're villains, fablers,
    You have knaves' chins and harlots'° tongues; you lie,
    And I will damn you with one meal a day!
1 SERVANT: O good my lord!
SPURIO: 'Sblood you shall never sup.
2 SERVANT: O, I beseech you, sir!
SPURIO: To let my sword   40
    Catch cold so long and miss him!
1 SERVANT: Troth, my lord,
    'Twas his intent to meet there.
SPURIO: Heart, he's yonder!
    Ha? What news here? Is the day out o' the socket,°
    That it is noon at midnight, the court up?
    How comes the guard so saucy with his elbows?°   45
LUSSURIOSO [*aside*]: The bastard here?
    Nay then the truth of my intent shall out. —
    My lord and father, hear me.
DUKE: Bear him hence.
LUSSURIOSO: I can with loyalty excuse —
DUKE: Excuse?
    To prison with the villain!   50
    Death shall not long lag after him.

SPURIO [*aside*]: Good i' faith, then 'tis not much amiss.
LUSSURIOSO: Brothers, my best release lies on your tongues;
    I pray persuade for me.
AMBITIOSO: It is our duties;
    Make yourself sure of us.°
SUPERVACUO: We'll sweat in pleading.   55
LUSSURIOSO: And I may live to thank you.   *Exit* [LUSSURIOSO *guarded*].
AMBITIOSO [*aside*]:   No, thy death
    Shall thank me better.
SPURIO [*aside*]:   He's gone. I'll after him,
    And know his trespass; seem to bear a part
    In all his ills — but with a Puritan° heart.   *Exit.*
AMBITIOSO: Now, brother, let our hate and love be woven   60
    So subtly together that in speaking
    One word for his life, we may make three for his death.
    The craftiest pleader gets most gold for breath.
SUPERVACUO: Set on, I'll not be far behind you, brother.
DUKE: Is't possible a son should be disobedient as far as the sword?   65
    It is the highest; he can go no farther.
AMBITIOSO: My gracious lord, take pity.
DUKE: Pity, boys?
AMBITIOSO: Nay, we'd be loth to move your grace too much;
    We know the trespass is unpardonable,
    Black, wicked and unnatural.   70
SUPERVACUO: In a son, O monstrous!
AMBITIOSO: Yet, my lord,
    A duke's soft hand strokes the rough head of law,
    And makes it lie smooth.
DUKE: But my hand shall ne'er do't.
AMBITIOSO: That as you please, my lord.
SUPERVACUO: We must needs confess
    Some° father would have entered into hate   75
    So deadly pointed, that before his eyes
    He would ha' seen the execution sound,°
    Without corrupted favour.
AMBITIOSO: But, my lord,
    Your Grace may live the wonder of all times
    In pard'ning that offence which never yet   80
    Had face° to beg a pardon.
DUKE: Honey,° how's this?
AMBITIOSO: Forgive him, good my lord; he's your own son,
    And — I must needs say — 'twas the vilelier done.
SUPERVACUO: He's the next heir; yet this true reason gathers,
    None can possess that dispossess their fathers.   85
    Be merciful —

DUKE [*aside*]:   Here's no stepmother's wit;°
 I'll try 'em both upon their love and hate.
AMBITIOSO: Be merciful — although —
DUKE: You have prevailed,
 My wrath, like flaming wax, hath spent itself.
 I know 'twas but some peevish moon° in him: 90
 Go, let him be released.
SUPERVACUO [*aside*]:   'Sfoot, how now, brother?
AMBITIOSO: Your Grace doth please to speak beside your spleen;°
 I would it were so happy.
DUKE: Why, go, release him.
SUPERVACUO: O, my good lord, I know the fault's too weighty
 And full of general loathing; too inhuman;   95
 Rather by all men's voices worthy death.
DUKE: 'Tis true too.
 Here then, receive this signet; doom shall pass.°
        [*He gives* SUPERVACUO *his signet ring.*]
 Direct it to the judges. He shall die
 Ere many days; — make haste.
AMBITIOSO: All speed that may be.   100
 We could have wished his burden not so sore;
 We knew your Grace did but delay before.
       Exeunt [AMBITIOSO *and* SUPERVACUO].
DUKE: Here's envy, with a poor thin cover o'er it,
 Like scarlet° hid in lawn,° easily spied through.
 This their ambition by the mother's side   105
 Is dangerous, and for safety must be purged.
 I will prevent° their envies;° sure it was
 But some mistaken fury in our son,
 Which these aspiring boys would climb upon.
 He shall be released suddenly.°   110

Enter NOBLES.

1 NOBLE: Good morning to your Grace.
DUKE: Welcome, my lords.
        [*The* NOBLES *kneel.*]
2 NOBLE: Our knees shall take away the office of our feet for ever,
 Unless your Grace bestow a father's eye
 Upon the clouded fortunes of your son,
 And in compassionate virtue° grant him that   115
 Which makes e'en mean men happy: liberty.
DUKE [*aside*]: How seriously their loves and honours woo
 For that which I am about to pray them do. —
 Rise, my lords, your knees sign his release:

We freely pardon him.   120
1 NOBLE: We owe your Grace much thanks, and he much duty.
                                                            Exeunt [NOBLES].
DUKE: It well becomes that judge to nod at crimes
     That does commit greater himself and lives.
     I may forgive a disobedient error,
     That expect pardon for adultery,   125
     And in my old days am a youth in lust.
     Many a beauty have I turned to poison
     In the denial,° covetous of all;
     Age hot is like a monster to be seen;
     My hairs are white, and yet my sins are green.°   [*Exit.*]

Act Three, Scene One

Enter AMBITIOSO *and* SUPERVACUO.

SUPERVACUO: Brother, let my opinion sway you once.°
     I speak it for the best to have him die
     Surest and soonest; if the signet come
     Unto the judges' hands, why then his doom
     Will be deferred till sittings and court-days,   5
     Juries and further. Faiths° are bought and sold;
     Oaths in these days are but the skin of gold.
AMBITIOSO: In troth 'tis true, too.
SUPERVACUO: Then let's set by° the judges,
     And fall° to the officers; 'tis but mistaking
     The duke our father's meaning, and where he named   10
     'Ere many days', 'tis but forgetting that,
     And have him die i' the morning.
AMBITIOSO: Excellent!
     Then am I heir — duke in a minute!
SUPERVACUO [*aside*]:   Nay,
     And he were once puffed out, here is a pin°
     Should quickly prick your bladder.
AMBITIOSO: Blest occasion!   15
     He being packed,° we'll have some trick and wile
     To wind our younger brother out of prison,
     That lies in for the rape. The lady's dead,
     And people's thoughts will soon be burièd.
SUPERVACUO:
     We may with safety do't and live and feed: 20
     The duchess' sons are too proud to bleed.

AMBITIOSO: We are, i' faith, to say true. — Come, let's not linger.
    I'll to the officers; go you before,
    And set an edge° upon the executioner.
SUPERVACUO: Let me alone to grind him.   *Exit.*
AMBITIOSO: Meet;° farewell.   25
    I am next now, I rise just in that place
    Where thou'rt cut off — upon thy neck, kind brother.
    The falling of one head lifts up another.   *Exit.*

Act Three, Scene Two

Enter, with the NOBLES, LUSSURIOSO *from prison.*

LUSSURIOSO: My lords, I am so much indebted to your loves
    For this, O this delivery.
1 NOBLE: But° our duties,
    My lord, unto the hopes that grow in you.
LUSSURIOSO: If e'er I live to be myself° I'll thank you.
    O liberty, thou sweet and heavenly dame!   5
    But hell, for prison, is too mild a name!   *Exeunt.*

Act Three, Scene Three

Enter AMBITIOSO *and* SUPERVACUO, *with* OFFICERS.

AMBITIOSO: Officers, here's the duke's signet, your firm warrant,
    Brings the command of present° death along with it
    Unto our brother, the duke's son. We are sorry
    That we are so unnaturally employed
    In such an unkind office, fitter far   5
    For enemies than brothers.
SUPERVACUO: But you know
    The duke's command must be obeyed.
1 OFFICER: It must and shall, my lord. This morning, then,
    So suddenly?
AMBITIOSO: Ay, alas, poor good soul,
    He must breakfast betimes;° the executioner   10
    Stands ready to put forth his cowardly valour.
2 OFFICER: Already?
SUPERVACUO: Already, i' faith; O, sir, destruction hies,
    And that° is least impudent, soonest dies.
1 OFFICER: Troth, you say true, my lord. We take our leaves.   15

Our office shall be sound,° we'll not delay
The third part of a minute.
AMBITIOSO: Therein you show
   Yourselves good men and upright officers.
   Pray let him die as private as he may.
   Do him that favour, for the gaping people   20
   Will but trouble him at his prayers,
   And make him curse and swear, and so die black.°
   Will you be so far kind?
1 OFFICER: It shall be done, my lord.
AMBITIOSO: Why, we do thank you; if we live to be,
   You shall have a better office.
2 OFFICER: Your good lordship.   25
SUPERVACUO: Commend us to the scaffold in our tears.
1 OFFICER: We'll weep, and do your commendations.°   *Exeunt* [OFFICERS].
AMBITIOSO: Fine fools in office!
SUPERVACUO: Things fall out so fit!
AMBITIOSO: So happily! Come, brother; ere next clock
   His head will be made serve a bigger block.°   *Exeunt.*

Act Three, Scene Four

Enter [the duchess' YOUNGER SON *and his prison* KEEPER].

YOUNGER SON: Keeper.
KEEPER: My lord.
YOUNGER SON: No news lately from our brothers?
   Are they unmindful of us?
KEEPER: My lord, a messenger came newly in,
   And brought this from 'em.   [*He gives him a letter.*]
YOUNGER SON: Nothing but paper comforts?
   I looked for my delivery before this,   5
   Had they been worth their oaths — prithee be from us.   [*Exit* KEEPER.]
   Now, what say you forsooth? Speak out I pray: [*He reads out the*] *letter.*
   'Brother be of good cheer' —° 'Slud,° it begins like a whore with
   good cheer! 'Thou shalt not be long a prisoner' — Not five and
   thirty year like a bankrupt, I think so! 'We have thought upon a
   device to get thee out by a trick' —° By a trick! Pox o' your trick   10
   and it be so long a playing. 'And so rest comforted, be merry and
   expect it suddenly' — Be merry, hang merry, draw and quarter
   merry, I'll be mad! Is't not strange that a man should lie in a whole
   month for a woman?° Well, we shall see how sudden our brothers
   will be in their promise, I must expect still a trick: I shall not be   15

long a prisoner. How now, what news?

[*Enter* KEEPER.]

KEEPER: Bad news, my lord, I am discharged of you.
YOUNGER SON: Slave, call'st thou that bad news? I thank you, brothers.
KEEPER: My lord, 'twill prove so; here come the officers   20
    Into whose hands I must commit you.   [*Exit* KEEPER.]
YOUNGER SON: Ha,
    Officers? What, why?

[*Enter* OFFICERS.]

1 OFFICER: You must pardon us, my lord;
    Our office must be sound. Here is our warrant,
    The signet from the duke; you must straight suffer.
YOUNGER SON: Suffer? I'll suffer you to be gone, I'll suffer you   25
    To come no more — what would you have me suffer?
2 OFFICER: My lord, those words were better changed to prayers.
    The time's but brief with you; prepare to die.
YOUNGER SON: Sure, 'tis not so!
3 OFFICER: It is too true, my lord.
YOUNGER SON: I tell you 'tis not, for the duke my father   30
    Deferred me till next sitting,° and I look
    E'en every minute, threescore times an hour,
    For a release, a trick, wrought by my brothers.
1 OFFICER: A trick, my lord? If you expect such comfort
    Your hope's as fruitless as a barren woman: 35
    Your brothers were the unhappy messengers
    That brought this powerful token for your death.
YOUNGER SON: My brothers! No, no!
2 OFFICER: 'Tis most true, my lord.
YOUNGER SON: My brothers to bring a warrant for my death?
    How strange this shows!
3 OFFICER: There's no delaying time.   40
YOUNGER SON: Desire 'em hither, call 'em up; my brothers?
    They shall deny it to your faces!
1 OFFICER: My lord,
    They're far enough by this, at least at court,
    And this most strict command they left behind 'em.
    When grief swum in their eyes they showed like brothers,   45
    Brim-full of heavy sorrow; but the duke
    Must have his pleasure.
YOUNGER SON: His pleasure?
1 OFFICER: These were their last words which my memory bears:

'Commend us to the scaffold in our tears'.
YOUNGER SON: Pox dry their tears: what should I do with tears?   50
    I hate 'em worse than any citizen's son
    Can hate salt water.° Here came a letter now,
    New bleeding from their pens, scarce stinted° yet —
    Would I'd been torn in pieces when I tore it —
    Look you officious whoresons, words of comfort: 55
    'Not long a prisoner'.
1 OFFICER: It says true in that, sir, for you must suffer presently.°
YOUNGER SON: A villainous Duns° upon the letter: knavish exposition!
    Look you then here sir: 'We'll get thee out by a trick', says he.
2 OFFICER: That may hold too sir, for you know a trick is commonly   60
    four cards,° which was meant by us four officers.
YOUNGER SON: Worse and worse dealing.°
1 OFFICER: The hour beckons us,
    The headsman waits: lift up your eyes to heaven.
YOUNGER SON: I thank you, faith; good, pretty, wholesome counsel!
    I should look up to heaven as you said,   65
    Whilst he behind me cozens me of° my head!
    Ay, that's the trick.
3 OFFICER: You delay too long, my lord.
YOUNGER SON: Stay, good authority's bastards. Since I must
    Through brothers' perjury° die, O let me venom
    Their souls with curses.
1 OFFICER: Come, 'tis no time to curse.   70
YOUNGER SON: Must I bleed then, without respect of sign?° Well —
    My fault was sweet sport which the world approves;
    I die for that which every woman loves.   *Exeunt.*

Act Three, Scene Five

Enter VINDICE [*disguised*], *with* HIPPOLITO *his brother.*

VINDICE: O sweet, delectable, rare, happy, ravishing!
HIPPOLITO: Why what's the matter, brother?
VINDICE: O, 'tis able
    To make a man spring up and knock his forehead
    Against yon silver ceiling.°
HIPPOLITO: Prithee tell me
    Why may not I partake with you? You vowed once   5
    To give me share to every tragic thought.
VINDICE: By th' mass, I think I did too.
    Then I'll divide it to° thee. The old duke,

Thinking my outward shape° and inward heart
Are cut out of one piece (for he that prates   10
His secrets, his heart stands o' the outside),
Hires me by price to greet him with a lady
In some fit place, veiled from the eyes o' the court,
Some darkened blushless angle° that is guilty
Of his forefathers' lusts, and great folks' riots;°   15
To which I easily, to maintain my shape,°
Consented, and did wish his impudent° Grace
To meet her here in this unsunnèd lodge
Wherein 'tis night at noon; and here the rather
Because unto the torturing of his soul   20
The bastard and the duchess have appointed
Their meeting too, in this luxurious° circle —°
Which most afflicting sight will kill his eyes
Before we kill the rest of him.
HIPPOLITO: 'Twill, i' faith; most dreadfully digested.°   25
    I see not how you could have missed me,° brother.
VINDICE: True, but the violence of my joy forgot it.
HIPPOLITO: Ay; but where's that lady now?
VINDICE: O, at that word
    I'm lost again; you cannot find me yet.
    I'm in a throng of happy apprehensions.°   30
    He's suited for a lady; I have took care
    For a delicious lip, a sparkling eye —
    You shall be witness, brother.
    Be ready; stand with your hat off.   *Exit.*
HIPPOLITO: Troth, I wonder
    What lady it should be. Yet 'tis no wonder,   35
    Now I think again, to have a lady
    Stoop to a duke, that stoops unto his men.°
    'Tis common to be common,° through the world,
    And there's more private-common shadowing vices
    Than those who are known both by their names and prices.°   40
    'Tis part of my allegiance to stand bare°
    To the duke's concubine — and here she comes.

Enter VINDICE, *with the skull of his love dressed up in tires*° [*and
masked*].

VINDICE: Madam, his Grace will not be absent long.
    Secret? Ne'er doubt us, madam. 'Twill be worth
    Three velvet gowns to your ladyship. Known?   45
    Few ladies respect that! Disgrace? A poor thin shell!°
    'Tis the best grace you have to do it well.

I'll save your hand that labour; I'll unmask you.

[VINDICE *reveals the skull.*]

HIPPOLITO: Why brother, brother!

VINDICE: Art thou beguiled now? Tut, a lady can   50
    At such, all hid,° beguile a wiser man.
    Have I not fitted the old surfeiter
    With a quaint° piece of beauty? Age and bare bone
    Are e'er allied in action. Here's an eye
    Able to tempt a great man — to serve God;   55
    A pretty hanging lip, that has forgot now to dissemble.
    Methinks this mouth should make a swearer tremble,
    A drunkard clasp his teeth, and not undo 'em
    To suffer wet damnation to run through 'em.
    Here's a cheek keeps her colour,° let the wind go whistle: 60
    Spout rain, we fear thee not, be hot or cold,
    All's one with us. And is not he absurd
    Whose fortunes are upon their faces set,
    That fear no other God but wind and wet?

HIPPOLITO: Brother you've spoke that right. Is this the form   65
    That, living, shone so bright?

VINDICE: The very same.
    And now methinks I could e'en chide myself
    For doting on her beauty, though her death
    Shall be revenged after no common action.
    Does the silkworm expend her yellow labours°   70
    For thee? For thee does she undo herself?
    Are lordships° sold to maintain ladyships
    For the poor benefit of a bewitching minute?
    Why does yon fellow falsify highways,°
    And put his life between the judge's lips   75
    To refine such a thing,° keeps horse and men
    To beat° their valours for her?
    Surely we're all mad people, and they,
    Whom we think are, are not: we mistake those.
    'Tis we are mad in sense,° they but in clothes.   80

HIPPOLITO: Faith, and in clothes too we, give us our due.

VINDICE: Does every proud and self-affecting° dame
    Camphor° her face for this, and grieve her maker
    In sinful baths of milk, when many an infant starves
    For her superfluous outside —° all for this?   85
    Who now bids twenty pound a night, prepares
    Music, perfumes and sweetmeats? All are hushed;
    Thou may'st lie chaste now! It were fine, methinks,
    To have thee seen at revels, forgetful feasts,
    And unclean brothels; sure, 'twould fright the sinner   90

And make him a good coward, put a reveller
Out of his antic amble°
And cloy an epicure with empty dishes.
Here might a scornful and ambitious woman
Look through and through herself;° see, ladies, with false forms   95
You deceive men, but cannot deceive worms.
Now to my tragic business. Look you, brother,
I have not fashioned this only for show
And useless property;° no, it shall bear a part°
E'en in its own revenge. This very skull,   100
Whose mistress the duke poisoned with this drug,
The mortal curse of the earth, shall be revenged
In the like strain,° and kiss his lips to death.
As much as the dumb thing can, he shall feel;
What fails in poison, we'll supply in steel.   105
HIPPOLITO: Brother, I do applaud thy constant vengeance,
    The quaintness° of thy malice, above thought.
                  [VINDICE *applies poison to the skull's mouth.*]
VINDICE: So 'tis laid on: now come and welcome, duke;
    I have her for thee. I protest it, brother,
    Methinks she makes almost as fair a sign°   110
    As some old gentlewoman in a periwig.   [*Puts a mask on the skull.*]
    Hide thy face now for shame; thou hadst need have a mask now.
    Tis vain° when beauty flows, but when it fleets°
    This would become graves better than the streets.
HIPPOLITO: You have my voice in that.   [*Noises within.*]
                 Hark, the duke's come.   115
VINDICE: Peace. Let's observe what company he brings,
    And how he does absent 'em,° for you know
    He'll wish all private. Brother, fall you back a little,
    With the bony lady.
HIPPOLITO: That I will.   [*He retires.*]
VINDICE: So, so —
    Now nine years' vengeance crowd into a minute.   120

[*Enter the* DUKE *and* GENTLEMEN.]

DUKE: You shall have leave to leave us, with this charge:
    Upon our lives, if we be missed by the duchess,
    Or any of the nobles, to give out
    We're privately rid forth.
VINDICE [*aside*]:   O happiness!
DUKE: With some few honourable gentlemen, you may say;   125
    You may name those that are away from court.
GENTLEMAN: Your will and pleasure shall be done, my lord.

[*Exeunt* GENTLEMEN.]

VINDICE [*aside*]: Privately rid forth?
    He strives to make sure work on't. — [*Advances.*] Your good Grace.
DUKE: Piato! well done. Hast brought her? What lady is't?   130
VINDICE: Faith, my lord, a country lady, a little bashful at first as most
    of them are, but after the first kiss, my lord, the worst is past with
    them. Your Grace knows now what you have to do. She's
    somewhat a grave° look with her, but —
DUKE: I love that best; conduct her.
VINDICE [*aside*]:   Have at all.°   135
DUKE: In gravest looks the greatest faults seem less;
    Give me that sin that's robed in holiness.
VINDICE [*aside to* HIPPOLITO]: Back with the torch;° brother, raise the
    perfumes.
DUKE: How sweet can a duke breathe? Age has no fault.°
    Pleasure should meet in a perfumèd mist.   140
    Lady, sweetly encountered: I came from court,
    I must be bold with you —   [*He kisses the skull.*]
              O! What's this? Oh!
VINDICE: Royal villain, white devil!°
DUKE: Oh!
VINDICE: Brother,
    Place the torch here, that his affrighted eyeballs
    May start into those hollows. Duke, dost know   145
    Yon dreadful vizard? View it well; 'tis the skull
    Of Gloriana,° whom thou poisonedst last.
DUKE: O 't'as° poisoned me!
VINDICE: Didst not know that till now?
DUKE: What are you two?
VINDICE: Villains all three! The very ragged° bone   150
    Has been sufficiently revenged.
DUKE: O, Hippolito! — Call treason! [*Falls.*]
HIPPOLITO: Yes, my good lord. Treason, treason, treason!   *Stamping on him.*
DUKE: Then I'm betrayed.
VINDICE: Alas poor lecher, in the hands of knaves,   155
    A slavish° duke is baser than his slaves.
DUKE: My teeth are eaten out.
VINDICE: Hadst any left?
HIPPOLITO: I think but few.
VINDICE: Then those that did eat are eaten.
DUKE: O, my tongue!
VINDICE: Your tongue? 'Twill teach you to kiss closer,°   160
    Not like a slobbering Dutchman.° You have eyes still:
    Look, monster, what a lady hast thou made me [*Throws off his disguise.*]
    My once betrothed wife.

DUKE: Is it thou, villain?
   Nay then —
VINDICE: 'Tis I, 'tis Vindice, 'tis I!
HIPPOLITO: And let this comfort thee. Our lord and father   165
   Fell sick upon the infection of thy frowns,
   And died in sadness. Be that thy hope of life.
DUKE: O!
VINDICE: He had his tongue, yet grief made him die speechless.
   Puh,° 'tis but early yet; now I'll begin   170
   To stick thy soul with ulcers; I will make
   Thy spirit grievous sore, it shall not rest
   But, like some pestilent° man, toss in thy breast.
   Mark me, duke,
   Thou'rt a renownèd, high, and mighty cuckold!   175
DUKE: Oh!
VINDICE: Thy bastard, thy bastard rides a-hunting in thy brow.°
DUKE: Millions of deaths!
VINDICE: Nay, to afflict thee more,
   Here in this lodge they meet for damnèd clips;°
   Those eyes shall see the incest of their lips.   180
DUKE: Is there a hell besides this, villains?
VINDICE: Villain?
   Nay, heaven is just, scorns are the hires of scorns;
   I ne'er knew yet adulterer without horns.°
HIPPOLITO: Once° ere they die 'tis quitted.°   [*Noises within.*]
VINDICE: Hark, the music;
   Their banquet is prepared, they're coming —   185
DUKE: O kill me not with that sight.
VINDICE: Thou shalt not lose that sight for all thy dukedom.
DUKE: Traitors, murderers!
VINDICE: What, is not thy tongue eaten out yet?
   Then we'll invent a silence. Brother, stifle° the torch.   190
DUKE: Treason! Murder!
VINDICE: Nay, faith, we'll have you hushed now with thy dagger. —
   Nail down his tongue, and mine shall keep possession
   About his heart. If he but gasp he dies;
   We dread not death to quittance° injuries.   195
   Brother, if he but wink, not brooking the foul object,°
   Let our two other hands tear up his lids
   And make his eyes, like comets, shine through blood.°
   When the bad bleeds, then is the tragedy good.
HIPPOLITO: Whist, brother, music's at our ear: they come.   200

Enter [SPURIO] *the Bastard meeting the* DUCHESS. [*They kiss.*
Attendants with lights stand apart.]

SPURIO: Had not that kiss a taste of sin, 'twere sweet.
DUCHESS: Why, there's no pleasure sweet but it is sinful.
SPURIO: True, such a bitter sweetness fate hath given;
    Best side to us, is the worst side to heaven.
DUCHESS: Push, come, 'tis the old duke thy doubtful° father;   205
    The thought of him rubs heaven° in thy way.
    But I protest by yonder waxen fire,°
    Forget him, or I'll poison him.
SPURIO: Madam, you urge a thought which ne'er had life.
    So deadly do I loathe him for my birth   210
    That, if he took me hasped° within his bed,
    I would add murder to adultery,
    And with my sword give up his years to death.
DUCHESS: Why, now thou'rt sociable: let's in and feast.
    Loudest music sound: pleasure is banquet's guest.   215
               Exeunt [SPURIO, DUCHESS, *and* Attendants.]
DUKE: I cannot brook —   [*Dies.*]
VINDICE: The brook is turned to blood.
HIPPOLITO: Thanks to loud music.
VINDICE: Twas our friend indeed;
    'Tis state,° in music for a duke to bleed.
    The dukedom wants° a head, though yet unknown;
    As fast as they peep up, let's cut 'em down.   *Exeunt.* 220

Act Three, Scene Six

Enter the duchess' two sons, AMBITIOSO *and* SUPERVACUO.

AMBITIOSO: Was not his execution rarely plotted?
    We are the duke's sons now.
SUPERVACUO: Ay, you may thank
    My policy° for that.
AMBITIOSO: Your policy
    For what?
SUPERVACUO: Why was't not my invention, brother,
    To slip° the judges, and, in lesser compass,   5
    Did not I draw the model° of his death,
    Advising you to sudden° officers,
    And e'en extemporal° execution?
AMBITIOSO: Heart, 'twas a thing I thought on too.
SUPERVACUO: You thought on't too! 'Sfoot,° slander not your thoughts 10
    With glorious untruth; I know 'twas from you.°
AMBITIOSO: Sir, I say 'twas in my head.

[SUPERVACUO:]   Ay, like your brains then;
    Ne'er to come out as long as you lived.
AMBITIOSO: You'd have the honour on't, forsooth, that your wit°
    Led him to the scaffold.
SUPERVACUO: Since it is my due   15
    I'll publish't — but I'll ha't, in spite of you.
AMBITIOSO: Methinks you're much too bold. You should a little
    Remember us, brother, next to be honest° duke.
SUPERVACUO [*aside*]: Ay, it shall be as easy for you to be duke
    As to be honest, and that's never, i' faith.   20
AMBITIOSO: Well, cold he is by this time; and because
    We're both ambitious, be it our amity,
    And let the glory be shared equally.
SUPERVACUO: I am content to that.
AMBITIOSO: This night our younger brother shall out of prison.   25
    I have a trick.
SUPERVACUO: A trick? Prithee, what is't?
AMBITIOSO: We'll get him out by a wile.
SUPERVACUO: Prithee, what wile?
AMBITIOSO: No, sir, you shall not know it till it be done,
    For then you'd swear 'twere yours.

[*Enter an* OFFICER *carrying a bleeding head.*]

SUPERVACUO: How now, what's he?
AMBITIOSO: One of the officers.
SUPERVACUO: Desired news.
AMBITIOSO: How now, my friend?   30
OFFICER: My lords, under your pardon, I am allotted
    To that desertless office, to present you
    With the yet bleeding head.
SUPERVACUO [*aside*]:   Ha! Ha! Excellent!
AMBITIOSO [*aside*]: All's sure our own. Brother, canst weep, thinkst thou?
    'Twould grace our flattery much; think of some dame,°   35
    'Twill teach thee to dissemble.
SUPERVACUO [*aside*]:   I have thought.
    Now for yourself.
AMBITIOSO: Our sorrows are so fluent
    Our eyes o'erflow our tongues. Words spoke in tears
    Are like the murmurs of the waters; the sound
    Is loudly heard, but cannot be distinguished.   40
SUPERVACUO: How died he, pray?
OFFICER: O, full of rage and spleen.
SUPERVACUO: He died most valiantly then; we're glad to hear it.
OFFICER: We could not woo him once to pray.

AMBITIOSO: He showed himself a gentleman in that,
    Give him his due.
OFFICER: But in the stead of prayer   45
    He drew forth oaths.
SUPERVACUO: Then did he pray, dear heart,
    Although you understood him not.
OFFICER: My lords,
    E'en at his last — with pardon be it spoke —
    He cursed you both.
SUPERVACUO: He cursed us? 'Las, good soul.
AMBITIOSO: It was not in our powers, but the duke's pleasure.   50
    [*Aside*] Finely dissembled o' both sides! Sweet fate,
    O happy opportunity!

Enter LUSSURIOSO.

LUSSURIOSO: Now, my lords —
AMBITIOSO *and* SUPERVACUO: Oh!
LUSSURIOSO: Why do you shun me brothers? You may come nearer now;
    The savour° of the prison has forsook me.   55
    I thank such kind lords as yourselves I'm free.
AMBITIOSO: Alive!
SUPERVACUO: In health!
AMBITIOSO: Released!
    We were both e'en amazed with joy to see it.
LUSSURIOSO: I am much to thank you.
SUPERVACUO: Faith, we spared no tongue unto my lord   60
    The duke.
AMBITIOSO: I know your delivery, brother,
    Had not been half so sudden but for us.
SUPERVACUO: O, how we pleaded.
LUSSURIOSO: Most deserving brothers;
    In my best studies I will think of it.   *Exit.*
AMBITIOSO: O, death and vengeance!
SUPERVACUO: Hell and torments!
AMBITIOSO: Slave!   65
    Cam'st thou to delude us?
OFFICER: Delude you, my lords?
SUPERVACUO: Ay, villain. Where's this head now?
OFFICER: Why here, my lord;
    Just after his delivery, you both came
    With warrant from the duke to behead your brother.
AMBITIOSO: Ay, our brother, the duke's son.
OFFICER: The duke's son,   70
    My lord, had his release before you came.

AMBITIOSO: Whose head's that, then?
OFFICER: His, whom you left command for —
  Your own brother's.
AMBITIOSO: Our brother's? O, furies!
SUPERVACUO: Plagues!
AMBITIOSO: Confusions!
SUPERVACUO: Darkness!
AMBITIOSO: Devils!
SUPERVACUO: Fell it out so accursedly?
AMBITIOSO: So damnedly?   75
SUPERVACUO: Villain, I'll brain thee with it!
OFFICER: O my good lord!   [*Exit.*]
SUPERVACUO: The devil overtake thee!
AMBITIOSO: O, fatal!
SUPERVACUO: O, prodigious to our bloods!°
AMBITIOSO: Did we dissemble?
SUPERVACUO: Did we make our tears women° for thee?
AMBITIOSO: Laugh and rejoice for thee?
SUPERVACUO: Bring warrant for   80
  Thy death?
AMBITIOSO: Mock off thy head?
SUPERVACUO: You had a trick,
  You had a wile, forsooth.
AMBITIOSO: A murrain° meet 'em!
  There's none of these wiles that ever come to good.
  I see now there is nothing sure in mortality, but mortality.°
  Well, no more words; shalt be revenged, i' faith.   85
  Come, throw off clouds now, brother; think of vengeance,
  And deeper settled hate. — Sirrah,° sit fast:
  We'll pull down all, but thou shalt down at last.   *Exeunt.*

Act Four, Scene One

Enter LUSSURIOSO, *with* HIPPOLITO.

LUSSURIOSO: Hippolito.
HIPPOLITO: My lord. Has your good lordship
  Aught to command me in?
LUSSURIOSO: I prithee leave us.
HIPPOLITO: How's this? Come, and leave us?
LUSSURIOSO: Hippolito.
HIPPOLITO: Your honour, I stand ready for any duteous employment.
LUSSURIOSO: Heart, what mak'st thou° here?
HIPPOLITO [*aside*]:   A pretty lordly humour: 5

He bids me to be present, to depart!
Something has stung his honour.
LUSSURIOSO: Be nearer, draw nearer;
   You're not so good, methinks; I'm angry with you.
HIPPOLITO: With me, my lord? I'm angry with myself for't.
LUSSURIOSO: You did prefer° a goodly fellow to me: 10
   'Twas wittily elected,° 'twas. I thought
   He'd been a villain, and he proves a knave!
   To me a knave!
HIPPOLITO: I chose him for the best, my lord.
   'Tis much my sorrow, if neglect in him
   Breed discontent in you.
LUSSURIOSO: Neglect? 'Twas will.   15
   Judge of it.
   Firmly to tell of an incredible act,
   Not to be thought, less to be spoken of,
   'Twixt my stepmother and the bastard — oh,
   Incestuous sweets between 'em!
HIPPOLITO: Fie, my lord.   20
LUSSURIOSO: I, in kind° loyalty to my father's forehead,°
   Made this a desperate arm, and in that fury
   Committed treason on the lawful bed,
   And with my sword e'en razed° my father's bosom,
   For which I was within a stroke of death.   25
HIPPOLITO: Alack, I'm sorry. [*Aside*] 'Sfoot, just upon the stroke
   Jars in° my brother: 'twill be villainous music !°

Enter VINDICE [*disguised*].

VINDICE: My honoured lord.
LUSSURIOSO: Away!
   Prithee, forsake us: hereafter we'll not know thee.
VINDICE: Not know me, my lord? Your lordship cannot choose.   30
LUSSURIOSO: Begone, I say, thou art a false knave.
VINDICE: Why, the easier to be known, my lord.
LUSSURIOSO: Push, I shall prove too bitter: with a word
   Make thee a perpetual prisoner
   And lay this iron age° upon thee.
VINDICE [*aside*]:   Mum,   35
   For there's a doom would make a woman dumb.°
   Missing the bastard, next him, the wind's come about;
   Now 'tis my brother's turn to stay, mine to go out.   *Exit.*
LUSSURIOSO: 'Has greatly moved me.
HIPPOLITO: Much to blame, i' faith.
LUSSURIOSO: But I'll recover, to his ruin. 'Twas told me lately,   40

I know not whether falsely, that you'd a brother.
HIPPOLITO: Who I? Yes, my good lord, I have a brother.
LUSSURIOSO: How chance the court ne'er saw him? Of what nature?
 How does he apply° his hours?
HIPPOLITO: Faith, to curse fates,
 Who, as he thinks, ordained him to be poor;   45
 Keeps at home, full of want and discontent.
LUSSURIOSO: There's hope in him, for discontent and want
 Is the best clay to mould a villain of.
 Hippolito, wish him repair° to us;
 If there be aught in him to please our blood,°   50
 For thy sake we'll advance him, and build fair
 His meanest fortunes; for it is in us
 To rear up towers from cottages.
HIPPOLITO: It is so, my lord.
 He will attend your honour, but he's a man
 In whom much melancholy dwells.
LUSSURIOSO: Why, the better: 55
 Bring him to court.
HIPPOLITO: With willingness and speed.
 [*aside*] Whom he cast off e'en now, must now succeed.°
 Brother, disguise must off;
 In thine own shape now I'll prefer thee to him.
 How strangely does himself work to undo him.   *Exit.* 60
LUSSURIOSO: This fellow will come fitly; he shall kill
 That other slave that did abuse my spleen,°
 And made it swell to treason. I have put
 Much of my heart° into him; he must die.
 He that knows great men's secrets, and proves slight,°   65
 That man ne'er lives to see his beard turn white.
 Ay, he shall speed° him: I'll employ thee brother,
 Slaves are but nails to drive out one another.
 He being of black condition,° suitable
 To want and ill content, hope of preferment   70
 Will grind him to an edge.

Enter NOBLES.

1 NOBLE: Good days unto your honour.
LUSSURIOSO: My kind lords,
 I do return the like.
2 NOBLE: Saw you my lord,
 The duke?
LUSSURIOSO: My lord and father, is he from court?

1 NOBLE: He's sure from court, but where, which way his pleasure took,   75
    we know not nor can we hear on't.

LUSSURIOSO: Here come those should tell. —

    [Enter two more] NOBLES.

    Saw you my lord and father?

3 NOBLE: Not since two hours before noon, my lord, and then he
    privately rid forth.

LUSSURIOSO: O, he's rode forth.

1 NOBLE: 'Twas wondrous privately.   80

2 NOBLE: There's none i' the court had any knowledge on't.

LUSSURIOSO: His Grace is old, and sudden;° 'tis no treason
    To say the duke my father has a humour,°
    Or such a toy,° about him. What in us
    Would appear light,° in him seems virtuous.   85

3 NOBLE: 'Tis oracle,° my lord.   *Exeunt.*

Act Four, Scene Two

Enter VINDICE *and* HIPPOLITO, [VINDICE *without his disguise*].

HIPPOLITO: So, so, all's as it should be, you're yourself.

VINDICE: How that great villain puts me to my shifts!°

HIPPOLITO: He that did lately in disguise reject thee,
    Shall, now thou art thyself, as much respect thee.

VINDICE: 'Twill be the quainter fallacy;° but brother,   5
    'Sfoot, what use will he put me to now, think'st thou?

HIPPOLITO: Nay, you must pardon me in that, I know not;
    H'as some employment for you, but what 'tis
    He and his secretary° the devil knows best.

VINDICE: Well, I must suit my tongue to his desires,   10
    What colour soe'er they be, hoping at last
    To pile up all my wishes on his breast.

HIPPOLITO: Faith, brother, he himself shows the way.

VINDICE: Now the duke is dead, the realm is clad in clay;°
    His death being not yet known, under his name   15
    The people still are governed. Well, thou his son
    Art not long-lived, thou shalt not 'joy° his death.
    To kill thee, then, I should most honour thee,
    For 'twould stand firm in every man's belief
    Thou'st° a kind child, and only diedst with grief.   20

HIPPOLITO: You fetch about well; but let's talk in present.°

How will you appear in fashion° different,
As well as in apparel, to make all things possible?
If you be but once tripped we fall for ever.
It is not the least policy to be doubtful;°   25
You must change tongue — familiar was your first.
VINDICE: Why, I'll bear me in some strain° of melancholy,
And string myself with heavy sounding wire,
Like such an instrument that speaks
Merry things sadly.
HIPPOLITO: Then 'tis as I meant;   30
I gave you out° at first in discontent.
VINDICE: I'll turn° myself, and then —
HIPPOLITO: 'Sfoot here he comes —
Hast thought upon't?
VINDICE: Salute him, fear not me.

[*Enter* LUSSURIOSO.]

LUSSURIOSO: Hippolito.
HIPPOLITO: Your lordship.
LUSSURIOSO: What's he yonder?
HIPPOLITO: 'Tis Vindice, my discontented brother,   35
Whom, 'cording to your will I've brought to court.
LUSSURIOSO: Is that thy brother? Beshrew me,° a good presence;
I wonder h'as been from the court so long. — Come nearer.
HIPPOLITO: Brother, lord Lussurioso, the duke's son.
LUSSURIOSO: Be more near to us. Welcome; nearer yet.   40
VINDICE: How don you? God you god den.°
                    [VINDICE] *snatches off his hat and makes legs* °*to him.*
LUSSURIOSO: We thank thee.
How strangely such a coarse, homely salute
Shows in the palace, where we greet in fire.
Nimble and desperate° tongues! Should we name God
In a salutation, 'twould ne'er be 'stood on't —° heaven!   45
Tell me, what has made thee so melancholy.
VINDICE: Why, going to law.
LUSSURIOSO: Why, will that make a man melancholy?
VINDICE: Yes, to look long upon ink and black buckram.° I went me to
law in *anno quadragesimo secundo*, and I waded out of it in *anno*   50
sextagesimo tertio.°
LUSSURIOSO: What, three and twenty years in law?
VINDICE: I have known those that have been five and fifty, and all about
pullen and pigs.°
LUSSURIOSO: May it be possible such men should breathe, to vex the   55
terms° so much?

VINDICE: 'Tis food to some, my lord. There are old men at the present
   that are so poisoned with the affectation of law words, having had
   many suits canvassed,° that their common talk is nothing but
   Barbary° Latin. They cannot so much as pray, but in law, that their   60
   sins may be removed with a writ of error,° and their souls fetched
   up to heaven with a sasarara.°
[LUSSURIOSO:] It seems most strange to me,
   Yet all the world meets round in the same bent:°
   Where the heart's set, there goes the tongue's consent.   65
   How dost apply thy studies, fellow?
VINDICE: Study? Why, to think how a great rich man lies a-dying, and a
   poor cobbler tolls the bell for him; how he cannot depart the world,
   and see the great chest° stand before him. When he lies speechless,
   how he will point you readily to all the boxes, and when   70
   he is past all memory, as the gossips° guess, then thinks he of
   forfeitures and obligations. Nay, when to all men's hearings he
   whirls° and rattles in the throat, he's busy threatening his poor
   tenants; and this would last me now some seven years thinking, or
   thereabouts! But I have a conceit° a-coming in picture upon this (I   75
   draw it myself) which i' faith la, I'll present to your honour. You
   shall not choose but like it, for your lordship shall give me nothing
   for it.
LUSSURIOSO: Nay, you mistake me then,
   For I am published° bountiful enough;   80
   Let's taste of your conceit.
VINDICE: In picture, my lord?
LUSSURIOSO: Ay, in picture.
VINDICE: Marry this it is:
   'A usuring father to be boiling in hell, and his son and heir with a
   whore dancing over him.'
HIPPOLITO [*aside*]: H'as pared him to the quick.°   85
LUSSURIOSO: The conceit's pretty i' faith —
   But take't upon my life, 'twill ne'er be liked.
VINDICE: No? Why I'm sure the whore will be liked well enough!
HIPPOLITO [*aside*]: Ay, if she were out o' the picture he'd like her then
   himself.   90
VINDICE: And as for the son and heir, he shall be an eyesore to no young
   revellers, for he shall be drawn in cloth of gold breeches.
LUSSURIOSO: And thou hast put my meaning in the pockets,
   And canst not draw° that out. My thought was this:
   To see the picture of a usuring father   95
   Boiling in hell, our rich men would ne'er like it.
VINDICE: O true, I cry you heartily mercy! I know the reason: for some
   of 'em had rather be damned indeed than damned in colours.°
LUSSURIOSO [*aside*]: A parlous° melancholy! H'as wit enough

To murder any man, and I'll give him means. —   100
   I think thou art ill-moneyed.
VINDICE: Money? Ho, ho!
   'T'as been my want so long 'tis now my scoff;
   I've e'en forgot what colour silver's of.
LUSSURIOSO [*aside*]: It hits as I could wish.
VINDICE: I get good clothes
   Of those that dread my humour,° and for table room   105
   I feed on those that cannot be rid of me.
LUSSURIOSO [*giving* VINDICE *money*]: Somewhat to set thee up withal.
VINDICE: O mine eyes!
LUSSURIOSO: How now, man?
VINDICE: Almost struck blind!
   This bright unusual shine to me seems proud;
   I dare not look till the sun be in a cloud.   110
LUSSURIOSO [*aside*]: I think I shall affect° his melancholy; —
   How are they° now?
VINDICE: The better for your asking.
LUSSURIOSO: You shall be better yet, if you but fasten
   Truly on my intent. Now you're both present,
   I will unbrace° such a close private villain   115
   Unto your vengeful swords, the like ne'er heard of,
   Who hath disgraced you much and injured us.
HIPPOLITO: Disgraced us, my lord?
LUSSURIOSO: Ay, Hippolito.
   I kept it here° till now, that both your angers
   Might meet him at once.
VINDICE: I'm covetous   120
   To know the villain.
LUSSURIOSO: You know him: that slave-pandar
   Piato, whom we threatened last
   With irons in perpetual prisonment.
VINDICE [*aside*]: All this is I!
HIPPOLITO: Is't he my lord?
LUSSURIOSO: I'll tell you —
   You first preferred him to me.
VINDICE: Did you, brother?   125
HIPPOLITO: I did indeed.
LUSSURIOSO: And the ungrateful villain
   To quit° that kindness, strongly wrought with° me,
   Being as you see a likely man for pleasure,
   With jewels to corrupt your virgin sister.
HIPPOLITO: O villain!
VINDICE: He shall surely die that did it.   130
LUSSURIOSO: I, far from thinking any virgin harm,

Especially knowing her to be as chaste
As that part which scarce suffers to be touched,
The eye, would not endure him. —
VINDICE: Would you not,
  My lord? 'Twas wondrous honourably done.   135
LUSSURIOSO: But with some fine frowns kept him out.
VINDICE: Out, slave!
LUSSURIOSO: What did me he, but in revenge of that,
  Went of his own free will to make infirm
  Your sister's honour, whom I honour with my soul,
  For chaste respect;° and, not prevailing there   140
  — As 'twas but desperate folly to attempt it —
  In mere spleen, by the way, waylays your mother,
  Whose honour being a coward as it seems,
  Yielded by little force.
VINDICE: Coward indeed.
LUSSURIOSO: He, proud of their advantage, as he thought,   145
  Brought me these news for happy;° but I — Heaven forgive me for't —
VINDICE: What did your honour?
LUSSURIOSO: In rage pushed him from me,
  Trampled beneath his throat, spurned him and bruised;
  Indeed I was too cruel, to say truth.
HIPPOLITO: Most nobly managed.
VINDICE [*aside*]:   Has not heaven an ear?   150
  Is all the lightning wasted?
LUSSURIOSO: If I now
  Were so impatient in a modest cause,°
  What should you be?
VINDICE: Full mad: he shall not live
  To see the moon change.
LUSSURIOSO: He's about the palace.
  Hippolito, entice him this way, that thy brother   155
  May take full mark of him.
HIPPOLITO: Heart! That shall not need, my lord;
  I can direct him so far.
LUSSURIOSO: Yet, for my hate's sake,
  Go, wind° him this way; I'll see him bleed myself.
HIPPOLITO [*aside*]: What now, brother?
VINDICE [*aside*]:   Nay, e'en what you will;
  You're put to't, brother.
HIPPOLITO [*aside*]:   An impossible task, I'll swear,   160
  To bring him hither that's already here.   *Exit* HIPPOLITO.
LUSSURIOSO: Thy name? I have forgot it.
VINDICE: Vindice, my lord.
LUSSURIOSO: 'Tis a good name, that.

VINDICE: Ay, a revenger.
LUSSURIOSO: It does betoken courage; thou shouldst be valiant,
    And kill thine enemies.
VINDICE: That's my hope, my lord.   165
LUSSURIOSO: This slave is one.
VINDICE: I'll doom him.
LUSSURIOSO: Then I'll praise thee.
    Do thou observe me° best, and I'll best raise thee.

Enter HIPPOLITO.

VINDICE: Indeed I thank you.
LUSSURIOSO: Now, Hippolito,
    Where's the slave-pandar?
HIPPOLITO: Your good lordship
    Would have a loathsome sight of him, much offensive.   170
    He's not in case° now to be seen, my lord;
    The worst of all the deadly sins is in him:
    That beggarly damnation, drunkenness.
LUSSURIOSO: Then he's a double slave.
VINDICE [*aside*]:   'Twas well conveyed,°
    Upon a sudden wit.°
LUSSURIOSO: What, are you both   175
    Firmly resolved? I'll see him dead myself!
VINDICE: Or else let not us live.
LUSSURIOSO: You may direct
    Your brother to take note of him.
HIPPOLITO: I shall.
LUSSURIOSO: Rise but in this, and you shall never fall.
VINDICE: Your honour's vassals.
LUSSURIOSO [*aside*]:   This was wisely carried.°   180
    Deep policy in us makes fools of such:
    Then must a slave die, when he knows too much.   *Exit* LUSSURIOSO.
VINDICE: O, thou almighty patience, 'tis my wonder
    That such a fellow, impudent and wicked,
    Should not be cloven° as he stood,   185
    Or with a secret wind burst open!
    Is there no thunder left, or is't kept up
    In stock for heavier vengeance? [*Thunder*]° There it goes!
HIPPOLITO: Brother, we lose ourselves.°
VINDICE: But I have found it,
    'Twill hold, 'tis sure, thanks, thanks to any spirit   190
    That mingled it 'mongst my inventions.
HIPPOLITO: What is't?
VINDICE: 'Tis sound and good; thou shalt partake it.

I'm hired to kill myself.
HIPPOLITO: True.
VINDICE: Prithee mark it;
    And the old duke being dead, but not conveyed,°
    For he's already missed too — and you know   195
    Murder will peep out of the closest husk —
HIPPOLITO: Most true!
VINDICE: What say you then to this device:
    If we dressed up the body of the duke —
HIPPOLITO: In that disguise of yours!
VINDICE: You're quick, you've reached° it.
HIPPOLITO: I like it wondrously.
VINDICE: And being in drink,   200
    As you have published him,° to lean him on his elbow,
    As if sleep had caught him, which claims most interest
    In such sluggy men.°
HIPPOLITO: Good yet; but here's a doubt.
    We, thought by th' duke's son to kill that pandar,
    Shall, when he is known, be thought to kill the duke.   205
VINDICE: Neither, O thanks! It is substantial;°
    For that disguise being on him which I wore,
    It will be thought I, which he calls the pandar,
    Did kill the duke and fled away in his apparel,
    Leaving him so disguised to avoid swift pursuit.   210
HIPPOLITO: Firmer and firmer.
VINDICE: Nay, doubt not, 'tis in grain,°
    I warrant it hold colour.
HIPPOLITO: Let's about it.
VINDICE: But by the way too, now I think on't, brother,
    Let's conjure° that base devil out of our mother.   *Exeunt.*

Act Four, Scene Three

Enter the DUCHESS *arm in arm with the bastard* [SPURIO]; *he
seemeth lasciviously to* [*look on*] *her. After them enter* SUPERVACUO
running with a rapier; his brother [AMBITIOSO] *stops him.*

SPURIO: Madam, unlock yourself; should it be seen,
    Your arm would be suspected.
DUCHESS: Who is't that dares suspect or this or these? [*Kisses* SPURIO.]
    May not we deal our favours where we please?
SPURIO: I'm confident you may.   *Exeunt* [SPURIO *and* DUCHESS].
AMBITIOSO: 'Sfoot, brother, hold!   5

SUPERVACUO: Would let the bastard shame us?
AMBITIOSO: Hold, hold, brother!
    There's fitter time than now.
SUPERVACUO: Now, when I see it!
AMBITIOSO: 'Tis too much seen already.
SUPERVACUO: Seen and known:
    The nobler she is, the baser is she grown.
AMBITIOSO: If she were bent° lasciviously — the fault   10
    Of mighty women that sleep soft —° O, death!
    Must she needs choose such an unequal° sinner
    To make all worse?
SUPERVACUO: A bastard! The duke's bastard!
    Shame heaped on shame!
AMBITIOSO: O, our disgrace!
    Most women have small waist the world throughout,   15
    But their desires are thousand miles about.
SUPERVACUO: Come, stay not here: let's after and prevent;
    Or else they'll sin faster than we'll repent.   *Exeunt.*

Act Four, Scene Four

Enter VINDICE *and* HIPPOLITO, *bringing out their mother*
[GRATIANA,] *one by one shoulder, and the other by the other, with*
daggers in their hands.°

VINDICE: O thou for whom no name is bad enough!
GRATIANA: What mean my sons? What, will you murder me?
VINDICE: Wicked, unnatural parent!
HIPPOLITO: Fiend of women!
GRATIANA: Oh! Are sons turned monsters? Help!
VINDICE: In vain.
GRATIANA: Are you so barbarous, to set iron nipples°   5
    Upon the breast that gave you suck?
VINDICE: That breast
    Is turned to quarlèd° poison.
GRATIANA: Cut° not your days for't; am not I your mother?
VINDICE: Thou dost usurp that title now by fraud,
    For in that shell of mother breeds a bawd.   10
GRATIANA: A bawd! O, name far loathsomer than hell!
HIPPOLITO: It should be so, knew'st thou thy office° well.
GRATIANA: I hate it.
VINDICE: Ah, is't possible, you powers on high,
    That women should dissemble° when they die?
GRATIANA: Dissemble?

VINDICE: Did not the duke's son direct   15
    A fellow of the world's condition° hither,
    That did corrupt all that was good in thee,
    Made thee uncivilly° forget thyself
    And work our sister to his lust?
GRATIANA: Who, I?
    That had been monstrous! I defy that man   20
    For any such intent. None lives so pure
    But shall be soiled with slander.
    Good son, believe it not.
VINDICE: O, I'm in doubt
    Whether I'm myself or no! Stay —
    Let me look again upon this face: 25
    Who shall be saved when mothers have no grace?°
HIPPOLITO: 'Twould make one half despair.
VINDICE: I was the man;
    Defy me now! Let's see: do't modestly.
GRATIANA: O, hell unto my soul!
VINDICE: In that disguise, I, sent from the duke's son,   30
    Trièd you, and found you base metal,
    As any villain might have done.
GRATIANA: O no;
    No tongue but yours could have bewitched me so.
VINDICE: O, nimble in damnation, quick in tune:°
    There is no devil could strike fire so soon!   35
    I am confuted in a word.
GRATIANA: O sons,
    Forgive me; to myself I'll prove more true;
    You that should honour me — I kneel to you.   [*She kneels and weeps.*]
VINDICE: A mother to give aim° to her own daughter!
HIPPOLITO: True, brother. How far beyond nature 'tis,   40
    Though many mothers do't.
VINDICE: Nay, and you° draw tears once, go you to bed;
    Wet will make iron blush, and change to red.°
    Brother, it rains; 'twill spoil your dagger, house it.
HIPPOLITO: 'Tis done.   [*They sheath their daggers.*] 45
VINDICE: I' faith, 'tis a sweet shower, it does much good;
    The fruitful grounds and meadows of her soul
    Has° been long dry. Pour down, thou blessed dew.
    Rise, mother; troth, this shower has made you higher.
GRATIANA: O you heavens,   50
    Take this infectious° spot out of my soul!
    I'll rinse it in seven waters of mine eyes;
    Make my tears salt enough to taste of grace.°
    To weep is to our sex naturally given;

But to weep truly — that's a gift from heaven!   55
VINDICE: Nay, I'll kiss you now. Kiss her, brother.
    Let's marry her to our souls, wherein's no lust,
    And honourably love her.
HIPPOLITO: Let it be.   [*Kisses* GRATIANA.]
VINDICE: For honest women are so seld° and rare,
    'Tis good to cherish those poor few that are.   60
    O you of easy wax,° do but imagine,
    Now the disease° has left you, how leprously
    That office would have clinged unto your forehead.°
    All mothers that had any graceful° hue
    Would have worn masks to hide their face at you.   65
    It would have grown to this: at your foul name,
    Green-coloured° maids would have turned red with shame.
HIPPOLITO: And then, our sister full of hire° and baseness —
VINDICE: There had been boiling lead° again!
    The duke's son's great concubine;   70
    A drab of state, a cloth o' silver slut,
    To have her train borne up, and her soul
    Trail i' the dirt: great!
HIPPOLITO: To be miserably great.
    Rich, to be eternally wretched.
VINDICE: O common madness.
    Ask but the thriving'st harlot in cold blood,°   75
    She'd give the world to make her honour good.
    Perhaps you'll say, but only to the duke's son
    In private — why, she first begins with one,
    Who afterward to thousand proves a whore:
    'Break ice in one place, it will crack in more.'   80
GRATIANA: Most certainly applied!
HIPPOLITO: O brother, you forget our business.
VINDICE: And well remembered. Joy's a subtle elf;°
    I think man's happiest when he forgets himself.
    Farewell once dried, now holy-watered mead;°   85
    Our hearts wear feathers that before wore lead.
GRATIANA: I'll give you this: that one I never knew
    Plead better for, and 'gainst the devil, than you.
VINDICE: You make me proud on't.
HIPPOLITO: Commend us in all virtue to our sister.   90
VINDICE: Ay, for the love of heaven, to that true maid.
GRATIANA: With my best words.
VINDICE: Why, that was motherly said.
                    Exeunt [VINDICE *and* HIPPOLITO].
GRATIANA: I wonder now what fury did transport me;
    I feel good thoughts begin to settle in me.

O, with what forehead can I° look on her   95
Whose honour I've so impiously beset?
— And here she comes.

[*Enter* CASTIZA.]

CASTIZA: Now, mother, you have wrought with me so strongly
    That what for° my advancement, as to calm
    The trouble of your tongue, I am content.   100
GRATIANA: Content to what?
CASTIZA: To do as you have wished me,
    To prostitute my breast to the duke's son,
    And put myself to common usury.°
GRATIANA: I hope you will not so.
CASTIZA: Hope you I will not?
    That's not the hope you look to be saved in.   105
GRATIANA: Truth but it is.
CASTIZA: Do not deceive yourself:
    I am, as you, e'en out of marble° wrought.
    What would you now; are ye not pleased yet with me?
    You shall not wish me to be more lascivious
    Than I intend to be.
GRATIANA: Strike not me cold.   110
CASTIZA: How often have you charged me, on your blessing,
    To be a cursèd° woman! When you knew
    Your blessing had no force to make me lewd,
    You laid your curse upon me. That did more.
    The mother's curse is heavy; where that fights,   115
    Sons° set in storm, and daughters lose their lights.°
GRATIANA: Good child, dear maid, if there be any spark
    Of heavenly intellectual° fire within thee,
    O let my breath revive it to a flame.
    Put not all out with woman's wilful follies,   120
    I am recovered of that foul disease
    That haunts too many mothers; kind,° forgive me,
    Make me not sick in health. If then
    My words prevailed when they were wickedness,
    How much more now, when they are just and good!   125
CASTIZA: I wonder what you mean. Are not you she
    For whose infect° persuasions I could scarce
    Kneel out my prayers, and had much ado
    In three hours' reading to untwist so much
    Of the black serpent as you wound about me?   130
GRATIANA: 'Tis unfruitful, held tedious, to repeat what's past:
    I'm now your present mother.°

CASTIZA: Push, now 'tis too late.
GRATIANA: Bethink° again, thou know'st not what thou say'st.
CASTIZA: No? Deny advancement, treasure, the duke's son?
GRATIANA: O see, I spoke those words, and now they poison me: 135
    What will the deed do then?
    Advancement? True: as high as shame can pitch.°
    For treasure? Who e'er knew a harlot rich,
    Or could build by the purchase° of her sin
    An hospital° to keep their bastards in?   140
    The duke's son? O, when women are young courtiers
    They are sure to be old beggars;
     To know the miseries most harlots taste,
    Thou'd'st wish thyself unborn when thou art unchaste.
CASTIZA: O mother, let me twine about your neck,   145
    And kiss you till my soul melt on your lips:
    I did but this to try you.
GRATIANA: O, speak truth!
CASTIZA: Indeed I did not; for no tongue has force
    To alter me from honest.
    If maidens would°, men's words could have no power;   150
    A virgin honour is a crystal tower,
    Which being weak is guarded with good spirits:
    Until she basely yields no ill inherits.°
GRATIANA: O happy child ! Faith, and thy birth, hath saved me.
    'Mongst thousand daughters happiest° of all others!   155
    Be thou a glass° for maids, and I for mothers.   *Exeunt.*

Act Five, Scene One

Enter VINDICE *and* HIPPOLITO [*with the duke's body* °*dressed in*
VINDICE'S *former disguise*].

VINDICE: So, so, he leans well; take heed you wake him not, brother.
HIPPOLITO: I warrant you, my life for yours.
VINDICE: That's a good lay,° for I must kill myself! [*Points to corpse*]
    Brother, that's I;° that sits for me; do you mark it. And I must stand
    ready here to make away myself yonder; I must sit to be killed, and   5
    stand to kill myself. I could vary it not so little as thrice over again;
    't'as° some eight returns, like Michaelmas term.
HIPPOLITO: That's enow,° o' conscience.
VINDICE: But sirrah, does the duke's son come single?
HIPPOLITO: No, there's the hell on't. His faith's° too feeble to go alone.   10
    He brings flesh-flies° after him, that will buzz against supper time,
    and hum for his coming out.

VINDICE: Ah, the fly-flop° of vengeance beat 'em to pieces! Here was the
      sweetest occasion, the fittest hour to have made my revenge
      familiar° with him: shown him the body of the duke his father, and   15
      how quaintly° he died, like a politician in hugger-mugger;° made
      no man acquainted with it, and in catastrophe° slain him over his
      father's breast! And, O, I'm mad to lose such a sweet opportunity.
HIPPOLITO: Nay push, prithee be content! There's no remedy present;
      may not hereafter times open in as fair faces as this?   20
VINDICE: They may, if they can paint so well.
HIPPOLITO: Come now, to avoid all suspicion let's forsake this room,
      and be going to meet the duke's son.
VINDICE: Content; I'm for any weather. Heart, step close;° here he
      comes!   25

                       Enter LUSSURIOSO.

HIPPOLITO: My honoured lord.
LUSSURIOSO: O me — you both present.
VINDICE: E'en newly, my lord, just as your lordship entered now. About
      this place we had notice given he should be, but in some loathsome
      plight or other.
HIPPOLITO: Came your honour private?   30
LUSSURIOSO: Private enough for this. Only a few
      Attend my coming out.
HIPPOLITO [*aside*]:   Death rot those few!
LUSSURIOSO: Stay — yonder's the slave.
VINDICE: Mass, there's the slave indeed, my lord;
      [*Aside*] 'Tis a good child, he calls his father slave!   35
LUSSURIOSO: Ay, that's the villain, the damned villain! Softly,
      Tread easy.
VINDICE: Puh, I warrant you my lord,
      We'll stifle in our breaths.
LUSSURIOSO: That will do well.
      Base rogue thou sleep'st thy last! [*Aside*] 'Tis policy
      To have him killed in's sleep, for if he waked   40
      He would betray all to them.
VINDICE: But my lord —
LUSSURIOSO: Ha? What say'st?
VINDICE: Shall we kill him now he's drunk?
LUSSURIOSO: Ay, best of all.
VINDICE: Why then he will ne'er live
      To be sober.
LUSSURIOSO: No matter; let him reel to hell.
VINDICE: But being so full of liquor, I fear he will   45
      Put out all the fire!

LUSSURIOSO: Thou art a mad beast!
VINDICE [*aside*]: And leave none to warm your lordship's gols° withall.
    — For he that dies drunk, falls into hell-fire
    Like a bucket o' water: qush, qush.
LUSSURIOSO: Come,
    Be ready, nake° your swords, think of your wrongs.   50
    This slave has injured you.
VINDICE: Troth so he has,
    [*Aside*] And he has paid well for't.
LUSSURIOSO: Meet with° him now.
VINDICE: You'll bear us out,° my lord?
LUSSURIOSO: Puh, am I a lord for nothing, think you?
    Quickly now!
VINDICE: Sa, sa, sa,° thump! [VINDICE *and* HIPPOLITO *stab the*
    body] There he lies!   55
LUSSURIOSO: Nimbly done. [*Approaches the corpse*] Ha! O villains, murderers,
    'Tis the old duke, my father!
VINDICE [*aside*]:   That's a jest.
LUSSURIOSO: What, stiff and cold already?
    O pardon me to call you from your names;°
    'Tis none of your deed. That villain Piato,   60
    Whom you thought now to kill, has murdered him,
    And left him thus disguised.
HIPPOLITO: And not unlikely.
VINDICE: O, rascal! Was he not ashamed
    To put the duke into a greasy doublet?
LUSSURIOSO: He has been cold and stiff — who knows how long?   65
VINDICE [*aside*]: Marry, that do I!
LUSSURIOSO: No words, I pray, of anything intended.
VINDICE: O, my lord.
HIPPOLITO: I would fain have your lordship think that we have small
    reason to prate.°   70
LUSSURIOSO: Faith, thou sayest true. I'll forthwith send to court
    For all the nobles, bastard, duchess, all —
    How here, by miracle, we found him dead,
    And, in his raiment,° that foul villain fled.
VINDICE: That will be the best way, my lord, to clear us all; let's cast   75
    about° to be clear.°
LUSSURIOSO: Ho! Nencio, Sordido, and the rest!

Enter [NENCIO, SORDIDO *and*] *all* [*his* Attendants].

SORDIDO: My lord.
NENCIO: My lord.
LUSSURIOSO: Be witnesses of a strange spectacle.

Choosing for private conference that sad room,
We found the duke my father 'gealed° in blood.   80
SORDIDO: My lord the duke! Run, hie thee, Nencio!
    Startle the court by signifying so much.   [*Exit* NENCIO.]
VINDICE [*aside*]: This much by wit a deep revenger can:°
    When murder's known, to be the clearest man.
    We're farthest off, and with as bold an eye   85
    Survey his body as the standers-by.
LUSSURIOSO: My royal father, too basely let blood
    By a malevolent slave!
HIPPOLITO [*aside*]:   Hark! He calls thee
    Slave again.
VINDICE [*aside*]: H'as lost, he may!
LUSSURIOSO: O sight!
    Look hither, see, his lips are gnawn with poison!   90
VINDICE: How? His lips? By the Mass, they be!
LUSSURIOSO: O villain! O rogue! O slave! O rascal!
HIPPOLITO [*aside*]: O good deceit; he quits him° with like terms.
1 VOICE WITHIN: Where?
2 VOICE WITHIN: Which way?   95

[*Enter* AMBITIOSO *and* SUPERVACUO *with* NOBLES *and* GENTLEMEN.]

AMBITIOSO: Over what roof hangs this prodigious comet°
    In deadly fire?
LUSSURIOSO: Behold, behold, my lords.
    The duke my father's murdered by a vassal
    That owes° this habit, and here left disguised.

[*Enter the* DUCHESS *and* SPURIO.]

DUCHESS: My lord and husband!
2 NOBLE: Reverend majesty.   100
1 NOBLE: I have seen these clothes often attending on him.
VINDICE [*aside*]: That nobleman has been in the country, for he does not
    lie.°
SUPERVACUO [*aside*]: Learn of our mother — let's dissemble too!
    I am glad he's vanished: so I hope are you.
AMBITIOSO [*aside*]: Ay, you may take my word for't.
SPURIO: Old dad dead?   105
    Ay, one of his cast sins will send the fates
    Most hearty commendations by his own son.
    I'll tug° in the new stream, till strength be done.
LUSSURIOSO: Where be those two that did affirm to us
    My lord the duke was privately rid forth?   110

1 [GENTLEMAN]: O pardon us, my lords, he gave that charge,
　　Upon our lives, if he were missed at court,
　　To answer so. He rode not anywhere,
　　We left him private with that fellow, here.
VINDICE [*aside*]: Confirmed.°
LUSSURIOSO: 　　　　　　　O heavens, that false charge was his death.　115
　　Impudent beggars! Durst you to our face
　　Maintain such a false answer? Bear him straight
　　To execution.
1 [GENTLEMAN]: 　My lord!
LUSSURIOSO: 　　　　　　Urge me no more.
　　In this, the excuse may be called half the murder.
VINDICE [*aside*]: You've sentenced well.
LUSSURIOSO: 　　　　　　　　　Away, see it be done.　　120
　　　　　　　　　　　[*Exit* 1 GENTLEMAN *under guard.*]
VINDICE [*aside*]: Could you not stick?° See what confession doth.
　　Who would not lie when men are hanged for truth?
HIPPOLITO [*aside*]: Brother, how happy° is our vengeance!
VINDICE [*aside*]: 　　　　　　　　　　　Why, it hits
　　Past the apprehension of indifferent wits.°
LUSSURIOSO: My lord, let post-horse be sent into all places　125
　　To entrap the villain.
VINDICE [*aside*]: 　　　　Post-horse!° Ha, ha!
[1] NOBLE: My lord, we're something bold to know our duty.
　　Your father's accidentally departed;°
　　The titles that were due to him meet you.
LUSSURIOSO: Meet me? I'm not at leisure, my good lord;　　130
　　I've many griefs to dispatch out o' the way. —
　　[*Aside*] Welcome, sweet titles! — Talk to me, my lords,
　　Of sepulchres and mighty emperors' bones;
　　That's thought for me.
VINDICE [*aside*]: 　　　　So, one may see by this
　　How foreign° markets go.　　　　　　　　　135
　　Courtiers have feet o' the nines and tongues o' the twelves;°
　　They flatter dukes, and dukes flatter themselves.
[2] NOBLE: My lord, it is your shine must comfort us.
LUSSURIOSO: Alas, I shine in tears like the sun in April.°
[1] NOBLE: You're now my lord's Grace.　　　　　140
LUSSURIOSO: My lord's Grace? I perceive you'll have it so.
[2] NOBLE: 'Tis but your own.
LUSSURIOSO: Then heavens give me grace to be so.
VINDICE [*aside*]: He prays well for himself!
[1] NOBLE: 　　　　　　　Madam, all sorrows
　　Must run their circles into joys. No doubt but time　145
　　Will make the murderer bring forth himself.

VINDICE [*aside*]: He were an ass then, i' faith!

[1] NOBLE: In the mean season
    Let us bethink° the latest funeral honours
    Due to the duke's cold body, and, withall
    Calling to memory our new happiness   150
    Spread in his royal son, — lords, gentlemen,
    Prepare for revels!

VINDICE [*aside*]:   Revels!

[1] NOBLE: Time hath several falls:°
    Griefs lift up joys, feasts put down funerals.

LUSSURIOSO: Come then, my lords, my favours to you all.
    [*aside*] The duchess is suspected foully bent;   155
    I'll begin dukedom with her banishment.
                             Exeunt [LUSSURIOSO], NOBLES *and* DUCHESS.

HIPPOLITO [*aside*]: Revels!

VINDICE [*aside*]:   Ay, that's the word. We are firm° yet:
    Strike one strain more, and then we crown our wit.°
                         Exeunt [VINDICE *and* HIPPOLITO].

SPURIO [*aside*]: Well, have at° the fairest mark —°
    So said the duke when he begot me —   160
    And if I miss his heart, or near about,
    Then have at° any; a bastard scorns to be out.   [*Exit.*]

SUPERVACUO: Not'st thou that Spurio, brother?

AMBITIOSO: Yes I note him, to our shame.

SUPERVACUO: We shall not live: his hair shall not grow much longer.   165
    In this time of revels tricks may be set afoot.
    Seest thou yon new moon? It shall outlive the new duke by much.
    This hand shall dispossess him, then we're mighty.
    A mask° is treason's licence: that build upon;
    'Tis murder's best face, when a vizard's on!   *Exit* SUPERVACUO. 170

AMBITIOSO: Is't so? 'Tis very good:
    And do you think to be duke then, kind brother?
    I'll see fair play: drop one, and there lies t'other.   *Exit* AMBITIOSO.

Act Five, Scene Two

Enter VINDICE *and* HIPPOLITO, *with* PIERO *and other* LORDS.

VINDICE: My lords, be all of music!°
    Strike° old griefs into other countries,
    That flow in too much milk and have faint livers,°
    Not daring to stab home their discontents.

Let our hid flames break out as fire, as lightning,   5
To blast this villainous dukedom vexed with sin;
Wind up your souls to their full height again.
PIERO: How?
1 LORD: Which way?
[2] LORD: Any way! Our wrongs are such,
We cannot justly be revenged too much.
VINDICE: You shall have all enough. Revels are toward,°   10
And those few nobles that have long suppressed you
Are busied to the furnishing of a masque
And do affect° to make a pleasant tale on't.
The masquing suits are fashioning; now comes in
That which must glad us all: we to take pattern   15
Of all those suits, the colour, trimming, fashion,
E'en to an undistinguished hair almost.
Then, entering first, observing the true form,°
Within a strain° or two we shall find leisure
To steal our swords out handsomely,   20
And when they think their pleasure sweet and good,
In midst of all their joys they shall sigh blood.
PIERO: Weightily, effectually!
3 LORD: Before the t'other° maskers come —
VINDICE: We're gone, all done and past.   25
PIERO: But how for the duke's guard?
VINDICE: Let that alone:
By one and one their strengths shall be drunk down.°
HIPPOLITO: There are five hundred gentlemen in the action,
That will apply themselves, and not stand idle.
PIERO: O let us hug your bosoms!
VINDICE: Come, my lords,   30
Prepare for deeds; let other times have words.   *Exeunt.*

Act Five, Scene Three

In a dumb show, the possessing of the young duke [LUSSURIOSO]
with all his NOBLES; then sounding music, a furnished table is
brought forth, then enters [LUSSURIOSO] and his NOBLES to the
banquet. A blazing star appeareth.°

1 NOBLE: Many harmonious hours and choicest pleasures
Fill up the royal numbers of your years.
LUSSURIOSO: My lords, we're pleased to thank you — though we know
'Tis but your duty now to wish it so.
[2] NOBLE: That shine° makes us all happy.

3 NOBLE [*aside*]:   His grace frowns.   5
2 NOBLE [*aside*]: Yet we must say he smiles.
1 NOBLE [*aside*]:   I think we must.
LUSSURIOSO [*aside*]: That foul incontinent° duchess we have banished;
    The bastard shall not live. After these revels
    I'll begin strange ones: he and the stepsons
    Shall pay their lives for the first subsidies.°   10
    We must not frown so soon, else 't'ad been now.
1 NOBLE: My gracious lord, please you prepare for pleasure;
    The masque is not far off.
LUSSURIOSO: We are for pleasure.   [*He sees the star.*]
    Beshrew thee, what art thou? Madest me start!
    Thou hast committed treason! — A blazing star!°   15
1 NOBLE: A blazing star? O where, my lord?
LUSSURIOSO: Spy out.°
2 NOBLE: See, see, my lords, a wondrous dreadful one!
LUSSURIOSO: I am not pleased at that ill-knotted fire,
    That bushing,° flaring star. Am not I duke?
    It should not quake° me now. Had it appeared   20
    Before it, I might then have justly feared:
    But yet they say, whom art and learning weds,°
    When stars wear locks° they threaten great men's heads.
    Is it so? You are read,° my lords.
1 NOBLE: May it please your Grace,
    It shows great anger.
LUSSURIOSO: That does not please our Grace.   25
2 NOBLE: Yet here's the comfort, my lord: many times,
    When it seems most,° it threatens farthest off.
LUSSURIOSO: Faith, and I think so too.
1 NOBLE: Beside, my lord,
    You're gracefully° established with the loves
    Of all your subjects; and for natural death,   30
    I hope it will be threescore years a-coming.
LUSSURIOSO: True. — No more but threescore years?
1 NOBLE: Fourscore I hope, my lord.
2 NOBLE: And fivescore, I.
3 NOBLE: But 'tis my hope, my lord, you shall ne'er die.
LUSSURIOSO: Give me thy hand; these others I rebuke.   35
    He that hopes so, is fittest° for a duke.
    Thou shalt sit next me. Take your places, lords,
    We're ready now for sports, let 'em set on.   [*Looks at the blazing star.*]
    You thing! We shall forget you quite anon.°
3 NOBLE: I hear 'em coming, my lord.

*Enter the masque of revengers (the two brothers [*VINDICE *and*
HIPPOLITO], *and two* LORDS *more*).

LUSSURIOSO: Ah, tis well!   40
  [*aside*] Brothers, and bastard, you dance next in hell!

*The revengers dance. At the end [they] steal out° their swords, and
these four kill the four at the table, in their chairs. It thunders.°*

VINDICE: Mark, thunder! Dost know thy cue, thou big-voiced crier?
  Duke's groans are thunder's watchwords.
HIPPOLITO: So, my lords,
  You have enough.
VINDICE: Come, let's away; no ling'ring.
HIPPOLITO: Follow — Go!   45
                                          Exeunt [all but VINDICE].
VINDICE: No power is angry when the lustful die;
  When thunder claps,° heaven likes the tragedy.   *Exit.*
LUSSURIOSO: Oh, oh!

*Enter the other masque of intended murderers, stepsons [*AMBITIOSO
and SUPERVACUO], *bastard [*SPURIO], *and a fourth man, coming in
dancing. [*LUSSURIOSO] *recovers a little in voice and groans; calls 'A
guard! Treason!' at which they all start out of their measure, and
turning towards the table they find them all to be murdered.*

SPURIO: Whose groan was that?
LUSSURIOSO: Treason! A guard!
AMBITIOSO: How now! All murdered!
SUPERVACUO: Murdered!
4 LORD: And those his nobles?
AMBITIOSO [*aside*]:   Here's a labour saved;   50
  I thought to have sped° him. 'Sblood, how came this?
[SUPERVACUO:] Then I proclaim myself. Now I am duke.
AMBITIOSO: Thou duke? Brother, thou liest.   [*He slays* SUPERVACUO.]
SPURIO: Slave! So dost thou.
                                          [*He slays* AMBITIOSO.]
4 LORD: Base villain, hast thou slain my lord and master?
                                          [*He slays* SPURIO.]

*Enter the first men [*VINDICE, HIPPOLITO *and the two* LORDS].

VINDICE: Pistols! treason! murder! help! guard   55
  My lord the duke!

[*Enter* ANTONIO *and* Guard].

HIPPOLITO: Lay hold upon these traitors!   [*Guard seizes* 4 LORD.]
LUSSURIOSO: O!
VINDICE: Alas, the duke is murdered.
HIPPOLITO: And the nobles.
VINDICE: Surgeons, surgeons! — [*Aside*] Heart, does he breathe so long?
ANTONIO: A piteous tragedy, able to make
     An old man's eyes bloodshot.°
LUSSURIOSO: O!   60
VINDICE: Look to my lord the duke. [*Aside*] A vengeance throttle him! —
     Confess thou murderous and unhallowed man,
     Didst thou kill all these?
4 LORD: None but the bastard, I.
VINDICE: How came the duke slain, then?
4 LORD: We found him so.
LUSSURIOSO: O, villain!
VINDICE: Hark.
LUSSURIOSO: Those in the masque did murder us.   65
VINDICE: Law you° now, sir:
     O marble impudence! will you confess now?
4 LORD: 'Sblood, 'tis all false!
ANTONIO: Away with that foul monster,
     Dipped in a prince's blood.
4 LORD: Heart, 'tis a lie!
ANTONIO: Let him have bitter° execution.   [*Exit* 4 LORD *guarded.*] 70
VINDICE [*aside*]: New marrow!° No, I cannot be expressed. —°
     How fares my lord the duke?
LUSSURIOSO: Farewell to all;
     He that climbs highest has the greatest fall.
     My tongue is out of office.
VINDICE: Air, gentlemen, air. —
     [*Whispers to* LUSSORIOSO] Now thou'lt not prate on't,° 'twas Vindice
     murdered thee!   75
LUSSURIOSO: O!
VINDICE: Murdered thy father!
LUSSURIOSO: O!
VINDICE: And I am he!
     Tell nobody. [LUSSURIOSO *dies*] — So, so. The duke's departed.°
ANTONIO: It was a deadly hand that wounded him;
     The rest, ambitious who should rule and sway
     After his death, were so made all away.   80
VINDICE: My lord was unlikely.°
HIPPOLITO: Now the hope
     Of Italy lies in your° reverend years.
VINDICE: Your hair will make the silver age° again,
     When there was fewer, but more honest men.

ANTONIO: The burden's weighty, and will press age down;   85
    May I so rule that heaven may keep° the crown.
VINDICE: The rape of your good lady has been 'quited°
    With death on death.
ANTONIO: Just is the law above.
    But of all things it puts me most to wonder
    How the old duke came murdered.
VINDICE: O, my lord.   90
ANTONIO: It was the strangeliest carried;° I not heard of the like.
HIPPOLITO: 'Twas all done for the best, my lord.
VINDICE: All for your Grace's good. We may be bold
    To speak it now: 'twas somewhat witty° carried,
    Though we say it. 'Twas we two murdered him!
ANTONIO: You two?   95
VINDICE: None else, i' faith, my lord. Nay 'twas well managed.
ANTONIO: Lay hands upon those villains.
VINDICE: How? On us?
ANTONIO: Bear 'em to speedy execution.
VINDICE: Heart! Was't not for your good, my lord?
ANTONIO: My good!
    Away with 'em! Such an old man as he;   100
    You that would murder him would murder me.
VINDICE: Is't come about?°
HIPPOLITO: 'Sfoot, brother, you begun.
VINDICE: May not we set as well as the duke's son?°
    Thou hast no conscience;° are we not revenged?
    Is there one enemy left alive amongst those?   105
    'Tis time to die, when we are ourselves our foes.
    When murderers shut deeds close this curse does seal 'em:
    If none disclose 'em, they themselves reveal 'em.
    This murder might have slept in tongueless brass°
    But for ourselves, and the world died an ass.   110
    Now I remember too, here was Piato
    Brought forth a knavish sentence° once:
    No doubt — said he — but time will make
    The murderer bring forth himself.
    'Tis well he died, he was a witch!°   115
    And now, my lord, since we are in° for ever,
    This work was ours, which else might have been slipped;°
    And, if we list,° we could have nobles clipped,°
    And go for° less than beggars. But we hate
    To bleed° so cowardly. We have enough, I' faith.   120
    We're well; our mother turned,° our sister true,
    We die after a nest of dukes! Adieu.
                Exeunt [VINDICE *and* HIPPOLITO, *guarded*].

ANTONIO: How subtly was that murder closed!° Bear up
　　Those tragic bodies; 'tis a heavy° season.
　　Pray heaven their blood may wash away all treason.　　[*Exeunt.*]　125

Finis

Notes to the Play

Dramatis Personae

2 LUSSORIOSO: 'lecherous, luxurious'

3 SPURIO: 'bastard, false'

4 AMBITIOSO: 'ambitious, seeking honour'

5 SUPERVACUO: 'superfluous, vain, useless'

7 VINDICE: 'revenger of wrongs'
PIATO: 'lying low, covered, hidden'

8 HIPPOLITO (also once named Carlo, see note to 1.1.108): The name may have been suggested by Hippolytus, the chaste young hero of tragedies by Euripides and Seneca, who resists seduction by his amorous step-mother. Seneca's play is quoted at 1.4.23.

11 NENCIO: 'fool, idiot'

12 SORDIDO: 'covetous wretch'

13 DONDOLO: 'foolish gull'

16 CASTIZA: 'chaste'

17 GRATIANA: 'full of grace, pardoned'

Act One, Scene One

1 grey-haired adultery: the old duke, as a personification of his own sin

4 do: copulate

5 characters: exemplary moral types

7 heat: with moisture the essential quality of a living body; contrasted with the heat (*infernal fires*) of lust

8 spendthrift veins: Since much blood was thought to be needed to produce semen, frequent intercourse was considered damaging to health.
dry: withered with age and disease

9 luxur: lecher

11 riot it: live extravagantly, recklessly

13 fret: agitation; with a play on the ring of gut used to mark out finger positions on a stringed instrument

14 sallow picture: the skull Vindice carries

15 study's ornament: a skull was a familiar symbol of the vanity of life and reminder of death. Vindice may refer to his room or his meditations on death.

19 heaven-pointed: directed towards heaven (cf. line 111)

20 unsightly: (1) ugly; (2) unseeing. The skull's empty eye-sockets are visualised as finger-rings set with jewel-like eyes.

27 patrimony: inherited wealth and property

28 years: pronounced as two syllables
told: counted in coin

29 cold: lacking passionate desire

34 palsy-lust: senile desire; a *palsy* was a shivering fever

36 Out-bid: overrated

37 vicious: trisyllabic

39 quit-rent: repayment; literally rent paid to a landlord in lieu of services

42 determined: judged

44 kept touch: kept her promise

45 thou terror: the fleshless skull, representing death

46 three-piled: fat, like best quality, thick velvet

48 great: (1) large; (2) important

50 vizard: face mask

52 braver: more splendidly dressed

55 bald: Opportunity was commonly imaged as a woman bald except for a forelock, to be seized at once or lost forever (cf. line 100).

56 happy: fortunate

62 hap: luck

69 policy: craft

71 wit: intelligence

71–2 keep...up: shut up securely (as in a castle keep)

76 strange-digested: oddly disposed

78 grooms: menial servants

79 blood: active, high-spirited person

81　base-coined: false (like counterfeit money) and immoral

82　reach: understand

85　vild: vilely

86　should be: would have to be

87　insurrection: (1) rising (in a physical sense); (2) revolt against the control of reason

91　spoke: described

93　put on: disguise myself as

94　right: (1) honest (spoken ironically); (2) right for the times

97　prefer: advance, bring forward

98　Occasion: opportunity

100　fast: tightly

101　French mole: syphilis (known as 'the French disease'), which causes loss of hair (as a mole destroys a lawn by tunnelling underneath it).

102　habit: costume
　　quaintly: ingeniously, finely

103　coin: (1) make counterfeit money; (2) pretend

106–7　Only...belief: With one exception, that, being women, they are credulous.

108　Carlo: This name for the character otherwise known as Hippolito may survive from the author's first draft for the play.

110　played: carried out, performed

113　If: even if
　　hopes: heirs to the throne

115　law's a woman: alluding to the figure of Justice as a blindfolded woman holding scales and a sword

117　travel: The original spelling (*travaile*) allows a pun on travel/work.

120　compelled: forced on me

123　estate: rank

124　deject: humble, deprive of high rank

129　secretary: confidant

132　wives: (1) women; (2) wives
　　feed: (1) satisfy their sexual appetites; (2) exploit their partner

Act One, Scene Two

4　forehead: brow (perceived as the seat of honour and shame, or shamelessness). Compare Revelation 17:5, where the shameful name of the Whore of Babylon is written 'upon her forehead'.

5　envious: malicious

10　closest: most secret

11　silver years: alluding to his white hair

13　insculption: carved inscription

14　'bowelled: disembowelled (in preparation for embalming)

15　cered: sealed in by being wrapped in cerecloths, or waxed winding sheets

19　doom: sentence

20　fact: crime

24　son-in-law: (1) stepson; (2) son, in a legal sense

29　Gilt: guilded, overlaid

36　corse: corpse

39　low metal: poor worth

41　doom: judgement

42　attempt: assault

46　general-honest: always chaste and upright

49　jest: joke about

50　law...serpent: alluding to Christ's injunction to his disciples, 'be ye therefore wise as serpents' (Matthew 10:16)

54　troth: truly, indeed

60　done: (1) finished with; (2) performed sexually

62　live: go on living; with the implication that he had to 'die' in the act of sexual intercourse. There is also an allusion to the story of the hunter Actaeon, who as a punishment for seeing the goddess Diana bathing was torn apart by his own hounds.

65　ceased: (1) deprived of life; (2) sentenced (assessed)

66　sport: (1) sexual pleasure; (2) a mere game

68　slip: (1) slide out; (2) be released (as hunting dogs were let slip)

75　performance: sexual activity

78	be abed: sit in bed, delay
79	wrongs: dishonours
80	too much right: excessive authority
86	makes for thee: works in your favour
96	easy: conniving
98	keep: attend (by being buried in the church)
100	at meat: while eating
104	durance: imprisonment
108	kill...forehead: kill him with grief by being unfaithful to him. The betrayed husband proverbially sprouted horns from his forehead.
114	kind: loving
122	ceremony: ceremonious respect
124	hatted dame: lower-class woman (such women were by law bound to wear hats to support their manufacture). Noblewomen did not wear hats.
125	But that: were it not that
130	't'as: it has
132	falsely: illegitimately
133	hard: difficult (with a *double entendre*, introducing a series of such sexual allusions)
137	ride a horse: sexual slang for 'engage in intercourse'
138–9	he...windows: he was so tall (also, 'with such a long penis') he could intrude on the private behaviour of people on holiday by looking over half-shuttered windows.
140	'light: dismount afoot: (1) on foot; (2) engaged in sexual intercourse
141	penthouse: (1) projecting upper storey of an Elizabethan house; (2) female genitals
142	check the signs: knock against the shop-sign boards hung out over the street (including the shaving basins used as such signs by barbers).
144	I...beggar: that is, like a beggar on horseback, who proverbially would 'ride' a gallop.
146	stand firm: be firmly established (with an allusion to male sexual erection)
148	bid fair: tried hard

149	cut...diamond: fashioned you as his legitimate son
152	collet: ring socket to hold a precious stone
155	of: on
157	injure: injury
161	the seventh commandment: the biblical prohibition against adultery (Exodus 20:1–17). 'Commandment' (spelled 'commandement' in the quarto) is pronounced as four syllables.
164	to: as
165	mad: madden make...rough: rouse the blood to anger
173	Earnest: foretaste, pledge (of more kisses)
176	arm: furnish (with heraldic arms); cf. line 201. woman's heraldry: horns, the sign of female deception (see line 108 and note)
180	stirring: aphrodisiac
183	Their tongues...heels: 'Their speech as wanton and agile as their bodies.' A licentious woman was described as 'short-heeled', so quick to 'fall'.
184–5	when...again: they were ready to lie with one man after another
193	mischief: wickedness
196	only: one legitimate
202	cuckolds: deceived husbands

Act One, Scene Three

1	far...myself: sufficiently disguised
3	wist: knew
9	turn: transform
14	get: acquire (as lovers' gifts)
16	Grace the bawd: possibly referring to an actual contemporary woman
17	reach...verge: go beyond the lawful limit
18	'Sfoot: by God's foot!
19	doubted: suspected
22	siftings: close questioning
23	rare: excellent
24–5	Time...hair: Time, like Occasion, was imaged as bald-headed.
28	blanks: worthless because

unvalidated documents, or metal blanks not yet stamped as current coin, or lottery tickets which fail to win prizes

31   give us leave: leave us

32   Push: Pish!

34   musk-cat: perfumed courtier or courtesan

37   ague: fever

40   remember me: remember my rank

41   conster: construe

46   scrivener: secretary, agent

47   Fool: foolish servant

49   not so little: to more than such petty wickedness

50   washed a-pieces: destroyed (as by a rough sea)

54   gravel a petition: serve as sand to dry the ink on a legal document seeking to recover lost property

57   Dutch: drunken, from the reputation of the Dutch, or Germans (the term could mean either), for 'fulsome' (excessive) drinking and lust.

60   cling: sexually embrace

63   rim: (1) edge, limit; (2) womb

70   Judas: one of the twelve disciples of Christ, and his betrayer

73   gaped: Hell was imaged as a beast-head with vast open mouth

74   Lucifer fell: Pride brought about Satan's fall from heaven.

76   estates: ranks and kinds of people

77   near employment: task intimately concerning me

80   o' the mother: (1) of talking too much (hysteria was known as 'the mother'); (2) from my mother

81   close: secretive

84   Your...morning: Doctors regularly examined their patients' urine to check their state of health.

85   confimed in me: established in my trust

86   enter: (1) record; (2) admit. The idea of demonic possession is also present.

Indian: from the West Indies, proverbial as a source of wealth

88   prevents: prevents, and anticipates

entering: admitting

93   waxed lines: sealed letters or poems

neatest spirit: purest ardour

98   phoenix: mythical Arabian bird, fabled to be the only one of its kind

99   repugnant: resistant

101   blood: family status

104   friend: mistress

110   luxurious day: licentious times

112   cozen: defraud, beguile

113   Enter...soul: take possession of, dispossess her of her soul's dowry. Lussorioso's speech continues to play on the legal, commercial and sexual senses of the idea of 'capture'. portion: birthright

115   expense: expenditure

118   given...tang: caught its very flavour

120   move it: urge Lussorioso's suit

123   raise: (1) lift up; (2) advance to higher rank

126   walk aside: Vindice turns away to privately express his horror.

129   bodkin: long hair-pin, or pointed instrument used to pierce holes in cloth

131   put you in: give you an opportunity to court her (with a secondary sexual sense)

137   close: hidden, secluded

138   simple age: innocent, foolish stage of life

141   wind up: incite

143   work: manipulate

153   puny: novice

155   name: title of bawd

164   'slud: by God's blood

166   Attend me: be my servant

169   fellows: partners

171   foul: debauch

179   overwraught: won over

183   touch: test

184   blood: (chaste) disposition

Act One, Scene Four

0 SD	*discovering*: revealing
4	glorious: overweening
14	confection: medicinal preservative
17	*Melius...vivere*: 'Better to die in virtue than live dishonoured.'
23	*Curae...stupent*: An inaccurate quotation from Seneca's play *Hippolytus*: 'small cares speak out, great griefs are silent'.
29	Putting...own: Masks were worn by participants in such courtly entertainments (cf. line 41).
31	moth: consumer, destroyer
32	room: place
33	wearing: apparel; metaphorically Antonio's honour and happiness
40	for relation: to complete my story
42	harried: raped
43	of both kinds: of themselves and their victims, or of both men and women
49	empress: (1) empress; (2) emblem of morality (*impressa*)
52	doom: sentence
71	court it: be shown at court

Act Two, Scene One

1	hardly...beset: fiercely besieged (by temptation)
3	child's-part: inheritance
8 SD	DONDOLO: There is a similar character, a 'bald fool', in Marston's play *The Fawn* (1606).
21	show myself: show off my capabilities place: office gentle-man usher: a gentleman attending on one of higher rank still
22	fancy: imagination
25	affects: loves
40	box: (1) blow; (2) sweeting-smelling box of perfumes
41	drawn-work cuff: (1) the mark left by Castiza's blow; (2) cuff decorated with patterned threads

43	take the wall: take superiority; from the practice of walking the narrow city streets where the inner wall-side was the safer, cleaner one
44	above my tongue: speechless (with joy)
52	siren's tongue: Sirens were fabulous creatures, part woman, part bird, whose singing lured sailors to destruction.
53	Mass: by the Mass!
55	next of Italy: heir to the dukedom
60	tide: moment, hour
63	save: except
65	seen in't: not be observed doing it
66	Marry: by the Virgin Mary!
69	this wheel: suggesting the turning of the Wheel of Fortune, bringing good luck.
71	white: white-headed, aged
79	vex: afflict, by adding to it
85	angels: (1) angelic spirits; (2) gold coins (which bore the figure of St Michael)
90	dejected: abased
92	Spring : grow, rise in rank
94	state: social rank
97	Take coach: Coaches were the privilege of only the most wealthy.
98	men after men: a crowd of servants
102	bring you home: make you wealthy
107	nearly: closely bate: diminish
109	my... edge: my eagerness is blunted
110	unmothered: lost her maternal feelings venture: Pronounced to rhyme with 'enter' in the following line.
123	the mother: (1) hysteria (thought of as a disease arising from displacement of the womb); (2) maternal affection and concern
126–8	with...myself: An inversion of Christ's miraculous healing of a blind man (Mark 8:22–6)
129	this: Gratiana either kisses

130 madam: (1) title of respect; (2) brothel-manager

131 move: persuade

136 dam: A contemptuous term for 'mother'; the phrase 'the Devil's dam' was used of a witch or an evil woman.

137 makes: is up to

142 honest: chaste

146 better: socially superior, with a play on morally superior

151 While...shades: 'While other women embrace the warmth of the life-giving sun (a common image for a human ruler), virgins embrace 'shadows' (that is, unreality, or possibly the spirits of the dead).'

153 come...fee: freely take possession of the 'paradise' (of sexual pleasure) within you (because only a man can provide the means)

159 coy: disdainful

163 I owe...hand: I should slap your face

168 ashore: from the shore

169 Gold...poor: the idea is that there would be an oversupply of virginity, and too few normal (sexual) transactions.

177 honesty: chastity

180 keep: support, maintain

181 keep less charge: (1) pay less heed; (2) incur less expense

182 intends: determines

187 petitionary people: those who bring requests to court

189 ravished: (1) carried away with delight; (2) raped

194 stirring meats: aphrodisiac foods

196 quicken: (1) stimulate; (2) impregnate

197 abroad: outside

198–9 Jacobean men commonly wore hats indoors, removing them in the presence of social superiors (cf. 3.5.34). Vindice suggests that their inferiority extended to the surrender of their wives ('hats') to the sexual embraces of greater men.

204 an: if

205 for his heart: in the extreme

207 Dealing: sharing out

210 with...backs: wearing enormously expensive clothes

211 foreparts: (1) ornamental stomachers covering the breasts; (2) park in front of a manor house

214 come up: rise socially, and come to court

216 mete: measured
rod: (1) measuring stick; (2) a land measure (=five and a half yards)

217 yard: (1) tailor's ruler; (2) a land measure; (3) penis

218 foretops: locks of hair at the front of the head

219 head-tires: head-dresses (wealthy Jacobean women wore elaborate wigs made of natural hair)
untold: unaccounted for

223 poorer profession: By implication, the professional prostitute could become wealthier than a chaste woman.

228 brook: endure its loss

229 look: seek

235 inward: deep within you

237 the mother: (1) parent; (2) hysteria

240 crystal plaudities: ringing applause from the crystalline 'heaven' (according to Ptolomaic astronomy, one of the heavenly spheres revolving between God's throne and the earth, and the dwelling place of the angels).

241 peevish: perverse

243 mine own: my own child

246 uncivil: barbarous

247 those...downward: there were travellers' tales of monstrous human beings lacking heads, but with eyes fixed in their shoulders and a mouth in their breast.

Act Two, Scene Two

1 fellow: companion
5 Knave...back: a proverbial saying. Hippolito means 'I'll call you a knave to your face — and make a fool of you behind your back'.
6 preferred: recommended
7 discourse: good conversational skills
9 season: (1) seasoning; (2) opportunity (for revenge)
    once: one day
14 remove: depart
18 toward: I can look forward to
19 Ravish: delight (but with Lussorioso's usual sexual suggestiveness)
    rare: exceptionally able
23 bate in courage: lose something of my desire for her
24 made...naught: corrupted a woman of average chastity
26 white money: silver coin (that is, prostitution)
27 turned to Mahomet: (1) abandoned Christianity for Islam; (2) lost her morals
30 flat: overthrow, lay flat for sexual intercourse
31 close: closed up, chaste
36 received me: welcomed me at birth
37 be true: speak honestly
    proclaim: make public my mother's shameful behaviour
42 did me straight: did I do at once
47 go foremost: preceed
50 beset: make an assault on
55 mad: (1) out of her wits; (2) maddened with desire
65 Knit: (1) knit together; (2) couple sexually
66 ravel: disentangle
67 make...now: release them from control (as former servants to Lussorioso's will)
68 precious fellow: valuable accomplice
69 revenue: accented on the second syllable, as usual in the period
    Beg, leg: bow (make a leg) and ask a favour
70 office: position, post

75 drab: whore
78 the fees...arras: Vindice wants a monopoly on the money spent to arrange illicit sexual encounters (the practice of awarding monopolies as court favours was much hated at this time). In Jacobean rooms tapestries (*arras*) were hung sufficiently far out from the wall to create a hiding place.
79 farthingales: hooped petticoats, underclothes
    plump: abruptly
80 the rushes: rush mats were used to cover the floors.
81 apprehensive: clever, perceptive
82 purchase: profit
89 back-biter: (1) traducer; (2) instrument used to attack from behind
94 lessen...days: Exodus 22:12 promised long life to those who honoured their father and mother.
95 by this...me: already I fear
96 use: sexual employment (cf. line 120)
98 lecherous hope: (1) hopeful lecher; (2) lustful heir to the dukedom
99 some...and all: many priests
102 ports: gates
107 pen: with a play on 'penis'
112 luxur: lecher
113 unbraced: with his clothing unfastened
126 passing out: departure
129 additions: 'honours'
130–1 Night...fitly: Vindice thinks of the darkness of night in terms of the black heraldic shields and other trappings displayed on the occasion of the death of a member of the aristocracy, and removed following the funeral.
130 fees: possibly 'tattered hangings' (feaze), or a compressed reference to the high charges imposed by the College of Heralds for providing such displays
131 betimes: early
133 full sea abed: high tide in sexual activity

134 juggling: deception
135 i' the toll-book: up for sale as prostitutes; the toll-book was the register of animals for sale at market, with the tax payable on each.
137 by water: suggesting surreptitious arrival by boat on the Thames
141 sisters: prostitutes, imaged as spider women
149 mischief: wickedness
154 cross: frustrate
156 start us: startle me
158 Shadows: covers
160 forehead: thought of as the seat of honour
161 horn-royal: a royal cuckold
162 two beds: adulterous behaviour
169 Wildfire: combustible material used in warfare
171 follow the event: go to see the outcome

Act Two, Scene Three

0 SD *curtained bed*: a four-poster bed with curtains drawn round it, concealing the identity of the actors from the audience. Such beds were common in wealthy Jacobean houses.
4 soft: gentle
5 spleen: rage
8 upper: inner, nearest the bedchamber
11 heaves: deep sighs
12 unclear: in my sins
16 nerves: sinews
17 SD Line 45 below suggests that here the guard immediately seizes Lussorioso.
19 myself: duke in my place
23 forfend: forbid
25 'file: defile
26 abused: deceived
32 frightful word: putting into words the terrible suggestion (that the duke be killed)
33 SD *dissemble a flight*: The phrase suggests an exaggerated stealing off stage.
34 Be...die: Some editors suggest

that the Duchess (who does not speak again in the scene) leaves the stage at this point.
35 Out...eye: not to be seen
37 harlots: rascals, villains
43 out...socket: disjointed
45 saucy...elbows: Lussorioso is standing with his arms pinned behind him by the guard.
55 Make...us: be confident of our support
59 Puritan: hypocritical
75 Some: some other
77 sound: thoroughly carried out
81 face: sufficient impudence
    Honey: 'sweetness' (instead of the condemnation of their brother the Duke expected)
86 Here's...wit: they're not as clever as their stepmother (Lussorioso's mother)
90 peevish moon: fit of lunacy. The moon was thought to be capable of deranging the mind.
92 beside your spleen: leaving your anger aside
97 doom shall pass: judgement will be carried out
104 scarlet: a deep red cloth
    lawn: fine (so partially transparent) white linen
107 prevent: forestall
    envies: malicious hatred
110 suddenly: immediately
115 virtue: authority, power
127–8 turned...denial: had poisoned when she refused me
130 green: those of a vigorous young man

Act Three, Scene One

1 once: for once
6 Faiths: depositions on oath
8 set by: disregard
9 fall: apply
14 pin: referring to his dagger
16 packed: sent on his way
24 set an edge: a play on 'whet the man', and 'sharpen his axe'
25 Meet: appropriate

Act Three, Scene Two

2 But: merely
4 myself: the rightful duke (cf. 3.3.24)

Act Three, Scene Three

2 present: immediate
10 betimes: early
14 that: whoever
16 sound: properly carried out (cf. 3.4.23)
22 black: in sin (swearing was regarded as sinful)
27 commendations: spoken as five syllables
30 a bigger block: the executioner's block, rather than the smaller block used in hat-making

Act Three, Scene Four

8 of good cheer: (1) cheerful; (2) well entertained
'Slud: by God's blood!
10 trick: (1) stratagem; (2) hand in a card game
13–14 lie in...woman: (1) be imprisoned for a crime against a woman; (2) be confined to bed like a pregnant woman
31 sitting: that is, of the court of law
52 salt water: travel by sea, which was notoriously dangerous
53 stinted: staunched, dried
57 presently: immediately
58 Duns: sophistical interpretation, from the name of Duns Scotus, a famous scholastic theologian
61 four cards: A possible allusion to the popular game of Primero, in which each player held four cards and the wining hand consisted of four cards of the same suit.
62 dealing: (1) dealing cards; (2) knavery
66 cozens me of : tricks me out of
69 perjury: violation of promise
71 without..sign: with nothing to mark the significance of the occasion

Act Three, Scene Five

4 yon silver ceiling: The ceiling of the canopy above the stage at the Globe Theatre, where this play was first performed, was known as 'the Heavens', and represented the sky, with the sun, moon and stars painted in gold and silver.
8 divide...to: share with
9 shape: outward appearance, costume
14 angle: corner
15 riots: wanton revelry
16 shape: disguise
17 impudent: shameless
22 luxurious: lecherous
circle: arena. The actor might indicate the sweep of the theatre, which was built as an octagonal structure.
25 dreadfully digested: fearfully worked out
26 missed me: left me out
30 apprehensions: anticipations
37 stoops...men: degrades himself to the level of his men
38 be common: prostitute oneself
39–40 there's...prices: 'There are more secretly wicked people, whose wickedness is both concealed and prevalent, than there are public prostitutes who advertise their name and price.'
41 bare: with hat removed. Hippolito removes his own hat as Vindice returns with Gloriana.
42 SD *tires*: a headdress, completed with a wig and mask (cf. line 49)
46 shell: husk without real substance
51 At such...hid: at such a game of hide-and-seek. 'All hid' was both the name of the game and the signal cry for it to begin. beguile: (1) allure; (2) deceive
53 quaint: dainty, fine
60 keeps her colour: retains its natural colour (unlike cosmetics)
70 yellow labours: the yellowish cocoon spun by the silkworm
72 lordships: whole estates
74 falsify highways: turn

highwayman (making the roads untrustworthy)

76 refine...thing: make a fine lady of such a common whore

77 beat: whip, wear out (in the act of robbery)

80 sense: brain, reason

82 self-affecting: self-loving

83 Camphor: apply perfumed soaps (camphor was used as a fragrance)

85 outside: clothing

92 antic amble: grotesque stride

95 Look...herself: look deeply into her own nature

99 property: stage accessory
bear a part: play a role

103 strain: manner (literally, melody)

107 quaintness: ingenuity

110 sign: outward appearance. It has been suggested that Vindice manipulates the skeleton to make it give a signal of invitation.

113 vain: pointless vanity
fleets: slips away

117 absent 'em: send them away

134 grave: (1) from the grave; (2) serious

135 Have at all: a call to indiscriminate combat

138 Back...torch: lower the light. Perhaps Hippolito acquires a blazing torch when he retires at line 119.

139 fault: physical inadequacy

143 white devil: a play on 'white-haired' and 'fair-seeming'. Proverbially, 'the white devil is worse than the black'.

147 Gloriana: a resonant name for the Jacobean audience, since it was one of the titles given to the dead Queen Elizabeth I

148 't'as: it has

150 ragged: tattered

156 slavish: (1) vile; (2) enslaved

160 kiss closer: kiss more intimately, with the tongue rather than on the lips

161 slobbering Dutchman: cf. 1.3.57 and note.

170 Puh: pish!

173 pestilent: plague-stricken

176 rides...brow: seeks to dishonour you (put horns on your brow) by 'riding' your wife

179 clips: lustful embraces

182 hires: rewards

183 without horns: who was not himself deceived by his wife

184 Once: at some time or other
quitted: paid back (by being cuckolded)

190 stifle: put out

195 quittance: repay

196 foul object: ugly sight

198 like comets...blood: comets, also known as 'blazing stars', were considered omens of disaster

205 doubtful: alluding to his uncertain parentage

206 rubs heaven: stirs up thoughts of morality

207 yonder waxen fire: the torches held by the attendants

211 hasped: in a sexual embrace

218 state: royal ceremony

219 wants: lacks

Act Three, Scene Six

3 policy: cunning

5 slip: evade

6 model: plan

7 sudden: quick-acting

8 extemporal: immediate

10 'Sfoot: by God's foot

11 from you: beyond you

14 wit: cleverness

18 honest: (1) legitimate; (2) honourable

35 dame: woman

55 savour: smell

78 prodigious...bloods: ominous to our family

79 women: and therefore deceitful, hypocritical

82 murrain: plague

84 mortality...mortality: human existence...death

87 Sirrah: spoken contemptuously to the absent Lussorioso

Act Four, Scene One

5	what mak'st thou: what are you doing?
10	prefer: put forward
11	wittily elected: intelligently chosen
21	kind: natural
	forehead: reputation
24	razed: grazed
27	Jars in: enters discordantly villainous music: (1) dreadful music; (2) the music of villains
35	this iron age: possibly Lussorioso indicates his sword; there is also an allusion to the Age of Iron, in Greek mythology the last and most savage of the four Ages.
36	doom...dumb: sentence which would silence even a woman (and therefore proverbially talkative)
44	apply: employ
49	repair: bring himself
50	blood: temper
57	succeed: (1) take his (own) place; (2) be successful
62	spleen: anger
64	heart: inmost secrets
65	slight: untrustworthy
67	speed: kill
69	black condition: melancholic disposition, thought to be caused by black bile, one of the four humours secreted in the spleen.
82	sudden: impulsive, rash
83	humour: caprice
84	toy: whim
85	light: frivolous
86	oracle: oraculous, absolutely true

Act Four, Scene Two

2	shifts: (1) disguisings; (2) cunning devices
5	quainter fallacy: more ingenious deception
9	secretary: aide
14	clad in clay: dressed in the livery of death
17	'joy: enjoy
20	Thou'st: you were
21	You...present: 'You're good at

	winding around in circles, but let's talk about what needs to be done now.'
22	fashion: manner
25	doubtful: open to suspicion
27	strain: tone (literally, melody)
31	gave you out: announced that you were
32	turn: transform
37	Beshrew me: Devil take me!
41	How...den: Vindice establishes his supposed long absence in the country by speaking a rustic form of greeting, 'How dost? God give you good evening.'
41 SD	*makes legs*: bows by drawing back one leg and bending the other
44	desperate: reckless, abandoned
45	stood on't: taken seriously
49	black buckram: the black bag carried by a lawyer
49–51	I went...*tertio*: 'I took up law in forty-two and left it in sixty-three.' The references are probably to such dates rather than to Vindice's personal age. Lussorioso calculates incorrectly.
54	pullen and pigs: insignificant matters (literally, poultry and pigs)
56	terms: the four terms of law-court sittings, Hilary, Easter, Trinity and Michaelmas
59	canvassed: brought before the courts
60	Barbary: barbarous, bad
61	writ of error: legal document overthrowing a judgement on the grounds of error
62	sasarara: writ of *certiorari* issued by a superior court to overturn the judgement of a lower court
64	bent: tendency, also 'curve'
69	the great chest: the equivalent to a modern safe
71	gossips: women attendants
73	whirls: rumbles
75	conceit: witty idea
80	published: given out to be
85	pared...quick: dug deep enough to hurt
94	draw: (1) pull; (2) sketch
98	in colours: (1) in the form of a

painting; (2) in mere appearances

99 parlous: dangerous, biting
105 humour: mood
111 affect: like
112 they: your eyes
115 unbrace: discover, lay open
119 here: possibly Lussorioso indicates his heart.
127 quit: pay back
wrought with: worked upon
140 For chaste respect: for her respect for her chastity
146 for happy: as welcome news of fortunate events
152 in...cause: with comparatively little provocation
158 wind: lure (metaphor from hunting)
167 observe me: attend to my needs
171 case: condition
174 conveyed: carried off, managed
175 wit: clever idea
180 carried: carried out
185 cloven: split open (by lightning, as a sign of God's judgement)
188 SD *Thunder*: taken as a sign of heavenly wrath
189 lose ourselves: forget what we are about. Vindice's reply puns on lose/find a way.
194 conveyed: disposed of
199 reached: grasped, understood
201 published him: given him out to be
203 sluggy: torpid
206 substantial: solid, convincing
211 in grain: fast dyed
214 conjure: exorcise

Act Four, Scene Three

10 bent: determined on behaving
11 soft: in luxury
12 unequal: socially inferior

Act Four, Scene Four

0 SD *daggers...hands*: From lines 5–6 it is clear that the daggers are

being held against Gratiana's breasts.

5 iron nipples: daggers
7 quarlèd: curdled
8 Cut: cut short (by being executed for murder)
12 office: moral obligations as a mother
14 dissemble...die: pretend, lie even at the point of death
16 of...condition: of the worldly, corrupted kind
18 uncivilly: barbarously
26 grace: virtue
34 nimble...tune: adroit in bringing damnation, so charmingly harmonious
39 give aim: direct an assault on, instruct in shooting at
42 and you: if you (addressed to Vindice's dagger)
43 red: rust (with an ominous suggestion of blood)
47–8 grounds...Has: such false agreements between subject and verb are common at this time (cf. *Spanish Tragedy*, 3.2.12–13)
51 infectious: diseased
53 grace: with a play on 'sweet savour'
59 seld: infrequent
61 of easy wax: of a (morally) pliable nature
62 the disease: hysteria (the 'mother')
63 forehead: thought of as the seat of honour and virtue
64 graceful: (1) pleasing; (2) full of virtue
67 Green-coloured: young and virginal
68 hire: payment (as a whore)
69 boiling lead: The punishment in hell for adultery
75 in cold blood: when she is seriously-minded
83 elf: spirit
85 mead: meadow (of Gratiana's soul; cf. lines 47–8)
95 with...can I: how may I dare
99 what for: as much for
103 common usury: (1) base money-dealing; (2) public prostitution ('use')

107 marble: that is, naturally hard to change, and sexually cold and chaste

112 cursèd: unchaste, and therefore damned

116 Sons: with a play on 'suns' lights: with a play on 'the guidance of heavenly bodies'

118 intellectual: as opposed to physical, of the senses

122 kind: Nature, though the word may mean 'dear' or 'daughter of mine'

127 infect: tainted

132 I...mother: I am really your mother now, ready to help you

133 Bethink: earnestly consider

137 pitch: climb (in falconry, the highest point of the falcon's ascent before it dives on its prey)

139 purchase: income

140 hospital: charitable institution

150 would: willed it so

153 no ill inherits: no evil takes over ownership

155 happiest: most blessed

156 glass: mirror, example

Act Five, Scene One

0 SD *the duke's body*: From lines 1 and 39 it is clear that the brothers place the corpse sitting leaning forward, as if asleep.

3 lay: bet

4 that's I: referring to the body of the duke

7 't'as...term: Michaelmas was a law term, with eight days on which the local sheriff could provide a 'return' or report on writs directed to him by the court. Vindice means there are eight ways of describing the same situation.

8 enow: enough

10 faith: self-confidence

11 flesh-flies: blow-flies (scavenging retainers)

13 fly-flop: fly-swat

15 familiar: (1) acquainted; (2) part of his family

16 quaintly: ingeniously like... hugger-mugger: like a devious intriguer (the early

sinister sense of 'politician'), in secret

17 in catastrophe: in conclusion (used of the end of a tragedy)

24 step close: keep out of sight

47 golls: hands

50 nake: unsheathe, bare

53 Meet with: encounter (as an enemy) bear us out: support our account

55 sa, sa: exclamation used by fencers when delivering a thrust (representing French 'ça, ça').

59 from your names: by names other than your own

70 prate: blab

74 raiment: clothing

75–6 cast about: devise means

76 clear: innocent, unsuspected

80 'gealed: congealed

83 can: is able to do

93 he quits him: Lussorioso repays his father the duke (who called him by such names, 2.3.14)

96 prodigious comet: comets were thought to be omens of disaster. Ambitioso expects to see such an omen; later a comet actually appears (5.3.0 SD).

99 owes: owns

102 That...lie: the country was proverbially associated with simplicity and truth, the court with sophistication and deceit.

108 tug: pull an oar, make my way

115 Confirmed: true, so establishing my innocence

121 stick: keep your mouth shut

123 happy: fortunate

124 indifferent wits: average intelligences

126 Post-horse: speedy mounted messengers

128 accidentally departed: died by mischance

135 foreign: other

136 Courtiers...twelves: courtiers' tongues are three sizes larger than their feet

139 April: known as a season of showery weather

148 bethink the latest: consider the last

152 several falls: different deaths, seasons of decline for each us

157 firm: secure, safe
158 wit: cleverness
159 have at: let us shoot at
     mark: target (Lussorioso)
162 be out: (1) miss, (2) miss out
169 mask: (1) disguise or vizard;
     (2) masque (an entertainment
     danced by masked performers
     at banquets and feasts)

Act Five, Scene Two

1   of music: 'in harmony'
2   Strike: (1) hit away; (2) strike
    up, as begin to play a melody
3   flow...livers: are too effeminate
    and cowardly (the liver was
    thought of as the seat of
    passion and courage)
10 toward: being prepared
13 affect: make pretence
18 form: pattern of the dance
19 strain: tune
24 t'other: other
27 drunk down: downed through
    drink

Act Five, Scene Three

0 SD This scene direction covers
      two successive entries and
      their following actions. First
      the 'possessing' or installation
      of the new duke, Lussorioso,
      on a throne; then Lussosioso
      and his court retire, to re-enter
      to the banquet, which is
      heralded by celebratory
      ('sounding') music. Since the
      'blazing star' (or comet) is not
      observed by the characters
      until line 13, that property,
      which in the Jacobean public
      theatres seems to have
      involved the use of flares or
      fireworks, may have been
      hung up but not lit
      immediately.
5   shine: smiling aspect (in
      contemporary symbolism,
      rulers were frequently
      equated with the sun and its
      light)
7   incontinent: lustful

10   subsidies: taxes levied by the
      ruler
15   blazing star: comet
      (considered an omen of death
      and disaster especially to
      rulers)
16   Spy out: look outside
19   bushing: referring to the tail of
      the comet
20   quake: cause me to tremble
22   whom...weds: who combine
      practical skill and theoretical
      knowledge
23   locks: long hair; another
      reference to the fiery tail of
      the comet
24   read: well-educated
27   most: to threaten mostly,
      closely to hand
29   gracefully: popularly
36   fittest: the most fitting
      companion
39   anon: shortly
41 SD *steal out*: quietly draw from
      their scabbards
      It thunders: A stage effect
      achieved by rolling a
      cannonball. Thunder was
      taken to be the voice of God
      speaking in judgement (cf.
      4.2.187, and line 47 below).
47   claps: (1) resonates, (2)
      applauds
48 SD *measure*: dance-pattern
51   sped: killed
60   bloodshot: (1) red with grief;
      (2) filled with the sight of
      blood
66   Law you: exclamation, 'la you!'
70   bitter: painful
71   marrow: food (for revenge)
      be expressed: put my feelings
      into words
75   prate on't: blab it out
77   departed: passed away
81   unlikely: unfit (to be duke)
82   your: spoken to Antonio
83   the silver age: Antonio is
      white-haired with age; his rule
      will bring back the Silver Age,
      in Greek mythology an age of
      order and civilisation (cf.
      4.1.35).
86   keep: protect
87   'quited: repaid, avenged

91 carried: carried out
94 witty: cleverly
102 come about: turned out,
   changed in this way
   'Sfoot: by God's foot!
103 set...son: a play on human death
   as the setting of the sun-king
   (cf. note to 5.3.5)
104 conscience: sense of what is
   right
109 brass: alluding to the memorial
   brasses placed on tombs
112 sentence: wise, proverbial saying
115 witch: wizard (endowed with
   foresight)

116 in: involved
117 been slipped: gone undetected
118 list: chose
   nobles clipped: (1) found noble
   accomplices; (2) raised money
   by shaving gold coins ('nobles'),
   a common criminal practice
119 go for: (1) pass as; (2) go to
   execution
120 bleed: die bloodily
121 turned: converted
123 closed: concealed
124 heavy: sorrowful

The Duchess of Malfi

JOHN WEBSTER

INTRODUCTORY NOTE

Authorship, date of composition and stage history

The Duchess of Malfi was written by John Webster (?1578–?1638) over
the period 1612-13, and was presented by the King's Men, London's
premier company, at both their public playhouse, the Globe, and
their indoors house, the Blackfriars Theatre, in the winter of 1613/14
or early in 1614. At least three revivals took place within Webster's
lifetime, the latest in 1630 before King Charles in the Cockpit Theatre
at Whitehall. A list of 'The Actors' Names' in the edition of 1623 (the
first such cast-list to be published in England) makes it possible to
reconstruct much of the original casting for the first production and
a subsequent revival. John Lowin, Richard Burbage, Henry Condell,
William Ostler, (probably) Richard Robinson and Richard Pallant
created the roles of Bosola, Ferdinand, the Cardinal, Antonio, the
Duchess and Cariola; in a later production, datable to shortly before
1623, John Taylor, Richard Robinson, Richard Benfield, Richard
Sharpe, John Thompson and Robert Pallant played the parts of
Ferdinand, the Cardinal, Antonio, the Duchess, Julia and Cariola. A
Venetian observer, writing in 1618, noted the splendid robes of the
Cardinal, the spectacle of his mistress sitting on his knee (2.4), the
erection of an altar on stage (for 3.4) and the Cardinal's ceremonial
preparations for war: 'He goes to war, first laying down his
cardinal's habit on the altar, with the help of his chaplains, with
great ceremoniousness; finally he has his sword bound on and dons
the soldier's sash with so much panache that you could not imagine

it better done.' This is a rare glimpse of the contemporary staging of
a Renaissance tragedy.

There were at least five Restoration productions (in one of them
Betterton and his wife played Bosola and the Duchess), and
occasional eighteenth-century adaptations. A modified version of
the play by Richard Horne held the nineteenth-century stage in
England, Australia and America, but following William Poel's
revival in 1892 the play has been regularly staged both by
professional and student companies, attracting such performers as
Edith Evans, Peggy Ashcroft, Judi Dench, Helen Mirren, Eleanor
Bron, Harriet Walter, John Gielgud, Eric Porter, Patrick Wymark and
Ian McKellen. In the authoritative Cambridge edition of the play
(see below), David Carnegie lists forty-one professional productions
between 1919, when the Phoenix Society first presented the full text
of the tragedy on the modern stage at the Lyric Theatre,
Hammersmith, and 1989, when the Royal Shakespeare Company
performed the play at both the Swan Theatre, Stratford-upon-Avon,
and later at the Pit, in the Barbican Centre, London, and Garland
Wright directed the Guthrie Theatre Company production in
Minneapolis. This record includes productions in America, Canada,
Australia and New Zealand. The play continues to hold the stage,
most recently in Philip Franks's 1995 Greenwich Theatre Company
London production, with Juliet Stevenson and Simon Russell Beale
as Ferdinand, and in Declan Donnellan's 1996 Cheek by Jowl
Company's international production. Here the play is given a 1930s
setting in Fascist Italy; Anastasia Hille's chain-smoking Duchess is a
woman of fierce sexuality, the Cardinal a sadistic sensualist and
Ferdinand a dependent but dangerous emotional adolescent. *The
Duchess of Malfi* received BBC radio productions in 1947 and 1954,
and BBC television productions in 1938, 1949 and 1972; CBC
broadcast the play on television in 1962.

Text

The present edition is based on the authoritative first quarto
published in 1623 by John Waterson, whose printer Nicholas Okes
probably worked from a professional transcript of the promptbook
for the play by Ralph Crane, an expert scribe long associated with
the King's Men. The title-page describes it as 'The perfect and exact
copy, with divers things printed that the length of the play would
not bear in the presentment' (that is, uncut for practical use in the

theatre). Webster himself seems to have checked and partly corrected the text in the printing-house. There was only one further reprint (1640) before the closing of the theatres.

Sources

Webster found the material for his tragedy in the historical life of a fifteenth-century Duchess of Amalfi who secretly married her major-domo, Antonio Bologna, in defiance of her brothers. His chief source was a translation by William Painter in his *Palace of Pleasure* (1567) of Matteo Bandello's account of the Duchess's tragic story in his *Novelle* (1554), already greatly elaborated by François de Belleforest in his *Histoires Tragiques* (1565). But Webster was an obsessively transformational writer: his own tragedies *The Duke of Florence* (known only in an untitled fragment discovered in 1986) and *The White Devil* (1612), as well as the anonymous *Second Maiden's Tragedy* (1611), Sidney's *Arcadia* (1590), and Simon Goulart's *Admirable and Memorable Histories* (1607) all contributed to the crafting of *The Duchess of Malfi*, and the text is studded with proverbial sayings and phrases culled from many other writers, to be recontextualised in the dense poetic texture typical of this writer.

Further reading

A facsimile of the 1623 text of the tragedy has been published by the Scolar Press (Menston, 1968). The fullest single-volume edition of *The Duchess of Malfi* is in the Revels series, edited by John Russell Brown (London, 1964). Other single-volume scholarly editions are edited by Elizabeth Brennan (New Mermaid, London, 1964), David Gunby, *John Webster: Three Plays* (Harmondsworth, 1972), and Jonathan Dollimore and Alan Sinfield, *The Selected Plays of John Webster* (Cambridge, 1983). A new standard old-spelling edition of the play, edited by David Gunby, David Carnegie and Antony Hammond, appears in volume one of *The Works of John Webster* (Cambridge, 1995). Contemporary performance of the tragedy is the subject of R. B. Graves' article '*The Duchess of Malfi* at the Globe and Blackfriars', *Renaissance Drama*, NS 9 (1978) 193–209. Modern productions of the tragedy are studied in R. V. Holdsworth's '*The White Devil' and 'The Duchess of Malfi': A Casebook* (London, 1975), Richard Allan Cave's '*The White Devil' and 'The Duchess of Malfi': Text and Performance* (London, 1988), and Kathleen McLuskie and

Jennifer Uglow's *The Duchess of Malfi* (Bristol, 1989). Book-length studies of Webster's tragic writing include Lee Bliss, *The World's Perspective: John Webster and the Jacobean Drama* (Brighton, 1983), Travis Bogard, *The Tragic Satire of John Webster* (Berkeley and Los Angeles, 1955), Gunnar Boklund, *The Duchess of Malfi: Sources, Themes, Characters* (Cambridge, Mass., 1962), Charles R. Forker, *The Skull Beneath the Skin: The Achievement of John Webster* (Carbondale, Ill., 1986), Christina Luckyj, *A Winter Snake: Dramatic Form in the Tragedies of John Webster* (Athens, Ga. and London, 1989), and Jaqueline Pearson, *Tragedy and Tragicomedy in the Plays of John Webster* (Manchester, 1980).

Dramatis Personae

FERDINAND, *Duke of Calabria, and twin brother to the* DUCHESS
The CARDINAL, *their elder brother*
DANIEL DE BOSOLA, *their spy; Provisor of the Horse° to the* DUCHESS
ANTONIO BOLOGNA, *Steward of the* DUCHESS's *household*
DELIO, *his friend.* 5
CASTRUCHIO,° *an elderly courtier, husband to* JULIA
The Marquis of PESCARA,° *a soldier*
Count MALATESTE,° *a Roman courtier*
SILVIO
RODERIGO } *courtiers at Amalfi* 10
GRISOLAN
The DOCTOR
FOROBOSCO,° *an official at the* DUCHESS's *court.*

The DUCHESS OF MALFI, *a widow, afterwards secretly married to* ANTONIO 15
CARIOLA,° *her waiting-woman*
JULIA, *wife of* CASTRUCHIO, *and mistress to the* CARDINAL
OLD LADY, *a midwife*

Two Pilgrims

Eight MADMEN, comprising an Astrologer, Broker, Doctor, English 20
Tailor, Farmer, Gentleman Usher,° Lawyer, and Priest

Court Officers; Attendants; Servants; Guards; Executioners; Churchmen

Ladies-in-Waiting

Scene: *Malfi, Rome, Loretto, the countryside near Ancona, and Milan.*

Act One, Scene One

[*Enter* ANTONIO *and* DELIO.]

DELIO: You are welcome to your country, dear Antonio;
　　You have been long in France, and you return
　　A very formal° Frenchman in your habit.°
　　How do you like the French court?
ANTONIO:　　　　　　　　　　I admire it.
　　In seeking to reduce both state° and people 5
　　To a fixed° order, their judicious king
　　Begins at home. Quits° first his royal palace

Of flatt'ring sycophants, of dissolute
And infamous persons, which he sweetly terms
His Master's master-piece, the work of heaven,   10
Consid'ring duly, that a prince's court
Is like a common° fountain, whence should flow
Pure silver-drops in general.° But if't chance
Some cursed example° poison't near the head,
Death and diseases through the whole land spread.   15
And what is't makes this blessèd government,
But a most provident° Council, who dare freely
Inform° him the corruption of the times?
Though some o'th' court hold it presumption
To instruct princes what they ought to do,   20
It is a noble duty to inform them
What they ought to foresee. Here comes Bosola,

[*Enter* BOSOLA.]

The only court-gall:° yet I observe his railing
Is not for simple love of° piety.
Indeed, he rails at those things which he wants;   25
Would be as lecherous, covetous, or proud,
Bloody, or envious,° as any man,
If he had means to be so. Here's the Cardinal.

[*Enter* CARDINAL.]

BOSOLA: I do haunt you still.
CARDINAL: So.   30
BOSOLA: I have done you better service than to be slighted thus.
   Miserable age, where only the reward° of doing well is the doing
   of it!
CARDINAL: You enforce° your merit too much.
BOSOLA: I fell into the galleys in your service, where, for two years   35
   together, I wore two towels instead of a shirt, with a knot on the
   shoulder, after the fashion of a Roman mantle. Slighted thus?
   I will thrive some way. Blackbirds° fatten best in hard weather:
   why not I, in these dog-days?°
CARDINAL: Would you could become honest —   40
BOSOLA: With all your divinity,° do but direct me the way to it. I have
   known many travel far for it, and yet return as arrant knaves° as
   they went forth; because they carried themselves always along
   with them.   [*Exit* CARDINAL.]
   Are you gone? Some fellows, they say, are possessed with the devil, 45
   but this great fellow were able to possess the greatest devil, and

make him worse.

ANTONIO: He hath denied thee some suit?°

BOSOLA: He and his brother are like plum trees that grow crooked over
standing° pools; they are rich, and o'erladen with fruit, but none but 50
crows, pies,° and caterpillars feed on them. Could I be one of their
flattering panders, I would hang on their ears like a horse-leech till I
were full, and then drop off. I pray leave me. Who would rely upon
these miserable dependences,° in expectation to be advanced°
tomorrow? What creature ever fed worse than hoping Tantalus;° nor 55
ever died any man more fearfully, than he that hoped for a pardon?
There are rewards° for hawks, and dogs, when they have done us
service; but for a soldier, that hazards his limbs in a battle, nothing
but a kind of geometry is his last supportation.°

DELIO: Geometry? 60

BOSOLA: Ay, to hang in a fair pair of slings, take his latter swing° in the
world, upon an honourable pair of crutches, from hospital to
hospital: fare ye well, sir. And yet do not you scorn us, for places
in the court are but like beds in the hospital, where this man's head
lies at that man's foot, and so lower and lower.   [*Exit* BOSOLA.] 65

DELIO: I knew this fellow seven years in the galleys
For a notorious murder, and 'twas thought
The cardinal suborned° it: he was released
By the French general, Gaston de Foix,
When he recovered Naples.°

ANTONIO: 'Tis great pity 70
He should be thus neglected; I have heard
He's very valiant. This foul melancholy
Will poison all his goodness, for, I'll tell you,
If too immoderate sleep be truly said
To be an inward rust unto the soul,° 75
It then doth follow want° of action
Breeds all black° malcontents, and their close° rearing,
Like moths in cloth, do hurt° for want of wearing.

Act One, Scene Two°

[*Enter* CASTRUCHIO, SILVIO, RODERIGO *and* GRISOLAN.]

DELIO: The presence° 'gins to fill. You promised me
To make me the partaker of the natures
Of some of your great courtiers.

ANTONIO: The Lord Cardinal's
And other strangers',° that are now in court?
I shall. Here comes the great Calabrian duke. 5

[*Enter* FERDINAND.]

FERDINAND: Who took the ring° oftenest?

SILVIO: Antonio Bologna, my lord.

FERDINAND: Our sister duchess' great Master of her Household? Give
    him the jewel; when shall we leave this sportive action,° and fall to
    action° indeed?   10

CASTRUCHIO: Methinks, my lord, you should not desire to go to war, in
    person.

FERDINAND [*aside*]: Now for some gravity: why, my lord?

CASTRUCHIO: It is fitting a soldier arise to be a prince, but not necessary
    a prince descend to be a captain.   15

FERDINAND: No?

CASTRUCHIO: No, my lord; he were far better do it by a deputy.

FERDINAND: Why should he not as well sleep, or eat, by a deputy? This
    might take idle, offensive, and base office° from him, whereas the
    other deprives him of honour.   20

CASTRUCHIO: Believe my experience: that realm is never long in quiet,
    where the ruler is a soldier.

FERDINAND: Thou told'st me thy wife could not endure fighting.°

CASTRUCHIO: True, my lord.

FERDINAND: And of a jest she broke,° of a captain she met full of   25
    wounds: — I have forgot it.

CASTRUCHIO: She told him, my lord, he was a pitiful fellow, to lie, like
    the children of Israel, all in tents.°

FERDINAND: Why, there's a wit were able to undo° all the chirurgeons° o'
    the city, for although gallants should quarrel, and had drawn their   30
    weapons, and were ready to go to it, yet her persuasions would
    make them put up.°

CASTRUCHIO: That she would, my lord.

FERDINAND: How do you like my Spanish jennet?°

RODERIGO: He is all fire.   35

FERDINAND: I am of Pliny's opinion, I think he was begot by the wind;°
    he runs as if he were ballasted° with quicksilver.°

SILVIO: True, my lord, he reels° from the tilt often.

RODERIGO *and* GRISOLAN: Ha, ha, ha!

FERDINAND: Why do you laugh? Methinks you that are courtiers   40
    should be my touchwood,° take fire when I give fire; that is, laugh
    when I laugh, were the subject never so witty —

CASTRUCHIO: True, my lord, I myself have heard a very good jest, and
    have scorned to seem to have so silly a wit as to understand it.

FERDINAND: But I can laugh at your fool,° my lord.   45

CASTRUCHIO: He cannot speak, you know, but he makes faces; my lady
    cannot abide him.

FERDINAND: No?

CASTRUCHIO: Nor endure to be in merry company; for she says too
much laughing, and too much company, fills her too full of the   50
wrinkle.°
FERDINAND: I would then have a mathematical instrument made for her
face,° that she might not laugh out of compass.° I shall shortly visit
you at Milan, Lord Silvio.
SILVIO: Your Grace shall arrive most welcome.   55
FERDINAND: You are a good horseman, Antonio, you have excellent
riders in France;° what do you think of good horsemanship?
ANTONIO: Nobly, my lord. As out of the Grecian horse° issued many
famous princes, so out of brave horsemanship arise the first sparks
of growing resolution, that raise the mind to noble action.   60
FERDINAND: You have bespoke it worthily.

[*Enter* DUCHESS, CARDINAL, CARIOLA *and* Attendant.]°

SILVIO: Your brother, the Lord Cardinal, and sister Duchess.
CARDINAL: Are the galleys come about?°
GRISOLAN: They are, my lord.
FERDINAND: Here's the Lord Silvio, is come to take his leave.   65
DELIO [*aside to* ANTONIO]: Now, sir, your promise. What's that cardinal?
I mean his temper.° They say he's a brave fellow, will play° his five
thousand crowns at tennis, dance, court ladies, and one that hath
fought single combats.
ANTONIO: Some such flashes° superficially hang on him, for form,° but   70
observe his inward character: he is a melancholy° churchman. The
spring° in his face is nothing but the engendering of toads.° Where he
is jealous° of any man, he lays worse plots for them than ever was
imposed on Hercules;° for he strews in his way flatterers, panders,
intelligencers,° atheists,° and a thousand such political° monsters. He 75
should have been Pope; but instead of coming to it by the primitive
decency° of the Church, he did bestow bribes, so largely, and so
impudently, as if he would have carried it away without heaven's
knowledge. Some good he hath done.
DELIO: You have given too much of him; what's his brother?   80
ANTONIO: The duke there? a most perverse and turbulent nature.
What appears in him mirth, is merely outside;
If he laugh heartily, it is to laugh
All honesty out of fashion.
DELIO: Twins?
ANTONIO: In quality:°
He speaks with others' tongues, and hears men's suits   85
With others' ears; will seem to sleep o'th' bench,°
Only to entrap offenders in their answers;
Dooms men to death by information,

Rewards by hearsay.
DELIO: Then the law to him
  Is like a foul black cobweb to a spider;   90
  He makes it his dwelling, and a prison
  To entangle those shall feed him.°
ANTONIO: Most true.
  He ne'er pays debts, unless they be shrewd turns,°
  And those he will confess that he doth owe.
  Last, for his brother, there, the cardinal,   95
  They that do flatter him most, say oracles°
  Hang at his lips: and verily I believe them,
  For the devil speaks in them.
  But for their sister, the right noble duchess,
  You never fixed your eye on three fair medals,°   100
  Cast in one figure,° of so different temper.°
  For her discourse, it is so full of rapture,°
  You only will begin then to be sorry
  When she doth end her speech; and wish, in wonder,
  She held it less vainglory° to talk much   105
  Than you penance° to hear her. Whilst she speaks,
  She throws upon a man so sweet a look
  That it were able to raise one to a galliard°
  That lay in a dead palsy,° and to dote
  On that sweet countenance; but in that look   110
  There speaketh so divine a continence,
  As cuts off all lascivious and vain hope.
  Her days are practised° in such noble virtue,
  That, sure her nights, nay more, her very sleeps,
  Are more in heaven° than other ladies' shrifts.°   115
  Let all sweet ladies break their flatt'ring glasses,°
  And dress themselves in her.°
DELIO: Fie, Antonio,
  You play the wire-drawer° with her commendations.
ANTONIO: I'll case the picture up;° only thus much.
  All her particular worth grows to this sum: 120
  She stains° the time past, lights the time to come.
CARIOLA: You must attend my lady, in the gallery,
  Some half an hour hence.
ANTONIO: I shall.
FERDINAND: Sister, I have a suit to you.
DUCHESS: To me, sir?
FERDINAND: A gentleman here, Daniel de Bosola;   125
  One that was in the galleys —
DUCHESS: Yes, I know him.
FERDINAND: A worthy fellow he's: pray let me entreat for

The provisorship of your horse.°
DUCHESS: Your knowledge of him
    Commends him, and prefers him.
FERDINAND: Call him hither.   [*Exit* Attendant.]
    We are now upon parting. Good Lord Silvio,   130
    Do us commend to all our noble friends
    At the leaguer.°
SILVIO: Sir, I shall.
DUCHESS: You are for Milan?
SILVIO: I am.
DUCHESS: Bring the caroches:° we'll bring you down to the haven.
                [*Exeunt all but the* CARDINAL *and* FERDINAND.]
CARDINAL: Be sure you entertain° that Bosola   135
    For your intelligence;° I would not be seen in't,
    And therefore many times I have slighted him
    When he did court our furtherance — as this morning.
FERDINAND: Antonio, the great Master of her Household,°
    Had been far fitter.
CARDINAL: You are deceived in him;   140
    His nature is too honest for such business.
    He comes: I'll leave you.   [*Exit.*]

[*Enter* BOSOLA.]

BOSOLA: I was lured to you.
FERDINAND: My brother here, the cardinal, could never
    Abide you.
BOSOLA: Never since he was in my debt.
FERDINAND: May be some oblique character in your face   145
    Made him suspect you.
BOSOLA: Doth he study physiognomy?
    There's no more credit° to be given to th'face,
    Than to a sick man's urine, which some call
    The physician's whore, because she cozens° him.
    He did suspect me wrongfully.
FERDINAND: ·   For that   150
    You must give great men leave to take their times:
    Distrust doth cause us seldom be deceived;
    You see, the oft° shaking of the cedar tree°
    Fastens it more at root.
BOSOLA: Yet take heed;
    For to suspect a friend unworthily   155
    Instructs him the next° way to suspect you,
    And prompts him to deceive you.
FERDINAND: There's gold.   [*Gives* BOSOLA *money.*]

BOSOLA: So:
    What follows? Never rained such showers as these
    Without thunderbolts i'th' tail of them;°
    Whose throat must I cut?   160
FERDINAND: Your inclination to shed blood rides post°
    Before my occasion to use you. I give you that
    To live i'th' court, here, and observe the duchess,
    To note all the particulars of her 'haviour:°
    What suitors do solicit her for marriage,   165
    And whom she best affects: —° she's a young widow,
    I would not have her marry again.
BOSOLA: No, sir?
FERDINAND: Do not you ask the reason; but be satisfied,
    I say I would not.
BOSOLA: It seems you would create me
    One of your familiars.°
FERDINAND: Familiar? what's that?   170
BOSOLA: Why, a very quaint° invisible devil in flesh:
    An intelligencer.°
FERDINAND: Such a kind of thriving thing
    I would wish thee; and ere long, thou mayst arrive
    At a higher place by't.
BOSOLA [*offers to return the money*]: Take your devils,
    Which hell calls angels!° these cursed gifts would make   175
    You a corrupter, me an impudent traitor,
    And should I take these they'd take me to hell.
FERDINAND: Sir, I'll take nothing from you that I have given.
    There is a place that I procured for you
    This morning, the Provisorship o'th' Horse;   180
    Have you heard on't?°
BOSOLA: No.
FERDINAND: 'Tis yours, is't not worth thanks?
BOSOLA: I would have you curse yourself now, that your bounty,
    Which makes men truly noble,° e'er should make
    Me a villain. O, that to avoid ingratitude
    For the good deed you have done me, I must do   185
    All the ill man can invent. Thus the devil
    Candies° all sins o'er; and what heaven terms vile,
    That names he complemental.°
FERDINAND: Be yourself:
    Keep your old garb of melancholy; 'twill express
    You envy those that stand above your reach,   190
    Yet strive not to come near 'em. This will gain
    Access to private lodgings, where yourself
    May, like a politic° dormouse —

BOSOLA: As I have seen some
    Feed in a lord's dish,° half asleep, not seeming
    To listen to any talk; and yet these rogues   195
    Have cut his throat in a dream. What's my place?°
    The Provisorship o'th' Horse? Say then my corruption
    Grew out of horse dung. I am your creature.°
FERDINAND: Away!
BOSOLA: Let good men, for good deeds, covet good fame,
    Since place and riches oft are bribes of shame;   200
    Sometimes the devil doth preach.   *Exit.*

                [*Enter* CARDINAL, DUCHESS *and* CARIOLA.]

CARDINAL: We are to part from you, and your own discretion
    Must now be your director.
FERDINAND: You are a widow.
    You know already what man is and therefore
    Let not youth, high promotion, eloquence —   205
CARDINAL: No, nor anything without the addition, honour,
    Sway your high blood.°
FERDINAND: Marry? they are most luxurious°
    Will wed twice.
CARDINAL: O fie!
FERDINAND: Their livers° are more spotted
    Than Laban's sheep.°
DUCHESS: Diamonds are of most value,
    They say, that have passed through most jewellers' hands.   210
FERDINAND: Whores, by that rule, are precious.
DUCHESS: Will you hear me?
    I'll never marry —
CARDINAL: So most widows say.
    But commonly that motion° lasts no longer
    Than the turning of an hourglass; the funeral sermon,
    And it, end both together.
FERDINAND: Now hear me.   215
    You live in a rank° pasture here, i'th' court;
    There is a kind of honey-dew° that's deadly:
    'Twill poison your fame. Look to't; be not cunning:
    For they whose faces do belie their hearts
    Are witches ere they arrive at twenty years,   220
    Ay, and give the devil suck.°
DUCHESS: This is terrible good counsel.
FERDINAND: Hypocrisy is woven of a fine small thread,
    Subtler than Vulcan's engine;° yet, believe't,
    Your darkest actions — nay, your privat'st thoughts —

Will come to light.
CARDINAL: You may flatter yourself,   225
    And take your own choice; privately be married
    Under the eaves° of night —
FERDINAND: Think't the best voyage
    That e'er you made; like the irregular° crab,
    Which, though't goes backward, thinks that it goes right,
    Because it goes its own way. But observe: 230
    Such weddings may more properly be said
    To be executed,° than celebrated.
CARDINAL: The marriage night
    Is the entrance into some prison.
FERDINAND: And those joys,
    Those lustful pleasures, are like heavy sleeps
    Which do forerun man's mischief.°
CARDINAL: Fare you well.   235
    Wisdom begins at the end: remember it.   [*Exit.*]
DUCHESS: I think this speech between you both was studied,
    It came so roundly° off.
FERDINAND [*draws a dagger*]: You are my sister;
    This was my father's poniard: do you see?
    I'd be loath to see't look rusty,° 'cause 'twas his.   240
    I would have you to give o'er these chargeable° revels;
    A visor and a mask are whispering-rooms°
    That were ne'er built for goodness. Fare ye well: —
    And women like that part, which, like the lamprey,°
    Hath ne'er a bone in't.°
DUCHESS: Fie, sir!
FERDINAND: Nay,   245
    I mean the tongue; variety of courtship.
    What cannot a neat knave° with a smooth tale°
    Make a woman believe? Farewell, lusty widow.   [*Exit* FERDINAND.]
DUCHESS: Shall this move me? If all my royal kindred
    Lay in my way unto this marriage,   250
    I'd make them my low foot-steps.° And even now,
    Even in this hate (as men in some great battles,
    By apprehending° danger, have achieved
    Almost impossible actions — I have heard soldiers say so,)
    So I, through frights and threat'nings, will assay   255
    This dangerous venture. Let old wives report
    I winked,° and chose a husband.— Cariola,
    To thy known secrecy I have given up
    More than my life, my fame.
CARIOLA: Both shall be safe;
    For I'll conceal this secret from the world   260

As warily as those that trade in poison
Keep poison from their children.
DUCHESS: Thy protestation
 Is ingenious° and hearty: I believe it.
 Is Antonio come?
CARIOLA: He attends° you.
DUCHESS: Good dear soul,   265
 Leave me; but place thyself behind the arras,°
 Where thou mayst overhear us. Wish me good speed,
 For I am going into a wilderness,
 Where I shall find nor path, nor friendly clue°
 To be my guide. [CARIOLA *goes behind the arras; the* DUCHESS *draws*
            the traverse to reveal ANTONIO.]°
     I sent for you. Sit down:
 Take pen and ink, and write. Are you ready?
ANTONIO [*sits*]:   Yes.   270
DUCHESS: What did I say?
ANTONIO: That I should write somewhat.
DUCHESS: O, I remember.
 After these triumphs° and this large expense
 It's fit, like thrifty husbands,° we inquire
 What's laid up for tomorrow.   275
ANTONIO: So please your beautous excellence.
DUCHESS: Beauteous?
 Indeed I thank you: I look young for your sake.°
 You have ta'en my cares° upon you.
ANTONIO [*rises*]:   I'll fetch your Grace
 The particulars of your revenue and expense.
DUCHESS: O, you are an upright° treasurer; but you mistook, 280
 For when I said I meant to make inquiry
 What's laid up for tomorrow, I did mean
 What's laid up yonder for me.
ANTONIO: Where?
DUCHESS: In heaven.
 I am making my will, as 'tis fit princes should,
 In perfect memory, and I pray, sir, tell me,   285
 Were not one better make it smiling, thus?
 Than in deep groans, and terrible ghastly looks,
 As if the gifts we parted with procured°
 That violent distraction?
ANTONIO: O, much better.
DUCHESS: If I had a husband now, this care were quit.° 290
 But I intend to make you overseer;°
 What good deed shall we first remember? Say.
ANTONIO: Begin with that first good deed began i'th' world,

After man's creation: the sacrament of marriage.
I'd have you first provide for a good husband,   295
Give him all.
DUCHESS: All?
ANTONIO: Yes, your excellent self.
DUCHESS: In a winding sheet?°
ANTONIO: In a couple.°
DUCHESS: Saint Winifred!° that were a strange will.
ANTONIO: 'Twere strange
If there were no will in you to marry again.
DUCHESS: What do you think of marriage?   300
ANTONIO: I take't, as those that deny purgatory,°
It locally contains or heaven, or hell;
There's no third place in't.
DUCHESS: How do you affect it?°
ANTONIO: My banishment, feeding my melancholy,
Would often reason thus.
DUCHESS: Pray let's hear it.   305
ANTONIO: Say a man never marry, nor have children,
What takes that from him? only the bare name
Of being a father, or the weak delight
To see the little wanton° ride a-cock-horse
Upon a painted stick, or hear him chatter   310
Like a taught starling.
DUCHESS: Fie, fie, what's all this?
One of your eyes is bloodshot;° use my ring to't,
They say 'tis very sovereign.° 'Twas my wedding ring,
                                        [*Gives him the ring.*]
And I did vow never to part with it,
But to my second husband.
ANTONIO: You have parted   315
With it now.
DUCHESS: Yes, to help your eyesight.
ANTONIO: You have made me stark blind.
DUCHESS: How?
ANTONIO: There is a saucy and ambitious devil
Is dancing in this circle.°
DUCHESS: Remove him.
ANTONIO: How?
DUCHESS: There needs small conjuration, when your finger   320
May do it: thus, is it fit?   [*She puts the ring on his finger.*] *He kneels.*
ANTONIO: What said you?
DUCHESS: Sir,
This goodly roof° of yours is too low built;
I cannot stand upright in't, nor discourse,

Without I raise it higher. Raise yourself,
Or if you please, my hand to help you: so.   [*Raises him.*]   325
ANTONIO: Ambition, madam, is a great man's madness,
That is not kept in chains, and close-pent rooms,
But in fair lightsome lodgings, and is girt°
With the wild noise of prattling visitants,°
Which makes it lunatic, beyond all cure.   330
Conceive not I am so stupid but I aim°
Whereto your favours tend. But he's a fool
That, being a-cold, would thrust his hands i'th' fire
To warm them.
DUCHESS: So, now the ground's broke,
You may discover what a wealthy mine   335
I make you lord of.
ANTONIO: O my unworthiness!
DUCHESS: You were ill to sell yourself;°
This dark'ning° of your worth is not like that
Which tradesmen use i'th' city; their false lights°
Are to rid bad wares off. And I must tell you,   340
If you will know where breathes a complete man
(I speak it without flattery), turn your eyes,
And progress° through yourself.
ANTONIO: Were there nor heaven, nor hell,
I should be honest: I have long served virtue,
And ne'er ta'en wages of her.
DUCHESS: Now she pays it.   345
The misery of us, that are born great!
We are forced to woo,° because none dare woo us;
And as a tyrant doubles° with his words,
And fearfully equivocates, so we
Are forced to express our violent passions   350
In riddles, and in dreams, and leave the path
Of simple virtue, which was never made
To seem the thing it is not. Go, go brag
You have left me heartless; mine is in your bosom,
I hope 'twill multiply love there. You do tremble: 355
Make not your heart so dead a piece of flesh
To fear, more than to love me. Sir, be confident;
What is't distracts you? This is flesh and blood, sir,
'Tis not the figure cut in alabaster
Kneels at my husband's tomb.° Awake, awake, man;   360
I do here put off all vain ceremony,
And only do appear to you, a young widow
That claims you for her husband, and like a widow,
I use but half a blush in't.

ANTONIO: Truth speak for me,
  I will remain the constant sanctuary   365
  Of your good name.
DUCHESS: I thank you, gentle love,
  And 'cause you shall not come to me in debt,
  Being now my steward, here upon your lips
  I sign your *Quietus est.*° [*Kisses him.*] This you should have begged now:
  I have seen children oft eat sweetmeats thus,   370
  As fearful to devour them too soon.
ANTONIO: But for your brothers?
DUCHESS [*embracing him*]:   Do not think of them:
  All discord, without this circumference,°
  Is only to be pitied, and not feared.
  Yet, should they know it, time will easily   375
  Scatter the tempest.
ANTONIO: These words should be mine,
  And all the parts you have spoke, if some part of it
  Would not have savoured° flattery.
DUCHESS: Kneel.

[*Enter* CARIOLA.]

ANTONIO: Ha?
DUCHESS: Be not amazed; this woman's of my counsel.°
  I have heard lawyers say a contract in a chamber,   380
  Per verba de presenti, is absolute marriage.° [DUCHESS *and* ANTONIO *kneel.*]
  Bless, Heaven, this sacred Gordian,° which let violence
  Never untwine.
ANTONIO: And may our sweet affections, like the spheres,
  Be still in motion.°
DUCHESS: Quickening,° and make   385
  The like soft music.
ANTONIO: That we may imitate the loving palms,°
  Best emblem of a peaceful marriage,
  That ne'er bore fruit divided.
DUCHESS: What can the Church force° more?   390
ANTONIO: That fortune may not know an accident,
  Either of joy or sorrow, to divide
  Our fixèd wishes.
DUCHESS: How can the Church build faster?
  We now are man and wife, and 'tis the Church
  That must but echo this. [*They rise.*] — Maid, stand apart,   395
  I now am blind.°
ANTONIO: What's your conceit° in this?
DUCHESS: I would have you lead your fortune by the hand,

Unto your marriage bed:
(You speak in me this, for we now are one).
We'll only lie, and talk together, and plot   400
T'appease my humorous° kindred; and, if you please,
Like the old tale,° in *Alexander and Lodowick,*
Lay a naked sword between us, keep us chaste.
O, let me shroud° my blushes in your bosom,
Since 'tis the treasury of all my secrets.
                              [*Exeunt* DUCHESS *and* ANTONIO.] 405
CARIOLA: Whether the spirit of greatness, or of woman
    Reign most in her, I know not, but it shows
    A fearful madness. I owe her much of pity.   *Exit.*

Act Two, Scene One

[*Enter* BOSOLA *and* CASTRUCHIO.]

BOSOLA: You say you would fain be taken for an eminent courtier?°
CASTRUCHIO: 'Tis the very main° of my ambition.
BOSOLA: Let me see, you have a reasonable good face for't already, and
    your nightcap° expresses° your ears sufficient largely;° I would have
    you learn to twirl the strings of your band° with a good grace; and in   5
    a set speech, at th' end of every sentence, to hum, three or four
    times, or blow your nose, till it smart again, to recover your
    memory. When you come to be a president° in criminal causes, if
    you smile upon a prisoner, hang him; but if you frown upon him,
    and threaten him, let him be sure to 'scape the gallows.   10
CASTRUCHIO: I would be a very merry president —
BOSOLA: Do not sup a nights; 'twill beget you an admirable wit.
CASTRUCHIO: Rather it would make me have a good stomach to quarrel,
    for they say your roaring boys° eat meat seldom, and that makes
    them so valiant. But how shall I know whether the people   15
    take me for an eminent fellow?
BOSOLA: I will teach a trick to know it: give out you lie a-dying, and if
    you hear the common people curse you, be sure you are taken for
    one of the prime nightcaps.°

[*Enter an* OLD LADY.]

You come from painting° now?   20
OLD LADY: From what?
BOSOLA: Why, from your scurvy face-physic: to behold thee not painted
    inclines somewhat near a miracle. These in thy face here, were

deep ruts and foul sloughs,° the last progress.° There was a lady in
France, that having had the smallpox, flayed the skin off her face   25
to make it more level; and whereas before she looked like a nutmeg
grater, after she resembled an abortive° hedgehog.

OLD LADY: Do you call this painting?

BOSOLA: No, no, but you call it careening of an old morphewed lady, to
make her disembogue again.° There's rough-cast phrase to your   30
plastic.°

OLD LADY: It seems you are well acquainted with my closet?

BOSOLA: One would suspect it for a shop of witchcraft, to find in it the
fat of serpents, spawn of snakes, Jews' spittle, and their young
children's ordure, and all these for the face. I would sooner eat a   35
dead pigeon, taken from the soles of the feet of one sick of the
plague,° than kiss one of you fasting. Here are two of you, whose sin
of your youth° is the very patrimony° of the physician, makes him
renew his footcloth° with the spring, and change his high-prized°
courtesan with the fall of the leaf.° I do wonder you do not loathe   40
yourselves. Observe° my meditation now:
What thing is in this outward form of man
To be beloved? We account it ominous
If nature do produce a colt, or lamb,
A fawn, or goat, in any limb resembling   45
A man; and fly from't as a prodigy.°
Man stands amazed to see his deformity,
In any other creature but himself.
But in our own flesh, though we bear diseases
Which have their true names only ta'en from beasts,   50
As the most ulcerous wolf,° and swinish measle,°
Though we are eaten up of lice, and worms,
And though continually we bear about us
A rotten and dead body, we delight
To hide it in rich tissue.° All our fear,   55
Nay, all our terror, is lest our physician
Should put us in the ground, to be made sweet.
Your wife's gone to Rome: you two couple, and get you
To the wells at Lucca,° to recover your aches.
                              [*Exeunt* CASTRUCHIO *and* OLD LADY.]
I have other work on foot. I observe our duchess   60
Is sick a-days; she pukes,° her stomach seethes,°
The fins° of her eyelids look most teeming° blue,
She wanes i'th' cheek, and waxes fat i'th' flank;
And, contrary to our Italian fashion,
Wears a loose-bodied° gown: there's somewhat in't.   65
I have a trick may chance discover° it,
A pretty one; I have bought some apricocks,°

The first our spring yields.

[*Enter* ANTONIO *and* DELIO, *talking apart.*]

DELIO: And so long since married?
  You amaze me.
ANTONIO: Let me seal your lips for ever,
  For did I think that anything but th' air   70
  Could carry these words from you, I should wish
  You had no breath at all. —
  [*To* BOSOLA.]   Now, sir, in your contemplation?
  You are studying to become a great wise fellow?
BOSOLA: O, sir, the opinion of wisdom is a foul tetter° that runs all over a
  man's body. If simplicity direct us to have no evil, it directs us to a   75
  happy being, for the subtlest folly proceeds from the subtlest
  wisdom. Let me be simply honest.
ANTONIO: I do understand your inside.
BOSOLA: Do you so?
ANTONIO: Because you would not seem to appear to th' world
  Puffed up with your preferment, you continue   80
  This out of fashion° melancholy; leave it, leave it.
BOSOLA: Give me leave to be honest in any phrase, in any compliment
  whatsoever. Shall I confess myself to you? I look no higher than I
  can reach: they are the gods, that must ride on winged horses; a
  lawyer's mule of a slow pace will both suit my disposition and   85
  business. For, mark me, when a man's mind rides faster than his
  horse can gallop, they quickly both tire.
ANTONIO: You would look up to heaven, but I think
  The devil, that rules i'th' air, stands in your light.
BOSOLA: O, sir, you are lord of the ascendant,° chief man with the   90
  duchess: a duke was your cousin-german, removed.° Say you were
  lineally descended from King Pippin,° or he himself, what of this?
  Search the heads of the greatest rivers in the world, you shall find
  them but bubbles of water. Some would think the souls of princes
  were brought forth by some more weighty cause than those of   95
  meaner persons; they are deceived, there's the same hand to them.
  The like passions sway them; the same reason that makes a vicar go
  to law for a tithe-pig,° and undo his neighbours, makes them spoil° a
  whole province, and batter down goodly cities with the cannon.

[*Enter* DUCHESS, *with* Attendants *and* Ladies.]

DUCHESS. Your arm, Antonio; do I not grow fat?   100
  I am exceeding short-winded. Bosola,
  I would have you, sir, provide for me a litter,

Such a one as the Duchess of Florence rode in.
BOSOLA: The duchess used one, when she was great with child.
DUCHESS: I think she did. — Come hither, mend my ruff,°   105
    Here; when?° thou art such a tedious° lady, and
    Thy breath smells of lemon peels. Would thou hadst done;
    Shall I sound° under thy fingers? I am
    So troubled with the mother.°
BOSOLA [*aside*]:   I fear too much.
DUCHESS: I have heard you say that the French courtiers   110
    Wear their hats on 'fore the king.°
ANTONIO: I have seen it.
DUCHESS: In the presence?°
ANTONIO: Yes.
DUCHESS: Why should not we bring up that fashion?
    'Tis ceremony more than duty, that consists
    In the removing of a piece of felt.   115
    Be you the example to the rest o'th' court;
    Put on your hat first.
ANTONIO: You must pardon me:
    I have seen, in colder countries than in France,
    Nobles stand bare° to th' prince; and the distinction
    Methought showed reverently.°   120
BOSOLA: I have a present for your Grace.
DUCHESS: For me, sir?
BOSOLA: Apricocks, madam.
DUCHESS: O sir, where are they?
    I have heard of none to-year.°
BOSOLA [*aside*]:   Good, her colour rises.
                                  [*Gives fruit to the* DUCHESS.]
DUCHESS: Indeed I thank you: they are wondrous fair ones.
    What an unskilful fellow is our gardener!   125
    We shall have none this month.   [*She eats.*]
BOSOLA: Will not your Grace pare them?
DUCHESS: No, they taste of musk,° methinks; indeed they do.
BOSOLA: I know not; yet I wish your Grace had pared 'em.
DUCHESS: Why?
BOSOLA: I forgot to tell you the knave gard'ner,   130
    Only to raise his profit by them the sooner,
    Did ripen them in horse-dung.
DUCHESS: O, you jest.
    [*to* ANTONIO] You shall judge: pray taste one.
ANTONIO: Indeed, madam,
    I do not love the fruit.
DUCHESS: Sir, you are loth
    To rob us of our dainties:° 'tis a delicate° fruit, —   135

They say they are restorative.
BOSOLA: 'Tis a pretty art,
    This grafting —°
DUCHESS: 'Tis so: a bett'ring of nature.
BOSOLA: To make a pippin grow upon a crab,°
    A damson on a black-thorn. [*Aside*] How greedily she eats them!
    A whirlwind strike off these bawd farthingales,°   140
    For, but for that, and the loose-bodied gown,
    I should have discovered apparently°
    The young springal cutting a caper° in her belly.
DUCHESS: I thank you, Bosola: they were right good ones, —
    If they do not make me sick.
ANTONIO: How now, madam?   145
DUCHESS: This green fruit and my stomach are not friends.
    How they swell me!
BOSOLA [*aside*]:   Nay, you are too much swelled already.
DUCHESS: O, I am in an extreme cold sweat.
BOSOLA: I am very sorry.   [*Exit.*]
DUCHESS: Lights° to my chamber! O, good Antonio,   150
    I fear I am undone.   [*Exeunt all but* ANTONIO *and* DELIO.]
DELIO: Lights there, lights!
ANTONIO: O my most trusty Delio, we are lost:
    I fear she's fall'n in labour; and there's left
    No time for her remove.
DELIO: Have you prepared
    Those ladies to attend her? and procured   155
    That politic° safe conveyance for the midwife
    Your duchess plotted?
ANTONIO: I have.
DELIO: Make use then of this forced occasion.
    Give out that Bosola hath poisoned her,
    With these apricocks; that will give some colour°   160
    For her keeping close.°
ANTONIO: Fie, fie, the physicians
    Will then flock to her.
DELIO: For that you may pretend
    She'll use some prepared antidote of her own,
    Lest the physicians should repoison her.
ANTONIO: I am lost in amazement: I know not what to think on't.
                                  Ex[eunt]. 165

Act Two, Scene Two

[*Enter* BOSOLA *and* OLD LADY.]

BOSOLA: So, so: there's no question but her tetchiness° and most

vulturous eating of the apricocks are apparent signs of breeding,°
now?

OLD LADY: I am in haste,° sir.

BOSOLA: There was a young waiting-woman had a monstrous desire to   5
see the glass-house —°

OLD LADY: Nay, pray let me go!

BOSOLA: And it was only to know what strange instrument it was
should swell up a glass to the fashion of a woman's belly.

OLD LADY: I will hear no more of the glass-house; you are still° abusing   10
women!

BOSOLA: Who, I? No; only, by the way now and then, mention your
frailties. The orange tree bears ripe and green fruit and blossoms
altogether. And some of you give entertainment° for pure love: but
more, for more precious reward. The lusty spring smells well; but   15
drooping autumn tastes well.° If we have the same golden showers
that rained in the time of Jupiter the Thunderer, you have the same
Danaes still, to hold up their laps to receive them.° Didst thou
never study the mathematics?

OLD LADY: What's that, sir?   20

BOSOLA: Why, to know the trick how to make a many lines meet in one
centre.° Go, go; give your foster-daughters good counsel: tell them,
that the devil takes delight to hang at a woman's girdle, like a false
rusty watch, that she cannot discern how the time passes.

[*Exit* OLD LADY.]

[*Enter* ANTONIO, DELIO, RODERIGO, GRISOLAN.]

ANTONIO: Shut up the court gates.

RODERIGO: Why, sir? what's the danger?   25

ANTONIO: Shut up the posterns° presently;° and call
All the officers o'th' court.

GRISOLAN: I shall instantly.   [*Exit.*]

ANTONIO: Who keeps the key o'th' park-gate?

RODERIGO: Forobosco.

ANTONIO: Let him bring't presently.   [*Exit* RODERIGO.]

[*Enter* SERVANTS, GRISOLAN, RODERIGO.]

1 SERVANT: O, gentlemen o'th' court, the foulest treason!   30

BOSOLA [*aside*]: If that these apricocks should be poisoned now —
Without my knowledge!

1 SERVANT: There was taken even now a Switzer° in the duchess'
bedchamber.

2 SERVANT: A Switzer?   35

1 SERVANT: With a pistol° in his great cod-piece.°

BOSOLA: Ha, ha, ha!

1 SERVANT: The cod-piece was the case for't.

2 SERVANT: There was a cunning traitor. Who would have searched his
    cod-piece?   40

1 SERVANT: True, if he had kept out of the ladies' chambers:° and all the
    moulds of his buttons were leaden bullets.

2 SERVANT: O, wicked cannibal! a fire-lock° in's cod-piece?

1 SERVANT: 'Twas a French plot,° upon my life.

2 SERVANT: To see what the devil can do.°   45

ANTONIO: All the officers here?

SERVANTS: We are.

ANTONIO: Gentlemen,
    We have lost much plate you know; and, but this evening,
    Jewels to the value of four thousand ducats
    Are missing in the duchess' cabinet.°
    Are the gates shut?

1 SERVANT: Yes.

ANTONIO: 'Tis the duchess' pleasure   50
    Each officer be locked into his chamber
    Till the sun-rising; and to send the keys
    Of all their chests, and of their outward doors,
    Into her bedchamber. She is very sick.

RODERIGO: At her pleasure.   55

ANTONIO: She entreats you take't not ill. The innocent
    Shall be the more approved° by it.

BOSOLA: Gentleman o'th' wood-yard,° where's your Switzer now?

1 SERVANT: By this hand, 'twas credibly reported by one o'th'
    black-guard.° [*Exeunt* BOSOLA, GRISOLAN, RODERIGO *and* SERVANTS.] 60

DELIO: How fares it with the duchess?

ANTONIO: She's exposed
    Unto the worst of torture, pain, and fear.

DELIO: Speak to her all happy comfort.

ANTONIO: How I do play the fool with mine own danger!
    You are this night, dear friend, to post° to Rome;   65
    My life lies in your service.

DELIO: Do not doubt° me.

ANTONIO: O, 'tis far from me; and yet fear presents me
    Somewhat that looks like danger.

DELIO: Believe it,
    'Tis but the shadow of your fear, no more.
    How superstitiously we mind our evils!   70
    The throwing down salt, or crossing of a hare,
    Bleeding at nose, the stumbling of a horse,
    Or singing of a cricket,° are of power
    To daunt whole man in us. Sir, fare you well.

I wish you all the joys of a blessed father;   75
And, for my faith, lay this unto your breast:
Old friends, like old swords, still° are trusted best.   [*Exit* DELIO.]

[*Enter* CARIOLA.]

CARIOLA: Sir, you are the happy father of a son;
    Your wife commends him to you.
ANTONIO: Blessed comfort!
    For heaven' sake tend her well. I'll presently   80
    Go set a figure for's nativity.°   *Exeunt.*

Act Two, Scene Three

[*Enter* BOSOLA *with a dark lantern.*]°

BOSOLA: Sure I did hear a woman shriek: list, ha?
    And the sound came, if I received it right,
    From the duchess' lodgings. There's some stratagem
    In the confining all our courtiers
    To their several wards.° I must have part° of it,   5
    My intelligence° will freeze else. List° again,
    It may be 'twas the melancholy bird,
    Best friend of silence, and of solitariness,
    The owl, that screamed so: — ha! Antonio?

[*Enter* ANTONIO, *with a horoscope.*]°

ANTONIO: I heard some noise: who's there? What art thou? Speak.   10
BOSOLA: Antonio! Put not your face nor body
    To such a forced expression of fear.
    I am Bosola; your friend.
ANTONIO: Bosola!
    [*Aside*] This mole does undermine me — heard you not
    A noise even now?
BOSOLA: From whence?
ANTONIO: From the duchess' lodging.   15
BOSOLA: Not I: did you?
ANTONIO: I did; or else I dreamed.
BOSOLA: Let's walk towards it.
ANTONIO: No. It may be 'twas
    But the rising of the wind.
BOSOLA: Very likely.

Methinks 'tis very cold, and yet you sweat.
You look wildly.
ANTONIO: I have been setting a figure°   20
For the duchess' jewels.
BOSOLA: Ah! and how falls your question?
Do you find it radical?°
ANTONIO: What's that to you?
'Tis rather to be questioned what design,
When all men were commanded to their lodgings,
Makes you a night-walker.°
BOSOLA: In sooth I'll tell you: 25
Now all the court's asleep, I thought the devil
Had least to do here; I come to say my prayers,
And if it do offend you I do so,
You are a fine courtier.
ANTONIO [*aside*]:   This fellow will undo me. —
You gave the duchess apricocks to-day;   30
Pray heaven they were not poisoned!
BOSOLA: Poisoned! a Spanish fig°
For the imputation.
ANTONIO: Traitors are ever confident,
Till they are discovered. There were jewels stol'n too.
In my conceit,° none are to be suspected
More than yourself.
BOSOLA: You are a false° steward.   35
ANTONIO: Saucy slave! I'll pull thee up by the roots.
BOSOLA: May be the ruin° will crush you to pieces.
ANTONIO: You are an impudent snake indeed, sir.
Are you scarce warm,° and do you show your sting?
BOSOLA: ...°   40
ANTONIO: You libel well, sir.
BOSOLA: No, sir; copy it out,
And I will set my hand to't.   ANTONIO *puts his handkerchief to his nose*.]
ANTONIO [*aside*]:   My nose bleeds.
One that were superstitious would count
This ominous, when it merely comes by chance.
Two letters, that are wrought° here for my name,   45
Are drowned in blood:
Mere accident. For you, sir, I'll take order;
I'th' morn you shall be safe. [*Aside*] 'Tis that must colour°
Her lying-in. —° Sir, this door you pass not:
I do not hold it fit that you come near   50
The duchess' lodgings, till you have quit° yourself. —
[*Aside*] The great are like the base; nay, they are the same,
When they seek shameful ways to avoid shame.   *Ex*[*it*].

BOSOLA: Antonio here about did drop a paper;
    Some of your help, false friend.° Oh, here it is.   55
    What's here? a child's nativity calculated?
    [*Reads*] *The Duchess was delivered of a son, 'tween the hours twelve and*
    one, in the night: Anno Dom: 1504 (that's this year), *decimo nono*
    Decembris° (that's this night), *taken according to the meridian of Malfi*
    (that's our Duchess: happy discovery). *The Lord of the first house,*   60
    being combust in the ascendant, signifes short life; and Mars being in a
    human sign, joined to the tail of the Dragon, in the eight house, doth
    threaten a violent death; °*cætera non scrutantur.* °
    Why, now 'tis most apparent. This precise° fellow
    Is the duchess' bawd: I have it to my wish.   65
    This is a parcel of intelligency°
    Our courtiers were cased up for! It needs must follow
    That I must be committed,° on pretence
    Of poisoning her; which I'll endure, and laugh at.
    If one could find the father now: but that   70
    Time will discover. Old Castruchio
    I'th' morning posts° to Rome; by him I'll send
    A letter that shall make her brothers' galls
    O'erflow their livers. This was a thrifty° way.
    Though lust do masque° in ne'er so strange disguise,   75
    She's oft found witty,° but is never wise.   [*Exit.*]

Act Two, Scene Four

[*Enter* CARDINAL *and* JULIA.]

CARDINAL: Sit.° Thou art my best of wishes; prithee tell me
    What trick didst thou invent to come to Rome,
    Without thy husband?
JULIA: Why, my lord, I told him
    I came to visit an old anchorite°
    Here, for devotion.°
CARDINAL: Thou art a witty false one: —   5
    I mean to him.
JULIA: You have prevailed with me
    Beyond my strongest thoughts; I would not now
    Find you inconstant.
CARDINAL: Do not put thyself
    To such a voluntary torture, which proceeds
    Out of your own guilt.

JULIA: How, my lord?

CARDINAL: You fear   10
   My constancy, because you have approved°
   Those giddy and wild turnings in yourself.

JULIA: Did you e'er find them?

CARDINAL: Sooth,° generally for women.
   A man might strive to make glass malleable,
   Ere he should make them fixèd.

JULIA: So, my lord.   15

CARDINAL: We had need go borrow that fantastic glass
   Invented by Galileo the Florentine,
   To view another spacious world i'th' moon,°
   And look to find a constant woman there.°

JULIA: This is very well, my lord.   [*Weeps.*]

CARDINAL: Why do you weep?   20
   Are tears your justification? The selfsame tears
   Will fall into your husband's bosom, lady,
   With a loud protestation that you love him
   Above the world. Come, I'll love you wisely —
   That's jealously —° since I am very certain   25
   You cannot me make cuckold.

JULIA: I'll go home
   To my husband.

CARDINAL: You may thank me, lady;
   I have taken you off your melancholy perch,
   Bore you upon my fist, and showed you game,
   And let you fly at it.° I pray thee, kiss me.   [*They kiss.*] 30
   When thou wast with thy husband, thou wast watched
   Like a tame elephant:° (still you are to thank me.)   [*They kiss.*]
   Thou hadst only kisses from him, and high feeding;°
   But what delight was that? 'Twas just like one
   That hath a little fing'ring° on the lute,   35
   Yet cannot tune it: (still you are to thank me.)   [*They kiss.*]

JULIA: You told me of a piteous wound i'th' heart,
   And a sick liver,° when you wooed me first,
   And spake like one in physic.°

CARDINAL: Who's that?

[*Enter* SERVANT.]

   Rest firm; for my affection to thee,   40
   Lightning moves slow to't.

SERVANT: Madam, a gentleman
   That's come post from Malfi desires to see you.

CARDINAL: Let him enter; I'll withdraw.   *Exit.*

SERVANT: He says
    Your husband, old Castruchio, is come to Rome,
    Most pitifully tired with riding post.

                      [*Exit* SERVANT.] 45

             [*Enter* DELIO.]

JULIA: Signior Delio! [*Aside*] 'tis one of my old suitors.
DELIO: I was bold to come and see you.
JULIA: Sir, you are welcome.
DELIO: Do you lie here?°
JULIA: Sure, your own experience
    Will satisfy you, no; our Roman prelates
    Do not keep lodging for ladies.
DELIO: Very well.   50
    I have brought you no commendations from your husband,
    For I know none by him.
JULIA: I hear he's come to Rome?
DELIO: I never knew man and beast, of a horse and a knight,
    So weary of each other. If he had had a good back,°
    He would have undertook to have borne his horse,   55
    His breach was so pitifully sore.
JULIA: Your laughter
    Is my pity.
DELIO: Lady, I know not whether
    You want° money, but I have brought you some.
JULIA: From my husband?
DELIO: No, from mine own allowance.   [*Offers a purse.*]
JULIA: I must hear the condition, ere I be bound to take it.   60
DELIO: Look on't,° 'tis gold, hath it not a fine colour?
JULIA: I have a bird more beautiful.
DELIO: Try the sound on't.
JULIA: A lute-string far exceeds it;
    It hath no smell, like cassia or civet,°
    Nor is it physical,° though some fond° doctors   65
    Persuade us seethe't in cullises.° I'll tell you,
    This is a creature bred by —

            [*Enter* SERVANT.]

SERVANT: Your husband's come;
    Hath delivered a letter to the Duke of Calabria,
    That, to my thinking, hath put him out of his wits.   [*Exit* SERVANT.]
JULIA: Sir, you hear: 70

Pray let me know your business and your suit,
   As briefly as can be.
DELIO: With good speed. I would wish you,
   At such time as you are non-resident
   With your husband, my mistress.
JULIA: Sir, I'll go ask my husband if I shall,   75
   And straight return your answer.   *Exit.*
DELIO: Very fine;
   Is this her wit, or honesty that speaks thus?
   I heard one say the duke was highly moved
   With a letter sent from Malfi. I do fear
   Antonio is betrayed. How fearfully   80
   Shows his ambition now; unfortunate Fortune!
   They pass through whirlpools, and deep woes do shun,
   Who the event weigh,° ere the action's done.   *Exit.*

Act Two, Scene Five

[*Enter*] CARDINAL, *and* FERDINAND, *with a letter.*

FERDINAND: I have this night digged up a mandrake.°
CARDINAL: Say you?
FERDINAND: And I am grown mad with't.
CARDINAL: What's the prodigy?°
FERDINAND: Read there, a sister damned; she's loose i'th' hilts,°
   Grown a notorious strumpet.
CARDINAL: Speak lower.
FERDINAND: Lower?
   Rogues do not whisper't now, but seek to publish't,   5
   As servants do the bounty of their lords,
   Aloud; and with a covetous searching eye,
   To mark who note them. O, confusion° seize her,
   She hath had most cunning bawds to serve her turn,°
   And more secure conveyances for lust,   10
   Than towns of garrison° for service.°
CARDINAL: Is't possible?
   Can this be certain?
FERDINAND: Rhubarb, O for rhubarb
   To purge this choler!° Here's° the cursèd day
   To prompt my memory, and here't shall stick,
   Till of her bleeding heart I make a sponge   15
   To wipe it out.
CARDINAL: Why do you make yourself
   So wild a tempest?

FERDINAND: Would I could be one,
That I might toss her palace 'bout her ears,
Root up her goodly forests, blast her meads,°
And lay her general territory as waste   20
As she hath done her honour's.
CARDINAL: Shall our blood,
The royal blood of Aragon and Castile,
Be thus attainted?°
FERDINAND: Apply desperate physic:°
We must not now use balsamum,° but fire,
The smarting cupping-glass,° for that's the mean   25
To purge infected blood, such blood as hers.
There is a kind of pity in mine eye,
I'll give it to my handkercher; and now 'tis here,

> [*Wipes his eyes with his handkerchief.*]

I'll bequeath this to her bastard.
CARDINAL: What to do?
FERDINAND: Why, to make soft lint for his mother's wounds,   30
When I have hewed her to pieces.
CARDINAL: Cursèd creature!
Unequal° nature, to place women's hearts
So far upon the left side.°
FERDINAND: Foolish men,
That e'er will trust their honour in a bark°
Made of so slight weak bulrush, as is woman,   35
Apt every minute to sink it!
CARDINAL: Thus ignorance, when it hath purchased° honour,
It cannot wield it.
FERDINAND: Methinks I see her laughing;
Excellent hyena!° Talk to me somewhat, quickly,
Or my imagination will carry me   40
To see her in the shameful act of sin.
CARDINAL: With whom?
FERDINAND: Happily,° with some strong-thighed bargeman;
Or one o'th' wood-yard, that can quoit the sledge°
Or toss the bar; or else some lovely squire,°
That carries coals up to her privy° lodgings.   45
CARDINAL: You fly beyond your reason.
FERDINAND: Go to, mistress!
'Tis not your whore's milk that shall quench my wild-fire,°
But your whore's blood.
CARDINAL: How idly° shows this rage! which carries you,
As men conveyed by witches, through the air,   50
On violent whirlwinds. This intemperate noise
Fitly resembles deaf men's shrill discourse,

Who talk aloud, thinking all other men
To have their imperfection.
FERDINAND: Have not you
    My palsy?°
CARDINAL: Yes, I can be angry,   55
    Without this rupture; there is not in nature
    A thing that makes man so deformed, so beastly,
    As doth intemperate anger. Chide yourself:
    You have divers° men who never yet expressed
    Their strong desire of rest but by unrest,   60
    By vexing of themselves. Come, put yourself
    In tune.
FERDINAND: So, I will only study to seem
    The thing I am not. I could kill her now,
    In you, or in myself, for I do think
    It is some sin in us heaven doth revenge   65
    By her.
CARDINAL: Are you stark mad?
FERDINAND: I would have their bodies
    Burnt in a coal-pit,° with the ventage stopped,
    That their cursed smoke might not ascend to heaven;
    Or dip the sheets they lie in in pitch or sulphur,
    Wrap them in't, and then light them like a match;   70
    Or else to boil their bastard to a cullis,°
    And give't his lecherous father, to renew
    The sin of his back.
CARDINAL: I'll leave you.
FERDINAND: Nay, I have done.
    I am confident, had I been damned in hell,
    And should have heard of this, it would have put me   75
    Into a cold sweat. In, in, I'll go sleep.
    Till I know who leaps° my sister, I'll not stir:
    That known, I'll find scorpions° to string my whips,
    And fix° her in a general° eclipse.   *Exeunt.*

Act Three, Scene One

[*Enter* ANTONIO *and* DELIO.]

ANTONIO: Our noble friend, my most belovèd Delio,
    O, you have been a stranger long at court;
    Came you along with the Lord Ferdinand?
DELIO: I did, sir, and how fares your noble duchess?
ANTONIO: Right fortunately well. She's an excellent   5

Feeder of pedigrees: since you last saw her,
She hath had two children more, a son and daughter.
DELIO: Methinks 'twas yesterday. Let me but wink,°
   And not behold your face (which to mine eye
   Is somewhat leaner): verily I should dream   10
   It were within this half hour.
ANTONIO: You have not been in law, friend Delio,
   Nor in prison, nor a suitor at the court,
   Nor begged the reversion° of some great man's place,
   Nor troubled with an old wife, which doth make   15
   Your time so insensibly hasten.
DELIO: Pray sir, tell me,
   Hath not this news arrived yet to the ear
   Of the Lord Cardinal?
ANTONIO: I fear it hath.
   The Lord Ferdinand, that's newly come to court,
   Doth bear himself right dangerously.
DELIO: Pray why?   20
ANTONIO: He is so quiet, that he seems to sleep
   The tempest out, as dormice do in winter;
   Those houses that are haunted are most still,
   Till the devil be up.
DELIO: What say the common people?
ANTONIO: The common rabble do directly° say   25
   She is a strumpet.
DELIO: And your graver heads,
   Which would be politic, what censure° they?
ANTONIO: They do observe I grow to infinite purchase°
   The left-hand° way, and all suppose the duchess
   Would amend it, if she could. For, say they,   30
   Great princes, though they grudge their officers
   Should have such large and unconfinèd means
   To get wealth under them, will not complain,
   Lest thereby they should make them odious
   Unto the people: — for other obligation,   35
   Of love, or marriage, between her and me,
   They never dream of.

[*Enter* FERDINAND, DUCHESS *and* BOSOLA.]

DELIO: The Lord Ferdinand
   Is going to bed.
FERDINAND: I'll instantly to bed,
   For I am weary: I am to bespeak°
   A husband for you.

DUCHESS: For me, sir! pray who is't?   40
FERDINAND: The great Count Malateste.
DUCHESS: Fie upon him;
   A count? He's a mere stick of sugar-candy;
   You may look quite thorough him. When I choose
   A husband, I will marry for your honour.
FERDINAND: You shall do well in't. How is't, worthy Antonio?   45
DUCHESS: But, sir, I am to have private conference with you,°
   About a scandalous report is spread
   Touching mine honour.
FERDINAND: Let me be ever deaf to't:
   One of Pasquil's paper bullets,° court calumny,
   A pestilent air, which princes' palaces   50
   Are seldom purged of. Yet, say that it were true,
   I pour it in your bosom, my fixed love
   Would strongly excuse, extenuate, nay, deny
   Faults, were they apparent in you. Go, be safe
   In your own innocency.
DUCHESS: O blessed comfort;   55
   This deadly air is purged.   *Exeunt* [DUCHESS, ANTONIO, DELIO].
FERDINAND: Her guilt treads on
   Hot burning coulters.° Now, Bosola,
   How thrives our intelligence?°
BOSOLA: Si r, uncertainly.
   'Tis rumoured she hath had three bastards, but
   By whom, we may go read i'th' stars.
FERDINAND: Why, some   60
   Hold opinion all things are written there.
BOSOLA: Yes, if we could find spectacles to read them.
   I do suspect there hath been some sorcery
   Used on the duchess.
FERDINAND: Sorcery, to what purpose?
BOSOLA: To make her dote on some desertless fellow   65
   She shames to acknowledge.
FERDINAND: Can your faith give way
   To think there's power in potions, or in charms,
   To make us love, whether we will or no?
BOSOLA: Most certainly.
FERDINAND: Away; these are mere gulleries,° horrid things   70
   Invented by some cheating mountebanks°
   To abuse us. Do you think that herbs, or charms
   Can force the will?° Some trials have been made
   In the foolish practice; but the ingredients
   Were lenative poisons,° such as are of force   75
   To make the patient mad; and straight the witch

Swears, by equivocation,° they are in love.
The witchcraft lies in her rank blood. This night
I will force confession from her. You told me
You had got, within these two days, a false key   80
Into her bed-chamber.
BOSOLA: I have.
FERDINAND: As I would wish.
BOSOLA: What do you intend to do?
FERDINAND: Can you guess?
BOSOLA: No.
FERDINAND: Do not ask then.
He that can compass me, and know my drifts,
May say he hath put a girdle 'bout the world,   85
And sounded all her quick-sands.
BOSOLA: _   I do not
Think so.
FERDINAND: What do you think then, pray?
BOSOLA: That you
Are your own chronicle° too much, and grossly
Flatter yourself.
FERD!NAND: Give me thy hand; I thank thee.
I never gave pension but to flatterers,   90
Till I entertained° thee. Farewell,
That friend a great man's ruin strongly checks,
Who rails into his belief all his defects.   *Exeunt.*

Act Three, Scene Two

[*Enter* DUCHESS, ANTONIO *and* CARIOLA.]

DUCHESS: Bring me the casket hither, and the glass;°
You get no lodging° here to-night, my lord.
ANTONIO: Indeed, I must persuade one.
DUCHESS: Very good:
I hope in time 'twill grow into a custom,
That noblemen shall come with cap and knee,°   5
To purchase a night's lodging of their wives.
ANTONIO: I must lie here.
DUCHESS: Must? You are a lord of mis-rule.°
ANTONIO: Indeed, my rule is only in the night.
DUCHESS: To what use° will you put me?
ANTONIO: We'll sleep together.
DUCHESS: Alas, what pleasure can two lovers find in sleep?   10

CARIOLA: My lord, I lie with her often; and I know
    She'll much disquiet you. —
ANTONIO: See, you are complained of.
CARIOLA: For she's the sprawling'st bedfellow.
ANTONIO: I shall like her the better for that.
CARIOLA: Sir, shall I ask you a question?   15
ANTONIO: I pray thee Cariola.
CARIOLA: Wherefore still,° when you lie with my lady,
    Do you rise° so early?
ANTONIO: Labouring men
    Count the clock oft'nest, Cariola;
    Are glad when their task's ended.
DUCHESS: I'll stop your mouth. [*Kisses him*]. 20
ANTONIO: Nay, that's but one. Venus had two soft doves
    To draw her chariot: I must have another.   [*Kisses her*].
    When wilt thou marry, Cariola?
CARIOLA: Never, my lord.
ANTONIO: O fie upon this single life! forgo it.
    We read how Daphne, for her peevish° flight,   25
    Became a fruitless bay-tree; Syrinx turned
    To the pale empty reed; Anaxarete
    Was frozen into marble:° whereas those
    Which married, or proved kind° unto their friends,°
    Were, by a gracious influence, transhaped   30
    Into the olive, pomegranate, mulberry;
    Became flowers, precious stones, or eminent stars.
CARIOLA: This is vain° poetry. But I pray you, tell me,
    If there were proposed me wisdom, riches, and beauty,
    In three several° young men, which should I choose?   35
ANTONIO: 'Tis a hard question. This was Paris' case,°
    And he was blind° in't, and there was great cause;
    For how was't possible he could judge right,
    Having three amorous goddesses in view,
    And they stark naked? 'Twas a motion°   40
    Were able to benight the apprehension°
    Of the severest counsellor of Europe.
    Now I look on both your faces, so well formed,
    It puts me in mind of a question I would ask.
CARIOLA: What is't?
ANTONIO: I do wonder why hard-favoured° ladies,   45
    For the most part, keep worse-favoured waiting-women
    To attend them, and cannot endure fair ones.
DUCHESS: O, that's soon answered.
    Did you ever in your life know an ill° painter
    Desire to have his dwelling next door to the shop   50

Of an excellent picture-maker? 'Twould disgrace
His face-making,° and undo° him. I prithee,
When were we so merry? My hair tangles.
ANTONIO [*aside to* CARIOLA]: Pray thee, Cariola, let's steal forth the room,
    And let her talk to herself. I have divers° times   55
    Served her the like, when she hath chafed extremely.
    I love to see her angry; softly, Cariola.   *Exeunt* [ANTONIO *and* CARIOLA].
DUCHESS: Doth not the colour of my hair 'gin to change?
    When I wax grey, I shall have all the court
    Powder their hair with arras,° to be like me.   60
    You have cause to love me; I entered° you into my heart.

                    [*Enter* FERDINAND, *unseen.*]

Before, you would vouchsafe° to call for the keys.
We shall one day have my brothers take you napping.
Methinks his presence, being now in court,
Should make you keep your own bed; but you'll say   65
Love mixed with fear is sweetest. I'll assure you,
You shall get no more children till my brothers
Consent to be your gossips.° Have you lost your tongue?
                                        [*She sees* FERDINAND.]°
'Tis welcome:
For know, whether I am doomed to live, or die,   70
I can do both like a prince.   FERDINAND *gives her a poniard.*°
FERDINAND: Die then, quickly.
    Virtue, where art thou hid? What hideous thing
    Is it, that doth eclipse thee?
DUCHESS: Pray sir, hear me —
FERDINAND: Or is it true, thou art but a bare name,
    And no essential thing?
DUCHESS: Sir —
FERDINAND: Do not speak.   75
DUCHESS: No, sir:
    I will plant my soul in mine ears, to hear you.
FERDINAND: O most imperfect light of human reason,
    That mak'st us so unhappy, to foresee
    What we can least prevent. Pursue thy wishes,   80
    And glory in them: there's in shame no comfort,
    But to be past all bounds and sense of shame.
DUCHESS: I pray sir, hear me! I am married —
FERDINAND: So!
DUCHESS: Happily° not to your liking; but for that,
    Alas, your shears do come untimely now   85

To clip the bird's wings, that's already flown.
Will you see my husband?
FERDINAND: Yes, if I could change°
Eyes with a basilisk.°
DUCHESS: Sure, you came hither
By his° confederacy.
FERDINAND: The howling of a wolf
Is music to thee,° screech-owl; prithee peace. —   90
Whate'er thou art, that hast enjoyed my sister,
(For I am sure thou hear'st me), for thine own sake
Let me not know thee. I came hither prepared
To work° thy discovery, yet am now persuaded
It would beget such violent effects   95
As would damn us both. I would not for ten millions
I had beheld thee; therefore use all means
I never may have knowledge of thy name.
Enjoy thy lust still, and a wretched life,
On that condition. — And for thee, vild° woman,   100
If thou do wish thy lecher may grow old
In thy embracements, I would have thee build
Such a room for him as our anchorites°
To holier use inhabit. Let not the sun
Shine on him, till he's dead. Let dogs and monkeys   105
Only converse with him, and such dumb things
To whom nature denies use to sound his name.
Do not keep a paraquito,° lest she learn it;
If thou do love him, cut out thine own tongue,
Lest it bewray° him.
DUCHESS: Why might not I marry?   110
I have not gone about, in this, to create
Any new world, or custom.
FERDINAND: Thou art undone;
And thou hast ta'en that massy sheet of lead
That hid thy husband's bones, and folded it
About my heart.
DUCHESS: Mine bleeds for't.
FERDINAND: Thine? thy heart?   115
What should I name't, unless a hollow bullet°
Filled with unquenchable wild-fire?°
DUCHESS: You are in this
Too strict; and, were you not my princely brother,
I would say too wilful.° My reputation
Is safe.
FERDINAND: Dost thou know what reputation is?   120
I'll tell thee, — to small purpose, since th'instruction

Comes now too late.
Upon a time, Reputation, Love and Death
Would travel o'er the world; and 'twas concluded°
That they should part, and take three several° ways.   125
Death told them they should find him in great battles,
Or cities plagued with plagues. Love gives them counsel
To inquire for him 'mongst unambitious shepherds,°
Where dowries were not talked of; and sometimes
'Mongst quiet° kindred, that had nothing left   130
By their dead parents. 'Stay', quoth Reputation,
'Do not forsake me; for it is my nature,
If once I part from any man I meet,
I am never found again.' And so, for you:
You have shook hands with Reputation,   135
And made him invisible. So fare you well.
I will never see you more.
DUCHESS: Why should only I,
    Of all the other princes of the world,
    Be cased up,° like a holy relic? I have youth,
    And a little beauty.
FERDINAND: So you have some virgins   140
    That are witches. I will never see thee more.   *Exit.*

Enter [CARIOLA, *and*] ANTONIO *with a pistol.*

DUCHESS: You saw this apparition?
ANTONIO: Yes; we are
    Betrayed. How came he hither? I should turn
    This to thee for that.
                                        [*He points the pistol at* CARIOLA.]
CARIOLA: Pray sir, do: and when
    That you have cleft my heart, you shall read there   145
    Mine innocence.
DUCHESS: That gallery gave him entrance.
ANTONIO: I would this terrible thing would come again,
    That, standing on my guard, I might relate
    My warrantable love.° Ha! what means this?
DUCHESS: He left this with me.   *She shows the poniard.*
ANTONIO: And it seems, did wish   150
    You would use it on yourself?
DUCHESS: His action seemed
    To intend so much.
ANTONIO: This hath a handle to't,
    As well as a point. Turn it towards him, and
    So fasten the keen edge in his rank gall.   [*Knocking within.*]

How now? Who knocks? More earthquakes?
DUCHESS: I stand　155
    As if a mine, beneath my feet, were ready
    To be blown up.
CARIOLA: 'Tis Bosola.
DUCHESS: Away!
    O misery! methinks unjust° actions
    Should wear these masks and curtains, and not we.
    You must instantly part hence; I have fashioned it already.
Exit ANTONIO.　160

Enter BOSOLA.

BOSOLA: The duke your brother is ta'en up in a whirlwind;
    Hath took horse, and's rid post to Rome.
DUCHESS: So late?
BOSOLA: He told me, as he mounted into th' saddle,
    You were undone.
DUCHESS: Indeed, I am very near it.
BOSOLA: What's the matter?　165
DUCHESS: Antonio, the master of our household,
    Hath dealt so falsely with me, in's° accounts:
    My brother stood engaged° with me for money
    Ta'en° up of certain Neapolitan Jews,
    And Antonio lets the bonds be forfeit. —°　170
BOSOLA: Strange. — [*Aside*] This is cunning.
DUCHESS: And hereupon
    My brother's bills° at Naples are protested°
    Against. Call up our officers.
BOSOLA: I shall. *Exit.*

[*Enter* ANTONIO.]

DUCHESS: The place that you must fly to is Ancona;
    Hire a house there. I'll send after you　175
    My treasure, and my jewels: our weak safety
    Runs upon enginous° wheels. Short syllables
    Must stand for periods.° I must now accuse you
    Of such a feigned crime as Tasso° calls
    Magnanima mensogna, a noble lie,　180
    'Cause it must shield our honours. Hark, they are coming.

[*Enter* BOSOLA *and* OFFICERS.]

ANTONIO: Will your Grace hear me?

DUCHESS: I have got well by you:° you have yielded me
    A million of loss; I am like to inherit
    The people's curses for your stewardship.   185
    You had the trick in audit time to be sick,
    Till I had signed your *Quietus;*° and that cured you
    Without help of a doctor. — Gentlemen,
    I would have this man be an example° to you all:
    So shall you hold my favour. I pray let him,°   190
    For h'as done that, alas! you would not think of,
    And, because I intend to be rid of him,
    I mean not to publish. — Use your fortune elsewhere.
ANTONIO: I am strongly armed to brook my overthrow,
    As commonly men bear with a hard year: 195
    I will not blame the cause on't, but do think
    The necessity° of my malevolent star
    Procures this, not her humour.° O, the inconstant
    And rotten ground of service, you may see;
    'Tis ev'n like him that, in a winter night,   200
    Takes a long slumber o'er a dying fire,
    As loth to part from't; yet parts thence as cold
    As when he first sat down.
DUCHESS: We do confiscate,
    Towards the satisfying° of your accounts,
    All that you have.
ANTONIO: I am all yours; and 'tis very fit   205
    All mine should be so.
DUCHESS: So, sir; you have your pass.°
ANTONIO: You may see, gentlemen, what 'tis to serve
    A prince with body and soul.   *Exit.*
BOSOLA: Here's an example for extortion;° what moisture is drawn out of
    the sea, when foul weather comes, pours down, and runs into the   210
    sea again.
DUCHESS: I would know what are your opinions of this Antonio.
SECOND OFFICER: He could not abide to see a pig's head gaping; I
    thought your Grace would find him a Jew.
THIRD OFFICER: I would you had been his officer,° for your own sake.   215
FOURTH OFFICER: You would have had more money.
FIRST OFFICER: He stopped his ears with black wool;° and to those came
    to him for money, said he was thick of hearing.
SECOND OFFICER: Some said he was an hermaphrodite, for he could not
    abide a woman.   220
FOURTH OFFICER: How scurvy proud he would look, when the treasury
    was full. Well, let him go.
FIRST OFFICER: Yes, and the chippings° of the buttery fly after him, to
    scour his gold chain.°

DUCHESS: Leave us.　　　　　　　　　*Exeunt* [OFFICERS].　225
　　What do you think of these?
BOSOLA: That these are rogues, that in's prosperity,
　　But to have waited° on his fortune, could have wished
　　His dirty stirrup riveted through their noses,
　　And followed after's mule, like a bear in a ring.°　　230
　　Would have prostituted their daughters to his lust;
　　Made their first-born intelligencers;° thought none happy
　　But such as were born under his blessed planet,
　　And wore his livery:° and do these lice drop off now?
　　Well, never look to have the like again;　　235
　　He hath left a sort° of flatt'ring rogues behind him;
　　Their doom must follow. Princes pay flatterers
　　In their own money. Flatterers dissemble their vices,
　　And they dissemble° their lies: that's justice.
　　Alas, poor gentleman!　　240
DUCHESS: Poor? He hath amply filled his coffers!
BOSOLA:　　　　　　　　　　　　　　Sure
　　He was too honest. Pluto, the god of riches,°
　　When he's sent by Jupiter to any man,
　　He goes limping, to signify that wealth
　　That comes on God's name, comes slowly; but when he's sent　　245
　　On the devil's errand, he rides post,° and comes in by scuttles.°
　　Let me show you what a most unvalued° jewel
　　You have, in a wanton° humour, thrown away,
　　To bless the man shall find him. He was an excellent
　　Courtier, and most faithful; a soldier, that thought it　　250
　　As beastly to know his own value too little,
　　As devilish to acknowledge it too much.
　　Both his virtue and form° deserved a far better fortune:
　　His discourse° rather delighted to judge itself, than show itself;
　　His breast was filled with all perfection,　　255
　　And yet it seemed a private whisp'ring room,°
　　It made so little noise of't.
DUCHESS:　　　　　　　　　But he was basely descended.
BOSOLA: Will you make yourself a mercenary herald,
　　Rather to examine men's pedigrees, than virtues?
　　You shall want° him.　　260
　　For know, an honest statesman to a prince
　　Is like a cedar, planted by a spring:
　　The spring bathes the tree's root, the grateful tree
　　Rewards it with his shadow. You have not done so.
　　I would sooner swim to the Bermudas° on　　265
　　Two politicians'° rotten bladders, tied
　　Together with an intelligencer's° heart-string,

Than depend on so changeable a prince's favour.
Fare thee well, Antonio; since the malice of the world
Would needs down with thee, it cannot be said yet   270
That any ill happened unto thee,
Considering thy fall was accomplished with° virtue.
DUCHESS: O, you render me excellent music.
BOSOLA: Say you?
DUCHESS: This good one that you speak of, is my husband.
BOSOLA: Do I not dream? Can this ambitious age   275
    Have so much goodness in't, as to prefer
    A man merely for worth: without these shadows°
    Of wealth, and painted honours? possible?
DUCHESS: I have had three children by him.
BOSOLA: Fortunate lady,
    For you have made your private nuptial bed   280
    The humble and fair seminary° of peace.
    No question but many an unbeneficed° scholar
    Shall pray for you for this deed, and rejoice
    That some preferment in the world can yet
    Arise from merit. The virgins of your land,   285
    That have no dowries, shall hope your example
    Will raise them to rich husbands. Should you want
    Soldiers, 'twould make the very Turks and Moors
    Turn Christians, and serve you for this act.
    Last, the neglected poets of your time,   290
    In honour of this trophy° of a man,
    Raised by that curious engine,° your white hand,
    Shall thank you in your grave for't; and make that
    More reverend° than all the cabinets°
    Of living princes. For Antonio,   295
    His fame shall likewise flow from many a pen,
    When heralds shall want coats,° to sell to men.
DUCHESS: As I taste comfort, in this friendly speech,
    So would I find concealment —
BOSOLA: O, the secret of my prince,
    Which I will wear on th'inside of my heart.   300
DUCHESS: You shall take charge of all my coin, and jewels,
    And follow him, for he retires himself
    To Ancona.
BOSOLA: So.
DUCHESS: Whither, within few days,
    I mean to follow thee.
BOSOLA: Let me think:
    I would wish your Grace to feign a pilgrimage   305
    To Our Lady of Loretto,° scarce seven leagues

From fair Ancona; so may you depart
Your country with more honour, and your flight
Will seem a princely progress, retaining
Your usual train about you.
DUCHESS: Sir, your direction   310
Shall lead me by the hand.
CARIOLA: In my opinion,
She were better progress to the baths
At Lucca,° or go visit the Spa
In Germany,° for, if you will believe me,
I do not like this jesting with religion,   315
This feigned pilgrimage.
DUCHESS: Thou art a superstitious fool!
Prepare us instantly for our departure.
Past sorrows, let us moderately lament them;
For those to come, seek wisely to prevent them.
                                        Exit [DUCHESS *with* CARIOLA].
BOSOLA: A politician° is the devil's quilted anvil: 320
He fashions all sins on him, and the blows
Are never heard. He may work in a lady's chamber,
As here for proof. What rests° but I reveal
All to my lord? O, this base quality
Of intelligencer! Why, every quality° i'th' world   325
Prefers but gain, or commendation.
Now for this act, I am certain to be raised,
And men that paint weeds, to the life, are praised.   *Exit.*

Act Three, Scene Three

[*Enter*] CARDINAL, FERDINAND, MALATESTE, PESCARA, SILVIO, DELIO.

CARDINAL: Must we turn soldier then?
MALATESTE: The Emperor,°
Hearing your worth that way ere you attained
This reverend garment, joins you in commission
With the right fortunate° soldier, the Marquis of Pescara,°
And the famous Lannoy.
CARDINAL: He that had the honour   5
Of taking the French king prisoner?°
MALATESTE: The same.
Here's a plot° drawn for a new fortification
At Naples.
FERDINAND: This great Count Malateste, I perceive,
Hath got employment.

DELIO: No employment, my lord;
   A marginal note in the muster book,° that he is   10
   A voluntary° lord.
FERDINAND: He's no soldier?
DELIO: He has worn gunpowder, in's hollow tooth, for the tooth-ache.
SILVIO: He comes to the leaguer° with a full intent
   To eat fresh beef, and garlic; means to stay
   Till the scent be gone, and straight° return to court.   15
DELIO: He hath read all the late service,°
   As the City chronicle relates it,
   And keeps two painters going, only to express°
   Battles in model.°
SILVIO: Then he'll fight by the book.
DELIO: By the almanac, I think,   20
   To choose good° days, and shun the critical.
   That's his mistress' scarf.
SILVIO: Yes, he protests
   He would do much for that taffeta.°
DELIO: I think he would run away from a battle
   To save it from taking prisoner.
SILVIO: He is horribly afraid   25
   Gunpowder will spoil the perfume on't.
DELIO: I saw a Dutchman break his pate° once
   For calling him pot-gun;° he made his head
   Have a bore° in't, like a musket.
SILVIO: I would he had made a touch-hole° to't.   30
   He is indeed a guarded sumpter-cloth,
   Only for the remove of the court.°

[*Enter* BOSOLA.]

PESCARA: Bosola arrived? What should be the business?
   Some falling out amongst the Cardinals?
   These factions amongst great men, they are like   35
   Foxes, when their heads are divided;
   They carry fire in their tails,° and all the country
   About them goes to wrack for't.
SILVIO: What's that Bosola?
DELIO: I knew him in Padua:° a fantastical° scholar, like such who study
   to know how many knots was in Hercules' club;° of what colour   40
   Achilles'° beard was, or whether Hector° were not troubled with
   the toothache. He hath studied himself half blear-eyed, to know
   the true symmetry of Caesar's° nose by a shoeing-horn, —° and
   this he did to gain the name of a speculative man.
PESCARA: Mark Prince Ferdinand;   45

A very salamander° lives in's eye,
To mock the eager violence of fire.
SILVIO: That cardinal hath made more bad faces with his oppression
than ever Michael Angelo° made good ones; he lifts up's nose, like
a foul porpoise before a storm.°   50
PESCARA: The lord Ferdinand laughs.
DELIO: — Like a deadly cannon, that lightens° ere it smokes.
PESCARA: These are your true pangs of death,
The pangs of life, that struggle with great statesmen.
DELIO: In such a deformed silence, witches whisper   55
Their charms.
CARDINAL: Doth she make religion her riding hood
To keep her from the sun and tempest?
FERDINAND: That:
That damns her. Methinks her fault and beauty,
Blended together, show like leprosy,
The whiter, the fouler. I make it a question   60
Whether her beggarly brats were ever christened.
CARDINAL: I will instantly solicit the state° of Ancona
To have them banished.
FERDINAND: You are for Loreto?
I shall not be at your ceremony; fare you well.
Write to the Duke of Malfi, my young nephew   65
She had by her first husband, and acquaint him
With's mother's honesty.°
BOSOLA: I will.
FERDINAND: Antonio!
A slave, that only smelled of ink and counters,°
And never in's life looked like a gentleman,
But in the audit time — go, go presently,°   70
Draw me out an hundred and fifty of our horse,
And meet me at the fort-bridge.   *Exeunt.*

Act Three, Scene Four

[*Enter*] *two* PILGRIMS *to the shrine of Our Lady of Loretto.*

1 PILGRIM: I have not seen a goodlier shrine than this,
Yet I have visited many.
2 PILGRIM: The Cardinal of Aragon
Is this day to resign his Cardinal's hat;
His sister duchess likewise is arrived
To pay her vow of pilgrimage. I expect   5
A noble ceremony.

1 PILGRIM: No question. They come.

Here the ceremony of the CARDINAL's *instalment in the habit° of a soldier:
performed in delivering up his cross, hat, robes, and ring at the shrine; and
investing him with sword, helmet, shield, and spurs. Then* ANTONIO, *the*
DUCHESS *and their Children, having presented themselves at the shrine, are
(by a form of banishment °in dumb-show expressed towards them by the*
CARDINAL, *and the state° of Ancona) banished. During all which ceremony
this ditty is sung to very solemn music, by divers churchmen; and then
exeunt [all, except the two* PILGRIMS.]

> Arms and honours deck thy story,
> To thy fame's eternal glory,
> Adverse fortune ever fly thee,
> No disastrous fate come nigh thee.   10
> I alone will sing thy praises,
> Whom to honour virtue raises;
> And thy study that divine° is,
> Bent to martial discipline is:
> Lay aside all those robes lie by thee,   15
> Crown thy arts with arms: they'll beautify thee.
> O worthy of worthiest name, adornèd in this manner,
> Lead bravely thy forces on, under war's warlike banner.
> O mayst thou prove fortunate in all martial courses, °
> Guide thou still by skill, in arts and forces.   20
> Victory attend thee nigh, whilst fame sings loud thy powers;
> Triumphant conquest crown thy head, and blessings pour down showers.

1 PILGRIM: Here's a strange turn of state: who would have thought
So great a lady would have matched herself   25
Unto so mean° a person? Yet the the cardinal
Bears himself much too cruel.
2 PILGRIM: They are banished.
1 PILGRIM: But I would ask what power hath this state°
Of Ancona to determine of° a free prince?
2 PILGRIM:They are a free state, sir, and her brother showed   30
How that the Pope, forehearing of her looseness,
Hath seized into th' protection of the Church
The dukedom which she held as dowager.
1 PILGRIM: But by what justice?
2 PILGRIM: Sure, I think by none;
Only her brother's instigation.   35
1 PILGRIM: What was it with such violence he took
Off from her finger?
2 PILGRIM: 'Twas her wedding-ring,
Which he vowed shortly he would sacrifice

To his revenge.
1 PILGRIM: Alas, Antonio!
If that a man be thrust into a well,   40
No matter who sets hand to't, his own weight
Will bring him sooner to th' bottom. Come, let's hence.
Fortune makes this conclusion general:
All things do help th'unhappy° man to fall. *Exeunt.*

Act Three, Scene Five

[*Enter* ANTONIO, DUCHESS, *three* Children, CARIOLA, Servants.]

DUCHESS: Banished Ancona?
ANTONIO: Yes, you see what power
Lightens° in great men's breath.
DUCHESS: Is all our train
Shrunk to this poor remainder?
ANTONIO: These poor men,
Which have got little in your service, vow
To take your fortune. But your wiser buntings°   5
Now they are fledged, are gone.
DUCHESS: They have done wisely.
This puts me in mind of death: physicians thus,
With their hands full of money, use to give o'er
Their patients.
ANTONIO: Right° the fashion of the world:
From decayed fortunes every flatterer shrinks;   10
Men cease to build where the foundation sinks.
DUCHESS: I had a very strange dream tonight.
ANTONIO: What was't?
DUCHESS: Methought I wore my coronet of state,
And on a sudden all the diamonds
Were changed to pearls.
ANTONIO: My interpretation   15
Is, you'll weep shortly; for to me, the pearls
Do signify your tears.
DUCHESS: The birds that live i'th' field
On the wild benefit° of nature live
Happier than we; for they may choose their mates,
And carol their sweet pleasures to the spring.   20

[*Enter* BOSOLA, *with a letter which he gives to the* DUCHESS.]

BOSOLA: You are happily o'erta'en.

DUCHESS: From my brother?
BOSOLA: Yes, from the lord Ferdinand, your brother;
    All love, and safety —
DUCHESS: Thou dost blanch° mischief;
    Wouldst make it white. See, see; like to calm weather
    At sea before a tempest, false hearts speak fair   25
    To those they intend most mischief.
    [*Reads*] *Send Antonio to me; I want his head° in a business.* —
    A politic equivocation —
    He doth not want your counsel, but your head;
    That is, he cannot sleep till you be dead.   30
    And here's another pitfall, that's strewed o'er
    With roses. Mark it, 'tis a cunning one:
    I stand engaged° for your husband for several debts at Naples. Let not
    that trouble him; I had rather have his heart than his money.
    And I believe so too.
BOSOLA: What do you believe?   35
DUCHESS: That he so much distrusts my husband's love
    He will by no means believe his heart is with him
    Until he see it. The devil is not cunning enough
    To circumvent us in riddles.
BOSOLA: Will you reject that noble and free league   40
    Of amity° and love which I present you?
DUCHESS: Their league is like that of some politic° kings —
    Only to make themselves of strength and power
    To be our after-ruin: tell them so.
BOSOLA: And what from you?
ANTONIO: Thus tell him: I will not come.   45
BOSOLA: And what of this?°
ANTONIO: My brothers° have dispersed
    Bloodhounds abroad, which till I hear are muzzled,
    No truce, though hatched with ne'er such politic skill,
    Is safe, that hangs upon our enemies' will.
    I'll not come at them.
BOSOLA: This proclaims your breeding.   50
    Every small thing draws a base mind to fear,
    As the adamant° draws iron. Fare you well, sir,
    You shall shortly hear from's.
DUCHESS: I suspect some ambush;
    Therefore by all my love, I do conjure° you
    To take your eldest son, and fly towards Milan.   55
    Let us not venture all this poor remainder
    In one unlucky bottom.°
ANTONIO: You counsel safely.
    Best of my life, farewell. Since we must part,

Heaven hath a hand in't; but no otherwise
Than as some curious artist° takes in sunder   60
A clock, or watch, when it is out of frame,
To bring't in better order.
DUCHESS: I know not which is best,
To see you dead, or part with you. Farewell, boy;
Thou art happy that thou hast not understanding
To know thy misery. For all our wit   65
And reading brings us to a truer sense
Of sorrow. In the eternal Church,° sir,
I do hope we shall not part thus.
ANTONIO: O, be of comfort!
Make patience a noble fortitude,
And think not how unkindly° we are used.   70
Man, like to cassia,° is proved best being bruised.
DUCHESS: Must I, like to a slave-born Russian,
Account it praise to suffer tyranny?
And yet, O heaven, thy heavy hand is in't.
I have seen my little boy oft scourge° his top,   75
And compared myself to't: nought made me e'er go right,
But heaven's scourge-stick.
ANTONIO: Do not weep.
Heaven fashioned us of nothing; and we strive
To bring ourselves to nothing. — Farewell, Cariola,
And thy sweet armful.° — [*To the* DUCHESS] If I do never see thee more,
Be a good mother to your little ones,   81
And save them from the tiger. Fare you well.
                                        Kisses the DUCHESS.]
DUCHESS: Let me look upon you once more, for that speech
Came from a dying father. Your kiss is colder
Than I have seen an holy anchorite°   85
Give to a dead man's skull.
ANTONIO: My heart is turned to a heavy lump of lead,
With which I sound° my danger. Fare you well. *Exit [with his elder* Son].
DUCHESS: My laurel° is all withered.
CARIOLA: Look, madam, what a troop of armèd men   90
Make toward us.

Enter BOSOLA *with a* Guard [*vizarded*].

DUCHESS: O, they are very welcome:
When Fortune's wheel is over-charged° with princes,
The weight makes it move swift. I would have my ruin
Be sudden. — I am your adventure,° am I not?
BOSOLA: You are; you must see your husband no more.   95

DUCHESS: What devil art thou, that counterfeits° heaven's thunder?
BOSOLA: Is that terrible? I would have you tell me whether
    Is that note worse that frights the silly° birds
    Out of the corn; or that which doth allure them
    To the nets? You have hearkened to the last too much.   100
DUCHESS: O misery! like to a rusty o'ercharged° cannon,
    Shall I never fly in pieces? Come: to what prison?
BOSOLA: To none.
DUCHESS: Whither then?
BOSOLA: To your palace.
DUCHESS: I have heard that Charon's° boat serves to convey
    All o'er the dismal lake,° but brings none back again.   105
BOSOLA: Your brothers mean you safety and pity.
DUCHESS: Pity!
    With such a pity men preserve alive
    Pheasants and quails, when they are not fat enough
    To be eaten.
BOSOLA: These are your children?
DUCHESS: Yes.
BOSOLA: Can they prattle?
DUCHESS: No: 110
    But I intend, since they were born accursed,
    Curses shall be their first language.
BOSOLA: _ Fie, madam!
    Forget this base, low fellow.°
DUCHESS: Were I a man,
    I'd beat that counterfeit face° into thy other —
BOSOLA: One of no birth.
DUCHESS: Say that he was born mean,°   115
    Man is most happy when's own actions
    Be arguments° and examples of his virtue.
BOSOLA: A barren, beggarly virtue.
DUCHESS: I prithee, who is greatest, can you tell?
    Sad tales befit my woe: I'll tell you one.   120
    A salmon, as she swam unto the sea,
    Met with a dog-fish; who encounters her
    With this rough language: 'Why art thou so bold
    To mix thyself with our high state of floods,°
    Being no eminent courtier, but one   125
    That for the calmest and fresh time o'th' year
    Dost live in shallow rivers, rank'st thyself
    With silly smelts° and shrimps? And darest thou
    Pass by our dog-ship without reverence?'°
    'O', quoth the salmon, 'sister, be at peace: 130
    Thank Jupiter, we both have passed the net!

Our value never can be truly known,
Till in the fisher's basket we be shown;
I'th' market then my price may be the higher,
Even when I am nearest to the cook, and fire.'   135
So, to great men, the moral may be stretchèd:
Men oft are valued high, when they're most wretched.
But come; whither you please. I am armed° 'gainst misery;
Bent to all sways° of the oppressor's will.
There's no deep valley, but near some great hill.   *Ex[eunt].* 140

Act Four, Scene One

[*Enter* FERDINAND *and* BOSOLA.]

FERDINAND: How doth our sister duchess bear herself
   In her imprisonment?
BOSOLA: Nobly: I'll describe her.
   She's sad, as one long used to't; and she seems
   Rather to welcome the end of misery
   Than shun it: a behaviour so noble,   5
   As gives a majesty to adversity.
   You may discern the shape° of loveliness
   More perfect in her tears, than in her smiles.
   She will muse four hours together; and her silence,
   Methinks, expresseth more than if she spake.   10
FERDINAND: Her melancholy seems to be fortified
   With a strange disdain.
BOSOLA: 'Tis so: and this restraint
   (Like English mastiffs, that grow fierce with tying)
   Makes her too passionately apprehend
   Those pleasures she's kept from.
FERDINAND: Curse upon her!   15
   I will no longer study in the book
   Of another's heart: inform her what I told you.   *Exit.*

[BOSOLA *draws the traverse to reveal the* DUCHESS, CARIOLA *and*
Servants.]°

BOSOLA: All comfort to your grace —
DUCHESS: I will have none.
   Pray thee, why dost thou wrap thy poisoned pills
   In gold and sugar?   20
BOSOLA: Your elder brother, the lord Ferdinand,
   Is come to visit you, and sends you word

('Cause once he rashly made a solemn vow
Never to see you more) he comes i'th' night;
And prays you, gently, neither torch nor taper   25
Shine in your chamber. He will kiss your hand,
And reconcile himself; but, for his vow,
He dares not see you.
DUCHESS: At his pleasure. —
Take hence the lights: he's come.   [*Exeunt* Servants *with lights.*]

[*Enter* FERDINAND.]

FERDINAND: Where are you?
DUCHESS: Here, sir.
FERDINAND: This darkness suits you well.
DUCHESS: I would ask your pardon.   30
FERDINAND: You have it;
    For I account it the honorablest revenge,
    Where I may kill, to pardon. Where are your cubs?
DUCHESS: Whom?
FERDINAND: Call them your children;   35
    For though our national law distinguish bastards
    From true legitimate issue, compassionate nature
    Makes them all equal.
DUCHESS: Do you visit me for this?
    You violate a sacrament o'th' Church°
    Shall make you howl in hell for't.
FERDINAND: It had been well   40
    Could you have lived thus always; for indeed
    You were too much i'th' light.° But no more;
    I come to seal my peace with you. Here's a hand,
                    [*He*] *gives her a dead man's hand.*
    To which you have vowed much love: the ring upon't
    You gave.
DUCHESS: I affectionately kiss it.   [*Kisses the hand.*] 45
FERDINAND: Pray do; and bury the print of it in your heart.
    I will leave this ring with you, for a love-token;
    And the hand, as sure as the ring; and do not doubt
    But you shall have the heart too. When you need a friend,
    Send it to him that owed° it: you shall see   50
    Whether he can aid you.
DUCHESS: You are very cold.
    I fear you are not well after your travel: —
    Ha! Lights! O, horrible!
FERDINAND: Let her have lights enough.   *Exit.*

[*Enter* Servants *with lights.*]

DUCHESS: What witchcraft doth he practise, that he hath left
    A dead man's hand here?   55

Here is discovered,° behind a traverse, the artificial figures of
ANTONIO *and his children, appearing as if they were dead.*

BOSOLA: Look you: here's the piece from which 'twas ta'en.
    He doth present you this sad spectacle,
    That now you know directly° they are dead,
    Hereafter you may, wisely, cease to grieve
    For that which cannot be recovered.   60
DUCHESS: There is not between heaven and earth one wish
    I stay for after this. It wastes me more
    Than were't my picture, fashioned out of wax,
    Stuck with a magical needle, and then buried
    In some foul dunghill; and yond's an excellent property°   65
    For a tyrant, which I would account mercy —
BOSOLA: What's that?
DUCHESS: If they would bind me to that lifeless trunk,
    And let me freeze to death.
BOSOLA: Come, you must live.
DUCHESS: That's the greatest torture souls feel in hell,
    In hell: that they must live, and cannot die.   70
    Portia,° I'll new kindle thy coals again,
    And revive the rare and almost dead example
    Of a loving wife.
BOSOLA: O fie! despair? remember
    You are a Christian.°
DUCHESS: The Church enjoins fasting:
    I'll starve myself to death.
BOSOLA: Leave this vain sorrow;   75
    Things being at the worst, begin to mend.
    The bee, when he hath shot his sting into your hand,
    May then play with your eyelid.
DUCHESS: Good comfortable fellow,
    Persuade a wretch that's broke upon the wheel°
    To have all his bones new set: entreat him live,   80
    To be executed again. Who must dispatch me?
    I account this world a tedious theatre,
    For I do play a part in't 'gainst my will.
BOSOLA: Come, be of comfort; I will save your life.
DUCHESS: Indeed I have not leisure to tend so small business.   85
BOSOLA: Now, by my life, I pity you.

DUCHESS: Thou art a fool then,
    To waste thy pity on a thing so wretched
    As cannot pity itself. I am full of daggers.°
    Puff! let me blow these vapours from me.

                    [*Enter* SERVANT.]

    What are you?
SERVANT: One that wishes you long life.   90
DUCHESS: I would thou wert hanged for the horrible curse
    Thou hast given me: I shall shortly grow one
    Of the miracles of pity. I'll go pray. No,
    I'll go curse.
BOSOLA: O fie!
DUCHESS: I could curse the stars. —
BOSOLA: O fearful!
DUCHESS: And those three smiling seasons of the year   95
    Into a Russian winter; nay, the world
    To its first chaos.
BOSOLA: Look you, the stars shine still.
DUCHESS: O, but you must
    Remember, my curse hath a great way to go.
    Plagues, that makes lanes through largest families,   100
    Consume them!
BOSOLA: Fie, lady!
DUCHESS: Let them, like tyrants,
    Never be remembered, but for the ill they have done:
    Let all the zealous prayers of mortified°
    Churchmen forget them —
BOSOLA: O uncharitable!
DUCHESS: Let heaven, a little while, cease crowning martyrs   105
    To punish them.
    Go, howl them this; and say I long to bleed.
    It is some mercy when men kill with speed.   *Exit* [*with* SERVANTS].

                    [*Enter* FERDINAND.]

FERDINAND: Excellent; as I would wish. She's plagued in art:
    These presentations are but framed in wax   110
    By the curious° master in that quality,°
    Vincentio Lauriola,° and she takes them
    For true substantial bodies.
BOSOLA: Why do you do this?
FERDINAND: To bring her to despair.
BOSOLA: 'Faith, end here;

And go no farther in your cruelty.   115
Send her a penitential garment,° to put on
Next to her delicate skin, and furnish her
With beads° and prayerbooks.
FERDINAND: Damn her! that body of hers,
While that my blood ran pure in't, was more worth
Than that which thou wouldst comfort, called a soul.   120
I will send her masques° of common courtesans,
Have her meat served up by bawds and ruffians,
And, 'cause she'll needs be mad, I am resolved
To remove forth° the common hospital
All the mad folk, and place them near her lodging.   125
There let them practise° together, sing, and dance,
And act their gambols to the full o'th' moon:°
If she can sleep the better for it, let her.
Your work is almost ended.
BOSOLA: Must I see her again?
FERDINAND: Yes.
BOSOLA: Never.
FERDINAND: You must.
BOSOLA: Never in mine own shape;°   130
That's forfeited by my intelligence,°
And this last cruel lie. When you send me next,
The business shall be comfort.
FERDINAND: Very likely;
Thy pity is nothing of kin to thee. Antonio
Lurks about Milan; thou shalt shortly thither,   135
To feed a fire as great as my revenge,
Which never will slack, till it have spent his fuel.
Intemperate agues° make physicians cruel.   *Exeunt.*

Act Four, Scene Two

[Enter DUCHESS *and* CARIOLA.*]*

DUCHESS: What hideous noise was that?
CARIOLA: 'Tis the wild consort°
Of madmen, lady, which your tyrant brother
Hath placed about your lodging. This tyranny,
I think, was never practised till this hour.
DUCHESS: Indeed I thank him: nothing but noise and folly   5
Can keep me in my right wits, whereas reason
And silence make me stark mad. Sit down;°
Discourse to me some dismal° tragedy.

CARIOLA: O, 'twill increase your melancholy.
DUCHESS: Thou art deceived;
   To hear of greater grief would lessen mine.   10
   This is a prison?
CARIOLA: Yes, but you shall live
   To shake this durance° off.
DUCHESS: Thou art a fool.
   The robin red-breast and the nightingale
   Never live long in cages.
CARIOLA: Pray dry your eyes.
   What think you of, madam?
DUCHESS: Of nothing.   15
   When I muse thus, I sleep.
CARIOLA: Like a madman, with your eyes open?
DUCHESS: Dost thou think we shall know one another
   In th'other world?
CARIOLA: Yes, out of question.
DUCHESS: O, that it were possible we might   20
   But hold some two days' conference with the dead,
   From them I should learn somewhat, I am sure,
   I never shall know here. I'll tell thee a miracle:
   I am not mad yet, to my cause of sorrow.
   Th'heaven o'er my head seems made of molten brass,   25
   The earth of flaming sulphur, yet I am not mad.
   I am acquainted with sad misery,
   As the tanned galley-slave is with his oar.
   Necessity makes me suffer constantly,
   And custom makes it easy. Who do I look like now?   30
CARIOLA: Like to your picture in the gallery:
   A deal of life in show,° but none in practice;
   Or rather like some reverend monument
   Whose ruins are even pitied.
DUCHESS: Very proper;
   And Fortune seems only to have her eyesight   35
   To behold my tragedy. —° How now!
   What noise is that?

[*Enter* SERVANT.]

SERVANT: I am come to tell you
   Your brother hath intended you some sport.
   A great physician, when the Pope was sick
   Of a deep melancholy, presented him   40
   With several° sorts of madmen, which wild object,
   Being full of change and sport, forced him to laugh,

And so th'impostume° broke: the selfsame cure
The duke intends on you.
DUCHESS: Let them come in.
SERVANT: There's a mad lawyer, and a secular priest,   45
    A doctor that hath forfeited° his wits
    By jealousy; an astrologian,
    That in his works said such a day o'th' month
    Should be the day of doom,° and, failing of't,
    Ran mad; an English tailor, crazed i'th' brain   50
    With the study of new fashion; a gentleman usher°
    Quite beside himself with care to keep in mind
    The number of his lady's salutations,
    Or 'How do you?' she employed him in each morning
    A farmer, too, an excellent knave in grain,°   55
    Mad, 'cause he was hindered transportation;°
    And let one broker,° that's mad, loose to these,
    You'd think the devil were among them.
DUCHESS: Sit, Cariola. — let them loose when you please,
    For I am chained° to endure all your tyranny.   60

[*Enter* MADMEN.]

Here, by a MADMAN, *this song is sung to a dismal° kind of music.*

    O, let us howl, some heavy note,
      Some deadly-doggèd° howl,
    Sounding, as from the threat'ning throat
      Of beasts, and fatal fowl.
    As ravens, screech-owls, bulls, and bears,   65
      We'll bell, and bawl our parts,
    Till yerksome° noise have cloyed° your ears,
      And corrosived° your hearts.
    At last, when as our quire wants° breath,
      Our bodies being blest,   70
    We'll sing like swans, to welcome death,°
      And die in love and rest.

MAD ASTROLOGER°: Doomsday not come yet? I'll draw it nearer by a
    perspective,° or make a glass,° that shall set all the world on fire
    upon an instant. I cannot sleep; my pillow is stuffed with a litter of   75
    porcupines.
MAD LAWYER: Hell is a mere glass-house,° where the devils are
    continually blowing up women's souls on hollow irons, and the
    fire never goes out.
MAD PRIEST:° I will lie with every woman in my parish the tenth night; I   80

will tithe them over like haycocks.°

MAD DOCTOR: Shall my pothecary° outgo me, because I am a cuckold? I
have found out his roguery: he makes alum° of his wife's urine,
and sells it to Puritans, that have sore throats with over-straining.°

MAD USHER: I have skill in heraldry.   85

MAD TAILOR: Hast?

MAD USHER: You do give for your crest a woodcock's° head, with the
brains pick't out on't. You are a very ancient° gentleman.

MAD PRIEST: Greek is turned Turk;° we are only to be saved by the
Helvetian translation.°   90

MAD LAWYER: Come on, sir, I will lay° the law to you.

MAD FARMER: O, rather lay a corrosive;° the law will eat to the bone.

MAD PRIEST: He that drinks but to satisfy nature is damned.

MAD ASTROLOGER: If I had my glass° here, I would show a sight should
make all the women here call me mad doctor.   95

MAD TAILOR [*indicating* MAD PRIEST]: What's he,° a rope-maker?°

MAD USHER: No, no, no, a snuffling knave,° that while he shows the
tombs, will have his hand in a wench's placket.°

MAD DOCTOR: Woe to the caroche° that brought home my wife from the
masque at three o'clock in the morning! it had a large feather bed   100
in it.

MAD FARMER: I have pared the devil's nails forty times, roasted them in
raven's eggs, and cured agues° with them.

MAD ASTROLOGER: Get me three hundred milch bats, to make possets°
to procure sleep.   105

MAD DOCTOR: All the college may throw their caps at me, I have made
a soap-boiler costive:° it was my masterpiece.

Here the dance, consisting of 8 MADMEN, *with music answerable
thereunto; after which* BOSOLA, *like an old man, enters.*

DUCHESS: Is he mad too?

SERVANT: Pray question him; I'll leave you.
                                   [*Exeunt* SERVANT *and* MADMEN.]

BOSOLA: I am come to make thy tomb.

DUCHESS: Ha! my tomb?
Thou speak'st as if I lay upon my death-bed,   110
Gasping for breath; dost thou perceive me sick?

BOSOLA: Yes, and the more dangerously, since thy sickness is insensible.°

DUCHESS: Thou art not mad, sure; dost know me?

BOSOLA: Yes.

DUCHESS: Who am I?   115

BOSOLA: Thou art a box of worm-seed,° at best; but a salvatory of green
mummy.° What's this flesh? a little crudded° milk, fantastical puff-
paste;° our bodies are weaker than those paper prisons boys use to

keep flies in; more contemptible, since ours is to preserve earth-
worms. Didst thou ever see a lark in a cage? such is the soul in the   120
body: this world is like her little turf of grass, and the heaven o'er
our heads, like her looking-glass, only gives us a miserable
knowledge of the small compass of our prison.

DUCHESS: Am not I thy duchess?

BOSOLA: Thou art some great woman, sure; for riot° begins to sit on thy   125
forehead (clad in grey hairs) twenty years sooner than on a merry
milkmaid's. Thou sleep'st worse than if a mouse should be forced
to take up her lodging in a cat's ear: a little infant, that breeds° its
teeth, should it lie with thee, would cry out, as if thou wert the
more unquiet bedfellow.   130

DUCHESS: I am Duchess of Malfi still.

BOSOLA: That makes thy sleeps so broken:
　　Glories, like glow-worms, afar off shine bright,
　　But looked to near, have neither heat nor light.

DUCHESS: Thou art very plain.   135

BOSOLA: My trade is to flatter the dead, not the living;
　　I am a tomb-maker.

DUCHESS: And thou com'st to make my tomb?

BOSOLA: Yes.

DUCHESS: Let me be a little merry; of what stuff° wilt thou make it?   140

BOSOLA: Nay, resolve° me first, of what fashion?°

DUCHESS: Why, do we grow fantastical in our death-bed?
　　Do we affect° fashion in the grave?

BOSOLA: Most ambitiously. Princes' images on their tombs
　　Do not lie as they were wont, seeming to pray   145
　　Up to heaven, but with their hands under their cheeks,
　　As if they died of the tooth-ache.° They are not carved
　　With their eyes fixed upon the stars; but as
　　Their minds were wholly bent upon the world,
　　The self-same way they seem to turn their faces.   150

DUCHESS: Let me know fully therefore the effect°
　　Of this thy dismal preparation,
　　This talk, fit for a charnel.°

BOSOLA: 　　　　　　　　　Now I shall;

[*Enter* EXECUTIONERS *with*] *a coffin, cords, and a bell.*

　　Here is a present from your princely brothers;
　　And may it arrive welcome, for it brings   155
　　Last benefit, last sorrow.

DUCHESS: 　　　　　　　　Let me see it.
　　I have so much obedience in my blood,
　　I wish it in their veins, to do them good.

BOSOLA: This is your last presence-chamber.°
CARIOLA: O my sweet lady!
DUCHESS: Peace; it affrights not me.   160
BOSOLA: I am the common bellman,°
    That usually is sent to condemned persons,
    The night before they suffer.
DUCHESS: Even now thou said'st
    Thou wast a tomb-maker?
BOSOLA: 'Twas to bring you
    By degrees to mortification.° Listen: [*He rings the bell.*] 165

> *Hark, now every thing is still,*
> *The screech-owl and the whistler° shrill*
> *Call upon our dame, aloud,*
> *And bid her quickly don her shroud.*
> *Much you had of land and rent,* °   170
> *Your length in clay's now competent.* °
> *A long war disturbed your mind;*
> *Here your perfect peace is signed.*
> *Of what is't fools make such vain° keeping?*
> *Sin their conception, their birth, weeping;*   175
> *Their life, a general mist of error,*
> *Their death, a hideous storm of terror.*
> *Strew your hair with powders sweet;*
> *Don clean linen, bathe your feet,*
> *And, the foul fiend more to check,*   180
> *A crucifix let bless your neck.*
> *'Tis now full tide 'tween night and day,*
> *End your groan, and come away.*

                                 [EXECUTIONERS *approach.*]

CARIOLA: Hence villains, tyrants, murderers! Alas!
    What will you do with my lady? Call for help.   185
DUCHESS: To whom, to our next° neighbours? They are mad-folks.
BOSOLA: Remove that noise.

                    [EXECUTIONERS *seize* CARIOLA, *who struggles.*]

DUCHESS: Farewell, Cariola,
    In my last will I have not much to give.
    A many hungry guests have fed upon me;
    Thine will be a poor reversion.°
CARIOLA: I will die with her.   190
DUCHESS: I pray thee look thou giv'st my little boy
    Some syrup, for his cold, and let the girl
    Say her prayers, ere she sleep.   [CARIOLA *is forced off.*]
                    Now what you please.
    What death?
BOSOLA: Strangling: here are your executioners.

DUCHESS: I forgive them: the apoplexy, catarrh,°   195
    Or cough o'th' lungs would do as much as they do.
BOSOLA: Doth not death fright you?
DUCHESS: Who would be afraid on't?°
    Knowing to meet such excellent company
    In th'other world.
BOSOLA: Yet, methinks,
    The manner of your death should much afflict you;   200
    This cord should terrify you.
DUCHESS: Not a whit.
    What would it pleasure me, to have my throat cut
    With diamonds? or to be smothered
    With cassia?° or to be shot to death, with pearls?
    I know death hath ten thousand several doors   205
    For men to take their exits; and 'tis found
    They go on such strange geometrical hinges
    You may open them both ways: — any way, for heaven sake,
    So I were out of your whispering. Tell my brothers
    That I perceive death, now I am well awake,   210
    Best gift is, they can give, or I can take.
    I would fain put off my last woman's fault;
    I'd not be tedious to you.
EXECUTIONERS: We are ready.
DUCHESS: Dispose my breath how please you, but my body
    Bestow upon my women, will you?
EXECUTIONERS: Yes.   215
DUCHESS: Pull, and pull strongly, for your able strength
    Must pull down heaven upon me. —
    Yet stay, heaven gates are not so highly arched
    As princes' palaces; they that enter there
    Must go upon their knees. [*She kneels.*] Come, violent death,   220
    Serve for mandragora° to make me sleep;
    Go tell my brothers, when I am laid out,
    They then may feed in quiet.   *They strangle her.*
BOSOLA: Where's the waiting woman?
    Fetch her. Some other strangle the children.   [*Exeunt* EXECUTIONERS.]

                [*Enter one with* CARIOLA.]

    Look you, there sleeps your mistress.
CARIOLA: O, you are damned   225
    Perpetually for this. My turn is next,
    Is't not so ordered?
BOSOLA: Yes, and I am glad
    You are well prepared for't.

CARIOLA: You are deceived, sir,
  I am not prepared for't. I will not die;
  I will first come to my answer,° and know   230
  How I have offended.
BOSOLA: Come, dispatch her. —
  You kept her counsel,° now you shall keep ours.
CARIOLA: I will not die, I must not, I am contracted
  To a young gentleman.
EXECUTIONER: Here's your wedding-ring.°
CARIOLA: Let me but speak with the duke. I'll discover   235
  Treason to his person.
BOSOLA: Delays: throttle her!
EXECUTIONER: She bites, and scratches.
CARIOLA: If you kill me now
  I am damned. I have not been at confession
  This two years.
BOSOLA: When!
CARIOLA: I am quick with child.
BOSOLA: Why then,
  Your credit's° sav'd. —   [CARIOLA *is strangled.*]
                        Bear her into th' next room.   240
  Let this lie still.   [*Exeunt* EXECUTIONERS *with* CARIOLA's *body.*]

[*Enter* FERDINAND.]

FERDINAND: Is she dead?
BOSOLA: She is what
  You'd have her. But here begin your pity.   *Shows the children strangled.*°
  Alas, how have these offended?
FERDINAND: The death
  Of young wolves is never to be pitied.
BOSOLA: Fix your eye here.°
FERDINAND: Constantly.
BOSOLA: Do you not weep?   245
  Other sins only speak; murder shrieks out.
  The element of water moistens the earth,
  But blood flies upwards, and bedews the heavens.°
FERDINAND: Cover her face.° Mine eyes dazzle: she died young.
BOSOLA: I think not so; her infelicity   250
  Seemed to have years too many.
FERDINAND: She and I were twins,
  And should I die this instant, I had lived
  Her time to a minute.
BOSOLA: It seems she was born first.
  You have bloodily approved° the ancient truth

That kindred commonly do worse agree   255
Than remote strangers.
FERDINAND: Let me see her face again.
Why didst not thou pity her? What an excellent
Honest man might'st thou have been
If thou hadst borne her to some sanctuary!°
Or, bold in a good cause, opposed thyself   260
With thy advancèd sword above thy head,
Between her innocence and my revenge!
I bade thee, when I was distracted of my wits,
Go kill my dearest friend, and thou hast done't.
For let me but examine well the cause;   265
What was the meanness° of her match to me?
Only I must confess, I had a hope,
Had she continued widow, to have gained
An infinite mass of treasure by her death;
And that was the main cause. Her marriage: 270
That drew a stream of gall, quite through my heart.
For thee (as we observe in tragedies
That a good actor many times is cursed
For playing a villain's part), I hate thee for't;
And, for my sake, say thou hast done much ill, well.   275
BOSOLA: Let me quicken your memory, for I perceive
You are falling into ingratitude. I challenge°
The reward due to my service.
FERDINAND: I'll tell thee,
What I'll give thee —
BOSOLA: Do.
FERDINAND: I'll give thee a pardon
For this murder.
BOSOLA: Ha?
FERDINAND: Yes; and 'tis   280
The largest bounty I can study° to do thee.
By what authority didst thou execute
This bloody sentence?
BOSOLA: By yours.
FERDINAND: Mine? Was I her judge?
Did any ceremonial form of law
Doom her to not-being? Did a complete° jury   285
Deliver her conviction up i'th' court?
Where shalt thou find this judgement registered,
Unless in hell? See: like a bloody fool
Th' hast forfeited thy life, and thou shalt die for't.
BOSOLA: The office of justice is perverted quite   290
When one thief hangs another. Who shall dare

To reveal this?
FERDINAND: O, I'll tell thee:
   The wolf shall find her grave, and scrape it up;°
   Not to devour the corpse, but to discover
   The horrid murder.
BOSOLA: You, not I shall quake for't.   295
FERDINAND: Leave me.
BOSOLA: I will first receive my pension.°
FERDINAND: You are a villain.
BOSOLA: When your ingratitude
   Is judge, I am so —
FERDINAND: O, horror!
   That not the fear of him which binds the devils
   Can prescribe man obedience.   300
   Never look upon me more.
BOSOLA: Why fare thee well.
   Your brother and yourself are worthy men;
   You have a pair of hearts are hollow graves,
   Rotten, and rotting others; and your vengeance,
   Like two chained bullets,° still goes arm in arm.   305
   You may be brothers, for treason, like the plague,
   Doth take much in a blood.° I stand like one
   That long hath ta'en a sweet and golden dream.
   I am angry with myself, now that I wake.
FERDINAND: Get thee into some unknown part o'th' world,   310
   That I may never see thee.
BOSOLA: Let me know
   Wherefore I should be thus neglected? Sir,
   I served your tyranny; and rather strove
   To satisfy yourself, than all the world;
   And though I loathed the evil, yet I loved   315
   You that did counsel it; and rather sought
   To appear a true servant, than an honest man.
FERDINAND: I'll go hunt the badger by owl-light:°
   'Tis a deed of darkness.   *Exit.*
BOSOLA: He's much distracted. Off my painted° honour!   320
   While with vain hopes our faculties we tire,
   We seem to sweat in ice and freeze in fire.
   What would I do, were this to do again?
   I would not change° my peace of conscience
   For all the wealth of Europe. She stirs; here's life.   325
   Return, fair soul, from darkness, and lead mine
   Out of this sensible° hell. She's warm, she breathes;
   Upon thy pale lips I will melt my heart
   To store them with fresh colour. Who's there?

Some cordial° drink! Alas! I dare not call.   330
So pity would destroy pity.° Her eye opes,°
And heaven in it seems to ope, that late was shut,
To take me up to mercy.
DUCHESS: Antonio!
BOSOLA: Yes, madam, he is living.
The dead bodies you saw were but feigned statues;   335
He's reconciled to your brothers: — the Pope hath wrought
The atonement.°
DUCHESS: Mercy.   *She dies.*
BOSOLA: O, she's gone again; there the cords of life broke.
O sacred innocence, that sweetly sleeps
On turtles'° feathers, whilst a guilty conscience   340
Is a black register, where is writ
All our good deeds and bad; a perspective°
That shows us hell! That we cannot be suffered
To do good when we have a mind to it!   [*He weeps.*]
This is manly sorrow.   345
These tears, I am very certain, never grew
In my mother's milk. My estate° is sunk
Below the degree of fear. Where were
These penitent fountains while she was living?
O, they were frozen up! Here is a sight   350
As direful to my soul as is the sword
Unto a wretch hath slain his father. Come,
I'll bear thee hence,
And execute thy last will; that's deliver
Thy body to the reverend dispose°   355
Of some good women. That the cruel tyrant
Shall not deny me. Then I'll post to Milan,
Where somewhat I will speedily enact
Worth my dejection.°   *Exit* [*with the body of the* DUCHESS].

Act Five, Scene One

[*Enter* ANTONIO *and* DELIO.]

ANTONIO: What think you of my hope of reconcilement
To the Aragonian brethren?
DELIO: I misdoubt it,
For though they have sent their letters of safe conduct
For your repair° to Milan, they appear
But nets to entrap you. The Marquis of Pescara,   5
Under whom you hold certain land in cheat,°

Much 'gainst his noble nature, hath been moved
To seize those lands, and some of his dependants°
Are, at this instant, making it their suit
To be invested° in your revenues.   10
I cannot think they mean well to your life,
That do deprive you of your means of life,
Your living.
ANTONIO: You are still an heretic°
To any safety I can shape myself.
DELIO: Here comes the Marquis. I will make myself   15
Petitioner for some part of your land,
To know whither it is flying.
ANTONIO: I pray do.

[*Enter* PESCARA.]

DELIO: Sir, I have a suit to you.
PESCARA: To me?
DELIO: An easy one.
This is the citadel of Saint Bennet,°
With some demesnes,° of late in the possession   20
Of Antonio Bologna; please you bestow them on me.
PESCARA: You are my friend. But this is such a suit
Nor fit for me to give, nor you to take.
DELIO: No, sir?
PESCARA: I will give you ample reason for't
Soon, in private. Here's the Cardinal's mistress.   25

[*Enter* JULIA.]

JULIA: My lord, I am grown your poor petitioner,
And should be an ill beggar, had I not
A great man's letter here, the cardinal's,
To court you in my favour.   [*She gives him a letter.*]
PESCARA: He entreats for you
The citadel of Saint Bennet, that belonged   30
To the banished Bologna.
JULIA: Yes.
PESCARA: I could not have thought of a friend I could
Rather pleasure with it: 'tis yours.
JULIA: Sir, I thank you;
And he shall know how doubly I am engaged,
Both in your gift, and speediness of giving,   35
Which makes your grant the greater.   *Exit.*
ANTONIO [*aside*]:   How they fortify°

  Themselves with my ruin!
DELIO: Sir, I am
 Little bound to you.
PESCARA: Why?
DELIO: Because you denied this suit to me, and gave't
 To such a creature.
PESCARA: Do you know what it was?   40
 It was Antonio's land: not forfeited
 By course of law, but ravished° from his throat
 By the cardinal's entreaty. It were not fit
 I should bestow so main a piece of wrong
 Upon my friend; 'tis a gratification   45
 Only due to a strumpet, for it is injustice.
 Shall I sprinkle the pure blood of innocents
 To make those followers I call my friends
 Look ruddier° upon me? I am glad
 This land, ta'en from the owner by such wrong, 50
 Returns again unto so foul an use,
 As salary° for his lust. Learn, good Delio,
 To ask noble things of me, and you shall find
 I'll be a noble giver.
DELIO: You instruct me well.
ANTONIO [*aside*]: Why, here's a man now, would fright impudence 55
 From sauciest beggars.
PESCARA: Prince Ferdinand's come to Milan,
 Sick, as they give out, of an apoplexy.
 But some say 'tis a frenzy;° I am going
 To visit him.   *Exit.*
ANTONIO: 'Tis a noble old fellow.
DELIO: What course do you mean to take, Antonio?   60
ANTONIO: This night I mean to venture all my fortune —
 Which is no more than a poor ling'ring life —
 To the cardinal's worst of malice. I have got
 Private access to his chamber, and intend
 To visit him about the mid of night,   65
 As once his brother did our noble duchess.
 It may be that the sudden apprehension
 Of danger (for I'll go in mine own shape),°
 When he shall see it fraught with love and duty,
 May draw the poison out of him, and work   70
 A friendly reconcilement. If it fail,
 Yet it shall rid me of this infamous calling;°
 For better fall once, than be ever falling.
DELIO: I'll second you in all danger; and, howe'er,°
 My life keeps rank with yours.   75

ANTONIO: You are still° my loved and best friend.   *Exeunt.*

Act Five, Scene Two

[*Enter* PESCARA *and* DOCTOR.]

PESCARA: Now, doctor, may I visit your patient?
DOCTOR: If't please your lordship: but he's instantly
    To take the air here in the gallery,
    By my direction.
PESCARA: Pray thee, what's his disease?
DOCTOR: A very pestilent disease, my lord,   5
    They call lycanthropia.°
PESCARA: What's that?
    I need a dictionary to't.
DOCTOR: I'll tell you:
    In those that are possessed with't, there o'erflows
    Such melancholy humour,° they imagine
    Themselves to be transformèd into wolves,   10
    Steal forth to churchyards in the dead of night,
    And dig dead bodies up: as two nights since,
    One met the duke, 'bout midnight in a lane
    Behind Saint Mark's church, with the leg of a man
    Upon his shoulder; and he howled fearfully: 15
    Said he was a wolf; only the difference
    Was, a wolf's skin was hairy on the outside,
    His on the inside; bade them take their swords,
    Rip up his flesh, and try. Straight I was sent for,
    And having ministered to him, found his Grace   20
    Very well recovered.
PESCARA: I am glad on't.
DOCTOR: Yet not without some fear of a relapse.
    If he grow to his fit again, I'll go
    A nearer° way to work with him than ever
    Paracelsus° dreamed of. If they'll give me   25
    Leave, I'll buffet° this madness out of him.
    Stand aside: he comes.

[*Enter* CARDINAL, FERDINAND, MALATESTE *and* BOSOLA, *who
remains in the background.*]

FERDINAND: Leave me.
MALATESTE: Why doth your lordship love this solitariness?

FERDINAND: Eagles commonly fly alone. They are crows, daws,° and   30
    starlings that flock together. Look, what's that follows me?

MALATESTE: Nothing, my lord.

FERDINAND: Yes.

MALATESTE: 'Tis your shadow.

FERDINAND: Stay° it; let it not haunt me.   35

MALATESTE: Impossible, if you move, and the sun shine.

FERDINAND: I will throttle it.   [*Throws himself upon his shadow.*]

MALATESTE: O, my lord; you are angry with nothing.

FERDINAND: You are a fool. How is't possible I should catch my shadow
    unless I fall upon't? When I go to hell, I mean to carry a bribe;° for   40
    look you, good gifts evermore make way for the worst persons.

PESCARA: Rise, good my lord.

FERDINAND: I am studying the art of patience.

PESCARA: 'Tis a noble virtue.

FERDINAND: To drive six snails before me, from this town to Moscow;   45
    neither use goad nor whip to them, but let them take their own
    time (the patient'st man i'th' world match me for an experiment!)
    and I'll crawl after like a sheep-biter.°

CARDINAL: Force him up.   [*They raise* FERDINAND *to his feet.*]

FERDINAND: Use me well, you were best.   50
    What I have done, I have done. I'll confess nothing.

DOCTOR: Now let me come to him! Are you mad, my lord?
    Are you out of your princely wits?

FERDINAND: What's he?

PESCARA: Your doctor.

FERDINAND: Let me have his beard sawed off, and his eyebrows   55
    Filed more civil.°

DOCTOR: I must do mad tricks with him,
    For that's the only way on't. I have brought
    Your Grace a salamander's skin,° to keep you
    From sun-burning.

FERDINAND: I have cruel° sore eyes.

DOCTOR: The white of a cockatrice's° egg is present° remedy.   60

FERDINAND: Let it be a new-laid one, you were best.
    Hide me from him! Physicians are like kings;
    They brook no contradiction.

DOCTOR: Now he begins
    To fear me; now let me alone with him.   [*Removes his gown.*]

CARDINAL: How now, put off your gown?   65

DOCTOR: Let me have some forty urinals filled with rosewater: he and
    I'll go pelt one another with them. Now he begins to fear me. —
    Can you fetch a frisk,° sir? — Let him go, let him go upon my peril.

                              [*They release* FERDINAND.]

I find by his eye, he stands in awe of me: I'll make him as tame as
a dormouse.   70
FERDINAND: Can you fetch your frisks, sir! I will stamp him into a cullis;°
flay off his skin, to cover one of the anatomies° this rogue hath set
i'th' cold yonder, in Barber-Chirurgeons'° Hall. Hence, hence! you
are all of you like beasts for sacrifice; [*Throws the* DOCTOR *down and
beats him*] there's nothing left of you but tongue and belly, flattery   75
and lechery.   [*Exit.*]
PESCARA: Doctor, he did not fear you throughly.°
DOCTOR: True, I was somewhat too forward.
BOSOLA [*aside*]: Mercy upon me, what a fatal judgement
        Hath fall'n upon this Ferdinand!
PESCARA: Knows your Grace   80
        What accident° hath brought upon the prince
        This strange distraction?
CARDINAL [*aside*]: I must feign somewhat. — Thus they say it grew:
        You have heard it rumoured for these many years
        None of our family dies, but there is seen   85
        The shape of an old woman, which is given
        By tradition, to us, to have been murdered
        By her nephews, for her riches. Such a figure
        One night, as the prince sat up late at's book,
        Appeared to him; when crying out for help,   90
        The gentlemen of's chamber° found his Grace
        All on a cold sweat, altered much in face
        And language. Since which apparition
        He hath grown worse and worse, and I much fear
        He cannot live.   95
BOSOLA: Sir, I would speak with you.
PESCARA: We'll leave your Grace.
        Wishing to the sick prince, our noble lord,
        All health of mind and body.
CARDINAL: You are most welcome.
                    [*Exeunt* PESCARA, MALATESTE *and* DOCTOR.]
        [*Aside*] Are you come? So: this fellow must not know
        By any means I had intelligence   100
        In° our duchess' death. For, though I counselled it,
        The full of all th'engagement° seemed to grow
        From Ferdinand. — Now sir, how fares our sister?
        I do not think but sorrow makes her look
        Like to an oft-dyed° garment. She shall now   105
        Taste comfort from me. — Why do you look so wildly?
        O, the fortune of your master here, the prince,
        Dejects you — but be you of happy comfort.
        If you'll do one thing for me I'll entreat,

Though he had a cold tombstone o'er his bones,   110
I'd make you what you would be.
BOSOLA: Any thing;
Give it me in a breath, and let me fly to't.
They that think long small expedition° win,
For musing much o'th' end, cannot begin.

[*Enter* JULIA.]

JULIA: Sir, will you come in to supper?
CARDINAL: I am busy, leave me.   115
JULIA [*aside*]: What an excellent shape° hath that fellow!   *Exit.*
CARDINAL: 'Tis thus. Antonio lurks here in Milan;
Inquire him out, and kill him. While he lives
Our sister cannot marry, and I have thought
Of an excellent match for her. Do this, and style° me   120
Thy advancement.
BOSOLA: But by what means shall I find him out?
CARDINAL: There is a gentleman called Delio,
Here in the camp, that hath been long approved°
His loyal friend. Set eye upon that fellow,
Follow him to mass. May be Antonio,   125
Although he do account religion
But a school-name,° for fashion of the world,
May accompany him; or else go inquire out
Delio's confessor, and see if you can bribe
Him to reveal it — there are a thousand ways   130
A man might find to trace him. As, to know
What fellows haunt the Jews for taking up°
Great sums of money, for sure he's in want;
Or else go to th' picture-makers,° and learn
Who brought her picture lately: — some of these   135
Happily may take.°
BOSOLA: Well, I'll not freeze i'th' business;
I would see that wretched thing, Antonio,
Above all sights i'th' world.
CARDINAL: Do, and be happy.   *Exit.*
BOSOLA: This fellow doth breed basilisks° in's eyes,
He's nothing else but murder; yet he seems   140
Not to have notice of the duchess' death.
'Tis his cunning: I must follow his example;
There cannot be a surer way to trace,
Than that of an old fox.

[*Enter* JULIA, *with a pistol.*]

JULIA: So, sir, you are well met.
BOSOLA: How now?
JULIA: Nay, the doors are fast enough.   145
   Now, sir, I will make you confess your treachery.
BOSOLA: Treachery?
JULIA: Yes, confess to me
   Which of my women 'twas you hired, to put
   Love-powder into my drink?
BOSOLA: Love-powder ?
JULIA: Yes, when I was at Malfi.   150
   Why should I fall in love with such a face else?
   I have already suffered for thee so much pain,
   The only remedy to do me good
   Is to kill° my longing.
BOSOLA: Sure, your pistol holds
   Nothing but perfumes or kissing-comfits:° excellent lady,   155
   You have a pretty way on't to discover°
   Your longing. Come, come, I'll disarm you,
   And arm° you thus:° yet this is wondrous strange.
JULIA: Compare thy form, and my eyes together,
   You'll find my love no such great miracle. [*Kisses him.*]
      Now you'll say   160
   I am a wanton. This nice° modesty in ladies
   Is but a troublesome familiar° that haunts them.
BOSOLA: Know you me, I am a blunt soldier.
JULIA: The better.
   Sure, there wants° fire where there are no lively sparks
   Of roughness.
BOSOLA: And I want compliment.°
JULIA: Why, ignorance   165
   In courtship cannot make you do amiss, °
   If you have a heart to do well.
BOSOLA: You are very fair.
JULIA: Nay, if you lay beauty to my charge,
   I must plead unguilty.
BOSOLA: Your bright eyes
   Carry a quiver of darts° in them, sharper   170
   Than sunbeams.
JULIA: You will mar me with commendation,
   Put yourself to the charge° of courting me,
   Whereas now I woo you.
BOSOLA [*aside*]: I have it, I will work upon this creature,
   Let us grow most amorously familiar. —   175
   If the great cardinal now should see me thus,
   Would he not count me a villain?

JULIA: No, he might count me a wanton,
    Not lay a scruple of offence on you;
    For if I see, and steal a diamond, 180
    The fault is not i'th' stone, but in me the thief
    That purloins it. I am sudden° with you;
    We that are great women of pleasure use to cut off
    These uncertain wishes and unquiet longings,
    And in an instant join the sweet delight 185
    And the pretty excuse together. Had you been i'th' street,
    Under my chamber window, even there
    I should have courted you.
BOSOLA: O, you are an excellent lady.
JULIA: Bid me do somewhat for you presently,°
    To express I love you.
BOSOLA: I will, and if you love me, 190
    Fail not to effect it.
    The cardinal is grown wondrous melancholy;
    Demand the cause, let him not put you off
    With feigned excuse; discover the main ground on't.
JULIA: Why would you know this?
BOSOLA: I have depended on him, 195
    And I hear that he is fall'n in some disgrace
    With the Emperor. If he be, like the mice
    That forsake falling houses, I would shift
    To other dependence.
JULIA: You shall not need follow the wars:
    I'll be your maintenance.
BOSOLA: And I your loyal servant; 200
    But I cannot leave my calling.°
JULIA: Not leave
    An ungrateful general for the love of a sweet lady?
    You are like some cannot sleep in feather-beds,
    But must have blocks for their pillows.
BOSOLA: Will you do this?
JULIA: Cunningly.
BOSOLA: Tomorrow I'll expect th'intelligence.° 205
JULIA: Tomorrow? get you into my cabinet,°
    You shall have it with you. Do not delay me,
    No more than I do you. I am like one
    That is condemned: I have my pardon promised,
    But I would see it sealed. Go, get you in; 210
    You shall see me wind my tongue about his heart
    Like a skein of silk.   [BOSOLA *withdraws*.]

[*Enter* CARDINAL, *with a book*.]

CARDINAL: Where are you?

[*Enter* SERVANTS.]

SERVANTS: Here.
CARDINAL: Let none, upon your lives,
　　Have conference° with the Prince Ferdinand,
　　Unless I know it. [*Aside*] In this distraction   215
　　He may reveal the murder.   [*Exeunt* SERVANTS.]
　　Yond's my lingering consumption:°
　　I am weary of her; and by any means
　　Would be quit of —
JULIA: How now, my lord?
　　What ails you?
CARDINAL: Nothing.
JULIA: O, you are much altered.   220
　　Come, I must be your secretary,° and remove
　　This lead from off your bosom. What's the matter?
CARDINAL: I may not tell you.
JULIA: Are you so far in love with sorrow,
　　You cannot part with part of it? Or think you   225
　　I cannot love your Grace when you are sad,
　　As well as merry? Or do you suspect
　　I, that have been a secret to your heart
　　These many winters, cannot be the same
　　Unto your tongue?
CARDINAL: Satisfy thy longing.   230
　　The only way to make thee keep my counsel
　　Is not to tell thee.
JULIA: Tell your echo this,
　　Or flatterers, that, like echoes, still° report
　　What they hear, though most imperfect, and not me;
　　For, if that you be true unto yourself,   235
　　I'll know.
CARDINAL: Will you rack me?
JULIA: No, judgement° shall
　　Draw it from you. It is an equal fault,
　　To tell one's secrets unto all, or none.
CARDINAL: The first argues° folly.
JULIA: But the last tyranny.
CARDINAL: Very well; why, imagine I have committed   240
　　Some secret deed, which I desire the world
　　May never hear of.
JULIA: Therefore may not I know it?
　　You have concealed for me as great a sin

As adultery. Sir, never was occasion
For perfect trial of my constancy   245
Till now. Sir, I beseech you.
CARDINAL: You'll repent it.
JULIA: Never.
CARDINAL: It hurries thee to ruin: I'll not tell thee.
Be well advised, and think what danger 'tis
To receive a prince's secrets: they that do,
Had need have their breasts hooped with adamant°   250
To contain them. I pray thee yet be satisfied.
Examine thine own frailty; 'tis more easy
To tie knots, than unloose them: 'tis a secret
That, like a ling'ring poison, may chance lie
Spread in thy veins, and kill thee seven year hence.   255
JULIA: Now you dally with me.
CARDINAL: No more; thou shalt know it.
By my appointment the great Duchess of Malfi
And two of her young children, four nights since
Were strangled.
JULIA: O heaven! Sir, what have you done?
CARDINAL: How now? How settles° this? Think you your bosom   260
Will be a grave dark and obscure enough
For such a secret?
JULIA: You have undone yourself, sir.
CARDINAL: Why?
JULIA: It lies not in me to conceal it.
CARDINAL: No?
Come, I will swear you to't upon this book.
JULIA: Most religiously.
CARDINAL: Kiss it.   [*She kisses the book.*] 265
Now you shall never utter it; thy curiosity
Hath undone thee; thou'rt poisoned with that book.
Because I knew thou couldst not keep my counsel,
I have bound thee to't by death.

[*Enter* BOSOLA.]

BOSOLA: For pity sake, hold.
CARDINAL: Ha, Bosola!
JULIA: I forgive you   270
This equal° piece of justice you have done,
For I betrayed your counsel° to that fellow.
He overheard it; that was the cause I said
It lay not in me to conceal it.
BOSOLA: O foolish woman,

Couldst not thou have poisoned him?

JULIA: 'Tis weakness,   275
    Too much to think what should have been done. I go,
    I know not whither.   [*Dies.*]

CARDINAL: Wherefore com'st thou hither?

BOSOLA: That I might find a great man, like yourself,
    Not out of his wits, as the Lord Ferdinand,
    To remember my service.

CARDINAL: I'll have thee hewed in pieces.   280

BOSOLA: Make not yourself such a promise of that life
    Which is not yours to dispose of.

CARDINAL: Who placed thee here?

BOSOLA: Her lust, as she intended.

CARDINAL: Very well;
    Now you know me for your fellow murderer.

BOSOLA: And wherefore should you lay fair marble colours°   285
    Upon your rotten purposes to me?
    Unless you imitate some that do plot great treasons,
    And when they have done,° go hide themselves i'th' graves
    Of those were actors in't.

CARDINAL: No more; there is a fortune attends° thee.   290

BOSOLA: Shall I go sue to Fortune any longer?
    'Tis the fool's pilgrimage.

CARDINAL: I have honours in store for thee.

BOSOLA: There are many ways that conduct to seeming honour,
    And some of them very dirty ones.

CARDINAL: Throw to the devil
    Thy melancholy. The fire burns well;   295
    What need we keep a stirring of't, and make
    A greater smother?° Thou wilt kill Antonio?

BOSOLA: Yes.

CARDINAL: Take up that body.

BOSOLA: I think I shall
    Shortly grow the common bier for churchyards!

CARDINAL: I will allow thee some dozen of attendants,   300
    To aid thee in the murder.

BOSOLA: O, by no means: physicians that apply horseleeches to any
    rank swelling use to cut off their tails, that the blood may run
    through them the faster. Let me have no train° when I go to shed
    blood, lest it make me have a greater, when I ride to the gallows.   305

CARDINAL: Come to me after midnight, to help to remove that body
    To her own lodging. I'll give out she died o'th' plague;
    'Twill breed the less inquiry after her death.

BOSOLA: Where's Castruchio her husband?

CARDINAL: He's rode to Naples, to take possession   310

Of Antonio's citadel.

BOSOLA: Believe me, you have done a very happy° turn.

CARDINAL: Fail not to come. There is the master-key
    Of our lodgings: and by that you may conceive
    What trust I plant in you.   *Exit.* [CARDINAL.]

BOSOLA: You shall find me ready.   315
    O poor Antonio, though nothing be so needful
    To thy estate° as pity, yet I find
    Nothing so dangerous. I must look to my footing;
    In such slippery ice-pavements men had need
    To be frost-nailed° well; they may break their necks else.   320
    The precedent's here afore me: how this man
    Bears up in blood!° seems fearless! Why, 'tis well:
    Security° some men call the suburbs of hell,
    Only a dead wall° between. Well, good Antonio,
    I'll seek thee out; and all my care shall be   325
    To put thee into safety from the reach
    Of these most cruel biters,° that have got
    Some of thy blood already. It may be
    I'll join with thee in a most just revenge.
    The weakest arm is strong enough, that strikes   330
    With the sword of justice. Still methinks the duchess
    Haunts me. There, there! 'tis nothing but my melancholy.
    O penitence, let me truly taste thy cup,
    That throws men down, only to raise them up.   *Exit.*

Act Five, Scene Three

[*Enter* ANTONIO *and* DELIO. *There is an*] ECHO (*from the* DUCHESS'
grave).°

DELIO: Yond's the cardinal's window. This fortification
    Grew from the ruins of an ancient abbey;
    And to yond side o'th' river lies a wall,
    Piece of a cloister,° which in my opinion
    Gives the best echo that you ever heard;   5
    So hollow, and so dismal, and withal
    So plain in the distinction of our words,
    That many have supposed it is a spirit
    That answers.

ANTONIO: I do love these ancient ruins:
    We never tread upon them but we set   10
    Our foot upon some reverend history.°
    And, questionless, here in this open court,

Which now lies naked to the injuries
Of stormy weather, some men lie interred
Loved° the church so well, and gave so largely° to't,   15
They thought it should have canopied their bones
Till doomsday.° But all things have their end.
Churches and cities, which have diseases like to men,°
Must have like death that we have.
ECHO: *Like death that we have.*
DELIO: Now the echo hath caught you.
ANTONIO: It groaned, methought, and gave   20
A very deadly accent.°
ECHO: *Deadly accent.*
DELIO: I told you 'twas a pretty one. You may make it
A huntsman, or a falconer, a musician
Or a thing of sorrow.
ECHO: *A thing of sorrow.*
ANTONIO: Ay, sure: that suits it best.
ECHO: *That suits it best.*   25
ANTONIO: 'Tis very like my wife's voice.
ECHO: *Ay, wife's voice.*
DELIO: Come, let's walk farther from't;
I would not have you go to th' cardinal's tonight:
Do not.
ECHO: *Do not.*
DELIO: Wisdom doth not more moderate wasting sorrow   30
Than time. Take time for't; be mindful of thy safety.
ECHO: *Be mindful of thy safety.*
ANTONIO: Necessity compels me:
Make scrutiny throughout the passages°
Of your own life; you'll find it impossible
To fly your fate.
ECHO: *O, fly your fate.*   35
DELIO: Hark: the dead stones seem to have pity on you
And give you good counsel.
ANTONIO: Echo, I will not talk with thee,
For thou art a dead thing.
ECHO: *Thou art a dead thing.*
ANTONIO: My duchess is asleep now,
And her little ones, I hope sweetly. — O Heaven,   40
Shall I never see her more?
ECHO: *Never see her more.*
ANTONIO: I marked not one repetition of the Echo
But that; and on the sudden, a clear light
Presented me a face folded° in sorrow.
DELIO: Your fancy, merely.

ANTONIO: Come: I'll be out of this ague;° 45
    For to live thus is not indeed to live.
    It is a mockery, and abuse of life.
    I will not henceforth save myself by halves;
    Lose all, or nothing.
DELIO: Your own virtue save you.
    I'll fetch your eldest son, and second you. 50
    It may be that the sight of his own blood,°
    Spread in so sweet a figure, may beget
    The more compassion.
ANTONIO: However, fare you well.
    Though in our miseries Fortune hath a part,
    Yet, in our noble sufferings she hath none. 55
    Contempt of pain, that we may call our own.   *Exeunt.*

Act Five, Scene Four

[*Enter*] CARDINAL, PESCARA, MALATESTE, RODERIGO, GRISOLAN.

CARDINAL: You shall not watch tonight by the sick prince;
    His Grace is very well recoverèd.
MALATESTE: Good my lord, suffer us.
CARDINAL: O, by no means.
    The noise, and change of object in his eye,
    Doth more distract him. I pray, all to bed, 5
    And though you hear him in his violent fit,
    Do not rise, I entreat you.
PESCARA: So, sir, we shall not —
CARDINAL: Nay, I must have you promise
    Upon your honours, for I was enjoined to't
    By himself; and he seemed to urge it sensibly.° 10
PESCARA: Let our honours bind this trifle.
CARDINAL: Nor any of your followers.
PESCARA: Neither.
CARDINAL: It may be to make trial of your promise
    When he's asleep, myself will rise, and feign
    Some of his mad tricks, and cry out for help, 15
    And feign myself in danger.
MALATESTE: If your throat were cutting,°
    I'd not come at you, now I have protested against it.°
CARDINAL: Why, I thank you. [*Withdraws.*]
GRISOLAN: 'Twas a foul storm tonight.
RODERIGO: The Lord Ferdinand's chamber shook like an osier.°
MALATESTE: 'Twas nothing but pure kindness in the devil, 20

To rock his own child.

Exeunt [RODERIGO, MALATESTE, PESCARA, GRISOLAN].

CARDINAL [*comes forward*]: The reason why I would not suffer these
    About my brother, is because at midnight
    I may with better privacy convey
    Julia's body to her own lodging. O, my conscience!   25
    I would pray now; but the devil takes away my heart
    For having any confidence in prayer.
    About this hour I appointed Bosola
    To fetch the body. When he hath served my turn,
    He dies.   *Exit.* 30

[*Enter* BOSOLA.]

BOSOLA: Ha! 'twas the cardinal's voice. I heard him name
    Bosola, and my death. Listen, I hear one's footing.

[*Enter* FERDINAND.]

FERDINAND: Strangling is a very quiet death.
BOSOLA: Nay, then, I see I must stand upon my guard.
FERDINAND: What say'st to that? Whisper, softly: do you agree to't?   35
    So it must be done i'th' dark: the cardinal
    Would not for a thousand pounds the doctor should see it.   *Exit.*
BOSOLA: My death is plotted; here's the consequence of murder.
    We value not desert, nor Christian breath,
    When we know black deeds must be cured with death.
    [*Withdraws.*] 40

[*Enter* ANTONIO *and a* SERVANT.]

SERVANT: Here stay, sir, and be confident, I pray.
    I'll fetch you a dark lantern.°   *Exit.*
ANTONIO: Could I take him
    At his prayers, there were hope of pardon.
BOSOLA: Fall right my sword!   [*Strikes* ANTONIO *down.*]
    I'll not give thee so much leisure as to pray.   45
ANTONIO: O, I am gone. Thou hast ended a long suit,°
    In a minute.
BOSOLA: What art thou?
ANTONIO: A most wretched thing,
    That only have thy benefit in death,
    To appear myself.

[*Enter* SERVANT, *with a dark lantern.*]

SERVANT: Where are you, sir?
ANTONIO: Very near my home. Bosola?
SERVANT: O, misfortune!   50
BOSOLA [*to* Servant]: Smother thy pity, thou art dead else. — Antonio!
   The man I would have saved 'bove mine own life!
   We are merely the stars' tennis-balls, struck and banded°
   Which way please them. O good Antonio,
   I'll whisper one thing in thy dying ear,   55
   Shall make thy heart break quickly. Thy fair duchess
   And two sweet children —
ANTONIO: Their very names
   Kindle a little life in me.
BOSOLA: Are murdered!
ANTONIO: Some men have wished to die
   At the hearing of sad tidings. I am glad   60
   That I shall do't in sadness.° I would not now
   Wish my wounds balmed, nor healed, for I have no use
   To put my life to. In all our quest of greatness,
   Like wanton° boys, whose pastime is their care,
   We follow after bubbles, blown in th'air.   65
   Pleasure of life, what is't? Only the good hours
   Of an ague;° merely a preparative to rest,
   To endure vexation. I do not ask
   The process of my death: only, commend me
   To Delio.
BOSOLA: Break, heart!   70
ANTONIO: And let my son fly the courts of princes.   [*Dies.*]
BOSOLA: Thou seem'st to have loved Antonio?
SERVANT: I brought him hither,
   To have reconciled him to the cardinal.
BOSOLA: I do not ask thee that.
   Take him up, if thou tender° thine own life,   75
   And bear him where the Lady Julia
   Was wont to lodge. — O, my fate moves swift.
   I have this cardinal in the forge already;
   Now I'll bring him to th' hammer. — O direful misprision!°
   I will not imitate things glorious,   80
   No more than base: I'll be mine own example. —
   On, on; and look thou represent, for silence,
   The thing thou bear'st.°   *Exeunt.*

Act Five, Scene Five

[Enter] CARDINAL, *with a book.*

CARDINAL: I am puzzled in a question about hell:
    He says, in hell there's one material fire,
    And yet it shall not burn all men alike.
    Lay him by.° How tedious° is a guilty conscience!
    When I look into the fishponds in my garden,   5
    Methinks I see a thing, armed with a rake,°
    That seems to strike at me. Now? Art thou come?

[Enter BOSOLA *and* SERVANT, *with* ANTONIO's *body.]*

    Thou look'st ghastly.
    There sits in thy face some great determination,
    Mixed with some fear.
BOSOLA: Thus it lightens° into action: 10
    I am come to kill thee.
CARDINAL: Ha? Help! our guard!
BOSOLA: Thou art deceived. They are out of thy howling.
CARDINAL: Hold! and I will faithfully° divide
    Revènues with thee.
BOSOLA: Thy prayers and proffers
    Are both unseasonable.°
CARDINAL: Raise the watch!   15
    We are betrayed!
BOSOLA: I have confined your flight.
    I'll suffer your retreat to Julia's chamber,
    But no further.
CARDINAL: Help! we are betrayed!

[Enter PESCARA, MALATESTE, RODERIGO *and* GRISOLAN, *above.]*

MALATESTE: Listen.
CARDINAL: My dukedom for rescue!
RODERIGO: Fie upon his counterfeiting.°
MALATESTE: Why, 'tis not the cardinal.
RODERIGO: Yes, yes, tis he;   20
    But I'll see him hanged, ere I'll go down to him.
CARDINAL: Here's a plot upon me; I am assaulted! I am lost,
    Unless some rescue!
GRISOLAN: He doth this pretty well,
    But it will not serve to laugh me out of mine honour.
CARDINAL: The sword's at my throat!

RODERIGO: You would not bawl so loud then.   25
MALATESTE: Come, come:
    Let's go to bed; he told us thus much aforehand.
PESCARA: He wished you should not come at° him; but believ't,
    The accent of the voice sounds not in jest.
    I'll down to him, howsoever, and with engines°   30
    Force ope the doors.   [*Exit.*]
RODERIGO: Let's follow him aloof,
    And note how the cardinal will laugh at him.   [*Exeunt above.*]
BOSOLA: There's for you first:
    'Cause you shall not unbarricade the door
    To let in rescue.   *He kills the* SERVANT. 35
CARDINAL: What cause hast thou to pursue my life?
BOSOLA: Look there.
CARDINAL: Antonio!
BOSOLA: Slain by my hand unwittingly.
    Pray, and be sudden.° When thou killed'st thy sister,
    Thou took'st from Justice her most equal balance,
    And left her naught but her sword.
CARDINAL: O, mercy!   40
BOSOLA: Now it seems thy greatness was only outward,
    For thou fall'st faster of thyself than calamity
    Can drive thee. I'll not waste longer time. There! [*Stabs the* CARDINAL.]
CARDINAL: Thou hast hurt me.
BOSOLA: Again.   [*Stabs him again.*]
CARDINAL: Shall I die like a leveret,°
    Without any resistance? Help, help, help!   45
    I am slain.

[*Enter* FERDINAND.]

FERDINAND: Th'alarum? give me a fresh horse!
    Rally the vaunt-guard,° or the day is lost.
    Yield, yield! I give you the honour of arms,°
    Shake my sword over you; will you yield?   50
CARDINAL: Help me, I am your brother.
FERDINAND: The devil?
    My brother fight upon the adverse party?
                     He wounds the CARDINAL *and, in the scuffle,*
                            gives BOSOLA *his death wound.*
    There flies your ransom.
CARDINAL: O, Justice!
    I suffer now for what hath former been:
    Sorrow is held the eldest child of sin.   55
FERDINAND: Now you're brave fellows. Caesar's fortune was harder°

than Pompey's: Caesar died in the arms of prosperity, Pompey at the
feet of disgrace;° you both died in the field. The pain's nothing. Pain
many times is taken away with the apprehension of greater, as the
toothache with the sight of a barber° that comes to pull it out: there's   60
philosophy for you.

BOSOLA: Now my revenge is perfect.   *He [fatally stabs]* FERDINAND.
                         Sink, thou main cause
Of my undoing; the last part of my life
Hath done me best service.

FERDINAND: Give me some wet hay, I am broken-winded.°   65
I do account this world but a dog-kennel.
I will vault credit,° and affect high pleasures
Beyond death.

BOSOLA: He seems to come to himself,
Now he's so near the bottom.

FERDINAND: My sister! O! my sister, there's the cause on't.   70
Whether we fall by ambition, blood,° or lust,
Like diamonds we are cut with our own dust.   [*Dies.*]

CARDINAL: Thou hast thy payment too.

BOSOLA: Yes, I hold my weary soul in my teeth;
'Tis ready to part from me. I do glory   75
That thou, which stood'st like a huge pyramid
Begun upon a large and ample base,
Shalt end in a little point, a kind of nothing.

          [*Enter* PESCARA, MALATESTE, RODERIGO *and* GRISOLAN.]

PESCARA: How now, my lord?

MALATESTE: O, sad° disaster!

RODERIGO: How comes this?

BOSOLA: Revenge, for the Duchess of Malfi, murdered   80
By th'Aragonian brethren; for Antonio,
Slain by this hand; for lustful Julia,
Poisoned by this man; and lastly, for myself,
That was an actor in the main° of all,
Much 'gainst mine own good nature, yet i'th' end   85
Neglected.

PESCARA: How now, my lord?

CARDINAL: Look to my brother.
He gave us these large wounds, as we were struggling
Here i'th'rushes.° And now, I pray, let me
Be laid by, and never thought of.   [*Dies.*]

PESCARA: How fatally, it seems, he did withstand   90
His own rescue!

MALATESTE: Thou wretched thing of blood,

How came Antonio by his death?
BOSOLA: In a mist: I know not how;
    Such a mistake as I have often seen
    In a play. — O, I am gone.   95
    We are only like dead° walls, or vaulted graves,
    That, ruined, yields no echo. Fare you well;
    It may be pain, but no harm to me, to die
    In so good a quarrel. O, this gloomy world!
    In what a shadow, or deep pit of darkness   100
    Doth womanish, and fearful mankind live!
    Let worthy minds ne'er stagger° in distrust
    To suffer death or shame for what is just:
    Mine is another voyage.   [*Dies.*]
PESCARA: The noble Delio, as I came to th'palace,   105
    Told me of Antonio's being here, and showed me
    A pretty gentleman, his son and heir.

            [*Enter* DELIO, *with* ANTONIO's *son.*]

MALATESTE: O sir, you come too late.
DELIO: I heard so, and
    Was armed° for't ere I came. Let us make noble use
    Of this great ruin; and join all our force   110
    To establish this young hopeful gentleman
    In's mother's right. These wretched eminent things
    Leave no more fame behind 'em, than should one
    Fall in a frost, and leave his print in snow;
    As soon as the sun shines, it ever melts   115
    Both form and matter. I have ever thought
    Nature doth nothing so great for great men,
    As when she's pleased to make them lords of truth.
    Integrity of life is fame's best friend,
    Which nobly, beyond death, shall crown the end.   *Exeunt.* 120

Finis

Notes to the Play

Dramatis personae

3   *Provisor...Horse*: manager of the ducal stables
6   CASTRUCHIO: named after an historical Cardinal of Sienna, but the word suggests 'castrated man' (*castrone*), glossed in a contemporary Italian-English dictionary as also meaning a cuckold and a fool
7   PESCARA: a distinguished Neapolitan general (1489–1525) in the service of Charles V of Spain
8   MALATESTE: the name of the ruling family of Rimini
13 FOROBOSCO: named as the keeper of the keys of the park gate (2.2.28), but without a walk-on part in the play as first printed.
16 CARIOLA: 'truckle-bed', an appropriate name for a personal attendant who would sleep in the Duchess' bedroom
21 Gentleman Usher: an official who preceded a member of the nobility

Act One, Scene One

3   formal: prim and precise
    habit: dress
5   state: ruling council
6   fixed: established
7   Quits: rids
12 common: public
13 in general: everywhere, to all
14 example: piece of behaviour
17 provident: foreseeing
18 Inform: make him familiar with
23 only court-gall: chief sore-spot, bitter critic of the court
24 simple love of: pure dedication to
27 envious: malicious

32 only the reward: the only reward
34 enforce: urge
38 Blackbirds: Bosola himself may be wearing black, the colour favoured by melancholy men (cf. 76 below)
39 dog-days: evil, oppressive times, associated with the hottest time of the year (August), when Sirius the dog-star is high in the sky
41 divinity: religion
42 arrant knaves: absolute villains
48 suit: request
50 standing: stagnant
51 pies: magpies
54 dependences: promised appointments or rewards
    advanced: promoted
55 hoping Tantalus: Tantalus's punishment in the underworld for an attempted rape was to be hungry and thirsty but never able to reach the food and drink set around him.
57 rewards: hunters rewarded their hawks and dogs with scraps from the prey
59 geometry...supportation: the crippled soldier on crutches is compared to the compasses or dividers used in geometrical measurement.
61 swing: (1) movement (on crutches); (2) fling
68 suborned: procured by bribery
69–70 Gaston...Naples: Naples was retaken from the Spanish by the French crown in 1501, but not by the distinguished general Gaston de Foix (1489–1512) who was then only a young adolescent.
74–5 If...soul: contemporary medical opinion held that excessive sleep harmed the body and the mind.
76 want: lack
77 black: the characteristic dress of melancholy young men

close: (1) secret; (2) confined (by lack of activity)

78   hurt: cause damage

Act One, Scene Two

SH   Although the Quarto marks this scene division, it is not strictly necessary, since Antonio and Delio remain on stage.

1   presence: ruler's audience-chamber

4   strangers: visitors

6   took the ring: a form of jousting in which riders attempted to spear a dangling ring with their lances

9   sportive action: play-game activity

10   action: warfare

19   office: duty, function

23   fighting: cf. line 29 and note. Ferdinand may be toying with the foolish husband of his brother's mistress, Julia.

25   jest she broke: joke she cracked

27–8   lie...in tents: (1) sleep, as did the Israelites in tents; (2) lie in bed like a Jew, wrapped up in surgical dressings ('tents')

29   undo: ruin
chirurgeons: surgeons (whose task it was to care for wounded duellists). There may also be an element of sexual innuendo, for surgeons also dealt with venereal disease, and 'fighting' was a common metaphor for sexual intercourse, followed up in 'drawn their weapons' and 'go to it'.

32   put up: (1) sheath their swords; (2) prepare for sex

34   jennet: a light sporting horse

36   Pliny's opinion...wind: the Roman writer Pliny, in his *Natural History*, tells of Portuguese mares that chose to be inseminated by the wind and produced unusually fleet offspring.

37   ballasted: weighed down
quicksilver: (1) mercury; (2) speed

38   reels...tilt: (1) rolls back to even keel (like a well-ballasted boat); (2) jibs at, reels back from a jousting encounter. Silvio's pun carries on Ferdinand's bawdy talk ('tilt' = copulate), and offends him.

41   touchwood: tinder

45   your fool: great families kept fools as part of their establishment, often, as here, congenitally simple-minded or deaf persons. What Castruchio does not perceive is that Ferdinand is hinting that he is a such a fool.

50–1   the wrinkle: (1) skin creases; (2) moral blemishes (a sense unintended by Castruchio)

52–3   mathematical...face: The phrase half-suggests a constrictive face-mask.

53   out of compass: (1) immoderately; (2) beyond the range of a 'compass'

57   riders in France: reputedly the best in Europe at this time

58   the Grecian horse: the Trojan Horse, which concealed a force of Greek warriors

61 SD   *Enter...Attendant*: the Cambridge editors suggest that the Duchess takes her seat in a chair of state since this is her court, not Ferdinand's.

63   come about: returned to port

67   temper: temperament
play: wager

70   flashes: superficial, transient shows
form: outward appearance's sake

71   melancholy: The term connoted moroseness, deep disaffection, envy, unsociableness, and disabling scepticism, as well as cowardice

72   spring: cf. the fountain image used by Antonio, 1.1.12ff. engendering of toads: birth-place of (poisonous) toads

73   jealous: suspicious

74   Hercules: Hera, queen of the gods, plotted to destroy the hero from his childhood.

75   intelligencers: informers, spies

	atheists: depraved persons
	political: scheming, cunning
77	decency: proper way (by election)
84	quality: social rank
86	bench: judge's bench
92	those..him: those who will become his food
93	shrewd turns: the result of injuries to himself
96	oracles: oraculous statements
100	medals: medallions, which often bore portrait-images of rulers and their consorts
101	figure: shape, form temper: character
102	rapture: delight
105	vainglory: pride, boastfulness
106	you penance: you consider it a painful punishment. The quarto reads 'your'.
108	galliard: lively, capering dance
109	dead palsy: complete paralysis
113	practised: exercised, spent
114–15	sleeps...heaven: implying that even her dreams were only of goodness
115	shrifts: spiritual acts of confession
116	glasses: mirrors
117	dress...in her: (1) use her as their mirror when dressing; (2) adopt her virtues
118	play the wire-drawer: go on too much about her
119	case...up: conclude, close up
121	stains: eclipses
128	provisorship...horse: position of manager of your stables
132	leaguer: siege-camp
134	caroches: large and fashionable coaches
135	entertain: receive, welcome
136	intelligence: secret information
139	Master...Household: steward who controlled domestic administration and household expenditure
147	credit: credibility, belief in
149	cozens: deceives; it was common practice for doctors to determine the state of patient's health from an inspection of their urine
153	oft: frequent

	cedar tree: a symbol of greatness
156	next: nearest
158–9	Never...of them: Jupiter, god of thunder, transformed himself into a shower of gold coins to gain access to Danäe, locked in a brazen tower.
161	post: in haste
164	'haviour: behaviour
166	affects: likes
170	familiars: (1) household members, intimates; (2) companion devils. The term was also used for an officer of the Spanish Inquisition responsible for arrests and the imprisonment of its victims.
171	quaint: cunning
172	intelligencer: spy
175	angels: gold coins ('nobles') bearing the image of St Michael slaying Satan were popularly called 'angels'
181	on't: about it
183	noble: with a possible play on 'noble', the gold coin
187	Candies: sugars
188	complemental: accomplished, refined
193	politic: cunning dormouse: known to hibernate, so an image for sleepiness
194	Feed...dish: dine at a lord's table
196	place: post
198	creature: devoted servant
207	your high blood: (1) one of your noble birth; (2) your passionate nature luxurious: lascivious
208	livers: considered to be the seat of love and violent passions
209	Laban's sheep: see Genesis 30:31–43; 'spotted' implies diseased, or defective
213	motion: resolve, impulse
216	rank: (1) over luxuriant (and therefore capable of harming feeding animals); (2) corrupt, festering
217	honey-dew: (1) sweet, sticky substance actually secreted by

aphids, but then supposed to be some kind of dew; (2) allusively suggesting the pleasures of sexual intercourse

221 give...suck: as witches were supposed to do, though Ferdinand also hints at young women falling pregnant

223 Vulcan's engine: the fine net in which Vulcan trapped his wife Venus with her lover Mars

227 eaves: cover, shelter

228 irregular: abnormal

232 executed: carried out, with the implication of punishment by death

235 forerun man's mischief: preceed human disasters

238 roundly: fluently

240 look rusty: with dried blood

241 chargeable: expensive

242 whispering-rooms: private places for intimate conversations

244–5 that part...in't: suggesting the penis

244 lamprey: a sinuous eel-like sucker-fish

247 neat knave: elegantly dressed, healthy rogue
tale: (1) story; (2) tail (penis)

251 foot-steps: stepping stones, rungs (to the altar)

253 apprehending: being made aware of

257 winked: closed my eyes (acted heedlessly)

263 ingenious: intelligent

264 attends: waits to meet

265 behind the arras: tapestries (*arras*) were hung out from the wall in wealthy Jacobean houses, and there are many references to illict behaviour behind them: cf. *The Revenger's Tragedy*, 2.2.78 and note. In the theatre, Cariola could retire behind the curtain (traverse) covering one of the rear entrance-doors.

268 clue: thread used to guide one through a labyrinth

269 SD *the* DUCHESS...ANTONIO: 1623 supplies no direction for Antonio's entry; it is likeliest

that the Duchess herself admits him.

273 triumphs: grand festivities

274 husbands: (1) husbands; (2) stewards

277 for your sake: (1) thanks to you; (2) for love of you

278 cares: financial responsibilities

280 upright: (1) virtuous; (2) standing

288 procured: purchased, brought on

290 quit: ended

291 overseer: an administrator of the will

297 winding-sheet: the wrappings of the dead
couple: (1) pair of (winding) sheets; (2) marriage; (3) sexual embrace

298 Saint Winifred: a Welsh saint, whose head was struck off when she refused the love of a chieftain's son

301 as...purgatory: as do those (Protestants) who deny the existence of purgatory

303 affect it: like the idea of marriage

309 wanton: playful child

312 bloodshot: (1) inflamed; (2) inflamed by sexual desire (*blood*)

313 sovereign: powerfully curative

319 dancing...circle: magicians might draw a magic circle in which to confine the spirits they called up; but there is also an allusion to the female and male organs of sex in *circle* and *finger* (line 320)

322 roof: that is, Antonio's bowed head

328 girt: surrounded, accompanied

329 prattling visitants: chatting visitors

331 but I aim: that I do not guess

337 You..yourself: you would do a bad job of marketing yourself

338 darkening: depreciation

339 false lights: deceitful illumination; shopkeepers were frequently accused of displaying shoddy or defective goods (*bad wares*) in darker parts of their shop

343 progress: make a royal tour

347 to woo: (1) into woe; (2) to woo.

In successive early editions of
the play, spellings vary
between these two forms.

348   doubles: acts deceitfully,
        evasively

359–60 the figure...tomb: Renaissance
        tombs often showed stone
        images or sculptures of the
        mourners.

369   *Quietus est*: formal discharge
        of debts; the phrase was also
        often used both to signify that
        accounts were correct, and to
        describe the 'release' offered
        by death.

373   without this circumference:
        outside this circle; the pair
        have embraced

377   parts: (1) words, parts of
        speech; (2) things spoken

378   savoured: had a taste of

379   of my counsel: in my
        confidence

380–1 I have...marriage: These
        words, spoken without
        witnesses, constituted a legal
        form of marriage, regarded by
        the church as valid but sinful,
        requiring a formal church
        ceremony for full ratification.
        Intercourse before such a
        religious ceremony was
        frequently practised, though
        regarded by puritans and
        some clergy as mere
        fornication.

382   Gordian: knot of marriage,
        from the knot tied by Gordius,
        King of Gordium in Phrygia,
        which signified the rule of
        Asia Minor. Alexander the
        Great undid it by cutting
        through it with his sword.

384–5 like...motion: in the old
        cosmology, the crystalline
        spheres carrying the planets
        around the earth were in
        perpetual movement (*still*
        means always), giving out a
        perfect music inaudible to
        human ears.

385   Quickening: stimulating,
        bringing new life (as of an
        unborn child)

387   loving palms: palm-trees were
        thought to need partner trees
        in order to fruit, and drooped
        amorously towards each other.

390   force: legally compel

396   I...blind: the Duchess may
        cover her eyes with one hand,
        signifying the conventional
        blindness of Love or Fortune.
        conceit: witty thought, fancy

401   humorous: ill-humoured

402   the old tale: the subject of an
        early play and a ballad, which
        relates how when Ludwicke
        married the Princess of
        Hungary in his companion
        Alexander's name, he laid a
        sword between himself and
        his bride each night to
        preserve their chastity.

404   shroud: (1) hide; (2) prepare
        for burial

Act Two, Scene One

1   courtier: legal or royal court
        attendant

2   main: goal, purpose

4   your...largely: that is,
        Castruchio has big, ass-like
        ears
        nightcap: the white skull-cap
        or coif worn by lawyers
        expresses: presses out

5   twirl...band: a courtier's or
        lawyers falling band or ruff
        was attached with ties; it was
        court fashion to play with
        these *strings*

8   president: presiding judge

14   roaring boys: street bullies

19   prime nightcaps: leading
        lawyers

20   painting: making up your face

24   sloughs: (1) muddy ditches or
        bogs; (2) layers of dead
        skin-tissue
        progress: official circuit (of her
        face)

27   abortive: half-formed

29–30 careening...again: 'scraping
        clean the hull of an old lady
        whose skin is crusted, covered
        with hard deposits, so that she
        can return to the open seas
        (*disembogue*)'; lustful women

31 were frequently compared to roving sea-vessels

31 plastic: fine, artistic modelling (implicitly, of the cosmetic plaster laid over your face)

36–7 dead...plague: one remedy for the plague required holding a bird to the plague-sore to draw the poison

37–8 sin of your youth: by implication, sexual immorality requiring expensive treatment by a doctor

38 patrimony: inheritable wealth

39 footcloth: a rich cloth laid over a horse's back to protect its rider; a sign of wealth and high rank
high-prized: expensive

40 fall of the leaf: autumn

41 Observe: pay attention to

46 prodigy: astonishing monstrosity

51 wolf: ulcers
measle: a skin disease in pigs, confused with the human ailment of the same name

55 tissue: rich cloth often interwoven with silver and gold thread

59 Lucca: famous Italian spa town, north-east of Pisa

61 pukes: vomits
seethes: is agitated

62 fins: rims
teeming: pregnant

65 loose-bodied: unwaisted; in England, a fashion normally reserved for older women, but also associated with prostitutes

66 discover: reveal

67 apricocks: apricots

74 tetter: skin eruption

81 out of fashion: inappropriate

90 lord of the ascendant: dominant planetary power

91 cousin-german, removed: first coursin once removed

92 King Pippin: Pepin, King of the Franks (died 768)

98 tithe-pig: an animal due as payment of a tenth of a farmer's income to support the church
spoil: despoil, lay waste

105 mend my ruff: put my collar right; a ruff was an elaborately gathered neck-piece

106 when: an exclamation of impatience
tedious: dilatory

108 sound: swoon

109 the mother: (1) hysteria; (2) motherhood

110–11 French...king: normally their hats (which men wore inside) would be doffed as a mark of respect. Antonio and the other courtiers have done so at the entry of the Duchess, who wishes to engineer a private signal of his equality with herself.

112 presence: audience-chamber

119 bare: bare-headed

120 reverently: respect

123 to-year: this year

128 taste of musk: a sought-after flavour in fruit

135 dainties: (1) choice foods; (2) delights (by implication, sexual pleasures)
delicate: delightful, exquisite

137 grafting: Bosola hints at the couple's liaison

138 pippin...crab: types of apple tree; but Bosola again hints at the social inferiority of the Duchess' secret husband

140 bawd farthingales: lewd hooped petticoats (because they concealed the pregnancy that might result from sexual intercourse)

142 apparently: openly

143 springal...caper: stripling frisking and leaping

150 Lights: A call for servants carrying torches

156 politic: cunning

160 colour: pretext

161 close: in seclusion

Act Two, Scene Two

1 tetchiness: irritability

2 breeding: pregnancy

4 I am in haste: she is in a hurry to act as midwife; she may carry a bag or some other property to make this clear to the audience.

6 glass-house: glass factory; there

was one near the Blackfriars theatre where the play was first presented

10 still: always

14 entertainment: receive lovers

15–16 The lusty...tastes well: whether young or old, women make good lovers

16–18 If...them: the god Jupiter came as a lover to Danäe in the form of a shower of gold; Bosola implies that there are always women willing to give themselves to lovers for money.

22 centre: that is, for one woman to receive many lovers

26 posterns: private or side gates
presently: immediately

33 Switzer: Swiss mercenary soldier

36 pistol: (1) gun; (2) penis (pizzle)
cod-piece: a pocket covering the male genitals, often stuffed out or used as an ordinary pocket. The cod-piece was out of fashion by the time this play was written but still good for a joke.

41 chambers: private rooms, with a *double entendre*

43 fire-lock: (1) the firing mechanism of a gun; (2) a musket

44 French plot: The French had a reputation for amorousness.

45 do: by way of sexual activity

49 cabinet: private apartment

57 approved: confirmed in their innocence

58 Gentlemen o'th' wood-yard: a mocking version of *gentlemen of the court* (line 30). The 'wood-yard' was the name given to an outlying and disreputable part of London.

60 black-guard: menial kitchen servants

65 post: take a fast horse

66 doubt: fear

71–3 The throwing...cricket: omens of the presence of evil or imminent death

77 still: always

81 set...nativity: cast his horoscope for the time of his birth; still a common practice in Webster's time

Act Two, Scene Three

0 SD *dark lantern*: lantern with a device for concealing its light

5 several wards: individual apartments
part: a share (in the secret)

6 intelligence: secret news-gathering
List: listen

9 SD Enter...horoscope: after the Cambridge Webster; the 1708 edition of the play marks Antonio's entry 'with a candle, his sword drawn', which may reflect earlier theatrical practice, resembling as it does Hieronimo's entry in *The Spanish Tragedy*, (2.4.63 SD and note).

20 setting a figure: casting a horoscope (as was commonly done to identify a thief and find stolen goods)

22 radical: able to be judged, when a certain astrological disposition took place

25 night-walker: (1) one who walks at night; (2) a nocturnal criminal

31 a Spanish fig: a contemptuous term, probably accompanied by an obscene phallic gesture; but figs were also a preferred means of poisoning

34 conceit: estimation

35 false: corrupt

37 ruin: fall of the tree

39 warm: (1) coming out of hibernation; (2) 'warmed' by promotion

40 Two successive speech-headings for Antonio at this point in 1623 imply the textual loss of a remark by Bosola.

45 wrought: worked, embroidered (on a handkerchief). In his concern

for the stained handkerchief,
Antonio drops the horoscope.

48 colour: give a pretext for
49 lying-in: bed-rest after giving
birth
51 quit: cleared
55 false friend: the dark lantern
58–9 *decimo nono Decembris*: the
nineteenth of December
60–3 *The Lord...death*: the technical
language of professional
astrology, clearly
prognosticating disaster.
'Combust' signifies that the
benign influence of the
dominant planet is nearly
destroyed by close conjunction
with the sun; 'a human sign' is
one of the four signs of the
zodiac with a human symbol
(Gemini, Virgo, Sagitarius and
Aquarius); the 'tail of the
Dragon' is the point where the
moon crosses the sun's ecliptic.
63 *caetera non scrutantur*: 'the
remainder is yet to be
examined'; this allows for the
turn in events by which the
couple's child survives.
64 precise: scrupulous, careful
66 intelligency: important secret
news
68 committed: jailed
72 posts: hurries back (by post
horse)
74 thrifty: economical and succesful
75 masque: conceal itself
76 witty: clever

Act Two, Scene Four

1 Sit: on a stool, or on the
Cardinal's knee, as in the
performance observed by a
Venetian visitor in 1618 (see the
Introductory Note, page 243)
4 anchorite: hermit
5 devotion: (1) piety; (2)
passionate love
11 approved: demonstrated
13 Sooth: truly
16–18 that...moon: an anachronistic
reference to the telescope
constructed by Galileo in 1609
19 look...there: in popular thought,

only the Man in the Moon
could be discovered there, and
the moon symbolised female
inconstancy.
25 jealously: ardently
28–30 I...fly at it: as if Julia was a
hunting falcon
32 a tame elephant: an elephant
being tamed (by being kept
awake to the point of
exhaustion)
33 high feeding: luxurious food
(supposed to generate restless
desire)
35 fing'ring: (1) skill in playing; (2)
sexual fumbling
38 sick liver: see 1.1.208 and note
39 in physic: under medical
treatment
48 lie: lodge
54 good back: (1) strong back; (2)
sexual vigour
58 want: are in need of
61 Look on't: Delio takes some
coins from the purse he has
offered.
64 cassia...civet: a kind of
sweet-smelling cinnamon; a
secretion of the civet cat used
for its strong musky perfume
65 physical: medicinal
fond: foolish
66 cullises: restorative broths (cf.
2.5.71–3)
83 the event weigh: seriously
consider the outcome

Act Two, Scene Five

1 mandrake: poisonous plant
with a forked root which gave it
a human-like appearance. There
was a belief that it had the
power to drive mad with its
shriek anyone who pulled it up.
2 prodigy: marvel
3 loose i'th' hilts: promiscuous
8 confusion: destruction; a term
frequently used in Ford's '*Tis
Pity She's a Whore*
9 turn: (sexual) purposes
11 towns of garrison: garrisoned
towns
service: (1) supplies; (2) sexual
gratification

12–13   Rhubarb...choler: choler (bile)
         was thought to be one of the
         four constituent humours
         making up the human
         temperament (the others were
         blood, phlegm and
         melancholy): in excess, it
         prompted vengeful thoughts.
         The purgative rhubarb was
         commonly prescribed for an
         excess of choler.

13   Here: perhaps Ferdinand has
         the horoscope in his hand

19   meads: meadows

22–3   shall...attainted: John Russell
         Brown points out that the
         Cardinal talks of a corrupted
         lineage; Ferdinand thinks of
         infection, and of *blood* in terms
         of passion and sensual
         appetite.

23   physic: medical treatment

24   balsamum: aromatic healing
         ointment

25   cupping-glass: a surgical
         vessel used to draw off blood

32   Unequal: unjust

33   the left side: conventionally,
         the 'wrong' side

34   bark: small vessel

37   purchased: obtained

39   hyena: the animal typified
         treachery, especially in
         women; its cry sounds like
         human laughter

42   Happily: perhaps

43   quoit the sledge: throw the
         sledge-hammer as a feat of
         strength

44   lovely squire: handsome
         young servant

45   privy: private; but 'carry coals
         up to her privy lodgings' also
         has the suggestive meaning
         'take the means to excite her
         genitally'

47   wild-fire: (1) uncontrollable
         fire; (2) (skin) disease

49   idly: ineffectually

55   palsy: shaking fever

59   divers: several

67   coal-pit: pit for making
         charcoal

71   cullis: see 2.4.66 and note

77   leaps: copulates with

78   scorpions: metal spikes

79   fix: place her forever
         general: total

Act Three, Scene One

8   wink: shut my eyes

14   reversion: right to succession

25   directly: openly

27   censure: judge

28   purchase: legitimate or
         criminal acquisition of wealth
         and property

29   left-hand: crooked, sinister (cf.
         2.5.33)

39   bespeak: name

46   The Duchess attempts to
         divert Ferdinand's
         questioning of Antonio.

49   Pasquil's paper bullets:
         pasquinades, satirical verses

57   coulters: plough-shares. An
         ordeal known under Old
         English law as a trial of
         chastity.

58   intelligence: news-gathering

70   gulleries: tricks, deceits

71   mountebanks: charlatans,
         quack-doctors
         will: appetite, carnal desire

75   lenative poisons: violent
         aphrodisiacs

77   equivocation: double-talk

88   chronicle: 'trumpet-blower',
         self-praiser

91   entertained: took into my
         service

Act Three, Scene Two

1   glass: mirror

2   lodging: here and at line 6 the
         word may be used with a
         secondary sense of sexual
         reception

5   with cap and knee: humbly,
         with cap in hand and on
         bended knee

7   lord of mis-rule: (1) master of
         revelry and disorder; (2) lord
         of the rule of mistresses
         (misses)

9   use: (1) practical purpose; (2)
         sexual employment

17   still: always
18   rise: (1) get out of bed; (2) become sexually erect
25–8   Daphne...marble: classical legends of the transformation of women who vainly tried to escape god-lovers (Daphne and Apollo, Syrinx and Pan), or were scornful of a lover (Anaxerete and Iphis)
25   peevish: perverse
29   kind: loving
       friends: lovers
33   vain: insubstantial, fictitious
35   several: different
36   Paris's case: The Trojan prince Paris was asked to judge between the naked charms of Juno, Minerva, and Venus.
37   blind: lacking in perception
40   motion: display
41   apprehension: clear thinking, perception
45   hard-favoured: ugly
49   ill: bad, second-rate
52   face-making: portrait work
       undo: ruin
55   divers times: on a number of occasions
60   arras: powdered iris root (*orris*), used to whiten and perfume the hair
61   entered: allowed entry
62   vouchsafe: be willing
68   your gossips: godparents of your children
68 SD   In some productions the Duchess turns and sees Ferdinand; in others she sights him in a mirror held as she combs her hair (cf. line 53 and 58ff.).
71 SD   *poniard*: small dagger
84   Happily: perhaps
87   change: exchange
88   basilisk: cockatrice; a fabulous reptile whose whose breath or sight could kill
89   his: Antonio's
90   to thee: compared to you (spoken to the Duchess)
94   work: bring about
100   vild: vile
103   anchorites: hermits
108   paraquito: parrot

110   bewray: betray
116   hollow bullet: explosive shell
117   wild-fire: (1) explosives; (2) conflagration
119   wilful: passionate
124   concluded: agreed
125   several: separate
128   shepherds: the shepherd lovers of pastoral myth
130   quiet: peaceable
139   cased up: enclosed. In Catholic practice, memorials of saints and other holy persons were kept as objects of veneration and often encased in elaborate reliquaries.
148–9   relate...warantable love: give a verbal defence of my legitimate love
158   unjust: faithless, dishonest
167   in's: in his
168   engaged: as security
169   Ta'en up: borrowed
170   be forfeit: to lapse (so making Ferdinand liable for the amount borrowed)
172:   bills: bills of exchange; the equivalent of modern cheques
       protested: publicly and formally declared invalid
174   Ancona: described in Webster's source as 'a city in the patrimony of the Roman Church'; then a semi-independent republic under papal protection and Authority
177   enginous: (1) of an elaborate mechanism or engine; (2) clever
178   periods: whole sentences
179   Tasso: Italian epic poet
183   got well by you: the first of a series of double meanings: (1) 'profited from your financial dealings' (spoken ironically); (2) 'found happiness through you'
187   signed your *Quietus*: (1) signed off your account books; (2) became your lover (cf. 1.2.369)
189   example: (1) of what happens to the guilty; (2) to be imitated
190   let him: (1) let him go; (2) remain to be an example
197   necessity: unavoidable influence

198	her humour: the Duchess's whim
204	satisfying: debt repayment
206	pass: (1) permission to leave; (2) approval (from me)
209	extortion: extortioners (as Antonio is said to be)
215	his officer: steward in place of him
217	stopped...wool: part of an old cure for deafness
223	chippings: fragments of bread crust (used to clean metal objects)
224	his gold chain: the steward's badge of office
228	waited: attended
230	in a ring: led by a ring
232	intelligencers: spies
234	livery: uniform
236	sort: company
238	dissemble: disguise
242	Pluto...riches: strictly Pluto was the ruler of the underworld, and Plutus the god of riches, but the two were often confused, as here.
246	post: in haste comes...scuttles: scuttles inside unvalued: (1) invaluable; (2) regarded as worthless
248	wanton: wilful
253	form: outward appearance
254	discourse: power of reason
256	whisp'ring room: see 1.2.242 and note
260	want: feel the lack of
265	Bermudas: islands in the North Atlantic, known as stormy and dangerous, especially after a famous wreck there in 1609
266	politicians: crafty schemers
267	intelligencer: spy, secret agent
272	with: through
277	shadows: empty appearances
281	seminary: nursery, seed bed
282	unbeneficed: without appointment to a church living
291	trophy: triumphant memorial
292	curious engine: exquisitely made instrument
294	reverend: admired cabinets: display of treasures
297	want coats: lack coats of arms

306	Our Lady of Loretto: a famous shrine, featuring a black Madonna and Child, fifteen miles southeast of Ancona, which drew pilgrims from all over Europe
313	Lucca: see 2.1.59 and note
313–14	Spa in Germany: a famous spa town in Belgium, south of Liège; to the Elizabethans all the Low Countries were known as 'Dutch' or 'German'
320	politician: crafty intriguer
323	rests: remains to do
324	quality: occupation

Act Three, Scene Three

1	The Emperor: Charles V of Spain (1516–56)
4	fortunate: successful Pescara: see Dramatis Personae, line 7 and note
5–6	Lannoy...prisoner: Charles de Lannoy, Viscount of Naples (1487–1527), to whom Francis I of France surrendered at the battle of Pavia in 1525. An anachronistic reference in this play.
7	plot: design, ground-plan
10	muster book: register of troops
11	voluntary: volunteer
13	leaguer: military camp
15	straight: immediately
16	late service: recent military operations
18	express: represent
19	model: scale drawings
21	good: lucky
23	taffeta: glossy silk
27	pate: head
28	pot-gun: braggart (from the name of a child's toy pop-gun)
29	bore: hole
30	touch-hole: flash point for igniting the charge in a firearm (possibly also 'anus')
31–2	guarded...court: ornamented sadle cloth for a pack-horse used in changing a court's place of residence
37	fire in their tales: alluding to the story of Samson, who tied foxes together by their tails

and attached firebrands to them, to destroy the Philistines' harvest (Judges 15:4–5)

39 Padua: a famous university, founded in 1238, was located there.
fantastical: eccentric

40 Hercules' club: Greek hero-god, whose weapon was a huge wooden club

41 Achilles: leading Greek warrior in the Trojan War
Hector: Trojan heroic warrior

43 Caesar: Julius Caesar, famous Roman general (100–44 BC)

43 shoeing-horn: ironically, an instrument without a straight edge

44 speculative: intellectually alert, given to theorising

46 salamander: a mythical lizard-like creature, supposed capable of living in fire

48 bad faces: the faces of his victims

49 Michael Angelo: the great Renaissance painter and sculptor (1475–1564)

49–50 lifts...a storm: acts haughtily, like an evil porpoise: proverbially, 'the porpoise plays before a storm'

52 lightens: flashes out

62 state: authorities

67 honesty: chastity, honour

68 counters: markers used in money calculation

70 presently: at once

Act Three, Scene Four

6 SD *habit*: dress
form of banishment: this must include the removal of the Duchess's wedding-ring (cf. lines 36–7 below)
state: ruler

13 *divine*: religious

19 *courses*: encounters

26 mean: of low social rank

28–9 state: territory; at this time Ancona was one of the Papal States and therefore subject to papal authority

29 determine of: make a judicial decision about

44 unhappy: unfortunate

Act Three, Scene Five

2 lightens: descends

5 buntings: small birds, related to larks but without song

9 Right: exactly

18 benefit: favour, kindness

23 blanch mischief: whitewash disaster

27 *head*: (1) advice, intelligence: (2) head (cut off)

28 politic equivocation: cunning piece of double talk

33 *engaged*: acting as security

41 amity: friendship

42 politic: scheming

46 this: Ferdinand's letter
brothers: brothers-in-law

52 adamant: magnetic loadstone

54 conjure: earnestly implore

57 bottom: ship's hold

60 curious artist: skilful artisan

67 eternal Church: fellowship of Christian believers, after death

70 unkindly: unnaturally

71 cassia: see 2.4.64 and note

75 scourge: whip. The word often carried the idea of divine chastisement, but refers here to the whip-stick used by children to spin their tops. Both ideas are present in *scourge-stick* (line 77).

80 sweet armful: Cariola is carrying the youngest child

85 anchorite: hermit

88 sound: test the depth of

89 laurel: triumphant garland; laurels were reputed to wither as an omen of the death of a ruler

92 over-charged: over-loaded

94 adventure: quarry (falconry)

96 counterfeits: imitates

98 silly: weak, defenceless, deserving pity

101 o'ercharged: (1) over loaded with an explosive charge; (2) too heavily burdened with grief

104 Charon: the ferryman of the underworld

105 the dismal lake: Acheron, the

fatal, dreadful (*dismal*) lake of hell

113 this...fellow: Antonio
114 counterfeit face: Bosola's mask
115 mean: of low social rank
117 arguments: demonstrations
124 high state of floods: majestic waters
128 silly smelts: lowly small fish
129 reverence: respect
138 armed: mentally fortified
139 sways: overmastering influences

Act Four, Scene One

7 shape: image
17 SD BOSOLA...*Servants*: 1623 marks no scene break here; on the Blackfriars stage the inner chamber might be used to indicate immediately the place of the Duchess's imprisonment. Although the theatre remained fully lit by candles, effects of light and darkness could be suggested by the bringing on or removal of torches.
39 a sacrament...Church: the Duchess's marriage
42 i'th' light: (1) in the public arena; (2) displaying wanton behaviour
50 owed: owned
55 SD *discovered*: revealed (by drawing back a curtain)
58 directly: plainly, immediately
65 property: (1) possession; (2) stage property
71 Portia: wife of the Roman republican hero Brutus, who on learning of his death committed suicide by eating hot coals
73–4 despair...Christian: despair (of God's grace and therefore of the possibility of salvation) was a damnable sin for a Christian
79 the wheel: an instrument of brutal torture
88 daggers: mental anguish
103 mortified: ascetic

111 curious: expert
     quality: occupation
112 Vincentio Lauriola: unidentified; probably an invented name
116 a penitential garment: as a hair-shirt, with a rough inner surface
118 beads: a rosary
121 masques: troupes
124 remove forth: empty of
126 practise: perform
127 to...moon: the moon's influence was thought to induce madness
130 shape: guise (a theatrical metaphor)
131 intelligence: acting as an informer
138 intemperate agues: immoderate fevers

Act Four, Scene Two

1 consort: group of musicians
7 sit down: implying that the Duchess is seated (repeated at line 59)
8 dismal: terrible
12 durance: imprisonment
32 show: outward appearance
35–6 Fortune...tragedy: conventionally, Fortune was blind (impartial)
41 several: different
43 impostume: abcess
46 forfeited: lost
49 day of doom: Judgement Day
51 gentleman usher: attendant on a person of rank
55 knave in grain: (1) thorough cheat; (2) crooked dealer in grains
56 hindered transportation: prevented from exporting produce. (Regulations prevented farmers from further exploiting a time of scarcity and high prices by exporting grain.)
57 broker: retailer
60 chained: restrained; it was customary to chain violent lunatics
60 SD *dismal*: doleful

62   *doggèd*: dog-like
67   *yerksome*: lashing
      cloyed: pierced
68   *corrosived*: eaten away, vexed
69   *quire wants*: choir lacks
71   *sing...death*: a popular belief (cf. the 'swansong')
73 SH   MAD ASTROLOGER: Although the text (lines 45–58) names eight madmen by their profession, for their speech headings 1623 simply numbers the madmen from one to four. There has been disagreement among scholars as to their correct identification, and it may be that Webster left the company to allocate roles appropriately. I follow the assignment of parts worked out by Frank B. Fieler, 'The Eight Madmen in *The Duchess of Malfi*', *Studies in English Literature*, vol. 7 (1967) 343–50. Fieler suggests that the Broker sings the song (lines 61–72).
74   perspective: magnifying glass, telescope
      glass: mirror
77   glass-house: glass factory
80 SH   MAD PRIEST: what follows is a satirical portrait of a Jacobean parson with Puritan sympathies
81   tithe...haycocks: take my tenth share of them as if they were stooks of hay (with a suggestion of 'turn them over')
82   pothecary: pharmacist
83   alum: an astringent mineral salt
84   over-straining: through too much preaching or singing
87   woodcock: thought to be a stupid bird
88   ancient: of ancient lineage
89   Greek...Turk: the Greek New Testament has gone Moslem. That is, this Puritan parson rejects both the Douay (1609–10) and King James (1611) versions of the Bible, associated with the Catholic and Anglican faiths respectively.
89–90   saved...Helvetian translation: the Calvinist Genevan Bible of 1560, which had a strong

Puritan bias in the translation and notes.
91   lay: expound
92   lay a corrosive: spread a caustic medicine
94   glass: perhaps a trick glass producing an indecent illusion
96   he: the mad parson
      rope-maker: that is, in league with the hangman
97   snuffling knave: alluding to the nasal sound of Puritan preachers
98   placket: (1) side-opening in a petticoat; (2) vulva
99   caroche: large, luxury coach
102   agues; fevers
104   possets: hot milk drinks, curdled with ale or wine and spiced
106   throw...me: acknowledge defeat by myself
106–7   made...costive: made a soap-maker constipated; the joke depends on the fact that diarrhoea was an occupational hazard in the industry
112   insensible: imperceptible
116   worm-seed: (1) a plant whose dried heads were used as a medicine against intestinal worms; (1) food for worms
116–17   salvatory..mummy: box of ointment made from rotting (*green*) mummified corpses ('mummia')
117   crudded: curdled
117–18   fantastical puff-paste: grotesque light pastry
125   riot: violent disorder
128   breeds: grows, cuts
140   stuff: material, cloth
141   resolve: inform
      fashion: style
143   affect: seek after
144–7   Princes' images...tooth-ache: Webster is describing contemporary English tomb imagery for royal and aristocratic families.
151   effect: purpose
153   charnel: cemetery, mortuary-chapel
159   presence-chamber: public anteroom, with a play on final living presence'

161   common bellman: a public
       bellman tolled his bell
       through the streets to attract
       attention to announcements of
       deaths and requests for
       prayers for the dead. Webster
       himself had been associated
       with the appointment of a
       church clerk to exhort
       condemned prisoners at
       Newgate prison on the eve of
       their execution, reminding
       them of their end and seeking
       God's mercy on their souls.
165   mortification: readiness for
       death
167   *whistler*: bird with a whistling
       cry, regarded as a bad omen
170   *rent*: income
171   *competent*: (1) all you need; (2)
       sufficient to provide a
       comfortable living
174   *vain*: futile
186   next: nearest
190   reversion: (1) left-overs from a
       meal; (2) entitlement from an
       estate
195   catarrh: cerebral haemorrhage,
       apoplexy
197   on't: of it
204   cassia: perfume; see 2.4.64 and
       note
221   mandragora: the mandrake
       plant, used as a narcotic
230   come...answer: make my legal
       defence
232   counsel: shared secrets
234   wedding-ring: the executioner
       offers a noose
240   credit: reputation
242 SD *Shows...strangled*: On the
       Jacobean stage, Bosola might
       draw a curtain to shock the
       audience with the sight of the
       children's bodies.
245   here: on the body of the
       Duchess
248   blood...heavens: that is,
       murder cries out for divine
       vengeance and calls forth
       tears of pity
249   Cover her face: Bosola does
       so, to uncover it again at line
       256.
254   approved: demonstrated

259   sanctuary: such as a church,
       where by ecclesiastical law a
       fugitive from justice could
       find protection against arrest
266   meanness: social inferiority
277   challenge: demand
281   largest...study: most generous
       reward I can consider
285   complete: competent, properly
       constituted
293   The wolf...up: There was a
       superstitious belief that
       wolves would uncover the
       bodies of victims of murder
       and leave them exposed; see
       5.2.9–12.
296   pension: reward; cf.
       Revelation 20:1–3
305   chained bullets: cannon-balls
       linked by a chain, principally
       used in naval warfare to
       destroy masts and rigging
307   blood: family group
318   owl-light: twilight, dusk
320   painted: false, specious
324   change: exchange
327   sensible: palpable
330   cordial: restorative
331   pity...pity: a cry of distress
       would bring Ferdinand back
       to kill the Duchess.
       opes: opens
337   atonement: reconciliation
340   turtles: turtle-doves, famous
       for the softness of their
       feathers
342   perspective: optical glass
347   estate: condition
355   reverend dispose: respectful
       disposal (for burial)
359   Worth my dejection: on a scale
       corresponding to my
       overthrow

Act Five, Scene One

4   repair: travel
6   in cheat: on condition that
       they would revert to the
       owner if a tenant died
       intestate without heirs, or was
       convicted of serious crime
8   dependants: hangers-on,
       followers

10	be invested...revenues: have your income allocated to them
13	still an heretic: always a disbeliever
19	Saint Bennett: St Benedict
20	demesnes: properties
36	fortify: strengthen
42	ravished: torn
49	ruddier: more warmly
52	salary: payment
58	frenzy: inflammation of the brain by an excess of choler, leading to completely irrational and changeable behaviour
68	in...shape: without wearing a disguise
72	calling: way of life
74	howe'er: whatever happens
76	still: forever

Act Five, Scene Two

6	lycanthropia: wolf-madness, the delusion that one is a wolf
9	melancholy humour: see 2.5.12–13 and note.
24	nearer: more direct
25	Paracelsus: a famous German Swiss doctor and philosopher (1493–1591), associated with stories of magic and strange cures
26	buffet: beat; whipping was a usual method of treating and controlling the insane
30	daws: jackdaws
35	Stay: stop
40	When...bribe: an allusion to the contemporary practice of bribing jailors to provide better accommodation. The worst room in a prison was known as the 'hell'.
48	sheep-biter: (1) dog which worries sheep; (2) sneak thief
56	civil: decently, politely
58	salamander's skin: see 3.3.46 and note. Salamanders could supposedly inhabit fire, or quench it.
59	cruel: painfully
60	cockatrice: a deadly serpent, the basilisk, which hatched from a cock's egg
	present: immediate

68	fetch a frisk: cut a caper (in dancing)
71	stamp...cullis: pound him into powder to make a broth
72	anatomies: skeletons
73	Barber-Chirurgeons' Hall: Dead bodies, especially of executed criminals, were brought to the Company of Barber-Surgeons' Hall, near Cripplegate in London, to be dissected or displayed as exhibits in the guild's anatomical museum.
77	throughly: entirely
81	accident: unexpected event
91	the gentlemen of's chamber: his personal attendants
100–1	intelligence In: secret information concerning
102	the full...engagement: the chief hand in his employment as a spy
105	dyed: with a possible play on 'died'
113	expedition: setting forth
116	shape: physical appearance
120	style: designate, name
123	approved: confirmed to be
127	a school-name: a merely academic suject
132	taking up: borrowing
134	picture-makers: portrait painters
136	Happily may take: possibly succeed
139	basilisks: see line 60 above and note
154	kill: destroy (by means of a sexual 'death' or orgasm)
155	kissing-comfits: lozenges to sweeten the breath
156	discover: reveal
157–8	I'll disarm...thus: Bosola seizes Julia, disarms and embraces her
158	arm: (1) embrace; (2) supply weapons
161	nice: fastidious
162	familiar: (evil) spirit
164	wants: lacks
	compliment: complimentary language, social conversation
166	do amiss: (1) act incorrectly; (2) make love ineptly
170	darts: arrows
172	charge: expense
182	sudden: abruptly amorous

189   presently: immediately
201   calling: occupation
205   intelligence: information
206   cabinet: private room
214   conference: conversation
217   consumption: wasting disease
221   secretary: confidant
233   still: always
236   judgement: (your own) sense
       of judgement
239   argues: evidences
250   adamant: impregnable
       hardness; applied to iron or
       steel
260   settles: sink down into your
       mind
271   equal: equitable, impartial
272   counsel: secrets
285   lay...colours: paint over to look
       like marble
288   done: (1) taken action; (2)
       finished
290   attends: is waiting for
297   smother: suffocating smoke
304   train: crowd of followers
312   happy: fortunate, clever
317   estate: condition
320   frost-nailed: wearing shoes
       with cleats to prevent slipping
       on ice
322   Bears...blood: (1) remains
       courageous; (2) continues a
       life of blood-shed
323   Security: careless freedom
       from anxiety
324   dead wall: (1) continuous
       wall; (2) wall of death
327   biters: bloodsuckers, or
       sheep-biters

Act Five, Scene Three

0 SD   ECHO...*grave*: probably spoken
       by the actor playing the
       duchess
4   cloister: covered walkway
11   reverend history: story to be
       respected
15   Loved: who loved
       largely: generously
17   doomsday: the end of time
       and the coming of the Last
       Judgement
18   like to men: just as human
       beings do

21   accent: sound
33   passages: eventful moments
44   folded: enveloped
45   ague: fever
51   his own blood: the Cardinal's
       own kin

Act Five, Scene Four

10   sensibly: in his right mind
16   cutting: being cut
17   protested against it: sworn not
       to do so
19   osier: willow tree
42   dark lantern: a lantern whose
       light could be hidden
46   suit: (1) petition; (2) chase
53   banded: bandied about
61   sadness: earnest, in reality
64   wanton: undisciplined
67   ague: recurrent fever
75   tender: are concerned for
79   misprision: mistake
82–3   look...bear'st: see that you act
       as silently as the dead man
       you carry

Act Five, Scene Five

4   Lay him by: the Cardinal puts
       the book down
       tedious: troublesome, painful
6   rake: traditiional tool of
       demons drawing souls into
       Hell
10   lightens: explodes, flashes out
13   faithfully: with complete
       honesty
14   unseasonable: at the wrong
       time
19   counterfeiting: pretence
28   come at: join
30   engines: tools, instruments
38   sudden: quick about it
44   leveret: young hare (not
       considered worth hunting)
48   vaunt-guard: vanguard
49   honour of arms: opportunity
       to surrender honourably as a
       soldier and be ransomed (cf.
       line 53)
56–8   Caesar's fortune...disgrace:
       Julius Caesar was assassinated
       in Rome at the height of his

political power; his rival Pompey was murdered in Egypt after his disastrous defeat in the Civil War with Caesar.

56 harder: unluckier

60 barber: barbers gave ordinary medical and dental care

65 wet...broken-winded: a recommended winter cure for horses with bronchial problems

67 vault credit: exceed belief, expectation

71 blood: violence

79 sad: grievous, terrible

84 main: principle events

88 rushes: fresh rushes were spread on the floors of rooms and on the stages of public theatres

96 dead: see 5.2.324 and note

102 stagger in distrust: falter in confidence

109 armed: prepared

The Changeling

THOMAS MIDDLETON AND WILLIAM ROWLEY

INTRODUCTORY NOTE

Authorship, date of composition and stage history

The Changeling was the collaborative creation of two dramatists, Thomas Middleton (1580–1627) and William Rowley (?1585-1626), who had acted in plays by Middleton and shared in the writing of at least four other Middleton plays. It was licensed for the stage on 7 May 1622, and was probably written shortly before this date, since one of the dramatists' sources was published in March of the same year. It is generally agreed that Rowley was responsible for the opening and closing scenes and the sub-plot, while Middleton wrote the rest of the main plot, that is, 2.1-3.2, 3.4-4.2, and 5.1-2. The tragedy was first performed by Lady Elizabeth's company at the Phoenix Theatre, Drury Lane. Success there is indicated by an early court performance at Whitehall, on 4 January 1624. Successive companies led by Christopher Beston, owner of the Phoenix, and later his son William, kept the play in their repertoire until the closing of the theatres, using both the Phoenix and the Salisbury Court playhouse in Whitefriars (built in 1629). Evidently it was the comic playing of the role of Antonio the Changeling by William Robbins and his successor Timothy Reade which particularly delighted contemporary audiences; the frontispiece to Francis Kirkman's *The Wits, or Sport upon Sport* (1672) shows a 'Changeling' among stage figures of several famous dramatic characters.

After the Restoration *The Changeling* was revived at the Phoenix, with Betterton and Sheppey as De Flores and Antonio; later performances are recorded in 1661–2 at Salisbury Court Theatre, Lincolns Inn Fields and the Cardinal's Cap, Cambridge. With the exception of a short-lived plagiarised version by William Hayley (*Marcella*, 1789), the play dropped into obscurity in the eighteenth and nineteenth centuries, to be revived in 1950 on stage by the First Folio Theatre Club and BBC radio. A number of academic and professional productions have marked its return to the classic repertory, including a notable television version broadcast by the BBC in 1974 with Helen Mirren and Stanley Baker as Beatrice-Joanna and De Flores. More than forty productions took place between 1950 and 1984, including a single performance given in 1954 by the Pegasus Society at Wyndham's Theatre and the Experimental Theatre Club production at Oxford in 1956. Mary Ure played Beatrice-Joanna and Robert Shaw De Flores in an important Royal Court Theatre production of 1961; the play was set in the period of Goya. There was a Cambridge student production in 1964, the Lycaeum Company performed *The Changeling* at the Edinburgh Festival in 1970, and a production was given at the Gardner Centre in 1971. In 1978 London saw two powerful versions of the tragedy, directed by Peter Gill at the Riverside Studios, Hammersmith, and Terry Hands working with the Royal Shakespeare Company at the Aldwych Theatre. In 1979 the play was staged at the Victoria Theatre, Stoke on Trent; in 1981 there were productions at the York Arts Centre and Nottingham University; and in 1983 the tragedy appeared at the Oxford Playhouse and the University Theatre, Manchester. In 1988 Richard Eyre directed a production at the National (Lyttleton) Theatre with Miranda Richardson as Beatrice-Joanna and a black actor, George Harris, as the alien De Flores. In 1989 Kelly Handerek directed the play for the Stratford (Ontario) Festival. In 1991 at the White Bear Theatre, London, Sophia Reed excised most of the subplot, as did Mark Rylance for a Chinese British Theatre production at Finborough, London, and later Robert Brustein in his 1995 American Repertory Theatre production, Cambridge, Massachusetts. In 1992 the full text of the tragedy was performed at Harrogate Theatre, and in the same year Cheryl Campbell and Malcolm Storry took the leads in a powerful revival by the Royal Shakespeare Company. In 1994 Simon Curtis directed a television film of the play, with Elizabeth McGovern as Beatrice-Joanna, Bob Hoskins as De Flores and Hugh Grant as Alsemero. Beyond Britain, there have been performances in the United States, Canada and New Zealand, such as the 1995

Renaissance Stage Company production at the Earl Street Theatre, Kingston, Ontario.

Text

This edition is based on the one seventeeth-century edition of the tragedy, printed by Thomas Newcomb for Humphrey Moseley in 1653. There are two imprints of this edition differing only in the title-page; unsold sheets were reissued in 1668 with yet another title-page. The 1653 text is free from major corruption, and is probably based on a careful scribal transcript from theatrical prompt-copy.

Sources

For the tragic story of Beatrice-Joanna and De Flores, Middleton and Rowley's main sources were a moralistic 'Tragical History' in Book 1 of John Reynolds's *The Triumphs of God's Revenge against the Crying and Execrable Sin of Murder* (1621), and a tale of a substituted bride in *Gerardo, the Unfortunate Spaniard*, translated from the Spanish of G. de Cespedes y Meneses by Leonard Digges in 1622. No substantial source for the sub-plot has as yet been found, though the story resembles parts of the plot of Middleton's earlier unaided play, *The Family of Love*, and there is a general resemblance between the institution directed by Alibius in the play and Bethlehem ('Bedlam'), the hospital for the insane in Jacobean London.

Further reading

The fullest single-volume edition of the play is in the Revels series, prepared by N. W. Bawcutt (London, rev. edn 1963); other scholarly editions are those of M. W. Black (Philadelphia, 1966), George Walton Williams in the Regents Renaissance Drama Series (London, 1967), David L. Frost in *The Selected Plays of Thomas Middleton* (Cambridge, 1978), and Joost Daalder, in the New Mermaids Series (London and New York, 2nd edn, 1990). The staging of plays at the Phoenix from 1617 to 1642 is the subject of a study by T. J. King, *Theatre Notebook*, vol. 19 (1965) 146–66. Modern performances are discussed in Michael Scott's *Renaissance Drama and a Modern Audience* (London and Basingstoke, 1982) and R. V. Holdsworth's *Three Jacobean Revenge Tragedies* (London, 1990). For general studies of Middleton's work as a tragic writer, see Samuel Schoenbaum, *Middleton's Tragedies: A Critical Study* (New York, 1955), R. H. Barker, *Thomas Middleton* (New York, 1958), David M. Holmes, *The Art of Thomas Middleton* (London, 1970), *'Accompaninge the Players': Essays Celebrating Thomas Middleton 1580–1980*, edited by K. Friedenreich (New York, 1982) and J. D. Jump, 'Middleton's Tragedies' in *The Age of Shakespeare*, edited by Boris Ford (rev. edn, Harmondsworth, 1982).

Dramatis Personae

VERMANDERO, *father to* BEATRICE
TOMAZO DE PIRACQUO, *a noble lord*
ALONZO DE PIRACQUO, *his brother, suitor to* BEATRICE
ALSEMERO, *a nobleman, afterwards married to* BEATRICE
JASPERINO, *his friend*   5

ALIBIUS,° *a jealous doctor*
LOLLIO,° *his man*
PEDRO, *friend to* ANTONIO
ANTONIO, *the Changeling*
FRANCISCUS, *the counterfeit madman*   10

DE FLORES,° *servant to* VERMANDERO
Madmen
Servants

BEATRICE-JOANNA,° *daughter to* VERMANDERO
DIAPHANTA, *her waiting-woman*   15

ISABELLA, *wife to* ALIBIUS

The Scene: *Alicant.°*

Act One, Scene One

Enter ALSEMERO.

ALSEMERO: 'Twas in the temple° where I first beheld her,
    And now again the same. What omen yet
    Follows of that? None but imaginary.
    Why should my hopes of fate be timorous?
    The place is holy, so is my intent: 5
    I love her beauties to the holy purpose,°
    And that, methinks, admits comparison
    With man's first creation,° the place° blest,
    And is his right home back,° if he achieve it.
    The church hath first begun our interview,°   10
    And that's the place must join us into one;
    So there's beginning and perfection too.

Enter JASPERINO.

JASPERINO: Oh, sir, are you here? Come, the wind's fair with you,
    You're like to have a swift and pleasant passage.
ALSEMERO: Sure, you're deceivèd, friend; 'tis contrary,   15
    In my best judgement.
JASPERINO: What, for Malta?
    If you could buy a gale amongst the witches,°
    They could not serve you such a lucky pennyworth
    As comes a' God's name.°
ALSEMERO: Even now I observed
    The temple's vane° to turn full in my face;   20
    I know 'tis against me.
JASPERINO: Against you?
    Then you know not where you are.
ALSEMERO: Not well, indeed.
JASPERINO: Are you not well, sir?
ALSEMERO: Yes, Jasperino;
    Unless there be some hidden malady
    Within me, that I understand not.
JASPERINO: And that   25
    I begin to doubt,° sir. I never knew
    Your inclinations to travels at a pause
    With any cause to hinder it, till now.
    Ashore you were wont° to call your servants up,
    And help to trap° your horses for the speed;   30
    At sea I have seen you weigh the anchor with 'em,
    Hoist sails for fear to lose the foremost breath,
    Be in continual prayers for fair winds,
    And have you changed your orisons?°
ALSEMERO: No, friend,
    I keep the same church, same devotion.   35
JASPERINO: Lover I'm sure you're none, the stoic° was
    Found in you long ago; your mother nor
    Best friends, who have set snares of beauty (ay
    And choice ones too), could never trap you that way.
    What might be the cause?
ALSEMERO: Lord, how violent°   40
    Thou art! I was but meditating of
    Somewhat I heard within the temple.
JASPERINO: Is this violence? 'Tis but idleness
    Compared with your haste yesterday.
ALSEMERO: I'm all this while a-going, man.   45

Enter SERVANTS.

JASPERINO: Backwards, I think sir. Look, your servants.

1 SERVANT: The seamen call; shall we board your trunks?
ALSEMERO: No, not today.
JASPERINO: 'Tis the critical° day, it seems, and the sign in Aquarius.°
2 SERVANT [*aside*]: We must not to sea today; this smoke will bring   50
    forth fire!
ALSEMERO: Keep all on shore; I do not know the end
    (Which needs I must do) of an affair° in hand
    Ere I can go to sea.
1 SERVANT: Well, your pleasure.
2 SERVANT [*aside*]: Let him e'en take his leisure too, we are safer on   55
    land.   *Exeunt* SERVANTS.

        Enter BEATRICE, DIAPHANTA, *and* Servants.
        [ALSEMERO *greets* BEATRICE *and kisses her.*]

JASPERINO [*aside*]: How now! The laws of the Medes° are changed, sure!
    Salute° a woman? He kisses too; wonderful! Where learnt he this?
    And does it perfectly too; in my conscience,° he ne'er rehearsed it
    before. Nay, go on, this will be stranger and better news at Valencia   60
    than if he had ransomed half Greece from the Turk.°
BEATRICE: You are a scholar, sir?
ALSEMERO: A weak one, lady.
BEATRICE: Which of the sciences is this love you speak of?
ALSEMERO: From your tongue, I take it to be music.
BEATRICE: You are skilful in't, can sing at first sight.°   65
ALSEMERO: And I have showed you all my skill at once.
    I want° more words to express me further,
    And must be forced to repetition:
    I love you dearly.
BEATRICE: Be better advised, sir.
    Our eyes are sentinels unto our judgements,   70
    And should give certain° judgement what they see;
    But they are rash sometimes and tell us wonders
    Of common things, which, when our judgements find,
    They then can check° the eyes and call them blind.
ALSEMERO: But I am further, lady; yesterday   75
    Was mine eyes' employment, and hither now
    They brought my judgement, where are both agreed.
    Both houses° then consenting, 'tis agreed;
    Only there wants the confirmation
    By the hand royal —° that's your part,° lady.   80
BEATRICE: Oh, there's one above me,° sir. [*Aside*] For five days past
    To be recalled! Sure, mine eyes were mistaken,
    This was the man was meant me. That he should come
    So near his time, and miss it!

JASPERINO [*aside*]: We might have come by the carriers° from Valencia, I   85
    see, and saved all our sea provision; we are at farthest,° sure.
    Methinks I should do something too; I meant to be a venturer° in
    this voyage. Yonder's another vessel; I'll board her. If she be lawful
    prize,° down goes her topsail!°   [*Approaches* DIAPHANTA.]

Enter DE FLORES.

DE FLORES: Lady, your father —
BEATRICE: Is in health, I hope.   90
DE FLORES: Your eye shall instantly instruct you, lady.
    He's coming hitherward.
BEATRICE: What needed then
    Your duteous preface?° I had rather
    He had come unexpected; you must stall°
    A good presence° with unnecessary blabbing;   95
    And how welcome for your part you are,
    I'm sure you know.
DE FLORES [*aside*]:   Will't never mend, this scorn,
    One side nor other? Must I be enjoined°
    To follow still° whilst she flies from me? Well,
    Fates do your worst, I'll please myself with sight   100
    Of her, at all opportunities,
    If but to spite her anger; I know she had
    Rather see me dead than living, and yet
    She knows no cause for't but a peevish will.
ALSEMERO: You seemed displeasèd, lady, on the sudden.   105
BEATRICE: Your pardon, sir, 'tis my infirmity;
    Nor can I other reason render you
    Than his or hers, of some particular thing
    They must abandon as a deadly poison,
    Which to a thousand other tastes were wholesome.   110
    Such to mine eyes is that same fellow there,
    The same that report speaks of, the basilisk.°
ALSEMERO: This is a frequent frailty in our nature;
    There's scarce a man among a thousand sound,°
    But hath his imperfection: one distastes°   115
    The scent of roses, which to infinites°
    Most pleasing is, and odoriferous;
    One oil, the enemy of poison;
    Another wine, the cheerer of the heart,
    And lively refresher of the countenance.   120
    Indeed, this fault, if so it be, is general:
    There's scarce a thing but is both loved and loathed.
    Myself, I must confess, have the same frailty.°

BEATRICE: And what may be your poison, sir? I am bold with you.
ALSEMERO: What might be your desire? perhaps, a cherry.°　　125
BEATRICE: I am no enemy to any creature
　　My memory has, but yon gentleman.
ALSEMERO: He does ill to tempt° your sight, if he knew it.
BEATRICE: He cannot be ignorant of that, sir,
　　I have not spared to tell him so; and I want　　130
　　To help myself,° since he's a gentleman
　　In good respect° with my father, and follows° him.
ALSEMERO: He's out of his place then now.　　　[*They talk apart.*]
JASPERINO: I am a mad wag, wench.
DIAPHANTA: So methinks; but for your comfort I can tell you, we have　135
　　a doctor in the city that undertakes the cure of such.°
JASPERINO: Tush, I know what physic° is best for the state of mine own
　　body.
DIAPHANTA: 'Tis scarce a well governed state, I believe.
JASPERINO: I could show thee such a thing° with an ingredience that we　140
　　two would compound° together, and if it did not tame the maddest
　　blood° i' th' town for two hours after, I'll ne'er profess physic
　　again.
DIAPHANTA: A little poppy,° sir, were good to cause you sleep.
JASPERINO: Poppy? I'll give thee a pop i' th' lips for that first, and begin
　　there. [*Kisses her.*] Poppy is one simple° indeed, and cuckoo (what　145
　　you call't)° another. I'll discover° no more now; another time I'll
　　show thee all.
BEATRICE: My father, sir.

Enter VERMANDERO *and* Servants.

VERMANDERO:　　　　　Oh, Joanna, I came to meet thee;
　　Your devotion's° ended?
BEATRICE:　　　　　　　For this time, sir.
　　[*Aside*] I shall change my saint,° I fear me; I find　　150
　　A giddy turning in me. — Sir, this while
　　I am beholding to this gentleman,
　　Who left his own way to keep me company,
　　And in discourse I find him much desirous
　　To see your castle. He hath deserved it, sir,　　155
　　If ye please to grant it.
VERMANDERO:　　　　With all my heart, sir.
　　Yet there's an article between:° I must know
　　Your country. We use not to give survey
　　Of our chief strengths to strangers; our citadels
　　Are placed conspicuous to outward view,　　160
　　On promonts'° tops; but within are secrets.

ALSEMERO: A Valencian, sir.
VERMANDERO: A Valencian?
    That's native, sir; of what name, I beseech you?
ALSEMERO: Alsemero, sir.
VERMANDERO: Alsemero? Not the son
    Of John de Alsemero?
ALSEMERO: The same, sir.   165
VERMANDERO: My best love bids you welcome.
BEATRICE [*aside*]:   He was wont
    To call me so, and then he speaks a most
    Unfeignèd truth.
VERMANDERO: Oh, sir, I knew your father;
    We two were in acquaintance long ago,
    Before our chins were worth Iulan down,°   170
    And so continued till the stamp of time
    Had coined us into silver.° Well, he's gone;
    A good soldier went with him.
ALSEMERO: You went together° in that, sir.
VERMANDERO: No, by Saint Jacques,° I came behind him;   175
    Yet I have done somewhat° too. An unhappy° day
    Swallowed him at last at Gibraltar°
    In fight with those rebellious Hollanders,
    Was it not so?
ALSEMERO: Whose death I had revenged,
    Or followed him in fate, had not the late league°   180
    Prevented me.
VERMANDERO: Ay, ay, 'twas time to breathe.
    — Oh, Joanna, I should ha' told thee news;
    I saw Piracquo lately.
BEATRICE [*aside*]:   That's ill news.
VERMANDERO: He's hot preparing for his day of triumph;
    Thou must be a bride within this sevennight.
ALSEMERO [*aside*]:   Ha!   185
BEATRICE: Nay, good sir, be not so violent;° with speed
    I cannot render satisfaction
    Unto the dear companion of my soul,
    Virginity, whom I thus long have lived with,
    And part with it so rude° and suddenly;   190
    Can such friends divide, never to meet again,
    Without a solemn farewell?
VERMANDERO: Tush, tush, there's a toy.°
ALSEMERO [*aside*]: I must now part, and never meet again
    With any joy on earth. — Sir, your pardon;
    My affairs call on me.
VERMANDERO: How, sir? By no means;   195

Not changed so soon, I hope. You must see my castle,
And her best entertainment,° ere we part;
I shall think myself unkindly used else.
Come, come, let's on; I had good hope your stay
Had been a while with us in Alicant;°   200
I might have bid you to my daughter's wedding.
ALSEMERO [*aside*]: He means to feast me, and poisons me beforehand.
   — I should be dearly glad to be there, sir,
Did my occasions° suit as I could wish.
BEATRICE: I shall be sorry if you be not there   205
   When it is done, sir; — but not so suddenly.
VERMANDERO: I tell you, sir, the gentleman's complete,
   A courtier and a gallant, enriched
   With many fair and noble ornaments;
   I would not change him for a son-in-law   210
   For any he in Spain, the proudest he,
   And we have great ones, that you know.
ALSEMERO: He's much
   Bound° to you, sir.
VERMANDERO: He shall be bound to me,
   As fast as this tie can hold him; I'll want
   My will else.
BEATRICE [*aside*]: I shall want° mine if you do it.   215
VERMANDERO: But come, by the way I'll tell you more of him.
ALSEMERO [*aside*]: How shall I dare to venture in his castle,
   When he discharges murderers° at the gate?
   But I must on, for back I cannot go.
BEATRICE [*aside*]: Not this serpent gone yet?   [*She drops her glove.*]
VERMANDERO: Look, girl, thy glove's fall'n. 220
   Stay, stay; — De Flores, help a little.   [*Exeunt* VERMANDERO, ALSEMERO,
                                                    JASPERINO *and* Servants.]
DE FLORES: Here, lady.   [*Offers the glove.*]
BEATRICE: Mischief on your officious forwardness!
   Who bade you stoop? They touch my hand no more.
   There! For t'other's sake I part with this;
        [*Takes off the other glove and throws it down.*]
   Take 'em and draw thine own skin off with 'em.   225
               Exeunt [BEATRICE *and* DIAPHANTA].
DE FLORES: Here's a favour come, with a mischief!° Now I know°
   She had rather wear my pelt tanned in a pair
   Of dancing pumps° than I should thrust my fingers
   Into her sockets here; I know she hates me,
   Yet cannot choose but love her.   230
   No matter; if but to vex her, I'll haunt° her still;
   Though I get nothing else, I'll have my will.   *Exit.*

Act One, Scene Two

Enter ALIBIUS *and* LOLLIO.

ALIBIUS: Lollio, I must trust thee with a secret,
    But thou must keep it.
LOLLIO: I was ever close to° a secret, sir.
ALIBIUS: The diligence that I have found in thee,
    The care and industry already past,   5
    Assures me of thy good continuance.
    Lollio, I have a wife.
LOLLIO: Fie, sir, 'tis too late to keep her secret, she's known to be
    married all the town and country over.
ALIBIUS: Thou goest too fast, my Lollio; that knowledge   10
    I allow no man can be barred it;
    But there is a knowledge° which is nearer,
    Deeper, and sweeter, Lollio.
LOLLIO: Well, sir, let us handle that between you and I.
ALIBIUS: 'Tis that I go about,° man. Lollio,   15
    My wife is young.
LOLLIO: So much the worse to be kept secret, sir.
ALIBIUS: Why, now thou meet'st the substance of the point;
    I am old, Lollio.
LOLLIO: No, sir, 'tis I am old Lollio.   20
ALIBIUS: Yet why may not this concord and sympathise?
    Old trees and young plants often grow together,
    Well enough agreeing.
LOLLIO: Ay, sir, but the old trees raise themselves higher and broader°
    than the young plants.   25
ALIBIUS: Shrewd application! There's the fear, man;
    I would wear my ring° on my own finger;
    Whilst it is borrowed it is none of mine,
    But his that useth it.
LOLLIO: You must keep it on still° then; if it but lie by,   30
    One or other will be thrusting into't.
ALIBIUS: Thou conceiv'st° me, Lollio; here thy watchful eye
    Must have employment; I cannot always be
    At home.
LOLLIO: I dare swear you cannot.   35
ALIBIUS: I must look out.°
LOLLIO: I know't; you must look out, 'tis every man's case.
ALIBIUS: Here, I do say, must thy employment be:
    To watch her treadings,° and in my absence
    Supply my place.   40

LOLLIO: I'll do my best, sir; yet surely I cannot see who you should have
    cause to be jealous of.

ALIBIUS: Thy reason for that, Lollio? 'Tis a comfortable° question.

LOLLIO: We have but two sorts of people in the house, and both under
    the whip,° that's fools and madmen; the one has not wit° enough to   45
    be knaves,° and the other not knavery enough to be fools.

ALIBIUS: Ay, those are all my patients, Lollio.
    I do profess the cure of either sort;
    My trade, my living 'tis, I thrive by it;
    But here's the care that mixes with my thrift:°   50
    The daily visitants,° that come to see
    My brainsick patients, I would not have
    To see my wife. Gallants I do observe
    Of quick enticing eyes, rich in habits,°
    Of stature and proportion very comely: 55
    These are most shrewd° temptations, Lollio.

LOLLIO: They may be easily answered, sir; if they come to see the fools
    and madmen, you and I may serve the turn, and let my mistress
    alone, she's of neither sort.

ALIBIUS: 'Tis a good ward;° indeed, come they to see   60
    Our madmen or our fools, let 'em see no more
    Than what they come for. By that consequent
    They must not see her; I'm sure she's no fool.

LOLLIO: And I'm sure she's no madman.

ALIBIUS: Hold that buckler° fast, Lollio; my trust   65
    Is on thee, and I account it firm and strong.
    What hour is't, Lollio?

LOLLIO: Towards belly-hour, sir.

ALIBIUS: Dinner time? Thou mean'st twelve o'clock?

LOLLIO: Yes, sir, for every part° has his hour: we wake at six and look   70
    about us, that's eye-hour; at seven we should pray, that's
    knee-hour; at eight walk, that's leg-hour; at nine gather flowers
    and pluck a rose,° that's nose-hour; at ten we drink, that's
    mouth-hour; at eleven lay about us for victuals, that's hand-hour;
    at twelve go to dinner, that's belly-hour.   75

ALIBIUS: Profoundly, Lollio! It will be long
    Ere all thy scholars learn this lesson, and
    I did look to have a new one entered; — stay,
    I think my expectation is come home.

Enter PEDRO, *and* ANTONIO *like an idiot.*°

PEDRO: Save you,° sir; my business speaks itself,   80
    This sight takes off the labour of my tongue.

ALIBIUS: Ay, ay, sir, 'tis plain enough; you mean him for my patient.

PEDRO: And if your pains prove but commodious,° to give but some
    little strength to his sick and weak part of nature in him, these are
    but patterns° [*gives him money*] to show you of the whole pieces that   85
    will follow to you, beside the charge° of diet, washing and other
    necessaries fully defrayed.
ALIBIUS: Believe it, sir, there shall no care be wanting.
LOLLIO: Sir, an officer in this place may deserve something; the trouble
    will pass through my hands.   90
PEDRO: 'Tis fit something should come to your hands then, sir.
                                           [*Gives him money.*]
LOLLIO: Yes, sir, 'tis I must keep him sweet, and read to him. What is his
    name?
PEDRO: His name is Antonio; marry, we use but half to him, only Tony.°
LOLLIO: Tony, Tony; 'tis enough, and a very good name for a fool. —   95
    What's your name, Tony?
ANTONIO: He, he, he! Well, I thank you, cousin; he, he, he!
LOLLIO: Good boy! Hold up your head. — He can laugh;
    I perceive by that he is no beast.°
PEDRO: Well, sir,   100
    If you can raise him but to any height,
    Any degree° of wit,° might he attain,
    (As I might say) to creep but on all four
    Towards the chair of wit, or walk on crutches,
    'Twould add an honour to your worthy pains,   105
    And a great family might pray for you,
    To which he should be heir, had he discretion
    To claim and guide his own; assure you,° sir,
    He is a gentleman.
LOLLIO: Nay, there's nobody doubted that. At first sight   110
    I knew him for a gentleman, he looks no other yet.
PEDRO: Let him have good attendance and sweet lodging.
LOLLIO: As good as my mistress lies in, sir; and as you allow us time
    and means, we can raise him to the higher degree of discretion.°
PEDRO: Nay, there shall no cost want,° sir.   115
LOLLIO: He will hardly be stretched up to the wit of a magnifico.°
PEDRO: Oh no, that's not to be expected, far shorter will be enough.
LOLLIO: I'll warrant you I make him fit to bear office in five weeks; I'll
    undertake to wind him up to the wit of constable.°
PEDRO: If it be lower than that it might serve turn.   120
LOLLIO: No, fie, to level him with a headborough,° beadle,° or
    watchman were but little better than he is; constable I'll able him.
    If he do come to be a justice afterwards, let him thank the keeper.
    Or I'll go further with you; say I do bring him up to my own pitch,
    say I make him as wise as myself.   125
PEDRO: Why, there I would have it.

LOLLIO: Well, go to; either I'll be as arrant° a fool as he, or he shall be as wise as I, and then I think 'twill serve his turn.

PEDRO: Nay, I do like thy wit passing well.

LOLLIO: Yes, you may; yet if I had not been a fool, I had had more wit   130
than I have too; remember what state you find me in.

PEDRO: I will, and so leave you; your best cares, I beseech you.   *Exit* PEDRO.

ALIBIUS: Take you none with you; leave 'em all with us.

ANTONIO: Oh, my cousin's gone! Cousin, cousin, oh!

LOLLIO: Peace, peace, Tony; you must not cry, child, you must be   135
whipped if you do. Your cousin is here still; I am your cousin, Tony.

ANTONIO: He, he! Then I'll not cry, if thou be'st my cousin; he, he, he!

LOLLIO: I were best try his wit° a little, that I may know what form° to place him in.

ALIBIUS: Ay, do, Lollio, do.   140

LOLLIO: I must ask him easy questions at first. — Tony, how many true° fingers has a tailor on his right hand?

ANTONIO: As many as on his left, cousin.

LOLLIO: Good; and how many on both?

ANTONIO: Two less than a deuce,° cousin.   145

LOLLIO: Very well answered. I come to you again, cousin Tony: how many fools goes to a wise man?

ANTONIO: Forty in a day sometimes, cousin.

LOLLIO: Forty in a day? How prove you that?

ANTONIO: All that fall out amongst themselves, and go to a lawyer to   150
be made friends.

LOLLIO: A parlous° fool! He must sit in the fourth form at least, I perceive that. I come again, Tony: how many knaves° make an honest man?

ANTONIO: I know not that, cousin.   155

LOLLIO: No, the question is too hard for you. I'll tell you, cousin, there's three knaves may make an honest man: a sergeant, a jailer, and a beadle; the sergeant catches him, the jailer holds him and the beadle lashes him; and if he be not honest then, the hangman must cure him.   160

ANTONIO: Ha, ha, ha! That's fine sport, cousin.

ALIBIUS: This was too deep a question for the fool, Lollio.

LOLLIO: Yes, this might have served yourself, though I say't. Once more, and you shall go play, Tony.

ANTONIO: Ay, play at push-pin,° cousin; ha, he!   165

LOLLIO: So thou shalt. Say how many fools are here.

ANTONIO: Two, cousin, thou and I.

LOLLIO: Nay, you're too forward there, Tony. Mark my question: how many fools and knaves are here? A fool before a knave, a fool behind a knave, between every two fools a knave; how many fools,   170
how many knaves?

ANTONIO: I never learnt so far, cousin.

ALIBIUS: Thou putt'st too hard questions to him, Lollio.

LOLLIO: I'll make him understand it easily. Cousin, stand there.°

ANTONIO: Ay, cousin.   175

LOLLIO: Master, stand you next the fool.

ALIBIUS: Well, Lollio.

LOLLIO: Here's my place. Mark now, Tony, there a fool
    before a knave.

ANTONIO: That's I, cousin.   180

LOLLIO: Here's a fool behind a knave, that's I; and between us two fools
    there is a knave, that's my master; 'tis but we three,° that's all.

ANTONIO: We three, we three, cousin.   MADMEN *within.*

1 MADMAN *within*: Put's head i' th' pillory, the bread's too little.°

2 MADMAN *within*: Fly, fly, and he catches the swallow.°   185

3 MADMAN *within*: Give her more onion, or the devil put the rope° about
    her crag.°

LOLLIO: You may hear what time of day it is, the chimes of Bedlam° goes.

ALIBIUS: Peace, peace, or the wire° comes!   190

3 MADMAN *within*: Cat whore, cat whore, her permasant,° her permasant!

ALIBIUS: Peace, I say! — Their hour's come, they must be fed, Lollio.

LOLLIO: There's no hope of recovery of that Welsh madman, was
    undone by a mouse that spoiled him a permasant; lost his wits
    for't.   195

ALIBIUS: Go to your charge,° Lollio, I'll to mine.

LOLLIO: Go to your madmen's ward, let me alone with
    your fools.

ALIBIUS: And remember my last° charge, Lollio.   *Exit.*

LOLLIO: Of which your patients do you think I am? Come, Tony, you   200
    must amongst your school-fellows now; there's pretty scholars
    amongst 'em, I can tell you, there's some of 'em at *stultus, stulta,*
    stultum.°

ANTONIO: I would see the madmen, cousin, if they would not bite me.

LOLLIO: No, they shall not bite thee, Tony.   205

ANTONIO: They bite when they are at dinner, do they not, coz?

LOLLIO: They bite at dinner, indeed, Tony. Well, I hope to get credit° by
    thee; I like thee the best of all the scholars that ever I brought up,
    and thou shalt prove a wise man, or I'll prove a fool myself.   *Exeunt.*

Act Two, Scene One

Enter BEATRICE *and* JASPERINO *severally.*°

BEATRICE: Oh sir, I'm ready now for that fair service
    Which makes the name of friend sit glorious on you.

Good angels and this conduct° be your guide;   [*Gives him a paper.*]
    Fitness of time and place is there set down, sir.
JASPERINO: The joy I shall return rewards my service.   *Exit.* 5
BEATRICE: How wise is Alsemero in his friend!
    It is a sign he makes his choice with judgement.
    Then I appear in nothing more approved
    Than making choice of him;
    For 'tis a principle, he that can choose   10
    That bosom well, who of his thoughts partakes,
    Proves most discreet in every choice he makes.
    Methinks I love now with the eyes of judgement,
    And see the way to merit, clearly see it.
    A true deserver like a diamond sparkles;   15
    In darkness you may see him° (that's in absence,
    Which is the greatest darkness falls on love),
    Yet he is best discernèd then
    With intellectual eyesight. What's Piracquo
    My father spends his breath for? And his blessing°   20
    Is only mine as I regard his name,°
    Else it goes from me, and turns head° against me,
    Transformed into a curse. Some speedy way
    Must be remembered; he's so forward, too,
    So urgent that way, scarce allows me breath   25
    To speak to my new comforts.°

                        Enter DE FLORES.

DE FLORES [*aside*]:   Yonder's she.
    Whatever ails me? Now a-late especially,
    I can as well be hanged as refrain seeing her.
    Some twenty times a day, nay, not so little,
    Do I force errands, frame ways and excuses   30
    To come into her sight, and I have small reason for't,
    And less encouragement; for she baits me still,°
    Every time worse than other, does profess herself
    The cruellest enemy to my face in town,
    At no hand° can abide the sight of me,   35
    As if danger or ill-luck hung in my looks.
    I must confess my face is bad enough,
    But I know far worse has better fortune,
    And not endured alone,° but doted on:
    And yet such pick-haired° faces, chins like witches',   40
    Here and there five hairs, whispering in a corner,
    As if they grew in fear one of another,

Wrinkles like troughs, where swine-deformity swills°
The tears of perjury that lie there like wash°
Fallen from the slimy and dishonest eye, —   45
Yet such a one plucked sweets° without restraint,
And has the grace of beauty to his sweet.°
Though my hard fate has thrust me out to servitude,
I tumbled into th'world a gentleman.
She turns her blessed eye upon me now,   50
And I'll endure all storms before I part with't.
BEATRICE [*aside*]: Again!
— This ominous ill-faced fellow more disturbs me
Than all my other passions.°
DE FLORES [*aside*]:   Now't begins again;
I'll stand this storm of hail, though the stones pelt me.   55
BEATRICE: Thy business? What's thy business?
DE FLORES [*aside*]:   Soft and fair,°
I cannot part so soon now.
BEATRICE [*aside*]:   The villain's fixed!
— Thou standing toad-pool!°
DE FLORES [*aside*]:   The shower falls amain° now.
BEATRICE: Who sent thee? What's thy errand? Leave my sight.
DE FLORES: My lord your father charged me to deliver   60
A message to you.
BEATRICE: What, another since?°
Do't and be hanged then; let me be rid of thee.
DE FLORES: True service merits mercy.°
BEATRICE: What's thy message?
DE FLORES: Let beauty settle but in patience,
You shall hear all.
BEATRICE: A dallying, trifling torment!   65
DE FLORES: Signior Alonzo de Piracquo, lady,
Sole brother to Tomazo de Piracquo —
BEATRICE: Slave, when wilt make an end?
DE FLORES: Too soon I shall.
BEATRICE: What all this while of him?
DE FLORES: The said Alonzo,
With the foresaid Tomazo —
BEATRICE: Yet again?   70
DE FLORES: Is new alighted.
BEATRICE: Vengeance strike the news!
Thou thing most loathed, what cause was there in this
To bring thee to my sight?
DE FLORES: My lord your father
Charged me to seek you out.
BEATRICE: Is there no other

To send his errand by?

DE FLORES: It seems 'tis my luck 75
To be i' th' way still.°

BEATRICE: Get thee from me!

DE FLORES: So;
[*Aside*] Why, am not I an ass to devise ways
Thus to be railed at? I must see her still!
I shall have a mad qualm° within this hour again,
I know't, and, like a common Garden-bull,° 80
I do but take breath to be lugged° again.
What this may bode I know not; I'll despair the less,
Because there's daily precedents of bad° faces
Beloved beyond all reason; these foul chops
May come into favour one day, 'mongst his fellows. 85
Wrangling has proved° the mistress of good pastime:
As children cry themselves asleep, I ha' seen
Women have chid themselves abed to men.   *Exit* DE FLORES.

BEATRICE: I never see this fellow, but I think
Of some harm towards me; danger's in my mind still; 90
I scarce leave trembling of° an hour after.
The next good mood I find my father in,
I'll get him quite discarded.° Oh, I was
Lost in this small disturbance, and forgot
Affliction's fiercer torrent that now comes 95
To bear down° all my comforts.

Enter VERMANDERO, ALONZO, TOMAZO.

VERMANDERO: You're both welcome,
But an especial one belongs to you, sir,
To whose most noble name our love presents
The addition° of a son,° our son Alonzo.

ALONZO: The treasury of honour cannot bring forth 100
A title I should more rejoice in, sir.

VERMANDERO: You have improved it well. — Daughter, prepare,
The day will steal upon thee suddenly.°

BEATRICE [*aside*]: Howe'er, I will be sure to keep° the night,
If it should come so near me.   [BEATRICE *and* VERMANDERO *talk apart*.]

TOMAZO: Alonzo.

ALONZO: Brother? 105

TOMAZO: In troth I see small welcome in her eye.

ALONZO: Fie, you are too severe a censurer
Of love in all points, there's no bringing on you;°
If lovers should mark everything a fault,°
Affection would be like an ill-set° book, 110

Whose faults might prove as big as half the volume.
BEATRICE: That's all I do entreat.
VERMANDERO: It is but reasonable;
  I'll see what my son says to't. — Son Alonzo,
  Here's a motion° made but to reprieve
  A maidenhead three days longer; the request   115
  Is not far out of reason, for indeed
  The former time is pinching.°
ALONZO: Though my joys
  Be set back so much time as I could wish
  They had been forward, yet since she desires it,
  The time is set as pleasing as before;   120
  I find no gladness wanting.°
VERMANDERO: May I ever
  Meet it in that point still. You're nobly welcome, sirs.

                              Exeunt VERMANDERO *and* BEATRICE.

TOMAZO: So: did you mark the dulness of her parting now?
ALONZO: What dulness? Thou art so exceptious still!°
TOMAZO: Why, let it go then, I am but a fool   125
  To mark your harms° so heedfully.
ALONZO: Where's the oversight?
TOMAZO: Come, your faith's cozened° in her, strongly cozened;
  Unsettle your affection with all speed
  Wisdom can bring it to, your peace is ruined else.
  Think what a torment 'tis to marry one   130
  Whose heart is leaped into another's bosom:
  If ever pleasure° she receive from thee,
  It comes not in thy name, or of thy gift;
  She lies but with another in thine arms,
  He the half-father unto all thy children   135
  In the conception; if he get 'em not,
  She helps to get 'em for him,° and how dangerous
  And shameful her restraint may go in time to,
  It is not to be thought on without sufferings.°
ALONZO: You speak as if she loved some other, then.   140
TOMAZO: Do you apprehend so slowly?
ALONZO: Nay, and that
  Be your fear only, I am safe enough.
  Preserve your friendship and your counsel, brother,
  For times of more distress; I should depart
  An enemy, a dangerous, deadly one,   145
  To any but thyself, that should but think
  She knew the meaning of inconstancy,
  Much less the use and practice; yet we're friends.
  Pray, let no more be urged; I can endure

Much, till I meet an injury to her,   150
    Then I am not myself. Farewell, sweet brother;
    How much we're bound to heaven to depart lovingly.°   *Exit.*
TOMAZO: Why, here is love's tame madness; thus a man
    Quickly steals into his vexation.   *Exit.*

Act Two, Scene Two

Enter DIAPHANTA *and* ALSEMERO.

DIAPHANTA: The place is my charge,° you have kept your hour,
    And the reward of a just meeting bless you.
    I hear my lady coming; complete gentleman,
    I dare not be too busy with my praises,
    They're dangerous things to deal with.   *Exit.*
ALSEMERO: This goes well;   5
    These women are the ladies' cabinets,°
    Things of most precious trust are locked into 'em.

Enter BEATRICE.

BEATRICE: I have within mine eye all my desires;
    Requests that holy prayers ascend heaven for,
    And brings° 'em down to furnish our defects,°   10
    Come not more sweet to our necessities
    Than thou unto my wishes.
ALSEMERO: We're so like
    In our expressions, lady, that unless I borrow
    The same words, I shall never find their equals.   [*Kisses her.*]
BEATRICE: How happy were this meeting, this embrace,   15
    If it were free from envy! This poor kiss,
    It has an enemy, a hateful one,
    That wishes poison to't; how well were I now
    If there were none such name known as Piracquo,
    Nor no such tie as the command of parents!   20
    I should be but too much blessed.
ALSEMERO: One good service
    Would strike off° both your fears, and I'll go near° it, too,
    Since you are so distressed. Remove the cause,
    The command ceases;° so there's two fears blown out°
    With one and the same blast.
BEATRICE: Pray, let me find you,° sir.   25
    What might that service be, so strangely happy?°
ALSEMERO: The honourablest piece 'bout man, valour.

I'll send a challenge to Piracquo instantly.
BEATRICE: How? Call you that extinguishing of fear,
　　When 'tis the only way to keep it flaming?　　　　　　　30
　　Are not you ventured° in the action,
　　That's all my joys and comforts? Pray, no more, sir.
　　Say you prevailed, you're danger's and not mine then;
　　The law would claim you from me, or obscurity
　　Be made the grave to bury you alive.　　　　　　　35
　　I'm glad these thoughts come forth; oh, keep not one
　　Of this condition,° sir; here was a course
　　Found to bring sorrow on her way to death;
　　The tears would ne'er ha' dried, till dust had choked 'em.
　　Blood-guiltiness becomes° a fouler visage.　　　　　　　40
　　[*Aside*] — And now I think on one. I was to blame,
　　I ha' marred so good a market° with my scorn;
　　'T° had been done questionless. The ugliest creature
　　Creation framed for some use,° yet to see
　　I could not mark so much where it should be!　　　　　　　45
ALSEMERO: Lady —
BEATRICE [*aside*]:　　Why, men of art make much of poison,
　　Keep one to expel another; where was my art?°
ALSEMERO: Lady, you hear not me.
BEATRICE:　　　　　　　　　I do especially, sir;
　　The present times are not so sure of our side°
　　As those hereafter may be; we must use 'em then　　　　　　　50
　　As thrifty fools their wealth, sparingly now
　　Till the time opens.°
ALSEMERO:　　　　　You teach wisdom, lady.
BEATRICE: Within there! Diaphanta!

Enter DIAPHANTA.

DIAPHANTA:　　　　　　　Do you call, madam?
BEATRICE: Perfect your service, and conduct this gentleman
　　The private way you brought him.
DIAPHANTA:　　　　　　　I shall, madam.　　　　　　　55
ALSEMERO: My love's as firm as love e'er built upon.
　　　　　　　　　　　　Exeunt DIAPHANTA *and* ALSEMERO.

Enter DE FLORES.

DE FLORES [*aside*]: I have watched this meeting, and do wonder much
　　What shall become of t'other.° I'm sure both
　　Cannot be served° unless she transgress; happily°
　　Then I'll put in for one:° for if a woman　　　　　　　60

Fly° from one point, from him she makes a husband,
She spreads and mounts then like arithmetic,
One, ten, a hundred, a thousand, ten thousand;
Proves in time sutler° to an army royal.
Now do I look to be most richly railed at,   65
Yet I must see her.
BEATRICE [*aside*]:   Why, put case° I loathed him
   As much as youth and beauty hates a sepulchre,
   Must I needs show it? Cannot I keep that secret
   And serve my turn upon him? —° See, he's here.
   [*To him*] De Flores!
DE FLORES [*aside*]:   Ha, I shall run mad with joy!   70
   She called me fairly by my name, De Flores,
   And neither rogue nor rascal.
BEATRICE: What ha' you done
   To your face a-late? You've met with some good physician;
   You've pruned° yourself, methinks; you were not wont
   To look so amorously.°
DE FLORES [*aside*]:   Not I;   75
   'Tis the same physnomy, to a hair and pimple,
   Which she called scurvy scarce an hour ago:
   How is this?
BEATRICE: Come hither; nearer, man.
DE FLORES [*aside*]: I'm up to the chin in heaven!
BEATRICE: Turn, let me see.
   Faugh, 'tis but the heat of the liver,° I perceiv't;   80
   I thought it had been worse.
DE FLORES [*aside*]:   Her fingers touched me!
   She smells all amber.°
BEATRICE: I'll make a water° for you shall cleanse this
   Within a fortnight.
DE FLORES: With your own hands, lady?
BEATRICE: Yes, mine own, sir; in a work of cure   85
   I'll trust no other.
DE FLORES [*aside*]:   'Tis half an act of pleasure
   To hear her talk thus to me.
BEATRICE: When we're used
   To a hard face, 'tis not so unpleasing;
   It mends still in opinion, hourly mends,
   I see it by experience.
DE FLORES [*aside*]:   I was blest   90
   To light upon this minute; I'll make use on't.°
BEATRICE: Hardness becomes° the visage of a man well;
   It argues° service, resolution, manhood,
   If cause were of employment.

DE FLORES: 'Twould be soon seen,
  If e'er your ladyship had cause to use it.   95
  I would but wish the honour of a service
  So happy as that mounts to.
BEATRICE: We shall try you —
  Oh, my De Flores!
DE FLORES [*aside*]: How's that? She calls me hers already, 'my De Flores'!
  — You were about to sigh out somewhat, madam?   100
BEATRICE: No, was I? I forgot. — Oh!
DE FLORES: _ There 'tis again,
  The very fellow on't.
BEATRICE: You are too quick, sir.
DE FLORES: There's no excuse for't now; I heard it twice, madam.
  That sigh would fain have utterance, take pity on't,
  And lend it a free word; 'las, how it labours   105
  For liberty! I hear the murmur yet
  Beat at your bosom.
BEATRICE: Would creation —
DE FLORES: Ay, well said, that's it.
BEATRICE: Had formed me man!
DE FLORES: Nay, that's not it.
BEATRICE: Oh, 'tis the soul of freedom!
  I should not then be forced to marry one   110
  I hate beyond all depths; I should have power
  Then to oppose my loathings, nay, remove 'em
  For ever from my sight.
DE FLORES [*aside*]:   O blest occasion!°
  — Without change to your sex, you have your wishes.
  Claim so much man in me.
BEATRICE: In thee, De Flores?   115
  There's small cause for that.
DE FLORES: Put it not from me;
  It's a service that I kneel for to you.   [*Kneels.*]
BEATRICE: You are too violent to mean faithfully;°
  There's horror in my service, blood and danger;
  Can those be things to sue for?
DE FLORES: If you knew   120
  How sweet it were to me to be employed
  In any act of yours, you would say then
  I failed, and used not reverence° enough
  When I receive the charge on't.
BEATRICE [*aside*]:   This is much, methinks;
  Belike his wants are greedy, and to such   125
  Gold tastes like angels' food. —° Rise.
DE FLORES: I'll have the work first.

BEATRICE [*aside*]:   Possible his need
   Is strong upon him. — There's to encourage thee;   [*Gives him money.*]
   As thou art forward° and thy service dangerous,
   Thy reward shall be precious.
DE FLORES: That I have thought on;   130
   I have assured myself of that beforehand,
   And know it will be precious; the thought ravishes.
BEATRICE: Then take him to thy fury!
DE FLORES: I thirst for him.
BEATRICE: Alonzo de Piracquo!
DE FLORES: His end's upon him; he shall be seen no more.   [*Rises.*] 135
BEATRICE: How lovely now dost thou appear to me!
   Never was man dearlier° rewarded.
DE FLORES: I do think of that.
BEATRICE: Be wondrous careful in the execution.°
DE FLORES: Why, are not both our lives upon the cast?°
BEATRICE: Then I throw all my fears upon thy service.   140
DE FLORES: They ne'er shall rise to hurt you.
BEATRICE: When the deed's done,
   I'll furnish thee with all things for thy flight;
   Thou may'st live bravely° in another country.
DE FLORES: Ay, ay, we'll talk of that hereafter.
BEATRICE [*aside*]:   I shall rid myself
   Of two inveterate loathings at one time: 145
   Piracquo, and his dog-face.   *Exit.*
DE FLORES: O my blood!°
   Methinks I feel her in mine arms already,
   Her wanton fingers combing out this beard,
   And, being pleased, praising this bad face.
   Hunger and pleasure, they'll commend sometimes   150
   Slovenly° dishes, and feed heartily on 'em;
   Nay, which is stranger, refuse daintier for 'em.
   Some women are odd feeders. — I'm too loud.
   Here comes the man goes supperless to bed,
   Yet shall not rise tomorrow to his dinner.   155

Enter ALONZO.

ALONZO: De Flores.
DE FLORES: My kind, honourable lord.
ALONZO: I am glad I ha' met with thee.
DE FLORES: Sir?
ALONZO: Thou canst show me
   The full strength of the castle?

DE FLORES: That I can, sir.
ALONZO: I much desire it.
DE FLORES: And if the ways and straits°
  Of some of the passages be not too tedious for you,   160
  I will assure you, worth your time and sight, my lord.
ALONZO: Puh, that shall be no hindrance.
DE FLORES: I'm your servant then.
  'Tis now near dinner time; 'gainst your lordship's rising°
  I'll have the keys about me.
ALONZO: Thanks, kind De Flores.
DE FLORES [*aside*]: He's safely° thrust upon me° beyond hopes. *Exeunt.* 165

Act Three, Scene One

Enter ALONZO *and* DE FLORES.
(*In the act-time°* DE FLORES *hides a naked rapier.*)

DE FLORES: Yes, here are all the keys. I was afraid, my lord,
  I'd wanted for the postern;° this is it.
  I've all, I've all, my lord: this for the sconce.°
ALONZO: 'Tis a most spacious and impregnable fort.
DE FLORES: You'll tell me more, my lord. This descent   5
  Is somewhat narrow; we shall never pass
  Well with our weapons, they'll but trouble us.
ALONZO: Thou say'st true.
DE FLORES: Pray let me help your lordship.
                                   [*They remove their swords.*]
ALONZO: 'Tis done. Thanks, kind De Flores.
DE FLORES: Here are hooks, my lord,
  To hang such things on purpose.   *He hangs up the swords.*
ALONZO: Lead, I'll follow thee.   10
                     Exeunt at one door and enter at the other.°

Act Three, Scene Two

DE FLORES: All this is nothing; you shall see anon
  A place you little dream on.
ALONZO: I am glad
  I have this leisure; all your master's house
  Imagine I ha' taken a gondola.
DE FLORES: All but myself, sir, — [*aside*] which makes up° my safety. — 5
  My lord, I'll place you at a casement° here

Will show you the full strength of all the castle.
Look, spend your eye awhile upon that object.
ALONZO: Here's rich variety, De Flores.
DE FLORES: Yes, sir.
ALONZO: Goodly munition.
DE FLORES: Ay, there's ordnance,° sir,   10
   No bastard° metal,° will ring you a peal like bells
   At great men's funerals. Keep your eye straight, my lord;
   Take special notice of that sconce before you,
   There you may dwell° awhile.   *[Takes up the rapier.]*
ALONZO: I am upon't.
DE FLORES: And so am I.   *[Stabs him.]*
ALONZO: De Flores! Oh, De Flores!   15
   Whose malice hast thou put on?
DE FLORES: Do you question
   A work of secrecy? I must silence you.   *[Stabs him.]*
ALONZO: Oh, oh, oh!
DE FLORES: I must silence you.   *[Stabs him.]*
   So here's an undertaking well accomplished.
   This vault serves to good use now. — Ha, what's that   20
   Threw sparkles in my eye? — Oh, 'tis a diamond
   He wears upon his finger; it was well found,
   This will approve° the work. What, so fast on?
   Not part in death? I'll take a speedy course then;
   Finger and all shall off. *[Cuts off the finger.]* So; now I'll clear   25
   The passages from all suspect° or fear.   *Exit with body.*

Act Three, Scene Three

Enter ISABELLA *and* LOLLIO.

ISABELLA: Why, sirrah?° Whence have you commission
   To fetter the doors against me? If you
   Keep me in a cage, pray whistle to me;
   Let me be doing something.
LOLLIO: You shall be doing,° if it please you; I'll whistle to you if you'll   5
   pipe after.°
ISABELLA: Is it your master's pleasure or your own,
   To keep me in this pinfold?°
LOLLIO: 'Tis for my master's pleasure, lest being taken in another man's
   corn, you might be pounded° in another place.   10
ISABELLA: 'Tis very well, and he'll prove very wise.
LOLLIO: He says you have company enough in the house,
   if you please to be sociable, of all sorts of people.

ISABELLA: Of all sorts? Why, here's none but fools and madmen.

LOLLIO: Very well; and where will you find any other, if you should go   15
    abroad? There's my master and I to boot° too.

ISABELLA: Of either sort one, a madman and a fool.

LOLLIO: I would ev'n participate of° both then, if I were as you; I know
    you're half mad° already, be half foolish too.

ISABELLA: You're a brave, saucy rascal! Come on, sir,   20
    Afford me then the pleasure of your bedlam.°
    You were commending once today to me
    Your last-come lunatic: what a proper°
    Body there was without brains to guide it,
    And what a pitiful delight appeared   25
    In that defect, as if your wisdom had found
    A mirth in madness. Pray, sir, let me partake,
    If there be such a pleasure.

LOLLIO: If I do not show you the handsomest, discreetest madman, one   30
    that I may call the understanding madman, then say I am a fool.

ISABELLA: Well, a match;° I will say so.

LOLLIO: When you have a taste of the madman, you shall, if you please,
    see Fools' College, o' th' side; I seldom lock there, 'tis but shooting
    a bolt or two,° and you are amongst 'em.   *Exit. Enter presently.*°
    — Come on, sir, let me see how handsomely you'll behave yourself   35
    now.

Enter FRANCISCUS.

FRANCISCUS: How sweetly she looks! Oh, but there's a wrinkle in her
    brow as deep as philosophy. Anacreon, drink to my mistress'
    health; I'll pledge it. Stay, stay, there's a spider in the cup!° No, 'tis
    but a grape-stone; swallow it, fear nothing, poet; so, so, lift higher.°   40

ISABELLA: Alack, alack, 'tis too full of pity°
    To be laughed at. How fell he mad? Canst thou tell?

LOLLIO: For love, mistress. He was a pretty poet too, and that set him
    forwards° first; the Muses then forsook him; he ran mad for a
    chambermaid, yet she was but a dwarf neither.°   45

FRANCISCUS: Hail, bright Titania!
    Why stand'st thou idle on these flow'ry banks?
    Oberon is dancing with his Dryades;°
    I'll gather daisies, primrose, violets,
    And bind them in a verse of poesy.°   50

LOLLIO: Not too near; you see your danger.   [*Shows the whip.*]

FRANCISCUS: Oh, hold thy hand, great Diomed!
    Thou feed'st thy horses well,° they shall obey thee;
    Get up,° Bucephalus° kneels.   [*Kneels.*]

LOLLIO: You see how I awe my flock; a shepherd has not his dog at   55 more obedience.

ISABELLA: His conscience is unquiet; sure that was
    The cause of this. A proper° gentleman.
FRANCISCUS: Come hither, Esculapius;° hide the poison.
LOLLIO: Well, tis hid.   [*Hides the whip.* FRANCISCUS *rises.*]   60
FRANCISCUS: Didst thou never hear of one Tiresias,° a famous poet?
LOLLIO: Yes, that kept tame wild-geese.°
FRANCISCUS: That's he; I am the man.
LOLLIO: No!
FRANCISCUS: Yes, but make no words on't; I was a man seven years ago.   65
LOLLIO: A stripling I think you might.
FRANCISCUS: Now I'm a woman, all feminine.
LOLLIO: I would I might see that.
FRANCISCUS: Juno struck me blind.
LOLLIO: I'll ne'er believe that; for a woman, they say, has an eye more°   70
    than a man.
FRANCISCUS: I say she struck me blind.
LOLLIO: And Luna° made you mad; you have two trades° to beg with.
FRANCISCUS: Luna is now big-bellied,° and there's room
    For both of us to ride with Hecate;°
    I'll drag thee up into her silver sphere,   75
    And there we'll kick the dog, and beat the bush,°
    That barks against the witches of the night;
    The swift lycanthropi° that walks the round,
    We'll tear their wolvish skins and save the sheep.
                               [*He tries to seize* LOLLIO.]
LOLLIO: Is't come to this? Nay then, my poison comes forth again.   80
    [*Shows the whip.*] Mad slave, indeed, abuse your keeper!
ISABELLA: I prithee, hence with him; now he grows dangerous.
FRANCISCUS *sings:*

    Sweet love, pity me.
    Give me leave to lie °with thee.   85

LOLLIO: No, I'll see you wiser first; to your own kennel.
FRANCISCUS: No noise, she sleeps, draw all the curtains round;
    Let no soft sound molest the pretty soul
    But love, and love creeps in at a mouse-hole.°
LOLLIO: I would you would get into your hole!   *Exit* FRANCISCUS. 90
    Now, mistress, I will bring you another sort, you shall be fooled°
    another while; Tony, come hither, Tony; look who's yonder, Tony.

Enter ANTONIO.

ANTONIO: Cousin,° is it not my aunt?°
LOLLIO: Yes, 'tis one of 'em, Tony.

ANTONIO: He, he! How do you, uncle?   95
LOLLIO: Fear him not, mistress, 'tis a gentle nidget;° you may play with
   him, as safely with him as with his bauble.°
ISABELLA: How long has thou been a fool?
ANTONIO: Ever since I came hither, cousin.
ISABELLA: Cousin? I'm none of thy cousins, fool.   100
LOLLIO: O mistress, fools have always so much wit as to claim their
   kindred.
MADMAN *within*: Bounce,° bounce, he falls, he falls!
ISABELLA: Hark you, your scholars in the upper room° are out of order.
LOLLIO: Must I come amongst you there? — Keep you the fool,   105
   mistress; I'll go up and play left-handed° Orlando amongst the
   madmen.
ISABELLA: Well, sir.
ANTONIO: 'Tis opportuneful now, sweet lady! Nay,
   Cast no amazing° eye upon this change.   110
ISABELLA: Ha!
ANTONIO: This shape° of folly shrouds your dearest° love,
   The truest servant to your powerful beauties,
   Whose magic had this force thus to transform me.
ISABELLA: You are a fine fool indeed.   115
ANTONIO: Oh, 'tis not strange:
   Love has an intellect that runs through all
   The scrutinous° sciences, and, like
   A cunning poet, catches a quantity
   Of every knowledge, yet brings all home   120
   Into one mystery, into one secret
   That he proceeds° in.
ISABELLA: You're a parlous° fool.
ANTONIO: No danger in me: I bring naught but love
   And his soft-wounding shafts to strike you with.
   Try but one arrow; if it hurt you,   125
   I'll stand you twenty back in recompense.   [*Kisses her.*]
ISABELLA: A forward fool too !
ANTONIO: This was love's teaching:
   A thousand ways he fashioned out my way,
   And this I found the safest and the nearest   130
   To tread the Galaxia° to my star.
ISABELLA: Profound, withal! Certain, you dreamed of this;
   Love never taught it waking.
ANTONIO: Take no acquaintance
   Of these outward follies; there is within
   A gentleman that loves you.
ISABELLA: When I see him,   135
   I'll speak with him; so in the meantime keep

Your habit,° it becomes you well enough.
As you are a gentleman, I'll not discover° you;
That's all the favour that you must expect.
When you are weary, you may leave the school,   140
For all this while you have but played the fool.

Enter LOLLIO.

ANTONIO: And must again. — He, he ! I thank you, cousin;
    I'll be your valentine° tomorrow morning.
LOLLIO: How do you like the fool, mistress?
ISABELLA: Passing well, sir.   145
LOLLIO: Is he not witty, pretty well for a fool?
ISABELLA: If he hold on as he begins, he is like to come to something.
LOLLIO: Ay, thank a good tutor; you may put him to't;° he begins to
    answer pretty hard questions. Tony, how many is five times six?
ANTONIO: Five times six is six times five.   150
LOLLIO: What arithmetician could have answered better?
    How many is one hundred and seven?
ANTONIO: One hundred and seven is seven hundred and one, cousin.
LOLLIO: This is no wit to speak on; will you be rid of the fool now?
ISABELLA: By no means, let him stay a little.   155
MADMAN *within*: Catch there, catch the last couple in hell!°
LOLLIO: Again! Must I come amongst you? Would my master were
    come home ! I am not able to govern both these wards together.   *Exit.*
ANTONIO: Why should a minute of love's hour be lost?
ISABELLA: Fie, out° again! I had rather you kept your other posture;° you   160
    become not your tongue° when you speak from your clothes.
ANTONIO: How can he freeze,
    Lives° near so sweet a warmth? Shall I alone
    Walk through the orchard of the Hesperides,°
    And cowardly not dare to pull° an apple?   165
    This with the red cheeks I must venture for.   [*Tries to kiss her.*]

Enter LOLLIO *above.*

ISABELLA: Take heed, there's giants keep 'em.°
LOLLIO [*aside*]: How now, fool, are you good at that?°
    Have you read Lipsius?° He's past *Ars Amandi;*° I believe
    I must put harder questions to him, I perceive that —   170
ISABELLA: You are bold; without fear too.
ANTONIO: What should I fear,
    Having all joys about me? Do you smile,°
    And love shall play the wanton on your lip,
    Meet and retire, retire and meet again;

Look you but cheerfully,° and in your eyes   175
I shall behold mine own deformity,
And dress myself up fairer. I know this shape
Becomes me not,° but in those bright mirrors
I shall array me handsomely.
LOLLIO: Cuckoo, cuckoo!°   *Exit.*   180

[*Enter*] Madmen *above, some as birds, other as beasts.*

ANTONIO: What are these?
ISABELLA: Of fear° enough to part us;
    Yet they are but our schools of lunatics,
    That act their fantasies in any shapes
    Suiting their present thoughts. If sad, they cry;
    If mirth be their conceit,° they laugh again.   185
    Sometimes they imitate the beasts and birds,
    Singing, or howling, braying, barking; all
    As their wild fancies prompt 'em.   [*Exeunt* Madmen.]

Enter LOLLIO.

ANTONIO: These are no fears.
ISABELLA: But here's a large one, my man.
ANTONIO: Ha, he! That's fine sport indeed, cousin.   190
LOLLIO: I would my master were come home, 'tis too much for one
    shepherd to govern two of these flocks; nor can I believe that one
    churchman can instruct° two benefices at once; there will be some
    incurable mad of the one side, and very fools on the other. Come,
    Tony.   195
ANTONIO: Prithee, cousin, let me stay here still.
LOLLIO: No, you must to your book° now, you have played sufficiently.
ISABELLA: Your fool is grown wondrous witty.
LOLLIO: Well, I'll say nothing; but I do not think but he will put you
    down° one of these days.   *Exeunt* LOLLIO *and* ANTONIO. 200
ISABELLA: Here the restrainèd current might make breach,
    Spite of the watchful bankers.° Would a woman stray,
    She need not gad abroad to seek her sin;
    It would be brought home one ways or other.
    The needle's point will to the fixèd north: 205
    Such drawing arctics° women's beauties are.

Enter LOLLIO.

LOLLIO: How dost thou, sweet rogue?
ISABELLA. How now?

LOLLIO: Come, there are degrees; one fool may be better than another.
ISABELLA: What's the matter? 210
LOLLIO: Nay, if thou giv'st thy mind to fool's-flesh,° have at thee!°

                                     [*He tries to kiss her.*]

ISABELLA: You bold slave, you!
LOLLIO: I could follow now as t'other fool did:
   'What should I fear,
   Having all joys about me? Do you but smile, 215
   And love shall play the wanton on your lip,
   Meet and retire, retire and meet again;
   Look you but cheerfully, and in your eyes
   I shall behold my own deformity,
   And dress myself up fairer; I know this shape 220
   Becomes me not'
   — and so as it follows; but is not this the more foolish way? Come,
sweet rogue; kiss me, my little Lacedemonian.° Let me feel how thy
pulses beat; thou hast a thing about thee° would do a man pleasure,
I'll lay my hand on't. 225
ISABELLA: Sirrah, no more! I see you have discovered
   This love's knight-errant,° who hath made adventure
   For purchase° of my love; be silent, mute,
   Mute as a statue, or his injunction
   For me enjoying° shall be to cut thy throat. 230
   I'll do it, though for no other purpose,
   And be sure he'll not refuse it.
LOLLIO: My share, that's all: I'll have my fool's part with you.
ISABELLA: No more! Your master.

                    Enter ALIBIUS.

ALIBIUS: Sweet, how dost thou?
ISABELLA: Your bounden° servant, sir.
ALIBIUS: Fie, fie, sweetheart, 235
   No more of that.
ISABELLA: You were best lock me up.
ALIBIUS: In my arms and bosom, my sweet Isabella,
   I'll lock thee up most nearly. Lollio,
   We have employment, we have task in hand;
   At noble Vermandero's, our castle-captain, 240
   There is a nuptial to be solemnized
   (Beatrice-Joanna, his fair daughter, bride)
   For which the gentleman hath bespoke° our pains:
   A mixture of our madmen and our fools,
   To finish (as it were) and make the fag° 245
   Of all the revels, the third night from the first.

KING ALFRED'S COLLEGE
LIBRARY

Only an unexpected passage over,°
To make a frightful pleasure,° that is all,
But not the all I aim at; could we so act it,
To teach it in a wild, distracted measure,°　　　　　　　　250
Though out of form and figure, breaking time's head,°
It were no matter; 'twould be healed again
In one age or other, if not in this.
This, this, Lollio, there's a good reward begun,
And will beget a bounty, be it known.　　　　　　　　255
LOLLIO: This is easy, sir, I'll warrant you. You have about you fools and
madmen that can dance very well; and 'tis no wonder your best
dancers are not the wisest men; the reason is, with often jumping
they jolt their brains down into their feet, that their wits° lie more
in their heels than in their heads.　　　　　　　　260
ALIBIUS: Honest Lollio, thou giv'st me a good reason,
And a comfort in it.
ISABELLA:　　　　　　　　You've a fine trade on't;
Madmen and fools are a staple° commodity.
ALIBIUS: Oh, wife, we must eat, wear clothes, and live:
Just at the lawyer's haven we arrive;°　　　　　　　　265
By madmen and by fools we both do thrive.　　　　　*Exeunt.*

Act Three, Scene Four

Enter VERMANDERO, ALSEMERO, JASPERINO, *and* BEATRICE.

VERMANDERO: Valencia speaks so nobly of you, sir,
I wish I had a daughter now for you.
ALSEMERO: The fellow of this creature were a partner
For a king's love.
VERMANDERO:　　　　　　　　I had her fellow once, sir,
But heaven has married her to joys eternal;　　　　　　　　5
'Twere sin to wish her in this vale° again.
Come, sir, your friend and you shall see the pleasures
Which my health chiefly joys in.
ALSEMERO: I hear the beauty of this seat° largely.°
VERMANDERO: It falls much short of that.　　　*Exeunt [all except]* BEATRICE.
BEATRICE:　　　　　　　　So, here's one step　　　　　　　　10
Into my father's favour; time will fix him.°
I have got him now the liberty of the house:°
So wisdom by degrees works out her freedom;
And if that eye be darkened that offends me°
(I wait but that eclipse), this gentleman　　　　　　　　15

Shall soon shine glorious in my father's liking,
Through the refulgent virtue of my love.

Enter DE FLORES.

DE FLORES [*aside*]: My thoughts are at a banquet. For the deed,
    I feel no weight in't, 'tis but light and cheap
    For the sweet recompense that I set down for't.   20
BEATRICE: De Flores.
DE FLORES: Lady?
BEATRICE: Thy looks promise cheerfully.
DE FLORES: All things are answerable:° time, circumstance,
    Your wishes, and my service.
BEATRICE: Is it done then?
DE FLORES: Piracquo is no more.
BEATRICE: My joys start at mine eyes; our sweet'st delights   25
    Are evermore born weeping.°
DE FLORES: I've a token° for you.
BEATRICE: For me?
DE FLORES: But it was sent somewhat unwillingly;
    I could not get the ring without the finger.   [*He shows the finger.*]
BEATRICE: Bless me! What hast thou done?
DE FLORES: Why, is that more
    Than killing the whole man? I cut his heart-strings.   30
    A greedy hand thrust in a dish at court
    In a mistake hath had as much as this.°
BEATRICE: 'Tis the first token my father made me send him.
DE FLORES: And I made him send it back again
    For his last token; I was loath to leave it,   35
    And I'm sure dead men have no use of jewels.
    He was as loath to part with't, for it stuck
    As if the flesh and it were both one substance.°
BEATRICE: At the stag's fall the keeper has his fees.°
    'Tis soon applied: all dead men's fees are yours, sir.   40
    I pray, bury the finger, but the stone
    You may make use on shortly; the true value,
    Take't of my truth, is near three hundred ducats.
DE FLORES: 'Twill hardly buy a capcase° for one's conscience, though,
    To keep it from the worm,° as fine° as 'tis.   45
    Well, being my fees, I'll take it;
    Great men have taught me that, or else my merit
    Would scorn the way on't.
BEATRICE: It might justly, sir;
    Why, thou mistak'st, De Flores, 'tis not given
    In state of recompense.

DE FLORES: No, I hope so, lady;   50
  You should soon witness my contempt to't then!
BEATRICE: Prithee, thou look'st as if thou wert offended.
DE FLORES: That were strange, lady; 'tis not possible
  My service should draw such a cause° from you.
  Offended? Could you think so? That were much   55
  For one of my performance, and so warm°
  Yet in my service.
BEATRICE: 'Twere misery in me° to give you cause, sir.
DE FLORES: I know so much; it were so, misery
  In her most sharp condition.
BEATRICE: 'Tis resolved then;   60
  Look you, sir, here's three thousand golden florins: [*Offers money.*]
  I have not meanly thought upon thy merit.
DE FLORES: What, salary? Now you move° me!
BEATRICE: How, De Flores?
DE FLORES: Do you place me in the rank of verminous fellows,
  To destroy things for wages? Offer gold?   65
  The life blood of man! Is anything
  Valued too precious for my recompense?
BEATRICE: I understand thee not.
DE FLORES: I could ha' hired
  A journeyman° in murder at this rate,
  And mine own conscience might have slept at ease   70
  And have had the work brought home.
BEATRICE [*aside*]:   I'm in a labyrinth;
  What will content him? I would fain be rid of him.
  — I'll double the sum, sir.
DE FLORES: You take a course
  To double my vexation, that's the good you do.
BEATRICE [*aside*]: Bless me! I am now in worse plight than I was;   75
  I know not what will please him. — For my fear's sake
  I prithee make away with all speed possible.
  And if thou be'st so modest not to name
  The sum that will content thee, paper blushes not;
  Send thy demand in writing, it° shall follow thee.   80
  But prithee take thy flight.
DE FLORES: You must fly too then.
BEATRICE: I?
DE FLORES: I'll not stir a foot else.
BEATRICE: What's your meaning?
DE FLORES: Why, are not you as guilty, in, I'm sure,
  As deep as I? And we should stick together.
  Come, your fears counsel you but ill; my absence   85
  Would draw suspect° upon you instantly;

There were no rescue for you.
BEATRICE [*aside*]:   He speaks home.°
DE FLORES: Nor is it fit we two, engaged so jointly,
    Should part and live asunder.   [*Tries to kiss her.*]
BEATRICE: How now, sir?
    This shows not well.
DE FLORES: What makes your lip so strange?°   90
    This must not be betwixt us.
BEATRICE [*aside*]:   The man talks wildly.
DE FLORES: Come, kiss me with a zeal now.
BEATRICE [*aside*]:   Heaven, I doubt° him!
DE FLORES: I will not stand so long to beg 'em shortly.
BEATRICE: Take heed, De Flores, of forgetfulness,°
    'Twill soon betray us.
DE FLORES: Take you heed first;   95
    Faith, you're grown much forgetful,° you're to blame in't.
BEATRICE [*aside*]: He's bold,° and I am blamed for't!
DE FLORES: I have eased
    You of your trouble, think on't; I'm in pain,
    And must be eased of° you; 'tis ⸱ charity;
    Justice invites your blood° to understand me.   100
BEATRICE: I dare not.
DE FLORES: Quickly!
BEATRICE: O, I never shall!
    Speak it yet further off that I may lose
    What has been spoken, and no sound remain on't.
    I would not hear so much offence again
    For such another deed.
DE FLORES: Soft,° lady, soft;   105
    The last is not yet paid for. Oh, this act
    Has put me into spirit;° I was as greedy on't°
    As the parched earth of moisture, when the clouds weep.
    Did you not mark, I wrought° myself into't,
    Nay, sued and kneeled for't? Why was all that pains took?   110
    You see I have thrown contempt upon your gold;
    Not that I want it not, for I do piteously.
    In order° I will come unto't, and make use on't.
    But 'twas not held so precious to begin with,
    For I place wealth after the heels of pleasure;   115
    And were I not resolved° in my belief
    That thy virginity were perfect in thee,
    I should but take my recompense with grudging,
    As if I had but half my hopes I agreed° for.
BEATRICE: Why, tis impossible thou canst be so wicked,   120
    Or shelter such a cunning cruelty,

To make his death the murderer of my honour!
Thy language is so bold and vicious,
I cannot see which way I can forgive it
With any modesty.
DE FLORES: Push,° you forget yourself!   125
   A woman dipped in blood, and talk of modesty!
BEATRICE: Oh misery of sin! Would I had been bound
   Perpetually unto my living hate
   In that Piracquo, than to hear these words.
   Think but upon the distance that creation   130
   Set 'twixt thy blood° and mine, and keep thee there.
DE FLORES: Look but into your conscience, read me there,
   'Tis a true book, you'll find me there your equal.
   Push! Fly° not to your birth, but settle you
   In what the act has made you, you're no more now;   135
   You must forget your parentage to me.°
   You're the deed's creature; by that name
   You lost your first condition,° and I challenge you,
   As peace and innocency has turned you out,°
   And made you one with me.
BEATRICE: With thee, foul villain?   140
DE FLORES: Yes, my fair murd'ress; do you urge° me?
   Though thou writ'st maid,° thou whore in thy affection!
   'Twas changed from thy first love, and that's a kind
   Of whoredom in thy heart; and he's changed° now,
   To bring thy second° on, thy Alsemero,   145
   Whom (by all sweets that ever darkness tasted)
   If I enjoy thee° not, thou ne'er enjoy'st.
   I'll blast the hopes and joys of marriage,
   I'll confess all; my life I rate at nothing.
BEATRICE: De Flores!   150
DE FLORES: I shall rest from all lovers' plagues then;
   I live in pain now: that shooting° eye
   Will burn my heart to cinders.
BEATRICE: Oh, sir, hear me.
DE FLORES: She that in life and love refuses me,
   In death and shame my partner she shall be.   155
BEATRICE: [*kneels*] Stay, hear me once for all. I make thee master
   Of all the wealth I have in gold and jewels;
   Let me go poor unto my bed with honour,
   And I am rich in all things.
DE FLORES: Let this silence thee:
   The wealth of all Valencia shall not buy   160
   My pleasure from me.
   Can you weep Fate from its determined° purpose?

So soon may you weep me.
BEATRICE: Vengeance begins;
 Murder, I see, is followed by more sins.
 Was my creation in the womb so cursed,   165
 It must engender with a viper first?°
DE FLORES: Come, rise, and shroud your blushes in my bosom;   [*Raises her.*]
 Silence is one of pleasure's best receipts;°
 Thy peace is wrought for ever in this yielding.
 'Las, how the turtle° pants! Thou'lt love anon   170
 What thou so fear'st and faint'st to venture on.   *Exeunt.*

Act Four, Scene One

[*Dumb show.*]

Enter Gentlemen, VERMANDERO *meeting them with action of wonderment at the flight of* PIRACQUO. *Enter* ALSEMERO, *with* JASPERINO *and Gallants;* VERMANDERO *points to him, the Gentlemen seeming to applaud the choice.* [*Exeunt in procession* VERMANDERO,] ALSEMERO, JASPERINO, *and Gentlemen;* BEATRICE *the bride following in great state, accompanied with* DIAPHANTA, ISABELLA, *and other Gentlewomen;* DE FLORES *after all, smiling at the accident.*° ALONZO'S *ghost appears to* DE FLORES *in the midst of his smile, startles him, showing him the hand whose finger he had cut off. They pass over in great solemnity.*

Enter BEATRICE.

BEATRICE: This fellow° has undone me endlessly;°
 Never was bride so fearfully distressed.
 The more I think upon th'ensuing night,
 And whom I am to cope° with in's embraces,
 One who's ennobled both in blood and mind,   5
 So clear in understanding (that's my plague now),
 Before whose judgement will my fault appear
 Like malefactors' crimes before tribunals —
 There is no hiding on't — the more I dive
 Into my own distress. How a wise man   10
 Stands for° a great calamity! There's no venturing
 Into his bed (what course soe'er I light upon)
 Without my shame, which may grow up to danger;°
 He cannot but in justice strangle me
 As I lie by him,° as a cheater use° me.   15
 'Tis a precious° craft to play with a false die°
 Before a cunning gamester.° Here's his closet,°

The key left in't, and he abroad i'th' park;°
Sure 'twas forgot; I'll be so bold as look in't.   [*She opens the closet.*]
Bless me ! A right° physician's closet 'tis,   20
Set round with vials; every one her mark too.
Sure he does practise physic° for his own use,
Which may be safely called your great man's wisdom.°
What manuscript lies here? 'The Book of Experiment,
Called Secrets in Nature'.° So 'tis, 'tis so;   25
'How to know whether a woman be with child or no'.
I hope I am not yet. If he should try, though!
Let me see, folio forty-five. Here 'tis;
The leaf tucked down upon't, the place suspicious.
'If you would know whether a woman be with child or not,   30
Give her two spoonfuls of the white water in glass C.
— Where's that glass C? Oh, yonder, I see't now. —
'And if she be with child she sleeps full twelve hours after; if not,
    not.'
None of that water comes into my belly;   35
I'll know you from a hundred. I could break you now,
Or turn you into milk, and so beguile
The master of the mystery,° but I'll look to you.°
Ha! That which is next is ten times worse:
'How to know whether a woman be a maid or not'.   40
If that should be applied, what would become of me?
Belike he has a strong faith° of my purity,
That never yet made proof;° but this he calls
'A merry sleight, but true experiment, the author Antonius
Mizaldus. Give the party you suspect the quantity of a spoonful of   45
the water in the glass M, which, upon her that is a maid, makes
three several° effects: 'twill make her incontinently° gape, then fall
into a sudden sneezing, last into a violent laughing; else dull,
heavy, and lumpish.'
Where had I been?°   50
I fear it, yet 'tis seven hours to bedtime.

Enter DIAPHANTA.

DIAPHANTA: Cuds,° madam, are you here?
BEATRICE [*aside*]:   Seeing that wench now,
    A trick comes in my mind; 'tis a nice piece°
    Gold cannot purchase. — I come hither, wench,
    To look my lord.   55
DIAPHANTA [*aside*]: Would I had such a cause
    To look him too! — Why, he's i' th' park, madam.
BEATRICE: There let him be.

DIAPHANTA: Ay, madam, let him compass
    Whole parks and forests, as great rangers° do;
    At roosting time° a little lodge° can hold 'em.   60
    Earth-conquering Alexander,° that thought the world
    Too narrow for him, in the end had but his pit-hole.°
BEATRICE: I fear thou art not modest, Diaphanta.
DIAPHANTA: Your thoughts are so unwilling to be known, madam;
    'Tis ever the bride's fashion towards bedtime   65
    To set light by her joys, as if she owed° 'em not.
BEATRICE: Her joys? Her fears, thou would'st say.
DIAPHANTA: Fear of what?
BEATRICE: Art thou a maid, and talk'st so to a maid?
    You leave a blushing business° behind,
    Beshrew your heart for't!
DIAPHANTA: Do you mean good sooth,° madam?   70
BEATRICE: Well, if I'd thought upon the fear at first,
    Man should have been unknown.
DIAPHANTA: Is't possible?
BEATRICE: I will give a thousand ducats to that woman
    Would try what my fear were, and tell me true
    Tomorrow, when she gets from't;° as she likes,   75
    I might perhaps be drawn to't.
DIAPHANTA: Are you in earnest?
BEATRICE: Do you get the woman, then challenge me,
    And see if I'll fly from't; but I must tell you
    This by the way, she must be a true maid,
    Else there's no trial, my fears are not hers else.   80
DIAPHANTA: Nay, she that I would put into your hands, madam,
    Shall be a maid.
BEATRICE: You know I should be shamed else,
    Because she lies° for me.
DIAPHANTA: 'Tis a strange humour;°
    But are you serious still? Would you resign
    Your first night's pleasure, and give money too?   85
BEATRICE: As willingly as live; [*aside*] alas, the gold
    Is but a by-bet to wedge in the honour.°
DIAPHANTA: I do not know how the world° goes abroad
    For faith or honesty; there's both required in this.
    Madam, what say you to me, and stray no further?   90
    I've a good mind, in troth,° to earn your money.
BEATRICE: You're too quick,° I fear, to be a maid.
DIAPHANTA: How? Not a maid? Nay, then you urge° me, madam;
    Your honourable self is not a truer°
    With all your fears upon you —
BEATRICE [*aside*]:   Bad enough then.   95

DIAPHANTA: Than I with all my lightsome° joys about me.
BEATRICE: I'm glad to hear't; then you dare put your honesty
    Upon an easy trial?
DIAPHANTA: Easy? Anything.
BEATRICE: I'll come to you straight.   [*Goes to the closet.*]
DIAPHANTA [*aside*]:   She will not search me, will she,
    Like the forewoman of a female jury?°   100
BEATRICE: Glass M; ay, this is it. — Look, Diaphanta,
    You take no worse than I do.   [*Drinks.*]
DIAPHANTA: And in so doing,
    I will not question what 'tis, but take it.   [*Drinks.*]
BEATRICE [*aside*]: Now if the experiment be true,° 'twill praise itself,
    And give me noble ease: — begins already;   [*DIAPHANTA gapes.*] 105
    There's the first symptom; and what haste it makes
    To fall into the second, there by this time!   [*DIAPHANTA sneezes.*]
    Most admirable secret! On the contrary,
    It stirs me not a whit, which most concerns it.°
DIAPHANTA: Ha, ha, ha!   110
BEATRICE [*aside*]: Just in all things and in order,
    As if 'twere circumscribed;° one accident°
    Gives way unto another.
DIAPHANTA: Ha, ha, ha!
BEATRICE: How now, wench?
DIAPHANTA: Ha, ha, ha! I am so, so light
    At heart — ha, ha, ha ! — so pleasurable.   115
    But one swig more, sweet madam.
BEATRICE: Ay, tomorrow;
    We shall have time to sit by't.
DIAPHANTA: Now I'm sad° again.
BEATRICE [*aside*]: It lays itself° so gently, too! — Come, wench,
    Most honest Diaphanta I dare call thee now.
DIAPHANTA: Pray tell me, madam, what trick call you this?   120
BEATRICE: I'll tell thee all hereafter; we must study
    The carriage° of this business.
DIAPHANTA: I shall carry't° well,
    Because I love the burthen.°
BEATRICE: About midnight
    You must not fail to steal forth gently,
    That I may use the place.
DIAPHANTA: Oh, fear not, madam,   125
    I shall be cool by that time. — The bride's place,
    And with a thousand ducats! I'm for a justice° now,
    I bring a portion° with me; I scorn small fools.   *Exeunt.*

Act Four, Scene Two

Enter VERMANDERO *and* SERVANT.

VERMANDERO: I tell you, knave,° mine honour is in question,
    A thing till now free from suspicion,
    Nor ever was there cause. Who of my gentlemen
    Are absent? Tell me and truly how many and who.
SERVANT: Antonio, sir, and Franciscus.   5
VERMANDERO: When did they leave the castle?
SERVANT: Some ten days since, sir, the one intending to
    Briamata,° th'other for Valencia.
VERMANDERO: The time accuses 'em. A charge of murder
    Is brought within my castle gate, Piracquo's murder;   10
    I dare not answer faithfully° their absence.
    A strict command of apprehension
    Shall pursue 'em suddenly,° and either wipe
    The stain off clear, or openly discover° it.
    Provide me winged warrants for the purpose.   *Exit* SERVANT. 15
    See, I am set on° again.

Enter TOMAZO.

TOMAZO: I claim a brother of you.
VERMANDERO: You're too hot;
    Seek him not here.
TOMAZO: Yes, 'mongst your dearest bloods,°
    If my peace find no fairer satisfaction;
    This is the place must yield account for him,   20
    For here I left him, and the hasty tie
    Of this snatched° marriage gives strong testimony
    Of his most certain ruin.
VERMANDERO: Certain falsehood!
    This is the place indeed; his breach of faith
    Has too much marred both my abusèd love,   25
    The honourable love I reserved for him,
    And mocked my daughter's joy; the prepared morning
    Blushed at his infidelity; he left
    Contempt and scorn to throw upon those friends
    Whose belief° hurt 'em. Oh 'twas most ignoble   30
    To take his flight so unexpectedly,
    And throw such public wrongs on those that loved him.
TOMAZO: Then this is all your answer?
VERMANDERO: 'Tis too fair

For one of his alliance;° and I warn you
That this place no more see you.   *Exit.*

Enter DE FLORES.

TOMAZO: The best is,   35
    There is more ground to meet a man's revenge on.
    — Honest De Flores?
DE FLORES: That's my name indeed.
    Saw you the bride? Good sweet sir, which way took she?
TOMAZO: I have blessed° mine eyes from seeing such a false one.
DE FLORES [*aside*]: I'd fain get off; this man's not for my company.   40
    I smell his brother's blood when I come near him.
TOMAZO: Come hither, kind and true one; I remember
    My brother loved thee well.
DE FLORES: Oh purely, dear sir!
    [*Aside*] Methinks I am now again a-killing on him,
    He brings it so fresh to me.
TOMAZO: Thou canst guess, sirrah   45
    (One honest friend has an instinct of jealousy),°
    At some foul guilty person?
DE FLORES: 'Las, sir,
    I am so charitable I think none
    Worse than myself. — You did not see the bride then?
TOMAZO: I prithee name her not. Is she not wicked?   50
DE FLORES: No, no, a pretty, easy, round-packed° sinner,
    As your most ladies are, else you might think
    I flattered her; but, sir, at no hand° wicked,
    Till they're so old their chins and noses meet,
    And they salute° witches. I am called, I think, sir.   55
    [*Aside*] His company ev'n o'erlays° my conscience.   *Exit.*
TOMAZO: That De Flores has a wondrous honest heart;
    He'll bring it out in time, I'm assured on't.
    Oh, here's the glorious° master of the day's joy;
    'Twill not be long till he and I do reckon.°   60

Enter ALSEMERO.

    Sir!
ALSEMERO: You are most welcome.
    TOMAZO: You may call that word back;
    I do not think I am, nor wish to be.
ALSEMERO: 'Tis strange you found the way to this house then.
TOMAZO: Would I'd ne'er known the cause! I'm none of those, sir,
    That come to give you joy and swill your wine;   65

'Tis a more precious liquor that must lay°
    The fiery thirst I bring.
ALSEMERO: Your words and you
    Appear to me great strangers.
TOMAZO: Time and our swords
    May make us more acquainted. This the business:
    I should have a brother in your place;   70
    How treachery and malice have disposed of him,
    I'm bound to inquire of him which holds his right,°
    Which never could come fairly.
ALSEMERO: You must look
    To answer for that word, sir.
TOMAZO: Fear you not,
    I'll have it° ready drawn at our next meeting.   75
    Keep your day solemn.° Farewell; I disturb it not.
    I'll bear the smart with patience for a time.   *Exit.*
ALSEMERO: 'Tis somewhat ominous this, a quarrel entered
    Upon this day. My innocence relieves me;

Enter JASPERINO.

    I should be wondrous sad else. — Jasperino,   80
    I have news to tell thee, strange news.
JASPERINO: I ha' some too,
    I think as strange as yours; would I might keep
    Mine, so my faith and friendship might be kept in't!
    Faith, sir, dispense a little with my zeal,°
    And let it cool in this.
ALSEMERO: This puts me on,°   85
    And blames thee for thy slowness.
JASPERINO: All may prove nothing;
    Only a friendly fear that leapt from me, sir.
ALSEMERO: No question it may prove nothing; let's partake° it, though.
JASPERINO: 'Twas Diaphanta's chance (for to that wench
    I pretend° honest love, and she deserves it)   90
    To leave me in a back part of the house,
    A place we chose for private conference.
    She was no sooner gone, but instantly
    I heard your bride's voice in the next room to me;
    And, lending more attention, found De Flores   95
    Louder than she.
ALSEMERO: De Flores? Thou art out° now.
JASPERINO: You'll tell me more anon.
ALSEMERO: Still I'll prevent thee:°
    The very sight of him is poison to her.

JASPERINO: That made me stagger° too, but Diaphanta
    At her return confirmed it.
ALSEMERO: Diaphanta!   100
JASPERINO: Then fell we both to listen, and words passed
    Like those that challenge interest° in a woman.
ALSEMERO: Peace! quench thy zeal; 'tis dangerous to thy bosom.
JASPERINO: Then truth is full of peril.
ALSEMERO: Such truths are.
    — Oh, were she the sole glory of the earth,   105
    Had eyes that could shoot fire into kings' breasts,
    And touched,° she sleeps not here! Yet I have time,
    Though night be near, to be resolved° hereof;
    And prithee,° do not weigh me by my passions.
JASPERINO: I never weighed friend so.
ALSEMERO: Done charitably.   110
    That key will lead thee to a pretty secret   [*Gives key.*]
    By a Chaldean° taught me, and I've made
    My study upon some. Bring from my closet
    A glass inscribed there with the letter M,
    And question not my purpose.
JASPERINO: It shall be done, sir.   *Exit.* 115
ALSEMERO: How can this hang together? Not an hour since,
    Her woman came pleading her lady's fears,
    Delivered her for the most timorous virgin
    That ever shrunk at man's name, and so modest,
    She charged her weep out her request to me   120
    That she° might come obscurely° to my bosom.

Enter BEATRICE.

BEATRICE [*aside*]: All things go well. My woman's preparing yonder
    For her sweet voyage, which grieves me to lose;
    Necessity compels it, I lose all else.
ALSEMERO [*aside*]: Push! Modesty's shrine is set in yonder forehead.   125
    I cannot be too sure though. — My Joanna!
BEATRICE: Sir, I was bold to weep a message to you;
    Pardon my modest fears.
ALSEMERO [*aside*]:   The dove's not meeker;
    She's abused,° questionless.

Enter JASPERINO [*with glass*].

                — O, are you come, sir?
BEATRICE [*aside*]: The glass, upon my life! I see the letter.   130
JASPERINO: Sir, this is M.

ALSEMERO: 'Tis it.
BEATRICE [*aside*]:   I am suspected.
ALSEMERO: How fitly our bride comes to partake with us!
BEATRICE: What is't, my lord?
ALSEMERO: No hurt.
BEATRICE: Sir, pardon me,
   I seldom taste of any composition.°
ALSEMERO: But this, upon my warrant,° you shall venture on.   135
BEATRICE: I fear 'twill make me ill.
ALSEMERO: Heaven forbid that!
BEATRICE [*aside*]: I'm put now to my cunning; th' effects I know,
   If I can now but feign 'em handsomely.   [*She drinks.*]
ALSEMERO [*to* JASPERINO]: It has that secret virtue,° it ne'er missed, sir,
   Upon a virgin.
JASPERINO: Treble qualitied?   [BEATRICE *gapes, then sneezes.*]   140
ALSEMERO: By all that's virtuous, it takes° there, proceeds!
JASPERINO: This is the strangest trick to know a maid by.
BEATRICE: Ha, ha, ha!
   You have given me joy of heart to drink, my lord.
ALSEMERO: No, thou hast given me such joy of heart   145
   That never can be blasted.
BEATRICE: What's the matter, sir?
ALSEMERO [*to* JASPERINO]: See, now 'tis settled in a melancholy,
   Keeps both the time and method. —° My Joanna,
   Chaste as the breath of heaven, or morning's womb
   That brings the day forth, thus my love encloses thee.   150
                         [*Embraces her.*] *Exeunt.*

Act Four, Scene Three

Enter ISABELLA *and* LOLLIO.

ISABELLA: Oh heaven! Is this the waxing° moon?
   Does love turn fool, run mad, and all at once?
   Sirrah, here's a madman, akin to the fool too,
   A lunatic lover.
LOLLIO: No, no, not he I brought the letter from?   5
ISABELLA: Compare his inside° with his out,° and tell me.
                        [*Gives him the letter.*]
LOLLIO: The out's mad, I'm sure of that; I had a taste on't. [*Reads.*] 'To
   the bright Andromeda,° chief chambermaid to the Knight of the
   Sun,° at the sign of Scorpio, in the middle region,° sent by the
   bellows-mender of Aeolus.° Pay the post.' This is stark madness.   10

ISABELLA: Now mark the inside.   [*Takes the letter and reads.*]
  'Sweet lady, having now cast off this counterfeit cover of a
  madman, I appear to your best judgement a true and faithful lover
  of your beauty.'
LOLLIO: He is mad° still.   15
ISABELLA: 'If any fault you find, chide those perfections in you which
  have made me imperfect; 'tis the same sun that causeth to grow
  and enforceth to wither, — '
LOLLIO: Oh rogue!
ISABELLA: '— Shapes and transhapes, destroys and builds again; I come   20
  in winter to you dismantled° of my proper ornaments;° by the
  sweet splendour of your cheerful smiles, I spring° and live a lover.'
LOLLIO: Mad rascal still!
ISABELLA: 'Tread him not under foot, that shall appear an honour to
  your bounties. I remain — mad till I speak with you, from whom I   25
  expect my cure. Yours all, or one beside himself, Franciscus.'
LOLLIO: You are like to have a fine time on't; my master and I may give
  over our professions.° I do not think but you can cure fools and
  madmen faster than we, with little pains too.
ISABELLA: Very likely.   30
LOLLIO: One thing I must tell you, mistress: you perceive that I am
  privy to your skill; if I find you minister once and set up the trade,°
  I put in for my thirds;° I shall be mad or fool else.
ISABELLA: The first place° is thine, believe it, Lollio, If I do fall —
LOLLIO: I fall upon you.   35
ISABELLA: So.
LOLLIO: Well, I stand to my venture.°
ISABELLA: But thy counsel now; how shall I deal with 'em?
LOLLIO: Why, do you mean to deal° with 'em?
ISABELLA: Nay, the fair understanding,° how to use 'em.   40
LOLLIO: Abuse 'em! That's the way to mad the fool, and make a fool of
  the madman, and then you use 'em kindly.°
ISABELLA: 'Tis easy, I'll practise;° do thou observe it. The key of thy
  wardrobe.
LOLLIO: There; fit yourself for 'em, and I'll fit 'em both for you.   45
                                                      [*Gives her the key.*]
ISABELLA: Take thou no further notice than the outside.°   *Exit.*
LOLLIO: Not an inch; I'll put you to the inside.°

                              Enter ALIBIUS.

ALIBIUS: Lollio, art there? Will all be perfect, think'st thou?
  Tomorrow night, as if to close up the solemnity,
  Vermandero expects us.   50

LOLLIO: I mistrust the madmen most; the fools will do well enough, I
have taken pains with them.

ALIBIUS: Tush, they cannot miss;° the more absurdity
The more commends it, so° no rough behaviours
Affright the ladies; they are nice° things, thou know'st. 55

LOLLIO: You need not fear, sir; so long as we are there with our
commanding pizzles,° they'll be as tame as the ladies themselves.

ALIBIUS: I will see them once more rehearse before they go.

LOLLIO: I was about it, sir; look you to the madmen's morris,° and let
me alone with the other. There is one or two that I mistrust their 60
fooling;° I'll instruct them, and then they shall rehearse the whole
measure.°

ALIBIUS: Do so; I'll see the music prepared. But Lollio,
By the way, how does my wife brook her restraint?
Does she not grudge at it? 65

LOLLIO: So, So; she takes some pleasure in the house, she would abroad
else. You must allow her a little more length, she's kept too short.

ALIBIUS: She shall go along to Vermandero's with us;
That will serve her for a month's liberty.

LOLLIO: What's that on your face, sir? 70

ALIBIUS: Where, Lollio? I see nothing.

LOLLIO: Cry you mercy, sir, 'tis your nose;° it showed like the trunk of
a young elephant.

ALIBIUS: Away, rascal! I'll prepare the music, Lollio. *Exit* ALIBIUS.

LOLLIO: Do, sir, and I'll dance the whilst. Tony, where art thou, Tony? 75

Enter ANTONIO.

ANTONIO: Here, cousin; where art thou?

LOLLIO: Come, Tony, the footmanship° I taught you.

ANTONIO: I had rather ride,° cousin.

LOLLIO: Ay, a whip take you; but I'll keep you out.
Vault in; look you, Tony: fa, la, la, la, la. [*Dances.*] 80

ANTONIO: Fa, la, la, la, la. [*Dances.*]

LOLLIO: There, an honour.°

ANTONIO: Is this an honour, cuz?° [*Bows.*]

LOLLIO: Yes, and it please your worship.°

ANTONIO: Does honour° bend in the hams,° cuz? 85

LOLLIO: Marry, does it, as low as worship, squireship, nay, yeomandry
itself sometimes, from whence it first stiffened.° There, rise; a caper.°

ANTONIO: Caper after an honour, cuz?

LOLLIO: Very proper; for honour is but a caper, rises as fast and high,
has a knee or two, and falls to th' ground again. You can remember 90
your figure,° Tony? *Exit.*

ANTONIO: Yes, cousin; when I see thy figure, I can remember mine.

[*Capers.*]

Enter ISABELLA [*like a madwoman*].

ISABELLA: Hey, how he treads the air!° Shough, shough,° t'other way!
    He burns his wings else. Here's wax enough below,°
    Icarus, more than will be cancelled these eighteen moons.

[ANTONIO *falls.*] 95

    He's down, he's down! What a terrible fall he had!
    Stand up, thou son of Cretan Dedalus,
    And let us tread the lower labyrinth;
    I'll bring thee to the clue.°   [ANTONIO *rises.*]
ANTONIO: Prithee, cuz, let me alone.   100
ISABELLA: Art thou now drowned?
    About thy head I saw a heap of clouds,
    Wrapped like a Turkish turban; on thy back
    A crooked chameleon-coloured rainbow hung
    Like a tiara° down unto thy hams.   105
    Let me suck out those billows in thy belly;°
    Hark how they roar and rumble in the straits!°
    Bless thee° from the pirates.°
ANTONIO: Pox upon you; let me alone!°
ISABELLA: Why shouldst thou mount so high as Mercury,°   110
    Unless thou hadst reversion° of his place?
    Stay in the moon with me, Endymion,°
    And we will rule these wild, rebellious waves,
    That would have drowned my love.
ANTONIO: I'll kick thee if again thou touch me,   115
    Thou wild unshapen antic;° I am no fool,
    You bedlam!°
ISABELLA: But you are, as sure as I am, mad.
    Have I put on this habit° of a frantic,
    With love as full of fury, to beguile
    The nimble eye of watchful jealousy,   120
    And am I thus rewarded?   [*She reveals herself.*]
ANTONIO: Ha, dearest beauty!
ISABELLA: No, I have no beauty now,
    Nor never had, but what was in my garments.
    You, a quick-sighted° lover? Come not near me!
    Keep your caparisons,° you're aptly clad;   125
    I came a feigner, to return stark mad.°   *Exit.*

Enter LOLLIO.

ANTONIO (*to* ISABELLA): Stay, or I shall change condition,
    And become as you are.

LOLLIO: Why, Tony, whither now? Why, fool?

ANTONIO: Whose fool, usher° of idiots? You coxcomb! 130
    I have fooled too much.

LOLLIO: You were best be mad another while then.

ANTONIO: So I am, stark mad. I have cause enough;
    And I could throw the full effects on thee,
    And beat thee like a Fury!° 135

LOLLIO: Do not, do not; I shall not forbear° the gentleman under the fool,
    if you do. Alas, I saw through your fox-skin° before now. Come, I can
    give you comfort; my mistress loves you, and there is as arrant a
    madman i' th' house as you are a fool, your rival, whom she loves
    not. If after the masque° we can rid her of him, you earn her love, she 140
    says, and the fool shall ride° her.

ANTONIO: May I believe thee?

LOLLIO: Yes, or you may choose whether you will or no.

ANTONIO: She's eased of him; I have a good quarrel on't.°

LOLLIO: Well, keep your old station yet, and be quiet. 145

ANTONIO: Tell her I will deserve her love.   [*Exit.*]

LOLLIO: And you are like to have your desire.

Enter FRANCISCUS.

FRANCISCUS [*sings*]: 'Down, down, down a-down a-down', and then
    with a horse-trick,°
    To kick° Latona's forehead, and break her bowstring. 150

LOLLIO: This is t'other counterfeit; I'll put him out of his humour.° [*Takes
    out letter and reads.*] 'Sweet lady, having now cast off this counterfeit
    cover of a madman, I appear to your best judgement a true and
    faithful lover of your heauty.' — This is pretty well for a madman.

FRANCISCUS: Ha! What's that? 155

LOLLIO: 'Chide those perfections in you which have made me imperfect.'

FRANCISCUS: I am discovered to the fool.

LOLLIO: I hope to discover the fool in you, ere I have done with you.
    'Yours all, or one beside himself, Franciscus.' — This madman will
    mend sure. 160

FRANCISCUS: What do you read, sirrah?

LOLLIO: Your destiny, sir; you'll be hanged for this trick,° and another
    that I know.

FRANCISCUS: Art thou of counsel with thy mistress?

LOLLIO: Next° her apron strings. 165

FRANCISCUS: Give me thy hand.

LOLLIO: Stay, let me put yours° in my pocket first. [*Puts away the letter.*]
    Your hand is true, is it not? It will not pick? I partly fear it, because I 170
    think it does lie.

FRANCISCUS: Not in a syllable.

LOLLIO: So; if you love my mistress so well as you have handled the
    matter here, you are like to be cured of your madness.

FRANCISCUS: And none but she can cure it.

LOLLIO: Well, I'll give you over° then, and she shall cast your water° next.

FRANCISCUS: Take for thy pains past. [*Gives him money*]   175

LOLLIO: I shall deserve more, sir, I hope; my mistress loves you, but
    must have some proof of your love to her.

FRANCISCUS: There I meet my wishes.

LOLLIO: That will not serve;° you must meet her enemy and yours.

FRANCISCUS: He's dead already!   180

LOLLIO: Will you tell me that, and I parted but now with him?

FRANCISCUS: Show me the man.

LOLLIO: Ay, that's a right course now. See him before you kill him in any
    case; and yet it needs not go so far neither, 'tis but a fool that
    haunts the house and my mistress in the shape° of an idiot. Bang°   185
    but his fool's coat well-favouredly,° and 'tis well.

FRANCISCUS: Soundly, soundly!

LOLLIO: Only reserve him till the masque be past; and if you find him
    not now in the dance yourself, I'll show you. In, in! My master!

FRANCISCUS: He handles° him like a feather. Hey!   [*Exit dancing.*] 190

Enter ALIBIUS.

ALIBIUS: Well said.° In a readiness, Lollio?

LOLLIO: Yes, sir.

ALIBIUS: Away then, and guide them in, Lollio;
    Entreat your mistress to see this sight.
    Hark, is there not one incurable fool
    That might be begged?° I have friends.   195

LOLLIO: I have him° for you, one that shall deserve it too.   [*Exit.*]

ALIBIUS: Good boy, Lollio.

[*Enter* ISABELLA, *then* LOLLIO *with* Madmen *and* Fools.]

The Madmen *and* Fools *dance.*

ALIBIUS: 'Tis perfect; well, fit we but once these strains,°
    We shall have coin and credit° for our pains.   *Exeunt.* 200

Act Five, Scene One

Enter BEATRICE. *A clock strikes one.*

BEATRICE: One struck, and yet she lies by't!° Oh my fears!
    This strumpet serves her own ends, 'tis apparent now,
    Devours the pleasure with a greedy appetite,

And never minds my honour° or my peace,
Makes havoc of my right. But she pays dearly for't: 5
No trusting of her life with such a secret,
That cannot rule her blood° to keep her promise.
Beside, I have some suspicion of her faith to me,
Because I was suspected of my lord,
And it must come from her. Hark! By my horrors,   10
Another clock strikes two.   [*A clock*] *strikes two.*

Enter DE FLORES.

DE FLORES: Pist! Where are you?
BEATRICE: De Flores?
DE FLORES: Ay. Is she not come from him yet?
BEATRICE: As I am a living soul, not.
DE FLORES: Sure the devil
    Hath sowed his itch within her. Who'd trust
    A waiting-woman?
BEATRICE: I must trust somebody.   15
DE FLORES: Push, they are termagants,°
    Especially when they fall upon their masters
    And have their ladies' first-fruits; they're mad whelps,
    You cannot stave 'em off from game royal.° Then
    You are so harsh and hardy,° ask no counsel;   20
    And I could have helped you to an apothecary's° daughter,
    Would have fall'n off° before eleven, and thanked you too.
BEATRICE: Oh me, not yet? This whore forgets herself.
DE FLORES: The rascal fares so well. Look, you're undone;
    The day-star, by this hand! See Phosphorus° plain yonder.   25
BEATRICE: Advise me now to fall upon some ruin;°
    There is no counsel safe else.
DE FLORES: Peace, I ha't now;
    For we must force a rising,° there's no remedy.
BEATRICE: How? Take heed of that.
DE FLORES: Tush, be you quiet
    Or else give over all.
BEATRICE: Prithee, I ha' done then.   30
DE FLORES: This is my reach:° I'll set some part a-fire
    Of Diaphanta's chamber.
BEATRICE: How? Fire, sir?
    That may endanger the whole house.
DE FLORES: You talk of danger when your fame's on fire?
BEATRICE: That's true; do what thou wilt now.
DE FLORES: Push! I aim   35
    At a most rich success, strikes all dead sure:

The chimney being a-fire, and some light parcels°
Of the least danger in her chamber only,
If Diaphanta should be met by chance then,
Far from her lodging (which is now suspicious),   40
It would be thought her fears and affrights then
Drove her to seek for succour. If not seen
Or met at all, as that's the likeliest,
For her own shame she'll hasten towards her lodging;
I will be ready with a piece high-charged,°   45
As 'twere to cleanse the chimney. There, 'tis proper,°
But she shall be the mark.
BEATRICE: I'm forced to love thee now,
   'Cause thou provid'st so carefully for my honour.
DE FLORES: 'Slid,° it concerns the safety of us both,
   Our pleasure and continuance.
BEATRICE: One word now, prithee: 50
   How for the servants?
DE FLORES: I'll despatch them,
   Some one way, some another in the hurry,
   For buckets, hooks, ladders. Fear not you;
   The deed shall find its time;° and I've thought since
   Upon a safe conveyance for the body too.   55
   How this fire purifies wit!° Watch you your minute.
BEATRICE: Fear keeps my soul upon't, I cannot stray from't.

Enter ALONZO'S *Ghost.*

DE FLORES: Ha! What art thou that tak'st away the light
   'Twixt that star and me? I dread thee not.
   'Twas but a mist of conscience — all's clear again.   *Exit.* 60
BEATRICE: Who's that, De Flores? Bless me! It slides by!   [*Exit Ghost.*]
   Some ill thing haunts the house; 't has left behind it
   A shivering sweat upon me. I'm afraid now.
   This night hath been so tedious. Oh, this strumpet!
   Had she a thousand lives, he should not leave her   65
   Till he had destroyed the last. — List! Oh my terrors!
                      [*A clock strikes*] *three o'clock.*
   Three struck by Saint Sebastian's!
[*Voice*] *within:* Fire, fire, fire!
BEATRICE: Already? How rare is that man's speed!
   How heartily he serves me! His face loathes° one,   70
   But look upon his care, who would not love him?
   The east is not more beauteous than his service.
[*Voice*] *within:* Fire, fire, fire!

Enter DE FLORES; Servants *pass over,°* ring *a bell.*

DE FLORES: Away, despatch! Hooks, buckets, ladders! — that's well said;
    The fire-bell rings, the chimney works;° my charge;°   75
    The piece is ready.   *Exit.*
BEATRICE: Here's a man worth loving —

Enter DIAPHANTA.

    Oh, you're a jewel.
DIAPHANTA: Pardon frailty, madam;
    In troth I was so well,° I ev'n forgot myself.
BEATRICE: You've made trim° work.
DIAPHANTA: What?
BEATRICE: Hie quickly to your chamber;
    Your reward follows you.
DIAPHANTA: I never made   80
    So sweet a bargain.   *Exit.*

Enter ALSEMERO.

ALSEMERO: O my dear Joanna,
    Alas, art thou risen too? I was coming,
    My absolute treasure.
BEATRICE: When I missed you,
    I could not choose but follow.
ALSEMERO: Th'art all sweetness!
    The fire is not so dangerous.
BEATRICE: Think you so, sir?   85
ALSEMERO: I prithee tremble not; believe me, 'tis not.

Enter VERMANDERO *and* JASPERINO.

VERMANDERO: O bless my house and me!
ALSEMERO: My lord your father.

Enter DE FLORES, *with a piece.*

VERMANDERO: Knave, whither goes that piece?
DE FLORES: To scour the chimney.   *Exit.*
VERMANDERO: Oh, well said,° well said;
    That fellow's good on all occasions.   90
BEATRICE: A wondrous necessary man, my lord.
VERMANDERO: He hath a ready wit, he's worth em all, sir;
    Dog° at a house of fire; I ha' seen him singed ere now. *The piece goes off.*

— Ha, there he goes.
BEATRICE: Tis done.
ALSEMERO: Come, sweet, to bed now;
    Thou wilt get cold.
BEATRICE: Alas, the fear keeps that out;   95
    My heart will find no quiet till I hear
    How Diaphanta, my poor woman, fares;
    It is her chamber, sir, her lodging chamber.
VERMANDERO: How should the fire come there?
BEATRICE: As good a soul as ever lady countenanced,°   100
    But in her chamber negligent and heavy;°
    She 'scaped a mine° twice.
VERMANDERO: Twice?
BEATRICE: Strangely° twice, sir.
VERMANDERO: Those sleepy sluts are dangerous in a house,
    And they be ne'er so good.

Enter DE FLORES.°

DE FLORES: O poor virginity,
    Thou hast paid dearly for't!
VERMANDERO: Bless us! What's that?   105
DE FLORES: A thing you all knew once — Diaphanta's burnt.
BEATRICE: My woman, oh my woman!
DE FLORES: Now the flames
    Are greedy of her; burnt, burnt, burnt to death, sir!
BEATRICE: Oh, my presaging soul!
ALSEMERO: Not a tear more;
    I charge you by the last embrace I gave you   110
    In bed before this raised us.
BEATRICE: Now you tie me;
    Were it my sister, now she gets no more.°

Enter SERVANT.

VERMANDERO: How now?
SERVANT: All danger's past; you may now take your rests, my lords, the
    fire is throughly° quenched. — Ah, poor gentlewoman, how soon   115
    was she stifled!
BEATRICE: De Flores, what is left of her inter,
    And we as mourners all will follow her;
    I will entreat that honour to my servant,
    Ev'n of my lord himself.
ALSEMERO: Command it, sweetness.   120
BEATRICE: Which of you spied the fire first?

DE FLORES: 'Twas I, madam.
BEATRICE: And took such pains in't too? A double goodness!
　　'Twere well he were rewarded.
VERMANDERO: He shall be;
　　De Flores, call upon me.
ALSEMERO: And upon me, sir. *Exeunt* [*all except* DE FLORES.]
DE FLORES: Rewarded? Precious! Here's a trick beyond me;   125
　　I see in all bouts, both of sport° and wit,
　　Always a woman strives for the last hit.   *Exit.*

Act Five, Scene Two

Enter TOMAZO.

TOMAZO: I cannot taste the benefits of life
　　With the same relish I was wont to do.
　　Man I grow weary of, and hold his fellowship
　　A treacherous, bloody friendship; and because
　　I am ignorant in° whom my wrath should settle,   5
　　I must think all men villains, and the next
　　I meet, whoe'er he be, the murderer
　　Of my most worthy brother. — Ha! What's he?

Enter DE FLORES, *passes over the stage.*

　　Oh, the fellow that some call honest De Flores;
　　But methinks honesty was hard bested°   10
　　To come there for a lodging — as if a queen
　　Should make her palace of a pest-house.°
　　I find a contrariety in nature
　　Betwixt that face and me: the least occasion
　　Would give me game upon him.° Yet he's so foul   15
　　One would scarce touch him with a sword he loved
　　And made account of;° so most deadly venomous,
　　He would go near to poison any weapon
　　That should draw blood on° him. One must resolve
　　Never to use that sword again in fight,   20
　　In way of honest manhood, that strikes him;
　　Some river must devour't, 'twere not fit
　　That any man should find it. What, again?

Enter DE FLORES.

　　He walks a' purpose by, sure, to choke me up,°

    To infect my blood.

DE FLORES: My worthy noble lord.   25

TOMAZO: Dost offer to come near and breathe upon me?   [*Strikes him.*]

DE FLORES: A blow!   [*Draws his sword.*]

TOMAZO: Yea, are you so prepared?

    I'll rather, like a soldier, die by th' sword.   [*Draws.*]

    Than like a politician° by thy poison.

DE FLORES: Hold, my lord, as you are honourable.   30

TOMAZO: All slaves that kill by poison are still° cowards.

DE FLORES [*aside*]: I cannot strike; I see his brother's wounds

    Fresh bleeding in his eye, as in a crystal. —°

    [*To* TOMAZO] I will not question this; I know you're noble;

    I take my injury with thanks given, sir,   35

    Like a wise lawyer; and as a favour

    Will wear it for the worthy hand that gave it. —

    [*Aside*] Why this from him that yesterday appeared

    So strangely loving to me?

    Oh, but instinct is of a subtler strain;   40

    Guilt must not walk so near his lodge again;

    He came near me now.   *Exit.*

TOMAZO: All league with mankind I renounce for ever,

    Till I find this murderer; not so much

    As common courtesy, but I'll lock up:°   45

    For in the state of ignorance I live in,

    A brother may salute° his brother's murderer,

    And wish good speed to th' villain in a greeting.

              Enter VERMANDERO, ALIBIUS *and* ISABELLA.

VERMANDERO: Noble Piracquo!

TOMAZO: Pray keep on your way, sir,

    I've nothing to say to you.

VERMANDERO: Comforts bless you, sir.   50

TOMAZO: I have forsworn compliment,° in troth I have, sir;

    As you are merely man, I have not left

    A good wish for you, nor any here.

VERMANDERO: Unless you be so far in love with grief

    You will not part from't upon any terms,   55

    We bring that news will make a welcome for us.

TOMAZO: What news can that be?

VERMANDERO: Throw no scornful smile

    Upon the zeal° I bring you, 'tis worth more, sir.

    Two of the chiefest men I kept about me

    I hide not from the law or your just vengeance.   60

TOMAZO: Ha!

VERMANDERO: To give your peace more ample satisfaction,
    Thank these discoverers.
TOMAZO: If you bring that calm,
    Name but the manner I shall ask forgiveness in
    For that contemptuous smile upon you;   65
    I'll perfect it with reverence that belongs
    Unto a sacred altar.   [*Kneels.*]
VERMANDERO: Good sir, rise;
    Why, now you overdo as much a' this hand
    As you fell short a' t'other. Speak, Alibius.
ALIBIUS: Twas my wife's fortune, as she is most lucky   70
    At a discovery, to find out lately
    Within our hospital of fools and madmen
    Two counterfeits slipped into these disguises:
    Their names, Franciscus and Antonio.
VERMANDERO: Both mine, sir, and I ask no favour for 'em.   75
ALIBIUS: Now that which draws suspicion to their habits,°
    The time of their disguisings agrees justly°
    With the day of the murder.
TOMAZO: O blest revelation!
VERMANDERO: Nay more, nay more, sir (I'll not spare mine own
    In way of justice), they both feigned a journey°   80
    To Briamata, and so wrought° out their leaves.
    My love was so abused in't.
TOMAZO: Time's too precious
    To run in waste now; you have brought a peace
    The riches of five kingdoms could not purchase.
    Be my most happy conduct;° I thirst for 'em;   85
    Like subtle lightning will I wind about 'em,
    And melt their marrow in 'em.°   *Exeunt.*

Act Five, Scene Three

Enter ALSEMERO *and* JASPERINO.

JASPERINO: Your confidence, I'm sure, is now of proof;°
    The prospect from the garden has showed
    Enough for deep suspicion.
ALSEMERO: The black mask°
    That so continually was worn upon't
    Condemns the face for ugly ere't be seen: 5
    Her despite° to him, and so seeming bottomless.
JASPERINO: Touch it home° then; 'tis not a shallow probe
    Can search this ulcer soundly; I fear you'll find it

Full of corruption. 'Tis fit I leave you;
She meets you opportunely from that walk.   10
She took the back door at his parting with her.   *Exit* JASPERINO.
ALSEMERO: Did my fate wait for this unhappy stroke
  At my first sight of woman? — She's here.

Enter BEATRICE.

BEATRICE: Alsemero!
ALSEMERO: How do you?
BEATRICE: How do I?
  Alas! How do you? You look not well.   15
ALSEMERO: You read me well enough; I am not well.
BEATRICE: Not well, sir? Is't in my power to better you?
ALSEMERO: Yes.
BEATRICE: Nay, then you're cured again.
ALSEMERO: Pray resolve me° one question, lady.
BEATRICE: If I can.
ALSEMERO: None can so sure. Are you honest?°   20
BEATRICE: Ha, ha, ha! That's a broad° question, my lord.
ALSEMERO: But that's not a modest answer, my lady.
  Do you laugh? My doubts are strong upon me.
BEATRICE: 'Tis innocence that smiles, and no rough brow
  Can take away the dimple in her cheek.   25
  Say I should strain a tear to fill the vault,°
  Which would you give the better faith to?
ALSEMERO: 'Twere but hypocrisy of a sadder colour,
  But the same stuff. Neither your smiles nor tears
  Shall move or flatter me from my belief: 30
  You are a whore!
BEATRICE: What a horrid sound it hath!
  It blasts a beauty to deformity;
  Upon what face soever that breath falls,
  It strikes it ugly: oh, you have ruined
  What you can ne'er repair again.   35
ALSEMERO: I'll all demolish, and seek out truth within you,
  If there be any left. Let your sweet tongue
  Prevent° your heart's rifling; there I'll ransack
  And tear out my suspicion.
BEATRICE: You may, sir,
  'Tis an easy passage.° Yet, if you please,   40
  Show me the ground° whereon you lost your love;
  My spotless virtue may but tread on that
  Before I perish.
ALSEMERO: Unanswerable!

A ground you cannot stand on; you fall down
Beneath all grace and goodness when you set   45
Your ticklish° heel on't. There was a visor°
O'er that cunning face, and that became you;
Now impudence in triumph rides upon't.
How comes this tender reconcilement else
'Twixt you and your despite,° your rancorous loathing,   50
De Flores? He that your eye was sore at sight of,
He's now become your arm's supporter,° your lip's saint!°
BEATRICE: Is there the cause?
ALSEMERO: Worse; your lust's devil,
    Your adultery!
BEATRICE: Would any but yourself say that,
    'Twould turn him to a villain.
ALSEMERO: 'Twas witnessed   55
    By the counsel of your bosom, Diaphanta.
BEATRICE: Is your witness dead then?
ALSEMERO: 'Tis to be feared
    It was the wages of her knowledge, poor soul;
    She lived not long after the discovery.
BEATRICE: Then hear a story of not much less horror   60
    Than this your false suspicion is beguiled with;
    To your bed's scandal I stand up innocence,°
    Which even the guilt of one black other deed
    Will stand for proof of: your love has made me
    A cruel murd'ress.
ALSEMERO: Ha!
BEATRICE: A bloody one;   65
    I have kissed poison for't, stroked a serpent:
    That thing of hate, worthy in my esteem
    Of no better employment, and him most worthy
    To be so employed, I caused to murder
    That innocent Piracquo, having no   70
    Better means than that worst, to assure
    Yourself to me.
ALSEMERO: Oh, the place itself e'er since
    Has crying been for vengeance, the temple
    Where blood° and beauty first unlawfully
    Fired° their devotion, and quenched the right one;   75
    'Twas in my fears at first, 'twill have it now.°
    Oh, thou art all deformed!
BEATRICE: Forget not, sir,
    It for your sake was done; shall greater dangers
    Make the less welcome?
ALSEMERO: Oh, thou shouldst have gone

A thousand leagues about° to have avoided   80
This dangerous bridge of blood; here we are lost.
BEATRICE: Remember I am true unto your bed.
ALSEMERO: The bed itself's a charnel,° the sheets shrouds
      For murdered carcasses. It must ask pause°
      What I must do in this; meantime you shall   85
      Be my prisoner only.° Enter my closet;   *Exit* BEATRICE.
      I'll be your keeper yet. Oh, in what part
      Of this sad story shall I first begin? — Ha!

                  Enter DE FLORES.

      This same fellow has put me in.° — De Flores!
DE FLORES: Noble Alsemero?
ALSEMERO: I can tell you   90
      News, sir; my wife has her commended° to you.
DE FLORES: That's news indeed, my lord; I think she would
      Commend me to the gallows if she could,
      She ever loved me so well. I thank her.
ALSEMERO: What's this blood upon your band,° De Flores?   95
DE FLORES: Blood? No, sure, 'twas washed since.
ALSEMERO: Since when, man?
DE FLORES: Since t'other day I got a knock
      In a sword-and-dagger school. I think 'tis out.
ALSEMERO: Yes, 'tis almost out, but 'tis perceived, though.
      I had forgot my message; this it is: 100
      What price goes murder?
DE FLORES: How sir?
ALSEMERO: I ask you, sir;
      My wife's behindhand° with you, she tells me,
      For a brave bloody blow you gave for her sake
      Upon Piracquo.
DE FLORES: Upon? 'Twas quite through him, sure.
      Has she confessed it?
ALSEMERO: As sure as death to both of you,   105
      And much more than that.
DE FLORES: It could not be much more;
      'Twas but one thing, and that — she's a whore.
ALSEMERO: It could not choose but follow. Oh cunning devils!
      How should blind men know you from fair-faced saints?
BEATRICE [*within*]: He lies, the villain does belie° me!   110
DE FLORES: Let me go to her, sir.
ALSEMERO: Nay, you shall to her.
      — Peace, crying crocodile,° your sounds are heard!
      — Take your prey to you, get you in to her, sir.   *Exit* DE FLORES.

I'll be your pander now; rehearse again
Your scene of lust, that you may be perfect   115
When you shall come to act it to the black audience°
Where howls and gnashings shall be music to you.
Clip° your adult'ress freely; 'tis the pilot
Will guide you to the Mare Mortuum,°
Where you shall sink to fathoms bottomless.   120

Enter VERMANDERO, ALIBIUS, ISABELLA, TOMAZO, FRANCISCUS *and*
ANTONIO.

VERMANDERO: Oh, Alsemero, I have a wonder for you.
ALSEMERO: No, sir, 'tis I, I have a wonder for you.
VERMANDERO: I have suspicion near as proof itself
    For Piracquo's murder.
ALSEMERO: Sir, I have proof
    Beyond suspicion for Piracquo's murder.   125
VERMANDERO: Beseech you, hear me; these two have been disguised
    E'er since the deed was done.
ALSEMERO: I have two other
    That were more close° disguised than your two could be
    E'er since the deed was done.
VERMANDERO: You'll hear me: these mine own servants —   130
ALSEMERO: Hear me: those nearer than your servants,
    That shall acquit them and prove them guiltless.
FRANCISCUS: That may be done with easy truth, sir.
TOMAZO: How is my cause bandied° through your delays!
    'Tis urgent in blood and calls for haste.   135
    Give me a brother alive or dead:
    Alive, a wife with him; if dead, for both
    A recompense for murder and adultery.
BEATRICE [*within*]: O, O, O!
ALSEMERO: Hark, 'tis coming to you.
DE FLORES [*within*]: Nay, I'll along for company.
BEATRICE [*within*]: O, O!   140
VERMANDERO: What horrid sounds are these?
ALSEMERO: Come forth, you twins of mischief.°

Enter DE FLORES, *bringing in* BEATRICE [*wounded*].

DE FLORES: Here we are; if you have any more
    To say to us, speak quickly, I shall not
    Give you the hearing else; I am so stout yet,°   145
    And so, I think, that broken rib of mankind.°
VERMANDERO: An host of enemies entered my citadel

Could not amaze like this: Joanna! Beatrice-Joanna!
BEATRICE: Oh, come not near me, sir, I shall defile you.
    I am that of your blood was taken from you   150
    For your better health;° look no more upon't,
    But cast it to the ground regardlessly:
    Let the common sewer take it from distinction.°
    Beneath the stars, upon yon meteor°
    Ever hung my fate, 'mongst things corruptible;   155
    I ne'er could pluck it from him. My loathing
    Was prophet to the rest, but ne'er believed;
    Mine honour fell with him, and now my life.
    Alsemero, I am a stranger to your bed.
    Your bed was cozened° on the nuptial night,   160
    For which your false bride died.
ALSEMERO: Diaphanta!
DE FLORES: Yes, and the while I coupled with your mate
    At barley-brake; now we are left in hell.°
VERMANDERO: We are all there; it circumscribes here.
DE FLORES: I loved this woman in spite of her heart;   165
    Her love I earned out of Piracquo's murder.
TOMAZO: Ha! my brother's murderer?
DE FLORES: Yes, and her honour's prize°
    Was my reward. I thank life for nothing
    But that pleasure; it was so sweet to me
    That I have drunk up all, left none behind   170
    For any man to pledge me.
VERMANDERO: Horrid villain!
    Keep life in him for further tortures.
DE FLORES: No!
    I can prevent° you; here's my penknife still;
    It is but one thread more. [*Stabs himself.*] — And now 'tis cut.
    Make haste, Joanna, by that token° to thee: 175
    Canst not forget, so lately put in mind,
    I would not go to leave thee far behind.   *Dies.*
BEATRICE: Forgive me, Alsemero, all forgive;
    'Tis time to die when 'tis a shame to live.   *Dies.*
VERMANDERO: Oh, my name is entered now in that record°   180
    Where till this fatal hour 'twas never read.
ALSEMERO: Let it° be blotted out; let your heart lose it,
    And it can never look you in the face,
    Nor tell a tale behind the back of life
    To your dishonour. Justice hath so right   185
    The guilty hit that innocence is quit
    By proclamation,° and may joy again.
    — Sir, you are sensible of what truth hath done;

'Tis the best comfort that your grief can find.
TOMAZO: Sir, I am satisfied; my injuries 190
　Lie dead before me. I can exact no more,
　Unless my soul were loose, and could o'ertake
　Those black fugitives° that are fled from thence,
　To take a second vengeance; but there are wraths°
　Deeper than mine, 'tis to be feared, about 'em. 195
ALSEMERO: What an opacous° body had that moon
　That last changed on us! Here's beauty changed
　To ugly whoredom; here, servant obedience
　To a master-sin, imperious murder;
　I, a supposed husband, changed° embraces 200
　With wantonness, but that was paid before:°
　Your change is come too, from an ignorant wrath
　To knowing friendship. Are there any more on's?°
ANTONIO: Yes, sir, I was changed too, from a little ass as I was to a great
　fool as I am, and had like to ha' been changed to the gallows, but that 205
　you know my innocence° always excuses me.
FRANCISCUS: I was changed from a little wit° to be stark mad,
　Almost for the same purpose.
ISABELLA [*to* ALIBIUS]:　　　　　　Your change is still behind°
　But deserve best your transformation;
　You are a jealous coxcomb, keep schools of folly, 210
　And teach your scholars how to break your own head.°
ALIBIUS: I see all apparent, wife, and will change now
　Into a better husband, and never keep
　Scholars that shall be wiser than myself.
ALSEMERO: Sir, you have yet a son's duty living; 215
　Please you accept it. Let that your sorrow,
　As it goes from your eye, go from your heart;
　Man and his sorrow at the grave must part.

Epilogue

ALSEMERO: All we can do to comfort one another,
　To stay° a brother's sorrow for a brother,
　To dry a child from the kind father's eyes,
　Is to no purpose, it rather multiplies;°
　Your only smiles° have power to cause relive 5
　The dead again, or in their rooms° to give
　Brother a new brother, father a child.
　If these appear, all griefs are reconciled.　　　　*Exeunt omnes.*

Finis

Notes to the Play

Dramatis Personae

6   ALIBIUS: 'elsewhere, absent in another place'

7   LOLLIO: The name suggests an idle person; one who lolls.

9   *Changeling*: (1) half-wit, fool; (2) ugly or mentally deficient child left by fairies in the place of a stolen child; (3) one who has been changed. There are other meanings – an inferior substitute, a waverer, an inconstant woman – variously applicable to other characters in the play.

10   FRANCISCUS: 'The Frenchman', connoting an amorous nature

11   DE FLORES: 'deflowers'

14   BEATRICE-JOANNA: Beatrice means (ironically) 'blessed one'

15   DIAPHANTA: 'heated with desire'

17   *Alicant*: a seaport south of Valencia, on the east coast of Spain

Act One, Scene One

1   temple: church

6   to...purpose: intending marriage

7–8   that...creation: Webster's Antonio, in *The Duchess of Malfi*, 1.2.293–4, similarly ranks marriage with the creation of man.

8   the place: Paradise, the Garden of Eden

9   right home back: true home (paradise) regained

10   interview: (1) meeting; (2) mutual sight of each other

17   buy...witches: witches were attributed with the power to call up storm winds

19   a' God's name: freely, as God's good gift

20   vane: wind-vane

26   doubt: suspect, fear

29   wont: accustomed

30   trap...speed: harness your horses yourself to hasten departure

34   your orisons: the subject of your prayers

36   the stoic: Stoic philosophers attempted to suppress all carnal desires.

40   violent: urgent, passionate

49   critical: astrologically crucial in Aquarius: the constellation of the Water-carrier, considered propitious for travel by water

52   affair: business matter

57   laws...Medes: immutable laws (see Daniel 6: 8)

58   Salute: greet (with a kiss)

59   in my conscience: truly, upon my word

61   ransomed...Turk: at this time Greece was under the rule of the Ottoman Turkish empire

65   sing...sight: (1) sight-read music; (2) express love at first sight

67   want: lack

71   certain: reliable, accurate

74   check: rebuke

78   Both houses: the eyes and the judgement as the two houses of Parliament, the Lords and the Commons

79–80   confirmation...royal: the signature of the King (required for a bill to become law)

80   part: role

81   one above me: the reference may be to Beatrice's father with God-like authority over his daughter, or God as supreme over kings

85   carriers: land transport

86   at farthest: at the limit of our journey

87   venturer: sharer in a commercial operation

88–9   lawful prize: a legitimate capture (that is, unmarried)

89   down...topsail: the signal of a vessel's surrender

93 duteous preface: dutiful introduction

94 stall: forestall, make stale

95 good presence: (1) welcome presence; (2) dignified bearing (of her father)

98 enjoined: commanded

99 still: always

112 basilisk: a fabulous lizard-like creature, that could kill at a glance

114 a thousand sound: a thousand healthy folk

115 distastes: dislikes

116 infinites: an infinite number of people

123 frailty: defect

125 a cherry: a lover's gift

128 tempt: try

130–1 I...myself: I am unable to do what I wish to do to assist myself (by dismissing De Flores)

132 respect: estimation
follows: attends on

136 such: madness. The doctor is Alibius.

137 physic: medicine, treatment

140 thing: (1) object; (2) penis

141 compound: mix

141–2 maddest blood: (1) wildest sexual passion (blood was considered to be the seat of the animal spirits); (2) greatest insanity

142 profess physic: declare myself to be a doctor

143 poppy: opium, commonly used to induce sleep

145 simple: herbal remedy

145–6 cuckoo...call't: Jasperino is being coy about naming the cuckoo-pintle, or wild arum, because 'pintle' meant penis

146 discover: reveal

149 devotion: act of worship

150 saint: object of religious (or sexual) devotion

157 article between: stipulation to be met first

161 promonts: high points of land

170 Iulan down: the first signs of a beard (after a young hero Iulus Ascanius in Virgil's *Aeneid*, 1.267, whose name in Greek means 'the first growth of the

beard'). *Iulan* is pronounced 'I-ul-an'.

172 silver: (1) silver coins; (2) white hair

174 went together: (1) left together; (2) matched each other

175 Saint Jacques: Saint James of Compostella, patron saint of Spain

176 done somewhat: have my military achievements
unhappy: unfortunate, sad

177 at Gibralter: the battle of Gibralter (1607), where the Dutch defeated a much larger Spanish fleet

180 the late league: the Treaty of the Hague (1609) which brought about a twelve-year cessation of hostilities

181 prevented: forestalled

186 violent: urgent

190 rude: roughly

192 toy: mere trifle

197 entertainment: hospitality

200 Alicant: see Dramatis Personae, 17 and note

204 occasions: circumstances

213 Bound: obliged

214 want: fail to achieve

218 discharges murderers: (1) dismisses killers; (2) fires small cannon

226 mischief: curse
Now I know: despite the fact that I know

228 pumps: slippers

231 haunt: hang about

Act One, Scene Two

3 close to: secretive, discreet about

12 knowledge: in the biblical sense of sexual intimacy and possession

15 go about: am discussing

24 higher and broader: alluding to the deceived husband's cuckold's horns

27 my ring: (1) my marriage ring; (2) my wife's vagina. The following bawdy exchange between Alibius and Lollio (*finger, useth, lie, thrusting into't, conceiv'st* all carry sexual

meanings) alludes to a folk story in which a husband is advised to keep his wife faithful by continually making love to her.

30   still: always

32   conceiv'st: understand

36   look out: (1) leave my house; (2(be vigilant

39   treadings: (1) movements; (2) sexual encounters

43   comfortable: comforting

44–5   under the whip: under control (flogging was used to treat the insane)

45   wit: intelligence

46   knaves: criminals

50   thrift: prosperity

51   daily visitants: It was regarded as entertainment to visit madhouses such as Bethleham Hospital in London (known as Bedlam) to watch the behaviour of patients.

54   habits: clothing

56   shrewd: keen, cunning

60   ward: defensive posture (in fencing)

64   madman: (1) lunatic; (2) insane male

65   buckler: shield

70   part: role, activity

73   pluck a rose: urinate

79 SD   *like an idiot*: an illustration published in 1672 shows a figure labelled 'Changeling' (possibly Middleton's Changeling) wearing a long-skirted coat and a tall pointed dunce's cap, and carrying at his wrist what may be a horn-book (or schoolchild's exercise-book).

80   Save you: God preserve you

83   commodious: effective, beneficial

85   patterns: examples (small coins)

86   charge: costs

94   Tony: During the seventeenth-century, the name came to mean 'fool' or 'madman'.

98–9   He...beast: according to Aristotle the faculty of laughter distinguished humans from animals.

102   degree: (1) degree of altitude; (2) academic award wit: rationality

108   assure you: be assured

114   discretion: Lollio may be hinting that Antonio will need to learn to conceal any future affair with Isabella.

115   there....want: all expenses will be covered

116   magnifico: wealthy nobleman

119   constable: a local officer of the law, notorious for stupidity

121   headborough: petty constable beadle: prison officer responsible for keeping order in church, and punishing minor offenders

127   arrant: outrageous

138   try his wit: test his intelligence form: school class

141   true: (1) real; (2) honest

145   deuce: pair; that is, none, since tailors had a reputation for dishonesty

152   parlous: dangerous

153   knaves: dishonest men

165   push-pin: (1) children's game in which the players attempt to push their pin across their opponent's; (2) sexual intercourse

174   Cousin, stand there: Lollio places Alibius between himself and Antonio, standing in a row. Ironically, Alibius, the master-knave, is set between two supposed knave-fools who will attempt to make a fool of him.

182   but we three: alluding to a popular comic picture showing two idiots, with an inscription' We three loggerheads be', so making the viewer the third fool.

183 SD   *within*: off-stage

184   Put's...little: a complaint against the patients' underfeeding by the keeper.

185   Fly...swallow: a proverbial saying, ironic because of the

famed agility of the swallow in flight

186 rope: (1) rope of onions; (2) hangman's noose

187 crag: neck

188 chimes of Bedlam: the cries of the insane at meal time in the madhouse

190 the wire: the wire whip

191–2 Cat-whore...permasent: a Welsh madman reviles his cat for not protecting his Parmesan cheese (*her* is stage-Welsh for 'my'). The Welsh were proverbially famous cheese-eaters.

196 your charge: Lollio's duties as guardian of Isabella

199 last: latest

202–3 at...*stultum*: put to learning how to decline the Latin word for 'fool'

207 credit: a reputation as a teacher

Act Two, Scene One

0 SD *severally*: from separate entrances

3 conduct: sheet of instructions

16 In...him: diamonds were supposed to be luminous

20 his blessing: Vermandero's parental blessing

21 as...name: ambiguously, her family's reputation, or the name of her proposed husband, Piracquo.

22 turns head: directs its power

26 my new comforts: Alsemero

32 still: always

35 At no hand: on no account

39 alone: only

40 pick-haired: sharp, hard-bristled

43 swills: gobbles up

44 wash: hog-wash

46 sweets: sweet-tasting sexual pleasures

47 has...sweet: gets a blessing as well as a dessert (or a sweetheart); enjoys the blessing of a beautiful mistress as well as his pleasure

54 passions: (1) emotions; (2) sexual desires

56 Soft and fair: proverbially, 'Soft and fair goes far'. De Flores

means to reply quietly to Beatrice-Joanna's abuse.

58 standing toad-pool: stagnant pond, where toads were thought to be bred by the action of the sun. The toad image implies that De Flores has a carbuncular skin, giving him a repulsive appearance.
amain: with full force

61 another since: cf. 1.1.90ff.

63 mercy: a coded word implying a lover's favour

76 i' th' way still: (1) always conveniently present; (2) an obstacle

79 qualm: fit of illness (lust)

80 Garden-bull: bulls were baited at the Paris Gardens in Southwark. The bull symbolised blind animal lust.

81 lugged: pulled about, baited

83 bad: ugly

86 proved: turned out to be

91 of: for

93 quite discarded: absolutely dismissed

96 bear down: overwhelm

99 addition: additional title
son: son-in-law

103 The day...suddenly: an echo of 1 Thessalonians 5:2–3: 'the day of the Lord so cometh as a thief in the night. For when they shall say peace and safety, then sudden destruction cometh upon them.'

104 keep: stay on watch, keep the night under my control.
Beatrice thinks of refusing to consummate her marriage.

108 bringing on you: (1) making you accede to the marriage; (2) rousing you to become a lover

109 fault: (1) defect; (2) printing error

110 ill-set: badly typeset

114 motion: plea

117 pinching: too tight

121 wanting: lacking

124 exceptious still: always quick to take offence

126 mark your harms: note what may injure you

127 cozened: deceived, cheated

132 pleasure: sexual pleasure

137 him: 1653 reads 'him, in his passions'. This may be a phrase marked for omission, or some loss of text may have taken place following the phrase, which many editors omit.

137–9 how...sufferings: 'It is painful to think of what dangerous and shameful consequences may eventuate from imposing restraints on her.'

152 depart lovingly: separate as loving friends. There is an allusion to Matthew 5:24, 'First be reconciled to thy brother, and then come and offer thy gift.'

Act Two, Scene Two

1 charge: responsibility

6 cabinets: jewel boxes

10 brings: The construction, common in the period, of a singular verb with a plural subject (*prayers*). furnish our defects: supply what we lack

22 strike off: remove, as fetters were removed; but *strike* also suggests the combat Alsemero has in mind. go near: hint at

23–4 remove...ceases: from the scholastic saying 'Once the cause is removed the effect ceases'; the *command* is Vermandero's instruction to Beatrice to marry Alonzo.

24 blown out: as candles are extinguished (cf. line 30)

25 find you: understand what you mean

26 happy: fortunate

31 ventured: put to risk

37 condition: kind

40 becomes: suits

42 ha'...market: have spoiled such a fine opportunity

43 'T: it (the killing of Alonzo)

44 Creation...use: the traditional doctrine that everything in nature has some use or purpose

47 art: (medical) learning, knowledge

49 of our side: favourable to us

52 opens: becomes more favourable

58 t'other: the other man (Alonzo)

59 served: supplied with their (sexual) needs happily: in that case

60 put in for one: apply for a share (with a sexual innuendo)

61 Fly: takes flight; the metaphor is sustained in *spreads* and *mounts* in the following line, though each word also carries an erotic meaning

64 sutler: camp-follower supplying provisions or, as here, sexual needs royal: of huge numbers

66 put case: suppose

69 serve...him: use him for my own purposes

74 pruned: preened, adorned (used of a bird cleaning and oiling its feathers)

75 amorously: attractive, loveable

80 heat of the liver: ironically correct, since the liver was regarded as the seat of violent passions such as love

82 amber: ambergris, used to make perfumes

83 water: medical lotion

91 use on't: use of it. The latent sexual sense of *use*, is present in much of the following conversation, where other terms such as *service, mount, blood, rise, act*, carry similar sexual meanings for speaker or listener.

92 becomes: suits

93 argues: suggests the presence of

107 creation: taken by De Flores to suggest 'procreation'

113 occasion: opportunity

118 faithfully: to offer honest service

123 reverence: dutiful respect

126 angels' food: the biblical bread of heaven, *panis angelorum*,

given in the form of manna to the Israelites in the wilderness. There is also a play on the gold coin known as an angel.

129 forward: bold and audacious
137 dearlier: (1) more richly (suggesting both money and sexual delight); (2) more costly
138 execution: (1) carrying out; (2) killing
139 cast: throw of the dice
143 bravely: finely, at ease
146 blood: sensual desire
151 Slovenly: nasty, disgusting
159 straits: narrow passages
163 'gainst...rising: in readiness for when your lordship leaves the dinner table
165 safely: with no danger of my being detected
thrust upon me: De Flores's language suggests his expectation of the act of murder (cf. *ravishes*, line 132)

Act Three, Scene One

0 SD *act-time*: interval between Acts 2 and 3. In the private theatres of the period this might be filled with orchestral music.
2 wanted...postern: lacked the key for the back door
3 sconce: small fort
10 SD *Exeunt...other*: The audience are to imagine that they have now descended to a different level of the castle

Act Three, Scene Two

5 makes up: increases
6 casement: recessed aperture; possibly, in the theatre, the inner alcove
10 ordnance: cannons
11 bastard: (1) impure, alloyed; (2) false, treacherous
metal: (1) metal; (2) mettle
14 dwell: (1) let your eye dwell; (2) remain as a corpse
I...upon't: (1) I have it in my eye; (2) I am in the act
23 approve: offer proof of
26 suspect: suspicion

Act Three, Scene Three

1 sirrah: used contemptuously
5 doing: (1) exercising; (2) making love
5–6 I'll...after: The metaphor of whistling to Isabella the caged bird if she will 'sing' (cry out) afterwards is used with a sexual innuendo.
8 pinfold: pen, pound; with a play on *pin* (penis)
10 pounded: (1) impounded; (2) 'pounded' sexually
16 to boot: as well
18 participate of: share in the nature of
19 mad: (1) insane; (2) mad with lust
21 bedlam: madhouse
23 proper: handsome
31 a match: a bargain
33–4 shooting...two: pulling back a few bolts; but there is also an allusion to the proverb 'A fool's bolt is soon shot'
34 SD *presently*: immediately
38–40 Anacreon...higher: There was a story that the Greek poet Anacreon choked to death on a grape-stone while drinking a cup of wine.
39 a spider...cup: Spiders were considered poisonous; to drink one in a cup was thought to be fatal.
41 'tis...pity: the fellow is too pitiful
44 forwards: on the way to madness
45 but...neither: no mere junior; Franciscus picks up the idea of dwarf as a small person, hence fairy.
46–8 Hail...Dryades: Oberon and Titania were King and Queen of the fairies; dryads were wood nymphs. Franciscus is hinting that since Alibius (*Oberon*) is absent, enjoying himself with other women (*Dryades*), Isabella (*Titania*) might as well console herself with him.
50 poesy: (12) poetry; (2) posy of flowers
52–3 Diomed...well: a Thracian king

whose horses were fed on human flesh.

54   Get up: mount; Franciscus kneels on all fours, inviting Lollio to mount him (*get up*). Bucephalus: the huge horse of Alexander the Great, which only he could ride

58   proper: handsome

59   Esculapius: the Greek god of medicine and healing, an ironic name for a keeper of the asylum
poison: that is, the whip. Whipping was a common treatment at the time for madness.

61   Tiresias: famous Theban soothsayer and prophet, who experienced male and female identity. He was blinded by Juno for revealing that sexual intercourse gave more pleasure to women than to men.

62   tame wild-geese: prostitutes

70   an eye more: the female organ of sex

72   Luna: the moon (which was thought to afflict humans with madness)
two trades: as madman and blindman, both qualifications for begging

73   big-bellied: (1) at the full; (2) pregnant

74   Hecate: Greek goddess of witchcraft and magic; an aspect of the moon

76   kick...bush: in folklore the man in the moon was accompanied by a dog and carried a bush

78   lycanthropi: humans suffering from wolf-madness, a derangement in which they suppose themselves to be wolves and might howl at the moon. Cf. *The Duchess of Malfi*, 5.2.6 and note.

85   *lie*: have sex

89   mouse-hole: (1) tiny entrance; (2) female organ of sex

91   fooled: provided with an amusing fool

93   Cousin: commonly used as a euphemism for 'lover'; which is why Isabella so angrily rejects the label (line 100)
aunt: with a play on 'whore'

96   nidget: idiot

97   bauble: (1) the fool's traditional stick tipped with a carved head with asses' ears; (2) penis

103   Bounce: boom! The sound of exploding guns or cannon firing.

104   upper room: suggesting the use of the upper gallery as the location of the madfolks' prison ward; cf. line 166 SD below

106   left-handed Orlando: 'dangerously mad or furious lover', after the name of the hero of Ariosto's Italian epic poem, *Orlando Furioso*

110   amazing: bewildered

112   shape: costume, outward appearance
dearest: most affectionate

118   scrutinous: scrutinizing

122   proceeds: takes a degree
parlous: dangerous

131   Galaxia: Milky Way

137   habit: disguise costume

138   discover: reveal

143   valentine: lover

148   put him to't: test him

156   Catch...hell: an allusion to the game of barley-break, played by pairs of men and women who held hands and were not allowed to separate. A chosen couple occupied a space in the centre of the field, called 'hell', and tried to catch other couples attempting to run through from each opposite end, who as they were caught in turn reinforced or replaced the original couple.

160   out: getting your spoken part wrong
other posture: as fool

161   become...tongue: speak unbecomingly
from your clothes: outside your adopted garb as fool

163   Lives: who lives

164   orchard...Hesperides: mythical garden of golden apples guarded by the daughters of Atlas and Hesperus and a hundred-headed dragon, offspring of the giant Tython

165   pull: pluck

167   keep 'em: guard (1) the apples of the Hesperides; (2) the rosy cheeks of Isabella

168   that: love-making

169   read Lipsius: studied the works of the Neo-Stoic scholar Justus Lipsius (1547–1606); playing on 'lips'
Ars Amandi: the Roman erotic poet Ovid's treatise on the Art of Love

172   Do you smile: a command to smile

175   cheerfully: favourably, encouragingly

177–8   this shape...not: this costume does not show me off well

180   Cuckoo, cuckoo!: the bird call associated with infidelity in love

181   Of fear: frightful

185   conceit: delusion

193   instruct...once: serve two church appointments simultaneously (a common and much criticised practice at the time)

197   book: classroom studies

199–200   put you down: (1) out-think you; (2) master you sexually

202   bankers: dyke-builders

206   drawing arctics: magnetic (north) poles; with a suggestion of the attraction of coldness on the woman's part

211   fool's-flesh: carnal behaviour with a fool
have at thee: the call of the fencer beginning a fight

223   Lacedemonian: Spartan, alluding to the faithless amorousness of Helen of Sparta; a cant-name for a prostitute

224   thing about thee: something (your sex organ) on your person

227   knight-errant: (1) roving champion; (2) deviant knight

228   purchase: winning

230   for me enjoying: in exchange for enjoying my sexual favours

235   bounden: (1) in duty bound: (2) imprisoned

243   bespoke: made a claim on

245   fag: conclusion

247   passage over: a theatrical term meaning a march across the stage; here an sudden irruption into the wedding celebration

248   frightful pleasure: entertaining fright

250   measure: dance form

251   breaking time's head: in an irregular rhythm

259   wits: brains

263   staple: basic, necessary

265   Just...arrive: we have exactly hit on the lawyers' port (source) of wealth

Act Three, Scene Four

6   vale: the world as a 'vale of tears', a place of tribulation

9   seat: dwelling
largely: widely expressed

11   fix him: establish him in Vermandero's favour

12   liberty of the house: permission to move about the house freely

14   if...offends me: meaning Alonzo, and alluding to the biblical injunction to pluck out the offending eye: 'it is better for thee to enter into life with one eye, rather than having two eyes to be cast into hell' (Matthew 18:9).

22   answerable: suitable

26   born weeping: as tears of joy
token: (1) proof (of the murder); (2) love-token

32   had...this: that is, losing a finger to a fellow diner's knife; there are contemporary references to the physical dangers of scrambling for food in common dishes on state occasions

38   As...substance: alluding to the biblical doctrine that husband and wife become one flesh. Beatrice-Joanna and Alonzo have gone through the binding contract of betrothal, a potential

39 union symbolized by the indivisibility of ring and finger.
    fees: the warden of a game park had rights to parts of the body of a hunted deer
44 capcase: protective covering
45 worm: (1) the pangs of remorse; (2) the sufferings of the damned in hell, 'where their worm dieth not, and the fire is never quenched' (Mark 9:48)
    as fine: however closely woven
54 cause: reason for offence
56 warm: energetic, active; though the language of *service* and *performance* also carries a latent sexual sense
58 'Twere misery in me: (1) I would feel wretched; (2) it would be mean of me
63 move: anger
69 journeyman: day labourer
80 it: the stated amount of money
86 suspect: suspicion
87 home: convincingly, reaching the heart of the matter
90 strange: unfriendly
92 doubt: fear
94 forgetfulness: forgetting your position
96 forgetful: forgetful of the service done you
97 bold: impudent, audacious
99 eased of : relieved, soothed by
100 blood: innate sexual desire
105 Soft: slowly
107 spirit: (1) vigour, vitality; (2) sexual desire
    on't: to have the commission to carry out the *act* (line 106)
109 wrought: worked
113 In order: in due course
116 resolved: certain
119 agreed: struck a bargain
125 Push: an exclamation of contempt
131 blood: social status
134 Fly: (1) take flight; (2) seek to escape
136 to me: in favour of
138 first condition: original innocence
139 turned you out: thrown you out of their dwelling-place

141 urge: provoke
142 writ'st maid: call yourself a virgin
144 changed: that is, from life to death
145 second: second love
147 enjoy thee: experience the pleasures of intercourse with you
152 shooting: (1) firing (an arrow or gun); a traditional metaphor for the effect of the sight of a beautiful woman); (2) burning like a comet
162 determined: fixed, settled
166 It...first: 'that I, so created, must have my first experience of sexual intercourse with a man of satanic evil, treachery and loathsome appearance'
168 receipts: recipes
170 turtle: turtle-dove

Act Four, Scene One

1.7 SD *accident*: incident
1   fellow: low-bred person; (2) companion
    undone me endlessly: (1) enjoyed sexual intercourse with me without remission; (2) destroyed me for ever
4   cope: (1) meet; (2 copulate
11 Stands for: represents
13 grow...danger: develop into personal danger for me
15 lie by him (1) lie beside him in bed; (2) tell him lies
    use: (1) deal with; (2) copulate with
16 precious: highly-skilled
    die: dice
17 cunning gamester: clever, skilful gambler
    closet: small private room; in the theatre located in the inner stage
18 park: game-park (cf. line 57 below)
20 right: true, real
22 physic: medicine
23 wisdom: prudence, since it protects him against poisoners
24–5 The Book...Nature: the title of a treatise by a French scholar,

Antonius Mizaldus (1520–78), *De Arcanis Naturae*. Mizaldus is named at line 44–5, and while this book does not contain the material Beatrice finds there, he was the author of another pseudo-scientific treatise, *Centuriae IX Memorabilium*, which does list similar virginity and pregnancy tests.

38 mystery: medical secret
look to you: watch out for you

42 faith: belief in

43 made proof: was put to the test

47 several: distinct
incontinently: immediately and ungovernably

50 Where...been: what would have happened to me (if I didn't know this)?

52 Cuds: a mild oath; a contraction of 'God save me'

53 nice piece: scrupulous wench

55 look: look for

59 great rangers: (1) keepers of royal parks and forests; (2) energetic wanderers

60 roosting time: the time for retiring to bed, and, in Diaphanta's excited imagination, for sexual activity
lodge: (1) dwelling; (2) female organ of sex

61 Alexander: the Macedonian king, Alexander the Great (356–323 BC)

62 pit-hole: (1) grave-pit; (2) lover's sex organ. Alexander married the famous beauty Roxana; cf. *Doctor Faustus*, Dramatis Personae 30 and note.

66 owed: owned

69 a blushing business: the embarassing matter of sexual intercourse

70 Do...sooth: are you speaking seriously?

75 gets from't: disengages from intercourse

83 lies: (1) lies in bed; (2) deceives
humour: whim

87 by-bet...honour: side-bet or extra inducement to ensure the preservation of Beatrice's reputation

88 the world...abroad: other people make a public search

91 in troth: indeed

92 quick: (1) pregnant; (2) smart, lively

93 urge: provoke

94 truer: that is, truer person

96 lightsome: light-hearted

100 Like...jury: probably an allusion to the notorious divorce trial in 1613 of the Countess of Essex, who claimed non-consummation of her marriage and was subjected to a physical examination by a group of matrons and noblewomen.

104 true: capable of discovering the truth

109 most concerns it: is the most relevant point of it

112 circumscribed: set out exactly
accident: event, symptom

117 sad: serious

118 lays itself: subsides

121–2 study/The carriage: plan the conduct

122 carry't: (1) perform; (2) physically support in intercourse

123 burthen: weight

127 justice: justice of the peace (as a husband to be fooled); with a latent ironic sense, 'to get my just deserts'

128 portion: dowry; the woman was required to bring wealth or property to a marriage

Act Four, Scene Two

1 knave: servant

8 Briamata: named as Vermandero's country house ten leagues from Alicant, in Middleton's major source, *The Triumphs of God's Revenge against the crying and Execrable Sin of Wilful and Premeditated Murder* (1621), by John Reynolds

11 answer faithfully: confidently account for

13 suddenly: immediately

14 discover: reveal

16 set on: harassed, attacked

18 dearest bloods: closest family

22 snatched: hasty
30 belief hurt 'em: trust (in Alonzo) caused them to be injured
34 alliance: kinship
39 blessed: guarded, protected
46 jealousy: suspicion
51 easy, round-packed: free with sexual favours, plump and well-fleshed
53 at no hand: in no way
55 salute: consort with
56 His...overlays: even being in his presence oppresses
59 glorious: boastful, arrogant
60 reckon: come to a reckoning
66 lay: allay
72 holds his right: possesses what is rightly his (Beatrice-Joanna)
75 it: Tomazo's sword
76 Keep...solemn: observe your wedding day with due solemnity
84 dispense...zeal: 'Allow me to show a little less zeal (in your service)'
85 puts me on: excites my curiosity
88 partake: share
90 pretend: offer
96 out: mistaken
97 prevent thee: forestall your making further mistakes
99 stagger: doubt, disbelieve
102 challenge interest: claim rights
107 touched: was corrupted, tainted
108 resolved: satisfied, decided
109 prithee: I pray you
112 Chaldean: astrologer, soothsayer (from the reputation ascribed to Chaldean astrologers in the book of *Daniel*)
121 she: Beatrice-Joanna obscurely: shrouded in darkness
129 abused: slandered
134 composition: made-up drink
135 warrant: assurance
139 virtue: quality

141 takes: works
148 time and method: temporal sequence and manner of operation

Act Four, Scene Three

1 waxing: increasing (in its effects)
6 inside: (1) interior nature; (2) the contents of his letter
out: (1) exterior appearance, guise; (2) the envelope
8 Andromeda: Isabella, as the maiden sacrificed to the sea-monster Alibius, whom Franciscus will rescue in the guise of the Greek hero Perseus.
8–9 chambermaid...Sun: that is, Isabella and Alibius again. Chambermaids had a reputation both for sexual looseness and an addiction to reading romances like *The Mirror of Princely Deeds and Knighthood*, by Diego Ortunez de Calahorra, translated from the Spanish in 1578–1601 and featuring as its hero the Knight of the Sun.
9 at...region: The address alludes to the genitals, which in astrology were governed by the constellation of the Scorpion.
10 bellows-mender of Aeolus: Aeolus was the god of winds; Middleton elsewhere associates bellows-makers with pimping; the shape of the instrument suggested the male phallus.
15 mad: (1) insane; (2) lustful
21 dismantled: stripped ornaments: adornments, dress
22 spring: grow up (with a play on the season of spring)
28 our professions: as doctors
32 minister...trade: administer healing and go into the business of (1) medicine; (2) adultery and prostitution
33 thirds: third share of Isabella's sexual favours, with Alibius

and Franciscus. A legal term for the share of the proceeds of a capture, or of certain fines and forfeitures which went to a private individual as distinct from the crown.

34   first place: the royal share (of two thirds), or the first right to my body

37   I...venture: I remain committed to this speculative transaction; a 'venturer' was an investor in a commercial voyage who took a commensurate share of the risks and profits.

39   deal: Isabella means 'cope'; Lollio deliberately misconstrues the word as meaning 'trade sexually'

40   the fair understanding: 'understand what I say in the decent and modest sense in which they are spoken'

42   kindly: (1) according to their natures; (2) gently

43   practise: deceive them

46   Take...outside: Isabella implies that Lollio can be sure of her virtue; he need only concern himself with exterior appearances.

47   put...inside: prepare you for copulation

53   miss: fail to please

54   so: provided that

55   nice: delicate

57   pizzles: (1) whips (made from the dried penises of bulls); (2) penises

59   morris: morris-dance; a vigorous country dance, in which the dancers, jingling small bells attached to their costumes, represented characters from the Robin Hood legends

61   fooling: (1) capacity to amuse with their clowning; (2) ability to behave with propriety

62   measure: dance

72   nose: a large nose was taken to be the sign of a large penis; but Lollio may also imply that Alibius is able to be led by the nose, that is, be grossly deceived.

77   footmanship: dance steps; taken by Antonio to mean 'capacity to walk'

78   ride: (1) ride a horse: (2) mount sexually

82   honour: ceremonious bow

83   cuz: cousin

84   your worship: (mock) courtesy title for a gentleman

85   honour: (1) bowing; (2) nobility bend...hams: (1) stoop; (2) copulate

86–7   low...stiffened: That is, nobly born women engage in liaisons with lower-born men, even from the very social rank (of yeomen) from which their family rose (*stiffened*; though the word also carries a sexual sense).

87   caper: (1) dance leap; (2) brief frolic

91   figure: (1) dance step; (2) face, appearance

93   he treads the air: Isabella pretends to see the leaping Antonio as Icarus, who in Greek myth, escaped from imprisonment in Crete with his father Dedalus (see line 97) by flying on wings fastened with wax. Icarus flew too near the sun and drowned in the Icarian Sea (see lines 101–2) when the wax melted and he lost his wings. He became a symbol for self-destructive ambition. Shough: shoo!

94   wax enough below: The image shifts to the wax on legal documents which may be rendered null and void ('killed').

98–9   tread...clue: A frank sexual invitation (*tread* suggests 'dance', 'walk' and 'copulate'), couched in terms of the famous Cretan Labyrinth, constructed by Dedalus to contain the Minotaur, slain by the hero Theseus, who made his way in and out again using a ball of thread given him by Ariadne as

	a *clue* (here used also in a indecent sense).
105	tiara: head-dress with a long tail
106	suck...belly: (1) revive the drowned man; (2) relieve Antonio's sexual frustrations
107	straits: (1) the sea between Crete and Greece; (2) Antonio's intestines
108	Bless thee: may God preserve you
	pirates: (1) pirates; (2) whores, predatory women
109	let me alone: Presumably Antonio is resisting passionate advances from Isabella.
110	Mercury: winged messenger of the gods
111	reversion: the right to succeed
112–13	Stay...Endymion: Isabella assumes the persona of the goddess of the moon, who fell in love with the beautiful youth Endymion, and who controlled the tides. Antonio, struggling to resist Isabella's advances, ironically is personified as *the wild, rebellious waves.*
116	unshapen antic: misshaped clown, grotesque figure
117	bedlam: lunatic
118	habit: costume
124	quick-sighted: Love is proverbially perceptive.
125	caparisons: coverings, trappings (strictly, of a horse)
126	stark mad: utterly and truly insane
130	usher: door-keeper
135	beat...Fury: the Greek Furies punished crime with their whips
136	forbear: spare
137	fox-skin: cunning disguise
140	the masque: the wedding-entertainment to be offered at Vermandero's house
141	ride: mount sexually
144	She's...on't: Isabella need not worry about Franciscus; Antonio will kill him in a duel.
149	horse: (1) horse; (2) whore's

150	kick...bowstring: that is, to lose her virginity. Latona is the mother of Diana, here confused with the huntress-goddess, goddess also of female chastity and the moon. The forehead was the symbolic location of personal honour: cf. *The Revenger's Tragedy*, 1.2.108 and note
151	humour: mood
161–2	this trick...know: that is, deceit and adultery
165	Next: nearest
167	yours: your hand; punning on *hand* as '(thief's) hand' and 'handwriting'
174	give you over: release you to Isabella for your 'cure'
	cast your water: diagnose your illness (by analysing your urine)
179	serve: be sufficient
185	shape: dress, appearance
	Bang: thump, beat
186	well-favouredly: soundly
190	handles him: handles himself (as a dancer)
191	Well said: well done
195–6	fool...begged: To beg a fool was to seek appointment as his guardian and so enjoy the profits of his estate.
207	him: Lollio may be thinking of Alibius or the two disguised lovers.
199	fit...strains: only get this musical entertainment ready for performance
200	credit: a favourable reputation

Act Five, Scene One

1	by't: engaged in intercourse
4	honour: reputation (for virtue)
7	blood: sensual desire
16	Push: expression of contempt, 'pish!'
	termagants: fierce, violent women
19	stave...royal: keep them from falling on game reserved for royal hunters
20	harsh and hardy: rough and daring

21 apothecary: druggist
22 fall'n off: ceased feeding
25 Phosporus: Lucifer, the morning star
26 fall...ruin: happen upon some destructive accident
28 force a rising: (1) compell Diaphanta to leave Alsemero's bed; (2) create a general disturbance
31 reach: plan
37 light parcels: insignificant items
45 piece high-charged: fully-loaded gun
46 There...proper: in that situation that (using a blast from a gun to extinguish the flames) is appropriate
49 'Slid: literally, by God's eyelid
54 time: proper occasion
56 purifies wit: concentrates quick-thinking
70 loathes: disgusts
73 SD *pass over*: cross the stage
75 works: is ablaze
charge: powder and shot for the gun
78 well: enjoying myself
79 trim: fine (ironic)
89 well said: well done
93 Dog: skilful, effective
100 countenanced: employed, favoured
101 heavy: slow, slovenly
102 mine: disastrous accident
strangely: surprisingly
104 SD *Enter* DE FLORES: Vermandero's response at line 105 suggests that De Flores is carrying a remnant of the dead girl: possibly a charred garment
112 gets no more: (1) receives no more grief; (2) gains no further sexual pleasure
115 throughly: completely
126 sport: (1) physical amusements; (2) sexual pleasure

Act Five, Scene Two

5 in: upon
10 hard bested: hard put to it
12 pest-house: hospital for victims of the plague

15 give...him: provide the opportunity to hunt him down
17 made account of: highly valued
19 on: from
24 choke me up: with rage
29 politician: ruthless schemer
31 still: always
33 crystal: crystal ball
45 lock up: shut away from use
47 salute: greet
51 compliment: formal courtesies
58 zeal: zealous service
76 habits: clothing
77 justly: exactly
80 both...journey: at 4.2.7–8 the pair plan separate destinations; a detail left unharmonised by the dramatists
81 wrought...leaves: craftily worked to get permission to go
85 conduct: guide
86–7 Like...in 'em: Lightning was thought capable of destroying a person without leaving a mark on the skin, and so became an image for sudden, undetectable murder.

Act Five, Scene Three

1 Your...of proof: your trust (in Beatrice-Joanna) is now on trial
3 the black mask: Beatrice's previous appearance of hatred for De Flores
6 despite: scorn
7 Touch it home: get to the bottom of the matter
19 resolve me: answer me
20 honest: chaste, virtuous
21 broad: (1) wide; (2) coarse, immodest
26 a tear...vault: sufficient tears to fill the heavens
38 Prevent: forestall
40 passage: access
41 ground: (1) ground; (2) evidence, reason
46 ticklish: (1) unsteady; (2) lecherous
visor: mask
50 despite: object of scorn
52 arm's supporter: (1) escort; (2) heraldic supporter to a coat of arms

lip's saint: the object of your (sensual) devotion; the one you kiss as a worshipper kisses the relic of a saint

62   To...innocence: I maintain my innocence of the deed which has dishonoured you

74   blood: sexual passion

75   Fired: set alight

76   'twill...now: now the temple will take its revenge

80   about: as a detour

83   charnel: a burial place

84   It...pause: I must take time to consider

86   only: in solitary confinement

89   put me in: given me the cue

91   her commended: commended herself

95   band: collar

102   behindhand with: indebted to

110   belie: slander

112   crocodile: The crocodile symbolised hypocrisy, since it was said to shed tears as it killed its victim.

116   black audience: the inhabitants of hell

118   Clip: embrace

119   Mare Mortuum: the Dead Sea, which was considered bottomless since it could not be reached, and which here also suggests the bottomless pit of hell

128   close: secretly

134   bandied: tossed aside

142   mischief: crime

145   so stout yet: still sufficiently strong

146   broken rib of mankind: Beatrice-Joanna, as the corrupted daughter of Eve, who was made from the rib of Adam (Genesis 2: 21–3)

150–1 I am...health: Beatrice sees herself as corrupted blood removed by the common medical practice of purging, for the sake of her father's health.

153   distinction: separate identity

154–5 Beneath...meteor: In Elizabethan cosmology, the stars were pure, fixed and eternal; meteors belonged to the sub-lunary world of change and decay, and commonly heralded disasters. De Flores is such a being.

160   cozened: deceived, betrayed

163   barley-break...hell: see 3.3.156 and note

167   her honour's prize: the prize of her honour

173   prevent: forestall

175   that token: his death wound

180   my name...record: my family name has now been entered in the heavenly record of misdeeds

182   it: Beatrice-Joanna's share in Vermandero's family name

185–7 Justice...proclamation: Justice has so exactly struck down the guilty that the innocent are acquitted by public declaration of the truth

193   those black fugitives: the damned souls of Beatrice and De Flores

194   wraths: the punishments of hell

196   opacous: darkened and therefore ominous

200   changed: exchanged

201   was paid before: has already been paid for (by Diaphanta's death)

203   on's: of us

206   innocence: (1) guiltlessness; (2) idiocy, simple-mindedness

207   little wit: fool, small brain

208   still behind: yet to come

211   break...head: beat you (by making a cuckold of you)

Epilogue

2   stay: put an end to, dry up

4   multiplies: increases grief

5   Your only smiles: only your favourable reception (of this play)

6   rooms: places

'Tis Pity She's a Whore

JOHN FORD

INTRODUCTORY NOTE

Authorship, date and stage history

'Tis Pity She's a Whore was written at some time before 1633 by John Ford (1586–c.1640); there is insufficient factual evidence to decide whether it was written well before or near that date. The first evidence of its performance, the quarto published in 1663, says it was 'Acted by the Queen's Majesty's Servants, at the Phoenix in Drury Lane' (a company formed in 1626), and an apology for misprints at the end of the text (which was probably written by Ford himself) refers ambiguously to 'The general commendation deserved by the actors in their presentment of this tragedy'. The play remained in the repertoire at the Phoenix until the closing of all theatres by the Puritans in 1642. After the Restoration, Pepys saw it at the Salisbury Court Theatre; 'a simple play and ill-acted'. The actors were probably George Jolly's company, who later took it to Norwich in 1663. Its subject-matter then kept it from the stage for the next two centuries until 1894, when Maurice Maeterlinck presented a cautious adaptation entitled *Anabella* at the Théâtre de L'Oeuvre, Paris, but academic and professional companies have since regularly proved its ability to challenge and grip modern audiences.

Private performances were first given by the Phoenix Society in 1923 at the Shaftesbury Theatre, London and by the Arts Theatre Club in London in 1925. Donald Wolfitt's company gave the first public performances in England since the seventeenth century at both the Cambridge Arts Theatre (1940) and the Strand Theatre,

London (1941); and it then began to appear more frequently, with performances at the Nottingham Playhouse (1955), Cambridge Arts Theatre (1958), the Mermaid Theatre, London (1961), the Vanbrugh Theatre, London (1967), the Bristol Old Vic (1968), the Cambridge Arts Theatre (1969) and the Old Vic (1972). In the same year, the Actors' Company took the play to Edinburgh, Oxford and Cambridge, with Mckellen and Dionisotti as Giovanni and Annabella. In 1976 boys from Alleyn's School, Dulwich, played the tragedy as it might have been performed by Beeston's Boys on the stage of the Phoenix; other productions took place at Bradford and Cambridge. The year 1977 saw a powerful Royal Shakespeare Company production at The Other Place, Stratford, and later at Newcastle upon Tyne and the Donmar Warehouse, London. Between 1978 and 1984 there were numerous productions by British provincial and university companies, from Exeter to Edinburgh. In 1988 there were performances at the Glasgow Citizens' Theatre, and a National (Olivier) Theatre production was directed by Alan Ayckbourn. In 1991 another impressive Royal Shakespeare Company production was mounted at the Swan Theatre, Stratford, with Jonathan Cullen, Saskia Reeves, Jonathan Hyde and Tim McInnery as Giovanni, Annabella, Vasques and Soranzo; it later transferred to the Pit, London. In 1995 *'Tis Pity* was produced at the Wimbleton Studio Theatre.

There have been a number of French productions (notably, Visconti's with Alain Delon and Romy Schneider in Paris in 1961, and an experimental Artaudian production at Vincennes in 1975), and German and American performances. Ford's play was broadcast on radio by the BBC in 1962 and 1970; in 1971 a film version was directed by Giuseppi Patroni Griffi, and there was an effective BBC television production broadcast in 1980.

Text

The present edition is based on the only seventeenth-century quarto of the play, printed by Nicholas Okes for Richard Collins and published in 1633. That the play was issued with the dramatist's approval is suggested by the fact that Ford supplied the printer with a dedication to John Mordant, first Earl of Peterborough, claiming the Earl's interest in the play 'in the action', that is, on stage. The text is relatively sound, with little sign of preparation for use in the playhouse; the printer's copy may well have been a fair copy of the play made by Ford himself.

Sources

There are many correspondences between Ford's tragic story and a story of incestuous love between a brother and a sister in François de Rosset's *Tragic Stories of Our Times (Les Histoires Tragiques de Nostre Temps*, Paris, 1615). But if Ford worked from this as his major source he drew on other materials as well: Ovid's tale of Canace and Macareus (*Heroides*, 11), and possibly for the death of Bergetto, a famous political assassination attempt on the life of Paolo Sarpi in Venice, 1607. There is good evidence that Ford turned to Beaumont and Fletcher's famous incest play, *A King and No King* (1611), and (still more extensively) to Shakespeare's equally famous story of tragic love, *Romeo and Juliet*, in constructing and organising his own tragedy.

Further reading

The fullest single-volume edition of *'Tis Pity She's a Whore* is in the Revels series, edited by Derek Roper (London, 1975); see also N. W. Bawcutt's Regents Renaissance Drama Series edition (Nebraska and London, 1966), the New Mermaid edition by Brian Morris (London, 1968), *John Ford: Three Plays*, edited by Keith Sturgess (Harmondsworth, 1970), The Selected Plays of John Ford, edited by Colin Gibson (Cambridge, 1986) and *'Tis Pity She's a Whore and Other Plays*, edited by Marion Lomax (Oxford, 1995). Information about modern productions of the tragedy is to be found in Lucette Andrieu's article in *Cahiers Élizabéthains*, vol. 3 (1973), and Michael Scott's *Renaissance Drama and a Modern Audience* (London, 1982). Donald K. Anderson surveys the dramatist's work in *John Ford* (New York, 1972), and there are a number of book-length studies including G. F. Sensabaugh, *The Tragic Muse of John Ford* (Stanford, 1944), Robert Davril, *Le Drame de John Ford* (Paris, 1954), Mark Stavig, *John Ford and the Traditional Moral Order* (Madison and London, 1968), H. J. Oliver, *The Problem of John Ford* (Melbourne, London and New York, 1955), Clifford Leech, *John Ford and the Drama of his Time* (London, 1957), Orbison Tucker, *The Tragic Vision of John Ford* (Salzburg, 1974), Ronald Heuber, *John Ford: Baroque English Dramatist* (Montreal and London, 1987), and Dorothy M. Farr, *John Ford and the Caroline Theatre* (London, 1979). See also, the essays on Ford gathered by D. K. Anderson, *'Concord in Discord': The Plays of John Ford 1586–1986* (New York, 1986) and by Michael Neill, in *John Ford: Critical Re-Visions* (Cambridge, 1988).

Dramatis Personae

BONAVENTURA,° *a friar*
A Cardinal, *Nuncio° to the Pope*
SORANZO, *a nobleman*
FLORIO,° *a citizen of Parma*
DONADO, *another citizen*   5
GRIMALDI, *a Roman gentleman*
GIOVANNI, *son to Florio*
BERGETTO,° *nephew to Donado*
RICHARDETTO, *a supposed physician*
VASQUES, *servant to Soranzo*   10
POGGIO,° *servant to Bergetto*
BANDITTI
OFFICERS, attendants

ANNABELLA, *daughter to Florio*
HIPPOLITA,° *wife to Richardetto*   15
PHILOTIS,° *his niece*
PUTANA,° *tutress to Annabella*
Ladies

Scene: *Parma*

Act One, Scene One

[*Enter*] FRIAR *and* GIOVANNI.

FRIAR: Dispute no more in this, for know, young man,
　　These are no school-points.° Nice° philosophy
　　May tolerate unlikely arguments,
　　But heaven admits° no jest: wits° that presumed
　　On wit too much, by striving how to prove   5
　　There was no God, with foolish grounds of art,°
　　Discovered first the nearest way to hell,
　　And filled the world with devilish atheism.
　　Such questions, youth, are fond;° for better 'tis
　　To bless the sun than reason why it shines;   10
　　Yet he thou talk'st of is above the sun.
　　No more! I may not hear it.
GIOVANNI:　　　　　　　　　　　　Gentle father,
　　To you I have unclasped my burdened soul,
　　Emptied the storehouse of my thoughts and heart,

Made myself poor of secrets; have not left   15
Another word untold, which hath not spoke
All what I ever durst or think or know;
And yet is here the comfort I shall have?
Must I not do what all men else may — love?
FRIAR: Yes, you may love, fair son.
GIOVANNI: Must I not praise   20
That beauty which, if framed anew, the gods
Would make a god of, if they had it there,
And kneel to it, as I do kneel to them?
FRIAR: Why, foolish madman!
GIOVANNI: Shall a peevish° sound,
A customary form, from man to man,°   25
Of brother and of sister, be a bar
'Twixt my perpetual happiness and me?
Say that we had one father, say one womb
(Curse to my joys!) gave both us life, and birth;
Are we not therefore each to other bound   30
So much the more by nature? by the links
Of blood,° of reason? nay, if you will have't,
Even of religion, to be ever one,
One soul, one flesh, one love, one heart, one all?
FRIAR: Have done, unhappy° youth, for thou art lost.   35
GIOVANNI: Shall then, for that I am her brother born,
My joys be ever banished from her bed?
No, father; in your eyes I see the change°
Of pity and compassion; from your age,
As from a sacred oracle, distils   40
The life° of counsel. Tell me, holy man,
What cure shall give me ease in these extremes?
FRIAR, Repentance, son, and sorrow for this sin;
For thou hast moved a Majesty above
With thy unrangèd,° almost, blasphemy.   45
GIOVANNI: O, do not speak of that, dear confessor.°
FRIAR: Art thou, my son, that miracle of wit°
Who once, within these three months, wert esteemed
A wonder of thine age, throughout Bononia?°
How did the university applaud   50
Thy government,° behaviour, learning, speech,
Sweetness, and all that could make up a man!
I was proud of my tutelage,° and chose
Rather to leave my books than part with thee.
I did so; but the fruits of all my hopes   55
Are lost in thee, as thou art in thyself.
O Giovanni! Hast thou left the schools

Of knowledge, to converse with lust and death?°
For death waits° on thy lust. Look through the world,
And thou shalt see a thousand faces shine   60
More glorious than this idol thou ador'st.
Leave her, and take thy choice; 'tis much less sin,
Though in such games as those they lose that win.
GIOVANNI: It were more ease to stop the ocean°
From floats° and ebbs, than to dissuade my vows.°   65
FRIAR: Then I have done, and in thy wilful flames
    Already see thy ruin; heaven is just.
    Yet hear my counsel.
GIOVANNI: As a voice of life.
FRIAR: Hie to thy father's house. There lock thee fast
    Alone within thy chamber, then fall down   70
    On both thy knees, and grovel on the ground;
    Cry to thy heart, wash every word thou utter'st
    In tears, and, if't be possible, of blood;°
    Beg heaven to cleanse the leprosy of lust
    That rots thy soul; acknowledge what thou art,   75
    A wretch, a worm, a nothing; weep, sigh, pray
    Three times a day, and three times every night.
    For seven days' space do this, then if thou find'st
    No change in thy desires, return to me:
    I'll think on remedy. Pray for thyself   80
    At home, whilst I pray for thee here. Away!
    My blessing with thee; we have need to pray.
GIOVANNI: All this I'll do, to free me from the rod
    Of vengeance; else I'll swear my fate's my god.   *Exeunt.*

Act One, Scene Two

Enter GRIMALDI *and* VASQUES *ready to fight.*

VASQUES: Come, sir, stand to your tackling.° If you prove craven I'll
    make you run quickly.
GRIMALDI: Thou art no equal match for me.°
VASQUES: Indeed, I never went to the wars to bring home news, nor
    cannot play the mountebank° for a meal's meat,° and swear I got my   5
    wounds in the field. See you these grey hairs? They'll not flinch for
    a bloody nose. Wilt thou to this gear?°
GRIMALDI. Why, slave, think'st thou I'll balance my reputation with a
    cast-suit?° Call thy master; he shall know that I dare —
VASQUES: Scold like a cot-quean —° that's your profession — thou poor   10

shadow of a soldier. I will make thee know my master keeps
servants thy betters in quality° and performance. Com'st thou to
fight, or prate?°

GRIMALDI. Neither, with thee. I am a Roman and a gentleman; one that
have got mine honour with expense of blood.   15

VASQUES: You are a lying coward, and a fool; fight, or by these hilts I'll
kill thee. — Brave my lord, —° you'll fight.

GRIMALDI: Provoke me not, for if thou dost —

VASQUES: Have at you!   *They fight;* GRIMALDI *hath the worst.*

Enter FLORIO, DONADO, SORANZO.

FLORIO: What mean these sudden° broils so near my doors?   20
Have you not other places but my house
To vent the spleen° of your disordered bloods?
Must I be haunted still with such unrest
As not to eat or sleep in peace at home?
Is this your love, Grimaldi? Fie, 'tis naught.°   25

DONADO: And Vasques, I may tell thee 'tis not well
To broach these quarrels; you are ever forward
In seconding° contentions.

Enter above° ANNABELLA *and* PUTANA.

FLORIO: What's the ground?°

SORANZO: That, with your patience, signiors, I'll resolve.°
This gentleman, whom fame reports a soldier   30
(For else I know not) rivals me in love
To Signior Florio's daughter; to whose ears
He still prefers° his suit, to my disgrace,
Thinking the way to recommend himself
Is to disparage me in his report.   35
But know, Grimaldi, though, may be, thou art
My equal in thy blood,° yet this bewrays°
A lowness in thy mind, which, wert thou noble,
Thou wouldst as much disdain as I do thee
For this unworthiness; and on this ground   40
I willed my servant to correct thy tongue,
Holding a man so base no match for me.

VASQUES: And had not your sudden coming prevented us, I had let my
gentleman blood under the gills;° I should have wormed you, sir,
for running mad.°   45

GRIMALDI: I'll be revenged, Soranzo.

VASQUES: On a dish of warm broth to stay your stomach —° do, honest

innocence,° do! Spoonmeat° is a wholesomer diet than a Spanish
blade.

GRIMALDI: Remember this!

SORANZO: I fear thee not, Grimaldi.   *Exit* GRIMALDI.   50

FLORIO: My lord Soranzo, this is strange to me,
  Why you should storm, having my word engaged.°
  Owing° her heart, what need you doubt her ear?°
  Losers may talk by law of any game.

VASQUES: Yet the villainy of words, Signior Florio, may be such as   55
  would make any unspleened dove° choleric; blame not my lord in
  this.

FLORIO: Be you more silent.
  I would not for my wealth my daughter's love
  Should cause the spilling of one drop of blood.   60
  Vasques, put up;° let's end this fray in wine.
                    Exeunt [FLORIO, DONADO, SORANZO *and* VASQUES].

PUTANA: How like you this, child? Here's threatening, challenging, quar-
  relling, and fighting, on every side, and all is for your sake. You had
  need look to yourself, charge; you'll be stolen away sleeping else
  shortly.   65

ANNABELLA: But tut'ress, such a life gives no content to me; my
  thoughts are fixed on other ends.° Would you would leave me.

PUTANA: Leave you? No marvel else;° leave me no leaving, charge, this
  is love outright. Indeed I blame you not; you have choice fit for the
  best lady in Italy.   70

ANNABELLA: Pray do not talk so much.

PUTANA: Take the worst with the best: there's Grimaldi the soldier, a very
  well-timbered° fellow. They say he is a Roman, nephew to the Duke
  Mount Ferratto;° they say he did good service in the wars against
  the Milanese, but faith, charge, I do not like him, an't° be for   75
  nothing but for being a soldier. One amongst twenty of your
  skirmishing° captains but have some privy° maim or other, that
  mars their standing upright. I like him the worse he crinkles so
  much in the hams;° though he might serve,° if there were no more
  men, yet he's not the man I would choose.   80

ANNABELLA: Fie, how thou prat'st.

PUTANA: As I am a very° woman, I like Signior Soranzo well. He is wise,
  and what is more, rich, and what is more than that, kind; and what
  is more than all this, a nobleman; such a one, were I the fair
  Annabella myself, I would wish and pray for. Then he is bountiful;   85
  besides he is handsome, and, by my troth, I think wholesome —°
  and that's news in a gallant of three-and-twenty. Liberal, that I
  know; loving, that you know; and a man sure, else he could never
  ha' purchased such a good name° with Hippolita the lusty
  widow, in her husband's lifetime: and 'twere but for that report,

sweetheart, would he were thine! Commend a man for his
qualities,° but take a husband as he is a plain-sufficient, naked   90
man. Such a one is for your bed, and such a one is Signior Soranzo,
my life for't.

ANNABELLA: Sure the woman took her morning's draught° too soon.

Enter BERGETTO *and* POGGIO.

PUTANA: But look, sweetheart, look what thing comes now; here's   95
another of your ciphers° to fill up the number. O, brave° old ape in
a silken coat! Observe.

BERGETTO: Didst thou think, Poggio, that I would spoil my new clothes,
and leave my dinner to fight?

POGGIO: No, sir, I did not take you for so arrant a baby.   100

BERGETTO: I am wiser than so; for I hope, Poggio, thou never heard'st
of an elder brother that was a coxcomb.° Didst, Poggio?

POGGIO: Never, indeed, sir, as long as they had either land or money left
them to inherit.

BERGETTO: Is it possible, Poggio? O, monstruous! Why, I'll undertake,   105
with a handful of silver, to buy a headful of wit at any time. But
sirrah, I have another purchase in hand; I shall have the wench
mine uncle says. I will but wash my face, and shift socks,° and then
have at her° i'faith! — Mark my pace, Poggio.   [*Walks affectedly.*]

POGGIO: Sir. I have seen an ass and a mule trot the Spanish pavin° with   110
a better grace, I know not how often.   *Exeunt* [BERGETTO *and* POGGIO].

ANNABELLA: This idiot haunts me too.

PUTANA: Ay, ay, he needs no description. The rich magnifico° that is
below with your father, charge, Signior Donado his uncle, for that he
means to make this his cousin° a golden calf,° thinks that you will   115
be a right Israelite, and fall down° to him presently: but I hope I
have tutored you better. They say a fool's bauble° is a lady's
play-fellow;° yet you having wealth enough, you need not cast
upon the dearth of flesh at any rate.° Hang him, innocent!°

Enter GIOVANNI.°

ANNABELLA: But see, Putana, see; what blessèd shape   120
    Of some celestial creature now appears?
    What man is he, that with such sad aspect
    Walks careless of himself?

PUTANA: Where?

ANNABELLA: Look below.

PUTANA: O, 'tis your brother, sweet —

ANNABELLA: Ha!

PUTANA: Tis your brother.
ANNABELLA: Sure, 'tis not he; this is some woeful thing   125
    Wrapped up in grief, some shadow of a man.
    Alas, he beats his breast, and wipes his eyes
    Drowned all in tears. Methinks I hear him sigh.
    Let's down, Putana, and partake° the cause;
    I know my brother, in the love he bears me,   130
    Will not deny me partage° in his sadness.
    My soul is full of heaviness and fear. *Exeunt* [ANNABELLA *and* PUTANA].
GIOVANNI: Lost! I am lost! My fates have doomed my death.
    The more I strive,° I love; the more I love,
    The less I hope. I see my ruin certain.   135
    What judgement or endeavours could apply
    To my incurable and restless wounds
    I throughly° have examined, but in vain.
    O, that it were not in religion sin
    To make our love a god, and worship it!   140
    I have even wearied heaven with prayers, dried up°
    The spring of my continual tears, even starved
    My veins with daily fasts. What wit or art°
    Could counsel, I have practised; but alas,
    I find all these but dreams, and old men's tales   145
    To fright unsteady youth; I'm still the same.
    Or I must speak, or burst; 'tis not, I know,
    My lust, but 'tis my fate that leads me on.
    Keep fear° and low faint-hearted shame with slaves!
    I'll tell her that I love her, though my heart   150
    Were rated at the price of that attempt.
    Oh me! she comes.

Enter ANNABELLA *and* PUTANA.

ANNABELLA: Brother!
GIOVANNI [*aside*]:   If such a thing
    As courage dwell in men, ye heavenly powers,
    Now double all that virtue in my tongue.
ANNABELLA: Why brother, will you not speak to me?
GIOVANNI: Yes;   155
    How d'ye, sister?
ANNABELLA: Howsoever I am,
    Methinks you are not well.
PUTANA: Bless us, why are you so sad, sir?
GIOVANNI: Let me entreat you leave us awhile, Putana, —
    Sister, I would be private with you.   160
ANNABELLA: Withdraw, Putana.

PUTANA: I will. [*Aside*] If this were any other company for her, I should
    think my absence an office of some credit;° but I will leave them
    together.   *Exit.*
GIOVANNI: Come, sister, lend your hand; let's walk together.   165
    I hope you need not blush to walk with me;
    Here's none but you and I.
ANNABELLA: How's this?
GIOVANNI: Faith, I mean no harm.
ANNABELLA: Harm?   170
GIOVANNI: No, good faith. How is't with ye?
ANNABELLA [*aside*]: I trust he be not frantic.°
    — I am very well, brother.
GIOVANNI: Trust me, but I am sick; I fear so sick
    'Twill cost my life.   175
ANNABELLA: Mercy forbid it! 'tis not so, I hope.
GIOVANNI: I think you love me, sister.
ANNABELLA: Yes, you know I do.
GIOVANNI: I know't, indeed. — You're very fair.
ANNABELLA: Nay, then I see you have a merry sickness.   180
GIOVANNI: That's as it proves.° The poets feign,° I read,
    That Juno° for her forehead did exceed
    All other goddesses; but I durst swear
    Your forehead exceeds hers, as hers did theirs.
ANNABELLA: Troth, this is pretty!
GIOVANNI: Such a pair of stars   185
    As are thine eyes would, like Promethean fire,°
    If gently glanced, give life to senseless stones.
ANNABELLA: Fie upon ye!
GIOVANNI: The lily and the rose, most sweetly strange,°
    Upon your dimpled cheeks do strive for change.°   190
    Such lips would tempt a saint; such hands as those
    Would make an anchorite° lascivious.
ANNABELLA: D'ye mock me, or flatter me?
GIOVANNI: If you would see a beauty more exact
    Than art can counterfeit, or nature frame,   195
    Look in your glass,° and there behold your own.
ANNABELLA: O, you are a trim° youth.
GIOVANNI: Here!   *Offers his dagger to her.*
ANNABELLA: What to do?
GIOVANNI: And here's my breast; strike home!
    Rip up my bosom; there thou shalt behold   200
    A heart in which is writ the truth I speak. Why stand ye?
ANNABELLA: Are you earnest?
GIOVANNI: Yes, most earnest.
    You cannot love?

ANNABELLA: ·   Whom?
GIOVANNI: Me. My tortured soul
   Hath felt affliction° in the heat of death.
   O Annabella, I am quite undone;   205
   The love of thee, my sister, and the view
   Of thy immortal beauty hath untuned
   All harmony both of my rest° and life.
   Why d'ye not strike?
ANNABELLA: Forbid it, my just fears;
   If this be true, 'twere fitter I were dead.   210
GIOVANNI: True, Annabella; 'tis no time to jest.
   I have too long suppressed the hidden flames
   That almost have consumed me. I have spent
   Many a silent night in sighs and groans,
   Ran over all my thoughts, despised° my fate,   215
   Reasoned against the reasons of my love,
   Done all that smoothed-cheek° virtue could advise,
   But found all bootless;° 'tis my destiny
   That you must either love, or I must die.
ANNABELLA: Comes this in sadness° from you?
GIOVANNI: Let some mischief°   220
   Befall me soon, if I dissemble° aught.
ANNABELLA: You are my brother, Giovanni.
GIOVANNI: You
   My sister, Annabella. I know this,
   And could afford you instance° why to love
   So much the more for this; to which intent   225
   Wise Nature first in your creation meant
   To make you mine: else't had been sin and foul
   To share one beauty to a double soul.
   Nearness in birth or blood doth but persuade°
   A nearer nearness in affection.   230
   I have asked counsel of the holy Church,
   Who tells me I may love you, and 'tis just
   That since I may, I should; and will, yes, will.
   Must I now live, or die?
ANNABELLA: Live. Thou hast won
   The field, and never fought; what thou hast urged,   235
   My captive heart had long ago resolved.°
   I blush to tell thee — but I'll tell thee now —
   For every sigh that thou hast spent for me,
   I have sighed ten; for every tear shed twenty.
   And not so much for that I loved, as that   240
   I durst not say I loved; nor scarcely think it.
GIOVANNI: Let not this music be a dream, ye gods,

For pity's sake I beg ye!
ANNABELLA: On my knees,   *She kneels.*
Brother, even by our mother's dust I charge you,
Do not betray me to your mirth or hate;   245
Love me, or kill me, brother.
GIOVANNI: On my knees,   *He kneels.*
Sister, even by my mother's dust I charge you,
Do not betray me to your mirth or hate;
Love me, or kill me, sister.
ANNABELLA: You mean good sooth° then?
GIOVANNI: In good troth I do,   250
And so do you I hope. Say; I'm in earnest.
ANNABELLA. I'll swear't; and I.
GIOVANNI: And I; and by this kiss —   *Kisses her.*
Once more, yet once more; now let's rise, by this —   *[They rise.]*
I would not change this minute for Elysium.
What must we now do?
ANNABELLA: What you will.
GIOVANNI: Come then;   255
After so many tears as we have wept,
Let's learn to court in smiles, to kiss and sleep.   *Exeunt.*

Act One, Scene Three

Enter FLORIO *and* DONADO.

FLORIO: Signior Donado, you have said enough;
I understand you, but would have you know
I will not force my daughter 'gainst her will.
You see I have but two, a son and her;
And he is so devoted to his book,   5
As I must tell you true, I doubt° his health.
Should he miscarry,° all my hopes rely
Upon my girl.° As for worldly fortune,
I am, I thank my stars, blessed with enough.
My care is how to match her to her liking;   10
I would not have her marry wealth, but love,
And if she like your nephew, let him have her.
Here's all that I can say.
DONADO: Sir, you say well,
Like a true father, and for my part, I,
If the young folks can like° ('twixt you and me)   15
Will promise to assure my nephew presently°
Three thousand florins yearly during life,

And after I am dead, my whole estate.
FLORIO: 'Tis a fair proffer, sir. Meantime your nephew
    Shall have free passage to commence his suit;   20
    If he can thrive, he shall have my consent.
    So, for this time I'll leave you, signior.   *Exit.*
DONADO: Well,
    Here's hope yet, if my nephew would have wit;°
    But he is such another dunce, I fear
    He'll never win the wench. When I was young   25
    I could have done't i'faith, and so shall he
    If he will learn of me; and in good time°
    He comes himself.

Enter BERGETTO *and* POGGIO.

How now, Bergetto, whither away so fast?
BERGETTO: O uncle, I have heard the strangest news that ever came out   30
    of the mint —° have I not, Poggio?
POGGIO: Yes indeed, sir.
DONADO: What news, Bergetto?
BERGETTO: Why, look ye, uncle, my barber told me just now that there is
    a fellow come to town, who undertakes to make a mill go without   35
    the mortal help of any water or wind, only with sandbags!° And
    this fellow hath a strange horse, a most excellent beast, I'll assure
    you, uncle (my barber says), whose head, to the wonder of all
    Christian people, stands just behind where his tail is —° is't not
    true, Poggio?
POGGIO: So the barber swore, forsooth.   40
DONADO: And you are running thither?
BERGETTO: Ay forsooth, uncle.
DONADO: Wilt thou be a fool still? Come, sir, you shall not go; you have
    more mind of° a puppet play than on the business I told ye. Why,
    thou great baby, wilt never have wit? Wilt make thyself a   45
    may-game° to all the world?
POGGIO: Answer for yourself, master.
BERGETTO: Why, uncle, should I sit at home still, and not go abroad to
    see fashions like other gallants?
DONADO: To see hobby-horses!° What wise talk, I pray, and you with   50
    Annabella, when you were at Signior Florio's house?
BERGETTO: O, the wench? Ud's sa' me,° uncle, I tickled° her with a rare
    speech, that I made her almost burst her belly with laughing.
DONADO: Nay I think so, and what speech was't?
BERGETTO: What did I say, Poggio?   55
POGGIO: Forsooth, my master said that he loved her almost as well as
    he loved parmasent,° and swore — I'll be sworn for him — that she

wanted° but such a nose as his was, to be as pretty a young woman
as any was in Parma.

DONADO: O, gross!   60

BERGETTO: Nay, uncle, then she asked me whether my father had any
more children than myself; and I said, 'No, 'twere better he should
have had his brains knocked out first.'

DONADO: This is intolerable!

BERGETTO: Then said she, 'Will Signior Donado, your uncle, leave you   65
all his wealth?'

DONADO: Ha! that was good; did she harp upon that string?

BERGETTO: Did she harp upon that string? Ay, that she did. I answered,
'Leave me all his wealth? Why, woman, he hath no other wit;° if he
had he should hear on't to his everlasting glory° and confusion. I   70
know', quoth I, 'I am his white boy,° and will not be gulled';° and with
that she fell into a great smile, and went away. Nay, I did fit° her.

DONADO: Ah sirrah, then I see there is no changing of nature. Well,
Bergetto, I fear thou wilt be a very ass still.   75

BERGETTO: I should be sorry for that, uncle.

DONADO: Come, come you home with me. Since you are no better a
speaker, I'll have you write to her after some courtly manner, and
enclose some rich jewel in the letter.

BERGETTO: Ay, marry, that will be excellent.

DONADO: Peace, innocent!   80
Once in my time I'll set my wits to school;
If all fail, 'tis but the fortune of a fool.

BERGETTO: Poggio, 'twill do, Poggio!   *Exeunt.*

Act Two, Scene One

Enter GIOVANNI *and* ANNABELLA, *as from their chamber.*°

GIOVANNI: Come, Annabella, no more sister now,
But love, a name more gracious; do not blush,
Beauty's sweet wonder, but be proud to know
That yielding thou hast conquered, and inflamed
A heart whose tribute is thy brother's life.   5

ANNABELLA: And mine is his. O, how these stolen contents
Would° print a modest crimson on my cheeks,
Had any but my heart's delight prevailed!

GIOVANNI: I marvel why the chaster of your sex
Should think this pretty toy° called maidenhead   10
So strange a loss, when being lost 'tis nothing,
And you are still the same.

ANNABELLA: 'Tis well for you;

Now you can talk.
GIOVANNI: Music as well consists
   In th'ear, as in the playing.°
ANNABELLA: O, you're wanton!
   Tell on't, you're best, do.
GIOVANNI: Thou wilt chide me, then?   15
   Kiss me: so; thus hung Jove on Leda's neck,°
   And sucked divine ambrosia° from her lips.
   I envy not the mightiest man alive,
   But hold myself, in being king of thee,
   More great than were I king of all the world.   20
   But I shall lose you, sweetheart.
ANNABELLA: But you shall not.
GIOVANNI: You must be married, mistress.
ANNABELLA: Yes; to whom?
GIOVANNI: Someone must have° you.
ANNABELLA: You must.
GIOVANNI: Nay, some other.
ANNABELLA: Now prithee do not speak so, without jesting.
   You'll make me weep in earnest.
GIOVANNI: What? You will not.   25
   But tell me, sweet, canst thou be dared to° swear
   That thou wilt live to me, and to no other?°
ANNABELLA: By both our loves I dare; for didst thou know,
   My Giovanni, how all suitors seem
   To my eyes hateful, thou wouldst trust me then.   30
GIOVANNI: Enough; I take thy word. Sweet, we must part:
   Remember what thou vow'st; keep well my heart.
ANNABELLA: Will you begone?
GIOVANNI: I must.
ANNABELLA: When to return?
GIOVANNI: Soon.
ANNABELLA: Look you do.
   GIOVANNI: Farewell.   *Exit.*
ANNABELLA: Go where thou wilt, in mind I'll keep thee here,   35
   And where thou art, I know I shall be there. —
   Guardian!

Enter PUTANA.

PUTANA: Child, how is't child? Well, thank heaven, ha?
ANNABELLA: O guardian, what a paradise of joy
   Have I passed over!°   40
PUTANA: Nay, what a paradise of joy have you passed under? Why, now
   I commend thee, charge; fear nothing, sweetheart. What though he

be your brother? Your brother's a man, I hope, and I say still, if a
young wench feel the fit° upon her, let her take anybody, father or
brother, all is one.   45

ANNABELLA: I would not have it known for all the world.

PUTANA: Nor I indeed, for the speech of the people;° else 'twere
nothing.

FLORIO [*within*]: Daughter Annabella!

ANNABELLA: O me, my father! — Here, sir! — Reach my work.°   50

FLORIO [*within*]: What are you doing?

ANNABELLA: So, let him come now.

    Enter FLORIO, RICHARDETTO *like a doctor of physic,*°
    and PHILOTIS *with a lute in her hand.*

FLORIO: So, hard to work, that's well; you lose° no time.
   Look, I have brought you company: here's one,
   A learned doctor, lately come from Padua,°
   Much skilled in physic; and for that I see   55
   You have of late been sickly, I entreated
   This reverend man to visit you some time.

ANNABELLA: You're very welcome, sir.

RICHARDETTO: I thank you, mistress.
   Loud fame in large report hath spoke your praise,
   As well for virtue as perfection;°   60
   For which I have been bold to bring with me
   A kinswoman of mine, a maid, for song
   And music one perhaps will give content.
   Please you to know her.

ANNABELLA: They are parts I love,
   And she for them most welcome.

PHILOTIS: Thank you, lady.   65

FLORIO: Sir, now you know my house, pray make not strange;°
   And if you find my daughter need your art,°
   I'll be your paymaster.

RICHARDETTO: Sir, what I am
   She shall command.

FLORIO: You shall bind me to you.
   Daughter, I must have conference with you   70
   About some matters that concerns us both.
   Good master doctor, please you but walk in,
   We'll crave a little of your cousin's cunning.°
   I think my girl hath not quite forgot
   To touch° an instrument; she could have done't;   75
   We'll hear them both.

RICHARDETTO: I'll wait upon you, sir.   *Exeunt.*

Act Two, Scene Two

Enter SORANZO *in his study, reading a book.*

SORANZO: 'Love's measure is extreme, the comfort pain,
　　The life unrest, and the reward disdain.'
　　What's here? Look't o'er again: 'tis so, so writes
　　This smooth licentious poet in his rhymes.
　　But Sannazar,° thou liest, for had thy bosom　　　　　　　　　5
　　Felt such oppression as is laid on mine,
　　Thou wouldst have kissed the rod that made thee smart.
　　To work then, happy Muse, and contradict
　　What Sannazar hath in his envy° writ.　　　　　　　　[*Writes.*]
　　'Love's measure is the mean,° sweet his annoys,°　　　　　10
　　His pleasures life, and his reward all joys.'
　　Had Annabella lived when Sannazar
　　Did in his brief encomium° celebrate
　　Venice, that queen of cities, he had left
　　That verse which gained him such a sum of gold,　　　　15
　　And for one only look from Annabell
　　Had writ of her, and her diviner cheeks.
　　O, how my thoughts are —
VASQUES [*within*]: Pray forbear; in rules of civility let me give notice
　　on't. I shall be taxed of° my neglect of duty and service.　　20
SORANZO: What rude intrusion interrupts my peace?
　　Can I be nowhere private?
VASQUES [*within*]: Troth, you wrong your modesty.
SORANZO: What's the matter, Vasques, who is't?

Enter HIPPOLITA *and* VASQUES.

HIPPOLITA:　　　　　　　　　　　　　　　　'Tis I.
　　Do you know me now? Look, perjured man, on her　　　　25
　　Whom thou and thy distracted° lust have wronged.
　　Thy sensual rage of blood° hath made my youth
　　A scorn to men and angels, and shall I
　　Be now a foil to thy unsated change?°
　　Thou know'st, false wanton, when my modest fame°　　30
　　Stood free from stain or scandal, all the charms
　　Of hell or sorcery could not prevail
　　Against the honour of my chaster bosom.
　　Thine eyes did plead in tears, thy tongue in oaths,
　　Such and so many, that a heart of steel　　　　　　　　35
　　Would have been wrought to pity, as was mine.
　　And shall the conquest of my lawful bed,

My husband's death urged on by his disgrace,
My loss of womanhood,° be ill-rewarded
With hatred and contempt? No; know Soranzo,   40
I have a spirit doth as much distaste°
The slavery of fearing thee, as thou
Doth loathe the memory of what hath passed.
SORANZO: Nay, dear Hippolita —
HIPPOLITA: Call me not 'dear',
Nor think with supple words to smooth the grossness   45
Of my abuses. 'Tis not your new mistress,
Your goodly Madam Merchant, shall triumph
On my dejection;° tell her thus from me,
My birth was nobler, and by much more free.°
SORANZO: You are too violent.
HIPPOLITA: You are too double   50
In your dissimulation. Seest thou this,
This habit,° these black mourning weeds° of care?
'Tis thou art cause of this, and hast divorced
My husband from his life and me from him,
And made me widow in my widowhood.   55
SORANZO: Will you yet hear?
HIPPOLITA: More of thy perjuries?
Thy soul is drowned too deeply in those sins;
Thou need'st not add to th'number.
SORANZO: Then I'll leave you;
You are past all rules of sense.
HIPPOLITA: And thou of grace.
VASQUES: Fie, mistress, you are not near the limits of reason: if my lord   60
had a resolution as noble as virtue itself, you take the course to
unedge° it all. — Sir, I beseech you do not perplex° her; griefs, alas,
will have a vent. I dare undertake Madam Hippolita will now
freely° hear you.
SORANZO: Talk to a woman frantic! Are these the fruits of your love?   65
HIPPOLITA: They are the fruits of thy untruth, false man!
Didst thou not swear, whilst yet my husband lived,
That thou wouldst wish no happiness on earth
More than to call me wife? Didst thou not vow
When he should die to marry me? For which   70
The devil in my blood, and thy protests,°
Caused me to counsel him to undertake
A voyage to Ligorne,° for that we heard
His brother there was dead, and left a daughter
Young and unfriended, who with much ado   75
I wished him to bring hither. He did so,
And went; and as thou know'st, died on the way.

Unhappy man, to buy his death so dear
With my advice! Yet thou for whom I did it
Forget'st thy vows, and leav'st me to my shame.   80
SORANZO: Who could help this?
HIPPOLITA: Who? Perjured man, thou couldst,
If thou hadst faith or love.
SORANZO: You are deceived.
The vows I made, if you remember well,
Were wicked and unlawful; 'twere more sin
To keep them than to break them. As for me,   85
I cannot mask my penitence. Think thou
How much thou hast digressed from honest shame
In bringing of a gentleman to death
Who was thy husband; such a one as he,
So noble in his quality,° condition,   90
Learning, behaviour, entertainment,° love,
As Parma could not show a braver° man.
VASQUES: You do not well; this was not your promise.
SORANZO: I care not; let her know her monstrous life.
Ere I'll be servile to so black a sin   95
I'll be accursed. — Woman, come here no more,
Learn to repent and die; for by my honour
I hate thee and thy lust; you have been too foul.   [*Exit.*]
VASQUES [*aside*]: This part has been scurvily played.
HIPPOLITA: How foolishly this beast contemns his fate,°   100
And shuns the use of that which I more scorn
Than I once loved, his love. But let him go;
My vengeance shall give comfort to his woe.°   *She offers to go away.*°
VASQUES: Mistress, mistress, Madam Hippolita, pray, a word or two!
HIPPOLITA: With me, sir?   105
VASQUES: With you, if you please.
HIPPOLITA: What is't?
VASQUES: I know you are infinitely moved now, and you think you have
cause. Some I confess you have, but sure not so much as you
imagine.   110
HIPPOLITA: Indeed!
VASQUES: O, you were miserably bitter, which you followed even to the
last syllable; faith, you were somewhat too shrewd.° By my life,
you could not have took my lord in a worse time since I first knew
him; tomorrow you shall find him a new man.   115
HIPPOLITA: Well, I shall wait his leisure.
VASQUES: Fie, this is not a hearty° patience, it comes sourly from you;
troth, let me persuade you for once.
HIPPOLITA [*aside*]: I have it, and it shall be so; thanks, opportunity! —
Persuade me to what?   120

VASQUES: Visit him in some milder temper.° O, if you could but master
    a little your female spleen, how might you win him!
HIPPOLITA: He will never love me. Vasques, thou hast been a too trusty
    servant to such a master, and I believe thy reward in the end will
    fall out like mine.   125
VASQUES: So, perhaps, too.
HIPPOLITA: Resolve thyself it will. Had I one so true, so truly honest, so
    secret to my counsels, as thou hast been to him and his, I should
    think it a slight acquittance,° not only to make him master of all I
    have, but even of myself.   130
VASQUES: O, you are a noble gentlewoman!
HIPPOLITA: Wilt thou feed always upon hopes? Well, I know thou art
    wise, and seest the reward of an old servant daily what it is.
VASQUES: Beggary and neglect.
HIPPOLITA: True; but Vasques, wert thou mine, and wouldst be private 135
    to° me and my designs, I here protest myself, and all what I can
    else call mine, should be at thy dispose.
VASQUES [*aside*]: Work you that way, old mole? Then I have the wind of
    you.° I were not worthy of it, by any desert that could lie within
    my compass. If I could —   140
HIPPOLITA: What then?
VASQUES: I should then hope to live in these my old years with rest and
    security.
HIPPOLITA: Give me thy hand. Now promise but thy silence,
    And help to bring to pass a plot I have,   145
    And here in sight of heaven, that being done,
    I make thee lord of me and mine estate.
VASQUES: Come, you are merry;° this is such a happiness that I can
    neither think or believe.
HIPPOLITA: Promise thy secrecy, and 'tis confirmed.   150
VASQUES: Then here I call our good genii° for witnesses, whatsoever
    your designs are, or against whomsoever, I will not only be a
    special° actor therein, but never disclose it till it be effected.
HIPPOLITA: I take thy word, and with that, thee for mine.
    Come then, let's more confer of this anon.   155
    On this delicious bane° my thoughts shall banquet;
    Revenge shall sweeten what my griefs have tasted.°   *Exeunt.*

Act Two, Scene Three

Enter RICHARDETTO *and* PHILOTIS.

RICHARDETTO: Thou seest, my lovely niece, these strange mishaps,
    How all my fortunes turn to my disgrace,

Wherein I am but as a looker-on,
Whiles others act° my shame and I am silent.
PHILOTIS: But uncle, wherein can this borrowed shape°   5
Give you content?
RICHARDETTO: I'll tell thee, gentle niece.
Thy wanton aunt in her lascivious riots°
Lives now secure, thinks I am surely dead
In my late journey to Ligorne for you,
As I have caused it to be rumoured out.   10
Now would I see with what an impudence°
She gives scope to her loose adultery,
And how the common voice allows hereof;°
Thus far I have prevailed.
PHILOTIS: Alas, I fear
You mean some strange revenge.
RICHARDETTO: O, be not troubled;   15
Your ignorance shall plead for you in all.°
But to our business: what, you learnt for certain
How Signior Florio means to give his daughter
In marriage to Soranzo?
PHILOTIS: Yes, for certain.
RICHARDETTO: But how find you young Annabella's love   20
Inclined to him?
PHILOTIS: For aught I could perceive,
She neither fancies him or any else.
RICHARDETTO: There's mystery in that which time must show.
She used you kindly?
PHILOTIS: Yes.
RICHARDETTO: And craved your company?
PHILOTIS: Often.
RICHARDETTO: 'Tis well; it goes as I could wish.   25
I am the doctor now, and as for you,
None knows you; if all fail not we shall thrive.
But who comes here?

Enter GRIMALDI.

                      I know him; 'tis Grimaldi,
A Roman and a soldier, near allied
Unto the Duke of Montferrato, one   30
Attending on the Nuncio of the Pope
That now resides in Parma, by which means
He hopes to get the love of Annabella.
GRIMALDI: Save you,° sir.
RICHARDETTO: And you, sir.

GRIMALDI: I have heard
Of your approvèd skill, which through the city 35
Is freely talked of, and would crave your aid.
RICHARDETTO: For what, sir?
GRIMALDI: Marry, sir, for this —
But I would speak in private.
RICHARDETTO: Leave us, cousin. *Exit* PHILOTIS.
GRIMALDI: I love fair Annabella, and would know
Whether in arts° there may not be receipts° 40
To move affection.
RICHARDETTO: Sir, perhaps there may;
But these will nothing profit you.
GRIMALDI: Not me?
RICHARDETTO: Unless I be mistook, you are a man
Greatly in favour with the Cardinal.
GRIMALDI: What of that?
RICHARDETTO: In duty to his Grace, 45
I will be bold to tell you, if you seek
To marry Florio's daughter, you must first
Remove a bar 'twixt you and her.
GRIMALDI: Who's that?
RICHARDETTO: Soranzo is the man that hath her heart,
And while he lives be sure you cannot speed.° 50
GRIMALDI: Soranzo? What, mine enemy! Is't he?
RICHARDETTO: Is he your enemy?
GRIMALDI: The man I hate
Worse than confusion;° I'll kill him straight.
RICHARDETTO: Nay, then take mine advice,
Even for his Grace's sake the Cardinal. 55
I'll find a time when he and she do meet,
Of which I'll give you notice, and to be sure
He shall not 'scape you, I'll provide a poison
To dip your rapier's point in. If he had
As many heads as Hydra° had, he dies. 60
GRIMALDI: But shall I trust thee, doctor?
RICHARDETTO: As yourself;
Doubt not in aught. [*Aside*] Thus shall the fates decree:
By me Soranzo falls, that ruined me. *Exeunt.*

Act Two, Scene Four

Enter DONADO, BERGETTO *and* POGGIO.

DONADO: Well, sir, I must be content to be both your secretary and your

messenger myself. I cannot tell what this letter may work, but as
sure as I am alive, if thou come once to talk with her, I fear thou
wilt mar whatsoever I make.

BERGETTO: You make, uncle? Why, am not I big enough to carry mine   5
    own letter, I pray?

DONADO: Ay, ay, carry a fool's head o' thy own. Why, thou dunce,
    wouldst thou write a letter, and carry it thyself?

BERGETTO: Yes, that I would, and read it to her with my own mouth; for
    you must think, if she will not believe me myself when she hears   10
    me speak, she will not believe another's handwriting. O, you think
    I am a blockhead, uncle. No, sir; Poggio knows I have indited° a
    letter myself, so I have.

POGGIO: Yes truly, sir, I have it in my pocket.

DONADO: A sweet one, no doubt; pray let's see't.   15

BERGETTO: I cannot read my own hand° very well, Poggio; read it,
    Poggio.

DONADO: Begin.

POGGIO [*reads*]: 'Most dainty and honey-sweet mistress, I could call you
    fair, and lie as fast° as any that loves you, but my uncle being the   20
    elder man I leave it to him, as more fit for his age, and the colour
    of his beard. I am wise enough to tell you I can board° where I see
    occasion, or if you like my uncle's wit better than mine, you shall
    marry me; if you like mine better than his, I will marry you in spite
    of your teeth.° So, commending my best parts° to you, I rest yours   25
    upwards and downwards, or you may choose,
    Bergetto.'

BERGETTO: Ah, ha! here's stuff, uncle!

DONADO: Here's stuff indeed to shame us all. Pray, whose advice did
    you take in this learned letter?   30

POGGIO: None, upon my word, but mine own.

BERGETTO: And mine, uncle, believe it, nobody's else; 'twas mine own
    brain, I thank a good wit for't.

DONADO: Get you home, sir, and look you keep within doors till I
    return.   35

BERGETTO: How! That were a jest indeed; I scorn it i'faith.

DONADO: What! You do not?

BERGETTO: Judge me, but I do now.

POGGIO: Indeed, sir, 'tis very unhealthy.

DONADO: Well, sir, if I hear any of your apish running to motions° and   40
    fopperies° till I come back, you were as good not;° look to't.   *Exit.*

BERGETTO: Poggio, shall's steal to see this horse° with the head in's tail?

POGGIO: Ay, but you must take heed of whipping.

BERGETTO: Dost take me for a child, Poggio? Come, honest Poggio.   *Exeunt.*

Act Two, Scene Five

FRIAR: Peace! Thou hast told a tale whose every word
　　Threatens eternal slaughter to the soul.
　　I'm sorry I have heard it; would mine ears
　　Had been one minute deaf before the hour
　　That thou cam'st to me. O young man cast away°　　　　　5
　　By the religious number° of mine order,
　　I day and night have waked my agèd eyes
　　Above my strength, to weep on thy behalf.
　　But heaven is angry, and be thou resolved,
　　Thou art a man remarked to taste a mischief.°　　　　　10
　　Look for't; though it come late, it will come sure.
GIOVANNI: Father, in this you are uncharitable;
　　What I have done, I'll prove both fit and good.
　　It is a principle, which you have taught
　　When I was yet your scholar, that the frame　　　　　15
　　And composition of the mind doth follow
　　The frame and composition of the body.
　　So where the body's furniture° is beauty,
　　The mind's must needs be virtue, which allowed,
　　Virtue itself is reason but refined,　　　　　20
　　And love the quintessence° of that.
　　This proves my sister's beauty, being rarely fair,
　　Is rarely virtuous; chiefly in her love,
　　And chiefly in that love, her love to me.
　　If hers to me, then so is mine to her;　　　　　25
　　Since in like causes are effects alike.
FRIAR: O ignorance in knowledge! Long ago,
　　How often have I warned thee, this before!
　　Indeed, if we were sure there were no deity,
　　Nor heaven nor hell, then to be led alone　　　　　30
　　By Nature's light — as were philosophers
　　Of elder° times — might instance° some defence.
　　But 'tis not so. Then, madman, thou wilt find
　　That Nature is in heaven's positions blind.°
GIOVANNI: Your age o'errules you; had you youth like mine,　　　　　35
　　You'd make her love your heaven, and her divine.
FRIAR: Nay, then I see th'art too far sold to hell,
　　It lies not in the compass of my prayers
　　To call thee back. Yet let me counsel thee:
　　Persuade thy sister to some marriage.　　　　　40
GIOVANNI: Marriage? Why, that's to damn her! That's to prove
　　Her greedy of variety of lust.
FRIAR: O fearful! If thou wilt not, give me leave

To shrive° her, lest she should die unabsolved.
GIOVANNI: At your best leisure,° father; then she'll tell you   45
    How dearly she doth prize my matchless love;
    Then you will know what pity 'twere we two
    Should have been sundered from each other's arms.
    View well her face, and in that little round
    You may observe a world of variety: 50
    For colour, lips, for sweet perfumes, her breath;
    For jewels, eyes; for threads of purest gold,
    Hair; for delicious choice of flowers, cheeks;
    Wonder in every portion of that throne.°
    Hear her but speak, and you will swear the spheres   55
    Make music to the citizens in heaven;°
    But father, what is else for pleasure framed,
    Lest I offend your ears, shall go unnamed.
FRIAR: The more I hear, I pity thee the more,
    That one so excellent should give those parts   60
    All to a second death.° What I can do
    Is but to pray; and yet I could advise thee,
    Wouldst thou be ruled.
GIOVANNI: In what?
FRIAR: Why, leave her yet,
    The throne of mercy° is above your trespass;
    Yet time is left you both —
GIOVANNI: To embrace each other,   65
    Else let all time be struck quite out of number.
    She is, like me, and I like her, resolved.
FRIAR: No more! I'll visit her. This grieves me most:
    Things being thus, a pair of souls are lost.   *Exeunt.*

Act Two, Scene Six

Enter FLORIO, DONADO, ANNABELLA, PUTANA.

FLORIO: Where's Giovanni?
ANNABELLA: Newly walked abroad,
    And, as I heard him say, gone to the friar,
    His reverend tutor.
FLORIO: That's a blessèd man,
    A man made up of holiness; I hope
    He'll teach him how to gain another world.   5
DONADO [*Offers a letter*]: Fair gentlewoman, here's a letter sent
    To you from my young cousin. I dare swear

He loves you in his soul; would you could hear
Sometimes, what I see daily, sighs and tears,
As if his breast were prison to his heart.   10
FLORIO: Receive it, Annabella.
ANNABELLA: Alas, good man!   [*Takes the letter.*]
DONADO: What's that she said?
PUTANA: And° please you, sir, she said — 'Alas, good man!' —
    [*Aside to* DONADO] Truly, I do commend him to her every night
    before her first sleep, because I would have her dream of him, and   15
    she hearkens to that most religiously.
DONADO: [*aside to* PUTANA] Say'st so?   [*Gives her money.*]
    Godamercy, Putana, there's something for thee, and prithee do what
    thou canst on his behalf; sha'not be lost labour, take my word for't.
PUTANA: [*aside to* DONADO] Thank you most heartily, sir; now I have a   20
    feeling° of your mind, let me alone to work.
ANNABELLA: Guardian!
PUTANA: Did you call?
ANNABELLA: Keep this letter.
DONADO: Signior Florio, in any case bid her read it instantly.   25
FLORIO: Keep it for what? Pray read it me here right.°
ANNABELLA: I shall, sir.   *She reads.*
DONADO: How d'ye find her inclined, Signior?
FLORIO: Troth, sir, I know not how; not all so well
    As I could wish.   30
ANNABELLA: Sir, I am bound to rest your cousin's debtor.
    The jewel I'll return, for if he love,
    I'll count that love a jewel.
DONADO: Mark you that? —
    Nay, keep them both, sweet maid.
ANNABELLA: You must excuse me;
    Indeed I will not keep it.
FLORIO: Where's the ring;   35
    That which your mother in her will bequeathed,
    And charged you on her blessing not to give't
    To any but your husband? Send back that.
ANNABELLA: I have it not.
FLORIO: Ha! Have it not? Where is't?
ANNABELLA: My brother in the morning took it from me;   40
    Said he would wear't today.
FLORIO: Well, what do you say
    To young Bergetto's love? Are you content
    To match with him? Speak.
DONADO: There's the point indeed.
ANNABELLA [*aside*]: What shall I do? I must say something now.
FLORIO: What say?° Why d'ye not speak?

ANNABELLA: Sir, with your leave,   45
    Please you to give me freedom?°
FLORIO: Yes, you have't.
ANNABELLA: Signior Donado, if your nephew mean
    To raise his better fortunes° in his match,
    The hope of me will hinder such a hope.
    Sir, if you love him, as I know you do,   50
    Find one more worthy of his choice than me.
    In short, I'm sure I sha'not be his wife.
DONADO: Why, here's plain dealing; I commend thee for't,
    And all the worst I wish thee, is heaven bless thee!
    Your father yet and I will still be friends,   55
    Shall we not, Signior Florio?
FLORIO: Yes, why not?
    Look, here your cousin comes.

Enter BERGETTO *and* POGGIO.

DONADO [*aside*]: O coxcomb, what doth he make° here?
BERGETTO: Where's my uncle, sirs?
DONADO: What's the news now?   60
BERGETTO: Save you, uncle, save you. You must not think I come for
    nothing, masters. And how, and how is't? What, you have read my
    letter? Ah, there I — tickled° you i'faith!
POGGIO [*aside to* BERGETTO]: But 'twere better you had tickled her in
    another place.   65
BERGETTO: Sirrah sweetheart, I'll tell thee a good jest; and riddle° what
    'tis.
ANNABELLA: You say you'd tell me.
BERGETTO: As I was walking just now in the street, I met a swaggering
    fellow would needs take the wall° of me; and because he did thrust   70
    me, I very valiantly called him rogue. He hereupon bade me draw.
    I told him I had more wit than so;° but when he saw that I would
    not, he did so maul me with the hilts of his rapier that my head
    sung whilst my feet capered in the kennel.°
DONADO [*aside*]: Was ever the like ass seen?   75
ANNABELLA: And what did you all this while?
BERGETTO: Laugh at him for a gull,° till I see the blood run about mine
    ears, and then I could not choose but find in my heart to cry; till a
    fellow with a broad beard — they say he is a new-come doctor —
    called me into this house, and gave me a plaster — look you, here   80
    'tis; and sir, there was a young wench washed my face and hands
    most excellently, i'faith I shall love her as long as I live for't — did
    she not, Poggio?
POGGIO: Yes, and kissed him too.

BERGETTO: Why la now, you think I tell a lie, uncle, I warrant.   85

DONADO: Would he that beat thy blood out of thy head, had beaten
    some wit into it; for I fear thou never wilt have any.

BERGETTO: O uncle, but there was a wench would have done a man's
    heart good to have looked on her; by this light, she had a face
    methinks worth twenty of you, Mistress Annabella.   90

DONADO [*aside*]: Was ever such a fool born?

ANNABELLA: I am glad she liked° you, sir.

BERGETTO: Are you so? By my troth, I thank you forsooth.

FLORIO: Sure 'twas the doctor's niece, that was last day with us here.

BERGETTO: 'Twas she, 'twas she!   95

DONALDO: How do you know that, simplicity?

BERGETTO: Why, does not he say so? If I should have said no, I should
    have given him the lie,° uncle, and so have deserved a dry° beating
    again; I'll none of that.

FLORIO: A very modest, well-behaved young maid,   100
    As I have seen.

DONADO: Is she indeed?

FLORIO: Indeed
    She is, if I have any judgement.

DONADO: Well, sir, now you are free, you need not care for sending letters
    now: you are dismissed, your mistress here will none of you.

BERGETTO: No? Why, what care I for that; I can have wenches enough   105
    in Parma for half-a-crown° apiece, cannot I, Poggio?

POGGIO: I'll warrant you, sir.

DONADO: Signior Florio,
    I thank you for your free recourse you gave
    For my admittance; and to you, fair maid,
    That jewel I will give you 'gainst° your marriage.   110
    Come, will you go, sir?

BERGETTO: Ay, marry will I. Mistress, farewell, mistress; I'll come again
    tomorrow. Farewell, mistress.

                        Exeunt DONADO, BERGETTO *and* POGGIO.

               Enter GIOVANNI.

FLORIO: Son, where have you been? What, alone, alone still?
    I would not have it so; you must forsake   115
    This over-bookish humour. Well, your sister
    Hath shook the fool off.

GIOVANNI: 'Twas no match for her.

FLORIO: 'Twas not indeed, I meant it nothing less;
    Soranzo is the man I only° like. —
    Look on him, Annabella. Come, 'tis supper-time,   120
    And it grows late.

GIOVANNI: Whose jewel's that?
ANNABELLA: Some sweetheart's.
GIOVANNI: So I think.
ANNABELLA: A lusty youth. —
   Signior Donado gave it me to wear
   Against my marriage.
GIOVANNI: But you shall not wear it;
   Send it him back again.
ANNABELLA: What, you are jealous?   125
GIOVANNI: That you shall know anon, at better leisure.
   Welcome, sweet night. The evening crowns the day.   *Exeunt.*

Act Three, Scene One

Enter BERGETTO *and* POGGIO.

BERGETTO: Does my uncle think to make me a baby still? No, Poggio, he
   shall know I have a sconce° now.
POGGIO: Ay, let him not bob° you off like an ape with an apple.
BERGETTO: 'sfoot,° I will have the wench, if he were ten uncles, in despite
   of his nose, Poggio.   5
POGGIO: Hold him to the grindstone, and give not a jot of ground. She
   hath in a manner promised you already.
BERGETTO: True, Poggio, and her uncle the doctor swore I should marry
   her.
POGGIO: He swore, I remember.   10
BERGETTO: And I will have her, that's more; didst see the codpiece-
   point° she gave me, and the box of marmalade?°
POGGIO: Very well; and kissed you, that my chops watered at the sight
   on't. There's no way but to clap up a marriage in hugger mugger.°
BERGETTO: I will do't, for I tell thee, Poggio, I begin to grow valiant   15
   methinks, and my courage° begins to rise.
POGGIO: Should you be afraid of your uncle?
BERGETTO: Hang him, old doting rascal; no! I say I will have her.
POGGIO: Lose no time then.
BERGETTO: I will beget a race of wise men and constables, that shall cart   20
   whores° at their own charges,° and break the Duke's peace ere I
   have done myself. Come away!   *Exeunt.*

Act Three, Scene Two

Enter FLORIO, GIOVANNI, SORANZO, ANNABELLA,
PUTANA, *and* VASQUES.

FLORIO: My lord Soranzo, though I must confess
    The proffers that are made me have been great
    In marriage of my daughter, yet the hope
    Of your still rising honours have prevailed
    Above all other jointures.° Here she is,   5
    She knows my mind, speak for yourself to her;
    And hear you, daughter, see you use him nobly.
    For any private speech I'll give you time.
    Come, son, and you, the rest, let them alone;
    Agree they as they may.
SORANZO: I thank you, sir.   10
GIOVANNI [*aside to* ANNABELLA]: Sister, be not all woman;° think on me.
SORANZO: Vasques!
VASQUES: My lord?
SORANZO: Attend me without.
                      Exeunt all but SORANZO *and* ANNABELLA.
ANNABELLA: Sir, what's your will with me?
SORANZO: Do you not know
    What I should tell you?
ANNABELLA: Yes, you'll say you love me.
SORANZO: And I'll swear it too; will you believe it?   15
ANNABELLA: Tis no point of faith.°

Enter GIOVANNI *above.*

SORANZO: Have you not will to love?
ANNABELLA: Not you.
SORANZO: Whom then?
ANNABELLA: That's as the fates infer.°
GIOVANNI [*aside*]: Of those I'm regent now.
SORANZO: What mean you, sweet?
ANNABELLA: To live and die a maid.
SORANZO: O, that's unfit.
GIOVANNI [*aside*]: Here's one can say that's but a woman's note.° 20
SORANZO: Did you but see my heart, then would you swear —
ANNABELLA: That you were dead.
GIOVANNI [*aside*]:   That's true, or somewhat near it.
SORANZO: See you these true love's tears?
ANNABELLA: No.

GIOVANNI [*aside*]:   Now she winks.°
SORANZO: They plead to you for grace.
ANNABELLA: Yet nothing speak.
SORANZO: O, grant my suit!
ANNABELLA: What is't?
SORANZO: To let me live —   25
ANNABELLA: Take it.
SORANZO: — still yours.
ANNABELLA: That is not mine to give.
GIOVANNI [*aside*]: One such another word would kill his hopes.
SORANZO: Mistress, to leave those fruitless strifes of wit,
 Know I have loved you long, and loved you truly;
 Not hope of what you have, but what you are   30
 Have drawn me on. Then let me not in vain
 Still feel the rigour of your chaste disdain.
 I'm sick, and sick to th'heart.
ANNABELLA: Help! Aqua-vitae!°
SORANZO: What mean you?
ANNABELLA: Why, I thought you had been sick.
SORANZO: Do you mock my love?
GIOVANNI [*aside*]:   There, sir, she was too nimble.   35
SORANZO [*aside*]: 'Tis plain; she laughs at me! — These scornful taunts
 Neither become your modesty or years.
ANNABELLA: You are no looking-glass; or if you were,
 I'd dress my language by you.
GIOVANNI [*aside*]:   I'm confirmed.°
ANNABELLA: To put you out of doubt, my lord, methinks   40
 Your common sense should make you understand
 That if I loved you, or desired your love,
 Some way I should have given you better taste.°
 But since you are a nobleman, and one
 I would not wish should spend his youth in hopes,   45
 Let me advise you here to forbear your suit,
 And think I wish you well, I tell you this.
SORANZO: Is't you speak this?
ANNABELLA: Yes, I myself; yet know —
 Thus far I give you comfort — if mine eyes
 Could have picked out a man amongst all those   50
 That sued to me, to make a husband of,
 You should have been that man. Let this suffice;
 Be noble in your secrecy, and wise.
GIOVANNI [*aside*]: Why now I see she loves me.
ANNABELLA: One word more.
 As ever virtue lived within your mind,   55
 As ever noble courses were your guide,

As ever you would have me know you loved me,
Let not my father know hereof by you:
If I hereafter find that I must marry,
It shall be you or none.
SORANZO: I take that promise.   60
ANNABELLA: O, O my head!
SORANZO: What's the matter? Not well?
ANNABELLA: O, I begin to sicken!
GIOVANNI [*aside*]:   Heaven forbid!   *Exit from above.*
SORANZO: Help, help, within there, ho! Look to your daughter,
Signior Florio.

Enter FLORIO, GIOVANNI, PUTANA.

FLORIO: Hold her up; she swoons.
GIOVANNI: Sister, how d'ye?
ANNABELLA: Sick; brother, are you there?   65
FLORIO: Convey her to her bed instantly, whilst I send for a physician;
quickly, I say.
PUTANA: Alas, poor child!   *Exeunt all but* SORANZO.

Enter VASQUES.

VASQUES: My lord.
SORANZO: Oh Vasques, now I doubly am undone,   70
Both in my present and my future hopes.
She plainly told me that she could not love,
And thereupon soon sickened, and I fear
Her life's in danger.
VASQUES [*aside*]: By'r Lady, sir, and so is yours, if you knew all. [*Aloud*]   75
'Las, sir, I am sorry for that; may be 'tis but the maid's sickness,° an
overflux° of youth — and then, sir, there is no such present°
remedy as present marriage. But hath she given you an absolute
denial?
SORANZO: She hath and she hath not; I'm full of grief,
But what she said I'll tell thee as we go.   *Exeunt.*

Act Three, Scene Three

Enter GIOVANNI *and* PUTANA.

PUTANA: O sir, we are all undone, quite undone, utterly undone, and
shamed forever; your sister, O your sister!
GIOVANNI: What of her? For heaven's sake speak, how does she?

PUTANA: O that ever I was born to see this day!

GIOVANNI: She is not dead, ha, is she?   5

PUTANA: Dead? No, she is quick.° 'Tis worse; she is with child. You
    know what you have done, heaven forgive ye! 'Tis too late to
    repent, now heaven help us!

GIOVANNI: With child? How dost thou know't?

PUTANA: How do I know't? Am I at these years ignorant what the   10
    meanings of qualms and water-pangs° be? Of changing of colours,
    queasiness of stomachs, pukings, and another thing that I could
    name?° Do not, for her and your credit's sake,° spend the time in
    asking how and which way 'tis so. She is quick, upon my word; if
    you let a physician see her water° you're undone.   15

GIOVANNI: But in what case is she?

PUTANA: Prettily amended;° 'twas but a fit, which I soon espied, and
    she must look for often henceforward.

GIOVANNI: Commend me to her, bid her take no care;°
    Let not the doctor visit her, I charge you,   20
    Make some excuse till I return. — O me,
    I have a world of business in my head! —
    Do not discomfort her. — How does this news
    Perplex me! — If my father come to her,
    Tell him she's recovered well; say 'twas   25
    But some ill diet. D'ye hear, woman? Look you to't.

PUTANA: I will, sir.   *Exeunt.*

Act Three, Scene Four

Enter FLORIO *and* RICHARDETTO.

FLORIO: And how d'ye find her, sir?

RICHARDETTO: Indifferent° well.
    I see no danger, scarce perceive she's sick,
    But that she told me she had lately eaten
    Melons, and as she thought, those disagreed
    With her young stomach.

FLORIO: Did you give her aught?   5

RICHARDETTO: An easy surfeit-water,° nothing else.
    You need not doubt her health; I rather think
    Her sickness is a fullness of her blood.° —
    You understand me?

FLORIO: I do; you counsel well,
    And once° within these few days will so order't   10
    She shall be married ere she know the time.

RICHARDETTO: Yet let not haste, sir, make unworthy choice;
    That were dishonour.
FLORIO: Master doctor, no,
    I will not do so neither; in plain words,
    My lord Soranzo is the man I mean.   15
RICHARDETTO: A noble and a virtuous gentleman.
FLORIO: As any is in Parma. Not far hence
    Dwells Father Bonaventure, a grave friar,
    Once tutor to my son; now at his cell
    I'll have 'em married.
RICHARDETTO: You have plotted wisely.   20
FLORIO: I'll send one straight to speak with him tonight.
RICHARDETTO: Soranzo's wise; he will delay no time.
FLORIO: It shall be so.

                Enter FRIAR *and* GIOVANNI.

FRIAR: Good peace be here, and love!
FLORIO: Welcome, religious friar, you are one
    That still bring blessing to the place you come to.   25
GIOVANNI: Sir, with what speed I could, I did my best
    To draw this holy man from forth his cell
    To visit my sick sister, that with words
    Of ghostly° comfort in this time of need
    He might absolve her, whether she live or die.   30
FLORIO: 'Twas well done, Giovanni; thou herein
    Hast showed a Christian's care, a brother's love.
    Come, father, I'll conduct you to her chamber,
    And one thing would entreat you.
FRIAR: Say on, sir.
FLORIO: I have a father's dear impression,°   35
    And wish, before I fall into my grave,
    That I might see her married, as 'tis fit.
    A word from you, grave man, will win her more
    Than all our best persuasions.
FRIAR: Gentle sir,
    All this I'll say, that heaven may prosper her.   *Exeunt.*

Act Three, Scene Five

                Enter GRIMALDI.

GRIMALDI: Now if the doctor keep his word, Soranzo,
    Twenty to one you miss your bride. I know

'Tis an unnoble act, and not becomes
A soldier's valour; but in terms° of love,
Where merit cannot sway, policy° must.   5
I am resolved: if this physician
Play not on both hands,° then Soranzo falls.

Enter RICHARDETTO.

RICHARDETTO: You are come as I could wish; this very night
    Soranzo, 'tis ordained, must be affied°
    To Annabella; and for aught I know,   10
    Married.
GRIMALDI: How!
RICHARDETTO: Yet your patience.
    The place, 'tis Friar Bonaventure's cell.
    Now I would wish you to bestow this night
    In watching thereabouts. 'Tis but a night;
    If you miss now, tomorrow I'll know all.   15
GRIMALDI: Have you the poison?
RICHARDETTO: Here 'tis in this box.   [*Gives him a box.*]
    Doubt nothing, this will do't; in any case,
    As you respect your life, be quick and sure.
GRIMALDI: I'll speed° him.
RICHARDETTO: Do; away, for 'tis not safe
    You should be seen much here. — Ever my love!   20
    GRIMALDI: And mine to you.   *Exit.*
RICHARDETTO: So, if this hit,° I'll laugh and hug revenge;
    And they that now dream of a wedding feast
    May chance to mourn the lusty bridegroom's ruin.
    But to my other business. Niece, Philotis!   25

Enter PHILOTIS.

PHILOTIS: Uncle?
RICHARDETTO: My lovely niece, you have bethought ye?
PHILOTIS: Yes, and as you counselled,
    Fashioned my heart to love him; but he swears
    He will tonight be married, for he fears
    His uncle else, if he should know the drift,°   30
    Will hinder all, and call his coz to shrift.°
RICHARDETTO: Tonight? Why, best of all! But let me see,
    Ay — ha — yes, — so it shall be; in disguise
    We'll early to the friar's, I have thought on't.

Enter BERGETTO *and* POGGIO.

PHILOTIS: Uncle, he comes!
RICHARDETTO: Welcome, my worthy coz.   35
BERGETTO: Lass, pretty lass, come buss,° lass; [*kisses her*] aha, Poggio!
POGGIO: There's hope of this yet.
RICHARDETTO: You shall have time enough; withdraw a little,
        We must confer at large.
BERGETTO: Have you not sweetmeats or dainty devices for me?   40
PHILOTIS: You shall have enough, sweetheart.
BERGETTO: Sweetheart! Mark that, Poggio; by my troth I cannot choose
        but kiss thee once more for that word 'sweetheart'. [*Kisses her*]
        Poggio, I have a monstrous swelling about my stomach,
        whatsoever the matter be.   45
POGGIO: You shall have physic° for't, sir.
RICHARDETTO: Time runs apace.
BERGETTO: Time's a blockhead!
RICHARDETTO: Be ruled; when we have done what's fit to do,
        Then you may kiss your fill, and bed her too.   *Exeunt.* 50

Act Three, Scene Six

Enter the FRIAR *in his study,° sitting in a chair,* ANNABELLA
kneeling and whispering to him, a table before them and wax lights;
she weeps, and wrings her hands.

FRIAR: I am glad to see this penance; for believe me
        You have unripped° a soul so foul and guilty,
        As I must tell you true, I marvel how
        The earth hath borne you up. But weep, weep on,
        These tears may do you good; weep faster yet,   5
        Whiles I do read a lecture.°
ANNABELLA: Wretched creature!
FRIAR: Ay, you are wretched, miserably wretched,
        Almost condemned alive. There is a place —
        List,° daughter! — in a black and hollow vault,
        Where day is never seen; there shines no sun,   10
        But flaming horror of consuming fires;
        A lightless sulphur, choked with smoky fogs
        Of an infected darkness. In this place
        Dwell many thousand thousand sundry sorts
        Of never-dying deaths: there damned souls   15
        Roar without pity; there are gluttons fed
        With toads and adders; there is burning oil
        Poured down the drunkard's throat; the usurer
        Is forced to sup whole draughts of molten gold;

There is the murderer forever stabbed,   20
Yet can he never die; there lies the wanton
On racks of burning steel, whiles in his soul
He feels the torment of his raging lust.
ANNABELLA: Mercy, O mercy!
FRIAR: There stands these wretched things
Who have dreamt out whole years in lawless sheets   25
And secret incests, cursing one another.
Then you will wish each kiss your brother gave
Had been a dagger's point; then you shall hear
How he will cry, 'O, would my wicked sister
Had first been damned, when she did yield to lust!'   30
But soft, methinks I see repentance work
New motions° in your heart. Say, how is't with you?
ANNABELLA: Is there no way left to redeem my miseries?
FRIAR: There is, despair not; heaven is merciful,
And offers grace even now. 'Tis thus agreed,   35
First, for your honour's safety that you marry
The Lord Soranzo; next, to save your soul,
Leave off this life, and henceforth live to him.
ANNABELLA: Ay me!
FRIAR: Sigh not; I know the baits of sin
Are hard to leave. O, 'tis a death° to do't.°   40
Remember what must come! Are you content?
ANNABELLA: I am.
FRIAR: I like it well; we'll take the time.°
Who's near us there?

Enter FLORIO, GIOVANNI.

FLORIO: Did you call, father?
FRIAR: Is Lord Soranzo come?
FLORIO: He stays° below.
FRIAR: Have you acquainted him at full?
FLORIO: I have,   45
And he is overjoyed.
FRIAR: And so are we;
Bid him come near.
GIOVANNI [*aside*]:   My sister weeping, ha!
I fear this friar's falsehood. I will call him. —
FLORIO: Daughter, are you resolved?
ANNABELLA: Father, I am.

Enter GIOVANNI, SORANZO, *and* VASQUES.

FLORIO: My lord Soranzo, here   50
    Give me your hand; for that I give you this.   *[Joins their hands.]*
SORANZO: Lady, say you so too?
ANNABELLA: I do, and vow
    To live with you and yours.°
FRIAR: Timely resolved.
    My blessing rest on both! More to be done,
    You may perform it on the morning sun.   *Exeunt.* 55

Act Three, Scene Seven

Enter GRIMALDI *with his rapier drawn, and a dark lantern.°*

GRIMALDI: 'Tis early night as yet, and yet too soon
    To finish such a work. Here I will lie
    To listen who comes next.   *He lies down.*

Enter BERGETTO *and* PHILOTIS *disguised, and after,°*
RICHARDETTO *and* POGGIO.

BERGETTO: We are almost at the place, I hope, sweetheart.
GRIMALDI [*aside*]: I hear them near, and heard one say 'sweetheart'.   5
    'Tis he; now guide my hand, some angry justice,
    Home to his bosom. [*Aloud*] Now have at you, sir!
                               Strikes BERGETTO *and exit.*
BERGETTO: O help, help! Here's a stitch fallen° in my guts. O for a
    flesh-tailor° quickly! Poggio!
PHILOTIS: What ails my love?   10
BERGETTO: I am sure I cannot piss forward and backward, and yet I am
    wet before and behind. Lights, lights, ho, lights!
PHILOTIS: Alas, some villain here has slain my love!
RICHARDETTO: O, heaven forbid it! — Raise up the next° neighbours
    instantly, Poggio, and bring lights.   *Exit* POGGIO. 15
    — How is't, Bergetto? Slain? It cannot be!
    Are you sure you're hurt?
BERGETTO: O, my belly seethes like a porridge pot; some cold water, I
    shall boil over else. My whole body is in a sweat, that you may
    wring my shirt; feel here — Why, Poggio!   20

Enter POGGIO *with* OFFICERS, *and lights and halberts.°*

POGGIO: Here. Alas, how do you?
RICHARDETTO: Give me a light. What's here? All blood! O sirs,

Signior Donado's nephew now is slain!
Follow the murderer with all thy haste
Up to the city; he cannot be far hence.   25
Follow, I beseech you!
OFFICERS: Follow, follow, follow!   *Exeunt* OFFICERS.
RICHARDETTO: Tear off thy linen, coz, to stop his wounds. —
    Be of good comfort, man.
BERGETTO: Is all this mine own blood? Nay then, good-night with me.   30
    — Poggio, commend me to my uncle, dost hear? Bid him for my
    sake make much of this wench. — O, I am going the wrong way
    sure, my belly aches so. — O, farewell, Poggio! — O! — O! —   *Dies.*
PHILOTIS: O, he is dead!
POGGIO: How! Dead?
RICHARDETTO: He's dead indeed.
    'Tis now too late to weep; let's have him home,
    And with what speed we may find out the murderer.   35
POGGIO: O my master, my master, my master!   *Exeunt.*

Act Three, Scene Eight

Enter VASQUES *and* HIPPOLITA.

HIPPOLITA: Betrothed?
VASQUES: I saw it.
HIPPOLITA: And when's the marriage-day?
VASQUES: Some two days hence.
HIPPOLITA: Two days? Why, man, I would but wish two hours   5
    To send him to his last and lasting sleep.
    And Vasques, thou shalt see, I'll do it bravely.°
VASQUES: I do not doubt your wisdom, nor, I trust, you my secrecy. I am
    infinitely yours.
HIPPOLITA: I will be thine in spite of my disgrace.   10
    So soon? O wicked man, I durst be sworn
    He'd laugh to see me weep.
VASQUES: And that's a villainous fault in him.
HIPPOLITA: No, let him laugh; I'm armed in my resolves,
    Be thou still true.   15
VASQUES: I should get little by treachery against so hopeful a
    preferment° as I am like to climb to.
HIPPOLITA: Even to my bosom, Vasques. Let my youth°
    Revel in these new pleasures. If we thrive,
    He now hath but a pair of days to live.   *Exeunt.*   20

Act Three, Scene Nine

Enter FLORIO, DONADO, RICHARDETTO, POGGIO, *and* OFFICERS.

FLORIO: 'Tis bootless° now to show yourself a child,
   Signior Donado; what is done, is done.
   Spend not the time in tears, but seek for justice.
RICHARDETTO: I must confess, somewhat I was in fault,
   That had not first acquainted you what love   5
   Passed 'twixt him and my niece; but as I live,
   His fortune grieves me as it were mine own.
DONADO: Alas, poor creature, he meant no man harm,
   That I am sure of.
FLORIO: I believe that too. —
   But stay, my masters, are you sure you saw   10
   The murderer pass here?
OFFICER: And it please you, sir, we are sure we saw a ruffian with a
   naked° weapon in his hand, all bloody, get into my lord Cardinal's
   Grace's gate. That we are sure of; but for fear of his Grace, bless us!
   [*they cross themselves*] we durst go no further.   15
DONADO: Know you what manner of man he was?
OFFICER: Yes, sure I know the man, they say he is a soldier; he that loved
   your daughter, sir, an't please ye, 'twas he for certain.
FLORIO: Grimaldi, on my life!
OFFICER: Ay, ay, the same.
RICHARDETTO: The Cardinal is noble; he no doubt   20
   Will give true justice.
DONADO: Knock someone at the gate.
   POGGIO: I'll knock, sir.   POGGIO *knocks*.
SERVANT [*within*]: What would ye?
FLORIO: We require speech with the lord Cardinal
   About some present° business; pray inform   25
   His Grace that we are here.

Enter CARDINAL *and* GRIMALDI.

CARDINAL: Why, how now, friends! What saucy mates° are you
   That know nor duty nor civility?
   Are we a person fit to be your host?
   Or is our house become your common inn,   30
   To beat our doors at pleasure? What such haste
   Is yours, as that it cannot wait fit times?
   Are you the masters of this commonwealth,°
   And know no more discretion?
   O, your news is here before you; you have lost a nephew,   35

Donado, last night by Grimaldi slain.
Is that your business? Well, sir, we have knowledge on't.
Let that suffice.
GRIMALDI: In presence of your Grace,
   In thought I never meant Bergetto harm.
   But Florio, you can tell with how much scorn   40
   Soranzo, backed with his confederates,
   Hath often wronged me. I, to be revenged
   (For that I could not win him else to fight),
   Had thought by way of ambush to have killed him,
   But was unluckily therein mistook;   45
   Else he had felt what late Bergetto did.
   And though my fault to him were merely chance,°
   Yet humbly I submit me to your Grace,   [*Kneels.*]
   To do with me as you please.
CARDINAL: Rise up, Grimaldi.   [*He rises.*]
   You citizens of Parma, if you seek   50
   For justice, know, as Nuncio from the Pope,
   For this offence I here receive Grimaldi
   Into his Holiness' protection.
   He is no common man, but nobly born;
   Of princes' blood, though you, sir Florio,   55
   Thought him too mean° a husband for your daughter.
   If more you seek for, you must go to Rome,
   For he shall thither. Learn more wit,° for shame.
   Bury your dead. — Away, Grimaldi; leave 'em.
                              Exeunt CARDINAL *and* GRIMALDI.
DONADO: Is this a churchman's voice? Dwells Justice here?   60
FLORIO: Justice is fled to heaven and comes no nearer.°
   Soranzo! Was't for him? O impudence!
   Had he the face to speak it, and not blush?
   Come, come, Donado, there's no help in this,
   When cardinals think murder's not amiss.   65
   Great men may do their wills; we must obey,
   But heaven will judge them for't another day.   *Exeunt.*

Act Four, Scene One

A banquet.° Hautboys.° Enter the FRIAR, GIOVANNI, ANNABELLA,
PHILOTIS, SORANZO, DONADO, FLORIO, RICHARDETTO, PUTANA, *and*
VASQUES.

FRIAR: These holy rites performed, now take your times,

To spend the remnant of the day in feast;
Such fit repasts are pleasing to the saints
Who are your guests, though not with mortal eyes
To be beheld. Long prosper in this day,   5
You happy couple, to each other's joy!
SORANZO: Father, your prayer is heard. The hand of goodness
Hath been a shield° for me against my death,
And, more to bless me, hath enriched my life
With this most precious jewel; such a prize   10
As earth hath not another like to this.
Cheer up, my love; and gentlemen, my friends,
Rejoice with me in mirth. This day we'll crown
With lusty cups to Annabella's health.
GIOVANNI [*aside*]: O, torture! Were the marriage yet undone,   15
Ere I'd endure this sight, to see my love
Clipped° by another, I would dare confusion,°
And stand the horror of ten thousand deaths.
VASQUES: Are you not well, sir?
GIOVANNI: Prithee, fellow, wait.°
I need not thy officious diligence.   20
FLORIO: Signior Donado, come, you must forget
Your late mishaps, and drown your cares in wine.
SORANZO: Vasques!
VASQUES: My lord?
SORANZO: Reach me that weighty bowl.
Here, brother° Giovanni, here's to you;
Your turn comes next, though now a bachelor.   25
Here's to your sister's happiness and mine!
                              [*Drinks, and offers him the bowl.*]
GIOVANNI: I cannot drink.
SORANZO: What?
GIOVANNI: 'Twill indeed offend° me.
ANNABELLA: Pray, do not urge him if he be not willing.   *Hautboys.*
FLORIO: How now, what noise° is this?
VASQUES: O sir, I had forgot to tell you. Certain young maidens of   30
Parma, in honour to Madam Annabella's marriage, have sent their
loves to her in a masque, for which they humbly crave your
patience and silence.
SORANZO: We are much bound to them, so much the more
As it comes unexpected; guide them in.   35

Enter HIPPOLITA *and* Ladies *in* [*masks and*] *white robes, with
garlands of willows.° Music, and a dance.*

SORANZO: Thanks, lovely virgins; now might we but know

To whom we have been beholding for this love,°
We shall acknowledge it.
HIPPOLITA: Yes, you shall know.   [*Unmasks.*]
What think you now?
ALL: Hippolita!
HIPPOLITA: 'Tis she.
Be not amazed, nor blush, young lovely bride: 40
I come not to defraud you of your man.
[*To* SORANZO] 'Tis now no time to reckon up the talk,
What Parma long hath rumoured of us both.
Let rash report° run on; the breath that vents it
Will, like a bubble, break itself at last.   45
[*To* ANNABELLA] But now to you, sweet creature; lend's your hand.
Perhaps it hath been said that I would claim
Some interest in Soranzo, now your lord;
What I have right to do, his soul knows best.
But in my duty to your noble worth,   50
Sweet Annabella, and my cares of you,
Here take, Soranzo, take this hand from me.
I'll once more join what by the holy Church
Is finished and allowed.° Have I done well?
SORANZO: You have much engaged° us.
HIPPOLITA: One thing more.   55
That you may know my single charity,°
Freely I here remit all interest
I e'er could claim, and give you back your vows;
And to confirm't — reach me a cup of wine.
My lord Soranzo, in this draught I drink   60
Long rest t'ye! — [*Aside*] Look to it, Vasques.
VASQUES [*aside*]:   _   Fear nothing.
                    He gives her a poisoned cup; she drinks.
SORANZO: Hippolita, I thank you, and will pledge
This happy union° as another life. —
Wine there!
VASQUES: You shall have none, neither shall you pledge her.   65
HIPPOLITA: How!
VASQUES: Know now, mistress she-devil, your own mischievous
    treachery hath killed you. I must not marry you.
HIPPOLITA: Villain!
ALL: What's the matter?   70
VASQUES: Foolish woman, thou art now like a firebrand, that hath
    kindled others and burnt thyself. *Troppo sperar, inganna;*° thy vain
    hope hath deceived thee. Thou art but° dead; if thou hast any
    grace, pray.
HIPPOLITA: Monster!   75

VASQUES: Die in charity,° for shame! — This thing of malice, this
woman, had privately corrupted me with promise of marriage,
under° this politic reconciliation to poison my lord, whiles she
might laugh at his confusion on his marriage day. I promised her
fair, but I knew what my reward should have been; and would 80
willingly have spared her life, but that I was acquainted with the
danger of her disposition — and now have fitted her a just
payment in her own coin. There she is, she hath yet — and end thy
days in peace, vile woman; as for life there's no hope, think not on't.

ALL: Wonderful justice!

RICHARDETTO: Heaven, thou art righteous.

HIPPOLITA: O, 'tis true, 85
I feel my minute° coming. Had that slave
Kept promise — O, my torment! — thou this hour
Hadst died, Soranzo. — Heat above hell-fire! —
Yet ere I pass away — cruel, cruel flames! —
Take here my curse amongst you: may thy bed 90
Of marriage be a rack unto thy heart;
Burn, blood, and boil in vengeance. — O my heart,
My flame's intolerable! — Mayst thou live
To father bastards, may her womb bring forth
Monsters, and die together in your sins, 95
Hated, scorned and unpitied! — O! — O! — *Dies.*

FLORIO: Was e'er so vile a creature?

RICHARDETTO: Here's the end
Of lust and pride.

ANNABELLA: It is a fearful sight.

SORANZO: Vasques, I know thee now a trusty servant,
And never will forget thee. — Come, my love, 100
We'll home, and thank the heavens for this escape.
Father and friends, we must break up this mirth;°
It is too sad a feast.

DONADO: Bear hence the body.

FRIAR [*aside to* GIOVANNI]: Here's an ominous change;
Mark this, my Giovanni, and take heed. 105
I fear the event;° that marriage seldom's good,
Where the bride-banquet so begins in blood. *Exeunt.*

Act Four, Scene Two

Enter RICHARDETTO *and* PHILOTIS.

RICHARDETTO: My wretched wife, more wretched in her shame
Than in her wrongs to me, hath paid too soon

The forfeit of her modesty and life.
And I am sure, my niece, though vengeance hover,
Keeping aloof yet from Soranzo's fall,   5
Yet he will fall, and sink with his own weight.
I need not — now my heart persuades me so
To further his confusion. There is One
Above begins to work, for, as I hear,
Debates° already 'twixt his wife and him   10
Thicken and run to head;° she, as 'tis said,
Slightens° his love, and he abandons hers.
Much talk I hear. Since things go thus, my niece,
In tender love and pity of your youth,
My counsel is that you should free your years   15
From hazard of these woes, by flying hence
To fair Cremona,° there to vow your soul
In holiness a holy votaress.°
Leave me to see the end of these extremes.
All human worldly courses are uneven;°   20
No life is blessed but the way to heaven.
PHILOTIS: Uncle, shall I resolve to be a nun?
RICHARDETTO: Ay, gentle niece, and in your hourly prayers
Remember me, your poor unhappy uncle.
Hie to Cremona now, as fortune leads,   25
Your home your cloister, your best friends your beads.°
Your chaste and single life shall crown your birth;
Who dies a virgin lives a saint on earth.
PHILOTIS: Then farewell, world, and worldly thoughts adieu!
Welcome, chaste vows; myself I yield to you.   *Exeunt.* 30

Act Four, Scene Three

Enter SORANZO *unbraced,° and* ANNABELLA *dragged in.*

SORANZO: Come, strumpet, famous° whore! Were every drop
Of blood that runs in thy adulterous veins
A life, this sword — dost see't? — should in one blow
Confound° them all. Harlot, rare, notable harlot,
That with thy brazen face maintain'st° thy sin,   5
Was there no man in Parma to be bawd
To your loose cunning whoredom else but I?
Must your hot itch and plurisy° of lust,
The heyday of your luxury,° be fed
Up to a surfeit, and could none but I   10

Be picked out to be cloak to your close° tricks,
Your belly-sports? Now I must be the dad
To all that gallimaufry° that's stuffed
In thy corrupted bastard-bearing womb!
Why must I?
ANNABELLA: Beastly man, why, 'tis thy fate.   15
I sued not to thee, for, but that I thought
Your over-loving lordship would have run
Mad on denial, had ye lent me time,
I would have told ye in what case° I was.
But you would needs be doing.°
SORANZO: Whore of whores!   20
Dar'st thou tell me this?
ANNABELLA: O yes, why not?
You were deceived in me: 'twas not for love
I chose you, but for honour.° Yet know this,
Would you be patient yet, and hide your shame,
I'd see whether I could love you.
SORANZO: Excellent quean!°   25
Why, art thou not with child?
ANNABELLA: What needs all this,
When 'tis superfluous? I confess I am.
SORANZO: Tell me by whom.
ANNABELLA: Soft, sir, 'twas not in my bargain.
Yet somewhat, sir, to stay° your longing stomach,
I'm content t'acquaint you with. The man,   30
The more than man that got this sprightly boy —
For 'tis a boy; that for your glory, sir;
Your heir shall be a son —
SORANZO: Damnable monster!
ANNABELLA: Nay, and° you will not hear, I'll speak no more.
SORANZO: Yes, speak, and speak thy last.
ANNABELLA: A match,° a match!   35
This noble creature was in every part
So angel-like, so glorious, that a woman
Who had not been but human, as was I,
Would have kneeled to him, and have begged for love.
You, why you are not worthy once to name   40
His name without true worship, or indeed,
Unless you kneeled, to hear another name him.
SORANZO: What was he called?
ANNABELLA: We are not come to that;
Let it suffice that you shall have the glory
To father what so brave a father got.   45
In brief, had not this chance fall'n out as't doth,

I never had been troubled with a thought
That you had been a creature.° But for marriage,
I scarce dream yet of that.
SORANZO: Tell me his name.
ANNABELLA: Alas, alas, there's all. Will you believe?   50
SORANZO: What?
ANNABELLA: You shall never know.
SORANZO: How!
ANNABELLA: Never; if you do, let me be cursed.
SORANZO: Not know it, strumpet! I'll rip up thy heart,
    And find it there.
ANNABELLA: Do, do!
SORANZO: And with my teeth
    Tear the prodigious° lecher joint by joint.   55
ANNABELLA: Ha, ha, ha, the man's merry!
SORANZO: Dost thou laugh?
    Come, whore, tell me your lover, or by truth
    I'll hew thy flesh to shreds! Who is't?
ANNABELLA [sings]: Che morte più dolce che morirei per amore?°
SORANZO: Thus will I pull out thy hair, and thus I'll drag   60
    Thy lust-belepered body through the dust.
    Yet tell his name.
ANNABELLA [sings]: Morendo in gratia a lui, morirei senza dolore.°
SORANZO: Dost thou triumph?° The treasure of the earth
    Shall not redeem thee; were there kneeling kings   65
    Did beg thy life, or angels did come down
    To plead in tears, yet should not all prevail
    Against my rage. Dost thou not tremble yet?
ANNABELLA: At what? To die? No, be a gallant hangman.°
    I dare thee to the worst; strike and strike home.   70
    I leave revenge behind, and thou shalt feel't.
SORANZO: Yet tell me ere thou diest, and tell me truly,
    Knows thy old father this?
ANNABELLA: No, by my life.
SORANZO: Wilt thou confess,° and I will spare thy life?
ANNABELLA: My life! I will not buy my life so dear.   75
SORANZO: I will not slack° my vengeance.   [Draws his sword.]

                    Enter VASQUES.

VASQUES: What d'ye mean, sir?
SORANZO: Forbear, Vasques; such a damned whore
    Deserves no pity.
VASQUES: Now the gods forfend!°

And would you be her executioner, and kill her in your rage too?
O, 'twere most unmanlike! She is your wife; what faults hath been   80
done by her before she married you, were not against you. Alas,
poor lady, what hath she committed which any lady in Italy in the
like case would not? Sir, you must be ruled by your reason, and not
by your fury; that were unhuman and beastly.

SORANZO: She shall not live.   85

VASQUES: Come, she must. You would have her confess the author of her
present misfortunes, I warrant ye; 'tis an unconscionable demand,
and she should lose the estimation that I, for my part, hold of her
worth, if she had done it. Why sir, you ought not of all men living to
know it. Good sir, be reconciled; alas, good gentlewoman!   90

ANNABELLA: Pish, do not beg for me; I prize my life
As nothing. If the man will needs be mad,
Why let him take it.

SORANZO: Vasques, hear'st thou this?

VASQUES: Yes, and commend her for it. In this she shows the nobleness
of a gallant spirit, and beshrew my heart but it becomes   95
her rarely.° [*Aside to* SORANZO] Sir, in any case° smother your
revenge; leave the scenting-out your wrongs to me. Be ruled, as you
respect your honour, or you mar all. [*Aloud*] Sir, if ever my service
were of any credit° with you, be not so violent in your distractions.
You are married now; what a triumph might the report of this give   100
to other neglected suitors! 'Tis as manlike to bear extremities,° as
godlike to forgive.

SORANZO: O Vasques, Vasques, in this piece of flesh,
This faithless face of hers, had I laid up
The treasure of my heart! — Hadst thou been virtuous,   105
Fair, wicked woman, not the matchless joys
Of life itself had made me wish to live
With any saint but thee. Deceitful creature,
How hast thou mocked my hopes, and in the shame
Of thy lewd womb even buried me alive!   110
I did too dearly love thee.

VASQUES *aside* [*to* SORANZO]: This is well. Follow this temper° with some
passion.° Be brief and moving; 'tis for the purpose.

SORANZO: Be witness to my words thy soul and thoughts,
And tell me, didst not think that in my heart   115
I did too superstitiously° adore thee?

ANNABELLA: I must confess, I know you loved me well.

SORANZO: And wouldst thou use me thus? O Annabella,
Be thou assured, whatsoe'er the villain was
That thus hath tempted thee to this disgrace,   120
Well he might lust, but never loved like me.
He doted on the picture that hung out

Upon thy cheeks, to please his humorous° eye;
Not on the part I loved, which was thy heart,
And, as I thought, thy virtues.
ANNABELLA: O my lord!   125
These words wound deeper than your sword could do.
VASQUES: Let me not ever take comfort, but I begin to weep myself, so
much I pity him; why, madam, I knew when his rage was
overpassed what it would come to.
SORANZO: Forgive me, Annabella. Though thy youth   130
Hath tempted thee above thy strength to folly,
Yet will not I forget what I should be,
And what I am, a husband; in that name
Is hid divinity. If I do find
That thou wilt yet be true, here I remit   135
All former faults, and take thee to my bosom.
VASQUES: By my troth, and that's a point of noble charity.
ANNABELLA: Sir, on my knees —   [*Kneels.*]
SORANZO: Rise up; you shall not kneel.
Get you to your chamber, see you make no show
Of alteration;° I'll be with you straight.   140
My reason tells me now that 'tis as common
To err in frailty° as to be a woman.
Go to your chamber.   *Exit* ANNABELLA.
VASQUES: So, this was somewhat to the matter; what do you think of
your heaven of happiness now, sir?   145
SORANZO: I carry hell about me; all my blood
Is fired in swift revenge.
VASQUES: That may be, but know you how, or on whom? Alas, to marry
a great woman,° being made great in the stock° to your hand,° is a
usual sport in these days; but to know what ferret it was that   150
haunted your cony-berry,° there's the cunning.°
SORANZO: I'll make her tell herself, or —
VASQUES: Or what? You must not do so. Let me yet persuade your
sufferance a little while. Go to her, use her mildly, win her if it be
possible to a voluntary,° to a weeping tune; for the rest, if all hit,° I   155
will not miss my mark. Pray, sir, go in; the next news I tell you shall
be wonders.
SORANZO: Delay in vengeance gives a heavier blow.   *Exit.*
VASQUES: Ah, sirrah, here's work for the nonce!° I had a suspicion of a
bad matter in my head a pretty whiles ago; but after my madam's   160
scurvy looks here at home, her waspish perverseness and loud
fault-finding, then I remembered the proverb, that where hens
crow and cocks hold their peace there are sorry houses.° 'Sfoot, if
the lower parts of a she-tailor's° cunning can cover such a

swelling in the stomach, I'll never blame a false stitch in a shoe
whiles I live again. Up, and up so quick?° And so quickly too?   165
'Twere a fine policy° to learn by whom. This must be known; and
I have thought on't.

Enter PUTANA.

Here's the way, or none. — What, crying, old mistress? Alas, alas,
I cannot blame ye; we have a lord, heaven help us, is so mad° as
the devil himself, the more shame for him.   170
PUTANA: O Vasques, that ever I was born to see this day! Doth he use
thee so too, sometimes, Vasques?
VASQUES: Me! Why, he makes a dog of me; but if some were of my
mind, I know what we would do. As sure as I am an honest man,
he will go near to kill my lady with unkindness. Say she be with   175
child, is that such a matter for a young woman of her years to be
blamed for?
PUTANA: Alas, good heart, it is against her will full sore.
VASQUES: I durst be sworn, all his madness is for that she will not
confess whose 'tis, which he will know, and when he doth know it,   180
I am so well acquainted with his humour,° that he will forget all
straight. Well, I could wish she would in plain terms tell all, for
that's the way indeed.
PUTANA: Do you think so?
VASQUES: Foh, I know't; provided that he did not win her to't by force.   185
He was once in a mind that you could tell, and meant to have
wrung it out of you, but I somewhat pacified him for that, yet sure
you know a great deal.
PUTANA: Heaven forgive us all, I know a little, Vasques.
VASQUES: Why should you not? Who else should? Upon my conscience,   190
she loves you dearly, and you would not betray her to any
affliction for the world.
PUTANA: Not for all the world, by my faith and troth, Vasques.
VASQUES: 'Twere pity of your life if you should; but in this you should
both relieve her present discomforts, pacify my lord, and gain   195
yourself everlasting love and preferment.
PUTANA: Dost think so, Vasques?
VASQUES: Nay, I know't. Sure 'twas some near and entire° friend.
PUTANA: 'Twas a dear° friend indeed; but —
VASQUES: But what? Fear not to name him; my life between you and   200
danger. Faith, I think 'twas no base° fellow.
PUTANA: Thou wilt stand between me and harm?
VASQUES: Ud's° pity, what else? You shall be rewarded too; trust me.
PUTANA: 'Twas even no worse than her own brother.

KING ALFRED'S COLLEGE
LIBRARY

VASQUES: Her brother Giovanni, I warrant ye!   205
PUTANA: Even he, Vasques; as brave° a gentleman as ever kissed fair
    lady. O, they love most perpetually.
VASQUES: A brave gentleman indeed; why, therein I commend her
    choice. [*Aside*] Better and better! — You are sure 'twas he?
PUTANA: Sure; and you shall see he will not be long from her too.   210
VASQUES: He were to blame if he would; but may I believe thee?
PUTANA: Believe me! Why, dost think I am a Turk or a Jew? No,
    Vasques, I have known their dealings too long to belie° them now.
VASQUES: Where are you? There within, sirs!

Enter BANDITTI.

PUTANA: How now, what are these?   215
VASQUES: You shall know presently.° Come, sirs, take me this old
    damnable hag, gag her instantly, and put out her eyes. Quickly,
    quickly!
PUTANA: Vasques, Vasques!
VASQUES: Gag her I say. 'Sfoot, d'ye suffer her to prate? What d'ye   220
    fumble about? Let me come to her. — I'll help your old gums, you
    toad-bellied bitch! [*He gags* PUTANA] — Sirs, carry her closely° into
    the coal-house and put out her eyes instantly. If she roars, slit her
    nose;° d'ye hear, be speedy and sure.   [*Exeunt* BANDITTI] *with* PUTANA.
    Why, this is excellent and above expectation. Her own brother? O   225
    horrible! To what a height of liberty° in damnation hath the devil
    trained° our age. Her brother, well! There's yet but a beginning; I
    must to my lord, and tutor him better in his points of vengeance.
    Now I see how a smooth° tale goes beyond a smooth tail. But soft
    — What thing comes next?   230

Enter GIOVANNI.

    Giovanni! As I would wish. My belief is strengthened; 'tis as firm
    as winter and summer.
GIOVANNI: Where's my sister?
VASQUES: Troubled with a new sickness, my lord; she's somewhat ill.
GIOVANNI: Took too much of the flesh,° I believe.   235
VASQUES: Troth, sir, and you I think have e'en hit it;° but my virtuous
    lady —
GIOVANNI: Where's she?
VASQUES: In her chamber. Please you visit her; she is alone.
                             [GIOVANNI *gives him money.*]
    Your liberality° hath doubly made me your servant, and ever shall,   240
    ever —   *Exit* GIOVANNI.

Enter SORANZO.

Sir, I am made a man,° I have plied my cue° with cunning and
success; I beseech you, let's be private.
SORANZO: My lady's brother's come, now he'll know all.
VASQUES: Let him know't; I have made some of them fast° enough. 245
How have you dealt with my lady?
SORANZO: Gently, as thou hast counselled. O, my soul
Runs circular in sorrow for revenge!
But Vasques, thou shalt know —
VASQUES: Nay, I will know no more, for now comes your turn to 250
know. I would not talk so openly with you. Let my young master
take time enough, and go at pleasure;° he is sold to death, and the
devil shall not ransom him. Sir, I beseech you, your privacy.
SORANZO: No conquest can gain glory of my fear.° [*Exeunt.*]

Act Five, Scene One

Enter ANNABELLA *above.*°

ANNABELLA: Pleasures farewell, and all ye thriftless° minutes
Wherein false joys have spun a weary life;
To these my fortunes now I take my leave.
Thou precious Time, that swiftly rid'st in post°
Over the world, to finish up the race 5
Of my last fate; here stay thy restless course,
And bear to ages that are yet unborn
A wretched woeful woman's tragedy.
My conscience now stands up° against my lust
With depositions charactered in guilt,° 10

Enter FRIAR [*below*].

And tells me I am lost. Now I confess
Beauty that clothes the outside of the face
Is cursed if it be not clothed with grace.
Here like a turtle,° mewed up° in a cage
Unmated,° I converse with air and walls, 15
And descant on° my vile unhappiness.
O Giovanni, that hast had the spoil°
Of thine own virtues and my modest fame,
Would thou hadst been less subject to those stars
That luckless reigned at my nativity! 20
O, would the scourge due to my black offence

Might pass from thee, that I alone might feel
The torment of an uncontrolled flame!
FRIAR [*aside*]: What's this I hear?
ANNABELLA: That man, that blessed friar,
Who joined in ceremonial knot my hand   25
To him whose wife I now am, told me oft
I trod the path to death, and showed me how.
But they who sleep in lethargies° of lust
Hug their confusion, making heaven unjust,
And so did I.
FRIAR [*aside*]:   Here's music to the soul!   30
ANNABELLA: Forgive me, my good genius,° and this once
Be helpful to my ends. Let some good man
Pass this way, to whose trust I may commit
This paper double-lined with tears and blood;
Which being granted, here I sadly° vow   35
Repentance, and a leaving of that life
I long have died° in.
FRIAR: Lady, heaven hath heard you,
And hath by providence ordained that I
Should be his minister for your behoof.°
ANNABELLA: Ha, what are you?
FRIAR: Your brother's friend, the friar;   40
Glad in my soul that I have lived to hear
This free confession 'twixt your peace and you.
What would you, or to whom? Fear not to speak.
ANNABELLA: Is heaven so bountiful? Then I have found
More favour than I hoped. Here, holy man —   *Throws a letter.* 45
Commend me to my brother, give him that,
That letter; bid him read it and repent.
Tell him that I — imprisoned in my chamber,
Barred of all company, even of my guardian,
Who° gives me cause of much suspect —° have time   50
To blush at what hath passed; bid him be wise,
And not believe the friendship of my lord.
I fear much more than I can speak. Good father,
The place is dangerous, and spies are busy;
I must break off — you'll do't?
FRIAR: Be sure I will,   55
And fly with speed. My blessing ever rest
With thee, my daughter; live to die more blest!   *Exit.*
ANNABELLA: Thanks to the heavens, who have prolonged my breath
To this good use. Now I can welcome death.   *Exit.*

Act Five, Scene Two

Enter SORANZO *and* VASQUES.

VASQUES: Am I to be believed now? First marry a strumpet that cast
    herself away upon you but to laugh at your horns,° to feast on
    your disgrace, riot° in your vexations, cuckold you in your
    bride-bed, waste your estate upon panders and bawds!
SORANZO: No more, I say, no more! 5
VASQUES: A cuckold is a goodly tame beast, my lord.
SORANZO: I am resolved; urge not another word.
    My thoughts are great,° and all as resolute
    As thunder. In mean time I'll cause our lady
    To deck herself in all her bridal robes, 10
    Kiss her, and fold her gently in my arms.
    Begone — yet hear you; are the banditti ready
    To wait in ambush?
VASQUES: Good sir, trouble not yourself about other business than your
    own resolution; remember that time lost cannot be recalled. 15
SORANZO: With all the cunning words thou canst, invite
    The states° of Parma to my birthday's feast;
    Haste to my brother rival and his father,
    Entreat them gently, bid them not to fail.
    Be speedy and return. 20
VASQUES: Let not your pity betray you. Till my coming back, think upon
    incest and cuckoldry.
SORANZO: Revenge is all the ambition I aspire;°
    To that I'll climb or fall: my blood's on fire.   *Exeunt.*

Act Five, Scene Three

Enter GIOVANNI.

GIOVANNI: Busy opinion° is an idle° fool,
    That, as a school-rod keeps a child in awe,
    Frights the unexperienced temper of the mind.
    So did it me; who, ere my precious sister
    Was married, thought all taste of love would die 5
    In such a contract. But I find no change
    Of pleasure in this formal law of sports.°
    She is still one° to me, and every kiss
    As sweet and as delicious as the first
    I reaped, when yet the privilege of youth 10
    Entitled her a virgin. O, the glory

Of two united hearts like hers and mine!
Let poring book-men dream of other worlds,
My world, and all of happiness, is here,
And I'd not change it for the best to come: 15
A life of pleasure is Elysium.°

Enter FRIAR.

Father, you enter on the jubilee°
Of my retired° delights. Now I can tell you,
The hell you oft have prompted° is nought else
But slavish and fond° superstitious fear;   20
And I could prove it, too —
FRIAR: Thy blindness slays thee.
Look there, 'tis writ to thee.   *Gives the letter.*
GIOVANNI: From whom?
FRIAR: Unrip the seals and see.
The blood's yet seething hot, that will anon   25
Be frozen harder than congealed coral.°
Why d'ye change colour, son?
GIOVANNI: 'Fore heaven, you make
Some petty devil factor° 'twixt my love
And your religion-maskèd sorceries.
Where had you this?
FRIAR: Thy conscience, youth, is seared,°   30
Else thou wouldst stoop° to warning.
GIOVANNI: 'Tis her hand,
I know't; and 'tis all written in her blood.
She writes I know not what. Death? I'll not fear
An armed° thunderbolt aimed at my heart.
She writes we are discovered — pox on dreams   35
Of low faint-hearted cowardice! Discovered?
The devil we are! Which way is't possible?
Are we grown traitors to our own delights?
Confusion take such dotage; 'tis but forged!
This is your peevish chattering, weak old man.   40

Enter VASQUES.

Now, sir, what news bring you?
VASQUES: My lord, according to his yearly custom keeping this day a
    feast in honour of his birthday, by me invites you thither. Your
    worthy father, with the Pope's reverend Nuncio and other
    magnificoes° of Parma, have promised their presence; will't please   45
    you to be of the number?

GIOVANNI: Yes, tell them I dare come.

VASQUES: Dare come?

GIOVANNI: So I said; and tell him more, I will come.

VASQUES: These words are strange to me.　　　　　50

GIOVANNI: Say I will come.

VASQUES: You will not miss?°

GIOVANNI: Yet more? I'll come! Sir, are you answered?

VASQUES. So I'll say. — My service to you.　　　　*Exit.*

FRIAR: You will not go, I trust.

GIOVANNI:　　　　　　　　Not go! For what?　　　　55

FRIAR: O do not go! This feast, I'll gage° my life,
　　Is but a plot to train° you to your ruin;
　　Be ruled, you sha'not go.

GIOVANNI:　　　　　　　Not go? Stood Death
　　Threat'ning his armies of confounding° plagues
　　With hosts of dangers hot as blazing stars,°　　　　60
　　I would be there. Not go! Yes; and resolve
　　To strike as deep in slaughter as they all.
　　For I will go.

FRIAR:　　　　　Go where thou wilt; I see
　　The wildness of thy fate draws to an end,
　　To a bad, fearful end. I must not stay　　　　65
　　To know thy fall; back to Bononia° I
　　With speed will haste, and shun this coming blow.
　　Parma farewell; would I had never known thee,
　　Or aught of thine! Well, young man, since no prayer
　　Can make thee safe, I leave thee to despair.　　　*Exit.* 70

GIOVANNI: Despair, or tortures of a thousand hells,
　　All's one to me; I have set up my rest.°
　　Now, now, work serious thoughts on baneful plots.
　　Be all a man, my soul; let not the curse
　　Of old prescription° rend from me the gall°　　　　75
　　Of courage, which enrols a glorious death.
　　If I must totter like a well-grown oak,
　　Some under-shrubs shall in my weighty fall
　　Be crushed to splits:° with me they all shall perish.　　　*Exit.*

Act Five, Scene Four

Enter SORANZO, VASQUES, *and* BANDITTI.

SORANZO: You will not fail, or shrink in the attempt?

VASQUES: I will undertake° for their parts. — Be sure, my masters, to be
　　bloody enough, and as unmerciful as if you were preying upon a

rich booty on the very mountains of Liguria.° For your pardons,
trust to my lord; but for reward you shall trust none but your own   5
pockets.

BANDITTI: We'll make a murder.

SORANZO [*gives money*]: Here's gold, here's more; want° nothing. What
    you do
Is noble, and an act of brave revenge.
I'll make ye rich, banditti, and all free.°   10

BANDITTI: Liberty, liberty!

VASQUES: Hold, take every man a vizard.° When ye are withdrawn,
keep as much silence as you can possibly. You know the
watchword, till which be spoken, move not, but when you hear
that, rush in like a stormy flood; I need not instruct ye in your own   15
profession.

BANDITTI: No, no, no!

VASQUES: In, then; your ends are profit and preferment — away!

                                    [*Exeunt*] BANDITTI.

SORANZO: The guests will all come, Vasques?

VASQUES: Yes, sir, and now let me a little edge° your resolution; you see   20
nothing is unready to this great work, but a great mind in you. Call
to your remembrance your disgraces, your loss of honour,
Hippolita's blood, and arm your courage in your own wrongs; so
shall you best right those wrongs in vengeance which you may
truly call your own.   25

SORANZO: 'Tis well; the less I speak, the more I burn,
And blood shall quench that flame.

VASQUES: Now you begin to turn Italian!° This beside; when my young
incest-monger comes, he will be sharp set on his old bit.° Give him
time enough, let him have your chamber and bed at liberty; let my   30
hot hare° have law° ere he be hunted to his death, that if it be
possible he may post° to hell in the very act of his damnation.

Enter GIOVANNI.

SORANZO: It shall be so; and see, as we would wish,
He comes himself first. — Welcome, my much loved brother.
Now I perceive you honour me; you're welcome.   35
But where's my father?

GIOVANNI: With the other states,°
Attending on the Nuncio of the Pope
To wait° upon him hither. How's my sister?

SORANZO: Like a good housewife, scarcely ready yet;
You're best walk to her chamber.

GIOVANNI: If you will.   40

SORANZO: I must expect° my honourable friends;
    Good brother, get her forth.
GIOVANNI: You are busy, sir.   *Exit.*
VASQUES: Even as the great devil himself would have it! Let him go and
    glut himself in his own destruction.   *Flourish.*
    Hark, the Nuncio is at hand; good sir, be ready to receive him.   45

    Enter CARDINAL, FLORIO, DONADO, RICHARDETTO, *and Attendants.*

SORANZO: Most reverend lord, this grace hath made me proud
    That you vouchsafe° my house; I ever rest
    Your humble servant for this noble favour.
CARDINAL: You are our friend, my lord; his Holiness
    Shall understand how zealously you honour   50
    Saint Peter's Vicar° in his substitute.
    Our special love to you.
SORANZO: Signiors, to you
    My welcome, and my ever best of thanks
    For this so memorable courtesy.
    Pleaseth your grace to walk near?
CARDINAL: My lord, we come   55
    To celebrate your feast with civil mirth,
    As ancient custom teacheth; we will go.
SORANZO: Attend his grace there! Signiors, keep° your way.   *Exeunt.*

Act Five, Scene Five

    Enter GIOVANNI *and* ANNABELLA *lying on a bed.*°

GIOVANNI: What, changed so soon? Hath your new sprightly lord
    Found out a trick in night-games more than we
    Could know in our simplicity? Ha, is't so?
    Or does the fit° come on you, to prove treacherous
    To your past vows and oaths?
ANNABELLA: Why should you jest   5
    At my calamity, without all sense
    Of the approaching dangers you are in?
GIOVANNI: What danger's half so great as thy revolt?
    Thou art a faithless sister, else, thou know'st,
    Malice, or any treachery beside,   10
    Would stoop° to my bent brows. Why, I hold fate
    Clasped in my fist, and could command the course
    Of time's eternal motion, hadst thou been
    One thought more steady than an ebbing sea.

And what? You'll now be honest, that's resolved?   15
ANNABELLA: Brother, dear brother, know what I have been,
      And know that now there's but a dining-time°
      'Twixt us and our confusion. Let's not waste
      These precious hours in vain and useless speech.
      Alas, these gay attires were not put on   20
      But to some end; this sudden solemn feast
      Was not ordained to riot° in expense;
      I that have now been chambered here alone,
      Barred of my guardian, or of any else,
      Am not for nothing at an instant freed   25
      To fresh access. Be not deceived, my brother,
      This banquet is an harbinger of death
      To you and me; resolve° yourself it is,
      And be prepared to welcome it.
GIOVANNI: Well then,
      The schoolmen° teach that all this globe of earth   30
      Shall be consumed to ashes in a minute.
ANNABELLA: So I have read too.
GIOVANNI: But 'twere somewhat strange
      To see the waters burn; could I believe
      This might be true, I could believe as well
      There might be hell or heaven.
ANNABELLA: That's most certain.   35
GIOVANNI: A dream, a dream; else in this other world
      We should know one another.
ANNABELLA: So we shall.
GIOVANNI: Have you heard so?
ANNABELLA: For certain.
GIOVANNI: But d'ye think
      That I shall see you there, you look on me?
      May we kiss one another, prate° or laugh,   40
      Or do° as we do here?
ANNABELLA: I know not that,
      But good,° for the present, what d'ye mean
      To free yourself from danger? Some way, think
      How to escape; I'm sure the guests are come.
GIOVANNI: Look up, look here; what see you in my face?   45
ANNABELLA: Distraction and a troubled countenance.
GIOVANNI: Death, and a swift repining° wrath. — Yet look,
      What see you in mine eyes?
ANNABELLA: Methinks you weep.
GIOVANNI: I do indeed. These are the funeral tears
      Shed on your grave; these furrowed up my cheeks   50
      When first I loved and knew not how to woo.

Fair Annabella, should I here repeat
The story of my life, we might lose time.
Be record, all the spirits of the air,
And all things else that are, that day and night,   55
Early and late, the tribute which my heart
Hath paid to Annabella's sacred love
Hath been these tears, which are her mourners now.
Never till now did Nature do her best
To show a matchless beauty to the world,   60
Which, in an instant, ere it scarce was seen,
The jealous Destinies required again.
Pray, Annabella, pray. Since we must part,
Go thou, white in thy soul, to fill a throne
Of innocence and sanctity in heaven.   65
Pray, pray, my sister.
ANNABELLA: Then I see your drift;
Ye blessed angels, guard me!
GIOVANNI: So say I.
Kiss me. If ever after-times should hear
Of our fast-knit affections, though perhaps
The laws of conscience and of civil use°   70
May justly blame us, yet when they but know
Our loves, that love will wipe away that rigour°
Which would in other incests be abhorred.
Give me your hand. How sweetly life doth run
In these well-coloured veins; how constantly   75
These palms do promise health! But I could chide
With Nature for this cunning flattery.
Kiss me again. — Forgive me.
ANNABELLA: With my heart.
GIOVANNI: Farewell.
ANNABELLA: Will you be gone?
GIOVANNI: Be dark, bright sun,
And make this midday night, that thy gilt rays   80
May not behold a deed will turn their splendour
More sooty than the poets feign° their Styx!°
One other kiss, my sister.
ANNABELLA: What means this?
GIOVANNI: To save thy fame,° and kill thee in a kiss.   *Stabs her.*
Thus die, and die by me, and by my hand.   85
Revenge is mine; honour doth love command.
ANNABELLA: O brother, by your hand?
GIOVANNI: When thou art dead
I'll give my reasons for't; for to dispute
With thy (even in thy death) most lovely beauty,

Would make me stagger to perform this act   90
   Which I most glory in.
ANNABELLA: Forgive him, heaven — and me my sins; farewell,
   Brother unkind,° unkind. — Mercy, great heaven! — O! — O! —   *Dies.*
GIOVANNI: She's dead, alas, good soul; the hapless° fruit
   That in her womb received its life from me,   95
   Hath had from me a cradle and a grave.
   I must not dally. This sad marriage-bed,
   In all her best, bore her alive and dead.
   Soranzo, thou hast missed thy aim in this;
   I have prevented° now thy reaching° plots,   100
   And killed a love for whose each drop of blood
   I would have pawned my heart. Fair Annabella,
   How over-glorious° art thou in thy wounds,
   Triumphing over infamy and hate!
   Shrink not, courageous hand; stand up, my heart,   105
   And boldly act my last and greater part!   *Exit with the body.*

Act Five, Scene Six

A Banquet. Enter CARDINAL, FLORIO, DONADO, SORANZO,
   RICHARDETTO, VASQUES, *and* Attendants; *they take their places.*

VASQUES [*aside to* SORANZO]: Remember, sir, what you have to do; be
   wise and resolute.
SORANZO: Enough, my heart is fixed. [*To the* CARDINAL] Pleaseth your Grace
   To taste these coarse confections?° Though the use
   Of such set entertainments more consists   5
   In custom than in cause,° yet, reverend sir,
   I am still° made your servant by your presence.
CARDINAL: And we your friend.
SORANZO: But where's my brother Giovanni?

Enter GIOVANNI *with a heart upon his dagger.*

GIOVANNI: Here, here, Soranzo! trimmed° in reeking blood   10
   That triumphs over death; proud in the spoil°
   Of love and vengeance! Fate, or all the powers
   That guide the motions of immortal souls,
   Could not prevent me.
CARDINAL: What means this?
FLORIO: Son Giovanni!
SORANZO [*aside*]:   Shall I be forestalled?   15

GIOVANNI: Be not amazed. If your misgiving hearts
    Shrink at an idle sight,° what bloodless fear
    Of coward passion would have seized your senses
    Had you beheld the rape of life and beauty
    Which I have acted? My sister, O my sister!   20
FLORIO: Ha! What of her?
GIOVANNI: The glory of my deed
    Darkened the midday sun, made noon as night.
    You came to feast, my lords, with dainty fare.
    I came to feast too, but I digged for food
    In a much richer mine than gold or stone   25
    Of any value balanced;° 'tis a heart,
    A heart, my lords, in which is mine entombed.
    Look well upon't; d'ye know't?
VASQUES: What strange riddle's this?
GIOVANNI:'Tis Annabella's heart, 'tis; why d'ye startle?   30
    I vow 'tis hers; this dagger's point ploughed up
    Her fruitful womb, and left to me the fame
    Of a most glorious executioner.
FLORIO: Why, madman, art thyself?
GIOVANNI: Yes, father, and that times to come may know   35
    How as my fate I honoured my revenge,
    List, father; to your ears I will yield up
    How much I have deserved to be your son.°
    FLORIO. What is't thou say'st?
GIOVANNI: Nine moons have had their changes
    Since I first throughly° viewed and truly loved   40
    Your daughter and my sister.
FLORIO: How! Alas,
    My lords, he's a frantic madman!
GIOVANNI: Father, no.
    For nine months' space, in secret I enjoyed
    Sweet Annabella's sheets; nine months I lived
    A happy monarch of her heart and her.   45
    Soranzo, thou know'st this; thy paler cheek
    Bears the confounding° print of thy disgrace,
    For her too fruitful womb too soon bewrayed°
    The happy passage° of our stol'n delights,
    And made her mother to a child unborn.   50
CARDINAL: Incestuous villain!
FLORIO: O, his rage belies him!°
GIOVANNI: It does not, 'tis the oracle of truth;
    I vow it is so.
SORANZO: I shall burst with fury;
    Bring the strumpet forth!

VASQUES: I shall, sir.   *Exit* VASQUES.
GIOVANNI: Do, sir; have you all no faith   55
    To credit yet my triumphs? Here I swear
    By all that you call sacred, by the love
    I bore my Annabella whilst she lived,
    These hands have from her bosom ripped this heart.

Enter VASQUES.

    Is't true or no, sir?
VASQUES: 'Tis most strangely true.   60
FLORIO: Cursed man ! — Have I lived to —
CARDINAL: Hold up Florio;
    Monster of children, see what thou hast done,
    Broke thy old father's heart! Is none of you
    Dares venture on him?
GIOVANNI: Let 'em. O, my father,
    How well his death becomes him in his griefs!   65
    Why, this was done with courage; now survives
    None of our house but I, gilt° in the blood
    Of a fair sister and a hapless father.
SORANZO: Inhuman scorn of men, hast thou a thought
    T'outlive thy murders?
GIOVANNI: Yes, I tell thee, yes;   70
    For in my fists I bear the twists° of life.
    Soranzo, see this heart which was thy wife's;
    Thus I exchange it royally for thine,   [*Stabs him.*]
    And thus, and thus; now brave revenge is mine.   [SORANZO *falls.*]
VASQUES: I cannot hold any longer. You, sir, are you grown insolent in   75
    your butcheries? Have at you!°
GIOVANNI: Come, I am armed to meet thee.
                        [*They*] *fight.* [GIOVANNI *is wounded.*]
VASQUES: No, will it not be yet? If this will not, another shall. Not yet?
    I shall fit you anon.° Vengeance!°

Enter BANDITTI.

GIOVANNI: Welcome! Come more of you, whate'er you be;   80
    I dare your worst. —   [*They attack and wound him.*]
    O, I can stand no longer; feeble arms,
    Have you so soon lost strength?   [*Falls.*]
VASQUES: Now you are welcome, sir! — Away, my masters, all is done.
    Shift for yourselves, your reward is your own; shift for yourselves.   85
BANDITTI: Away, away!   *Exeunt* BANDITTI.
VASQUES: How d'ye, my lord? See you this? How is't?

SORANZO: Dead; but in death well pleased that I have lived
    To see my wrongs revenged on that black devil.
    O Vasques, to thy bosom let me give   90
    My last of breath; let not that lecher live — O! —   *Dies.*
VASQUES: The reward of peace and rest be with him, my ever dearest
    lord and master.
GIOVANNI: Whose hand gave me this wound?
VASQUES: Mine, sir, I was your first man; have you enough?   95
GIOVANNI: I thank thee; thou hast done for me but what
    I would have else done on myself. Art sure
    Thy lord is dead?
VASQUES: O impudent slave! As sure as I am sure to see thee die.
CARDINAL: Think on thy life and end, and call for mercy.   100
GIOVANNI Mercy? Why, I have found it in this justice.
CARDINAL: Strive yet to cry to heaven.
GIOVANNI: O, I bleed fast!
    Death, thou art a guest long looked-for; I embrace
    Thee and thy wounds. O, my last minute comes!
    Where'er I go, let me enjoy this grace,   105
    Freely to view my Annabella's face.   *Dies.*
DONADO: Strange miracle of justice!
CARDINAL: Raise up the city; we shall be murdered all!
VASQUES: You need not fear, you shall not. This strange task being
    ended, I have paid the duty to the son which I have vowed to the   110
    father.
CARDINAL: Speak, wretched villain, what incarnate fiend
    Hath led thee on to this?
VASQUES: Honesty, and pity of my master's wrongs. For know, my lord,
    I am by birth a Spaniard,° brought forth my country in my   115
    youth by Lord Soranzo's father; whom, whilst he lived, I served
    faithfully; since whose death I have been to this, as I was to him.
    What I have done was duty, and I repent nothing but that the loss
    of my life had not ransomed his.
CARDINAL: Say, fellow, know'st thou any yet unnamed   120
    Of counsel° in this incest?
VASQUES: Yes, an old woman, sometimes° guardian to this murdered
    lady.
CARDINAL: And what's become of her?
VASQUES: Within this room° she is; whose eyes, after her confession, I   125
    caused to be put out, but kept alive, to confirm what from
    Giovanni's own mouth you have heard. Now, my lord, what I have
    done you may judge of, and let your own wisdom be a judge in
    your own reason.
CARDINAL: Peace! First this woman, chief in these effects;°   130
    My sentence is that forthwith she be ta'en

Out of the city, for example's sake,
There to be burnt to ashes.
DONADO: 'Tis most just.
CARDINAL: Be it your charge, Donado, see it done.
DONADO: I shall.   135
VASQUES: What for me? If death, 'tis welcome. I have been honest to the
    son, as I was to the father.
CARDINAL: Fellow, for thee, since what thou didst was done
    Not for thyself, being no Italian,
    We banish thee for ever, to depart   140
    Within three days; in this we do dispense
    With grounds of reason,° not of thine offence.
VASQUES: 'Tis well; this conquest is mine, and I rejoice that a Spaniard
    outwent an Italian in revenge.   *Exit* VASQUES.
CARDINAL: Take up these slaughtered bodies; see them buried;   145
    And all the gold and jewels, or whatsoever,
    Confiscate by the canons of the Church,
    We seize upon to the Pope's proper° use.
RICHARDETTO [*discovers himself*]: Your grace's pardon. Thus long I
        lived disguised,
    To see the effect of pride and lust at once°   150
    Brought both to shameful ends.
CARDINAL: What? Richardetto, whom we thought for dead?
DONADO: Sir, was it you —
RICHARDETTO: Your friend.
CARDINAL: We shall have time
    To talk at large° of all; but never yet
    Incest and murder have so strangely met.   155
    Of one so young, so rich in Nature's store,
    Who could not say, *'Tis pity she's a whore?*   *Exeunt.*

Finis

Notes to the Play

Dramatis Personae

1 BONAVENTURA: the name of a famous Franciscan friar and scholar (1221–74), who taught at the University of Paris
2 *Nuncio*: ambassador
4 FLORIO: taken from the name of a English scholar John Florio (1553–1625) who authored an Italian dictionary, *A World of Words* (1598) used by Ford and other Renaissance writers
8 BERGETTO: 'little shepherd'; the name suggests the innocent simplicities of pastoral love
11 POGGIO: the name of a famous fifteenth-century Italian humanist
15 HIPPOLYTA: the name of the Queen of the Amazons, and of the lustful wife of Acastus (Hippolyte)
16 PHILOTIS: 'love', 'affection'
17 PUTANA: 'whore'

Act One, Scene One

2 school-points: topics for academic argument
Nice: (1) hair-splitting, (2) dangerous
4 admits: allows, tolerates
wits: clever people
6 art: academic learning
9 fond: foolish
24 peevish: trifling
25 customary...man: mere human convention
32 blood: (1) kinship, (2) passion, since blood was thought to be the locus of sexual impulse
35 unhappy: ill-fated
38 change: substitution
41 life: essence
45 unrangèd: deranged, beyond all limits
46 confessor: accented on the first syllable
47 wit: intelligence
49 Bononia: Bologna, the site of a famous university

51 government: prudent conduct
53 tutelage: guardianship
58 death: of the soul (and, ironically, the body)
59 waits:.attends
64 ocean: pronounced as three syllables
65 floats: risings of the incoming tide
vows: desires
73 tears...of blood: expressions of the profoundest sorrow

Act One, Scene Two

1 tackling: weapons
3 Thou...me: it was considered dishonourable to fight a social inferior.
5 mountebank: travelling salesman
a meal's meat: food for one meal
7 Wilt...gear: are you willing to fight?
9 cast-suit: servant (who might wear his master's secondhand clothing)
10 cot-quean: vulgar, abusive woman (literally a cottage woman)
12 quality: birth and character
13 prate: talk idly
17 Brave my lord: my brave lord. Vasques taunts Grimaldi and threatens him physically (the dashes may indicate intervals of provocative sword play) until he draws his sword (at line 18), and is immediately attacked by Vasques.
20 sudden: violent
22 spleen: fit of anger
25 naught: worthless
28 seconding: stirring up
28 SD *above*: on the upper stage, from which they descend at line 132
28 ground: subject (of the quarrel)
29 resolve: answer
33 prefers: advances
37 blood: lineage
bewrays: reveals
43–4 let...gills: cut Grimaldi's throat;

doctors commonly let blood to 'cool' their patients

44–5   wormed...mad: treated you like a mad dog; 'worming' involved cutting out a small ligament under a dog's tongue, called the 'worm', to prevent rabies

45   mad: (1) insane, (2) enraged

47   stay your stomach: satisfy your appetite for (1) food; (2) fighting

48   innocence: harmless fool
        Spoonmeat: baby food (like soup)

52   engaged: pledged

53   Owing: possessing
        ear: willingness to listen to you alone (cf. line 32)

56   unspleened dove: the proverbially mild dove was believed to be incapable of anger, since it secreted no gall (in contemporary science, the location of the emotion of anger)

61   put up: sheath your sword

67   ends: matters

68   No marvel else: 'Indeed I don't wonder that you ask me to go'

73   well-timbered: physically well-built

74   Duke Mount Ferrato: the Duke of Monferat, since 1565 an Italian duchy under the rule of the Gonzagas of Mantua.

75   an't: if it

77   skirmishing: weapon-flourishing
        privy: (1) secret, (2) in the groin, leading to the sexual implication of 'standing upright', in line 78.

78–9   crinkles...the hams: (1) curtsies, (2) cringes away so much

79   serve: (1) suffice; (2) give sexual satisfaction

82   very: true, real

86   wholesome: free from sexual disease

89   purchased...name: acquired such favour

90   qualities: accomplishments

94   morning's draught: drinks of ale or spirits were often taken early in the morning or at mid-morning.

96   ciphers: nonentities
        brave: richly dressed; proverbially, 'An ape is an ape though clad in scarlet'.

102   coxcomb: simpleton

108   shift socks: change my stockings, or light shoes

109   have at her: make our thrust at her (a fencing expression)

110   pavin: pavane, a stately dance

113   magnifico: nobleman

115   cousin: kinsman (actually Bergetto is Donado's nephew)
        golden calf: (1) wealthy fool; (2) biblical idol (the story is told in Exodus 32)

116   fall down...presently: prostrate yourself immediately in (1) sexual invitation; (2) worship

117   They...play-fellow: proverbially, 'Fools and little dogs are ladies' play-fellows'.
        bauble: (1) baton carried by professional fools; (2) penis

118–19 cast...rate: take a reckless gamble (by accepting Bergetto) for lack of male suitors

119   innocent: simpleton that he is

119 SD *Enter* GIOVANNI: Giovanni enters on the main stage below, where he joined by Annabella and Putana, at line 152.

129   partake: be informed of

131   partage: share

134   strive: resist the impulse

138   throughly: thoroughly

141   dried up: exhausted

143   wit or art: intelligence or medical knowledge

149   Keep fear : let fear dwell

163   office of some credit: (1) post of honour; (2) service deserving some reward

172   frantic: lunatic

181   proves: turns out
        feign: relate the legend (see Homer's *Iliad*, Book 16)

182	Juno: sister as well as wife of Jupiter, king of the gods
186	Promethean fire: in Greek mythology, Prometheus stole fire from heaven to give life to the humans he had created from clay.
189	strange: opposed to each other
190	change: mutual interchange
192	anchorite: hermit
196	glass: mirror
197	trim: fine
204	affliction...death: suffering of deadly intensity
208	rest: peace of mind
215	despised: defied
217	smoothed-cheek: young and innocent
218	bootless: unavailing
220	sadness: seriousness mischief: disaster
221	dissemble: pretend
224	instance: reasons
229	persuade: encourage
236	resolved: decided on
250	sooth: faith and truth

Act One, Scene Three

6	doubt: fear for
7	miscarry: come to harm
8	girl: pronounced as two syllables throughout this text
15	like: find mutual love
16	presently: immediately
23	wit: some brains
27	in good time: at the right moment
30–1	out...mint: fresh, new
35–6	undertakes...sandbags: an early attempt at a perpetual-motion machine
37–9	horse...tail is: this was a popular side-show at fairs of the time; the horse's tail was tied to the manger.
44	have...mind of: show more interest in
46	may-game: laughing-stock
50	hobby-horses: performers, dressed as a rider on a horse, who took part in morris dances and other entertainments.
52	Ud's sa' me: God save me tickled: amused

57	parmasent: Parmesan cheese
58	wanted: lacked
69	wit: thought
70	glory: malapropism for 'shame'
71	white boy: favourite gulled: tricked
72	fit: answer aptly

Act Two, Scene One

0 SD	*chamber*: bedroom. The actors probably entered on the upper stage.
10	toy: trifle
13–14	Music...playing: 'Music is composed of the act of hearing as much as it is of the act of performance'; but 'music' is also a metaphor for love-making, and 'ear' alludes to the female organ of sex.
16	thus...neck: Giovanni imagines himself as the king of the gods, who took the form of a swan to seduce the maiden Leda. From this act stemmed the destructive Trojan War.
17	ambrosia: the sweet, scented food of the gods, which gave immortality to those who ate it
23	have: (1) possess in marriage; (2) have intercourse with
26	dared to: so daring as to
27	thou...no other: the language of the marriage ceremony
40	passed over: experienced; Putana applies the adverb literally to the couple's love-making
44	fit: sexual impulse
47	for...people: to avoid scandalous gossip
50	Reach my work: hand me my needlework
51 SD	*physic*: medicine
52	lose: waste
54	Padua: Italian city famous for its medical school.
60	perfection: perfect beauty or accomplishments. But because of the previous scene of love-making between Giovanni and Annabella, much of the language of this passage is given an ironic, sexual

colouring. Such charged words include 'perfection' (by sexual experience), 'music, content' (63), 'know, parts' (accomplishments *and* sex organs) (64), 'touch an instrument' and 'done't' (75).

66   make not strange: do not act with formal reserve
67   art: medical skill
73   cousin's cunning: niece's musical skill
75   To touch: (1) how to play upon; (2) to touch intimately

Act Two, Scene Two

5   Sannazar: Jacopo Sannazaro (1455–1530), a famous Neapolitan pastoral and love poet. He received a lavish reward for a brief Latin poem praising the city of Venice (see lines 12–15 below).
9   envy: ill-will
10   mean: the golden mean, moderation
        annoys: pains
13   encomium: poem of praise
20   taxed of: blamed for
26   distracted: changeable, fickle
27   blood: sexual passion
29   change: promiscuity
30   modest fame: reputation for modesty (cf. 5.1.18)
39   womanhood: womanly modesty
41   distaste: dislike
47–8   triumph...dejection: exult over my humiliation
49   free: high-born
52   habit: costume
        weeds: clothes
62   unedge: blunt
        perplex: drive to distraction
64   freely: uninterruptedly
71   protests: protestations
73   a voyage...Ligorne: a journey (by land) to the sea-port of Leghorn, about one hundred miles from Parma. The route was mountainous and infested with brigands (cf. 5.4.2–4).

90   quality, condition: social class and position
91   entertainment: hospitality
92   braver: finer
100   contemns his fate: scorns his approaching doom
103   his woe: the grief he has caused
103 SD *offers...away*: moves to leave
113   shrewd: sharp, abusive
117   hearty: genuine, heart-felt
121   temper: mood
129   slight acquittance: mean payment of a debt
135–6   be private to: keep secrecy about
138–9   have...you: scent what you intend; a hunting metaphor
148   merry: joking
151   good genii: guardian spirits
152   special: leading
156   bane: poison
157   tasted: given a (salt) taste to

Act Two, Scene Three

4   act: (1) display, put on stage; (2) actively contribute to
5   borrowed shape: disguise; 'shape' was a theatrical term for an actor's costume.
7   riots: orgies
11   impudence: shamelessness
13   how...hereof: what popular opinion makes of her conduct
16   plead...in all: clear you of all responsibility
34   Save you: 'God save you'; a customary greeting, but ironic in the circumstances.
40   arts: medical knowledge
        receipts: prescriptions (for love-potions)
50   speed: succeed
53   confusion: total ruin, destruction
60   Hydra: a many-headed monster, which grew two heads for every one it lost. It was one of the labours of Hercules to destroy it.

Act Two, Scene Four

13	indited: written
16	hand: handwriting
20	fast: much
22	board: (1) approach a girl; (2) jest (bourd)
24–5	in spite...teeth: despite your resistance
25	parts: points, accomplishments
40	motions: puppet shows (regarded as childish amusements)
41	fopperies: follies
	you...good not: you had better not have done so
42	this horse: see 1.3.37–9 and note

Act Two, Scene Five

5	cast away: rejected and considered damned
6	religious number: orthodox members
10	remarked...mischief: marked out to experience calamity
18	furniture: outward features
21	quintessence: purest manifestation
32	elder: older, pre-Christian instance: adduce
34	is...blind: can offer no insights into the tenets of religion
44	shrive: administer the rite of confession
45	At...leisure: whenever it suits you
54	throne: seat of divinity; or angel (thrones were one of the nine orders of angelic beings).
55–6	the spheres...heaven: in medieval science (now discredited by the discoveries of Copernicus and Galileo), the concentric spheres carrying the planets and stars made in their motions a perfectly harmonious music, inaudible to human beings.
61	a second death: eternal damnation, following natural death
64	the throne of mercy: God, as supreme ruler and merciful judge

Act Two, Scene Six

13	And: if it
21	feeling: (1) understanding; (2) monetary indication
26	here right: at once
45	What say: what do you have to say?
46	freedom: free choice of a husband
48	raise...fortunes: improve his rank and wealth
58	what....make: what is his business?
63	tickled: pleased
66	riddle: guess
70	take the wall: take the position next the wall, the cleanest part of the street. Quarrels over this privileged place were frequent and sometimes bloody.
72	more...so: more intelligence than to do so
74	kennel: gutter
77	gull: fool, dupe
92	liked: pleased
98	given...lie: accused him of lying, the usual preliminary to a duel dry: severe
106	half-a-crown: the usual price for an English prostitute
110	'gainst: in anticipation of
119	only: particularly

Act Three, Scene One

2	sconce: head, brain
3	bob: fob
4	'Sfoot: by God's foot
11	codpiece-point: lace fastening for the codpiece, an item of male clothing well out of date by 1633
11–12	marmalade: fruit conserve
14	clap...mugger: conclude a secret marriage
16	courage: (1) bravery; (2) sexual desire
20–1	cart whores: Prostitutes were frequently punished by being paraded through the streets in carts or wagons, exposed to public ridicule.
21	charges: expense

Act Three, Scene Two

5	jointures: marriage settlements
11	all woman: Giovanni fears stereotypical female inconstancy.
16	point of faith: article of belief considered essential for salvation
17	infer: contrive
20	but...note: a typical female remark
23	winks: turns a blind eye
33	Aqua-vitae: Annabella pretends to call for medicinal spirits.
39	confirmed: sure of her loyalty
43	taste: experience of welcome
76	maid's sickness: green sickness (chlorosis); an anaemic disease affecting young women especially at puberty
77	overflux: overflow present: immediate

Act Three, Scene Three

6	quick: alive
11	qualms and water-pangs: fits of sickness and frequent impulses to urinate
12–13	another...name: an end to menstruation
13	credit's sake: sake of her good name
15	see her water: the usual method of diagnosis of illness or pregnancy
17	Prettily amended: pretty well recovered
19	take no care: not to worry

Act Three, Scene Four

1	Indifferent: reasonably
6	easy surfeit-water: mild cure for indigestion
8	a fullness...blood: a case of sexual frustration
10	once: at some time
29	ghostly: spiritual
35	dear impression: loving notion

Act Three, Scene Five

4	terms: circumstances
5	policy: cunning
7	Play...hands: does not double-cross me
9	affied: betrothed
19	speed: dispatch, kill
22	hit: succeed
30	drift: intention, plan
31	call...shrift: summon his nephew (*coz*) to confession
36	buss: kiss
46	physic: remedy

Act Three, Scene Six

0 SD	*in his study*: There is some textual uncertainty about the location of this scene, and some editors substitute Annabella's bedroom for the Friar's study, on the grounds that the room is upstairs (line 44), and the Friar has previously been directed to Annabella's 'chamber' (3.4.33). However, the whole stage direction is clearly authorial, and in the preceding scene Grimaldi and Richardetto speak of a betrothal in the Friar's cell (3.5.12), which might be imagined as an upstairs room in a larger building belonging to a religious order.
2	unripped: torn out, exposed
6	read a lecture: deliver a rebuke
9	List: attend
16	there are gluttons: What follows is a traditional description of the torments of the damned in hell.
32	motions: impulses
40	death: death to the soul, final damnation; though the word can also refer to the moment of orgasm
	do't: (1) do as you are doing; (2) engage in sexual activity
42	take the time: seize the opportunity
44	stays: waits

50–3 My lord...yours: This exchange constitutes a legally binding betrothal, to be followed by a church service (as indicated in lines 54–5).

Act Three, Scene Seven

0 SD *dark lantern*: one whose light could be concealed by a shutter
3 SD *after*: that is, following Berghetto and Philotis
8 fallen: burst
8–9 flesh-tailor: surgeon
14 next: nearest
20 SD *halberts*: lances with axe blades; the usual weapon carried by officers of the city watch

Act Three, Scene Eight

7 bravely: handsomely
16–17 against...preferment: in exchange for such a promising promotion
18 my youth: Soranzo (cf. 1.2.87)

Act Three, Scene Nine

1 bootless: useless
13 naked: unsheathed
25 present: urgent
27 mates: fellows
33 masters...commonwealth: magistrates of this community
47 chance: an accidental one
56 mean: undistinguished
58 wit: common sense
61 Justice...nearer: a reference to the end of the Greek Golden Age, when Astraea, goddess of justice, fled to the heavens and was placed there as the constellation Virgo.

Act Four, Scene One

0 SD *banquet*: not necessarily a feast; the word could also mean light refreshment or wine-drinking (which took place after a wedding)
Hautboys: oboes, instruments

often associated with solemn celebration
7–8 The hand...shield: biblical language for the protecting power of God
17 Clipped: embraced confusion: utter ruin
19 wait: attend on the guests
24 brother: brother-in-law
27 offend: (1) make me ill; (2) displease
29 noise: sound of music
35 SD *willows*: symbolising disappointment in love
37 love: act of kindness
44 rash report: swift-spreading gossip
54 allowed: approved
55 engaged: (1) laid under an obligation; (2) betrothed
56 single charity: sincere love
63 union: agreement
72 *Troppo sperar, inganna*: 'Too much hope deceives.'
73 but: as good as
76 charity: a state of forgiveness and love (cf. line 56)
78 under: under the cloak of
86 minute: moment of death
102 mirth: celebration
106 event: outcome

Act Four, Scene Two

10 Debates: arguments, quarrels
11 Thicken...head: multiply and come to bursting point (as a boil might do)
12 Slightens: disdains
17 Cremona: a town dominated by its cathedral, and within forty miles of Parma
18 votaress: nun
20 uneven: unjust, difficult
26 beads: the nun's prayer rosary

Act Four, Scene Three

0 SD *unbraced*: with his clothing (here, probably his doublet) unfastened
1 famous: notorious
4 Confound: destroy
5 maintain'st: (1) persists in; (2) defends

8   plurisy: excess
9   heyday...luxury: heat of your
       lustfulness at its height
11   close: (1) physically close; (2)
       secret
13   gallimaufry: hodge-podge,
       jumble. The word expresses
       Soranzo's horror at the
       thought of the mixture of his
       blood-line.
19   case: condition (of pregnancy)
20   doing: sexually active
23   honour: my reputation's sake
25   Excellent quean: excelling
       whore
29   stay: satisfy, appease
34   and: if
35   A match: agreed; a bargain
       struck
48   had been a creature: existed
55   prodigious: monstrous
59   *Che...amore*: 'What death is
       sweeter than to die for love?'
63   *Morendo...dolore*: 'Dying in his
       favour I would die without
       pain.'
64   triumph: exult
69   hangman: executioner
74   confess: admit your lover's
       name
76   slack: delay, mitigate
78   forfend: forbid
95–6   beshrew...rarely: curse my
       heart if it doesn't grace her
       remarkably well
96   in any case: by any means
99   credit: esteem
101   extremities: hardships
112   temper: attitude
113   passion: display of emotion
116   superstitiously: idolatrously,
       extravagantly
123   humorous: capricious
140   alteration: (emotional)
       disturbance
142   in frailty: through human
       weakness
149   great woman: (1) woman of
       high rank; (2) pregnant woman
       stock: (1) body; (2) family; (3)
       rabbit burrow (that is, female
       sex organ)
       to your hand: already
151   haunted your cony-berry:
       frequented your 'rabbit

       burrow'
       cunning: hunter's skill
155   voluntary: (1) extempore piece
       of music; (2) free confession
       hit: goes well (an archery
       metaphor)
159   nonce: present occasion
162–3 the proverb...houses: This
       proverb is found in an Italian
       phrase book used by the
       dramatist, John Florio's *Florio
       His First Fruits* (1578).
164   she-tailor's: with an indecent
       pun on 'tail' (cf. line 229)
165   quick: (1) fast; (2) in an
       advanced stage of pregnancy
166   policy: piece of cunning
169   mad: raging furiously
181   humour: temperament
198   entire: devoted, intimate
199   dear: (1) beloved; (2) costly
201   base: of low birth
203   Ud's: God's
206   brave: splendid
213   belie: lie about
216   presently: instantly
222   closely: secretly
223   slit her nose: both a savage
       threat, and a not uncommon
       punishment for sexual offences
226   liberty: licence
227   trained: lured
229   smooth: deceitful
235   flesh: (1) meat; (2) sexual
       activity
236   hit it: (1) discovered the true
       reason; (2) enjoyed sexual
       intercourse
240   liberality: (1) generosity; (2)
       licentiousness
242   made a man: a made man,
       assured of success
       plied my cue: played my part
245   fast: securely imprisoned
252   go at pleasure: visit
       (Annabella) when he pleases
254   No...fear: my fear will not
       contribute to any other man's
       success

Act Five, Scene One

0 SD   *above*: Annabella speaks from
       her bedchamber, above the
       street where the Friar passes
       by.

1	thriftless; profitless
4	in post: at the utmost speed (using post horses)
9	stands up against: opposes (the metaphor is of a legal witness for the prosecution)
10	charactered in guilt: (1) of a guilty nature; (2) written in gilt lettering
14	turtle: turtle-dove, proverbially devoted to its mate
	mewed up: imprisoned
15	Unmated: deprived of its mate
16	descant on: sing and talk about
17	spoil: (1) plunder; (2) despoliation
28	lethargies: states of morbid drowsiness
31	good genius: guardian spirit
35	sadly: (1) solemnly; (2) sorrowfully
37	died: in a spiritual sense, lived a life doomed to final damnation
39	behoof: benefit
50	Who: which
	suspect: fear, suspicion

Act Five, Scene Two

2	horns: the conventional attributes of the deceived husband
3	riot: revel
8	great: full of wrath
17	states: dignitaries
23	aspire: ardently seek

Act Five, Scene Three

1	Busy opinion: officious common belief
	idle: futile
7	formal law of sports: conventional legal regulation of sexual activities (that is, marriage)
8	one: perfectly united
16	Elysium: paradise, realm of the blessed spirits
17	jubilee: joyful celebration
18	retired: hidden
19	prompted: proposed in argument
20	fond: foolish
26	congealed coral: coral was

	thought to harden into its usual form on being taken from the water; red coral provides an image of frozen blood.
28	factor: intermediate agent
30	seared: cauterised, incapable of feeling
31	stoop: humble yourself (as a hawk 'stoops' to its trainer's lure)
34	armed: prepared for delivery
45	magnificoes: great men, nobles
52	miss: fail to come
56	gage: pledge, stake
57	train: lure
59	confounding: destructive
60	blazing stars: comets, generally taken as omens of disaster (cf. *The Revenger's Tragedy*, 5.3.15), and here associated with signs reminiscent of the biblical Last Judgement
66	Bononia: Bologna (cf. 1.1.49 and note)
72	set up my rest: finally committed myself. In the card game Primero, to 'set up one's rest' was to decide to venture the outcome of the game on the cards in one's hand.
74–5	the curse...prescription: the ancient biblical condemnations of incest; see Deuteronomy 27:22, and Leviticus 20:17
75	gall: audacity, bitterness of spirit. The common use of oak-galls in the manufacture of ink leads to the idea of writing down in a roll of honour (line 76) Giovanni's intended action.
79	splits: splinters

Act Five, Scene Four

2	undertake: give an assurance
4	Liguria: mountainous region between Parma and Genoa in north-west Italy
8	want: lack
10	free: safe from the law
12	vizard: mask
20	edge: sharpen
28	turn Italian: Italians had a reputation for ferocious revenge-taking.

29	sharp...bit: hungry and eager for his former (sexual) food	6	cause: logical purpose
31	hot hare: an animal associated with excessive and unnatural lustfulness	7	still: always
		10	trimmed: adorned
		11	spoil: plunder and destruction
	have law: follow the rules, by being given the usual start before the chase began	17	idle sight: insignificant spectacle
		26	balanced: established by weighing
32	post: speed	38	son: son-in-law (as Annabella's 'husband')
36	states: dignitaries		
38	wait: attend	40	throughly: utterly, fully
41	expect: wait for	47	confounding: shaming, disconcerting
47	vouchsafe: deign to visit		
51	Saint Peter's Vicar: the Pope	48	bewrayed: revealed
58	keep: continue on	49	passage: course
		51	belies him: makes him a liar

Act Five, Scene Five

		67	gilt in: (1) smeared with; (2) made guilty by
0 SD	Enter...bed: the bed may have been pushed out onto the stage, or 'discovered' by the drawing of the curtain across the inner stage.	71	twists: threads. Giovanni imagines himself as one of the Greek Fates, holding the spun threads of others' lives in his hands.
4	fit: caprice	76	Have at you: the duellist's challenge. Vasques and Giovanni draw their swords and prepare to fight.
11	stoop: submit		
17	dining-time: period of the mid-day meal		
22	riot: indulge extravagantly	79	I...anon: I'll deal with you shortly
28	resolve yourself: be assured		Vengeance: the agreed watchword to summon the bandits
30	schoolmen: medieval theologians		
40	prate: talk casually	115	a Spaniard: the Spanish had a contemporary reputation for cunning, pride and ferocious enmity.
41	do: (1) behave; (2) make love		
42	good: good brother		
47	repining: discontented	121	Of counsel: involved in
70	civil use: civilised custom	122	sometimes: formerly
72	rigour: offensive violence	125	Within this room: In some productions, Putana is brought on stage for the audience to see and the Cardinal to condemn, but Vasques may simply gesture off-stage towards the coalhouse where she had been taken (see 4.3.222–3).
82	More sooty...Styx: in Greek mythology, the black waters of the river Styx surrounded the underworld.		
	feign: falsely imagine		
84	fame: good name		
93	unkind: (1) cruel; (2) unnatural		
94	hapless: unfortunate		
100	prevented: forestalled	130	effects: events
	reaching: clutching	141–2	dispense...reason: offer a dispensation on the grounds of your motivation
103	over-glorious: beautiful beyond all measure		

Act Five, Scene Six

		148	proper: personal
4	coarse confections: homely dishes	150	at once: together
		154	at large: fully, in detail

Appendix I

The Spanish Tragedy (1602)

The 'Painter Scene'

Ten years after the appearance of the first surviving edition of *The Spanish Tragedy* the publisher Thomas Pavier brought out a fresh edition of the play, advertising it as 'Newly corrected, amended, and enlarged with new additions of the Painter's part, and others, as it hath of late been divers times acted'.

The Pavier text contains five new passages, totalling some 320 lines, interpolated (1) in Act Two, Scene Four, between lines 108 and 109; (2) replacing lines 64 and part of 65 in Act Three, Scene Two; (3) interpolated in Act Three, Scene Eleven, between lines 1 and 2; (4) introduced as a new scene between Act Three, Scene Eleven and Scene Twelve (the 'Painter scene'); and (5) replacing lines 168–189 in Act Four, Scene Four.

The author of these passages is unknown (it cannot have been Kyd, who died in 1594), and the metrical roughness of much of the verse suggests that the source of the additions may have been an unofficial transcript of writing intended to replace earlier passages by then thought to be defective, or to give further development to material already found effective in the theatre. Surviving theatrical records show that it was not uncommon to commission such revisions and additions to a popular and frequently performed text; both *The Spanish Tragedy* and *The Tragical History of Doctor Faustus* were revised in this way. However, Pavier apparently simply added the new material into his reprint of the original text with a minimum of editing, leaving the original passages intended to be replaced uncut; it is most unlikely that the full Pavier text, now of excessive length, was ever acted in its existing state.

The first, second and fifth additions are of little literary merit or interest. The third addition, not printed here, introduces a moving set-piece, a 'character' of a son (Horatio). The fourth addition powerfully develops the theme of Hieronimo's madness, translating to the stage the popular subject in poetry of instructions to a painter; whoever its author was, it was good enough to attract contemporary parodies and lead the advertising for a new edition of the tragedy. Lines 133–5 offer interesting evidence for the way in which Elizabethan actors may have staged the famous scene of Hieronimo's discovery of his son's body, and may be compared with the visual evidence provided in a 1615 woodcut illustration of the same moment (see 2.4.63 SD and the commentary note).

Act Three, Scene Twelve A

Enter JAQUES *and* PEDRO [*carrying torches*].

JAQUES: I wonder, Pedro, why our master thus
    At midnight sends us with our torches' light,
    When man and bird and beast are all at rest,
    Save those that watch for° rape and bloody murder.
PEDRO: O Jaques, know thou that our master's mind   5
    Is much distraught since his Horatio died,
    And, now his aged years should sleep in rest,
    His heart in quiet, like a desperate man,
    Grows lunatic and childish for his son.
    Sometimes, as he doth at his table sit,   10
    He speaks as if Horatio stood by him,
    Then starting° in a rage, falls on the earth,
    Cries out, 'Horatio! Where is my Horatio?'
    So that, with extreme grief and cutting sorrow,
    There is not left in him one inch of man.   15
    See where he comes.

Enter HIERONIMO.

HIERONIMO: I pry through every crevice of each wall,
    Look on each tree, and search through every brake,°
    Beat at the bushes, stamp our grandam earth,
    Dive in the water, and stare up to heaven,   20
    Yet cannot I behold my son Horatio.
    How now? Who's there? Sprites?° sprites?
PEDRO: We are your servants that attend you, sir.
HIERONIMO: What make you° with your torches in the dark?
PEDRO: You bid us light them, and attend you here.   25
HIERONIMO: No, no, you are deceived; not I, you are deceived.
    Was I so mad to bid you light your torches now?
    Light me your torches at the mid of noon,
    Whenas the sun-god rides in all his glory;°
    Light me your torches then.
PEDRO: Then we burn daylight.°   30
HIERONIMO: Let it be burnt. Night is a murderous slut

That would not have her treasons to be seen;
And yonder pale-faced Hecate° there, the moon,
Doth give consent to that is done in darkness;
And all those stars that gaze upon her face   35
Are aglets° on her sleeve, pins° on her train;
And those that should be powerful and divine,
Do sleep in darkness when they most should shine.
PEDRO: Provoke them not, fair sir, with tempting words.
The heavens are gracious, and your miseries   40
And sorrow makes you speak you know not what.
HIERONIMO: Villain, thou liest, and thou doest naught
But tell me I am mad. Thou liest; I am not mad.
I know thee to be Pedro, and he Jaques.
I'll prove it° to thee, and were I mad, how could I?   45
Where was she that same night when my Horatio
Was murdered? She should have shone: search thou the book.°
Had the moon shone, in my boy's face there was a kind of grace
That I know, nay, I do know, had the murderer seen him,
His weapon would have fall'n and cut the earth,   50
Had he been framed of naught but blood and death.
Alack, when mischief° doth it knows not what,
What shall we say to mischief?

Enter ISABELLA.

ISABELLA: Dear Hieronimo, come in a-doors;
O seek not means so to increase thy sorrow.   55
HIERONIMO: Indeed, Isabella, we do nothing here.
I do not cry— ask Pedro, and ask Jaques—
Not I, indeed, we are very merry, very merry.
ISABELLA: How? be merry here, be merry here?
Is not this the place, and this the very tree,   60
Where my Horatio died, where he was murdered?
HIERONIMO: Was — do not say what; let her weep it out.
This was the tree; I set° it of a kernel,
And when our hot Spain could not let it grow,
But that the infant and the human° sap   65
Began to wither, duly twice a morning
Would I be sprinkling it with fountain water.
At last it grew, and grew, and bore and bore,
Till at length
It grew° a gallows, and did bear° our son.   70
It bore thy fruit and mine: O wicked, wicked plant.
                              One knocks within at the door.
See who knock there.
PEDRO: It is a painter, sir.

HIERONIMO: Bid him come in and paint some comfort,
    For surely there's none lives but painted° comfort.
    Let him come in. One knows not what may chance.   75
    God's will that I should set this tree. — But even so
    Masters ungrateful servants rear from naught,
    And then they hate them that did bring them up.

Enter the PAINTER.

PAINTER: God bless you, sir.
HIERONIMO: Wherefore?° Why, thou scornful villain,
    How, where, or by what means should I be blessed?   80
ISABELLA: What wouldst thou have, good fellow?
PAINTER: Justice, madam.
HIERONIMO: O ambitious beggar, wouldst thou have that
    That lives not in the world?
    Why all the undelved° mines cannot buy
    An ounce of justice, 'tis a jewel so inestimable.   85
    I tell thee,
    God hath engrossed° all justice in his hands,
    And there is none, but what comes from him.
PAINTER: O then I see
    That God must right me for my murdered son.°   90
HIERONIMO: How, was thy son murderèd?
PAINTER: Ay, sir. No man did hold a son so dear.
HIERONIMO: What, not as thine? That's a lie
    As massy° as the earth. I had a son,
    Whose least unvalued hair did weigh   95
    A thousand of thy sons; and he was murdered.
PAINTER: Alas, sir, I had no more but he.
HIERONIMO: Nor I, nor I; but this same one of mine
    Was worth a legion. But all is one.°
    Pedro, Jaques, go in a-doors; Isabella   100
    Go, and this good fellow here and I
    Will range° this hideous orchard up and down,
    Like to two lions reaved° of their young.
    Go in a-doors, I say.   *Exeunt* [ISABELLA, PEDRO, JAQUES].

The PAINTER *and he sits down.*

    Come, let's talk wisely now. Was thy son murdered?   105
PAINTER: Ay, sir.
HIERONIMO: So was mine. How dost take it? Art thou not sometimes
    mad? Is there no tricks that comes before thine eyes?
PAINTER: O Lord, yes sir.

HIERONIMO: Art a painter? Canst paint me a tear, or a wound, a   110
  groan, or a sigh? canst paint me such a tree as this?
PAINTER: Sir, I am sure you have heard of my painting; my name's
  Bazardo.
HIERONIMO: Bazardo! afore God, an excellent fellow! Look you sir,
  do you see, I'd have you paint me in my gallery, in your oil   115
  colours matted,° and draw me five years younger than I am — do
  you see, sir, let five years go, let them go — like the Marshal of
  Spain, my wife Isabella standing by me, with a speaking° look to
  my son Horatio, which should intend to this or some such like
  purpose: 'God bless thee, my sweet son,' and my hand leaning   120
  upon his head, thus sir, do you see? May it be done?
PAINTER: Very well, sir.
HIERONIMO: Nay, I pray mark me, sir. Then, sir, would I have you
  paint me this tree, this very tree. Canst paint a doleful cry?
PAINTER: Seemingly, sir.°   125
HIERONIMO: Nay, it should cry; but all is one. Well, sir, paint me a
  youth, run through and through with villains' swords, hanging
  upon this tree. Canst thou draw a murderer?
PAINTER: I'll warrant you, sir: I have the pattern of the most
  notorious villains that ever lived in all Spain.   130
HIERONIMO: O let them be worse, worse. Stretch thine art, and let
  their beards be of Judas his own colour,° and let their eyebrows
  jutty° over; in any case observe that. Then, sir, after some violent
  noise, bring me forth in my shirt, and my gown under mine arm,
  with my torch in my hand, and my sword reared up thus, and   135
  with these words: 'What noise is this? who calls Hieronimo?' May
  it be done?
PAINTER: Yea, sir.
HIERONIMO: Well, sir, then bring me forth, bring me through alley
  and alley, still with a distracted countenance going along, and let   140
  my hair heave up my night-cap. Let the clouds scowl, make the
  moon dark, the stars extinct, the winds blowing, the bells tolling,°
  the owl shrieking, the toads croaking,° the minutes jarring,° and the
  clock striking twelve. And then at last, sir, starting, behold a man
  hanging, and tottering° and tottering, as you know the wind will   145
  weave° a man, and I with a trice° to cut him down. And looking
  upon him by the advantage of my torch, find it to be my son
  Horatio. There you may show a passion, there you may show a
  passion. Draw me like old Priam of Troy,° crying, 'The house is a-
  fire, the house is a-fire, as the torch over my head.' Make me curse, 150
  make me rave, make me cry, make me mad, make me well again,
  make me curse hell, invocate heaven, and in the end, leave me in a
  trance — and so forth.
PAINTER: And is this the end?

HIERONIMO: O no, there is no end; the end is death and madness. As   155
 I am never better than when I am mad; then methinks I am a
 brave° fellow, then I do wonders. But reason abuseth me, and there's
 the torment, there's the hell. At the last, sir, bring me to one of the
 murderers. Were he as strong as Hector,° thus would I tear and drag
 him up and down.   160

He beats the PAINTER *in, then comes out again with a book in his
hand.*

Notes

4	watch for: wait to commit
12	starting: starting up
18	brake: thicket
22	Sprites: spirits, demons
24	What make you: what are you doing?
29	the sun-god...glory: in Greek mythology, Apollo, the god of the sun, drove his chariot across the sky
30	burn daylight: (1) burn up the light of day; (2) waste our time
33	Hecate: Greek goddess associated with night and the underworld; in Elizabethan thought associated with witches and the moon.
36	aglets: metal tag-ends on a lace pins: ornamental pins
45	it: refering back to lines 32-33
47	the book: the almanac, indicating the phases of the moon
52	mischief: deliberate evil
63	set: planted
65	human: naturally frail
69	grew: grew into, became did bear: (1) grew as a fruit; (2) carried suspended
74	painted: (1) on canvas; (2) false, spurious
79	Wherefore: why?
84	undelved: remaining to be dug out
87	engrossed: taken control of

90	God...son: a reference to the biblical teaching (Deuteronomy 32:25) that vengeance is the prerogative of God.
94	massy: huge and weighty
99	all is one: no matter
102	range: wander
103	reaved: robbed, forcibly deprived
116	matted: mounted, set in a mat
118	speaking: eloquent, expressive
125	Seemingly: with a life-like appearance
132	Judas...colour: traditionally, Judas, the betrayer of Christ, was painted with red hair and beard, signifying a violent and irascible temperament
133	jutty: project
142–3	bells tolling: church bells were rung for a funeral
143	the owl...croaking: both owls and toads were considered to be creatures of ill-omen jarring: ticking away
145	tottering: dangling, swinging
146	weave: cause to swing with a trice: immediately
149	Priam of Troy: King Priam of Troy, imagined as grieving over the destruction of his city by the Greeks
157	brave: splendid
159	Hector: the greatest of the Trojan warriors

Appendix II

The Tragical History of Doctor Faustus (1616)

Act Five

The existence of two early but substantially different versions of the text of *The Tragical History of Doctor Faustus,* known as the A text (1603) and the B text (1616), has led to considerable variation in editorial practice since modern editorial work on the tragedy began with C. W. Dilke in 1814. The first editors generally choose the B text as the basis for their editions; from the nineteenth to the early twentieth century the A text was favoured. Beginning with Boas (1932) and including such distinguished scholars as Greg (1950), Bowers (1952, 1973), Jump (1962) and Gill (1965), many mid-century editors reverted to the B text, taking the view that the A text was a 'bad quarto', a rough memorial reconstruction by actors of the text of original performances. However, since C. L. Barber's 1964 edition of *Doctor Faustus,* a succession of editors have again chosen the 1603 (A text) printing of the play as their copy-text, on the grounds set out most fully in Eric Rasmussen's *A Textual Companion to 'Doctor Faustus'* (Manchester, 1993) that the A text was set in print from an authorial manuscript consisting of inter-leaved scenes by Marlowe and another dramatist, while the B text reflects a mixture of authorial and theatrical provenances, including substantial revisions by William Birde and Samuel Rowley introduced in 1602.

The present edition is based on the A text as its copy-text, but the B text remains of interest because of the way it shows the typical development in the Renaissance theatre of a much-performed script. This Appendix prints the whole of the 1616 print version of Act Five of *Doctor Faustus.* Comparison with the A text version will quickly show the expansion of the earlier text (the B text version of the Act is 90 lines longer than its predecessor), its adaptation for theatrical venues offering more elaborate technical resources (evidenced in the new stage effects required for demonic appearances and the thrones of heaven and hell), and the addition of further sensations (as in the discovery by the scholars of Faustus's dismembered body). In general, as the new Revels editors put it, 'the B text additions call for more characters on stage, more props and special effects, and more for more characters on stage, more props and special effects, and more exploitation of physical space'. The B text also shows the intervention of a censor removing sensitive theological material and references; it is significant that in 1606 an act of parliament forbade the use on the stage of the name of God, Christ, the Holy Spirit or the Trinity, and that in passages such as 5.2.150–1 and 168–9 the lines in the 1616 version are emasculated by the removal of just such terms. More importantly, the B text alterations seriously diminish the audience's sense of Faustus's freedom of choice, not least by the introduction of a speech by Mephostophilis (5.2.98–101) in which the demon claims responsibility for and control over Faustus's fatally selective reading of the Scriptures. Here and elsewhere, the original ironic and ambiguous study of human ambition and its relation to divine powers in the universe is skewed towards a cautionary moral tale, a tragedy of determinism.

Act Five, Scene One

> *Thunder and lightning. Enter* Devils *with covered dishes.*
> MEPHOSTOPHILIS *leads them into Faustus's study.° Then enter*
> WAGNER.

WAGNER: I think my master means to die shortly.
    He has made his will and given me his wealth:
    His house, his goods, and store of golden plate,
    Besides two thousand ducats ready coined.
    I wonder what he means. If death were nigh,   5
    He would not frolic thus. He's now at supper
    With the scholars, where there's such belly-cheer
    As Wagner in his life ne'er saw the like.
    And see where they come. Belike° the feast is done.   *Exit.*

> *Enter* FAUSTUS, MEPHOSTOPHILIS, *and two or three* SCHOLARS.

FIRST SCHOLAR: Master Doctor Faustus, since our conference° about fair   10
    ladies — which was the beautifullest in all the world — we have
    determined with ourselves that Helen of Greece° was the admirablest
    lady that ever lived. Therefore, Master Doctor, if you will do us so
    much favour as to let us see that peerless dame° of Greece, whom
    all the world admires for majesty, we should think ourselves much   15
    beholding unto you.
FAUSTUS: Gentlemen,
    For that I know your friendship is unfeigned,
    It is not Faustus' custom to deny

The just request of those that wish him well.   20
You shall behold that peerless dame of Greece,
No otherwise for pomp or majesty
Than when Sir Paris° crossed the seas with her,
And brought the spoils to rich Dardania.°
Be silent, then, for danger is in words.   [*Exit* MEPHOSTOPHILIS.] 25

    Music [*sounds*]. MEPHOSTOPHILIS *brings in* HELEN. *She passeth*
                over the stage.°

2 SCHOLAR: Was this fair Helen, whose admirèd worth
    Made Greece with ten years' wars afflict poor Troy?
3 SCHOLAR: Too simple is my wit° to tell her worth,
    Whom all the world admires for majesty.
1 SCHOLAR: Now we have seen the pride of nature's work,   30
    We'll take our leaves, and for this blessed sight
    Happy and blest be Faustus evermore.
FAUSTUS: Gentlemen, farewell. The same wish I to you.   *Exeunt* SCHOLARS.

           Enter an OLD MAN.

OLD MAN: O gentle Faustus, leave this damnèd art,
    This magic, that will charm the soul to hell   35
    And quite bereave thee of salvation!
    Though thou hast now offended like a man,
    Do not persever in it like a devil.
    Yet, yet thou hast an amiable° soul,
    If sin by custom grow not into nature.   40
    Then, Faustus, will repentance come too late;
    Then thou art banished from the sight of heaven.
    No mortal can express the pains of hell.
    It may be this my exhortation°
    Seems harsh and all unpleasant. Let it not,   45
    For, gentle son, I speak it not in wrath,
    Or envy of° thee, but in tender love
    And pity of thy future misery;
    And so have hope that this my kind rebuke,
    Checking° thy body,° may amend thy soul.   50
FAUSTUS: Where art thou, Faustus? Wretch, what hast thou done?
    Hell claims his right, and with a roaring voice
    Says, 'Faustus, come! Thine hour is almost come.'
              MEPHOSTOPHILIS *gives him a dagger.*°
    And Faustus now will come to do thee right.
               [FAUSTUS *goes to stab himself.*]
OLD MAN: O stay, good Faustus, stay thy desperate steps!   55

I see an angel hover o'er thy head,
And with a vial full of precious grace
Offers to pour the same into thy soul.
Then call for mercy and avoid despair.
FAUSTUS: O friend, I feel thy words to comfort my distressèd soul.   60
    Leave me a while to ponder on my sins.
OLD MAN: Faustus, I leave thee, but with grief of heart,
    Fearing the enemy of thy hapless soul.   Ex*it.*
FAUSTUS: Accursèd Faustus, wretch, what hast thou done?
    I do repent, and yet I do despair.   65
    Hell strives with grace for conquest in my breast.
    What shall I do to shun the snares of death?
MEPHOSTOPHILIS: Thou traitor, Faustus, I arrest thy soul
    For disobedience to my sovereign lord.
    Revolt,° or I'll in piecemeal tear thy flesh.   70
FAUSTUS: I do repent I e'er offended him.
    Sweet Mephostophilis, entreat thy lord
    To pardon my unjust presumption,
    And with my blood again I will confirm
    The former vow I made to Lucifer.   75
MEPHOSTOPHILIS: Do it then,° Faustus, with unfeignèd heart,
    Lest greater dangers do attend thy drift.°
FAUSTUS: Torment, sweet friend, that base and agèd man
    That durst dissuade me from thy Lucifer,
    With greatest torment that our hell affords.   80
MEPHOSTOPHILIS: His faith is great. I cannot touch his soul.
    But what I may afflict his body with
    I will attempt, which is but little worth.
FAUSTUS: One thing, good servant, let me crave of thee
    To glut the longing of my heart's desire: 85
    That I may have unto my paramour°
    That heavenly Helen, which I saw of late,
    Whose sweet embraces may extinguish clear°
    Those thoughts that do dissuade me from my vow,
    And keep my vow I made to Lucifer.   90
MEPHOSTOPHILIS: This, or what else my Faustus shall desire,
    Shall be performed in twinkling of an eye.

Enter HELEN *again* [*brought in by* MEPHOSTOPHILIS], *passing over
between two* Cupids.

FAUSTUS: Was this the face that launched a thousand ships°
    And burnt the topless° towers of Ilium?°
    Sweet Helen, make me immortal with a kiss.   [*They kiss.*] 95
    Her lips suck forth my soul. See where it flies!°

Come, Helen, come, give me my soul again.   [*They kiss again.*]
Here will I dwell, for heaven is in these lips,
And all is dross that is not Helena.
I will be Paris, and for love of thee   100
Instead of Troy shall Wittenberg° be sacked,
And I will combat with weak Menelaus,°
And wear thy colours on my plumèd crest.
Yea, I will wound Achilles in the heel,°
And then return to Helen for a kiss.   105
O, thou art fairer than the evening's air,
Clad in the beauty of a thousand stars.
Brighter art thou than flaming Jupiter
When he appeared to hapless Semele,°
More lovely than the monarch of the sky   110
In wanton Arethusa's azure arms;°
And none but thou shalt be my paramour.   *Exeunt.*

Act Five, Scene Two

Thunder. Enter LUCIFER, BEELZEBUB, *and* MEPHOSTOPHILIS [*above*].

LUCIFER: Thus from infernal Dis° do we ascend
    To view the subjects of our monarchy,
    Those souls which sin seals the black sons of hell,
    'Mong which as chief, Faustus, we come to thee,
    Bringing with us lasting damnation   5
    To wait upon° thy soul. The time is come
    Which makes it forfeit.
MEPHOSTOPHILIS: And this gloomy night
    Here in this room will wretched Faustus be.
BEELZEBUB: And here we'll stay
    To mark him how he doth demean° himself.   10
MEPHOSTOPHILIS: How should he, but in desperate lunacy?
    Fond° worldling, now his heart-blood dries with grief;
    His conscience kills it,° and his labouring brain
    Begets a world of idle° fantasies
    To overreach° the Devil. But all in vain.   15
    His store of pleasures must be sauced with pain.
    He and his servant Wagner are at hand;
    Both come from drawing° Faustus' latest will.
    See where they come.

Enter FAUSTUS *and* WAGNER.

FAUSTUS: Say, Wagner. Thou hast perused my will;   20
　　How dost thou like it?
　　WAGNER:　　　　　　　Sir, so wondrous well
　　As in all humble duty I do yield
　　My life and lasting service for your love.

Enter the SCHOLARS.

FAUSTUS: Gramercies,° Wagner. — Welcome, gentlemen.   [*Exit* WAGNER.]
1 SCHOLAR: Now, worthy Faustus, methinks your looks are changed.   25
FAUSTUS: O gentlemen!
2 SCHOLAR: What ails Faustus?
FAUSTUS: Ah, my sweet chamber-fellow!° Had I lived with thee, then
　　had I lived still, but now must die eternally. Look, sirs, comes he
　　not? Comes he not?   30
1 SCHOLAR: O my dear Faustus, what imports° this fear?
2 SCHOLAR: Is all our pleasure turned to melancholy?
3 SCHOLAR [*to the other* SCHOLARS: He is not well with being over-
　　solitary.
2 SCHOLAR: If it be so, we'll have° physicians, and Faustus shall be cured.   35
FAUSTUS: A surfeit° of deadly sin, that hath damned both body and soul.
2 SCHOLAR: Yet, Faustus, look up to heaven, and remember mercy is
　　infinite.
FAUSTUS: But Faustus' offence can ne'er be pardoned. The serpent that
　　tempted Eve may be saved,° but not Faustus. O gentlemen, hear with
　　patience, and tremble not at my speeches. Though my heart pant° and   40
　　quiver to remember that I have been a student here these thirty years, O,
　　would I had never seen Wittenberg, never read book! And what
　　wonders I have done, all Germany can witness, yea, all the world,
　　for which Faustus hath lost both Germany and the world;° yea,
　　heaven itself—heaven, the seat of God, the throne of the blessed, the   45
　　kingdom of joy—and must remain in hell for ever. Hell, O, hell for
　　ever! Sweet friends, what shall become of Faustus, being in hell for
　　ever?
2 SCHOLAR: Yet, Faustus, call on God.
FAUSTUS: On God, whom Faustus hath abjured? On God, whom   50
　　Faustus hath blasphemed? O my God, I would weep, but the devil
　　draws in my tears.° Gush forth blood instead of tears, yea, life and
　　soul. O, he stays my tongue! I would lift up my hands, but see, they
　　hold 'em, they hold 'em.
ALL: Who, Faustus?   55
FAUSTUS: Why, Lucifer and Mephostophilis. O gentlemen, I gave them
　　my soul for my cunning.°
ALL: O, God forbid!

FAUSTUS: God forbade it indeed, but Faustus hath done it. For the vain
    pleasure of four-and-twenty years hath Faustus lost eternal joy and   60
    felicity. I writ them a bill° with mine own blood. The date is
    expired. This is the time, and he will fetch me.
1 SCHOLAR: Why did not Faustus tell us of this before, that divines°
    might have prayed for thee?
FAUSTUS: Oft have l thought to have done so, but the Devil threatened   65
    to tear me in pieces if I named God, to fetch me body and soul if I
    once gave ear to divinity.° And now 'tis too late. Gentlemen, away,
    lest you perish with me.
2 SCHOLAR: O, what may we do to save Faustus?
FAUSTUS: Talk not of me, but save yourselves and depart.   70
3 SCHOLAR: God will strengthen me. I will stay with Faustus.
1 SCHOLAR [*to the third* SCHOLAR]: Tempt not God,° sweet friend, but let
    us into the next room and pray for him.
FAUSTUS: Ay, pray for me, pray for me! And what noise soever you hear,
    come not unto me, for nothing can rescue me.   75
2 SCHOLAR: Pray thou, and we will pray that God may have mercy upon
    thee.
FAUSTUS: Gentlemen, farewell. If I live till morning, I'll visit you; if not,
    Faustus is gone to hell.
ALL: Faustus, farewell.   *Exeunt* SCHOLARS.°   80
MEPHOSTOPHILIS: Ay, Faustus, now thou hast no hope of heaven;
    Therefore despair. Think only upon hell,
    For that must be thy mansion,° there to dwell.
FAUSTUS: O thou bewitching fiend, 'twas thy temptation
    Hath robbed me of eternal happiness.   85
MEPHOSTOPHILIS: I do confess it, Faustus, and rejoice.
    'Twas I that, when thou wert i'the way to heaven,
    Dammed° up thy passage. When thou took'st the book
    To view the Scriptures, then I turned the leaves
    And led thine eye.   90
    What, weep'st thou?° 'Tis too late. Despair, farewell!
    Fools that will laugh on earth must weep in hell.   *Exit.*

Enter the GOOD ANGEL *and the* BAD ANGEL *at several° doors.*

GOOD ANGEL: O Faustus, if thou hadst given ear to me,
    Innumerable joys had followed thee.
    But thou didst love the world.
BAD ANGEL: —Gave ear to me,   95
    And now must taste hell's pains perpetually.
GOOD ANGEL: O, what will all thy riches, pleasures, pomps°
    Avail thee now?
BAD ANGEL: Nothing but vex thee more,

To want in hell, that had on earth such store.

                         Music while the throne descends.°

GOOD ANGEL: O, thou hast lost celestial happiness,   100
    Pleasures unspeakable, bliss without end.
    Hadst thou affected° sweet divinity,
    Hell or the devil had had no power on thee.
    Hadst thou kept on that way, Faustus, behold
    In what resplendent glory thou hadst set°   105
    In yonder throne, like those bright shining saints,
    And triumphed over hell. That hast thou lost.
    And now, poor soul, must thy good angel leave thee.
    The jaws of hell are open to receive thee.

                 [*The throne ascends.*] *Exit* [GOOD ANGEL].

                            Hell is discovered.°

BAD ANGEL: Now, Faustus, let thine eyes with horror stare 110
    Into that vast perpetual torture-house.
    There are the Furies° tossing damnèd souls
    On burning forks; their bodies boil in lead.
    There are live quarters° broiling on the coals,
    That ne'er can die. This ever-burning chair   115
    Is for o'er-tortured° souls to rest them° in.
    These that are fed with sops° of flaming fire
    Were gluttons, and loved only delicates,°
    And laughed to see the poor starve at their gates.
    But yet all these are nothing. Thou shalt see   120
    Ten thousand tortures that more horrid be.
FAUSTUS: O, l have seen enough to torture me!
BAD ANGEL: Nay, thou must feel them, taste the smart of all.
    He that loves pleasure must for pleasure fall.
    And so I leave thee, Faustus, till anon;   125
    Then wilt thou tumble in confusion.°   *Exit.°*

                        The clock strikes eleven.

FAUSTUS: O Faustus, now hast thou but one bare hour to live,
    And then thou must be damned perpetually.
    Stand still, you ever-moving spheres° of heaven,
    That time may cease and midnight never come!   130
    Fair nature's eye,° rise, rise again, and make
    Perpetual day; or let this hour be but
    A year, a month, a week, a natural day,
    That Faustus may repent and save his soul!
    O lente, lente currite noctis equi!°   135
    The stars move still; time runs; the clock will strike;
    The Devil will come, and Faustus must be damned.
    O, I'll leap up to heaven! Who pulls me down?
    One drop of blood° will save me. O, my Christ!

Rend not my heart for naming of my Christ! 140
Yet will I call on him. O, spare me, Lucifer!
Where is it now? 'Tis gone;
And see, a threat'ning arm, an angry brow.
Mountains and hills, come, come and fall on me,°
And hide me from the heavy wrath of heaven! 145
No? Then will I headlong run into the earth.   [*Flings himself down.*]
Gape, earth! O, no, it will not harbour me.
You stars that reigned at my nativity,°
Whose influence° hath allotted death and hell,
Now draw up Faustus like a foggy mist 150
Into the entrails of yon labouring° cloud,
That when you vomit forth° into the air,
My limbs may issue from your smoky mouths,
But let my soul mount and ascend to heaven.   [*Rises.*]
The watch° strikes. O, half the hour is past!   [*The watch strikes.*] 155
'Twill all be past anon. O, if my soul must suffer for my sin,
Impose some end to my incessant pain.
Let Faustus live in hell a thousand years,
A hundred thousand, and at last be saved.
No end is limited° to damnèd souls. 160
Why wert thou not a creature wanting° soul?
Or why is this immortal that thou hast?
O, Pythagoras' metempsychosis,° were that true,
This soul should fly from me and I be changed
Into some brutish beast. All beasts are happy,° for, when they die, 165
Their souls are soon dissolved in elements;°
But mine must live still° to be plagued in hell.
Curst be the parents that engendered me!
No, Faustus, curse thyself. Curse Lucifer,
That hath deprived thee of the joys of heaven. 170
                         The clock strikes twelve.

It strikes, it strikes! Now, body, turn to air,
Or Lucifer will bear thee quick° to hell.
O soul, be changed into small waterdrops,
And fall into the ocean, ne'er be found!

          Thunder, and enter the Devils.

O, mercy, heaven, look not so fierce on me! 175
Adders and serpents,° let me breathe a while!
Ugly hell, gape not. Come not, Lucifer!
I'll burn my books.° O, Mephostophilis!   *Exeunt.*

Act Five, Scene Three

Enter the SCHOLARS.

1 SCHOLAR: Come, gentlemen, let us go visit Faustus,
    For such a dreadful night was never seen
    Since first the world's creation did begin.
    Such fearful shrieks and cries were never heard.
    Pray heaven the doctor have escaped the danger. 5
2 SCHOLAR: O, help us, heaven! See, here are Faustus' limbs,°
    All torn asunder by the hand of death.
3 SCHOLAR: The devils whom Faustus served have torn him thus.
    For, 'twixt the hours of twelve and one, methought
    I heard him shriek and call aloud for help, 10
    At which self° time the house seemed all on fire
    With dreadful horror of these damnèd fiends.
2 SCHOLAR: Well, gentlemen, though Faustus' end be such
    As every Christian heart laments to think on,
    Yet, for° he was a scholar, once admired 15
    For wondrous knowledge in our German schools,
    We'll give his mangled limbs due burial;
    And all the students, clothed in mourning black,
    Shall wait upon° his heavy° funeral. *Exeunt.*

Epilogue

Enter CHORUS.

CHORUS: Cut is the branch that might have grown full straight,
    And burned is Apollo's laurel bough°
    That sometime° grew within this'learnèd man.
    Faustus is gone. Regard his hellish fall,
    Whose fiendful° fortune may exhort the wise 5
    Only to wonder° at unlawful things,
    Whose deepness doth entice such forward wits°
    To practise more than heavenly power permits. [*Exit.*]

Terminat hora diem; terminat author opus.°

Finis

Notes

Act Five, Scene One

0 SD *Thunder...study*: the Devils'
      entrance may have been up
      through a trapdoor in the floor
      of the stage. Since concealed
      access is needed by the actors to
      prepare for Faustus' and his
      companions' entrance from the
      study (line 9 SD), in the
      Elizabethan theatre, the central
      alcove or one of the two stage
      doors on either side of the
      alcove, covered by a hanging,
      might have been used for the
      purpose.

9   Belike: in all likelihood
10   conference: discussion
12   Helen of Greece: the beautiful
      daughter of Leda and Jupiter
      and wife of Menelaus, King of
      Sparta, whose abduction by the
      Trojan prince Paris led to the
      Trojan War
14   dame: lady
23   Sir Paris: the title presents Paris
      as the knight-hero of a medieval
      romance
24   Dardania: the city of Troy,
      founded by Dardanus
25 SD *She...stage*: a common stage
      direction for the Elizabethan
      theatre, calling for an entry at
      one stage door and an exit by
      another, or for a movement
      from the yard up over the stage
      and out through the yard on the
      other side. (See also 92 SD.)
28   wit: intellect
39   amiable: able to be loved by God
44   exhortation: pronounced as five
      syllables
47   envy of: enmity towards
50   Checking: restraining,
      reproving.
      body: Faustus's physical body
      (the Old Man may lay hands on
      Faustus); or body in the sense
      of physical appetites
53 SD *a dagger*: traditional symbol of
      suicidal despair, the deadly sin
      against hope in God's mercy

70   Revolt: return (to your
      allegiance to the devil)
76   Do it then: some editors
      introduce a stage direction for
      Faustus to cut his arm again (cf.
      2.1.52 SD)
77   drift: wavering
86   unto my paramour: as my lover
88   clear: 'completely', with a
      quible on 'purified'
93   a thousand ships: traditionally
      the size of the Greek fleet that
      sailed to Troy to begin the War
94   topless: immeasurably high
      Ilium: Troy, so named after its
      founder Ilos
95–6 Sweet...flies: the hyperbolic
      language of love poetry
      becomes ironic, given Faustus's
      imminent damnation and final
      loss of soul.
101   Wittenberg: see Prologue 13 and
      note
102   weak Menelaus: husband of
      Helen and King of Sparta.
      Faustus is boasting that he will
      out-do Paris, who in the *Iliad*,
      Book 3, fought with Menelaus
      and was only saved by the
      Intervention of his protector, the
      goddess Aphrodite.
104   wound...heel: Achilles, the
      greatest warrior among the
      Greeks, was made invulnerable
      by his goddess-mother Thetis,
      except for one heel, where he
      was shot by Paris.
108–9 flaming Jupiter...Semele: when
      Semele, one of Jupiter's human
      mistresses, presumptuously
      asked her divine lover to
      appear in his full glory, she was
      destroyed by his fire.
110–11 the monarch...arms: in classical
      myth, the nymph Arethusa
      excited the river-god Alpheus's
      lust when she bathed in his
      stream; she fled him and was
      transformed into a fountain by
      Diana. No classical myth links
      Arethusa with Jupiter or the
      sun god, as Marlowe does here,

in an image of sunlight
reflected in water.

111   azure: blue

Act Five, Scene Two

1   Dis: the kingdom of the
         underworld ruled by Dis
         Pater or Pluto
6   wait upon: (1) act as a servant;
         (2) lie in wait for
10   demean: conduct
12   Fond: foolish
13   it: ? Faustus' potentially
         saving grief
14   idle: useless
15   overreach: outsmart
18   drawing: preparing
24   Gramercies: thanks
28   chamber-fellow: room-mate; it
         was usual at this time for two
         or more university students to
         share a college room
31   imports: signifies
35   have: call in
36   surfeit: over-indulgence, excess
38–9   The serpent...saved: the
         reference is to the biblical
         story of the primal Fall into
         sin, through the agency of the
         serpent (Genesis 3)
40   pant: may throb, palpitate
44   Faustus...world: Cf. Mark 8:36,
         'For what shall it profit a man,
         if he shall win the world, and
         lose his own soul?'
51–2   O...my tears: the inability to
         shed tears was taken as a sign
         of hardness of heart and a
         witch's nature.
57   cunning: knowledge
61   bill: deed
63   divines: priests, ministers of
         heaven
67   divinity: (1) religion; (2) God
72   Tempt not God: do not test or
         try the patience of God; cf.
         Christ's rejection of the devil's
         temptation in the wilderness,
         'Thou shalt not tempt the
         Lord thy God' (Matthew 4:7)
80 SD   *Exeunt* SCHOLARS: while the
         departure of the scholars is
         indicated in both the A and B
         text at this point, the staging

of Mephostophilis's
intervention is unclear in the
B text. He might descend from
the upper stage to join
Faustus at this point, or
remain there speaking down
to Faustus until his exit at line
92, reappearing on stage
among the devils at the end of
the play to receive Faustus
into hell.

83   mansion: dwelling-place, with
         an allusion to the dwelling
         places of blest souls in heaven
         (John 14:2)
88   Dammed: with a play on
         'damned' (the word is spelled
         Damb'd in the B text).
91   weep'st thou: cf. lines 51–2.
92 SD   *several*: different
97   pomps: ostentatious displays
99 SD   *Music...descends*: this presumes
         an elaborately-equipped
         theatre with machinery to let
         down a throne from the
         'heavens' above the stage,
         using winches and pulleys.
         Line 106 suggests that the
         throne contained a painted
         representation of enthroned
         saints.
102   affected: aspired to, been
         drawn to
105   set: sat
109, SD The jaws...*discovered*: the Good
         Angel exits, perhaps using the
         rising throne to do so. A
         vision of hell might have been
         displayed on a painted
         backcloth (perhaps revealed
         by drawing a curtain), or a
         hell-mouth construction raised
         through the trapdoor in the
         stage flooring. The Admiral's
         Men owned such a property,
         which probably showed
         fanged jaws gaping open to
         reveal the images of horror
         described in the text and
         might have been accompanied
         by smoke and terrifying
         sound effects.
112   the Furies: Greek female
         deities who avenged wrong
         and punished crime; cf. *The*

Spanish Tragedy, 1.1.65 and note.

114 live quarters: still living quartered human bodies

116 o'er-tortured: tortured beyond the limits of endurance
rest them: (1) remain; (2) enjoy a 'respite'; (3) wrest, twist themselves

117 sops: food dipped in liquid (usually wine)

118 delicates: delicacies

126 tumble in confusion: fall into destruction or perdition

126 SD *Exit*: the stage business is unclear at this point. The Bad Angel may exit independently, leaving the hellmouth to sink out of sight, or exit via the hellmouth. Alternatively the property may remain on stage throughout Faustus's soliloquy.

129 ever-moving spheres: cf. 2.3.35 and note

131 Fair nature's eye: the sun

135 *O lente...equi*: 'O gallop slowly, slowly, you horses of the night.' From the Roman erotic poet Ovid's *Amores*, 1.13.40; in its original context spoken by a lover asking the goddess of the dawn to think of her own reluctance to leave the arms of her lover Tithonus, and so to grant him more time with his Corinna.

139 One... blood: in Christian thought, blood as the symbol of the crucified Christ's power to save all believers

144 Mountains...me: the language of terrified humanity at the time of the Last Judgement; '[They] said to the mountains and rocks, Fall on us, and hide us from the face of him that sitteth on the throne, and from the wrath of the Lamb' (Revelation 6:16–17)

148 stars...nativity: the dominant planetary powers at the time of Faustus's birth

149 influence: an etherial fluid streaming from the heavenly bodies to act upon the characters and destinies of human beings

151 labouring: convulsing in the act of emission

152 vomit forth: in the form of a thunderbolt. Renaissance science (based on Aristotle's *Metaphysics*) held that lightning resulted from an exhalation exploding within a enclosing cloud. Faustus asks for his body to be utterly destroyed, so releasing his soul to rise to heaven.

155 watch: clock

160 limited: appointed

161 wanting: lacking

163 Pythagoras' metempsychosis: the sixth-century BC Greek philosopher Pythagoras's doctrine of the transmigration of souls, which argued that at the moment of death the human soul assumed some alternate life-form

165 happy: fortunate (in that they have no afterlife, so no experience of hell)

166 in elements: into their constituent elements

167 still: for ever

172 quick: alive

176 Adders and serpents: creatures associated with the demonic, and possibly incorporated in the costumes of Lucifer and his companion devils

178 burn my books: so renouncing the magic arts

Act Five, Scene Three

6 here...limbs: on the Elizabethan stage, the discovery space, opened by drawing back a curtain, could have been used to reveal Faustus's torn body.

11 self: same

15 for: because

19 wait upon: attend
heavy: sorrowful

Epilogue

2 Apollo's laurel bough: the laurel

was sacred to Apollo, god of
light, prophecy, the healing
arts, poetry and music. Laurel
wreaths were symbols of
eminence in the arts.

3   sometime: previously
5   fiendful: (1) terrible; (2) full of
    devils

6   Only to wonder: to be content
    with wondering
7   forward wits: the clever and
    daring
9   *Terminat...opus*: 'The hour ends
    the day; the author finishes
    his work.' A conventional
    motto which may have been
    added by the printer.

Further Reading

Reference Works and Histories

Bowers, Fredson (ed.), *Dictionary of Literary Biography*, vol. 62: *Elizabethan Dramatists*; vol. 58: *Jacobean and Caroline Dramatists* (Detroit, 1987).

Braunmuller, A. R. and Hattaway, Michael, *The Cambridge Companion to English Renaissance Drama* (Cambridge, 1990).

Greg, W. W., *A Bibliography of the English Printed Drama to the Restoration*, 4 vols (London, 1939–59).

Harbage, Alfred B., *Annals of English Drama 975–1700*, rev. edn Samuel Schoenbaum and S. Wagonheim (London and New York, 1989).

Hawkins-Dady, M. (ed.), *International Dictionary of Theatre*, vol. 1: *Plays* (Chicago and London, 1992); vol. 2: *Playwrights* (Detroit, London and Washington, 1994).

Hunter, G. K., *English Drama 1586–1642* (Oxford, 1997).

Leech, Clifford and Craik, T. W. (general eds), *The Revels History of Drama in English*, vol. 3: *1576–1613*; vol. 4: *1613–1660* (London, 1975–81).

Companies, Playhouses and Performances

Bentley, Gerald Eades, *The Jacobean and Caroline Stage*, 7 vols (Oxford, 1941–68).

Bentley, Gerald Eades, *The Profession of Dramatist in Shakespeare's Time 1590–1642* (Princeton, 1971).

Chambers, E. K., *The Elizabethan Stage*, 4 vols (Oxford, 1923).

Dressen, Alan C., *Elizabethan Stage Conventions and Modern Interpreters* (Cambridge, 1984).

Foakes, R. A., *Illustrations of the English Stage 1580–1652* (London, 1985).

Griswold, Wendy, *Renaissance Revivals: City Comedy and Revenge Tragedy in the London Theatre, 1576–1980* (Chicago, 1986).

Gurr, Andrew, *Playgoing in Shakespeare's London* (Cambridge, 1987).

Gurr, Andrew, *The Shakespearean Stage, 1574–1642* (Cambridge, 1980).

Gurr, Andrew, *The Shakespearean Playing Companies* (Oxford, 1996).

Harbage, Alfred, *Shakespeare's Audience* (New York, 1941).

Hattaway, Michael, *Elizabethan Popular Theatre: Plays in Performance* (London, 1982).

King, T. J., 'Staging of Plays at the Phoenix', *Theatre Notebook*, vol. 19 (1965).

Leacroft, Richard, *The Development of the English Playhouse* (London, 1973).

Neill, Michael, '"Wit's most accomplished Senate": The Audience of the Caroline Private Theatres', *Studies in English Literature* vol. 18 (1978).

Lomax, Marion, *Stage Images and Traditions: Shakespeare to Ford* (Cambridge, 1987).

Scott, Michael, *Renaissance Drama and a Modern Audience* (London and Basingstoke, 1982).

Southern, Richard, *The Open Stage* (London, 1953).

Sturgess, Keith, *Private Playhouses* (London and New York, 1987).

Trussler, Simon, *The Cambridge Illustrated History of British Theatre* (Cambridge, 1994).

General Studies

Adams, Henry Hitch, *English Domestic or Homiletic Tragedy, 1575–1642* (New York, 1943).

Babb, Lawrence, The *Elizabethan Malady: A Study of Melancholia* (East Lancing, Mich., 1951).

Barber, C. L., *Creating Elizabethan Tragedy: The Theater of Marlowe and Kyd*, ed. Richard P. Wheeler (Chicago, 1988).

Belsey, Catherine, *The Subject of Tragedy: Identity and Difference in Renaissance Tragedy* (London, 1985).

Bowers, Fredson, *Elizabethan Revenge Tragedy, 1587–1642* (Princeton, 1940).

Bradbrook, M. C., *Themes and Conventions of Elizabethan Tragedy* (New York, 1980).

Braden, Gordon, *Renaissance Tragedy and the Senecan Tradition: Anger's Privilege* (New Haven, Conn., 1985).

Brooke, Nicholas, *Horrid Laughter in Jacobean Tragedy* (London, 1979).

Callaghan, Dympna, *Woman and Gender in Renaissance Tragedy* (Atlantic Highlands, NJ, 1989).

Champion, L. S., *Tragic Patterns in Jacobean and Caroline Drama* (1977).

Clemen, W. H., *English Tragedy before Shakespeare* (London, 1961).

Dollimore, Jonathan, *Radical Tragedy: Religion, Ideology and Power in the Drama of Shakespeare and his Contemporaries* (Brighton, 1989).

Ellis-Fermor, Una, *The Jacobean Drama* (London, 1955).

Farnham, Willard, *The Medieval Heritage of Elizabethan Tragedy* (New York, 1956).

Hallett, Charles A. and Elaine S., *The Revenger's Madness: A Study of Revenge Tragedy Motifs* (Lincoln, Nebr. and London, 1980).

Jacoby, Susan, *Wild Justice: the Evolution of Revenge* (London, 1983).

Jardine, Lisa, *Still Harping on Daughters: Women and Drama in the Age of Shakespeare* (Brighton, 1983).

Lever, J. W., *The Tragedy of State* (London, 1987).

Levin, Richard, *The Multiple Plot in English Renaissance Drama* (Chicago, 1971).

McAlindon, Thomas, *English Renaissance Tragedy* (London, 1986).

McCabe, Richard A, *Incest, Drama and Nature's Law 1550–1700* (Cambridge, 1993).

McLuskie, Kathleen, *Renaissance Dramatists: Feminist Readings* (London, 1989).

Margeson, J. M. R., *The Origins of English Tragedy* (Oxford, 1967).

Mendell, Clarence, *Our Seneca* (New Haven, Conn., 1941).

Ornstein, Robert, *The Moral Vision of Jacobean Tragedy* (Madison, Wis., 1965).

Prior, Moody E., *The Language of Tragedy* (Bloomington, Ind., 1966).

Ribner, Irving, *Jacobean Tragedy: The Quest for Moral Order* (London, 1962).

Spenser, Theodore, *Death and Elizabethan Tragedy: A Study of Convention and Opinion in the Elizabethan Drama* (Cambridge, Mass., 1936).

Stilling, Roger, *Love and Death in English Renaissance Tragedy* (Baton Rouge, La., 1976).

Tomlinson, T. B., *A Study of Elizabethan and Jacobean Tragedy* (Cambridge, 1964).

Wymer, Roland, *Suicide and Despair in the Jacobean Drama* (Brighton, 1986).

KING ALFRED'S COLLEGE
LIBRARY